Mannó

BYZANTINE MISSIONS
AMONG THE SLAVS
SS. Constantine-Cyril and Methodius

RUTGERS BYZANTINE SERIES

PETER CHARANIS
GENERAL EDITOR

BYZANTINE MISSIONS AMONG THE SLAVS

SS. Constantine-Cyril and Methodius

FRANCIS DVORNIK

RUTGERS UNIVERSITY PRESS
New Brunswick *New Jersey*

197069

To John Seymour Thacher

CONTENTS

LIST OF ILLUSTRATIONS

All illustrations will be found following page 234.

MAPS

A. Great Moravian Empire.
B. Kingdom of Dioclea *ca.* 1080.

PLANS

C. Mikulčice, Churches. No. 1, remnant; Nos. 2, 3, 4, 5; Nos. 6 and 7, Rotundas; No. 8; No. 9, Rotunda; No. 10.
D. 11. Modrá; 12. Osvětimany; 13. Pohansko by Břeclav; 14. Sady ("Episcopal" Church); 15. Staré Město, Valy; 16. Staré Město, Špitálky; 17. Staré Město (Rotunda, St. Michael).

PHOTOGRAPHS

1. Mikulčice. Gilded Bronze Ornaments. From the Tomb of a Nobleman (No. 44).
2. Mikulčice. Silver Belt-end. Found near Church #3 (Plate C).
3. Mikulčice. Silver Belt-ends. Found near Church #3 (Plate C).
4. Mikulčice. Silver Gilt Belt-end. Found near Church #2 (Plate C).
5. Mikulčice. Silver Belt-end, with the Figure of a Nobleman Orant.
6. Mikulčice. Gold Earrings, Buttons, and Pendant. Found near Church #3 (Plate C).
7. Mikulčice. Bone Medallion, with an Archer. From Tomb 251, near Church #3 (Plate C).
8. Mikulčice. Gilded Bronze Reliquary. From Tomb 505, near Church #3 (Plate C).
9. Pohansko. Rings, Buckles, and Ornaments. From Tombs near the Church (Plate D, No. 13).
10. Pohansko. Unique Silver Earrings.
11. Kourim (Bohemia). Earrings and Reliquary. From the Tomb of a Noblewoman.

LIST OF ABBREVIATIONS

BZ   *Byzantinische Zeitschrift,* Leipzig, 1892–1943, Munich, 1949–

DO   *Dumbarton Oaks Papers,* Cambridge, Mass., Washington, D.C., 1940–

JGOE   *Jahrbücher für Geschichte Osteuropas,* Breslau, 1936–1941, Munich, 1953–

Loeb   *The Loeb Classical Library,* Cambridge, Mass.

Mansi   *Sacrorum conciliorum nova et amplissima collectio,* ed. G. D. Mansi, 31 vols., Florence, Venice, 1759–1798.

MGH   *Monumenta Germaniae historica. Dip,* Diplomata; *Ep,* Epistolae; *in us schol,* in usum scholarum; *Leg,* Leges; *Ns,* Nova Series; *Ss,* Scriptores; *Ss rer Lang,* Scriptores rerum Langobardicarum.

PG   *Patrologiae cursus completus,* ed. J. Migne: *Patrologia Graeca,* 161 vols., Paris, 1844–1866.

PL   *Patrologiae cursus completus,* ed. J. Migne: *Patrologia Latina,* 221 vols., Paris, 1844–1864.

Teubner   *Bibliotheca Teubneriana,* Leipzig.

Foreword

An important feature of the Byzantine Empire as a political and cultural entity was its transmittal of its own cultural forms to the surrounding barbarians, thereby bringing these barbarians within the orbit of civilization. This it did not so much by force of arms as by its missionary activity. Conversion to Christianity was, of course, the immediate objective of that activity but meant a great deal more than just the exchange of one religion for another. It meant the introduction, among those converted, of the Graeco-Roman cultural tradition as that tradition had crystallized in Christianity, with some additional elements drawn from Judaism. The dissemination of Christianity meant, therefore, the dissemination of forms of art, of literature, of law, even of government.

The missionary activity of the Byzantine Empire is the subject matter of the present book by Francis Dvornik. Dvornik is no newcomer to scholarship; for over forty years he has explored the history of the Slavs and various problems relating to Christianity and the Church. At least three of his books have become classics. Byzantium as the civilizing agent among the Slavs attracted his attention very early. Byzantium, he wrote once, "moulded the undisciplined tribes of Serbs, Bulgars, Russians, Croats even, and made nations out of them; it gave to them its religion and institutions, taught their princes how to govern, transmitted to them the very principles of civilization — writing and literature." The Byzantine mission has been, therefore, one of Dvornik's principal objects of investigation. Much of what the present volume contains, Dvornik is saying here for the first time. He has also wisely drawn upon much that he established in earlier work. Thus the book as a whole is an important contribution to Byzantine scholarship. It is important because of its integrating qualities, of the synthesis which it makes of the missionary activities, of the Byzantines and the political and cultural repercussions that these activities entailed. It is a pleasure indeed to publish it and a further satisfaction to add it to the Rutgers Byzantine Series.

Peter Charanis
General Editor
Rutgers Byzantine Series

Preface

In 1963, the Slavic world celebrated the eleven hundredth anniversary of the arrival in Moravia of SS. Constantine-Cyril and Methodius. At that time, I was asked to contribute to this anniversary with a new work, but I declined to do so, as I had already treated the problems concerning the activities of the two Greek brothers, and their contributions to the Slavic culture, in two earlier publications: first, in my thesis at the Sorbonne, *Les Slaves, Byzance et Rome au IXe siècle* (1926), which was awarded a prize by the French Academy, and again in 1933, in *Les Légendes de Constantin et de Méthode vues de Byzance*. Both works are being reprinted in 1970 by Academic International (Hattiesburg, Miss.), with the addition of extensive introductions in English to complement the texts.

The unexpected archaeological discoveries made in Moravia from 1949 to 1963, which I was able to study when I visited my native country after twenty-five years, consist of the remains of sixteen stone churches from the ninth century, and rich finds of jewelry, together with other objects from the surrounding cemeteries. These have shown me that this new and surprisingly rich archaeological material gives a clearer picture of that period, and that the history of the Byzantine mission in Moravia should be re-examined in the light of these new discoveries. However, I did not want to limit myself just to problems concerning the history of Great Moravia and of the activity of its Greek missionaries, SS. Constantine-Cyril and Methodius. I have approached the problems raised by the new discoveries from the Byzantine point of view, and have tried to illustrate what Byzantium did toward the Christianization of the Slavic nations, exposing in this framework not only what the two brothers did in Great Moravia but also stressing the importance of their religious and literary activities in the cultural and religious development of the Slavic nations during the early Middle Ages.

The successful excavations made by Serbian archaeologists in ancient Praevalis, modern Montenegro, helped me to re-evaluate the role of the Latin coastal cities and of Byzantine Dalmatia in the Christianization of the Croats and the Serbs. The excavations have also revealed similarities between Moravian church architecture and that of Byzantine Dalmatia and Istria in that same period. In the present book I have completed the research begun in my previous works, and I have reviewed some of the publications issued at the time of the eleven hundredth anniversary of the two brothers.

I wish to express my thanks to J. V. Richter, Professor at the University of Brno, for his permission to reproduce the sketches of the foundations of the sixteen churches discovered in Moravia, and published by him in *Magna Moravia* (Prague, 1965); I also thank the Czechoslovak archaeologists J. Filip and V. Hrubý, J. Poulik and A. Točík, for providing me with reproductions of archaeological material discovered by them, which is in part published in this book. I am especially obliged to Dr. V. Vavřínek for the many useful suggestions he gave me during our discussions of Cyrilo-Methodian problems throughout his stay in Washington in 1967 as Visiting Fellow at Dumbarton Oaks. I am indebted to Professor Peter Charanis, who included this work in the Rutgers Byzantine Series, and who has provided a foreword for the reader. My sincere thanks also go to the Director of the Dumbarton Oaks Center for Byzantine Studies, the Honorable William R. Tyler, for granting a subsidy toward its publication.

I am dedicating this work to John S. Thacher, in gratitude for his understanding and support of my scholarly activity at Dumbarton Oaks, where he functioned as Director from 1940 to 1969.

Francis Dvornik
February 1970
Washington, D. C.

BYZANTINE MISSIONS
AMONG THE SLAVS

I. Byzantine, Roman, and Frankish Missions among the Southern Slavs

Establishment of the Slavs in Central Europe, Pannonia, and Illyricum—The Emperor Heraclius, Rome, and the Christianization of the Croats—First results—The role of the coastal cities of Zara and Split and of Aquileia—Foundation of the bishopric of Nin by Pope Nicholas I in 860—Christianization of the Serbs and of the Slavs on Byzantine territory—First traces of ·Christianity in Bulgaria—The Bulgars and the Franks.

For many centuries Byzantium, capital of the eastern part of the Roman Empire, had a difficult Slavic problem on its hands. It was one of many problems, deriving from the upheaval caused by the great migration of nations. First there was the Germanic wave which swept over the Roman fortifications on the lower Morava and Vag rivers and on the Danube. Death prevented Marcus Aurelius in A.D. 180 from subjugating the German and Sarmatian tribes on the left bank of the Danube, and from extending the Roman Empire to the Carpathian Mountains. Because of this the Roman provinces of Pannonia and Dacia were exposed to constant danger from the wandering Germanic tribes. The Goths conquered the Greek cities on the Black Sea coast and, in the middle of the third century A.D., Dacia became their prey. The short-lived Gothic empire was completely destroyed by the new invaders, the Huns, (A.D. 370), and modern Hungary became the center of their empire under Attila (435–453).

At that time, there were already a few Slavic tribes in Hungary

1

and in Southern Russia; these tribes had also followed the Goths from their primitive habitats in the region between the Vistula and Dnieper rivers. The main Slavic influx into Central Europe and modern Hungary began during the fifth century and the beginning of the sixth, when the Germanic tribes, who occupied these regions, moved westward and southward to other lands after the collapse of the Hunnic empire. Thus Bohemia, Moravia, and Slovakia were definitively settled by the Slavs, and the Slovenes pushed through the Alps towards Istria. It was then that the real Slavic problem began for Byzantium. These tribes reached the river Danube and, after 517, according to Byzantine writers, they crossed the Danube to raid Macedonia, Thessaly, and Epirus.

Justinian (527-565) seems to have fought against them, and forced the tribes established beyond the lower Danube, under the leadership of the Antes, probably of Sarmatian origin, to become federates of the Empire. This success added to Justinian's titles that of Anticus. In spite of this, the invasions of Illyricum continued, becoming more and more dangerous as the Slavs occupied the invaded territory.[1]

These incursions were violent, but a slow assimilation of the newcomers by the natives in lands with a high level of culture seemed possible. The example of the Antes demonstrates this. But these chances were spoiled by the arrival of new invaders, the Avars, a nomadic Turkic tribe. They first destroyed (after 558) the loose political formation of the Antes, allied themselves with the Lombards (c. 565), with the help of their allies exterminated the Gepids in what was previously Dacia, and occupied the whole of modern Hungary after the Lombards had left for northern Italy (after 573). All the Slavic tribes in Central Europe became their subjects. Then serious trouble began for the Byzantines. With their Slavic subjects, the Avars invaded Illyricum and Dalmatia.[2] All the cities of Pannonia[3] and western Illyricum were destroyed, only those on the Adriatic Sea managed to survive, and the Slavs took definitive possession of what is today Yugoslavia. As a consequence of this, almost all traces of Christian life disappeared in Pannonia, Dalmatia, and the western part of Illyricum. These provinces, which once possessed flourishing Christian cities and bishoprics, were once again pagan territory.

There was great danger that even Macedonia and Greece

would meet with a similar fate. Both lands were invaded, and by about 578 the Slavs had penetrated as far as the Peloponnesus, where two of their tribes, the Milingues and the Ezerites, established themselves.[4] In the last quarter of the sixth century, further Slavic colonies were founded in Greece, even in the neighborhood of the famous classical cities of Thebes, Demetrias, and Athens.[5] In 597 Thessalonica was unsuccessfully besieged by the Avars and Slavs. The citizens attributed their deliverance to the intervention of their patron saint, Demetrius, but the environs of the city were to a great extent Slavicized.

The situation was growing more dangerous as the Empire was also menaced by the Persians. The Emperor Heraclius looked for allies among the neighbors of the Avars. In 619 he concluded an alliance with Kuvrat (Kurt), Khagan of the Bulgars, then established north of the lower Danube.[6] It is not impossible that Byzantine diplomacy also sponsored the uprising of the Slavs north of the upper Danube in Moravia and Bohemia.[7] The rebellious Slavs found an able leader in the person of Samo, a Frankish merchant,[8] who became the head of the first Slavic political state, which lasted until his death thirty-five years later (658).

The year 626 was extremely critical, as Constantinople was besieged by the Persians, Avars, and Slavs. Their defeat under the walls of the capital signalled the growing decline of Avar power. Another diplomatic move by Heraclius speeded up the decline— an invitation to the White Croats to help defeat the Avars in Dalmatia and Illyricum, and then to settle in those provinces. Originally the Croats were most probably a Sarmatian tribe who had been forced by the Huns to flee from their settlements near the Caucasus towards the northwest. They settled among the Slavic tribes in modern Galicia, Silesia, and southern Bohemia. The Slavs accepted the leadership of these warriors, who soon lost their national character and were Slavicized. They had escaped Avar supremacy and accepted the emperor's invitation.

It is difficult to say by which route they had reached Dalmatia. It is generally thought that they travelled through the Moravian Gates, Pannonia, and the former Noricum. The way through Moravia was perhaps open, after the successful insurrection led by Samo. Pannonia was, however, still in Avar hands, and the way through that country was certainly well guarded.

However, it seems more logical to suppose that Heraclius

wanted them near the capital, which was besieged by the Avars in 626. A safe and easy route could be found along the great rivers behind the Carpathian Mountains, towards the lower Danube, and thence along the coast to Byzantine territory. It should be recalled that at that time the lands from the lower Don southwards to the Caucasus—the Old Great Bulgaria—were under the rule of Kuvrat (Kurt), who had liberated himself from the Avars with the help of the Byzantines and was an ally of Heraclius.

The cities of the former Roman provinces of Scythia, Moesia, and Thrace were destroyed during the invasions, but the old Roman road along the coast still existed. It can be imagined that the approach of a new allied army from the North accelerated the retreat of the Avars, who were pursued by the liberated Byzantine army and the emperor's new allies. In this way we can perhaps explain how the Byzantines succeeded in reoccupying Singidunum—Belgrade. Constantine Porphyrogenitus relates that a number of White Serbs, another Sarmatian tribe which had been overtaken by the same fate as the Croats and had settled among the Slavs in modern Saxony, left their country and asked Heraclius for a new home. The emperor settled them in the *thema* of Thessalonica, but the majority of them were dissatisfied and decided to return to their original place. They got as far as Belgrade, but were persuaded by the Byzantine commander there to settle in the land which became the nucleus of the future Serbia. This must have happened soon after the liberation of the besieged capital.

It could be imagined that the Byzantines directed the Croats from Macedonia to the coast. They could reach Dyrrhachium along the old Via Egnatia and begin the war against the Avars from the province of Epirus and the Adriatic coast, where remnants of Byzantine possessions still existed. With the help of the Slavic subjects of the Avars, and the remnants of the Greek and Latin population, aided perhaps by the Byzantine navy, the Croats succeeded, after a fight which lasted several years, in expelling the Avars from Dalmatia. Constantine relates that, after this achievement, some of them also occupied lower Pannonia and Epirus, which was at that time called Illyricum. One tribe also seems to have liberated the Slovenes of Carinthia. The Croats settled in the liberated countries, and assumed the overlordship of the Slavs living there.[9]

* * *

According to the Emperor Constantine Porphyrogenitus (913–959), Heraclius thought that after this success it was necessary to Christianize the Slavs. He describes Heraclius' plan as follows:[10] "By command of the Emperor Heraclius, these same Croats defeated and expelled the Avars from these parts, and by mandate of the Emperor Heraclius they settled down in that same country of the Avars, where they now dwell. These same Croats had at that time for prince the father of Porgas. The Emperor Heraclius sent and brought priests from Rome, and made of them an archbishop and a bishop and elders and deacons, and baptized the Croats; and at that time these Croats had Porgas for their prince."

This report by Constantine is rejected by most subsequent historians, including the best Serbian historian, C. Jireček.[11] It was thought that Byzantium and Rome were not on good terms, and that, if Heraclius had desired to reintroduce Christianity into Illyricum, he would have sent Byzantine missionaries. However, there is no reason why Constantine's report should not be accepted. Byzantium and Rome were not always quarrelling, as is so often believed under the shadow of the later schism. On the contrary, Pope Honorius, to whom Heraclius may have addressed his request to send missionaries, was on very good terms with the emperor. We must not forget that the whole of Illyricum, which embraced all the provinces from Pannonia through Greece to the Peloponnesus, with their Latin and Greek populations, were subject ecclesiastically to the Roman patriarchate.[12] This situation was only changed in 732 when the iconoclastic Emperor Leo III, in order to punish Pope Gregory III for his condemnation of iconoclasm, detached what was left of Illyricum from Roman jurisdiction and subordinated it to the Byzantine patriarchate.[13] This explains Heraclius' move. He could not overlook this fact, and was bound to acknowledge the right of Rome to send missionaries to Dalmatia and the reconquered part of Illyricum.

This was the first attempt at the Christianization of the Slavs, and it was initiated by Byzantium. Unfortunately, we have no

direct information about the progress of Christianity among the
Croats at this early period. However, the emperor's statement
must have been founded on some facts.[14] It seems most probable
that Heraclius, after the liberation of Dalmatia from the Avars,
reorganized the ecclesiastical situation in the Dalmatian cities on
the Adriatic. There is a local tradition in Split (Spalato) which
attributes the erection of an archbishopric in this city to this
period. Split claimed the inheritance of Salona, the metropolis of
Dalmatia, which was destroyed by the Avars in 614. Thomas the
Archdeacon, who died in 1268, the author of a history of Salona,[15]
even mentions the name of the first archbishop of Split—John of
Ravenna. He says that the pope had sent him as his legate to
Dalmatia and Croatia on a special mission to reinforce Christianity among the surviving natives. John is said to have fulfilled his
mission well. He encouraged the Christians to conserve the ancient ecclesiastical organization by transferring the metropolitan
see from Salona to Spalato (Split). He was elected archbishop by
the local population and confirmed in this dignity by the pope.

Some scholars have thought, however, that Thomas confused
this archbishop with Pope John IV, a native Dalmatian (640–642),
or with Pope John X (914–929), who, in his reorganization of the
Dalmatian and Croatian clergy, subordinated the whole country
to Split.[16] There may, however, be some good reasons which explain this intimate connection of Byzantine Dalmatia with
Ravenna, and which would seem to justify the choice of a priest
from Ravenna for a special mission to Dalmatia.

First of all, the place of Dalmatia in the organization of the
Roman provinces should be re-examined. It is generally assumed
that it was a part of Eastern Illyricum.[17] This opinion appears to
be confirmed by the letter sent in 592 by Pope Gregory the Great
to Jobinus, prefect of Eastern Illyricum, in which the pope asked
the prefect not to give any support to Natalis, the Bishop of
Salona, who was accused of an uncanonical attitude and was
unwilling to obey papal orders.[18] The main object of this letter
was the recommendation of an envoy to administer the papal
patrimony in Illyricum. The pope only mentioned Natalis because
his case was foremost in his mind at that time, as is shown by
several papal letters concerning this bishop, written in the same
year. There was a danger that Natalis might seek the prefect's
support at the imperial court.

There are, however, in the papal register several letters concerning the affair of Natalis' successor Maximus (594–620), who, with the support of Marcellinus, the proconsul of Dalmatia, had ousted Honoratus, the archdeacon who had been canonically elected. Maximus had made himself archbishop of Salona and was then confirmed in office by the emperor on the recommendation of Marcellinus, and was accepted by all the suffragans, with one exception, as their metropolitan. The pope protested this action and forbade Maximus to exercise his episcopal functions.[19] Gregory wanted first to learn whether the imperial sanction really had been granted. The Emperor Maurice replied to Gregory that Maximus should not have been ordained without the pope's permission. This the pope disclosed in the letter to the deacon Sabinus, his representative in Constantinople.[20] In the same letter Gregory directly accused the distinguished men (*gloriosi viri*) of Romanus, exarch of Ravenna, of having accepted bribes from Maximus and allowing him to be ordained metropolitan of Salona. The pope probably meant the proconsul Marcellinus of Dalmatia and certain high functionaries of Dalmatia and of Ravenna.

Gregory's envoy at the court obtained from the emperor an order that Maximus, who had invoked the emperor's intervention, should appear in Rome and justify himself in the presence of the pope.[21] The affair was becoming increasingly annoying for both the court and the pope. The new exarch Callinicus asked the pope to accept Maximus as the legitimate metropolitan,[22] but Gregory persisted in his demand that Maximus should first be judged for his deeds according to Canon Law. Callinicus and Marcellinus made a further attempt to change the pope's attitude, but in vain. [23] Finally, Marcellinus himself convinced Maximus that he should give some satisfaction to the pope. Because Maximus refused to go to Rome, the pope ordered the metropolitans of Ravenna, and of Milan, to act as his representatives and to pronounce judgment in Ravenna where Maximus was willing to appear. Again the pope informed the exarch of this decision.[24] After submitting to penance, Maximus was accepted by the pope as the legitimate metropolitan of Salona. In his letter announcing this Gregory again stressed that he had shown his benevolence toward the metropolitan because of the intervention of the exarch Callinicus.[25]

All this would appear to indicate that intimate relations must have existed between Dalmatia and the exarchs of Ravenna. It seems to be established that in 549, and in 579, Dalmatia was not a part of Illyricum. This is confirmed by Procopius and Menander who separate Dalmatia very clearly from Illyricum.[26] We have seen that the argument derived from the letter of Gregory the Great to Jobinus, prefect of Illyricum, cannot be regarded as proving conclusively that in 592 Dalmatia was a province of Illyricum. The letters of Gregory I on the affairs of Maximus, which reveal the prominent role played in Dalmatian ecclesiastical affairs by the exarchs of Ravenna, Romanus and Callinicus, seem rather to indicate that in the seventh century Dalmatia formed a part of the exarchate of Ravenna.

This would further indicate that Justinian, having liberated Dalmatia from the Goths in 538, had reinstated the old status. According to all this, from the time of Diocletian's reforms, Dalmatia—with the exception of a very short period in the fifth century[27]—formed a part of the prefecture of Italy.

Unfortunately, no trace of this is found in Justinian's legislation. Since Dalmatia was adminstered by a proconsul in Gregory the Great's time, as is attested by his correspondence, E. Stein[28] has advanced the theory that Justinian instituted the proconsulate of Dalmatia after 538, probably at the time when the exarchate of Ravenna was established. The existence of the latter is only attested for the year 584 by a letter of Pope Pelagius II to the deacon Gregory.[29] But Stein's opinion that Dalmatia was incorporated into Illyricum[30] some time before 592 cannot be accepted, as we have seen. If one hesitates to think of Dalmatia as a part of the exarchate, one should, at least, conclude from all this that Dalmatia was directly subject to Constantinople, without the intermediary of the prefecture of Illyricum. Such is the opinion of J. Ferluga who, however, rejects the thesis that Dalmatia belonged to the exarchate of Ravenna.[31] What we have found in Gregory's letters seems to contradict this opinion. On the other hand, the fact that Dalmatia was governed by a proconsul does not exclude the possibility that a proconsul could be subject to a prefect. Peter the Patrician,[32] a contemporary of Justinian, speaks of a proconsul of Achaia who was subject to the prefect of Illyricum. A similar situation might have existed in the exarchate. The proconsul of Dalmatia could have been responsible to the exarch. The interest of the exarchs in the ecclesiastical affairs of Dalmatia can be explained in this way.[33]

If we accept this, then we are entitled to suppose that this situation continued until the end of the exarchate in 751, when the Lombards took Ravenna. We also find an echo of this old tradition in Constantine Porphyrogenitus' work *De thematibus*. When speaking of Dalmatia, the emperor simply says that it is a part of Italy.[34] He probably had the geographical location in mind, but this suggests that, because of the geographical factor, Dalmatia had been included in the administrative system of Italy.

There is yet another fact which seems to support the close connection of Dalmatia with Italy, Rome and the exarchate of Ravenna. In his ecclesiastical organization Justinian respected the special position of Dalmatia and, although it was a Latin province, he did not subordinate its bishops to Justiniana Prima. Only the bishops of the two Dacies, of Illyria, Dardania, Praevalis, and Pannonia were subject to the metropolitan of Justiniana Prima,[35] who also became the pope's vicar in Western Illyricum. The metropolitan of Thessalonica continued to represent the Roman patriarch in Eastern Illyricum with its Greek population. This explains why the clergy of Milan, in its letter concerning Vigilius' attitude to ecclesiastical policy,[36] distinguished very clearly between the clergy of Illyricum and that of Dalmatia. So also did the African bishop Facundus.[37] All this seems to indicate that Justinian had restored Dalmatia to the prefecture of Italy, or the Exarchate of Ravenna. This also explains why Gregory the Great dealt with the bishops of Dalmatia directly, as he did with the bishops of Italy.

If this was so, then the request of Heraclius to the pope to Christianize the new inhabitants of Dalmatia, who were regarded as the allies of the Empire, becomes more logical. The sending of a native of Ravenna to the Croats on a special mission can also be explained in the light of the relations between Ravenna and Dalmatia in the past.

If we accept the testimony of Constantine Porphyrogenitus that the initiative for the re-establishment of a Dalmatian hierarchy and the Christianization of the Croats came from Heraclius, there are three popes who may be thought of as executors of the imperial will, namely, Honorius I (625–638), Severinus (638–640), and

John IV (640–642). Honorius enjoyed friendly relations with
Heraclius, who granted him permission to use the gilt bronze roof
tiles of the temple of Venus and Rome for the basilica of St.
Peter.[38] If it was Honorius who was asked by the emperor to send
priests to Dalmatia, he could hardly have done so before 630.
Assuming that the Croats had arrived at the invitation of the
emperor in 626, or soon afterwards, their fight with the Avars had
lasted several years, according to Porphyrogenitus. During that
time the question of converting them could hardly have existed.

Also it seems that, after the settlement of the Croats in the conquered land, there were conflicts of interest between the new
masters and the remnants of the native Christian population. Such
conflicts are mentioned by Archdeacon Thomas in his history of
Salona and Spalato.[39] According to him, the remnants of the
population of Salona first took refuge on the Adriatic Islands and
only began to return to the mainland later. They were molested
by the Slavs, who prevented them from leaving the palace of
Diocletian (Spalato), where they had settled. The citizens then
sent an embassy to the emperor who gave them permission to
take up their abode in the palace, and through a "sacrum rescriptum" ordered the Slavs to leave the native population in peace.
The Slavs obeyed and, from that time on, there was peaceful
coexistence.

There is no reason for us not to accept this report of the archdeacon. His information is certainly based on local tradition. The
expression he uses when speaking of the emperor's order—*sacrum
rescriptum dominorum principum*—emphasizes this. It could
hardly have been invented in the thirteenth century. Also the
words *dominorum principum* aptly describe the political situation
in Byzantium. In 613, Heraclius made his infant son Constantine
co-emperor.[40] The rescript was therefore really sent in the name
of two emperors—Heraclius and Constantine.

If all these events took place during the reign of Heraclius, the
peaceful coexistence between the Croats and the natives could
only have begun during the last years of the pontificate of Honorius. He could, thus, have been the pope to whom the emperor
made the request to initiate the Christianization of the Croats. His
successor Severinus (638–640) could hardly have done anything
in this respect because he was only confirmed in his dignity by
Heraclius in 640. [41] John IV was confirmed and consecrated as

early as December 640. During his pontificate the situation in Dalmatia was already stabilized, and it could be accepted that he was the pontiff who implemented the request of Heraclius and re-established the hierarchy in Dalmatia.

John IV was born in Dalmatia, and showed his interest in his native land by sending Abbot Martin there, and to Istria, with the mission of collecting the relics of the saints in the ruined churches, and of redeeming the Christian prisoners. [42] The Croats, being the emperor's allies, were not supposed to hold the native population in slavery, but they certainly kept the prisoners taken by the Avars after the defeat of the latter. The pope gave the abbot a large sum of money, and great numbers of Christian prisoners were freed. They settled on the coast among those of their countrymen who had escaped captivity. The abbot collected the relics of the saints and brought them to Rome; they were deposited by the Pope in an oratory near the basilica of St. John in the Lateran Palace.

This indicates that the situation in Dalmatia was not only peaceful, but that friendly relations already existed between the new settlers and the remnants of the Latin population. Such an atmosphere was very favorable to the realization of Heraclius' plans. It could thus be accepted that, if there is any truth in Thomas' statement concerning the transfer of the metropolitan status from Salona to Spalato, it was effected by John IV in 640, the last year of the reign of Heraclius.

There is one objection which may be made against this supposition, namely, that it is vain to search in the *Liber Pontificalis* for any mention of any pope re-establishing hierarchical order in Dalmatia. However, a perusal of the short biographies of Honorius I, Severinus, and John IV leaves the impression that the author of the *Liber Pontificalis* was interested only in the deeds of those popes in Rome itself. He goes into detail describing the erection or restoration of churches by the popes, or of complications with the local militia, or the exarchs. But he limits himself in regard to the ordinations of bishops, quoting only the number of ordinations which each pope had held and the number of bishops and priests he had ordained "for different places." It is probable that not even the mission of Abbot Martin would have attracted the attention of the biographer of John IV, if the relics collected in Dalmatia had not been deposited in a special oratory in Rome, constructed and decorated by John IV for the purpose. Of course, it would have been a great help to historians had the author given us the names of the bishops ordained, and of the bishoprics they were to occupy, but, unfortunately, the writer of the *Liber Pontificalis* was more interested in other matters less relevant to Church historians.

Fortunately, an archaeological discovery has come to the aid of the historians. A sarcophagus discovered in the Cathedral of Spalato bears an inscription which testifies that it contained the body of the "feeble, useless sinner, Archbishop John".[43] The archaeologists were not unanimous as to the date of the sarcophagus. L. Karaman[44] dated it as being of the second half of the eighth century. Its plastic decoration could point to this period, but its archaic form suggests that it may also be from an earlier period. The recent discovery of a church portal in Sućurac, in the vicinity of the former Salona, helped to make further progress in the dating of the sarcophagus.[45] Its simple plastic decoration is definitely archaic, pointing to the last phase of antiquity, and this style of decoration was not used after the seventh century.

The epigraphy of the two documents is almost identical. Both monuments must be from the same period, although the sarcophagus may be one or two decades later than the portal. This eliminates the opinion that Thomas of Spalato had confused John of Ravenna with John IV, or John X, and confirms that there did exist in the seventh or eighth century a prelate John who called himself archbishop. He could only have been the archbishop of Salona-Spalato.

The dating of the sarcophagus as being of the end of the seventh century is more probable. This confirms the testimony of Thomas of Spalato that John of Ravenna became the first archbishop of Spalato, successor to the metropolitans of ancient Salona. The supposition that John IV had been instrumental in transferring the metropolitan status from Salona to Spalato also becomes most probable, thanks to these two archaeological discoveries. This, of course, does not exclude the possibility that Heraclius' request to re-establish the hierarchy in the reconquered lands, was accomplished by one of the successors of John IV. In any case, John of Ravenna did exist and he was the first archbishop of Spalato.

The discovery of the church portal in Sućurac also confirms Thomas' other information, namely that John of Ravenna, when ordained by the pope, began to restore the ruined churches and to preach the Gospel to the new inhabitants.[46] The restoration of a church in Sućurac indicates also that the conversion of the Croats was making progress in the seventh century. Sućurac was not situated in the part of Dalmatia which belonged to the territory of Spalato, but was on Croat soil, and later became a royal domain.

A further archaeological discovery made in Spalato in 1958 reveals another deed of the same archbishop of Ravenna. This is the finding of the sarcophagus of St. Domnius (Dujan) in the Cathedral of Spalato. The inscription on the sarcophagus says that "the body of the blessed Domnius, archbishop of Salona, disciple of St. Peter, the prince of the Apostles, was transferred from Salona to Spalato by John, the archipresul of the same see."[47]

This again seems to confirm the report by Thomas in the *History* of the transfer of the remains of Domnius and of Anastasius from Salona to Spalato. This transfer must have taken place in the early years of John's bishopric, because Thomas says that the discoverers of the relics hurried to Spalato, being afraid that the Slavs might interfere with their operation. The relics of St. Anastasius are also said to have been transferred by him.

It was generally believed that the relics of Domnius were brought to Rome by Abbot Martin. If this is true, then we should suppose that Spalato later acquired a part of those relics from Rome,[48] or that the relics found by the citizens of Spalato in the ruins of Salona were not genuine. The inscription on the sarcophagus recalls, however, the epigraphic style of the two inscriptions mentioned above. It should also be noted that the name of Domnius is not mentioned among the relics brought by Martin. On the mosaic representing the Saints whose relics had been deposited by John IV in the oratory of St. Venantius, Domnius is also shown, although his relics were not transferred to Rome. John IV desired to have him represented there because he was the first bishop of Salona, the pope's native city, and the patron saint of Dalmatia. It is quite logical to think that the Spalatans wished to keep the body of the founder of the metropolitan see of Salona which had been transferred to Spalato. It is quite possible also that the moving of the relics of Domnius to Spalato was made in agreement with Abbot Martin.

We have thus sufficient reason to believe that the reorganization of the Dalmatian hierarchy was really effected in the first half of the seventh century, on the initiative of the Emperor Heraclius, who was responsible for the settlement of the Croats in that province. It was, most probably, Pope John IV who established the first metropolitan in Spalato, considered to be the heir of Salona. The choice of a cleric from Ravenna is explained by the fact that Dalmatia was still, in the seventh century, a part of the exarchate of Ravenna. The exarch Isacius most probably influenced this choice. He had declared his interest in Christian refugees from the territories invaded by the Lombards, by constructing a cathedral in Torcello in 639 for the new bishopric created for them.[49] He tried to use the Croats also in his struggle with the Lombards. Desiring to obtain a direct connection between the exarchate and the Byzantine possessions in southern Italy, he was, most probably, the initiator of the maritime expedition of the Croats against Siponto.[50] Their attack was, however, unsuccessful. It was the second time that the Croats had acted as imperial allies against the enemies of the Empire.

We can also accept another statement by Porphyrogenitus, namely, that the Croats were converted under their ruler Porgas. He says that the Croats fought against the Avars under the leadership of Porgas' father, whose name he does not give. The latter was, most probably, one of the five brothers who came with their nation to Dalmatia, perhaps Kloukas, who is first mentioned by Porphyrogenitus, or Chrobatos.[51] The first generation of the Croats fought against the Avars and ensured their leadership of the Slavs whom they found in the country. The second generation was more inclined to listen to the Christian message.

Rome continued to manifest its interest in the Christianization of the Croats. This can be concluded from the letter which Pope Agatho sent to the Emperor Constantine IV in 680.[52] There he discloses that many of his *"confamuli"* were working among the Lombards, Slavs, Franks, Gauls, Goths, and Britons. The Slavs mentioned in the letter can only be the Croats. If the "confamuli" should be bishops—and the context seems rather to indicate it— then we can see in it a reference to the newly re-established Latin hierarchy in the Adriatic cities which was charged with the conversion of the Croats.

This would seem to be confirmed also by another report of Constantine's. In the same chapter he writes that the "baptized Croats will not fight foreign countries outside the borders of their own; for they received a kind of oracular response and promise from the pope of Rome, who in the time of Heraclius, emperor of the Romans, sent priests and baptized them. For after their baptism the Croats made a covenant, confirmed with their own hands and by oaths sure and binding in the name of St. Peter the apostle, that never would they set upon a foreign country and make war on it, but would rather live at peace with all who were willing to do so; and they receive from the same pope of Rome a benediction to this effect, that if any of the pagans should come against the country of these same Croats and bring war upon it, then might the God of the Croats fight for the Croats and protect them, and Peter the disciple of Christ give them victories."

The account has a strong legendary aspect. In spite of that, it must be based on something real. It seems to indicate that peaceful relations between the Latin coastal cities and the Croats were established thanks to the missionary activity of Roman priests among them.[53] We are entitled to go even further and suppose that Constantine may have found in the imperial archives a report sent to Heraclius by Honorius or John IV, announcing that the first result of the missions—the establishment of a hierarchy and of peaceful relations between the coastal cities and the Croats of the hinterland—had been realized. The repeated mention of Peter in Constantine's report sounds like an extract from or an echo of a papal letter. Constantine had no special reason to mention St. Peter in this connection. His name was, however, repeatedly invoked in papal documents[54].

After the disappearance of the exarchate in 751, and during the eighth century, the Croats were politically directly under Byzantine supremacy, which was rather nominal. Ecclesiastically, however, Dalmatian Croatia remained under direct Roman jurisdiction, as before. Although no reports are extant on the progress of Christianization among the Croats, we can suppose that, during the second half of the seventh and the eighth century, churches had already been constructed, or ruined churches restored, by Latin missionaries from the coastal cities to the Croats, especially those from Zadar (Zara) and Split.

One should imagine that this first wave of Christianization could reach only the tribes in the neighborhood of the coastal cities. Their Latin population had first to recover from the onslaught and increase the number of its priests. In this, the citizens were most probably assisted by their compatriots from Italy and by the papacy. The penetration of Christianity into the interior of Dalmatia must have been slower and could be accelerated only in the second half of the eighth and the beginning of the ninth centuries.

* * *

The city of Zara, which had not suffered during the invasion, seems always to have had a bishop.[55] According to Porphyrogenitus even the great islands of Arbe (Rab), Vekla (Krk), and Opsara, (Osor) remained intact, and many Latin Dalmatians found a refuge there. Rab possessed a bishopric in 530 and 533. It is listed in the *Acts* of synods held in Salona in these years.[56] Because Rab had not been invaded, it is legitimate to suppose that its bishopric continued to exist. The *Chronicle* of Grado [57] records that Elias, the Patriarch of Grado, had announced at his synod in 579 the foundation of sixteen new bishoprics in Istria and Dalmatia, and among them were the bishoprics of Vekla (Krk) and Opsara (Osor). Even if the existence of the synod is questioned by some specialists, it seems certain that these two bishoprics were founded in the second half of the sixth century. It appears that this foundation is connected with the opposition of the metropolitan of Aquileia-Grado to the condemnation by the fifth general council (553), at the request of Justinian, of the three Chapters containing the writings of Ibas of Edessa, Theodoret of Kyros, and Theodore of Mopsuestia. The bishop of Rab joined the patriarch, who founded new bishoprics in order to strengthen his position. It is probable that when Candianus, the Patriarch bishop of Grado (607–612), had ended the schism with Rome,[58] the bishoprics of Rab, of Vekla, and Opsara—both situated on the territory of Rab— returned for a short time to Salona before the city was destroyed.

We can thus name five bishops in the neighborhood of the Croat territory whose prime interest was to work on the conversion of the Croats. The higher civilization displayed by the Latin cities must naturally have attracted the Croats. The missionaries sent to the mainland by the bishops of the coastal cities and islands were aided in their work by the remnants of the Christian population which had found refuge in the mountains. These survivors of Christianity in Croat lands are mentioned in the chronicle of the

Priest of Duklja[59] and also in some documents published by G. Marini.[60] The existence of such Christian islands in the pagan sea cannot be doubted.

It is also possible that all the churches in Dalmatia were not completely destroyed and that some of them could be used by the remnants of the Christian population and by the new converts. Archdeacon Thomas mentions such a church in Delmis (Duvno) where a church, consecrated in 518 by Bishop Germanus of Capua, on his way to Constantinople, was still in use in the thirteenth century.[61] Croat archaeologists may find more cases of this kind.

Unfortunately, we have no information on the progress of the Christianization of the Croats during the eighth century. It has been thought that the subordination of Dalmatian bishoprics under Constantinople in 732 by the Emperor Leo III had hampered this. There is still a lively controversy among historians concerning this change in Dalmatian religious status. In order to punish Pope Gregory III (731–741) for his opposition to the emperor's iconoclastic decrees, Leo III confiscated the patrimony of St. Peter in the prefecture of Illyricum, in the exarchate of Sicily, and in the duchy of Calabria. At the same time he detached all the bishoprics of these countries from the Roman patriarchate and subordinated them to the patriarchs of Constantinople.

Because it was believed that Dalmatia had been a part of Illyricum, it was concluded that, from 732 on, the bishops of Dalmatia were under the jurisdiction of the patriarchate of Constantinople.[62] We have seen, however, that Dalmatia was not a part of Illyricum, but, down to the year 751, of the exarchate of Ravenna. Because of this, the decree of Leo III in 732 did not affect the Dalmatian bishoprics. This seems to be confirmed by the letter of Nicholas I to Michael III in 860[63] in which the pope demanded the return of the detached provinces under his jurisdiction. Dalmatia is not mentioned, which shows that it had never been detached from the jurisdiction of Rome. It should be stressed also that Dalmatia never appeared in the Byzantine *Tactica*, the lists of bishoprics under the patriarchate of Constantinople.[64] After the disappearance of the exarchate, Dalmatia was directly under Constantinople, probably as an *archontia*[65] with an *archon-dux* who resided in Zara. Zara was chosen to become the political center of Byzantine Dalmatia because the city was the best preserved and best developed of the Latin coastal cities and, perhaps, also because it was nearer to Istria and Venice, which were still in Byzantine hands.

The Croats also were nominally under Byzantine supremacy. Constantine Porphyrogenitus says that "from the Croats who came to Dalmatia a part split off and possessed themselves of Illyricum and Pannonia."[66] It is not quite clear if the emperor here means only Pannonia, which used to be part of Western Illyricum or, if besides Pannonia, he hints at Epirus which was in the later period identified with Illyricum. The circumstance in which Constantine speaks only of one "sovereign prince, who used to maintain friendly contact, though through envoys only, with the prince of Croatia," would indicate that he had in mind only the prince of Pannonia of the ancient western Illyricum.[67] It is however, quite possible that the Croats had extended their sway over all the Slavic tribes of former Praevalis and parts of Epirus.[68] This would be most probable if we could assume that the Croats had begun their struggle against the Avars from these provinces which were still partly in Byzantine possession. We know that these lands had suffered heavily during the invasions and almost all the bishoprics in Praevalis and Epirus had disappeared.[69] It is thus quite possible that some of the Croat people went there and subjugated the Slavs living there.

The Byzantines were in no position to reinforce their authority in the lands freed from the Avars by the Croats. But the bishoprics of the coastal cities were under direct Byzantine rule, although under Roman jurisdiction, and Byzantium enjoyed friendly relations with Rome after the liquidation of the first phase of iconoclastic quarrels (787). Therefore, there was no reason why the progress of Christianity among the Croats could not have continued during the eighth century. There is a report by the chronicler of Duklja, written between 1149 and 1153,[70] of a national assembly held in the plain near the former Delminium (Duvno), in the presence of the representatives of the Byzantine emperor and of the pope. If this event is dated in the year 753, as was recently proposed,[71] we would have here new documentary evidence of the development of Christianity among the Croats. Unfortunately, the report is highly unreliable and so full of confusing reminiscences, that it cannot be taken as evidence that Croatia was already completely Christianized by the middle of

the eighth century. There is, however, further evidence showing
that at least some of the Croat chiefs were Christians by the end
of the eighth century. There is the inscription which the Župan
Godeslav (780–800) ordered to be made in the Church of the Holy
Cross in Nin (ancient Nona), which he had constructed. Nin was
also the residence of the first known Croat prince—Višeslav (about
800), who was certainly a Christian.[72]

Moreover, certain Croatian words from the realm of Christian
terminology indicate that Christianity came to the Croats at an
early stage from the coastal cities, where the Latin terminology
formerly used in Dalmatia and Illyricum had survived. The patron saints of the coastal cities were also popular among the
Croats.[73] Other saints whose cults were favored by the coastal
cities and later by the Croats include names which indicate that
Eastern, Italian, and Roman influences were prominent in the
primitive Christian community in Dalmatian Croatia. The cults
of Moses, Daniel, Elias, Demetrius, Michael, St. Sophia, Sergius,
George, Theodore, Stephen, Cosmas and Damian, Plato, Zoilus,
Andrew, and others could only have been imported from the East.
The cult of Peter, Appollinaris, Vitalis, Alexander, Benedict, Cas-
sian, Cyprian, Dominicus (=Dinko), Isidore, and others came
from Rome, Ravenna, and Italy in general.[74] This influence is also
documented by the transformation of the Latin *sanctus* into *sut* in
Dalmatia (in Istria also *sat*). In this way we encounter in the Dalmatian popular calendar and toponomy curious combinations,
like *Sutpetar* (St. Peter), Stugjuragj, Sujuraj (St. Georgius), Sut-
vara, Sveta Vara (Sancta Barbara), Sutikla (Sancta Thecla),
Sutomiscica (Sancta Eufemia), Stošija (Sancta Anastasia), etc.[75]

It is also important to note that at this early stage of its history
the Croatian Church was unaware of the system of proprietary
churches, according to which ecclesiastical institutions became
the property of the founders, who claimed certain rights in the
appointment of priests in these institutions. This system was a
Frankish invention, and the fact that the Croats did not accept it
indicates that knowledge of Christianity must have reached them
at an early stage from another center, which ignored this system.
This can only be the area of the Adriatic coastal cities, or Rome
itself.

All this leads us to believe that Christianity penetrated into

Slavic Dalmatia from Rome and Italy, through the intermediary of the Latin coastal cities. Rome never lost its interest in the new-comers to Dalmatia and in what was left of Illyricum.

On the other hand, however, a new power was rising on the northern frontier of Dalmatia—the Frankish Empire under Charlemagne. In 788 Bavaria was added to the Empire, and Byzantium lost Istria. The Slavs of the former Noricum became Frankish subjects. The Pannonian Croats, with their prince Vojnomir, accompanied Charlemagne in his campaign against the Avars (791; 795–796) and became his subjects. The Margrave Eric of Friuli, whose territory also comprised Noricum, Istria, and Croatian Pannonia, made an attempt in about 797 to subjugate the Dalmatian Croats, but the vain attempt cost him his life.[76] The war between Byzantium and the Franks, which started after Charlemagne's "usurpation" of the imperial title in 800 permitted the successor of Eric, Cadolah, to intervene in Dalmatia and to force the Croats to recognize Frankish sovereignty (803). In 805 even Paul "dux Jaderae," and Donatus, bishop of the same city, appeared before Charlemagne at Diedenhofen (Thionville), to plead for their country.[77] The peace of Aix-la-Chapelle in 812 finally confirmed the Byzantines in the possession of Venice and of the Dalmatian coastal cities. The Croats, however, remained under Frankish suzerainty.

From the beginning of the ninth century on our information about Dalmatia is more precise, and it is still often believed that the Christianization of the Croats only began seriously during this perod, and that the conversion of the Croats was effected by Frankish missionaries, sent especially by the patriarchs of Aquileia,[78] the nearest Christian center in Frankish territory. The metropolitans, and later the patriarchs of Aquileia, extended their jurisdiction over Venetia, Istria, western Illyricum, Noricum, and Raetia Secunda in the fifth century, and then, after the destruction of Sirmium, as far as the frontiers of Pannonia and Savia. The barbarian invasions restricted their influence, but their missionary zeal may have been awakened at the beginning of the eighth century, when they were definitively reconciled with Rome; but their quarrels with their rivals of Grado seem to have consumed most of their energies.

In any event, we have no information concerning the missionary activity of Aquileia among the Slovenes living between the Drava and the Adriatic coast, although Salzburg, which had inherited jurisdiction over Pannonia and Raetia, had developed considerable activity among the Slovenes of Carinthia. Only after Charlemagne had conquered Lombardy and Istria, or rather after his destruction of Avar power in 796, did the Patriarch Paulinus, at the request of Alcuin,[79] manifest an interest in missions among the Slavs. In spite of this, we have not learned of any results of Aquileia's missions under Paulinus and his successor Ursus. Only after Charlemagne had definitely fixed the frontier between Salzburg and Aquileia on the Drava in 811, did Aquileia appear to be interested in missions among the Slovenes within its jurisdiction.[80] This seems to suggest that Aquileia could only have manifested an interest in Croatia after 803, when Charlemagne, at war with the Byzantines, had forced the Dalmatian Croats to accept Frankish supremacy.

In reality, Aquileia found easy access to the territory of the Pannonian Croats. Vojnomir, the prince of the Pannonian Croats, accepted baptism between the years 805 and 811. His successor Ljudevit was also a Christian. The work of Aquileian missionaries among the Croats was interrupted by the insurrection of Ljudevit in 819. The Frankish army was defeated, and the Dalmatian Croats were forced to recognize Ljudevit as their ruler after his victory over the army of their prince Borna, and even the Slovenes of Istria joined his realm. Only in 822 did the Franks succeed in forcing Ljudevit out of Dalmatia. In the next year he was assassinated, perhaps on the orders of Vladislav, successor to Borna.[81]

The rivalry between Aquileia and Grado was evident even during these events. Fortunatus, the Patriarch of Grado, supported Ljudevit, furnishing him with Italian specialists for the construction of his fortresses. After Ljudevit's defeat, Fortunatus left Grado and found refuge in Constantinople. This incident seems to reveal that Byzantium had not lost all support in Istria.

The fact that Borna remained faithful to the Franks indicates that Frankish influences had begun to penetrate into Dalmatian Croatia, as is shown by the spread of the cult of certain Frankish saints among the Croats.[82] These influences are especially traceable in the western part of Dalmatia.

On the other hand, the princes Mislav (about 835–845) and

Trpimir (845–864) entertained cordial relations with archbishops Justin and Peter I of Spalato. Trpimir, when introducing the Benedictines into his realm and building the first monastery in Croatia, addressed himself not to Aquileia or to other Frankish religious centers, but to Peter, the archbishop of Split, with the request that he supply him with the necessary silver for the making of sacred vases. Giving thanks for this service, Trpimir not only confirmed the donations made to the archbishop by his father Mislav, but considerably increased them.[83]

In his deed confirming the donations, Trpimir quotes a passage from a letter addressed to him by the archbishop asking for the confirmation of the donations. In this Peter I calls his see a metropolis over lands as far as the river Danube, almost over the whole Croat kingdom.[84] These words are often regarded as an interpolation from the tenth century when Spalato was seeking the recognition of its supremacy over the whole of Croatia.[85] From what we have seen, these words may be perfectly genuine. Spalato was the metropolis of Croatia, and the two rulers treated the archbishop as their metropolitan. This explains also why they did not think it necessary to have new dioceses erected in their realm. The bishops of the coastal cities were their hierarchs.

The main objection to this interpretation is the erection of a Croat bishopric in Nin (Nona). Its creation is often regarded as a result of the efforts of Frankish missionaries among the Croats. It is said to have been founded from Aquileia and to have been subject to the patriarchate. The problems connected with this foundation therefore need to be re-examined.

The erection of a bishopric in Nin was preceded by the construction of the Church of the Holy Cross, which was built by the Župan Godeslav between 780 and 800. However, even the construction of this first known Croatian sanctuary seems to be linked not with Aquileia but with Zara. M. M. Vasić, in comparing the architecture of this church with that of St. Vid (Vitus) at Zara, stated that the architecture of the church in Nin followed the pattern of that in Zara (now destroyed), which was older than that of Nin.[86]

He found a similarity between the pattern of the church in Zara and that of St. Catherine in Pulj (Pola), which dated from the sixth century.[87] This again shows the intimate connection of the Byzantine coastal cities with Istria.

The date of the foundation of the bishopric of Nin has not yet been clearly established. The document, by which in 892 the Croat prince Mutimir confirmed Peter II, archbishop of Split, in the possession of the Church of St. George in Putalj, is claimed by F. Šišić [88] to provide proof that the bishopric of Nin existed before 852. In this document Mutimir spoke of the dispute between Aldefred, bishop of Nin, and Peter II of Split, and the manner in which the quarrel is described [89] seems to suggest, according to Šišić, that the church in Putalj, which had belonged to the bishopric of Nin before 852, was given by Trpimir to Peter I of Split, but that after the death of Peter I about 860 it was again claimed by Nin.

This interpretation, although suggestive, can be questioned. It is not clear from Trpimir's description whether Nin had reclaimed possession of the church after Peter I's death, or whether the church had been in the possession of the bishopric of Nin before it had been donated to Split by Trpimir in 852. Although the words with which Aldefred defended his rights, suggest that at the time of the complaint he was in possession of the disputed church and its property, the bishopric of Nin could have come into possession of it upon the death of Peter I, or on another occasion.

Such an occasion occurred in 887, when Theodosius, bishop of Nin, was elected archbishop of Split. During his episcopacy, the properties of both dioceses were in his possession until his death. His successor in Nin, Aldefred, may have taken possession of the church, pretending that Trpimir's donation was meant only for the lifetime of Peter I.[90] This supposition explains more clearly why the dispute started in 892 and not earlier, for thirty-two years had passed since the death of Peter I. We conclude therefore that this document can hardly be used as proof that the bishopric of Nin already existed before 852.

Only one official document is extant to indicate the existence of this bishopric—the fragment of a letter from Nicholas I to the clergy and people of Nin.[91] In it, the pope defends his rights to erect bishoprics. To stress this, he points out that not even basilicas can be consecrated without papal authorization.

It should be noted that the letter is addressed not to the bishop of the city, but to its clergy and people. This suggests that when the letter was sent Nin had no bishop, which could mean that the pope was announcing to the clergy and people of Nin his intention of erecting a bishopric in their city. The reason why the pope stressed his exclusive right to found a bishopric is also easily understandable. In Nicholas' time, the influence of the Frankish clergy in Croatia must have been considerable, and Aquileia may already have considered the possibility of creating a bishopric in Croatia, to be subject to itself. The patriarch of Aquileia may have thought that, because of the work of his missionaries in that area, he had a right to harvest the results. Therefore, the pope thought it necessary to stress that it was his exclusive privilege to erect new bishoprics.

Could Pope Nicholas have conceived this idea at that time? The most favorable moment was the year 860. The letter [92] sent in September of that year to Emperor Michael III, in which he expressed his suspicions concerning the legitimacy of Photius' elevation to the patriarchal throne, indicates that the pope was very much concerned about regaining jurisdiction over the whole of Illyricum, which the papacy had lost in 732. He requested Michael to restore to him his right, and enumerated all those provinces which had been detached from the Roman patriarchate. The struggle over Illyricum started with this request.

We must not forget that Dalmatia was always under Roman jurisdiction. The pope could not accept the loss of a part of it to a see under Frankish influence. In order to prevent the danger, he founded the bishopric of Nin and subordinated it directly to Rome. The foundation of this bishopric, most probably in 860, marked the first success of the papacy over the expansion of the jurisdiction of Frankish hierarchy in territories which had been directly subject to Rome. It was a warning indicating that Rome would extend its claims to other lands which had been part of the former Illyricum. [93]

The fact that the first Croatian bishopric was erected not near Split but in the neighborhood of Zara, nearer to the Frankish border, cannot be invoked as proof that Frankish missionaries were mainly responsible for the preaching of the Gospel to the Croats. [94] It is true that Split claimed the inheritance of Salona and the ecclesiastical leadership of the coastal cities and of Croatia, but the political leadership under Byzantine supremacy belonged to Zara, [95] and Nin [96] was, at the beginning of the ninth century, the residence of Prince Višeslav, considered to be the first known Christian Croat prince.

The fact that Nicholas subordinated the new bishopric not to Spalato but directly to Rome can be explained by the apprehensions harbored by the pope at that time, concerning his relations with Byzantium. The bishoprics of the coastal cities, although under Roman jurisdiction, were under Byzantine supremacy. By subordinating the new bishopric directly to Rome, Nicholas issued a warning not only to the Franks but also to Spalato, in case ecclesiastical relations between Rome and Byzantium should deteriorate with the opening of the antiphotian offensive. Spalato may have resented this, and if so, it would explain why, in 945, when the reorganization of the Croatian bishoprics was under way during the famous Spalatan synod, the archbishop requested and obtained the suppression of the first national Croatian bishopric in Nin.

Nicholas was correct in foreseeing a danger to papal interests from the complicated political affairs of Dalmatian Croatia by supporting the claims of Zdeslav, son of Trpimir, who, deprived of the succession by Domagoj, had found refuge in Constantinople. The bishops of the coastal cities seem not only to have supported Zdeslav, but also to have recognized the authority of the patriarch of Constantinople. The situation was saved for Rome by Theodosius, the bishop-elect of Nin, and by the Croat aristocracy, which did not like the supremacy of a foreign power. The revolt, led by Branimir, was successful and Zdeslav was killed (879).

Theodosius and Branimir informed the pope, and John VIII expressed his relief and thanks in his letters. He addressed a long missive also to the Church of Spalato whose see appears to have been vacant in 879, and to the Dalmatian bishops, exhorting them to return to the Roman obedience following the example of their predecessors. He exhorted the clergy and people of Spalato to elect an archbishop who would come to Rome where he would obtain the pallium "more pristino," which implied according to the custom of his predecessors.

The pope's exhortation seems to have had its effect, the more so as Byzantine political intervention had met with a reverse. The elected archbishop of Spalato might have been Marinus who, however, seems to have asked Walpertus of Aquileia to consecrate him. But he was succeeded by Theodosius of Nin, who held both dioceses initially but, after the protest of Stephen V, retained the archbishopric of Spalato and obtained the pallium from Rome.[97]

❧ ❧ ❧

According to information given us by Constantine Porphyrogenitus, Heraclius made the first attempt to Christianize the Serbs. After enumerating the parts of modern Serbia occupied by five Slavic tribes, he says,[98] "and since these countries had been made desolate by the Avars (for they had expelled from those parts the Romans who now live in Dalmatia and Dyrrhachium), therefore the Emperor settled these same Serbs in these countries, and they were subject to the Emperor of the Romans; and the Emperor brought elders from Rome and baptized them and taught them fairly to perform the works of piety and expounded to them the faith of the Christians."

Constantine regards all Slavic tribes in ancient Praevalis and Epirus—the Zachlumians, Tribunians, Diocletians, Narentans— as Serbs. This is not exact. Even these tribes were liberated from the Avars by the Croats who lived among them. Only later, thanks to the expansion of the Serbs, did they recognize their supremacy and come to be called Serbians.[99]

We have no reason to doubt Heraclius' initiative in the Christianization of these Slavic tribes and of the Serbians. Their country was a part of Western Illyricum and was under Roman jurisdiction. Unfortunately, we have almost no information as to the progress of this work. The nearest center whence Christianity could have begun to spread to the Slavic tribes was Ragusa, founded by the Christian refugees from the Roman city of Epidaurum, destroyed by the Avars during the seventh century. It is most probable that the episcopal see was transferred from Epidaurum to Ragusa when the refugees began to reorganize their life. Because Epidaurum seems to have depended on Salona, even the re-established episcopal see of Ragusa depended on Spalato—heir of Salona. There exists a false Bull, attributed to Pope Zacharias (741–752),[100] which pretends that the pope had promoted Andrew, bishop of Epidaurum, to metropolitan rank with jurisdiction over the kingdoms of Zachlumlja, Serbia, and

Travunje, with bishoprics in Cattaro (Kotor) Risan, Budva, Bar, Ulcinj, Skadar, Drivasto, and Pulati. The forgery was made in the eleventh century and was invoked by the bishops of Ragusa from the end of the twelfth century to support their claim to metropolitan status.

The only documents which confirm the existence of a bishopric at Ragusa (Dubrovnik) are the *Acts* of the Spalatan synods of 925 and 928.[101] At that time Ragusa was subject to the archbishops of Spalato. It can be supposed, however, that an operation was enacted here similar to that accomplished in Spalato, on the initiative of Heraclius, about the year 640. The bishopric of Epidaurum was transferred to Ragusa, whence the first knowledge of Christianity could have penetrated to the Slavs of ancient Praevalis.

All this shows us that the first attempts to Christianize the Slavs in Dalmatia and in Western Illyricum were made by the Byzantines in the seventh century in close collaboration with Rome. The first missionaries came from the Latin cities of Byzantine Dalmatia. There was yet another power, with Latin traditions but under Byzantine supremacy, which was interested in strengthening Christianity in Dalmatia and in sending missionaries to the Slavs—namely, Venice. One of the Slavic tribes—the Narentans, who settled on the river Neretva and along the coast—were dangerous pirates, interfering in the commerce of Venice with Southern Italy. Before 830, the Venetians sent a maritime expedition against them with some success, for, as we learn from John the Deacon, and from the *Chronicle* of Dandolus,[102] the Narentans sent an envoy to Doge John asking for peace. At the exhortation of the Doge the pagan envoy accepted baptism. This was the first success of Venetian missionaries amongst the Slavs. However, it must have been very limited, because both sources complain that in 834–835 the Narentans captured a Venetian commercial delegation returning from Benevento.

So it happened that Dalmatia and the western part of Illyricum were pacified to a great extent and thus, even when the territory of the Croats could not be kept under Byzantine supremacy, no immediate danger threatened Byzantium from that side. But there still remained the problem of those Slavs who had invaded the eastern part of Illyricum—Epirus Nova, Epirus Vetus, Macedonia, Thessaly, Hellas, the Peloponnesus, Moesia, Dacia, and even Thrace. The Byzantines called the regions occupied by them simply Sclavinia. Various emperors tried in vain to stop, or push back, this wave. Justinian II (685–695) was partially successful in 688. He took thirty thousand prisoners on his expedition and moved them to Asia Minor. The transplantation of these Slavs permitted the Byzantines to bring the Slavs of Macedonia into a more dependent position. In order to strengthen his position in Central Greece, Justinian II raised Hellas to *thema* with a *strategos*, a military and civil governor. Leontius, *strategos* of Hellas, is mentioned in 695. This was the second *thema* to have been created in Europe aside from that of Thrace, which was elevated most probably by Constantine IV (668–685) against the Bulgarian and Slavic menace.[103]

The invasions created great havoc in Byzantine ecclesiastical organization even in these provinces. In Epirus Nova only Dyrrhachium survived the onslaught and her bishopric never seems to have been vacant. Nicephorus, bishop of Dyrrhachium, was present at the Seventh Oecumenical Council (787).[104] He is the only bishop from the end of the eighth century whose name is known to us. His immediate successor is not recorded, but we learn of a bishop of Dyrrhachium, who must have lived during the first half of the ninth century, from a letter of St. Theodore of Studios.[105] Theodore calls him Anthony, and in another letter he speaks of an archbishop of Dyrrhachium, but does not name him.[106] Most probably he has the same person in mind. In the *Life* of St. Theodora of Thessalonica we also find mentioned an archbishop of Dyrrhachium called Anthony,[107] who is said to be Theodora's brother. According to the *Life*, he must have governed the Church of Dyrrhachium up to the time that Leo V, the Armenian, reopened the iconoclastic controversy (815). Anthony was ordered to appear before the emperor and to profess iconoclasm, but he defended the cult of images in a long discourse. The emperor exiled him, but, unfortunately, the author of the *Life* does not tell us where. The ban was lifted by Michael II (820–829), but Anthony was ordered to live privately. He may have returned to Dyrrhachium, but we are not told when, nor for how long. After the victory of the iconodoules, he was elected metropolitan of Thessalonica but died soon after, on November 2, 843.

It is most probable that Theodore's Anthony is identical with the brother of St. Theodora. They both lived in the same period and were opponents of iconoclasm. It is strange that both documents refer to an archbishop in Dyrrhachium and not a metropolitan. Dyrrhachium had been a metropolis with seven suffragan bishops, all of whom disappeared, with the possible exception of Aulindos, during the Avar and Slavic invasions into Epirus. However, this does not mean that the metropolitan of Dyrrhachium, left alone in Epirus, became archbishop, without suffragans, under the direct jurisdiction of the patriarch. It would seem rather that the metropolitans were sometimes called archbishops. In the *Acts* of the Seventh Oecumenical Council, for example, even metropolitans are called quite simply bishops. The existence of a metropolitan in Dyrrhachium at the beginning of the ninth century shows us that ecclesiastical life in the provinces was becoming normal. This normalization was effected also in the political organization. St. Theodore, in one of his letters, speaks of a *chartularius* in Dyrrhachium whose name was Thomas.[108] The office of *chartularius* was held by one of the most prominent members on the staff of a *strategos*.[109] The *chartularius* of a *thema*, with the title of *hypatos*, or consular order of the Senate, was in charge of the military rolls, and was responsible for the payment of officers and men, and, as such, was responsible also to the central government. The reference to such an officer in Dyrrhachium by Theodore shows that Epirus was reorganized into a *thema* with a *strategos* in Dyrrhachium. Since Theodore died in 826, this reorganization must have been effected before that date, and his letter seems to have been written during the reign of Michael II (820–829) after the iconoclastic persecution subsided. Theodore's other letter,[110] in which he speaks of the monk Dionysius who, although absolved by the archbishop of Dyrrhachium from his lapse into the iconoclastic heresy, asked for absolution from Theodore, should also be dated in the reign of Michael, probably from 821, when the exiled bishop Anthony may have returned to his see.

However, this does not mean that the *thema* of Dyrrhachium was founded by Michael. Nicephorus, bishop of the city, spoke of himself, in the *Acts* of the Seventh Oecumenical Council, as bishop of the province of Dyrrhachium of the eparchy of Illyricum.[111] This could mean that he still considered himself the head of the ecclesiastical province of Epirus which had been destroyed, but since he uses the word *"chora"* of Dyrrhachium, part of the Illyrian eparchy, this may indicate that in 787 Dyrrhachium and

its surrounding territory were regarded as an autonomous part of
Illyricum, governed probably by an archon. Archontes of Dyrrhachium are mentioned in the *Tacticon of Uspenskij*.[112] This first
attempt at the reorganization of the province can be attributed
to the Empress Irene (780–802) who in 783 sent the logothete
Stauracius to fight against the Slavs in Hellas.[113] His victory was
of great importance in the pacification of the Slavs and in the
reorganization of the European provinces of the Empire. It made
possible the foundation of the Macedonian *thema* (between 789
and 802), and it seems that even the *thema* of the Peloponnesus
was created after this success, the see of the *strategos* being in
Corinth.[114]

Having this in mind, it is unlikely that Irene and Stauracius
would overlook the need to strengthen the position of the Empire
in the Epirus region where Dyrrhachium was the most important
outpost. It is thus quite possible that the *archontia* of Dyrrhachium was founded at the same time as the *themata* of Macedonia
and of the Peloponnesus. We could, of course, attribute this first
attempt at stabilizing the situation in Epirus to Constantine IV
(668–685) who is said to have introduced or, at least, strengthened the system of *themata* in Asia Minor and in Thrace, leaving
the rest of the European provinces under the prefecture of Illyricum.[115] Anyhow, in 787, judging from the *Acts* of the Seventh
Oecumenical Council, Dyrrhachium was still a part of the eparchy
of Illyricum, although probably governed by an *archon*.

It is not easy to determine when Dyrrhachium and its territory
was promoted to a *thema* with a *strategos*.[116] If it did not take
place in the last years of the reign of Irene, we might attribute its
foundation to the Emperor Nicephorus (802–811), or to Leo V
(813–820). Nicephorus can also be considered the founder of the
thema of Cephalonia. Its existence at the end of the eighth century does not seem warranted,[117] but we know that in 809 the
strategos of Cephalonia, Paul, commanded the Byzantine naval
operations against Pepin in Venice.[118] The *thema* must thus have
existed before this date. Not only the danger from the Arabs, but
also the expansion of the Franks in Istria and in the Adriatic had
forced the Byzantines to build a solid naval base in the Adriatic.
This could only be Cephalonia.

One is tempted to date the establishment of the *thema* of
Dyrrhachium, not during the reign of Leo V, but rather at the

same time as that of Cephalonia. Dyrrhachium was an important outpost, not only against Slavic expansion, but also against Arab and Frankish attempts to gain a foothold in Dalmatia. It is thus quite probable that the *archontia* of Dyrrhachium was elevated to a *thema* by Nicephorus at the beginning of the ninth century. The reorganization of the *thema* of Dyrrhachium was very important, not only in strengthening the Byzantine rule over ancient Praevalis and Epirus Nova with its important coastal region, but also for the re-Christianization of the coastal region and of both Slavs and Illyrians who occupied most of this territory.

The former province of Praevalis, now a part of Montenegro, was invaded by the Avars and Slavs at the end of the sixth and the beginning of the seventh centuries. Its ecclesiastical organization, of course, perished with the destruction of its main cities— Scodra, Dioclea, and Elissus (Lissus). The last mention of a bishop of Elissus, John, is from 592 and of a metropolitan in Scodra from 602.[119] The Christian population was scattered, but many had found refuge in the fortress and city of Decatera (Kotor), as is testified by Constantine Porphyrogenitus in his *De administrando imperio*,[120] and in other city fortresses on the coast which had survived the first onslaught. This may have been the case with the ancient city of Licinium (Ulcinj), which seems to have reorganized its municipal life in the eighth century. Others may have followed the last bishop of Lissus, who took refuge in Italy and was transferred by Gregory the Great to an Italian bishopric.

These remnants of the Roman population seem to have found a new chance for survival during the reign of Heraclius (610–641), who had settled the Serbs in the devastated regions. Some kind of arrangement concerning the newcomers and the natives must have been made by the emperor, because Porphyrogenitus attributes to him the Christianization of the new inhabitants by priests called from Rome. This may also mean that the emperor helped the remaining Latin Christians to reorganize their religious life. One may presume that the refugees started to return and to build new cities in their former home. It appears that in this way the city of Antibari (Bar), opposite the Italian city of Bari, was founded, probably by the refugees from Doclea (Dioclea). Old Olcinium (Licinium, Italian Dulcigno, Slavic Ulcinj), which was situated between Antibari and the river Bojana, was also revived,

along with Elissus (Lissus, Alessio, Ljes) on the Drin, near Scodra
(Skadar). Budua (Budva), between Kotor and Ulcinj, must also
have been resurrected from ruins in the seventh century. Many
of its native inhabitants might have survived the invasion, because
the old city was built on an island which was not connected to the
mainland until years later. Even the Roman Risinium (Risan)
seems to have found new inhabitants.

As for Budua and Risan, the two cities must have been rehabilitated, at least during the last half of the eighth century,
because the Arabs, when attacking the littoral of ancient Praevalis in 840, thought it worthwhile to pillage and destroy them.
Heraclius must also have made a change in the political organization of the former Praevalis with its remnant of Christian
population. It became a part of Byzantine Dalmatia. Only much
later did Dyrrhachium start claiming part of it. The Slavic tribes
continued to be ruled by their own Župans who were nominally
under Byzantine suzerainty.

We do not know if Heraclius had taken any measures for the
reorganization of the ecclesiastical order in the former province.
The only bishopric which may have survived the catastrophe was
that of Cataro (Kotor). However, its existence from the sixth
century is not well documented. The only evidence is the signature of bishop Victor who assisted at the synod of Salona in 530.
He called himself bishop *ecclesiae Martaritanae*. As such a city is
unknown in the provinces under the jurisdiction of Salona, one
may be entitled to read Cateritanae or Decateritanae which means
Catara (Kotor).[121] It is probable that, if there was a bishopric in
Catara before the invasion, it may have survived the onslaught
with the city. Heraclius can be supposed to have stabilized its
existence, or if there was no bishopric, to have established it. It is
also quite possible that Heraclius had transferred the bishopric
of Doclea (Dioclea) to Antibari (Bar), where the refugees from
the destroyed city seem to have gathered. This could explain why
later (see below, p. 256) the bishops of Antibari, claiming a
metropolitan status, pretended to be successors of the bishops
of Dioclea. They were wrongly giving to Dioclea a metropolitan
status, since Scodra and not Dioclea had been a metropolis in
Praevalis.

It could also be presumed that the Italian hierarchy, especially
the bishops of Bari, the capital of Byzantine Apulia, were espe-

cially interested in the re-Christianization of the coastal regions on the other side of the Adria. It is probably from this region that Heraclius obtained the Roman priests for the Christianization of the Serbs as it is mentioned by Porphyrogenitus. Thanks to this help coming from Byzantine Apulia, and perhaps also to new immigrants from that province and the return of refugees, the remnants of the Latin population in former Praevalis were able to reorganize their municipal life during the eighth century.

Their vital interest was to live in peace with the Župans of the Slavic tribes in their neighborhood. This may have been facilitated by the fact that the newcomers were, at least nominally, subjects of Byzantium. The second stage of their reorganization were attempts at the Christianization of the Slavs. In reality the Christianization of the Serbian tribes did start from the remnants of the Latin population of these cities.

Thanks to recent archaeological discoveries made by Serbian specialists in modern Montenegro, at least some traces of this activity can be detected in the ruins of a number of churches dating from the beginning of the ninth century. Latin inscriptions found there testify to the Latin character of their founders. Let us enumerate the most important discoveries shedding more light on these first attempts.[122]

In 809, during the episcopacy of John in Kotor, a wealthy citizen named Andreaci built a church of St. Tryphun which became a cathedral church. Andreaci also built a sepulchral chapel of St. Mary for himself. The church of St. Peter in Bijela, between Risan (Risinium) and Dračevica, also dates from the beginning of the ninth century (between 797 and 809). Some reliefs and a Latin inscription mentioning a bishop—probably John—are preserved. Pre-Romanesque reliefs were also found near the Gothic Church of St. Andrew near Zelenica. It seems to indicate that an ecclesiastical building had existed there, probably in the ninth century. In the former župa of Ston the pre-Romanesque church of St. Michael also testifies to the missionary activity of the Latins which must have continued during the reign of the Nemanjids. The constructions of the churches of St. Jurij in Janina on Peljašac and of St. Ivan in Lopud must be dated to the beginning of the ninth century. This seems confirmed by remnants of reliefs and of a Latin inscription by the founder. A most interesting example of ecclesiastical architecture is revealed by the foundations of a church discovered in Ošlje dating from the ninth century. It was a centralized structure in the form of eight half-circular apses. In Dioclea the Church of Our Lady should also be dated in the beginning of the ninth century. It was constructed on the ruins of an early Christian basilica. The same can be said of the Church of St. Peter in Bijela. The Church of St. Stephen in Ragusa, built about 815, also replaced a destroyed early Christian basilica.

In ancient Licinium (Olcinium, Ulcinj) the foundations of a small church with an apse were excavated. The Latin inscriptions on the ciborium indicate that the church was built between 813 and 820. Northwest of Bar (Antibari) in the ruins of the Benedictine Abbey St. Mary of Ratac, which had flourished during the early Middle Ages, two reliefs have been found which should be dated to the beginning of the ninth century. This does not mean that a Benedictine abbey had existed there at such an early period, but the find presupposes the existence of an ecclesiastical structure from that time.

A Latin inscription found on the ruins of the Church of Our Lady in Budua testifies that this church was constructed in 840. Later the Benedictines built around this church their Abbey, called Sancta Maria de Punta. The Church of St. Stephen in Vranoviči probably should also be dated in the beginning of the ninth century. Near Tival was a Church of SS. Sergius, Nicholas, and Demetrius, founded by the deacon Alberinus, son of Bergolinus. According to the Latin inscription, the foundation should be dated in the second half of the ninth century. The cruciform Church of St. Thomas in Prčanj probably was also constructed in the ninth century.

As for the founders of these churches, most of them were built by wealthy citizens of the Latin cities. Bishop John of Cattaro seems to have been particularly active in the Christianization of the Serbs. He is probably the founder of the church in Bijala. The founder of the church in Vranoviči calls himself Churog and his wife Dana. His family name seems to be Turkic or rather Avar. If it is so, we have here an evidence that some of the Avars had advanced as far as the Latin littoral and been absorbed by the native populations. If the name of his wife Dana should be regarded as Slavic, we can see in this case an indication that Slavic elements were penetrating into the Latin cities already at that early period. There is no trace in these foundations of the Ger-

manic practice of proprietary churches, as we have also stated
concerning the early Croat Christian life.

Although remaining Latin and under the ecclesiastical supremacy of Rome, the citizens were loyal to Byzantium. This is confirmed by the construction dates of two of the churches. The
founder of the Church of St. Tryphun in Cattaro mentions the
name of the Emperor Nicephorus I (802–811), and the ciborium
of the church in Ulcinj bears the date *"Sub temporibus domini
nostri PIS PERPETUO AGUSTI DN LEO ET DN CONSTAN..."*
This could mean only the reign of Leo V and of his son Constantine (813–820).

Also, the names of the founders and of the saints venerated in
the Latin cities present a mixture of Latin and Greek hagiology:
John, Thomas, Tryphun, Sergius, Nicholas, Demetrius, Stephen,
George, Michael, Spirido (Greek Spiridon), and Guzma (Slavic
form of Latin Cosma, but a female name). The locality of Sus-
tiepan near Herzeg-Novog reveals the same Slavization of the
name *Sanctus* as we have noticed in Croatian Dalmatia.

Besides the Latin coastal cities, Dyrrhachium was also active in
the Christianization of the Slavs residing in the territory of its
thema. The first results of the Greek missionaries are revealed by
the *Notitia* of bishoprics, compiled under Leo the Wise (886–
912).[123] Nearest to the Latin coastal cities was the bishopric of
Lissus (Ljes) which had disappeared at the end of the sixth century. The bishopric was restored in the ninth century and,
although it had been under the jurisdiction of Rome before the
city's destruction, it was now subject to its new founder, the metropolitan of Dyrrhachium. The same *Notitia* enumerates three
more bishoprics revived during the ninth century by Dyrrhachium,
that of Kroja, of Stephaniakia, and that of Chunabia. The latter
bishopric is certainly a new foundation in a region of the *thema*
occupied predominantly by Slavs.

The metropolitans of Dyrrhachium continued their missionary
activity during the tenth century. Moreover, they tried to extend
their jurisdiction also over the bishoprics of the Latin cities. A
Notitia dating from the eleventh century enumerates, besides the
four bishoprics indicated in the *Notitia* of Leo the Wise, the following Latin bishoprics: Dioclea, Scutari (Skadar), Drivasto,
Pulati, and Antibari. In addition to these sees, Dyrrhachium
counted six more: Glavinitsa (or Acrokeraunia), Auloneia (Va-

lona), Lychnidos (probably Olcinium, Dulcigno), Tsernikios (perhaps in the region of Čerminika, near El-basan), Pulcheri-opolis (perhaps Belgrad, modern Berat), and Graditzios. Gla-vinitsa, Tsernikios, and Graditzios recall Slavic names and may be regarded as new foundations in regions inhabited by a Slavic population.[124] The *Notitia* reveals that great changes had been made in the re-Christianization of the *thema* of Dyrrhachium and in the coastal regions since the reign of Leo the Wise. The *Notitia* dating from his reign, as we have seen, counted only four bishop-rics under Dyrrhachium.

It is difficult to say when these new sees were created.[125] We can attribute this lively activity of re-Christianization to the initia-tive of the Emperor Basil I. Constantine Porphyrogenitus gives us interesting information on how this happened.[126] He says that the Roman Empire "through the sloth and inexperience of those who then governed it and especially in the time of Michael from Amorion, the Lisper (820–829), had declined to the verge of total extinction, the inhabitants of the cities of Dalmatia became inde-pendent, subject neither to the Emperor or the Romans nor to anybody else, the natives of those parts, the Croats and Serbs and Zachlumites, Terbunites and Kanalites and Diocletians and the Pagani, shook off the reins of the empire of the Romans and became self-governing and independent, subject to none." Con-stantine here enumerates the Slavic tribes which inhabited South Dalmatia, former Praevalis, and Epirus Nova. They were gov-erned, "not by princes but by Župans"; moreover, the majority of these Slavs were not even baptized, and remained unbaptized for a long time. "But in the time of Basil, the Christ-loving Emperor, they sent diplomatic agents, beseeching him that those of them who were unbaptized might receive baptism and that they might be, as they had originally been, subject to the empire of the Romans; and that glorious Emperor, of blessed memory, gave ear to them and sent out an imperial agent and priests with him and baptized all of them that were unbaptized of the aforesaid nations, and after baptizing them he then appointed for them princes whom they themselves approved and chose, from the family which they themselves loved and favored." Then Constan-tine reports that even the pagan Narentans who had remained unbaptized, "sent to the same glorious Emperor and begged that they too might be baptized, and he sent and baptized them."

Constantine oversimplifies the history of the conversion and subjection of the Slavs of this part of Eastern Illyricum, presenting it as effected by the initiative of the Slavs themselves. The actual motivation is not so simple. It was rather the attack by the Arabs on Dalmatia and on the *thema* of Dyrrhachium in 866 which brought about these events. In the same chapter Constantine describes how the Arabs from Africa appeared in the Adriatic with thirty-six ships, taking the cities of Budva and Rossa. The fortress of Decatero (Kotor) seems to have been left untouched, but the lower city was taken. The Arabs then blockaded Ragusa for fifteen months; the citizens asked for help, and Basil sent a fleet of one hundred ships to the Adriatic Sea. The appearance of such an imposing armada not only forced the Arabs to abandon their blockade of Ragusa but persuaded the Slavic Župans to seek friendship with the emperor.

Constantine admits that although the majority of the Slavs were unbaptized, there were a few who had been converted previously. These may have been the remnants of the first efforts of Christianization made by Heraclius, and of further attempts made by the Latin coastal cities in the eighth century and in the first half of the ninth century. Of course, this activity increased after the naval demonstration and the initiative taken by Basil to bring the Slavic tribes closer to the Empire and to the Church.

However, the Latin missionaries must have penetrated even earlier into the land which was to be Serbia. The first Christian names in the dynasty of the Višeslavić ruling over Raška, the cradle of the Serbians, are Stephen, son of Mutimir, and Peter, son of Gojnik. Both names were very familiar in the coastal cities and the župas of ancient Praevalis. Peter is said by Porphyrogenitus to have ruled between 892 and 897. He may have been baptized about 874. Stephen with his brother Bran defeated Vladimir, the son of the Bulgarian Khagan Boris in 860.[127] Stephen may have been born and baptized between 830 and 840. These are the years when the missionary activity of the Latin citizens had started to flourish. It is thus quite possible that their activity had reached even the ruling family of Raška. There are some other indications showing that the central region of Serbia started to be Christianized about the end of the first half of the ninth century. Already Mutimir who, with his brothers Strojmir and Gojnik, had succeeded Vlastimir (about 830–860) appears to have been Christian.[128] This seems to be confirmed by a letter sent to Mutimir by Pope John VIII in 873.[129] The pope exhorted him to join with his people the metropolis of Pannonia, as a new metropolitan (Methodius; see below, p. 150) had been ordained by the pope. The letter is interesting, as it reveals the policy of the papacy concerning ancient Illyricum and the religious situation in the lands forming the cradle of the Serbians, later called Raška. Thus, exhorting the prince to join the diocese of Pannonia as his predecessors had done, the pope reveals a poor knowledge of the situation in this part of the ancient Illyricum. He regards Mutimir and his people as ancient inhabitants of these parts, ignoring the fact that they were new arrivals who had replaced the autochthonous inhabitants. All of Mutimir's predecessors—Višeslav, Radoslav, Prosigoj, and Vlastimir—were pagans. When the pope castigates the prince, saying that his land is full of priests coming from everywhere, with no superiors, and conducting religious services contrary to the canon laws, he thus discloses the religious situation in Serbian lands. It was a missionary territory, not yet ecclesiastically organized. The words seem to reveal also the rivalry between the missionaries. This is quite understandable, because Greek priests from the metropolis of Dyrrhachium were as zealous in their Christianizing missions as the Latins, who came from the coastal cities and perhaps also from Dalmatian and Pannonian Croatia.

The presence of Latin missionaries in the cradle of the Serbian race is further revealed by the early religious architecture of this region. Some of the early churches of this region recall the architecture characteristic of the Latin coastal cities, thus revealing the influence of early missionaries who had begun their work in the ninth century and continued it in the tenth.[130] For example, the Church of St. Peter in Ras is circular in plan, with the cupola resting on pendentives, and with an apse. It is dated from the ninth to the beginning of the tenth century. Other churches of a very early period can also be found. In Stará Pavlica there is a cruciform church, and although that of Zaton is ruined, it nevertheless reveals a threefold plan.[131] This region has not yet been completely examined by Serbian archaeologists. It is possible that, in the future, the ruins of other churches will be found to document further the activities of the Latin missionaries from the coastal cities who—on orders from the Emperor Basil I and supported by the *strategos* of Dyrrhachium and the emperor's envoys —penetrated into the land which is now modern Serbia and Christianized the inhabitants. Constantine describes Basil's rule over the Župans in the years that followed as being a lenient one.

In the Roman province of Epirus Vetus, the ecclesiastical situation was normal during the reign of Pope Gregory the Great (590–604), as we learn from his letter to the bishops of Epirus.[132] The province had suffered heavily during the time of the invasions, but the see of Nicopolis survived. We find the name of Anastos of Nicopolis in the *Acts* of the Seventh Council, which are also signed by Philip of Corcyra.[133] These appear to be the only two sees which survived up to the ninth century without interruption. It is possible that the bishopric of Hadrianopolis of the ancient province also survived, since we find the name of Cosmas of that see in the *Acts* of the Council of 870.[134]

Nicopolis must have suffered further setbacks during the eighth century. It lost the metropolitan see, which was transferred to Naupactos, but we do not know when this occurred. The list of bishoprics composed during the reign of Leo the Wise (886–911) does not even mention a bishopric of Nicopolis among the eight suffragans of Naupactos.[135] Even the political reorganization of this part of Epirus seems to have been effected later than that of Dyrrhachium. This *thema* is listed in the *Tacticon of Uspenskij* (compiled between 845 and 856), while the *thema* of Nicopolis does not appear. However, this does not mean that the *thema* of Nicopolis could not have been established during the regency of Theodora. Her prime minister Theoctistus was very much preoccupied with the situation in Hellas and the Peloponnesus, where the Slavs continued to be restless. In 842 he sent a military expedition into the Peloponnesus and succeeded in subjugating the rebellious Slavic tribes. In order to strengthen the Byzantine position in these provinces, he transplanted those fierce warriors, the Mardaites, from Syria, to the *themata* of the Peloponnesus and Cephalonia and also into the territory of ancient Epirus Vetus. By this manoeuvre he hoped to prevent the danger of an Arab invasion and to keep the Slavic tribes subjugated.[136] It is, thus, quite possible that it was Theoctistus who had created the *thema* of Nicopolis. This could have happened after 853. If the *Tacticon* of Uspenskij was composed in this year, or some year after this date, this would explain why the *thema* of Nicopolis was not listed by its author. But the *thema* must have been established during the ninth century, for we have a seal belonging to the *strategos* Leo from this period, and one of Constantine's, also from the ninth or the beginning of the tenth century.[137] The ecclesiastical reorganization of this territory followed the political stabilization. The metropolis was established in Naupactos. Among its eight suffragans who are enumerated in the list of Leo the Wise, we find the see of Bounditsa. The name seems to reveal that it was founded for the new Slavic converts, perhaps by Michael III, or more probably by Basil I, as a result of the definite Christianization of the Slavs settled in the ancient province of Epirus.

The reorganization of Macedonia was ended by the foundation of the *thema* of Thessalonica. This seems to have been effected during the reign of Theophilus (829–842), since a *strategos* of Thessalonica is already mentioned in 836.[138] This reorganization was very important because the Slavs were settled in the very neighborhood of the city. The region of the river Strymon was a part of the *thema*, governed most probably by an *archon*. This area was almost completely inhabited by Slavic tribes and was elevated to a *thema* at the end of the ninth century.[139] The land between the mountains of Rhodope and the Aegean Sea was called Boleron [140] and seems to have enjoyed a kind of autonomous status under the *strategos* of Strymon. This meant the end of the political reorganization of the European provinces.

This reorganization was followed by a complete reorganization of the episcopal sees in these provinces. This was accomplished at the beginning of the ninth century, as is revealed in the list of bishoprics compiled by a certain Basil.[141] Only then could serious attempts at the Christianization of the Slavs in Greece be made. The superior culture which these Slavs had found in their new home attracted them, and facilitated their Christianization. Unfortunately, we have only two documents which give information as to the progress of this work among the Slavs, namely, the list of bishops who attended the union councils of 879–880, and the list of bishoprics compiled during the reign of Leo the Wise (886–912). Among the bishops who attended the Union Council was Agathon, bishop of Morava, Damaius, bishop of Ezero, and Peter of Drugubitia.[142] All three sees were established in Slavic territory. Moravia can only be a small city at the confluence of the rivers Morava and Danube, in modern Serbia.[143] The Ezerites

were a Slavic tribe, the majority of whom founded settlements in
the Peloponnesus. Some of them must have stayed in Hellas.
The Drugubites settled in Macedonia.

During the reign of Leo the Wise [144] there is listed among the
bishoprics of Hellas, under the metropolitan of Larissa, a bishopric
of the Ezerites. The same catalogue lists under Thessalonica two
Slavic dioceses, that of the Drugubites and that of the Serbs.
The latter bishopric must have been erected for the White Serbs,
who had preferred to stay there after they had reached the Byzantine borders under Heraclius. Constantine Porphyrogenitus says
that the majority of them were not satisfied with the territory
allotted to them by the emperor, and that they left to return home
(which is now Saxony), but were persuaded by the *strategos* of
Singidunum (Belgrade) to settle with the Croats, fighting against
the Avars.[145] It seems thus that some of them preferred to stay in
the territory given to them by the emperor.

The conversion of the Slavs in Macedonia must have started
after their defeat by Justinian II. The catalogue of Leo the Wise
lists two bishoprics with Slavic names under the metropolitan of
Philippi, that of Velikia and that of the Smoljans. Other bishoprics
listed in the same catalogue—that of the Ljutici, of Velikia, of
Ioannitsa, and of Dramitsa in Thrace (under Philippopolis)—also
had Slavic populations.

Among the bishoprics of Greece itself,[146] we do not find names
which can be regarded with certainty as Slavic, but the complete
reorganization of its ecclesiastical provinces indicates that the
Christianization of the Slavs settled there must have been completed by the ninth century.

In this respect, it seems that the Slavs who most resisted Christian influence were the Milingues and Ezerites in the Peloponn-
nesus. Only in the fourteenth century was a special bishopric for
the Ezerites founded. This can be explained by the fact that those
tribes had settled in the mountainous region of Taygetus.[147] The
Christianization of the Slavs transported by Justinian II to Asia
Minor seems to have been more rapid. A catalogue of bishoprics
dating from the seventh century lists among the sees of Bithynia
at least one whose name is Slavic, that of the Gordoserbs.[148]

Of course, the Christianization of the Slavs in Greek territory
meant also their assimilation and Hellenization. This process had
already begun in the seventh century. On several occasions the

Byzantines used Slavic troops in their armies, and the names of a few Slavic generals are known.[149] The most famous of these was Thomas, a Slav from Asia Minor,[150] who led the revolution against the iconoclastic Emperor Michael II (820–829). The Patriarch Nicetas of Constantinople (766–780) was also of Slavic origin, and the domestic staff of the Emperor Michael III included a certain Damian, of Slavic extraction.[151] This assimilation and Hellenization was a natural process. The Slavs in the purely Greek provinces did not form large, homogeneous groups, and they were unable to resist the attraction of a higher cultural environment. The situation was different in the lands of future Serbia, fully occupied by Slavic tribes. But, at least, after their conversion, these Slavs were won over to the Byzantine religious tradition and civilization. These events took place between 867 and 874.[152]

Byzantine influence would probably also have reached the Slavs between the Danube and the Black Sea, if their resistance had not been strengthened by the appearance of the Bulgars. The pressure of a new Asiatic invader, the Khazars, a Turkic tribe, had forced Asparuch, the son of Kuvrat, to move south, and about the year 679 he appeared with his horsemen on the Danube.[153] He was welcomed by the Slavs, who inhabited this region, and thus the foundations of a new Slavic state, Bulgaria, were laid. The Bulgars, not being numerous, were gradually Slavicized. Political disorders in Byzantium helped the successors of Asparuch to consolidate their new political structure to such an extent that not even Constantine V (741–775), despite eight successful campaigns, was able to destroy this menace.

From that time on, Bulgaria presented a difficult problem for the Byzantines. Reciprocal hostility made the penetration of Christianity into Bulgaria very difficult. Khagan Krum (c. 802–815) reorganized Bulgaria and became the most dangerous foe of Byzantium. Two emperors lost their thrones through disastrous expeditions against Bulgaria. Nicephorus (802–811) was killed on the battlefield, and his skull, mounted in silver, later served as a cup for the khagan at solemn banquets. The emperor's son Stauracius, severely wounded, escaped, but died soon after. The Emperor Michael I (811–813) was deposed after a calamitous battle. Krum extended his sway over more Byzantine territory, destroyed Serdica (the modern Sofia), and caused great havoc in Byzantine territory, devastating the land and destroying the cities. He died suddenly while facing the walls of Constantinople with his armies. Only when his successor Omortag (814–831) had concluded peace with Leo the Armenian did the situation become more propitious for the penetration of Byzantine influence into Bulgaria.[154]

The native Greek population had not completely disappeared after the Slavs took possession of the land. These groups formed the first Christian islands in the pagan sea. They were augmented by numerous war prisoners, whom Krum had brought from various areas after his victorious expeditions. There were many priests among them, even bishops, from the cities taken by the khagan. They worked not only among their compatriots, but also among the Slavic population. They must have been successful, because Omortag, seeing that Christianity was taking firmer root in his lands, began to persecute the Christians. He is said to have put to death four bishops and three hundred and seventy-seven prisoners. Their memory was celebrated yearly in Constantinople on January 22, and their martyrdom is vividly described in the Greek *Synaxarium*.[155]

This report is completed by the *Menologium* of Basil II [156] and in a Slavic prologue to the translation of the *Menologium*.[157] According to this information, the first persecutors of the Christians were the boyars Tsok and Ditzeng, who seem to have risen to power after the death of Krum, before his son Omortag was able to assert his succession. It was Ditzeng who ordered the mutilation of Bishop Manuel's arms. Tsok is said to have invited all Christian prisoners—"officers, priests, deacons, and laymen"— to abjure their faith. After their refusal to do so, he had some of them decapitated and others killed after prolonged torture. The chief victim of this persecution was the metropolitan of Adrianople, Manuel, who had already been maimed by the boyar Ditzeng. The Continuator of Theophanes [158] confirms that Manuel died as a martyr under Omortag.

This indicates that the most determined enemies of Christianity were the Bulgar boyars. The Slavic population was more responsive to Christian propaganda emanating from the original Christians who had survived invasion, and with whom the Slavic lower and middle classes were mingling.

The discovery of a short office in honor of the Bulgarian martyrs in the Vatican Greek manuscript 2008 throws more light on the persecution of the Christians by Omortag.[159] It was written by an hymnographer called Joseph. Two authors of this name lived in the ninth century, one called Joseph of Studios, who died in 832, and Joseph the Hymnographer, who flourished in the second half of the ninth century.[160] One is inclined to attribute this office to Joseph of Studios, because his monastery seems to have been particularly interested in the history of the Bulgarian martyrs. We shall see that St. Theodore of Studios spoke of this persecution in his *Little Catechism*. At any rate, the office was composed by an author of the ninth century who used a contemporary source for his hymn.

The hymnographer mentions all the names listed in the *Synaxarium*, with the exception of Sisinius. Instead of Marinus, he speaks of Martinus. This may be the same person. He pays special homage to a layman named Peter, to his wife Mary, and their children. About twenty-five other names listed by the hymnographer were currently used by the Byzantines of this period. The martyr Arabios was probably one of the Arabs in the army of Nicephoros mentioned by Theophanes.[161] Artabazos and Bardanes were members of the Armenian colony which is known to have existed in the region of Adrianopolis.[162] More interesting are four other names: Aspher and Cupergo recall strangely those of Aspar, Asparuch, Isperich, and Kuber, used by the proto-Bulgars.[163] This should indicate that the Christian missionaries had converted even some of the Bulgar boyars. Two other names, Lubomeros and Chotiameros, are evidently Slavic, i.e. Lubomir and Hotomir. This, again, is an indication that the Byzantine missionaries were successful among the Slavic population. The two martyrs mentioned by the hymnographer were most probably men of some standing, perhaps Župans of Slavic tribes under the Bulgars.[164]

The episode related by Theodore of Studios [165] must have taken place during the reign of Omortag. He describes how the Christians in Bulgaria were forced to break the Church's regulation on fasting and were made to eat meat in Lent. Fourteen souls refused to do so. One of them was killed by the khagan, and his wife and children sold into slavery. But even this example did not induce the rest to break the rule of fasting, and they were all executed.

In spite of their hostility to the Christian religion, the Khagans were unable to resist the attraction of the higher culture of their enemies. Krum was not particularly anti-Christian, and he appreciated the services rendered to the State by the Greek artisans among the prisoners and the remainder of the Christian population. Omortag also availed himself of their services to a large extent. Inscriptions recording his deeds were composed in Greek and inscribed in stone by the Greeks. He even acceptd the Byzantine title of "ruler (archon) established by God."[166] His palace in Pliska reveals a marked relationship to Slavic structures in Byzantium.[167]

Despite the fact that he was at peace with the Byzantines, Omortag looked unfavorably on the spread of Christianity among the Slavic population, for he had to reckon with the strongly anti-Christian attitude of the non-Slavic boyars. It was only natural that the prisoners and the Christian subjects should consider the Byzantine emperor as their liberator and religious leader. The khagan thus felt he had sufficient reason to doubt their loyalty. His persecution was dictated more by political than by religious motives.

Theophylactus, archibishop of Ochrid,[168] relates an interesting story which illustrates the missionary zeal of the Greek prisoners. One of them, Cinamon, who was particularly able, was given by Krum to his son Omortag. The latter became very much attached to him, but because Cinamon refused to renounce his faith, he was imprisoned by Omortag.

Omortag was survived by his sons, Enravotas, Svinitse, and Malamir. The Slavic names of the last two, although Enravotas seems to have had a Slavic name also, that of Vojna, make it clear that the Slavic element had penetrated into the khagan's court and his family. Omortag favored those Slavic nobles who were inclined to foster his autocratic tendencies, rather than the non-Slavic boyars. But, after his death, the boyars demonstrated their influence in state affairs. Neither Enravotas nor Svinitse was given the succession. The boyars, fearing that the elder sons of Omortag would continue their father's policy, chose the youngest son, Malamir (831–836), as khagan, hoping that they would more easily be able to control him. In fact, during Malamir's reign, one of them, Isboulos, seems to have exercised the greatest influence on state affairs.

It is possible that there was also another reason which influenced the boyars in their choice of the inexperienced youngest son. Enravotas and Svinitse may have been suspected of being less hostile to the Greeks and their religious beliefs than was their father. This happened to be true concerning Enravotas. Theophylactus says in his story that the latter asked his brother to release Cinamon from prison and to give him to him as a slave. Cinamon must have been a very able man and a zealous Christian. Enravotas not only became very attached to him, but Cinamon even succeeded in converting the prince to Christianity.

Malamir was alarmed when he learned of his brother's conversion. The pagan boyars saw it as a betrayal of the national cause. The conversion of a prince would certainly encourage the Christians in Bulgaria. In vain Malamir exhorted his brother to renounce the Christian faith, and finally he felt obliged to put him to death.[169]

✽ ✽ ✽

The mistrust of the Bulgarian rulers toward Christianity is quite understandable. Thus far they knew Christianity only in the Byzantine form and were constantly more or less hostile towards the emperor, who was regarded as the head of orthodox Christians. This hostile attitude could be tempered only if the Bulgars were in touch with other Christians free from any influence of the Byzantine emperor in religious matters. This became possible only when the Bulgarian rulers began to expand their realm toward the West, where they came into contact with the Christian Franks.

The defection of the Slavs of the Timok Valley and of the Abodrites to the north of the Danube, who looked to the Franks for help, and the affirmation of Frankish rule over the whole of Dalmatian and Pannonian Croatia after the defeat of Ljudevit, induced Omortag to negotiate with the Franks in order to limit the frontiers of their realms. The evasive answers given by Louis the Pious to the embassies of 824, 825, and 826[170] exasperated Omortag, and in 827 he invaded Pannonian Croatia, which was under Frankish sovereignty, and forced the Slavs to accept his authority.[171] Louis the German tried in vain to reverse the situation in 828. The war dragged on under Malamir (831–836), and was only concluded under Presjam (836–852) to the advantage of the Bulgars. The Peace of Paderborn (845)[172] left the region of Sirmium, and a part of Pannonian Croatia, in Bulgarian possession.

Malamir remained on good terms with the ranks until the end of his reign. About 839 the Bulgarian army, led by Presjam,[173] whom the Serbs called khagan, invaded the Serbian territory governed by Vlastimir under nominal Byzantine sovereignty, but had to withdraw without success.[174]

A successor of Presjam, Boris, son of Svinitse, renewed the treaty of 845 when he sent an embassy in 852 to Louis the German, who held a Reichstag in Mainz.[175] But according to the *Annales Bertiniani*,[176] he seems to have soon afterwards attacked the territory of Louis the German. The attack appears to have been supported unsuccessfully by some of the Slavs. This can only have affected Pannonian Croatia, then under Frankish sovereignty.

Prudentius, the author of the second part of the *Annales Bertiniani*, chronicled certain rumors, according to which Boris' attack against the territory under Louis the German's sovereignty was made at Frankish instigation. If this is true, the initiative could have come only from Charles the Bald, then king of Western Francia, which would indicate that Boris was on rather intimate terms with the Franks. The Slavs who supported Boris' attack cannot be the Moravians, as was thought by Zlatarski [177] and Bury,[178] for they were too well known to the annalist, and he would hardly have called them simply "Sclavi", as we read in his report.[179] He could only have had in mind a local Slavic tribe discontented with Frankish supremacy. Theophylactus of Ochrida [180] probably had this defeat in mind when writing that at the beginning of Boris' reign a Frankish cloud had covered the whole of Bulgaria.

Boris tried his luck also in Dalmatian Croatia, which he was able to reach through the territory of Sirmium, which formed part of his realm. The Croatian prince Trpimir (845–864) successfully defended his lands with the result that, as Constantine Porphyrogenitus stresses, the Croats were never subjugated by the Bulgarian forces. He can mean only Dalmatian Croatia, because Pannonian Croatia was for some time under Bulgarian supremacy during the reign of Omortag prior to the conclusion of the treaty of Paderborn, probably from 827 to 838.[181] Boris was also unsuccessful in his attempt to annex Serbia, probably in 860.

Prince Mutimir, with his brothers Strojmir and Gojnik, defeated the army of Boris, and even captured his son, Vladimir, together with twelve boyars.[182] This incident ended amicably, and from that time on Boris continued on good terms with Mutimir and the Serbs.

By concluding peace with the Serbs, Boris at least secured the boundary of his realm in the southwest. He extended his kingdom to the mountains of Albania and to the Pindus, including all the lands around Lake Ochrid and Lake Prespa. He was now free to pay more attention to events developing in the northeastern part of his vast territory.

II. Byzantium, the Russians, the Khazars, the Arabs, and Constantine's Early Career

Appearance of Russians under Constantinople's walls—The Khazars, the Jews, and Byzantium—Youth of Constantine and Methodius—Constantine's stay in the capital—Methodius, civil servant and monk—Constantine at the university, and his definition of philosophy—Constantine's disputation with the iconoclastic ex-patriarch, and the Arab mission—Constantine and the political upheaval in Byzantium—The brothers' stay in Cherson, and the relics of St. Clement—The Khazar mission—Constantine at the patriarchal academy.

Suddenly the Byzantines were faced with another Slavic problem, that of the Russians.[1] On June 18, 860 "this sudden hailstorm of barbarians burst forth," according to one of the homilies of Photius. Their hordes landed on the shores near the capital, destroying and plundering cities and villages and encircling Constantinople. It was the first invasion by the Russians, called Rhôs by the Byzantines. The attack was completely unexpected and was made in strength. Over two hundred small vessels appeared on the sea of Marmara, some of them landing on the islands. In his two homilies the Patriarch Photius left a vivid description of the devastating effect resulting from the apparition of unknown barbarians under the walls of the capital.[2]

"A nation dwelling somewhere far from our country, barbarous, nomadic, armed with arrogance, unwatched, unchallenged, leaderless, has so suddenly, in the twinkling of an eye, like a wave of the sea, poured over our frontiers, and as a wild boar has

49

devoured the inhabitants of the land like grass, or straw, or a crop . . . sparing nothing from man to beast . . . but boldly thrusting their sword through persons of every age and sex."

The danger was all the greater since the Emperor Michael III and his army were in Asia Minor on an expedition against the Arabs. The inhabitants, frightened by this sudden danger, invoked the protection of Our Lady whose garment—a most venerated relic—the Patriarch carried in procession along the walls of Constantinople. Fortunately, the invaders did not stay under the walls, but took to their vessels loaded with booty and returned whence they had come. They seem to have sailed into a violent storm which destroyed many of their small vessels.

Although there are still some scholars who think that the attack was made by Russians established near the Crimea at Tmutorakan, it seems certain that the attackers came from "far away," from their center at Kiev on the Dnieper. This also seems confirmed by the description given by Photius. The Byzantines still had some possessions in the Crimea centering on Cherson. If there had existed such a powerful Russian center near the Crimea, the Byzantines could have learned about it from their own people in Cherson and they would not have been so much surprised by the sudden attack by a foreign nation. An expedition sailing from Kiev down the Dnieper to the Black Sea and, following its shores to Constantinople would naturally escape the attention of the Chersonese and the Byzantines.

The attack against Constantinople was a last link in a chain of events taking place in Eastern Europe, between the Baltic and the Black Sea. Numerous Slavic tribes had preceded and followed the Goths along the Dnieper and Dniester rivers toward the frontiers of the Eastern Roman Empire on the lower Danube. They came into touch with the many nations which had established themselves in what is today southern Russia—the Scythians and the Sarmatians, both of Iranian stock, then the Goths, the Huns, the Avars, and finally the Khazars. The latter were a Turkic tribe which occupied the Caucasus region in the second half of the seventh century and founded a political structure which extended from the Sea of Azov to the Aral Sea with its capital at Itil, on the delta of the Volga. They replaced the Avars in South Russia and extended their domination over the Slavs settled in the Dnieper region. The Poljane, the most important of these

Slavic tribes, had already developed an important center at Kiev on the Middle Dnieper and were engaged in lively commercial transactions with Greek colonies which had survived on the shores of the Black Sea and the Sea of Azov and in the interior. The Khazars saw the importance of this Slavic center and of the commerce with the Crimean cities and the Near East, and occupied Kiev.

Soon, however, another enterprising nation, the Scandinavians, discovered the importance of commercial relations with the Arabic Near East. In this case it was the Swedes who, exploring the Baltic coast and the Gulf of Finland, found easy access to the Volga via Lakes Ladoga and Beloozero, hauling their boats over the portages. Soon a lively commercial intercourse was established by the Swedes with the Bulgars on the Middle Volga, with the Khazars and, through the Caspian Sea, with the Arabs of Bagdad.

More important, later, was the discovery of another route, from the Baltic Sea to the Dnieper and to Kiev, then in Khazar hands. Since the Khazars were not able to offer sufficient protection to the Slavs against the marauding nomadic tribes, the Slavs welcomed the Swedes, concluding protective treaties with them or simply accepting their political leadership. Once established in Kiev, the Swedes and their Slav protégés coveted the riches which were accumulating in the Byzantine cities on the Black Sea and especially in Constantinople. The attack of 860 was their first direct contact with Byzantium.[3]

❊ ❊ ❊

The appearance of a new nation under the walls of the capital naturally alerted Byzantine diplomacy and forced it to take prompt action. The last Byzantine possessions in the Crimea were in danger. There was, in these regions, only one possible ally who could also regard himself as endangered by the Rhôs, the Khazars.

The Byzantines had been in touch with the Khazars since the sixth century.[4] The Emperor Heraclius concluded an alliance with them against the Persians and a strong Khazar contingent placed at his disposal, contributed considerably to the emperor's famous victory over the Persians in 627. Then the Arab danger, threatening both the Khazars and the Byzantines, brought them together once more. During the reign of Justinian II the Khazars played an important role in Byzantine politics. The alliance was renewed by Leo III the Isaurian, whose son Constantine V married a Khazar princess. His son Leo IV was called simply the Khazar.

In spite of some tension at the end of the eighth century, the alliance continued to exist. Under the Emperor Theophilus the Khazars, menaced by perhaps the Magyars or the Petchenegues, asked the Byzantines to help them to strengthen their defensive measures. Theophilus, who reorganized the Byzantine possessions in the Crimea, sent Greek architects who constructed for the Khazars the fortress of Sarkel at the mouth of the Don (c. 833).

Thanks to these friendly relations with Byzantium Christianity penetrated the lands of the Khazars. But Christian missionaries encountered very serious competition from the Arabs and Jews. The Abbasid dynasty of Caliphs at Baghdad (from 750 on) brought Arab power to new heights. Their influence grew not only in the political, but also in the cultural field. A kind of cultural renaissance under the first Abbasid Caliph, of course, also encouraged religious propaganda among the neighboring nations. Through the Caspian Sea and the Volga this penetrated among the Turkic Bulgars on the middle Volga. The Bulgars began to embrace the religion of Mohammed during the ninth century. The conversion of the whole nation was achieved at the beginning of the tenth century.

Mohammedan propaganda also reached the Khazars, and many of them embraced the religion of the Prophet. There, however, the Mohammedan proselytizers encountered serious competition from the Jews. In the many Greek colonies on the coast of the Sea of Azov there had always lived numerous Jews engaged in commerce, serving as intermediaries between the Byzantines and Arabs and the interior of Russia. The Jewish communities in these regions were always zealous proselytizers for their religion among the pagans. Their religious zeal and success in their missionary activity seem to have attracted the Apostle Andrew. He is said to have preached in Scythia, which can only mean modern southern Russia with the Crimea (see below, Chapter VII, p. 261).

Thanks to their commercial relations with the Khazars, the Jewish proselytizers were successful in Khazaria and seem even to have won over the Khagan of the Khazars to the teaching of Moses. The date and the circumstances of their conversion are still under discussion.[5] Jewish sources date this conversion at about

730 and call the first Khagan who became a Jew Bulan. Arab sources date this event from the reign of Harun-al-Rašid (786–809), and this date also seems to be indicated by the biographer of the Georgian Saint Abo. It seems that, in the first half of the ninth century, the upper class of the Khazars had been won over to Judaism.

This situation was well known in Byzantium. When it was decided to send a new embassy to the Khazars to renew the alliance in view of the fresh danger coming from the Russians, it was thought that the ambassadors should be accompanied by one or several scholars, well versed in theology. Because three religions were competing in Khazaria it was to be assumed that the embassy might also be involved in religious disputations. For this mission the Emperor Michael III, his uncle the regent Bardas, and the Patriarch Photius chose the young scholar Constantine and his brother Methodius. Before examining the historicity of this embassy, let us see who were the men chosen as companions for the official ambassador and why they were chosen for such a task.

* * *

Fortunately, two important documents are extant which give us ample information on the activity of Constantine-Cyril and his brother Methodius. These documents, whose authenticity has been definitely established,[6] were the so-called Pannonian Legends, the *Life of Constantine* and the *Life of Methodius*.[7]

They were natives of Thessalonica, Constantine being born in 826 or 827 and his older brother about the year 815. Their father Leo was a high-ranking officer—*drungarios*—a rank corresponding to that of colonel. Thessalonica was a very important outpost of the Empire and the second city after Constantinople. We have seen that masses of Slavs had settled in its neighborhood. During the political and ecclesiastical reorganization of the Empire after the pacification of the Slavs, Thessalonica, as we have seen above, became a *thema* headed by a *strategos*, who exercised not only administrative power but also military command. This reorganization was effected before 832 and the *strategos* mentioned in the *Life of Constantine* is an historical person.

It is also quite probable that this military governor of Thessalonica with his *drungarios* Leo participated about 836 in the

campaign against the Bulgars. These, taking advantage of some
troubles among the Slavs in the neighborhood of Thessalonica,
seemed to menace the city itself. The Bulgars occupied the territory of the Slavic tribe of the Smoljans, but the Byzantine army,
commanded by the Caesar Alexis, prevented them from penetrating towards the coast of the Aegean Sea.[8]

This incident shows clearly how important the Slavic problem
was for the *thema* of Thessalonica and also explains why the two
brothers were so familiar with the Slavic language.

The author of the *Life of Constantine* was well versed in Byzantine hagiography. All his remarks (in chapters two and three of the
Life) on his hero's youth reflect the mentality of Byzantine hagiographers. For example, the baby refused to take the milk of the
nurse. This had to happen in order that a child of such parentage
should be nourished only by the milk of his pious mother. Inspired by the story of St. Plakidas, who was converted while hunting a stag, the biographer shows how Constantine made a decision to reject all earthly things when he had lost his falcon during
a hunting expedition. His parents had seven children, and, after
the birth of the last—Constantine—they lived as brother and sister,
in mutual abstinence for fourteen—that is, twice seven—years.
This predilection for the number of seven, the sacred number,
preferred by the hagiographers, should make us a little hesitant
to accept all the numerical indications without serious scrutiny.[9]

The choice of Sophia, in the dream of the boy, as his bride
among the beautiful girls of Thessalonica assembled by the military governor, can be explained by the custom at the Byzantine
court of assembling young ladies of the best families so that the
future emperor should choose his wife from among them.[10] St.
Gregory of Nazianzus, who became the favorite saint and doctor
of Constantine, also had a vision in a dream of two beautiful
ladies, Chastity and Temperance, whom he chose for himself.[11]
He relates in his poem how he left to other people all the beauties
of nature, all entertainment, "the neighing of the horses and the
barking of hunting dogs," and accepted the yoke of temperence.[12]
One can see how easy it was for Constantine's biographer to find
inspiration in Byzantine customs and hagiography to illustrate
the exemplary life of his hero.

The stressing of the great piety of the parents was also a commonplace in hagiographic writings. This does not mean that all

that the biographer relates about Constantine's youth was unsub-
stantiated. It is quite understandable that St. Gregory of Nazianzus should have become his favorite doctor. He was extremely
popular in Byzantium and his poems attracted Constantine—and
other young men—and it must be his poems which Constantine is
supposed to have learned by heart. The short encomium which
Constantine is said to have composed in his honor seems to have
been the young man's first literary achievement.[13]

Both brothers obtained their elementary education in Thessalonica. Constantine is said to have endeavored vainly to persuade
a grammarian to give him a more solid training in scholarship.
This he only obtained in Constantinople at the invitation of the
Logothete (Theoctistus)—equivalent to a modern prime minister—
and he was educated with the young emperor Michael III.

This statement of the biographer needs some investigation. This
invitation was apparently issued after the death of Constantine's
father. It must have happened when Constantine was fourteen
years old. This may be exact but it is also possible that the biographer adjusted the dates slightly, in order to obtain the holy
number, seven plus seven.

One is tempted to admit that the *drungarios* Leo died from a
wound inflicted on a battlefield. In reality we learn from Constantine Porphyrogenitus[14] that the Peloponnesian Slavs became
independent during the reign of the Emperor Theophilus (829–
842), and that "in the reign of Michael, the son of Theophilus, the
protospatharius Theoctistus, surnamed Bryennius, was sent as military governor to the province of Peloponnesus with great power
and force, viz., of Thracians and Macedonians and the rest of the
western provinces, to war upon and subdue them." His expedition
was successful and the Slavs were forced to pay tribute to the
Empire.

The revolt must have happened in 841. Michael was born in
January of 840 and crowned co-emperor towards September of
the same year. He became emperor nominally in 842, after the
death of his father, under the regency of his mother Theodora.
Theoctistus' expedition may be dated in this year. According to
Porphyrogenitus, the military contingents from Thrace and Macedonia especially participated in this expedition, but also those
from "the rest of the western provinces," thus equally from the
thema of Thessalonica. If the death of Leo can be dated in 842,

it is admissible that he died from wounds received during the campaign. If this was the case, it is more easily comprehensible why, when dying, he sought to relieve the anxiety of his wife concerning the education of their youngest son, by saying that he "who governs, all Christians" will take care of him (chapter two). This can only be the emperor, who regarded it as his duty to take care of the orphans of officers who died on active service.

Of course, it is also possible that Leo's family had some connections with Theoctistus, the *Logothete,* prime minister for the Empress Theodora. In any event, the government took the young orphan under its protection and gave him the opportunity to obtain a higher education.[15] We can, however, hardly accept the biographer's note that Constantine was to be educated together with the young Emperor Michael III. Even if Michael's birth could be dated not from 840 but from 836,[16] which is now disproved, he would have been only six years old in 842. It is, however, quite possible that Constantine was accommodated in the imperial palace, because the highest official was interested in his education.

* * *

It is evident that Constantine was to study at the imperial university in whose reorganization Theoctistus was personally interested. The biographer describes (chapter four) Constantine's studies in the following manner: "After having learned grammar there ... in three months, he turned his attention to other sciences. He studied Homer and geometry and equally—with Leo[17] and Photius—dialectics and all other philosophical disciplines. Moreover, he also learned rhetoric, arithmetic, astronomy, music, and the other hellenic arts."

The biographer's statement corresponds with the facts we know from other Byzantine sources about the university and Byzantine scholarship. The university had existed since the reign of Constantine the Great. It was enriched by his son Constantius and reorganized by Theodosius II. Contrary to what has been thought, it was not suppressed by the iconoclastic emperors, and flourished again in the ninth century. The emperors were necessarily interested in its prosperity, since its main object was to train able personnel for imperial offices.

Constantine was also destined to enter the imperial service. In chapter four the biographer describes how much the *logothete* liked and trusted the talented young man. He offered him the hand of his spiritual daughter—he had no children, being an eunuch—and he promised him a high post in the imperial service. "You will attain even more," he said, "because you will quickly become a *strategos.*" However, Constantine desired to continue his scholarly career. After consulting the empress, Theoctistus decided to let Constantine take holy orders and be appointed librarian to the patriarch.

It is now established that Constantine was not ordained a priest, but only deacon. The post of librarian *(bibliothecarius)* in Rome—the hagiographer employs here the title used in the western Church—corresponded in Byzantium to that of the *chartophylax*. It was the most important function in the offices of the patriarch's entourage.[18] The *chartophylax* represented the patriarch at all important functions which the latter did not attend personally and, because of that, when exercising his function, he enjoyed precedence over the bishops, although only a deacon. When the patriarch desired to get rid of his *chartophylax* it was necessary to raise him to the priesthood for, as such, he could not continue to be *chartophylax*.

One can understand why Theoctistus and the empress desired to have at the court of the patriarch someone they trusted. The Patriarch Ignatius was appointed by the Empress Theodora in June 847 without the customary election by the local synod and presentation to the emperor for approval. The liquidation of iconoclasm by Theodora in 842 did not immediately pacify the Byzantine Church. Two parties were trying to influence ecclesiastical life in Byzantium. The intransigents asked for severe measures against the former heretics, but the moderates advised more benevolent treatment of the penitent iconoclasts. The Patriarch Methodius (843–847) excommunicated some of the intransigents who criticized his benevolent treatment of the returning heretics. Fearing new complications, the empress thought she was entitled to dispense with the ordinary procedure and herself appointed Ignatius, son of the former Emperor Michael I. The appointment, however, did not help to establish peace among the two factions. It is understandable that, in these conditions, the post of the *chartophylax* became all the more important, and it was natural that the government wished to appoint to this post someone in their confidence.

✤ ✤ ✤

Contrary to Constantine's biographer, Methodius' biographer gives very little data on his subject's early years. He was also predestined to a career in the imperial administration. The biographer says (chapter two) that when the emperor learned of his capacities, he appointed him *archon* of a Slavic territory. The information deserves credit. The Byzantine list of functionaries enumerates several *archons* in different territories—for example, those of Cherson, of Dyrrhachium, of Dalmatia, or of Crete. Some of these *archontiai* became *themata,* others seem to have been part of a *thema,* preserving, however, some local autonomy.

It seems logical to look for the Slavic territory of which Methodius became *archon* in the neighborhood of Thessalonica. It can be assumed that it was situated in the region of the river Strymon. This region was in danger of being absorbed by the progress of the Bulgars, a fact which, probably, warranted its special position in the administration. It could have formed a part of the *thema* of Thessalonica, but, because of its importance, was raised to an *archontia.* As stated before, in the second half of the ninth century this territory became a *thema.*[19]

Methodius seems to have occupied this post during the years 843 and 856. In the short third chapter of his biography we read that Methodius, after some years, resigned his post and became a monk in a monastery on Mount Olympus in Asia Minor which was, at that time, the most important center of Byzantine monasticism. The biographer gives as a reason for his resignation Methodius' desire for things eternal.

There exists, however, a liturgical panegyric in honor of St. Methodius, called *canon,* which gives some new details about his decision to become a monk. Its anonymous author apostrophizes Methodius in the following way:[20] "Holy and most glorious Teacher, when you had decided to leave your family and your native country, your spouse and your children, you chose to go away into the wilderness in order to live there with the Holy Fathers."

Is this information to be credited? We do not know, but it

should not be completely neglected. Cases were not rare in Byzantium where a husband and wife decided to renounce their common life and to retire into a monastery and a convent. The existence of children would complicate such a mutual arrangement, but it is possible that this is an addition of the author of the *canon,* who desired to make this separation even more painful for his hero. In any case it seems clear that Methodius' decision was freely taken and that it was not politically motivated.

* * *

His brother Constantine also resigned his high post at the *patriarcheion.* If we may believe the hagiographer (chapter four) this happened in a rather spectacular fashion. Constantine is said simply to have disappeared after a short time and to have been found only six months later in a monastery on the Bosphorus.

What was the real reason for this resignation? Most probably the office of a *chartophylax* did not suit the nature of the young scholar. He preferred scholarship to an administrative office. Ignatius himself was a saintly man, but we know from other sources that he did not favor scholarship. He belonged to the group of monks who were hostile to profane studies. Many hagiographers have left us descriptions showing to what extent their heroes disliked and underestimated profane learning.[21] Moreover, in his religious policy Ignatius did not fulfill the hopes the government had nurtured when it had appointed him. He liquidated the schism of the intransigent monks, but his strict attitude toward the repentant iconoclasts evoked bitter criticism among the partisans of a more liberal policy. Constantine could not feel at home in such an atmosphere and it is understandable that he acted as his biographer indicates.

Again Theoctistus intervened and, because Constantine refused to go back to the *patriarcheion,* he appointed him professor of philosophy at the university he had himself reorganized. There Constantine gave courses on philosophy "to natives and to foreigners." This happened most probably in 850, or at the beginning of 851.

At the university Constantine most probably succeeded his teacher Photius. The latter was the most prominent scholar in Byzantium at this time.[22] His family enjoyed high esteem there, which was only enhanced by the exile which his parents had suffered under the Iconoclasts. Photius was related to the reigning family, and his brother had married a daughter of Theodora. Photius was appointed to the university by Theoctistus, together with Leo, the former iconoclastic bishop of Thessalonica, also famous for his learning. In about 850 Photius abandoned his teaching career to become chancellor of the Empire, a promotion which he owed again to Theoctistus. This explains why the chair of philosophy was offered to Constantine and accepted by him.

Constantine is called, by all our sources, the Philosopher. We do not know the origin of this title. It may have been that of the professor of philosophy at the imperial university. There is no doubt that Constantine obtained this chair. We know that the rector of the university was called "oecumenical teacher", a title which was later given to the rector of the patriarchal academy. But we do not know if the other professors had special titles. Such a title may have been given to Constantine because of his achievements in this discipline. Both explanations are possible.[23]

What did philosophy mean to Constantine himself? We know that it had a double meaning in Byzantine intellectual and religious life. A philosopher was supposed to be a man well versed in the teaching of the great classical age, using this knowledge for a deeper understanding of Christian teaching. On the other hand, the man who abandoned all wordly goods and led an ascetic life as a monk was called a true philosopher.

In chapter four of the *Life* of Constantine we find a definition of philosophy given by Constantine himself. Theoctistus is said to have told Constantine that he would like to know what philosophy was. The young graduate from the university answered "with a quick mind." "Knowledge of things divine and human, as much as man is able to approach God, for it teaches man by deeds to be the image and after the likeness of the One who created him."

This definition goes back to the Stoic teaching that wisdom consisted in the knowledge of things divine and human. The second part of Constantine's definition recalls Plato's idea that man has to approach God according to his ability.

An attempt has been made to show that Constantine was influenced in this respect by his favorite master, St. Gregory of Nazianzus.[24] This is, however, an exaggeration. Gregory was not alone in using such a definition. The Stoic and Platonic understanding of the meaning of philosophy is frequently used in Byzantine literature and by many Greek Fathers. The source of Constantine's definition might better be sought in the standard Byzantine textbook for the study of dialectic, the *Isagoge* of Porphyry (died *c.* 305), and in the numerous commentaries on it, especially those of Ammonius (late fifth century), Elias (sixth century) and David (sixth or seventh century).[25] The definition by David is especially suggestive: "Philosophy is the knowledge of things divine and human, the becoming like God according to the ability of man."[26] Among the many definitions given in these textbooks, Constantine had evidently chosen the best. This reveals his originality.

The biographer presented the interrogation by Theoctistus as a kind of examination of the young man before he was offered a post in the imperial administration. This may be an addition by the hagiographer, who thus wished to place his hero in the best possible light and to exhibit his scholarship.

Constantine's definition of philosophy is thus well in accord with what he had learned at the university from his master Photius. The handbooks from which he derived this definition were also the basis of his teaching at the university.

This, of course, does not mean that Constantine did not try to give to his commentaries on philosophical treatises and disciplines a more profoundly Christian character. He was an intellectual like his master, and in Byzantium all science was connected with Christian teaching. Constantine's biographer shows this in the same chapter, when he lets Constantine say that he preferred to go on with his scholarship "in order to recover the honor of the ancestors," meaning, probably, Adam and Eve, who had lost honor through their sin.[27]

In chapter five the biographer describes a disputation between the young philosopher and the former iconoclastic patriarch John VII, called Grammaticus because of his great learning. John was deposed in 843 and interned in the monastery of Kleidion on the Bosphorus. It is quite possible that the young Constantine had a discussion with the ex-patriarch at this place during the six months he was in hiding in a monastery. Kleidion may have been that monastery, or one of the other monasteries which Constantine visited during this time.

There may thus be some truth in the description of this disputation. However, the discussion is presented as a kind of public examination. Hitherto this passage has been interpreted as a promise to Constantine that if he defeated the ex-patriarch, he would obtain the chair of philosphy at the imperial university. However, some specialists in Slavic philology have shown convincingly that the passage should be translated and interpreted as a challenge to the ex-patriarch: "If you can defeat this young man in disputation, you will get back your chair," namely, the patriarchal throne.[28]

This is, however, once again an imaginative presentation of a private disputation, with details added by the biographer in order to glorify his hero. The situation in Byzantium about the year 850 was not ripe for a public disputation with a deposed patriarch who was a stubborn iconoclast. There was still danger of a renewal of the iconoclastic movement and it would have been inexpedient to offer the heretics an opportunity to defend their doctrine.[29]

The story, however, reflects well the mentality in Byzantium after 843. The biographer was a Byzantine, who wrote his biography under the direction of Constantine's brother Methodius. His interest in the ex-patriarch John and in iconoclasm shows clearly that this problem was still of lively importance in Byzantium at that period. There was no danger of iconoclasm among the Moravians for whom the *Life* was written, but the biographer, although far from his homeland, used this opportunity to refute the main objections of the iconoclasts against the worship of images and the Holy Cross. He still sensed the tense atmosphere which prevailed in Byzantium after the defeat of iconoclasm, and was anxious to preserve his new converts from any iconoclastic danger. It should be stressed that a discussion with the famous iconoclastic patriarch was a kind of commonplace in the hagiographic literature of the ninth century.

In the next chapter the biographer describes how the Arabs sent an embassy to Constantinople asking for a religious disputation in their land. The emperor thereupon convoked the Senate to deliberate as to what should be done and he asked Constantine to go in person to the Arabs for this discussion. Constantine is said to have been at that time twenty-four years old (851).

Because the historicity of this embassy has been questioned by some authors, I have devoted to it a special study which is reprinted in Appendix One of this book: I came to the conclusion that there are good reasons for accepting the historicity of a Byzantine embassy to the Arabs in 851 when Constantine was twenty-four years old, and that he did not participate in the embassy of 855–56, to which his former teacher Photius had been attached.

Thus, there is no evidence for the supposition that Constantine had accompanied Photius during the embassy of 855–856. The author of the *Life* has in mind a different embassy, and, as we have seen, we are entitled to accept the historicity of an embassy to the Arabs in 851, although it is not mentioned in any historical document other than the *Life*.

✤ ✤ ✤

After recounting the events during the Arab embassy, the author of the *Life* reports in chapter seven that Constantine suddenly renounced all he possessed and took refuge, first in a peaceful spot, and then with his brother Methodius in his monastery on Mount Olympus.

What had provoked this new escapade? If Constantine desired only to "converse with books," as the biographer has it, he could have indulged his desire in Constantinople at the university. Photius' *Bibliotheca*, in which he describes the works in all disciplines which he had read, reveals the immense wealth of literature on philosophy, theology, and other related disciplines which could be found in Constantinople's libraries. A monastery at Mount Olympus could hardly compete with Constantinople in this respect. There must have been another and more serious reason which compelled the Philosopher to abandon his teaching and take refuge in a monastery.

This reason could only have been the political upheaval which took place in the capital in 856.[31] The *Logothete* Theoctistus, murdered by the supporters of Theodora's brother, the ambitious Bardas, with the consent of the young emperor, had been Constantine's greatest benefactor. There was a danger that the friends of the unfortunate prime minister would be persecuted. In such a case a monastery was the safest place in which to mourn the death of a fatherly friend and await the passing of the political storm.

Other events followed. The Senate put an end to the regency of

Theodora in the same year. To prevent a counter-revolution by her partisans, she was expelled from the palace at the end of the summer of 857. The patriarch Ignatius, a supporter of Theodora, became involved in trouble with the new regent Bardas, to whom he is said to have refused Holy Communion, accusing him of incest with his widowed daughter-in-law. Ignatius, a pious, simple, and inexperienced man, may have believed the barely substantiated stories[32] of Bardas' misbehavior propagated by his enemies. But this regrettable incident put the Church in a difficult situation. In order to avoid an open clash between the Church and the new government, the bishops advised Ignatius to resign his office. He did so in 858. The local synod elected as his successor Photius, the chancellor of the Empire. The choice of a layman was made in order to avoid the struggle for power in the Church between the two factions—the intransigents, whose majority favored Ignatius, and the moderates who stood for the "economy," a word which the Byzantines used for compromise in difficult and delicate situations. The consent of all the bishops was given to the election of the new patriarch, even by those who most fervently supported Ignatius, their attitude having been influenced by the fact that Photius was not involved in any way in the upheaveal of 856, since he was absent from the city and on his way back from the embassy to the Arabs. He may not have returned until the early part of 857, thus giving the followers of Theodora time to become reconciled to the idea of Photius as the successor of Ignatius. Had he been present in Constantinople at the time of the disturbance, it is possible that the reactionary members of the clergy would have refused to accept Bardas' proposal to elevate him to the patriarchate, for it was Bardas who was responsible for the changes in the government, and who was favorably inclined to the intellectual circle of which Photius was the center.

Although the bishops had unanimously consented to the election of the new patriarch, the intransigents, for reasons unknown, revolted against Photius two months afterwards, declaring that Ignatius was the only legitimate patriarch. The revolt had a political aspect, namely, the restoration of Theodora's régime, and the imperial police intervened against organized noisy demonstrations when the intransigents refused to accept the decision of a local council convoked by the patriarch in order to pacify the Church.

All this took place before the attack of the Russian fleet. Constantine was certainly not an intransigent. His resignation from the highest office in the *patriarcheion* shows clearly that Constantine did not share Ignatius' disdain of scholarship and, perhaps, that he disapproved of Ignatius' methods in the government of the Church. He was not a fanatic, however, and abhorred being involved in party intrigues. It is therefore quite probable that he stayed with his brother in the monastery all this time, although his biographer does not say so explicitly. Before joining his brother he appears to have been in material difficulties, but the sudden appearance of a benefactor (chapter seven) provided him with the necessary means.

* * *

The biographer himself seems to suggest that Constantine was still on Mount Olympus when the decision was made to send an embassy to the Khazars. He speaks first of an embassy sent by the Khazar Khagan asking for a theologian capable of explaining Christian doctrine to the Khazars, who were hesitating between paganism, Judaism, and Islam. Then, he says, "the emperor searched for Constantine and after finding him, he communicated to him the message of the Khazars." If Constantine had been in the city teaching philosophy, it would hardly have been necessary to search for him.[33]

The sending of a Khazar embassy could be an invention of the biographer, although an exchange of embassies is not impossible. The aim of the supposed Khazar embassy was, however, certainly an invention of the biographer.[34] Religious discussions at the court of the khagan were to be expected, and, therefore, the presence of a good theologian was necessary, although this was not the sole, or even principal, aim of the embassy as it is presented by the biographer.

If Photius had not been elected patriarch, he would probably have been the man whom the government would have chosen to represent Christian theological scholarship in Khazaria. Because he was not available for such a mission, the emperor and Bardas chose his disciple and successor at the university—Constantine. The acceptance of the embassy by the latter also marked his

reconciliation with the new régime. It can be imagined that his
former teacher acted as intermediary, recommending his disciple
for this important mission.

The ambassadors, with Constantine and his brother Methodius
—his presence is attested by the author of the *Life* of Methodius
(chapter four)—spent the winter in Cherson, the Byzantine possession in the Crimea (chapter four, *Life* of Constantine). Constantine profited from this occasion to make further progress in
the Hebrew language in preparation for his encounter with the
Jewish scholars. He had a discussion with a Samaritan, was able
to learn that language, and to read a Samaritan Bible. The biographer also says (chapter eight) that he found in Cherson a psalter
written with "rus'skymi" letters and a man speaking this language.
Many scholars thought that Constantine had found a Russian
alphabet in Cherson, but this was impossible, since at that time
the Russians could not have possessed any kind of literature.
Others thought that he had found a Gothic translation of the
psalter made by Ulphila. Both solutions proved to be wrong. It
has been established that the word is corrupted and that we
should read "sur'skymi" which means "Syriac."[35] All this shows
that Constantine was a very good philologist.

The most important event during the stay in Cherson was the
discovery of relics believed to be those of St. Clement of Rome.
Constantine and all his contemporaries were convinced that
Clement, the second successor to St. Peter, was exiled in Cherson
and died a martyr's death there. This was described in his *Life*,
which was composed in the fourth, or at the beginning of the fifth
century, and was well known in both West and East. The author
of the descriptions of Clement's martyrdom, however, confused
Clement with another saint who may have been martyred in the
Crimea. The whole tradition concerning Clement is legendary. It
is not even certain that St. Clement died a martyr's death. The
first Church historian, Eusebius, ignores it in his *History* (Book 3,
chapter 15). But, because his relics were not in the church built in
his house in Rome, the statement of the anonymous author concerning Clement's martyrdom was generally accepted, and it was
thought that his relics were still hidden in the ruins of a church
on a small island near Cherson, which was not easily accessible
because it was flooded by the sea. Constantine was honestly convinced that he had found the relics of St. Clement of Rome. This

discovery was highly regarded by all his contemporaries, and the finding of these relics later played a great role in the Slavic mission.

The discovery, made on January 30, 861, was described by Constantine in a special discourse, which was translated into Latin by Anastasius Bibliothecarius in Rome, but which is partly preserved only in Old Slavonic.[36]

A short story about the discovery, composed in Greek by Constantine, is known in an Old Slavonic translation. The hymn composed by him on the saint seemed so artistic to Anastasius that he did not dare translate it, and it is not preserved even in Old Slavonic.[37]

During their stay in Cherson the ambassadors found it necessary to intervene officially in a border incident. A Khazar general was besieging a Christian city. Constantine is said to have gone to the general and to have persuaded him to withdraw. This story may not have been invented, however; it was probably not Constantine alone who intervened, but the imperial official, representing the emperor, who led the embassy.

The other incident reported by the biographer also has an historical background. Probably when returning to Cherson from their expedition, the envoys were surprised by a horde of Magyars who "shouted like wolves," threatening to kill Constantine. The latter did not interrupt his prayers, and his attitude calmed the interlopers who let him go free, together with his companions. The Magyars, before invading Central Europe during the ninth century, stayed for some time in the territory of the Lower Don. It is quite possible that one horde made an incursion into the Crimea.[38]

* * *

From Cherson the embassy sailed through the Strait of Kerch, formerly known as Panticapaeum, to the Sea of Azov.[39] The legend does not say expressly when Constantine and his companions met the khagan of the Khazars. The Khazars evidently expected them, because they sent an emissary to meet them and, probably, to conduct them to where the Khagan was staying with his court. This emissary most probably met the envoys at Sarkel on the Don. The khagans had their winter quarters at Itil on the Volga delta. Their summer residence was at Semender (Samander) near the pass of Derbend on the Caspian Sea, called by the biographer, *Kaspiskaja vrata.*[40] It is there that they met the Khagan. All these details must have been prepared in advance as is indicated by the sending of an emissary to act as guide. These arrangements could have been made during the prolonged stay of the envoys in Cherson.

The embassy was well received at the khagan's court and was invited to a banquet. The master of ceremonies is said to have asked Constantine what rank he held in order to give him his proper place at the table (chapter nine). This cannot be regarded simply as a stylistic phrase used by the author to introduce Constantine's clever answer that "he was Adam's grandson." This reply was intended to show the Khazars that the noble origin of Adam superseded that of Abraham, whose sons the Jews called themselves. We know that the Khazars observed a strict ceremonial on such occasions.[41] This indicates also that Constantine was not the head of the embassy, for had he been the emperor's representative there would have been no need to enquire about his rank.

The first subjects of discussion were the Trinity, the Incarnation, and the Redemption. Constantine defended the doctrine of the Trinity by quoting certain passages of the Old Testament on the Word and the Spirit. Concerning the Incarnation he asked the Jews why God could not have appeared in human form when he appeared as a burning bush to Moses. Then they discussed the law of Moses which was abrogated by the law of the New Testament. With numerous quotations from the Prophets, Constantine proved that Jesus was the expected Messiah. He justified also the veneration of pictures of the Saints. During the third meeting Constantine defended the superiority of Christian morality.

Constantine (chapter ten) is said to have described the disputations in detail in a special report which was later translated into Old Slavonic by his brother, and divided into eight chapters. The Legend contains a part of this composition.[42]

The whole presentation of the discussions makes a good impression. It is quite realistic and it can be compared favorably with other Byzantine writings against the Jewish and Mohammedan doctrines. Constantine was a good theologian.

One can conclude from the description of the disputations that the khagan had already embraced the Jewish creed, and that Judaism had many adherents at his court. Islam seems to have held a much weaker position in Khazaria. Constantine mentions the Moslems only toward the end of the disputation when explaining why the Christians cannot venerate Mohammed, although the latter recognized Christ as a Prophet. The majority of the Khazars still seem to have been pagan, and about two hundred of them demanded to be baptized as the result of the discussions.

The khagan is said to have written to the emperor thanking him for having sent him such a man, and announcing that he had given permission to those who wished to be baptized.

There is a phrase at the end of the letter which seems to confirm that the purpose of the embassy encompassed more than discussions on religion. The khagan writes, "We are friends of the Empire and we are ready to be at your service wherever you may wish it." These words indicate the renewal of the Byzantine-Khazar alliance, a renewal which seemed to be necessary to both because of the threat of new danger from the Russians on their common frontier.

The Philosopher is then said to have returned to Cherson with two hundred Greek prisoners whom the khagan had released. En route through Khazaria the expedition had trouble finding drinking water. The biographer, of course, cannot refrain from seeing a miracle in their manner of finding it. In the same chapter twelve we read how Constantine had learned that in a Christian city in the peninsula, called Phoullae, the men of that place venerated a huge oak tree, even bringing sacrifices to it, especially in times of drought, but that no woman could come near. The Philosopher went to the city and persuaded the men to abandon this idolatrous custom. They obeyed, felled the tree and burned it. That same night the Lord sent rain.[43]

In his harangue Constantine quoted abundantly from Isaiah who spoke of Tärshish and Pul (Isa. 66:19). The Greek text reads Phud instead of Pul. E. H. Mins[44] rightly concluded from this that Constantine knew and was using the Hebrew text. This confirms the biographer's statement concerning Constantine's Hebrew studies in Cherson (chapter eight). He is also said to have translated eight parts of a Hebrew grammar, which again testifies to his keen interest in philology.

❋ ❋ ❋

When returning from Cherson to Constantinople, the Philosopher is said (chapter thirteen) to have seen the emperor and afterwards to have lived in peace, praying to God and "sitting in the Church of the Holy Apostles."[45]

It is interesting to note that Constantine did not resume his teaching at the imperial high school. Nor did he go back to the *patriarcheion* where his former master and friend, Photius, was then presiding. Why should he have taken up his residence at the Church of the Holy Apostles? And why does the biographer describe him as "sitting in the Church of the Holy Apostles"?

Only one explanation of this strange behavior on the part of the Philosopher seems feasible. After such a great success in Khazaria, and after having rendered great service to the Empire and the Church, it could be expected that his new function would be an honorable one serving the interests of the Church. This leads us to seek an explanation in the religious situation in Byzantium.

After the envoys returned from Khazaria, the new Patriarch Photius seems to have affirmed his position by confirming the deposition of ex-Patriarch Ignatius, pronounced by the papal legates in a council held in the summer months of 861.[46] Important measures were voted to improve the religious situation and to remove abuses which had crept into monastic institutions, especially during and after the iconoclastic persecutions. It can be imagined that Photius, the greatest scholar of his time, now head of the Byzantine Church, would devote his attention in the first place to the education of the clergy.

A special institution existed for this purpose, a kind of patriarchal Academy. It had its headquarters in, or near, the Church of Holy Wisdom (Hagia Sophia)), and there were branches in different ecclesiastical institutions. We have some information as to their existence before the ninth century, but more complete data are available for later periods.[47] A high school in the Church of the Holy Apostles is especially mentioned by Mesarites, in the twelfth century, in his description of the church. According to the eulogies with which he exalts its teaching, the school must have been very famous and had a long-established tradition. In chapters seven to twelve[48] he describes the elementary curriculum, corresponding to the *trivium,* and the behavior of the young students in the different classes, which were not held in the church itself but in an adjacent building.

In chapters forty-two and forty-three, Mesarites describes the more advanced courses corresponding to the *quadrivium*. He dwells especially on the courses in grammar, dialectics, physiology and medicine, and arithmetic and geometry.[49] It is evident from his words that he is not describing the courses given at the imperial university, but at a school which was under the supervision of the patriarch. It is clear then that the liberal arts were also taught at the patriarchal Academy, and that this teaching was given in classes adjoining the Church of the Holy Apostles. Theological courses seem to have been held near the Church of St. Peter, in the neighborhood of Hagia Sophia.[50]

All this shows us that the patriarchal Academy possessed several kinds of colleges where both profane and theological instruction was given. It was certainly reformed after the victory over the Iconoclasts, and further reorganization was needed when Photius became patriarch, because secular scholarship was most probably neglected during the patriarchate of Ignatius. This permits us to suppose that Photius reorganized the Academy and introduced the teaching of philosophy and other profane disciplines, corresponding to the *trivium* and *quadrivium* in the schools surrounding the Church of the Holy Apostles where, perhaps, this teaching had been given previously.

As professor of philosophy he appointed his former student, Constantine. This is indicated by the description of Constantine's activities in this church by his biographer, "he was sitting in the Church of the Holy Apostles." In antiquity teachers were represented as "sitting."[51] In the New Testament, Christ, when teaching, is said to have "sat down."[52] Only twice, in Luke 21:35 and in the Apocalypse 14:06, is the word *Kathizein* employed to indicate "staying," or "living in." In early Christian art, Christ as Teacher was represented sitting.[53]

Constantine's biographer was a Byzantine well acquainted with ecclesiastical and other usages. If Constantine had held an ecclesiastical position in the church he would have used another expression. But what kind of function could he have fulfilled, since he was only a deacon? Besides, sitting during liturgical office was not customary in the Eastern Church.

Constantine's office can then be compared to that of George Choiroboskos who, in the first half of the seventh century, was deacon, grammarian, and *chartophylax*, who gave courses in gram-

mar and dialectics at the patriarchal Academy. He seems also to
have been called "Oecumenical Teacher".[54]

Knowledge of the Hebrew and Samaritan languages helped
Constantine to solve a puzzling inscription on a precious chalice
which was believed to have belonged to Solomon, and which was
kept in the treasury of Hagia Sophia. The three verses of the
inscription were interpreted as a prophecy about Christ, but they
could also have echoed Christian apocryphal tradition concerning
the Messiah and his reign.[55] This is all that we learn of the activities of Constantine after his return from the Khazarian mission.

III. Moravia Before the Byzantine Mission

Formation of the Moravian State— Annexation of Nitra—Irish or Frankish (Bavarian) missionaries in Moravia and Slovakia?— Priests from Greece in Moravia?—Moravian churches built in the first half of the ninth century—Prototypes of those churches in the Adriatic sphere?—Political and economic organization of Moravia —Cultural background of Moravia in the light of recent archaeological discoveries—The Avar civilization, Byzantium and Moravia —Mojmír, Pribina, Rastislav—Franco-Bulgarian and Moravo-Byzantine alliance?—Cultural and religious objects of the Moravian embassy in Byzantium—Invention of the Slavic alphabet— How the Byzantine embassy reached Moravia.

Constantine did not follow the career of his probable predecessor George Choiroboskos, because of an event which changed completely the lives of the two brothers. Prince Rastislav of the Moravians sent an embassy to the emperor in 862. Constantine's biographer recounts this in the following words: "Rastislav, the Prince of Moravia, impelled by God, took advice with his princes and with the Moravians and sent to the Emperor Michael, saying: "Our people has renounced paganism and is observing the Christian law, but we do not have a teacher to explain to us the true Christian faith in our own language in order that other nations even, seeing this, may imitate us. Send us therefore, Master, such a bishop and teacher, because from you emanates always, to all sides, the good law."

The author of the *Life* of Constantine's brother Methodius describes this event in the following way in chapter five: "It happened then in those days, Ratislav, the Slavic prince with Svatopluk had sent from Moravia to the Emperor Michael (an embassy) speaking as follows: 'Thanks to the grace of God, we are well. And many Christian teachers have come to us from Italy and from Greece and from Germany teaching us in different way. We Slavs are simple people, and we have nobody who would lead us to the truth and interpret its meaning. Thus hark, Master, send us such a man who would teach us all law.'"

Before examining the reasons which prompted the Moravian prince to address himself to the Byzantine emperor, and the real aim of this embassy, the political and cultural development of Moravia must be reviewed in order to understand Rastislav's move.

This country, which suddenly came into contact with Byzantium, lay outside the boundaries of the Roman Empire, of which Byzantium was the heir. An important Slavic political structure developed very early in the fertile valley of the river Morava, and pressure from the Avars accelerated this process.

New archaeological discoveries in the valleys of the Thaya (Dyje) and Morava rivers are today supplementing the meagre literary sources concerning the history of this region. Historians are finding sufficient evidence—whch, however, does not seem conclusive—to place the center of the first Slavic political structure, erected by the Frankish Samo against the Avars, in Moravia and in the region between the Danube and the Thaya, abandoning the old theory which placed it in Bohemia.[1] This formation could hardly be called a state in the true sense, although Samo extended his sway not only over Moravia and Lower Austria, but also over Bohemia and White Serbia, whose prince Drvan voluntarily joined him. Although Samo was able to defend his independence against the Frankish King Dagobert also,[2] this structure disintegrated after Samo's detah, about 658. But new archaeological evidence again shows that the direct political influence of the Avars stopped on the Thaya and in lower Morava.

Charlemagne's campaigns against the Avars must have been welcomed in Bohemia and Moravia. Einhard's *Annals*[3] relate that one of his armies marched through Bohemia, indicating that the Slavic tribes in that country were on good terms with the Franks. Charlemagne's victory over the Avars (795–796) resulted in the extension of Frankish rule over the whole of ancient Pannonia as far as the river Tisza. The Bulgars, on the other hand, occupied ancient Dacia as far as that river.

The Slavs in Moravia and Bohemia were unable to escape Frankish political influence. It seems that submission by the Slavs in Bohemia to the Frankish empire met with resistance. Einhard,[4] the *Chronicle of Moissac*,[5] and the *Annals of Metz*[6] certainly speak of expeditions against the Slavs in Bohemia in 805.

The situation was clarified in 822 under Louis the Pious. According to Einhard[7] the emperor received in Frankfurt the envoys not only of Polabian Slavs, but also of the Slavs from Bohemia and Moravia. Submission naturally implied Christianization, and this was a slow process in Bohemia. Only in 845 did fourteen Bohemian princes present themselves at Ratisbon to express to Louis the German their willingness to be baptized,[8] and they were, most probably, the chiefs of clans living near the Bavarian frontier. Christianity began to spread among the Czech tribes of Central Bohemia only toward the end of the ninth century.

The regrouping of the Slavic tribes in Moravia must have started in the seventh century. The wars with the Avars in the eighth century accelerated this process and strenthened the position of the tribal chiefs who, with their retinues, defended their territories against Avar incursions. The report of Einhard[9] tells us that, in 822, the process was finished and that the tribes in the valleys between the Danube and around the rivers Thaya and Morava had acknowledged the supremacy and name of the most important tribe, that of the Moravians.

Although these tribes are mentioned for the first time only in 822 as being united under the Moravians, it is possible that they were included in the report in the *Annales Laurissenses*, which tells us that in 803[10] the Slavs of Pannonia, together with the Avars, subjected themselves to Charlemagne. Besides this, political formations *(regna)* of the Slavs in the neighborhood of Pannonia are mentioned.[11] These *regna* may be those of the Slavs on the northern side of the river Danube.

The existence of such *regna* appears to be confirmed by the report of 811,[12] which mentions chiefs and princes living in the territory around the river Danube, who addressed themselves to the emperor asking for support in their troublesome relations with the Avars. Besides the Slavs of Pannonia, the writer may also have had in mind those chiefs living north of the Danube.

The concentration of these Slavs into a political group seems also to be attested by the so-called Bavarian Geographer.[13] The

dating of his *Descriptio* is still debated by specialists, but it seems
most probable that the first redaction of this document was written in one of the Bavarian monasteries about the year 817 when
Louis the Pious, in dividing the Empire, assigned Bavaria, Pannonia, and the Slavs with the Avars east of Bavaria, to Louis the
German. This was the moment when detailed knowledge of Bavaria's neighbors seemed important and necessary.

The author mentions the Marharii as neighbors of the Beheimi
(Slavs of Bohemia). After them he placed the Vulgarii—who are
certainly the Bulgarians who had extended their rule over modern
central Hungary to the river Tisza, after the defeat of the Avars.
But then he adds: "There is a people who are called Merehani."
The meaning of this passage is still disputed. It was proposed by
L. Havlík [14] that the author, after writing of the Beheimi, thought
to describe, not two different tribes, but their political formation
around two centers. The Marharii should be those between the
Danube, Thaya (Dyje), Morava, and the White Carpathian
Mountains united under the chief of the Moravians—Mojmír, or
his predecessor, and the Merehani, their kinsmen, between the
middle Danube and the Carpathian Mountains, united by Prince
Pribina, or his predecessor, around their center, which was most
probably Nitra.

It is true that the political organization of the Slavic tribes East
of the Danube, in the territory mentioned above, was proceeding
independently in two formations, but it is doubtful that the Merehani are the Slavic tribes of modern Slovakia. The passage concerning them may have been added by another scribe after the
union of the two groups was effected in about 833, as we shall see.
This would explain why the Geographer assigned only eleven
cities *(civitates)* to the Marharii, meaning the economic and political centers of the united tribes, and to the Merehani, thirty *civitates*. This number could indicate the increase in strength of the
Moravian political formation after its expansion toward the northeast.[15]

Anyhow, the Marharii of the *Descriptio* are Moravian tribes;
their unification must have been achieved by the unknown predecessor of Mojmír, their first ruler whose name is known to us.

Mojmír was an able ruler. He was on good terms with the
Franks, although we do not know when and to what extent he
acknowledged their supremacy. He or his predecessor might have

been among the chiefs who submitted to Charlemagne in 803, but
it should be stressed that Moravia is not mentioned among the
lands which Louis the German was to inherit according to the
arrangement made in 817.[16] Besides Bavaria, only Bohemia, and
the lands of the Slavs and the Avars east of Bavaria and Pannonia,
are expressly listed. Were the Moravians included among the Slavs
East of Bavaria? It is probable, although it is possible that only
the Slavic tribes in the Eastern Mark could have been meant.

Anyhow, Mojmír lived in peace with the Franks. His realm was
solidly organized and he did not oppose the missionary work of
Frankish priests in his country. The information given us by the
Bavarian Geographer concerning the eleven *civitates* which existed in his realm was confirmed recently by archaeological discoveries in Moravia. Most probably the fortified settlements of
Staré Město, Mikulčice, Pohansko, Rajhrad, Hradiště near Znojmo,
Strachotín, Olomouc, Pohansko near Nejdek, Staré Zámky near
Líšeň (outskirts of Brno), and Kirchberg in Austria, the existence
of which is confirmed by archaeological finds, were already known
to the Geographer in 817 as well as to some others.[17]

❋ ❋ ❋

As already indicated, the Slavic tribes in modern Slovakia were
also grouped around another center, probably Nitra, and this unification must also have been achieved at the end of the eighth
century. The first ruler of this new political group whose name is
known to us was Prince Pribina, who resided in Nitra.

He too enjoyed good relations with the Franks and, although
still a pagan, did not object to the activities of Frankish missionaries in his territory. There seems to have been at his court an
important colony of Frankish merchants [18] for whom a church was
built. Adalwin, the archbishop of Salzburg, is said to have consecrated it,[19] probably in 828.[20] It appears that he accompanied
Louis the German on his military expedition against the Bulgarian
Khagan Omortag and took advantage of this occasion to visit the
important Frankish missionary center at Nitra.[21]

It is probable that the missionaries were successful even among
the native Slavic population. However, the fact that the prince
himself was still a pagan, excludes the possibility of a mass conversion. Adalram wished to encourage his missionaries in their

work and perhaps even to convert their ruler. In this he did not succeed, for Pribina remained a pagan.

The prince's reluctance to accept the Christian faith appears to have cost him his dukedom. Mojmír of Moravia attacked him, chased him from Nitra and added the territory to his own realm,[22] thus ending the inclination of the Slavic tribes to gather around this political center. The annexation most probably took place in 833.[23]

Pribina fled across the Danube to Margrave Ratbod, governor of the Frankish East Mark. He was probably seeking Frankish intervention against Mojmír, as he considered himself a vassal. Ratbod introduced him to Louis the German, but the latter did nothing to restore him to his possessions. He simply ordered him to be instructed in the Christian faith and baptized.

The fact that the Empire refused to intervene against Mojmír, although the latter's territory was considerably enlarged by this annexation, clearly indicates the Mojmír was already a Christian and on excellent terms with the Franks. His own country, Moravia, was also, at that time to a great extent already Christianized, thanks mainly to Frankish missionaries supported by him.

Although the presence of Moravian envoys at a Reichstag is first mentioned in 822, the submission of Moravia to the Franks must have been realized much earlier, perhaps already by the end of the eighth century, or in 803 as mentioned above. We do not hear of any Frankish expeditions against Moravia. We hear only of Bohemian Slavs in the accounts of expeditions which took place in 805, which means, of course, that Christianity had already begun to spread in Moravia toward the end of the eighth century.

* * *

The discovery (in 1953-55) of the foundations of a stone church with a rectangular presbytery in Modrá in southern Moravia, which seems to recall early Iro-Scottish architecture, gave occasion to a discussion on Iro-Scottish monks following the rule of St. Columban, and led some scholars to the conclusion that the first missionaries in Moravia were Iro-Scottish monks established in their own monasteries in Bavaria.[24] The wandering Iro-Scottish monks came to Bavaria at the beginning of the seventh century, but their activities were concentrated mostly in the territory inhabited by the Slovenes in former Noricum, and in Lower Pannonia. The Iro-Scottish missions in these lands flourished especially in the years from 745 to 784 under the direction of St. Virgil, the Irish bishop of Salzburg, who is rightly called the Apostle of Carinthia.[25] Passau also had at that time a bishop—Sidonius—who may have been of Irish descent.

In the eighth century the Anglo-Saxon mission worked in Bavaria, and its main representative—St. Boniface—was an outspoken adversary of Iro-Scottish missionary practices, one of which was that a bishop accepted orders from his abbot. After Virgil's death Charlemagne appointed as his successor the Benedictine Abbot Arn and, in 798 raised the see of Salzburg to that of an archbishopric. On Charlemagne's orders the Iro-Scottish monasteries were made to accept the Benedictine rule. The missions among the Slavs in Noricum, Pannonia, and on the left border of the Danube were directed, from the end of the eighth century on, by the Frankish clergy.

It is quite possible that some of the traditions of the missionary practice of the Iro-Scottish monks had survived in some of the Bavarian monasteries after they had abandoned St. Columban's rule—especially in that of Kremsmünster—and that some of these monks continued their activities even after the missions had come under the direction of the Frankish clergy who followed the Roman and Anglo-Saxon methods introduced by St. Boniface. But even so, their work should rather have centered around ancient Noricum and Lower Pannonia, among the Slovene population. In spite of this, the presence of some Irish missionaries in southern Moravia at the end of the eighth century could be postulated. Any systematic continuation of such missions in Moravia, however, can not be accepted.[26]

We have thus to conclude that the Irish-Scottish missionaries from Bavaria could not have played any noticeable role in the Christianization of the Moravian Slavs. The principal missionaries in Moravia were Frankish priests, and the claims which Passau later voiced that Moravia was part of its diocese, point out that most of the Frankish missionaries were sent to Moravia by the bishops of Passau. The most active in this work was Bishop Reginhar (818-838). A much later tradition attributes the conversion of all Moravians to him.[27] Although this tradition cannot be fully trusted, it remains certain that Bishop Reginhar had become very

active in Moravia. The claim that he had himself visited the
country and had there held synods with the missionary clergy (a
claim put forward in the letter of 900 [28] from the Bavarian hierarchy, protesting against the hierarchical reorganization of Moravia by Pope John IX) cannot be completely rejected. The primitive organization of the Moravian Christians headed by archpriests [29] should also be attributed to Reginhar.

When we take all this into consideration, we may go even
further and date the baptism of Mojmír after 818. It is probable
that the embassy to Louis the Pious in 822 may have been connected with Mojmír's decision to accept Christianity, together
with his tribal chiefs.

*   *   *

The presence in Moravia of missionaries from Germany is attested also by the *Life of Methodius,* as we have seen. The author
also speaks, however, of priests from Greece and Italy. The presence of priests from Greece in Moravia at the beginning of the
ninth century has presented an enigma to many historians of this
period. It has been suggested that during the persecution of the
Christians in Bulgaria by Omortag, some Greek priests escaped
into Moravia.[30] Although not absolutely impossible, this supposition appears less probable when we remember that the Christian
Greek prisoners were concentrated in the region between Drava
and Sava, and in cities in the conquered territories of Macedonia
and Thrace. It would have been easier for them to escape to
Byzantine territory, as many of them did in 836, or to find refuge
in the lands of the Croats.

However, Greek priests had much easier access to Slavic territories through the Byzantine possessions in Dalmatia. The Dalmatian *ducate* and later *thema* was "Greece" to its Slavic neighbors. The Latin cities of Byzantine Dalmatia had commercial,
religious, and cultural relations, not only with Byzantium, but also
with Italy, especially with Istria, a former Byzantine possession,
Venice, still under Byzantine sovereignty, and Ravenna. Ecclesiastically, they were under the jurisdiction of Rome. Thus, the
native clergy of these cities could easily be reinforced, and probably was, by clergy from Constantinople and especially from Italy.
Let us remember that Rome had never lost interest in Dalmatia.

Moreover, the Byzantine Adriatic cities could provide Slavic speaking missionaries. When we keep in mind, as was shown in the first chapter, that at the beginning of the ninth century the Christianization of the Croats, which had started not from Aquileia but from the Latin coastal cities under their bishops, had already made great progress, it is quite probable that some of the Latin or even Greek missionaries, who had worked among the Croats, ventured further toward the northeast.

Naturally, they avoided the territories claimed by Aquileia and Salzburg, where priests sent by the patriarch and the archbishop were working. They went to another Slavic territory which was neither under Aquileia nor Salzburg, nor Passau—namely Moravia. They spoke the Slavic language and were welcomed by its ruler Mojmír, as they did not present the political danger the Frankish missionaries did. The presence of missionaries other than Frankish is attested also by a letter of 900 of the Bavarian clergy, since we read there that the Bishop of Passau's synods held in Moravia comprised not only his own clergy but all the other missionary priests as well.[31]

* * *

The affirmation by Rastislav's embassy that their country "had already rejected paganism and now observed the Christian law," is also confirmed by the existence of stone churches in Moravia erected during the first half of the ninth century, before the arrival of the Byzantine mission. Their foundations have been discovered only in recent years.

Archaeological research in Moravia and Slovakia began on a large scale only in 1948; it is directed by the Archaeological Institute of the Czechoslovak Academy in Prague, which has branches in Brno and in Nitra. It has at its disposal a small army of specialists, the most prominent of this group being J. Filip, the director of the Archaeological Institute of the Academy, J. Poulík, V. Hrubý, F. Kalousek and T. Točík.

The excavations led to some remarkable discoveries, the most surprising among them being the disclosure of the foundations of sixteen churches built of stone;[32] up until now it was thought that all early constructions in Moravia were of wood. Ten of these churches were excavated in and near the settlement of Mikulčice.

A lively discussion continues among Czech archaeologists concerning the style and origin of these churches, and the nationality of the missionaries and architects who built them.

The most disputed church, rediscovered by V. Hrubý in 1953, is that in Modrá mentioned above, of small size, without a narthex, but with a rectangular presbytery. J. Cibulka has dated it from about 808, and compared it to the churches built by the Iro-Scottish monks in the lands of their mission. As already mentioned, his dating and theory of its Iro-Scottish origin has been rejected by almost all specialists. Hrubý[33] dates this church to the end of the first quarter of the ninth century or about 840, therefore still long before Rastislas had dispatched his embassy to Byzantium.

Foundations of similar constructions have been discovered in Mikulčice. One was excavated by J. Poulík in 1954, of which only the ruins of two walls joined in a rectangle are preserved. They seem to be the remains of a church which was destroyed or perhaps not finished. The excavator called them the remnants of the First Church of Mikulčice. This church was replaced by another construction with sturdy walls. It measured 12.60 meters in length, with an oblong nave and a rectangular presbytery. A kind of square construction was added to the presbytery. Under its floor, four graves were found. The floor of the church was covered with flat stones. This church is called the Second Church of Mikulčice. Under it were found remains of an earlier building, the true purpose of which has yet to be revealed. J. Cibulka thinks that there stood a church with a rectangular presbytery, with rather thin walls—he calls it Church Two B of Mikulčice—which was later replaced on the same foundations by Church Two A. The excavator has his well-founded doubts about this theory. He thinks that Church Number Two was the first stone church built in Moravia. This is not impossible, if we accept the idea that the fortified large settlement of Mikulčice was the political center of Great Moravia and the residence of its prince.

This church was surrounded by 138 tombs containing some very interesting objects, the finding of which permits us to date the building of this church to the years 840 to 860, that is, again in the period before the arrival of the Byzantine mission. The rectangular presbytery was rounded up in the interior.[34]

A little different from these constructions is the Fifth Church discovered in Mikulčice. Its rectangular presbytery, also rounded in the interior, is somehow contracted, which might have been caused by the unevenness of the terrain. No tombs were found near the church, and therefore the date of its construction cannot be established. Another similar sanctuary, with a rectangular presbytery and rather strong walls, is called the Eighth Church of Mikulčice; it was discovered in 1961, and can be dated from the second half of the ninth century, as indicated by the objects found in the twenty-six graves which surrounded the sanctuary. The presbytery is rectangular (six by five meters). The Tenth Church, discovered in 1963, also has a rectangular presbytery. The walls of the nave were strengthened by two pilasters; two pillars in the interior seem to indicate the existence of a tribune. Only six graves, without any objects, were found around the church. The exact date of its construction cannot be determined.[35]

These are the churches which are regarded by Cibulka as being in an Iro-Scottish style.[36] However, several objections have been raised against his conclusion.[37] Only the church in Modrá has the elongated presbytery which is a common feature of the Iro-Scottish sanctuaries. None of the Moravian churches had a narrowing triumphal arch, the most characteristic mark of Irish churches. Irish church architecture did not have any supports in the navě, such as were found in the Modrá church. These are to be seen only in the church of Bretigny, whose Irish origin, moreover, has not been proved.[38]

We must, therefore, conclude that the church in Modrá was not a prototype for other constructions of this kind in Moravia. The First Church of Mikulčice seems to be even older than that of Modrá. This type of construction was the simplest and easiest form of architecture in a country where Christianity was only just beginning and which lacked skilled masons and architects. It was practiced not only in the eighth and the ninth century, but even later in the tenth and eleventh, by the Irish, Anglo-Saxon, and other missionaries in Europe. We also find several churches of this kind in Dalmatia. Dyggwe has made a special study of early Croatian church architecture; after studying the ground plans of some of the churches from Solin and Otok, excavated mostly by himself, he concludes that "The round apse . . . is rare in early Croatian time, where the main form is vigorously rectangular."[39] The only religious building in Salona which survived the destruction of the city by the Avars in 614 was the Oratory of St. Anastasius in the cemetery at Marušinac.[40] It was used for divine service as late as the early Middle Ages. This building "with its remarkable Syro-Mesopotamian style has exercised," says Dyggwe,[41] "a formal influence not only on the early Croatian church building at Solin and its surroundings, but on the whole of Central Dalmatia." He reproduces the ground plans of several Croatian churches in which the unmistakable influence of the Oratory of Anastasius can be detected. The two oldest of them, that of St. Jure at Kastel Stari and *Gospa od prikraj mora* (Our Lady by the Sea), each have a rectangular presbytery. There has never been any connection whatsoever between this part of Yugoslavia and the Irish or Bavarian missions.

Particular attention should be paid to the architectural complex excavated in 1959 by V. Hrubý at Sady, near Staré Město.[42] The oldest building on this site is a cruciform church. Another construction with some kind of apse was later added to its western side. Toward the end of the ninth century a small sanctuary with a semi-circular apse was built on the north side of the main church. The main earliest structure has a rectangular presbytery (3.8 meters long and 4 meters wide), and its nave (7.8 meters long and 6.8 meters wide) is divided into three by two stone walls. The excavator dates the oldest part of this cruciform church to about 825. A wide transept connecting the nave and the chancel makes it similar to the transept-type, three-aisled basilicas. The church seems to have been built in quite a sumptuous fashion. Remains of Roman roofing were found in the rubble and even fragments of rich, green polished porphyrite of Peloponnesian origin, and of gray marble, probably used for the altar decoration. Some big sandstone blocks were preserved in their original positions, on the floor, covered with tiles of moss-colored marble.

The most spectacular examples of old Moravian church architecture are the three rotundas discovered in the territory of Mikulčice, and the fourth rotunda found under the presbytery of the church of St. Michael in Staré Město. Of these the most interesting is the rotunda with two apses which was uncovered in 1960.[43] It is almost 15 meters long and 7.30 meters wide. It is known as Church Number Six of Mikulčice. The archaeological finds in one of the 190 graves around this church must be dated to about 825. Therefore, the church must have been built in the first quarter of the ninth century. The rotunda was adorned inside with frescoes

in vivid colors. Many remnants of them were found in the ruins
of the church. Unfortunately, no larger fragment has been re-
covered, although it can be seen from some of the pieces that
human figures were represented.

About the year 860, a round building was constructed on the
same site—Church Number Seven of Mikulčice—the foundations
of which are rather badly preserved. It was probably a wooden
structure, although rough cast on the inside. The altar was in a
polygonal apse built of sandstone joined with mortar. A piece of
greenish porphyrite found in the apse served, probably, as a cover
for the altar. The discoverer of this rotunda thinks that it is a sim-
plified copy of the rotunda with two apses and dates it to the second half of the ninth century.

The third rotunda—the Ninth Church of Mikulčice—excavated
in 1961, is a round building ten meters in diameter with four
niches. It seems that it was used as a baptistery.

The fourth rotunda, excavated beneath the presbytery of the
church in Staré Město, dates to the middle of the ninth century.[44]

✳ ✳ ✳

The number of churches built before the arrival of the Byzantine mission is considerable, and shows that Christianity must
have been well implanted in Moravia during the first half of the
ninth century. The question arises as to where the missionaries
and the architects who built the churches came from. There are
different opinions concerning their origin. The cruciform structure
of Sady has been compared to the Carolingian "Eglises cloi-
sonnées" in Reichenau, Corvey, and elsewhere, but even those
scholars who are inclined to accept this solution confess that there
is a great difference between the Carolingian churches and the
Moravian sanctuaries. J. Cibulka sees in it another phase in the
development of Great Moravian architecture, originating from the
combination of different architectural forms.[45] However, there are
many objections to this interpretation, especially if we take into
consideration that the main part of the church of Sady, according
to the archaeologist, should be one of the oldest structures yet
found in Moravia.

The existence of rotundas in Moravia at such an early date
poses many problems as to their origin. J. Cibulka, who would like

to find their counterpart in Carolingian structures and who mentioned in this connection the rotunda of Marienberg near Würzburg, had to admit that such an attempt should be abandoned, and he declared that he knew of no prototype for these Moravian churches.[46]

There is, however, a region which has not yet been sufficiently examined by Czech archaeologists, although the *Life of Methodius* points quite clearly to it—namely, Italy (with Istria) and Greece, which can also mean Byzantine Dalmatia with its Latin coastal cities. We have seen that the eighth-century cruciform church of St. Vid in Zara was to become the prototype for the church of the Holy Cross in Nin. The structure of St. Vid in Zara was copied from St. Catherine's church in Pula (Pola) which is dated from the sixth century. San Vitale in Ravenna was the prototype for the church of St. Donatus in Zara, built at the beginning of the ninth century.[47]

There are, however, also other churches in Zadar which deserve to be studied in connection with the origin of Moravian architecture. The church of Petar Stari, with its irregular rectangular form, was divided by two columns and one pillar into two naves which were vaulted with cruciform arches; the church has two apses. Sveti Lovro, of small dimensions, with three naves, had a cupola and was vaulted with two cruciform arches. The church of Sveta Nediljica had a basilica form, cruciform vaults, and apses. The circular church of St. Ursula, called Stomorica, has six conches. The entrance section was rectangular. We shall see that there were different variants of such a church style in Dalmatia during the so-called pre-Romanesque period, from the end of the eighth through the ninth centuries.

One of them is the church of St. Nicholas near Nin, and another that of Sveti Krševan on the island of Krk. The latter church is cruciform. Of a similar cruciform type is the church of St. Dunat on the island. That of St. Lovro had three naves and dates also from the pre-romanesque period.[48]

Rotundas were also known in Byzantine Dalmatia at an early period. A rotunda with six apses was built in the eighth or ninth century near Split. It is the church of the Holy Trinity in Poljud.[49] Although the rotunda of Sveta Gospa on the island of Vis is surprisingly similar to one of the rotundas of Mikulčice, it cannot be grouped with the Moravian rotundas, because it should be dated, not from the eleventh century as has been thought, but from about 1500. Its presence on the island, even at this late period, can perhaps be cited as an indication that this type of church building was popular in Dalmatia.[50]

This seems to be confirmed by the excavation of the foundations of a rotunda with eight conches in Pridraz, near Novigrad, by Stephen Gunjača, Director of the Museum of Antiquities in Split, in the year 1939–40. Remnants of another church with six conches were excavated by the same archaeologist in 1947 in Brnazi near Sinj.[51] The church of Our Lady of Trogir is also a construction with six apses.[52]

One should also take into consideration the architectural forms introduced into future Serbia by the missionaries from the Latin coastal cities of the southern part of Byzantine Dalmatia. New archaeological discoveries in ancient Praevalis (modern Montenegro), seem to indicate that their study may bring some satisfactory results. Among the early churches built by the missionaries of the coastal cities, mentioned above on p. 33 ff., two at least belong to the type of cruciform churches. First, the church of Our Lady in Duklja, which was constructed in the middle of the ninth century on the ruins of an early Christian basilica. Another church of this kind, that of St. Thomas in Prčanj, may be from the end of this period. Its plan is similar to that of Germigny des Prés in France, constructed in 813, and to that of San Satiro in Milan, built by the Archbishop Ampert in 876. The church of St. Peter the Great or Old in Dubrovnik (Ragusa) also represents the cruciform type. A new basilica with three naves ending with apses was excavated in Suranj near Kotor. The apse of the main nave is rectangular on the outside. It was, most probably, built soon after 840 during the reconstruction of the low city of Kotor, destroyed by the Arabs in 840. Another church, with a rounded apse inside and outside and one nave, was excavated in Ulcinj.[53]

Rotundas were also known in ancient Praevalis in the ninth century. It seems that there was a rotunda over the church of St. Tryphun in Kotor, which is described above, p. 35.[54] The church in Ošlje with eight conches reminds one of the rotunda of Church Number Nine in Mikulčice.[55] We have seen above, p. 38, that the church of St. Peter in Ras had a circular plan with an apse and a cupola resting on pendentives. It was built soon after the conversion of the Serbs of Raška, probably at the end of the ninth century. A cruciform church is found in Stará Pavlica.

These are, of course, only the results of the most recent archaeological discoveries. It is to be expected that Serbian and Croatian archaeologists will discover some other interesting remains which will help them and the historians to solve some problems concerning the origins of this architecture and its spread toward the northeast. We should keep in mind that even the region of ancient Praevalis was a part of Byzantine Dalmatia, although inhabited by Latins and Illyrians. The Latin priests were in touch with the priests of other coastal cities in northern Dalmatia with whom they exchanged their experiences in missionary activities. Many of them had at least an elementary knowledge of Slavic, as did their confrères from the northern part of Byzantine Dalmatia.

The architecture of Istria and the Quarnero should also be taken into consideration and be studied more thoroughly, because among the missionaries in Moravia there were most probably also priests from the patriarchates of Aquileia and Grado[56] who had also some knowledge of the Slavic language, since Slavic tribes were still numerous in Istria.

It should be imagined that the influx of priests from Istria and Byzantine Dalmatia into Moravia must have increased from 850, and especially from 855 on, when Rastislav had closed his lands to Bavarian clergy. He broke his relations with the Empire, but since he wanted his land to remain Christian, he was anxious to replace the expelled Bavarian clergy with missionaries from other lands, not hostile to Moravia.

These facts have been overlooked so far, as it was thought that the Croats had not been Christianized until the ninth century by missionaries from Aquileia and by the Frankish clergy. Because of this, it was even assumed that the church of St. Donatus in Zara was modelled on the basilica of Aix-la-Chapelle, rather than on San Vitale in Ravenna. The possibilities of influences from Aquileia and Istria coming to Moravia have not been excluded, but according to the new findings concerning the role played by the Dalmatian coastal cities in the Christianization of the Slavs, we cannot regard the non-Frankish missionaries in Moravia as originating exclusively from Aquileia and Istria. Aquileia's missionaries were fully occupied with the conversion of the Slavs in

Istria and lower Pannonia–modern Carinthia—and in Pannonian Croatia. Moravia was not Aquileia's missionary land, although some Aquileian priests did reach that country.[57] Then, we must not forget that churches were not built by the missionaries, but by architects, masons, and other technicians who accompanied them.[58] The costs were borne by the Christianized princes who regarded the churches according to Frankish custom, as their property. Architects could travel freely, and with their workshops they could reach any land to the northeast from Italy, Istria, or the coastal cities, independently of the missionaries. It is probable that even Salzburg employed architects from Istria. These factors must be kept in mind when studying the provenance and style of Moravian architecture. Fortunately, Czech specialists are becoming more and more aware of the fact that the prototypes of early Moravian architecture should be looked for in the Adriatic sphere of Istria, Dalmatia, and Ravenna.[59]

* * *

The excavations have given us a clearer picture of the political organization of the country. The numerous strongholds with suburban settlements were also economic centers, and seats of tribal chiefs. The settlements of Staré Město and of Mikulčice are particularly important in this respect. At Staré Město, a large Slavic settlement already existed in the seventh and eighth centuries, which grew considerably in the ninth, during the Great Moravian period.[60] At that time it was fortified by palisades surrounded with a deep moat. The remains of numerous workshops, foundries, and pottery kilns show that on this side a great center of manufacture and commerce existed which had the character of an urban community. The inhabitants depended for their provisions on the products of small agricultural settlements, traces of which are apparent in the neighborhood. So far, no trace of the residence of a prince has been found.

The settlement at Mikulčice was of different character, being centered on the prince's residence. There were stone walls and a stone palace with adjacent buildings. Around the prince's residence were grouped other compounds and the mansions of various nobles. They, too, were heavily fortified. The whole settlement had the character of an urban community more advanced

than that of Staré Město. In one place, the ruins of more than fifty
dwellings were found, separated by narrow streets. The neighboring villages provided the urban population with agricultural
products. The remains of workshops for the processing of gold,
bronze, and iron have also been discovered. The place was the
residence of a prince with a military retinue and was fortified with
a wooden stockade as early as the seventh and eighth centuries.
An outer stone wall was erected at the beginning of the ninth
century. The excavations made so far indicate an estimated population of 2,000 inhabitants in this huge settlement, which covered
an area of almost one hundred hectares. At that time this represented a considerable concentration of population in one place—
a kind of town with a castle in the middle.[61]

J. Poulík, director of the excavations in Mikulčice, believes that
"the indescribable fortress" of Rastislav, which was admired by
the annalist of Fulda and which, in 869, stopped the progress of
the Frankish army, can be identified with the fortified compound
of Mikulčice. The same chronicler in 871 also makes a reference
to the city of Rastislav.[62] The settlement of Mikulčice presents a
strongly urban character; thus, both these descriptions can be
applied.

The stronghold of Pohansko,[63] fortified with palisades, was the
seat of a feudal lord. The houses, the remains of which have been
found, had floors of mortar. The church which had existed there
was built by a feudal lord and was a proprietary church. A similar
fortified settlement, with the residence of a feudal lord, is supposed to have been built in the ninth century near the village of
Strachotín. The remains of a church have not yet been discovered.
Other fortified settlements whose existence in the ninth century
is ascertained have not yet been examined by Czech archaeologists.

The Slovak archaeologists concentrated their research in two
places, Děvín and Nitra. It is now established that Děvín was a
frontier fortress called Dovina by the Franks. Many specialists
have identified Rastislav's "indescribable fortress" with Děvín, but
this view must now be abandoned because of new archaeological
evidence. Slavic settlements can be traced in the region of Nitra
from the fifth century on. The concentration of tribes in the region
ended in the eighth century, as already indicated. It has not yet
been established where the fortified residence of Pribina and

Svatopluk was. It seems that it was situated on one side of the modern city of Nitra where, of course, excavations can be made only on special and rare occasions. The church built by Pribina was most probably also nearby.[64] Foundations of a church have been discovered.

Two important forts have been detected near Nitra. The one below the hill of Zobor has not yet been explored, but a settlement on the southeast slope of Zobor has been excavated. Several dwellings of different construction have been laid bare, with broad stone-paved paths separating them. The objects found indicate that the fort was a center of trade. Both finished and semi-finished products and raw materials attest to a large iron production. The other, smaller fort was located on the Lupka hill. The excavations made in the settlements around it show that the place was a Slavic pottery center. Thirteen kilns were found concentrated in three groups. The building of the pottery kilns confirms the gradual development of this industry, documenting early introduction of the potter's wheel, and points to the specialization in certain regions of ceramic production both for domestic use and for export.

Near another fortified hill called Borina several hearths were discovered which attest the existence of another trade, that of glassmaking. Some local names seem to indicate the existence of groups of artisans of different trades who produced their wares both for domestic consumption and export. Although the excavations have only been started, the results seem to indicate that Nitra was not only a political but particularly an important economic center of Great Moravia.[65]

The archaeological discoveries made in Moravia shed more light not only on the political but also on the social character of the Slavic state, and confirm what the envoys of Rastislav said in the presence of the Emperor Michael III. The biographer of Constantine has them declare that Rastislav, "on God's inspiration and having consulted his chiefs and Moravians," had sent them to the emperor. On the other hand, the biographer of Methodius says that the embassy was sent by Rastislav and Svatopluk.

This last information is important. It confirms what we have seen before, that the country of the tribes which had been united in a type of political formation by Pribina's predecessor was regarded as a kind of appendage of Moravia, and had kept its particular character, which it had before, even after the conquest by Mojmír. Rastislav appointed his nephew Svatopluk as successor to Pribina, residing in Nitra, of course, under his supremacy.

The large cemeteries with numerous tombs which have been opened confirm the existence of chieftains and disclose a certain social differentiation among the Moravian population. In many graves lords with swords and spurs were buried. Some were even entombed in masonry crypts in churches. Even boys were buried with their spurs, although they would have been too young to ride horses. This shows that they were descendants of the upper class. The graves of ladies with silver and gold jewels buried with them also testify that quite a wealthy upper class existed in Moravia. On the other hand, graves with fewer and simpler objects, although from the same period, show the existence of simple folk governed by the rulers of the upper class. These social differences were not as noticeable in Slavic graves from the pre-Moravian period. On the other hand, a class of freemen must have existed and was still influential in political life, because the biographer of Constantine tells us that, before sending his embassy to Constantinople, Rastislav thought it necessary to consult not only the chieftains, but also the Moravians, which can only mean a kind of assembly of free men. Because of this one can characterize the Moravians of the first half of the ninth century as living in a semi- or early-feudal society.[66] Slow development toward the feudal system was evident, and was certainly accelerated during the second half of that period. It would probably have reached the same form as in other western states in the high middle ages, if the Moravian State had existed longer.

❊ ❊ ❊

Although the main occupation of the population was agriculture and cattle raising, certain kinds of crafts were well advanced. The ruins of many primitive iron foundries point out that metal work was already well developed in Moravia in the eighth century. Moravian blacksmiths were skilled craftsmen. Perfect agricultural implements of all kinds have been found in graves and in the remains of workshops, among which are assymetrical ploughshares. Some of the tools found in the graves of peasants testify that the Moravians cultivated orchards and vineyards as early as the eighth century.

Blacksmiths equipped the Moravian warriors with their arms. Besides lances and bows, their chief weapons were not swords but axes of a peculiar shape, particularly characteristic of ninth-century Moravia.[67] Different kinds of knives were common, but swords were scarce. Some were acquired by various means from the Carolingian Empire, but the Moravian smiths were quite capable of producing swords. Swords are found only in the graves of feudal lords. It is a known fact that in the Frankish Empire it was forbidden by imperial law to export arms into any Slavic country,[68] but this prohibition was not strictly observed. Some of the swords found in Moravia were also part of war-booty. Spurs were likewise produced in Moravia by native blacksmiths and were usually modelled on those imported from neighboring Germany. No Avar influence in this sphere could have existed, since they did not use spurs. The Moravian artisans produced remarkable specimens of this art, as is illustrated by some bronze-gilt spurs, one bearing a human face, found in the grave of a wealthy man in Mikulčice, near the Second Church.[69]

In the same grave were also found gilt buckles. The nomadic peoples had introduced the wearing of belts to Europe. Even the Byzantines had borrowed this custom in the sixth century, probably from the nomadic Bulgars. The Byzantine buckles, however, are rather smaller in size, and their plates are of an oval, triangular, or horse-shoe form with palmette or leaf decoration. The Moravian Slavs must have adopted this practice from the Avars. Many objects of this kind are to be found in the South Slovakian cemeteries where there are both Avar and Slavic graves.[70]

The Moravian Slavs, after taking over this custom from the Avars, developed still further the practice of decorating the clasps and tabs of belts, adapting it to their taste. Avar and other influences can be seen in these decorations, but differences between the Avar and Moravian fashions can also be detected. Some of them may have been inspired by Byzantine models. This may be the case with a silver-gilt tongue-piece from the grave of a boy buried near the Second Church in Mikulčice. It represents a crude figure effigy of a priest, or saint, in the attitude of an Orans.[71] The figure of a man in the same attitude can be seen on another object of a similar kind. Another specimen represents a nobleman displaying the insignia of his rank and with his hands raised in prayer.[72] This shows that similar ornamentation of belt plates appears to have been popular in Moravia. Several plaques found in the graves testify that Moravian artisans often used bones and antlers to make domestic and other implements as well as for decoration.[73]

The most unusual decorative object is a silver medallion with the relief of a rider holding a falcon. It was found in a grave in Staré Město and is one of the earliest known representations of a hunting scene with a falcon. It has been studied by K. Benda,[74] who looked for the prototype of this scene in post-Sassanian art. The manner in which the eyes, the horse, and the rider's clothing are represented betrays features typical of the late Avar and Moravian period. The original of this representation must have reached the Danubian basin from the East in the second half of the eighth century. The origin of this silver medallion is not certain. If it came from an Avar workshop it could have been produced in the second half of the eighth century. But if it was the work of a Moravian artisan, it may be dated to the second half of the ninth century.

A great variety of pots, dishes, and vases were produced by the Moravian potters. All of them display simple ornamental motifs, characteristic of Slavic ceramic art.[75] Some of the vessels discovered in the graves resemble late antique pieces. It was thought that they were imported into Moravia, but after examination of the remains of the Moravian pottery kilns, especially in Sady near Staré Město and around Nitra, Czech archaeologists are inclined to admit that even these pieces, which resemble antique Roman amphoras and flasks, could have been produced by native artisans. It seems that the glass blowers around Nitra were producing glass buttons, glass pearls, and glass vases. Fragments of glass vases found in Staré Město indicate that glassware was also imported from the Rhineland factories to Moravia.

Remarkable achievements were realized by Moravian gold- and silversmiths. A great quantity of different kinds of jewelry was found in the graves. The most typical ornaments of the Moravians were copper-gilt, silver, and gold buttons, used by them instead of the clasps and fibulas characteristic of Roman and Byzantine fashion. Although the Slavic name for button—*gomb, gumb*—is derived from the Byzantine *kombos,* this Moravian model does not seem to have been an import from Byzantium. We are not very familiar with the history of Byzantine costume, but it seems that buttons, instead of (or in addition to) clasps were used in Byzantium in the ninth century. There are several types of buttons in Moravia which were classified by V. Hrubý, who found more than 178 specimens in the graves around Staré Město. A great number of buttons was also found in Mikulčice and at Pohansko.[76]

Most numerous are metal buttons of copper-gilt; some are of silver and in some rare cases of gold. The surface is punched and incised, displaying, as a rule, plant motifs, sometimes geometric patterns and, more rarely, fantastic birds. Another type of button has a granulated design giving it the aspect of a raspberry. They are mostly of silver, seldom of gold. The granulated ornaments often varied. Other buttons were made in an oval shape with a granulated design and with the addition of colored glass decoration. Some of them may have been copies of Byzantine or other models and designs, but executed in workshops in a rather barbaric environment with a less perfect technique.

It is almost impossible to determine the origin of the many glass necklaces found in the graves of Moravian ladies of the ninth century.[77] It was a current and popular glass product which was exported to the whole continent from workshops in Egypt, Syria, the Danubian basin, and Byzantium. Most of these objects found in Moravia were imported from the East or from the Byzantine glass factories, perhaps also from workshops in the Rhineland. It is probable, however, that glass necklaces were also produced in Moravia in imitation of the imports. One of the necklaces found in the vicinity of Staré Město is particularly interesting. It is ornamented with a topaz and a shell prevalent in the area of the Adriatic Sea.[78] This find furnishes additional proof of contacts between Moravia and Dalmatia, and points out the fact that at least some of the jewelry probably came to Moravia from Byzantine cities on the Adriatic coast. Rings[79] are not very numerous among the finds in the Moravian cemeteries. The oldest type so far discovered is a simple circle; they are often of bronze, which would link them to Roman provincial models. Rings with the bezel decorated with granular or incised geometrical and plant motifs seem to have been popular. Some of them are inset with small pieces of colored glass. The form of the ring often recalls Byzantine patterns, but the workmanship does not. This seems to indicate that some of the rings were produced in Moravian workshops by both native and foreign artisans.

The earrings[80] which have been found deserve special study. They were a particularly popular ornament in Moravia. In the graves around Staré Město 687 specimens have been discovered, and a great number of them was also found in other Moravian places, especially in Mikulčice. Many of these earrings, usually of a very simple design, came from the Danubian workshops which supplied the nomadic invaders—Huns, Langobards, Avars—with this kind of jewelry. They were very numerous in all Slavic lands, and are found in graves which date from the seventh and eighth to the eleventh centuries.

The more attractive examples of these earrings have been identified by the archaeologists as having been modelled on Oriental or Byzantine patterns. The oldest type is represented by earrings of one or several beads suspended from a ring. They date from the first quarter of the ninth century. Others represent a further stage in the development of the art of earring manufacture, and have been found in graves of the second half of the ninth century. Similar jewelry was also found in Dalmatia together with some coins of Constantine V (741–775).[81] We may assume that this form of earring came to Moravia from Dalmatia in the ninth century, and was reproduced in native workshops.

Another type is characterized by small granulated pendants of globular or barrel shape with four or more little globes. They are mostly of gold or silver. Similar earrings have been found in Slovenia in a cemetery at Ptuj[82] dating from the tenth and eleventh century, which may indicate that this kind of ornament came to Moravia by way of Aquileia through former Noricum in the ninth or tenth century. Another type of earring is represented by some 42 specimens found in Staré Město, characterized by a barrel-shaped (pendant) element between two granulated beads. Jewelry with a lunar motif, common in Byzantium and copied by foreign workshops, was also reproduced by Moravian artisans.

* * *

We have to confess that among the examples of Moravian minor arts few of the objects so far discovered can be safely thought of as having been imported from Byzantium. This applies particularly to the first half of the ninth century. Because of this fact, it seemed to many specialists almost inexplicable how the Moravian Slavs had been able to reach such a high level of culture and where Rastislav had obtained such detailed information about Byzantium, as is evident from the request made by his ambassadors to Michael III. The distance between Moravia and Byzantium seemed too far to allow commercial and other contacts between them. It was also thought that the provincial Roman culture which had flourished in Pannonia and Noricum, Roman provinces neighboring on Moravia, did not survive the devastations made by the invaders (Germanic tribes, Huns, Avars, and Slavs), and that the Slavs in Moravia were completely cut off from the remnants of this cuture.

However, this opinion has to be radically changed. As is shown in Appendix II, the Roman provincial culture did not disappear completely from the Danubian provinces, and the Slavs on the left of the Danube had many occasions to become acquainted with old Roman traditions in the production of many objects of Roman material culture. The contact of these lands with Byzantium had not completely been cut off either, continuing through the intermediary of the new conquerors of Pannonia. These new discoveries sketched in Appendix II show that this new state, which had been slowly formed in the eighth century and which had begun to play an important role in the political and cultural life of Central Europe in the ninth century, was not an isolated phenomenon, and that its origin and growth was not alien to the cultural and political trends of that period. It fitted well into European evolution. Not only was it connected with contemporary Europe, but it had benefited from the achievements of all the cultures which had enriched the life of the peoples in the Danubian region for centuries. Although its peoples had lived outside the *Limes* of the Roman Empire, it was able to improve its primitive civilization with what was left of Roman accomplishments in Noricum and Pannonia. It fell heir to the Avar culture, which was also made up of Asiatic and Byzantine elements. It was in commercial contact with the Franks from the time of Samo[83] and, although profiting from the Carolingian renaissance, fought for its political and cultural independence. Indirect contacts with the Byzantine civilization which came from Pannonia, and from Byzantine possessions

on the Adriatic through the ancient Amber Road, informed
Rastislav and his people of the great cultural center on the
Bosphorus and stirred his ambitions for more intimate relations
with Byzantium.

There was, however, another reason which prompted Rastislav
to send an embassy to Byzantium. In order to understand it we
must examine in more detail the political development of Moravia
after Mojmír's conquest of the territory ruled by Pribina.

*   *   *

Pribina is said to have stayed with Ratbod for some time after
his baptism. However, having quarreled with him, he left Frankish
territory and reached Bulgaria, probably in 836.[84] If he hoped to
induce the Bulgars to intervene in his favor against Mojmír, he
was deceived in his expectations. Omortag might have ventured
to intervene, but Malamir was a weak ruler disinclined to hazard-
ous enterprises. Then the unfortunate prince tried his chances
with Ratimir, who ruled over Pannonian Croatia, at that time
under Bulgarian sovereignty. But he was again disappointed. In
838, Louis the German ordered Ratbod to invade Ratimir's territory and to restore Frankish supremacy.[85] Ratimir was unable to
stop the Franks and escaped, probably to Bulgaria; Pribina, with
his son Kocel and his retinue, took refuge in the Frankish territory
beyond the Sava river, administered by Count Salacho. The latter
succeeded in reconciling Pribina with Ratbod. About 840 Louis
the German entrusted Pribina with the administration of a part
of Upper Pannonia around Lake Balaton. In this region Pribina
built his stronghold called Mosaburg, and worked intensively to
strengthen Christianity by building many new churches. In reward for his pro-Frankish sentiments and Christian zeal, this
territory was conferred on him by Louis as an hereditary dominion
in 847.[86]

Mojmír of Moravia seems to have died in 845. It appears that
his policy of peaceful relations with the Franks was not approved
of by all his subjects, and some of the tribal chiefs advocated a
more independent attitude. The core of this opposition may have
been the chieftains who were still pagans and who objected to the
missionary activity of the Frankish clergy, which they regarded
as a danger to national traditions. The opposition seems to have

won over the successor of Mojmír, whose name is unknown, and provoked the military intervention of Louis the German in 846.[87] He found the Moravians militarily unprepared, and it was easy for him to pacify the country. Deposing the unfaithful but un-named successor of Mojmír, he appointed Mojmír's nephew Rastislav as ruler. Rastislav may have been known to Louis from his visit to the court, where he became acquainted with Louis' son, Carloman. This supposition, for which there is, however, no evidence, would explain not only Louis' choice of Rastislav as Mojmír's successor but also Rastislav's support of Carloman when the latter rebelled against his father.

Rastislav took advantage of his good relations with the Franks and further consolidated the Moravian tribes. His power and influence grew steadily and the ties with the Empire loosened as a consequence. From 850 on he could regard himself as a ruler independent of the Empire. This situation is illustrated not only by the absence of Moravian envoys from the Reichstags, but also by the cessation of missionary work by the Frankish clergy in his lands. Only those priests who had won the sympathies of the pop-ulation, and missionaries from other lands—we hear of priests from Italy and Greece—continued to work in Moravia.

The deterioration in relations between Louis the German and Rastislav can be explained not only by the consolidation of Rastislav's power, but also by complications in the relations of the Franks with other Slavs. Louis himself suffered heavy losses in Bohemia when he returned from Moravia in 846, which resulted in a loosening of the ties of the Bohemian Slavs with the Empire.

Louis tried to repair the situation in 847 and 848, but with little result. The Bohemian Slavs revolted again in 849 and, thanks to disunity among the Frankish counts who led the army, emerged victorious. The Slavs of Bohemia became independent.[88] In 851 Louis himself had to lead an army against the revolt of the Serbs.[89]

He was able to intervene against Rastislav only in 855,[90] but his army was stopped under the walls of Rastislav's main fortress. The retiring Frankish army was pursued by Rastislav, whose warriors devastated the Frankish lands on the Danube. Complications with his brother Charles the Bald prevented Louis from paying more attention to events taking place on his eastern boundary. The Moravians took advantage of this and invaded the territory of

Pribina in 860. Pribina was killed and his son Kocel succeeded him.[91]

Then, in 861, Carloman rebelled against his father and turned to Rastislav for support. In the following year he submitted to his father, but soon started another revolt, again counting on Rastislav's support.

* * *

All this forced Louis the German to look for an ally against the mighty Moravian ruler whose growing power so awed the Frankish annalists that they called him "king."[92] He found an ally in the Bulgarian Khagan Boris. The latter must have watched the growth of the Moravian power with some apprehension. Mojmír and Rastislav extended their territory to the middle Tisza,[93] and Moravia became a neighbor of Bulgaria. The Bulgars had never been allies of the Moravians, as has hitherto been thought. Even when they became Christians they manifested enmity towards the Moravians, as is documented by the complaints of Rastislav's successor, Svatopluk, that the Bulgarians had attacked his territory in 882; he accused Arnulf, Carloman's successor, of conniving in this attack.[94]

We know little of the negotiations between Louis and Boris, and therefore hypercritical scholars[95] have rejected the idea of a Franco-Bulgarian alliance, as direct evidence is lacking. However, there is enough indirect evidence to allow us to admit the possibility of the conclusion of such an alliance. The most eloquent indication that a kind of negotiation must have been in progress between Louis and Boris is given by the annalist of Fulda.[96] When speaking of Louis' attack on Carloman in 863, he says that, in order to surprise Carloman, who had taken refuge in Carinthia, Louis feigned an expedition "against Rastislav, the duke of the Moravian Slavs, with the help of the Bulgarians, coming from the East, as was said." His ruse was successful. Rastislav left his ally without help and Carloman had again to give allegiance to his father.

Why should Louis have pretended that the Bulgarians were his allies and were marching against Rastislav from the East if there had not been any attempt at a rapprochement between him and Boris a short time previously? The *Annales Bertiniani*[97] report of the year 864 says that the Bulgarian Khagan had made a promise expressing his desire to become a Christian. The annalist mentions this when speaking of a hostile expedition sent by Louis against the Khagan. Louis' initiative can be interpreted in the sense that, after having obtained the promise of Boris to become Christian— this presupposes previous negotiations between the two rulers— Louis grew impatient and began to threaten his supposed ally, who was hesitating to keep his promise.

This threat, if there was one, resulted well for Louis. We learn this from the letter sent in the middle of the year 864 by Pope Nicholas I to Bishop Salomon of Constance, in which the pope says:[98] "Because you report that the faithful king has the intention to go to Tulln and then to confirm the peace with the king of the Bulgars, and afterwards to subjugate to himself Rastislav willingly or unwillingly, we pray the almighty Lord, that the angel who was with the Patriarch Jacob be also with him and with all his men and that he direct well his operation in order that he may return with peace and joy to his own. Then because you say that the most Christian king is hoping that even the king of the Bulgarians desires to be converted to the faith and that many of them had become Christians, we express our thanks to God. . . ."

We can only conclude from this document that Boris, at last, no longer hesitated to fulfill his pledge to Louis, declared his willingness to meet him in Tulln where the alliance was to be confirmed and arrangements made for Boris' promise to be carried out. The pope speaks not of a conclusion of peace, but only of its confirmation *(pacem confirmare)* which indicates that the peaceful relations which existed before between Louis and Boris remained unbroken by the threat of military pressure referred to in the *Annales Bertiniani.*

On the other hand, should we hesitate to conclude from this information that the alliance reaffirmed in Tulln was directed against Rastislav, and that the king relied on Bulgarian help in his anti-Moravian manoeuvres, we have to admit that Louis was anxious to remain on good terms with Bulgarians—Moravian neighbors—and to secure, at least, their neutrality.

The bishop of Constance told the pope that Christianity had already reached Bulgaria, which confirms what we have said already about the Christianization of Bulgaria. Boris' initiative to turn to the Franks reveals that, at last, he saw how unwise it would be to oppose the Christianization of his country. Friendly relations with the Franks revealed to him another kind of Christianity less dangerous to the national sentiments of the Bulgarian boyars than the Byzantine form. It was a weighty decision and, had it been carried out, Latin culture and Frankish influence would have reached the frontiers of the Byzantine Empire.

* * *

The initiative taken by the Moravian ruler Rastislav and the prompt Byzantine response to it changed everything. Rastislav seems to have turned first to Rome with a request to regularize the ecclesiastical situation in his country. This is indicated in the letter of Pope Hadrian II to Rastislav, Svatopluk, and Kocel dating from 868–869, in which he approved the use of the Slavonic language in the liturgy. The letter is preserved only in Old Slavonic; its genuineness is now, however, generally accepted. The pope says there that Rastislav had addressed himself also to Rome to send him "a teacher."[99] There is no reason why this information should not be accepted. Nicholas, however, did not dare to interfere in such a delicate situation, preferring to keep on good terms with Louis the German, whose support he valued.

Not having obtained a satisfactory reply from Rome, and observing that the Franco-Bulgarian alliance was becoming a reality, and was aimed at him, Rastislav turned to Byzantium.

Let us now examine what the other objects of the Moravian embassy were. According to the authors of the *Vitae* they were, above all, cultural and religious.

After his break with the Franks, Rastislav could no longer expect any further cultural benefits from them and he did not want them, being convinced that any cultural or religious influence emanating from that quarter endangered the freedom of his realm. However, his young nation needed such influences and he knew it.

In this way one of Rastislav's requests was fulfilled. The emperor's reaction, after he had received the Moravian embassy, seems to indicate that the Moravian prince really asked for cultural and religious help. The emperor is said to have called on Constantine (chapter fourteen), saying that all Thessalonicians spoke Slavic (*Life of Methodius*, chapter five), but Constantine's first problem was to discover if a Slavic alphabet existed. From the reply of the emperor one can judge that, in their dealings with the Slavs, the Greeks encountered difficulties arising from the transliteration of Slavic words into the Greek alphabet, because of the peculiarities of the Slavic language.

※ ※ ※

This, and the task which awaited him in Moravia, prompted Constantine to invent the first Slavic alphabet, called glagolithic. It was a new creation, different from all other alphabets known at that time. In some cases Constantine may have been inspired by the Hebrew alphabet or by Greek cursive writing, but it is evident that he desired to produce something new and original and was influenced by the fact that all the civilized nations known to him —namely the Latins, Greeks, Copts, Hebrews, Syrians, Armenians, Persians, Arabs—each had their own alphabet by which their cultural standard was documented.

This idea is also expressed in the same chapter of the *Legend*, in the emperor's letter to Rastislav in which he extols the importance of this discovery. God himself had revealed to Constantine a Slavic alphabet "in order that you too may be counted among the great nations which praise God in their own language." The author of the *Life of Methodius* (chapter five) also stresses the fact that God himself had revealed the Slavic alphabet to Constantine.

All this suggests that the alphabet composed by Constantine was something completely new and bore no resemblance to existing alphabets. The author of the two *Lives* would hardly have used such strong words if Constantine's invention had been a mere adaptation of the Greek letters, such as the script now used by the orthodox Slavs which is called cyrillic. The manner in which the biographers speak of the discovery is rightly cited by the defenders of the thesis that the letters invented by Constantine were not cyrillic, but glagolitic. This fact is now generally accepted by almost all Slavic scholars, but only after a protracted discussion.[100] Slavic philologists are unanimous in praising the glagolitic alphabet because of its originality, and because it expresses perfectly all the sounds of the Old Slavic language, which reveals that Constantine was a highly talented philologist and linguist.

The *Legend*, of course, speaks only of Constantine as the inventor of the new letters. His and Methodius' biographers mention, however, that others joined Constantine in his prayer for inspiration, which indicates that there were in Constantinople many young clerics interested in such an enterprise. It may be that they were working among the Slavs, or were themselves of Slavic extraction. Among them Constantine found able companions for his missionary work in Moravia. However, it was his brother Methodius who became his most intimate collaborator.[101]

Methodius' biographer reports that, after his hero had returned from the Khazarian mission, he was offered the administration of an important diocese by the patriarch. Methodius refused this episcopal dignity, but undertook instead the direction of the Polychron monastery, one of the most important on Mount Olympus. This again shows that both brothers acknowledged the legitimacy of the patriarchate of Photius.

Constantine had already begun his preparations for his missionary work in Constantinople. The first literary works in Slavic were the perikopes, or readings, from the Holy Writ for Sundays *(Aprakos)*, translated by him before leaving for Moravia.

His biographer naturally mentions Constantine as the only envoy of the emperor to Rastislav. Methodius' biographer (chapter five) speaks only of the two brothers. The reference to many presents sent by the emperor to the Moravian prince suggests that the embassy which left Constantinople in the early spring of 863 was large. The brothers were accompanied by clerics of Slavic origin, and we are entitled to suppose that these clerics, who were expelled from Moravia after Methodius' death, were Byzantine subjects. The *Life of Clement* mentions particularly Clement, Laurentius, Naum, Angelarius, "and others" (chapter twelve).[102] It was not the custom in Byzantium to send unaccompanied clerics on imperial missions. High functionaries, leading the embassy, were responsible for the security of its members and were charged to discuss with Rastislav matters consequent on the conclusion of some kind of alliance.

As is shown in detail in Appendix III, the Byzantine embassy traveled most probably by the Roman Via Egnatia leading from Constantinople through Thessalonica to Dyrrhachium, where the brothers with their companions and imperial officers embarked. Sailing near the coast of Byzantine Dalmatia, the boats reached Venice, the last Byzantine possession in Istria, from where the members of the embassy reached Moravia by taking the old Amber Road, in the autumn of 863.

IV. The Byzantine Mission in Moravia

Reasons for not sending a bishop to Moravia—Byzantine liturgy in Moravia—The Three Folios of Sinai and the Euchologium of Sinai—The Leaflets of Kiev—The liturgy of St. Peter—The Leaflets of Vienna and of Prague—When did the liturgy of St. Peter replace the liturgy of Chrysostom?—Character of the Slavonic translation of the Euchologium—Constantine's method in the translation of the Gospels—Constantine's Proglas to the Gospels—Pastoral activity of the brothers—Moravian churches with semi-circular apses built by the Byzantine mission?—Development of "missionary" churches during the conversion of the Slavs in Greece and of the Alans; their introduction into Moravia?—Conversion of the Bulgars and the Russians—The brothers in Pannonia and in Venice.

Constantine's biographer describes very simply (chapter fifteen) how the emissaries were received by Rastislav. A more enthusiastic description is to be found in the Italian Legend. Its author says that when the Moravians learned that the new missionaries were bringing the relics of St. Clement—he was particularly interested in their discovery—and that Constantine had translated the Gospel into their language, they went to meet them and "received them with honor and great jubilation."

From the description of Constantine's activity in Moravia, it seems evident that the main object of the Byzantine mission was not conversion but instruction. Rastislav is said to have assembled disciples whom he entrusted to Constantine for instruction. This shows that Christianity was well advanced in Moravia because there were already numerous young natives preparing themselves for the priesthood.[1]

It should be stressed that the Byzantine missionaries were not led by a bishop, although, according to Constantine's biographer, Rastislav asked for a bishop and priests. In this respect the emperor and his prime minister Bardas—he is also mentioned in chapter fourteen—did not fulfill Rastislav's request.

The following reason could explain this omission. Moravia had been the object of missionary work by Latin priests and could be regarded as belonging to the sphere of the Roman patriarchate. The relationship between the Patriarch Photius, who was certainly one of the organizers of the mission, and Pope Nicholas, who was hesitating whether to recognize the legitimacy of Photius' patriarchate, was extremely delicate. However, after the synod of 861, Photius could assume that the situation had improved, and in 863, when the embassy left Constantinople, he was unaware that the pope had refused to recognize the decision of the Synod, had condemned his legates, and excommunicated him. It is thus possible that the patriarch did not wish to deepen this misunderstanding by sending a bishop to a country where Latin missionaries had hitherto been working.

On the other hand, however, the Byzantines were perfectly entitled to send missionaries to a land in which there was no hierarchical organization, the more so as it was done at the request of its ruler. Moravia was still a missionary land, and, besides Latins, Greeks are also said to have been working there. Thus it seems more natural to suppose that Photius was putting into practice here a method which he later applied also to the Bulgarians. After the conversion of Boris, he did not establish a hierarchy in Bulgaria, but sent there priests to give religious instruction to the boyars as well as to the people. He intended to introduce a hierarchical order in Bulgaria after the missionaries had prepared the ground. As concerns Moravia, it could have been presumed that the preparation for an ecclesiastical organization would take some time, because of the innovations in the missionary practice which Constantine was about to introduce. The first object of the mission was instruction in the Slavic language, the translation of liturgical books into Slavic, and the education of a native clergy in the reading and understanding of the translated liturgical texts. It was assumed that the introduction of a hierarchical organization would be delayed until after this first task was completed. It was well meant, but Photius later most probably regretted that he had not strengthened the position of Byzantium in Moravia and Bulgaria by sending them bishops.

✥ ✥ ✥

In Moravia Constantine, with his brother and other assistants, continued his literary activities. The question arises as to whether the Byzantine or the Roman liturgy was used and translated by the brothers after their arrival in Moravia.

It is natural to presume that the members of the Byzantine mission continued to celebrate the liturgy according to their own rite. Methodius was only a deacon and we are uncertain as to whether Constantine had been ordained a priest, but even so we are entitled to assume that there were some priests among their companions. This would rather imply that the liturgical books translated by Constantine were of the Byzantine rite.

Specialists in Slavonic liturgy point out that in reality there exist Slavonic translations of almost all the liturgical books used at that time in Byzantium. Many of the manuscripts containing the translations are from the tenth century, which shows us that the translators were anxious to give to the Slavs the whole body of Byzantine liturgical texts in their own language. This seems to be suggested also by the author of the *Life of Constantine* when we read (chapter fifteen) that Constantine had soon translated the whole ecclesiastical order into Slavonic.

We can deduce from this that the author of the *Life* had in mind the Greek liturgical order. After that we read: "He taught them (his disciples) the office of matins and of other hours, of vespers, of complete and of the holy liturgy (Mass)." For the complete he uses the word *navečernica* which is a translation of the Greek term *apodeipnon,* not of the Latin *completorium.* This suggests that at least the Office, or the breviary for the clergy, was translated from the Greek original. Some specialists have read in this passage instead of *prělož* (translated), *priim* (accepted),[2] and deduced from this reading that Constantine accepted the Roman rite. However, the reading *prelož* is preferable according to the manuscript tradition. The variant *priim* can, thus, not be used as a proof that the brothers accepted the Latin rite after their arrival in Moravia.

Of the manuscripts containing these translations there are two which seem to be most important for the appreciation of what Constantine had really done. One is the so-called *Euchologium of Sinai*[3] containing non-liturgical prayers (trebnik), and the other is *Three Folios of Sinai*[4] which were primitively a part of the *Euchologium* and which contain a considerable section of the liturgy of St. John Chrysostom. Some prayers of the *Euchologium* reveal great similarity with the style and vocabulary used by Constantine. This would imply that the brothers had translated into Slavonic a Byzantine *Euchologium* as well as the *Liturgy of St. John Chrysostom,* which had become more popular in Byzantium in the ninth century than had the liturgy of St. Basil.[5]

The first folio of the *Leaflets of Sinai* is of special interest. It contains some of the prayers which precede the Byzantine Mass—the *proskomidion*—which are common to the Liturgies of St. Chrysostom and of St. Basil. These prayers of the *proskomidion* have their own history. They presented many variations and were changed from time to time. The *proskomidion* in its present form was definitely stabilized only in the fourteenth century by the Patriarch Philotheus (1354–1376) and it was soon translated into Slavonic in Bulgaria and in Russia. However, the prayers of the *Leaflets of Sinai* do not correspond to the liturgical tradition of Byzantium or of the Slavic Orthodox Church. They reveal some western features and seem to be an original creation of the translator. Did Constantine intend to adapt these Byzantine prayers to the western atmosphere in which his mission had to work? As these prayers were not yet stabilized in Byzantine liturgy, he could regard himself as entitled to an original interpretation which would be more congenial to the new environment.

The *Leaflets of Sinai* do not give the whole text of Chrysostom's liturgy. Three double folios which would have contained the text of the main parts of the Mass are missing.

The third folio contains the final prayers recited by the priest at the end of Mass. Another characteristic feature of Constantine's translation should be pointed out. As some of the prayers used to be loud-voiced or chanted, they were composed according to certain prosodic rules. Constantine, respecting this custom, arranged his translation of the prayers in syllabic units of sentences (*kola*) with a syllabical structure. Some specialists see in this device the first poetic attempts of Constantine in the Slavic language.[6] We have seen that he had composed several poetical works in Greek.[7]

The translation of the Byzantine liturgy of St. John Chrysostom can thus be attributed without hesitation to Constantine. As concerns the *Euchologium* of Sinai, it should not be overlooked that many prayers have a vocabulary pointing to the post-Moravian era. We must deduce from this that the brothers may have had the intention to translate the whole *Euchologium,* but first chose the formulars and prayers which they regarded as the most important for their mission in Moravia. Their disciples completed the work in Bulgaria after the destruction of Great Moravia.

The attempt to introduce the Byzantine liturgy into Moravia seems logical and may have been welcomed by Rastislav, who had broken with the Franks and who wished to preserve his land from any political and cultural influence coming from them. If he had accepted Byzantine missionaries, why could he not accept the Byzantine rite, not in Greek, but in the language of his people? All this gave him and his people more self-confidence. It should also be noted that the Byzantine Mass liturgy was, at that time, much shorter than it is today. Additions to it began to be made at the end of the ninth century[8] and were later translated into Slavonic by St. Clement, the disciple of the brothers in Bulgaria, and by orthodox priests in Russia. We can thus conclude that the brothers did introduce the Byzantine liturgy into Moravia and did translate into Slavonic the most important Byzantine liturgical books—selected formulars and prayers from the *Euchologium* and the Mass liturgy of St. John Chrysostom.

* * *

On the other hand, the brothers must have learned already from Rastislav's envoys that the Moravians were accustomed to the Roman rite which had been introduced there by Frankish and Latin missionaries. Because of this many specialists think that it would not have been good policy to impose the Byzantine Mass formulary on the native priests and people, who were unaccustomed to it. They, therefore, see in the so-called *Leaflets of Kiev* the oldest known old Slavonic manuscript, which has been found in Jerusalem, and which on its seven folios contains the translation of a fraction of a Roman Mass formulary, a kind of Mass order introduced by Constantine in Moravia.[9] This is regarded as proof that the brothers had accepted the Roman liturgy. However, the *Leaflets* do not contain the whole Mass formulary and cannot even be regarded as a part of a Roman sacramentary. They present a complete section of the category called *libelli missae*, extracts from Latin sacramentaries which were used by missionaries and chosen according to the liturgical needs of their missions.[10] They are translated most probably from a Latin original, and contain ten Mass formulas, altogether thirty-eight prayers. C. Mohlberg devoted a special study to the *Leaflets* and discovered a sacramentary dated by him from the sixth or seventh century, in a manuscript belonging to the chapter of Padua (Codex Padovanus D47) which seems to have been the prototype of the Slavonic translation.

There is still controversy among Slavic philologists concerning the author of this translation. Because in the translation can be detected the use of some expressions current only in the Byzantine liturgy, it is thought that the translator must have been a Byzantine.[11] Since some of the vocabulary of the *Leaflets* is similar to that found in other translations made by Constantine—especially in the Gospels—it is assumed that the translator of the *Leaflets* was Constantine himself.[12] The manner in which the translation was made is also regarded as pointing to him. It is rather a free translation, partly paraphrasing the original text, especially in the prefaces, revealing in its rhythmic flow the poetic nature of Constantine.[13]

There are, however, serious objections to this attribution. The similarity of certain vocabulary with that used by Constantine cannot be regarded as proof of his authorship.[14] Moreover, the *Leaflets* contain also words and expressions which could not have been used in ninth-century Moravia, but only in Bohemia in the tenth century.[15] Of course, this latter objection could be eliminated by the admission that the *Leaflets* were copied in Bohemia in the tenth century from an original brought from Moravia. The scribe could have replaced some of the words which sounded strange to him by others which were more familiar. One can also ask how could the *Sacramentary* of Padua have become known in Moravia. Therefore, K. Gamber[16] thought that Constantine had used a formulary of Salzburg which may have been composed by

Paulinus II, Patriarch of Aquileia, and which may have been used in Salzburg and by the Bavarian missionaries in Pannonia and Moravia.[17]

Gamber's theory has, however, its weakness. He tries to minimize the similarity of the Kievan *Leaflets* to the Paduan *Sacramentary,* but he cannot deny it. He does not pay sufficient attention to the fact that not only Bavarian priests were working in Moravia but also priests from Italy. It is quite possible that some of them had brought the copy of the old *Sacramentary* from the sixth or seventh century which is preserved in the Paduan manuscript. Thus, the Kievan *Leaflets* could present a Slavonic translation of a part of this *Sacramentary.*

In spite of this, however, it is not proved that this translation was made by Constantine. A more thorough philological study of this document and a more critical examination of the similarity of its vocabulary and style with that of other works of Constantine is necessary in order to solve the problem of its authorship. But there is another piece of important evidence concerning the liturgy introduced into Moravia which calls for our attention.

❖ ❖ ❖

The *Leaflets of Kiev* do not contain the most important part of a Mass formulary, i.e. the canon. J. Vajs has shown in two studies that the glagolitic missals used in Dalmatia and especially that contained in a Vatican manuscript from the early fourteenth century which reproduces a Roman Mass order, reveal, especially in the canon, many lexical and morphological archaisms echoing forms and words of the oldest Slavonic period in Moravia.[18] He saw in these findings a proof that a translation of a Roman Mass liturgy must have existed in Moravia in the ninth century, from where it was brought by Methodius' disciples into Dalmatia where this glagolitic Missal is still in use. Because some of the expressions did not conform to the Latin norm of the canon and sounded like translations from Greek, J. Vašica came to the conclusion that the canon was translated not from a Latin original but from a Greek translation of the Roman Mass liturgy.[19]

It has been found that there existed a Greek translation of the Latin Mass order which was called by the Greeks the Liturgy of St. Peter.[20] The manuscript tradition of this translation can so far

be traced only to the eleventh century. Some Byzantine prayers
were added with time to the primitive translation, as is witnessed
by the oldest manuscripts from the eleventh and twelfth centuries. The original Greek translation seems to be reflected in the
Georgian version of the Peter liturgy,[21] made from the Greek most
probably by St. Hilarion (822–875), a Georgian monk who had
spent six years in a monastery of Olympus in Bithynia, and two
years in Rome. He died in Thessalonica. The Georgian version
gives a short account of liturgical actions from the reading of the
Gospel up to the confession of faith. It appears to follow the
Greek archetype which reflected its Latin original. In preserved
Greek manuscripts a longer text from the liturgy of St. James was
added to this part of the Peter liturgy. The main part of the Peter
liturgy is the Mass canon, translated from a Roman *Sacramentary.*
All Greek manuscripts have a common Latin basis and must have
followed the copy of the first original translation.[22]

A Slavonic translation of the Peter liturgy was discovered in the
monastery of Chilandar on Mount Athos by P. Uspenskij in a manuscript of the eighteenth century.[23] It shows many Byzantine features, reflecting the process of gradual Byzantinization of the
primitive text in preserved Greek manuscripts. It is a copy of an
older Slavonic manuscript which, however, has not yet been
traced.

As we have seen, the Greek manuscript tradition of the Peter
liturgy can be traced so far only to the eleventh century, but the
Georgian translation presupposes its existence in the first half of
the ninth century. It is, however, quite probable that it was known
in the eighth century or earlier among the Greeks of southern Italy
and of the eastern part of Illyricum. We must not forget that the
whole of Illyricum was, down to the year 732, under the jurisdiction of Rome. Because the metropolitan of Thessalonica was the
pope's vicar for the Greek part of Illyricum, we can assume that
the liturgy of St. Peter was known, and perhaps also used on some
occasions, in that city. If this was so, it would indicate that the
two brothers were acquainted with this liturgy. It could be also
presumed that they took a copy of this liturgy with them to
Moravia and translated it for the Moravians.

The archaic language of some parts of the canon in the glagolitic Missal from the fourteenth century and its linguistic character
revealing that it had been translated not from the Latin but from

the Greek, show that the main part of the Peter liturgy—the canon or *anaphora*—was known in Moravia in the ninth century and was translated into old Slavonic. The canon must have been contained in a kind of *libellus Missae* as were the *Leaflets of Kiev.*

❊ ❊ ❊

It should be stressed that there must have been used in Moravia another *libellus* which seems to be preserved in two glagolitic folia, called the *Leaflets of Vienna.*[24] They were copied in Dalmatia in the eleventh or twelfth century and contain fragments of prayers from a Mass in honor of one or two Apostles called in the Roman Missal *commune apostolorum.* Although they are of Croatian origin, they betray a very archaic prototype. This indicates that they were translated in Moravia in the ninth century and shows at the same time that a Slavonic Mass liturgy was used in Dalmatia in the eleventh and twelfth centuries. This supposes also the use of the canon which is preserved in the glagolitic manuscript from the fourteenth century and which also betrays its Moravian origin.

There exists yet another old Slavonic document written in the glagolitic alphabet—the so-called *Fragments of Prague.* They contain only two folia which were discovered in the library of the chapter of Prague in 1885.[25] It contains a part of the *Kalendarium,* indicating the festivals from the twenty-fifth day after Easter to the Assumption of the Virgin Mary. It is an old Slavonic translation from a Greek original, according to all the specialists who have studied this document. The language, however, does not reveal such an archaic character as do the *Leaflets of Vienna, of Kiev,* and *of Sinai.* It might have been copied from a prototype in Bulgaria or in Russia, but the Moravian origin of the prototype is more than doubtful. It contains also a Byzantine prayer called *lychnikos* which cannot be traced in any Western Mass formular. The Greek original of this translation has not been found. Was it another *libellus* which may have been brought in connection with the Peter liturgy? This does not seem likely, and the *Fragment of Prague* can hardly have been a part of the liturgy introduced into Moravia by the two brothers.[26]

In resuming the discussion concerning the liturgy introduced into Moravia by the two brothers, we have to conclude that they had first translated the Byzantine liturgy of John Chrysostom and parts of the Byzantine ritual, the *Euchologium*. On the other hand, however, the glagolitic missals used in Dalmatia testify that a translation of the most important part of the Roman Mass order—the canon—must have existed in Moravia in the ninth century. It is probable that this translation was made from the liturgy of St. Peter, a Greek translation of the Roman Mass order. The Slavonic translation of this part of the Missal could be attributed to Constantine.

What about the *Leaflets of Kiev?* Is it possible that they originated in Moravia? We should not exclude the possibility that the translation was made by Constantine, but his authorship is questionable. This problem calls for a more thorough investigation by Slavic philologists, as we have seen.

✣ ✣ ✣

Supposing that the brothers did translate the Greek liturgy of St. Peter, when did they decide to introduce the Roman Mass liturgy in Moravia? Some think that the brothers became acquainted with the Greek translation of the Latin Mass—the liturgy of St. Peter—only in Rome in 869. They are supposed to have found it in Greek monasteries in Rome, where this liturgy was in use as well as the Byzantine liturgy. The translation would thus have been made in Rome.[27] This theory cannot, however, be accepted. When the brothers left Moravia, after activities there lasting about three years, they did not intend to return, as we shall see, to that country.

They were leaving Moravia for good because they had done all that was necessary for the young Church there to carry on an independent existence. This means that they had translated not only the Office and the Gospels, the ritual (*Euchologium*), but also the Mass in Old Slavonic. If the Latin liturgy was also among these translations, then it must have been done before they had left Moravia. How could one imagine that this translation, made in Rome, would have been introduced into Moravia in the absence of the two brothers?

If the translation of a Roman Mass formulary was made by Constantine, when was it done? We have seen that the brothers had first translated the Byzantine liturgy of St. Chrysostom and a

Byzantine *Euchologium.* Thus the Byzantine liturgy was celebrated in Moravia from 863 to the year 865. It was in August 864
that Louis the German carried out his previously planned Moravian expedition, perhaps in agreement with Boris of Bulgaria. This
time Rastislav was unable to repulse the massive Frankish attack.
Surrounded by the Frankish army in the fortress of Dovina, he
submitted to Louis the German, recognizing the supremacy of the
Empire, and gave hostages to the King.[28] One of the conditions
imposed on his surrender must have been the readmittance of
Frankish priests into Moravia. The latter naturally restored the
Latin liturgy and began to criticize the liturgical novelties introduced by the brothers.

Constantine is said to have carried on polemics against his opponents who declared that the liturgy could be performed only in
the three ancient languages, Hebrew, Latin, and Greek, in which
Pilate had ordered the composition of the inscription placed on
Christ's Cross.[29] Constantine called them Pilate's disciples.

The biographer's mention of "archpriests, priests, and disciples"
opposing the Byzantines is important. It reveals an ecclesiastical
organization introduced into Moravia by the Franks before the
expulsion of their missionaries. Archpriests were appointed by
Frankish bishops in missionary territories when Christianization
had made a certain progress. They represented the bishops to
whose dioceses the new lands belonged, and the missionaries were
subject to them. We know of some cases of this kind in the lands
of the Slovenes under the jurisdiction of the archbishop of Salzburg.[30] The passage of the *Vita* in question suggests that Moravia
had its archpriestly ecclesiastical organization before the arrival of
the Byzantines and that this system was renewed in 864.

It would seem a good policy if Constantine, in order to thwart
these attacks and confuse the new "invaders," had decided, at that
moment, to introduce the Roman Mass formulary, translated into
Slavonic, and abandon the Byzantine liturgy of St. Chrysostom.
In this way a certain uniformity in liturgical practice would have
been introduced in Moravia, and the activity of the Frankish
clergy would have been dampened, since the people were more
attracted by the Slavic than the Latin Mass, both celebrated according to the same Roman rite. This supposition seems to be
probable, and in this case the translation of the Roman Mass formulary contained in the Greek translation called the *Liturgy of St.*

Peter should be attributed to Constantine himself. Of course, as we have mentioned several times, his authorship of the translation of the *Leaflets of Kiev* can be proved definitely only by a more thorough investigation by Slavic philologists. In his translation Constantine could have used another Mass *Libellus* which is unknown.

* * *

The change from the Byzantine Mass liturgy of St. Chrysostom to the Latin one of St. Peter, however, does not mean that all Byzantine ritual was abandoned by the missions. Some prayers and formulars of the Byzantine *Euchologium* almost certainly continued to be used in Moravia. This seems to be shown by the fact that one of these prayers was known and used in Bohemia in the tenth century, namely the prayer recited by the priest when cutting the hair of a boy who was, by this ceremony, initiated into manhood. Such a ceremony was performed in Prague on the young prince St. Wenceslas (died in 929). Although there existed a Latin prayer for such an occasion, the ceremony for St. Wenceslas was performed according to the Byzantine rite, as we find it in the *Euchologium Sinaiticum.*[31] As the Czechs of Bohemia have inherited Slavonic books from Moravia, the *Euchologium* appears to have been introduced and used also in Bohemia.

The *Euchologium* in its Slavonic translation contains also a formular of confession (or *de poenitentia*) which must have been used in Moravia before the arrival of the Byzantine mission.

Although no Latin parallel has been found so far to this formular, it reveals an obviously western character.[32] Only one part of this formular, called the *Prayer of St. Emmeram,* is preserved in manuscripts in the Old High German dialect.[33] A similar prayer was preserved in the so-called *Fragments of Freisingen,* translated for the use of Slovene converts.[34] This shows that the brothers also used prayers and formulars translated into Slavonic by Frankish missionaries, which were popular among the Moravians. But even here, the originality of Constantine is to be seen. Into this formular are inserted prayers and psalms taken from a Byzantine prototype. Thus, even in the translation of the *Euchologium* Constantine manifested his creative thought. His translation is in many ways an adaptation to the particular genius of the Slavic idiom, elevated to a literary language and to the needs of the young Moravian Church. He also adapted to his purpose prayers translated from the Old High German and the Latin by Latin missionaries.[35] We can, thus, characterize the liturgy introduced by the brothers as a combination of the Byzantine and Roman liturgical practices.

* * *

The translation of liturgical books was soon followed by the translation of the four Gospels. In Constantinople Constantine had already translated these parts of the Gospels called *aprakos* or *evangeliar* read during the liturgical action. Constantine tried to justify the translation of the Gospels into the Slavic language and to explain the method which he intended to use in his translation in a special treatise composed originally in Greek, of which, however, only one folio in the Slavonic translation is preserved, unfortunately in a very corrupt state. The Bulgarian ecclesiastical writer John the Exarch quoted a part of Constantine's treatise in the introduction to his translation of the work of True Faith by St. John of Damascus.[36] Using this quotation A. Vaillant was able to reconstruct partially the corrupted text of the folio which was written in Macedonia in the eleventh or twelfth century.[37] We can gather from this reconstruction that Constantine was well acquainted with the translations of the Gospels into other eastern languages. He seemed to have in mind especially the Syriac translation used by the Nestorians, thus justifying his translation into the Slavonic language. He stressed his intention of translating the Gospels as accurately as possible, respecting, however, the differences in expression and in meaning of certain words of both languages. In such cases he thought himself entitled to a more independent rendering of some of the passages in order to be able to explain the true meaning of the original.

In his translation Constantine followed the principles expounded in his treatise. Slavic philologists recognize the excellent qualities of his translation, which reveals a very deep knowledge of the Greek and Slavic languages and of their character. The translation is sometimes not verbal, as Constantine tried to make the Greek expressions more understandable to the Slavic Christians.[38] The original text he had used seems to have been copied from a

Greek codex of Lucian's recension common in Constantinople which, however, contained some variants used in the West and in Palestine; some of these variants were taken also from the Alexandrian recension.[39]

Constantine introduced his translation of the four Gospels in a special poetic composition, called *Proglas.* Its text was discovered in 1858 in a Serbian parchment manuscript from the fourteenth century where the composition is ascribed to Constantine the Philosopher.[40] Later it was found to have a special rhythmic character and is really a poem. Although some specialists were inclined to attribute this composition to a disciple of the brothers, especially to Constantine the Bulgarian,[41] it was shown recently that it is a very characteristic poetical composition of great value, reflecting very well the main ideas which had inspired Constantine. We read there a passionate appeal to the Slavs to cherish books written in their own language.[42] This appeal is all the more pathetic, since this was the first translation of the Gospels into a vernacular language to appear in the West.[43]

❖ ❖ ❖

The authors of the *Lives* do not give us much information on the activities of the brothers in Moravia. They are said to have found it necessary to defend the sanctity of marriage and to combat certain pagan customs and usages which the Latin priests were unable to exterminate. Among the false teachings, belief in the existence of antipodes with large heads is especially singled out. This doctrine was propagated by the learned Bishop of Salzburg, St. Virgil, who taught that the earth was of spherical shape, which naturally presupposed the existence of antipodes. It is possible that in Bavaria this was combined with an old Germanic pagan belief in the existence of an underworld in the environs of Salzburg (*Untersberg*). St. Boniface may have seen that Virgil's teaching gave new support in the eyes of many to this old pagan belief and, as he was anxious to exterminate all pagan customs, he threatened Virgil with an accusation of heresy.[44]

The spread of such a belief in Moravia can hardly be regarded as proof that the Irish missionaries, disciples of Virgil, had been preaching in Moravia. Frankish missionaries from Bavaria could also have held similar ideas. In any case, this passage is rightly regarded as a confirmation of the historical reliability of the *Life of Constantine*.[45]

The question arises whether the Byzantine mission had also initiated a new style in ecclesiastical architecture. We have seen that a number of churches were constructed before the arrival of the Byzantine missions.

There is, however, another group of churches discovered in Moravia, of different architecture from the churches we studied before. These buildings are characterized by elongated semi-circular apses. In 1949 the foundations of a small church were unearthed at Valy, near Staré Město, revealing an oblong nave whose internal dimensions were 8.50 X 7.25 meters. The apse in the shape of a horse-shoe was separated from the nave by a triumphal arch. It was most probably a burial church, because 954 graves were unearthed around it. A great quantity of richly ornamented gold and silver jewelry was discovered, together with vessels, knives, spears, and iron axes. This archaeological material permits us to date the construction of this church to the second half of the ninth century.[46]

The same year another and much larger church was discovered, but unfortunately not until a mechanical excavator had destroyed half of its foundations. The apse had an outside diameter of approximately three and a half meters. It was attached to the oblong nave by a transept. In the nave three piers were discovered and a screen partition separating the narthex from the nave. Part of the exterior surface was made of rods and wattles. It was roughcast on the inside, and there were traces of wall paintings. The reconstruction of this church presents great difficulties. We cannot definitely say whether there was a dome or a barrel-vault. Only forty-two graves were discovered near this church. It seems most probable that members of the early feudal upper class were buried in its narthex. The construction dates from the last quarter of the ninth century. A wooden annex seems to have surrounded the church. The building was destroyed by fire in the first years of the tenth century.[47]

A very interesting find was made in 1957 in Mikulčice. The foundations of what is now known as the Third Church of Mikulčice were discovered, with a long apse, three naves, and a narthex. The church had a total inside length of 34 meters, and the nave was 9 meters wide. The narthex was partitioned probably sometime after the completion of the building. The archaeological finds in the 350 graves—some of the stone tombs were built inside the church—permit us to conclude that the church, the largest so far discovered in Moravia, was built soon after the arrival of the Byzantine mission.[48] Another church which has been excavated, known as the Fifth Church of Mikulčice, also has an apse and resembles in shape the first church in Staré Město.[49]

Similar in style was yet another church, the foundations of which were uncovered in Pohansko near Břeclav in 1959. It is 20 meters long and seven and a half meters wide. It has a hemispherical apse and a rectangular sacristy. The oblong nave shows traces of having been divided by a transverse partition: this may represent a wall which was added to the nave to provide a narthex; or it may be the remains of a west wall knocked down at a later stage to extend the original nave.[50] We have to add to these structures also the presbytery of the Church of St. Clement in Osvětimany.[51]

The above dating of the churches with apses was proposed by the archaeologists who had excavated their foundations, and is based on the nature of the jewelry and other objects found in the graves in the vicinity of these sanctuaries.

The accuracy of their conclusions has been questioned by the Czech art historian J. Cibulka. He thinks that these churches belong to the second stage in the development of Great Moravian architecture and were all constructed before the arrival of the Byzantine mission.[52] One of his arguments against Byzantine influence on Moravian ecclesiastical architecture is the fact that none of the discovered churches possessed a *pastoforium*, the small additional building in which the Greek priests prepared the offerings for the liturgy and whence the procession with the offerings to the altar began.[53] However, this argument has no solid ground. It is natural that the churches built by Latin missionaries and their architects did not have *pastoforia* because the Roman liturgy does not require it. When the Byzantine mission arrived, its priests naturally celebrated their liturgy in the existing churches, accommodating their liturgical customs to the available facilities. This possibility is also admitted by J. Cibulka. When we accept the proposed solution that the liturgical change to the Roman rite was inaugurated by the brothers after 864, then in the ecclesiastical constructions which they may have initiated there was no need for *pastoforia*. At the same time the fact that no Moravian churches had this special additional construction cannot be used as an argument that the Byzantine liturgy could not have been introduced into Moravia.

In order to explain the existence of churches with rounded apses, J. Cibulka looks for prototypes in Bulgaria, pointing to the small apsidal church of Hagia Sophia discovered under the present Cathedral in Sofia.

According to his theory, this kind of early Christian architecture had survived in Bulgaria and Pannonia and was imported into Moravia by Greek and Latin priests who had taken refuge in Moravia during the persecution of Christians by the Khagan Omortag (814–831).[54] However, the church of Hagia Sophia was from the fourth century, and no such constructions are known to have been erected in Bulgaria in the first half of the ninth century. We have seen that the theory attributing the importation of such a church style into Moravia by Greek priests escaping the persecution of Omortag is preposterous [55] and cannot be accepted.

Another specialist, the architect J. Pošmourný, thinks that these churches were built with the use of a common unit of measure— i.e. the antique Roman *modulus*—and sees in them an example of simple missionary churches of the type introduced to Moravia by the Byzantine mission.[56] Even this theory, although more probable, has its weak point. The system of *modulus* originated in antiquity and no proof has been put forward to show that it was ever introduced into Moravia from Byzantium.[57]

In one matter Cibulka is right, when he points out that this church style is connected with early Christian architecture and that it was imported from the East. However, it did not come from Bulgaria, but from Byzantium. We are able to point to some indications which show that this new type of church was inspired by early Christian architects, and that it was adopted by Byzantine missionaries among the Slavic people in Greece at the end of the eighth and the beginning of the ninth century.

We have seen how important it was for Byzantium to rechristianize the Greek provinces occupied or at least infiltrated by the Slavs. Great progress was made, especially in the first half of the ninth century, in the political and ecclesiastical reorganization of Greece and the Peloponnesus. The most telling example of how the Byzantines reconstructed the churches destroyed by the invad-

ers can be found in Epidaurus. This city, famous in the classical
time for its cult of Asclepius, must have kept some importance
also after the Christianization of Greece. The catalogue of Greek
bishoprics dating from the iconoclastic period counts Epidaurus
among the six episcopal sees of Argolis under the metropolitan
of Corinth.[58] The information given by the author of these *Notitiae*
is not reliable, as is well known. Anyhow, Epidaurus had an early
Christian basilica which can be dated from the end of the fourth
century.[59] For its construction material from the temple of Asclepius was used. This basilica was destroyed during the Slavic invasions. Its apse survived the destruction, and in the Byzantine
period was used for the construction of a small church dedicated
to St. John. This could have happened only when the danger from
the Slavs had subsided, perhaps after their defeat at Patras. The
building of a new church inside the ruins of an early Christian
basilica shows that the rechristianization of the Peloponnesus
had begun. It illustrates, at the same time, the method used during this process—rebuilding the ruined sanctuaries from the early
Christian period, although in a more modest way—and accommodating the new constructions to the style of early Christian
architecture.

The Greeks of Epidaurus were not alone in following such
practice. We find another example in Eleusis.[60] The basilica was
constructed in the fifth century. On the ruins, inside the presbytery, was later built a small church dedicated to St. Zacharias. It
had an oblong nave with an apse similar in form to the apse of
the destroyed basilica.

On the island of Lemnos [61] two early Christian basilicas had
existed dating from the fifth or sixth century. Over the ruins of
the second basilica another church was constructed during the
Byzantine period, again with three small apses. Special attention
should be called to the little early Christian basilica of Alimoun-
tos, near Athens. It was built in the fifth century, and was one
of the few churches which had survived the troubled times. Probably in the sixth century it was enlarged and readjusted. Its apse
was left untouched, but no other apse was added to the *diakonion*
at that period. The *diakonion* was adorned with an apse sometime
during the Byzantine period.[62]

Perhaps we could add to these examples also that of the ruins
of the old Christian basilica of Thebes in Thessalia. Soteriou, who

describes the ruins of the basilica which must have been destroyed by the Slavs during their siege of Thessalonica, shows that a great part of the building was occupied by the Slavs who had constructed their small dwellings nearby, but he admits that a part of the basilica may have been used for worship in the Byzantine period. His plan of this part of the basilica, with a new construction inside the old building, using its apse and columns for a small nave, recalls that of Epidaurus. The Slavs who conquered and occupied Thebes were the Velegezites, subjected during the reign of Irene, whose General Stauracius had defeated them in the neighborhood of Saloniki, and in Hellas. If there was any new use of this part of the old basilica, it should have been after this period, in connection with the Christianization of the Velegezites.[63]

We can quote a similar case from Macedonia. Between the years 1931–1937 the ruins of an old Christian basilica were discovered in Suvodol, near Bitolj. The basilica seems to have been built at the end of the fifth, or at the very beginning of the sixth century. It was destroyed during the Slavic invasions, probably at the end of the sixth century. Later, after or during the Christianization of the Slavs, the church was readapted for worship in a diminished form. Only the middle nave was used with the bema and the septum. The partitions between the columns were filled in with the ruins of the old basilica and a small apse seems to have been added in imitation of the apse of the old basilica. Even this church was destroyed during the Turkish invasion, and only a small modern chapel recalls the existence of an old Christian basilica of the past.[64]

The excavation of a church with an apse and one small nave, near the confluence of the river Giljac with the river Kuban in the Caucasian region, shows clearly that Byzantine missionaries actually used this new style in the lands of their missions. T. M. Minajeva, who excavated its ruins,[65] shows clearly that this kind of architecture was used in the construction of small churches in this region from the ninth to the eleventh centuries. The small church should be dated from the ninth century; its discovery shows that at the same time the Byzantine Church had expanded its missionary activity as far as the Caucasus to the Alanic population, reviving an interest in these countries which earlier had been manifested by Justinian.[66] Kulakovskij has shown that the whole nation was Christianized in the tenth century by the monk Euthymius and Bishop Peter under the Patriarch Nicholas Mysticus.[67] He admits, however, that sporadic Christianization had begun earlier. The first attempts can be attributed to the initiative of the Patriarch Photius, and his disciple Nicholas Mysticus successfully concluded that which his master had started.

These few examples which have so far been unnoticed are of great importance. They show that the missionary activity among the Slavic population in Greece started to develop after their pacification, and that the missionaries and their architects were following the traditions of early Christian architecture in the building of new churches. They were unable to build great monuments such as those whose ruins were to be seen in their cities, but the modest sanctuaries which they constructed were serving the new faithful and the native population, who had survived the storm as well as could be expected.

The examples quoted above were hardly exceptions. They reveal a method which was most probably also accepted in other places in Greece, and show the emergence of a new type of Byzantine missionary architecture. Because of its simplicity, this architecture was best fitted for the mission lands and, at the same time, kept a link with early Christian artistic traditions.

All this entitles us to presume that this type of architecture was brought into Moravia by the Byzantine mission. There is no reason why churches with an apse—the church of Pohansko included —should be dated from the period before the arrival of Constantine and Methodius, the less so as the archaeological findings discovered in the burial grounds surrounding those churches should be dated, with some exceptions, from the second half of the ninth century.

These observations also help to solve the problem concerning the largest church, the third of Mikulčice. J. Cibulka [68] saw in this structure a partition-wall church, a kind of *église cloisonnée*. He compared it rightly with the Greek church at Skripou. This church was built in 873–74 in the reign of Basil I, when his sons Alexander and Leo had become co-emperors, and is still in use. Its construction shows that this kind of architecture, related to early Christian types, was known in Byzantium certainly before the church was constructed, and could have been imported into Moravia after 863.

Besides these constructions, we can also date from the Byzantine period in Moravia the addition to the cruciform church of Sady, which is one of the oldest sacral constructions in that region.[69] This apsidal addition may have also served as a school for catechumens or for the instruction of clerics. We have seen that theological schools were often erected in Byzantium in and outside the churches.[70]

There are points in his review of Moravian architecture on which Cibulka is right. Not one of the discovered churches resembles the monuments which adorned Constantinople and Thessalonica at that period, but this does not mean that the Byzantine mission could not have used simpler architectural types better suited to a newly converted land. He also rightly points out the difference in building material used in Byzantium and in Moravia. But it was certainly more practical for the architects who came with or after the Byzantine mission to accommodate themselves to the material used in local construction—ashlar and mortar—than to teach the primitive workers how to cut stone blocks or to fabricate bricks, the current material in Byzantine architecture. It is also true that Moravians could have learnt the basic principles of old Roman architecture from ruins of Roman constructions. They did not, however, have to go to Pannonia. They found ruins of Roman forts in their own country. They also used bricks from these ruins for their own constructions. Cibulka is also right in admitting that the Moravian architects often had their own ideas, and changed the types imported by foreign builders to their own taste. In this way, the forms of Moravian apses and narthexes could perhaps be explained. He is also right in saying that Moravian architecture was influenced by that of the limitrophe countries; but why go as far as Bulgaria in imagining a continuation of the early Christian type represented by the church of the Holy Wisdom in Sofia in Bulgaria, and the Danubian region? When Bulgaria became Christian, the first churches were built in that country not by native, but by Byzantine architects. If it is true that this Bulgarian architecture came back to the local forms of the late Roman period, thus erecting churches with apses of the same breadth and depth, then this adaptation was made by Byzantine architects. Let us remember here the attempts of Greek missionaries to adapt the ruins of old Christian basilicas with apses for the worship of their new converts, simply by the addition of a nave. Why exclude the possibility that this new simple style was introduced into Moravia by Greek artisans? On the other hand, why not take into consideration a similar development in another former Roman province—Dalmatia? There, too, we see that the building activity in the ninth century was inspired not by Byzantine models, but rather that the builders went back to late Roman and early Christian traditions. Let us recall, also, the remnants of the small church in Ulcinj, very similar to Moravian churches with an apse. The artisans who came to Moravia from the South remained in that country after the arrival of the Moravian mission, and continued their building activity with or without the inspiration of their colleagues from Byzantium.

It will be the task of art historians to compare these affinities and differences in order to present a clearer picture of the development of Moravian architecture. However, to exclude the possibility of any architectural activity by the Byzantine mission in Moravia is preposterous.

The question has been raised as to whether the Byzantine mission had introduced monachism into Moravia. This is possible. Methodius was Abbot of Polychron on Mount Olympus in Asia Minor and, as we will see, he certainly intended to return to his monastery. There seems to be some indication that the settlement of Osvětimany, near Staré Město, was chosen by Methodius for a monastic institution.[71] This is possible, but we have to wait for more archaeological evidence to verify this supposition.

✻ ✻ ✻

The situation of Rastislav and the chances for the success of his Byzantine project were improved by events in Bulgaria. It appears that the political aspect of the Moravo-Byzantine alliance was not forgotten by the Byzantines. In the same year that the Franco-Bulgarian alliance was due to show its first positive results, a Byzantine army invaded Bulgaria and the fleet made a demonstration on the Danube. The Bulgarian people were starving because of a bad harvest and tried to get provisions by invading the Byzantine territory. Boris himself seems to have been making preparations to join Louis the German in the campaign against Rastislav, which had been jointly planned. The reaction of the Byzantines was swift and unexpected. Boris capitulated, abandoned the Franks and promised to accept the Byzantine form of Christianity.

It has been believed hitherto that all this happened in 864, and that Boris' envoys were baptized in Constantinople in that year, and Boris himself in 865.[72] It appears that these dates should be changed, as has been shown by A. Vaillant and M. Lascaris.[73] A new examination of sources by them shows that the defeat of the Bulgarians should be dated after the decisive victory of the Byzantines over the Arab army in Asia Minor which took place on September 3, 863. Boris' envoys were baptized soon afterwards and Boris himself became a Christian in 864. In the light of this new evaluation, the effectiveness of the Moravo-Byzantine alliance very soon became evident. Louis the German was deprived of his ally and had to postpone his planned attack until 864.

Boris took the Christian name of Michael, that of his imperial godfather. As a present from his godfather Boris most probably obtained the recognition of his former conquests in Byzantine Macedonia, including the territory around Lake Ochrida and Lake Prespa.[74]

The news of Boris' conversion caused a great sensation in Byzantium. Different stories circulated in attempts to explain its sudden occurrence.[75] The story of the monk Methodius and his pictorial representation of the last judgment, which was reputed to have frightened Boris,[76] is certainly apocryphal. There may be, however, some truth in another story of the influence of a Greek slave Capharas on Boris, and of Boris' sister who, according to the Continuator of Theophanes, had become a Christian during her captivity in Constantinople. After being exchanged for Capharas, she persuaded her brother to follow her. This story may contain a grain of truth, although it resembles too closely the genuine story of Cinamon and Enravotas.

This important victory of the Empire and its Church, strengthened considerably the position of the Byzantine mission in Moravia. Rastislav also became bolder in supporting the two brothers and their work.

It appears probable that, during their stay in Moravia, the brothers learned of a further success of their Mother Church, namely, the conversion of the Russians of Kiev. This happened between 864 and 866. We learn about it from the encyclical letters sent by Photius to the oriental patriarchs to convoke a council for

867.[77] This first Christianization of Kievan Russia did not last. However, this could not have been anticipated in 864–866, and the news of this further success must have inspired the Byzantine missionaries in Moravia to new deeds. These events may have enlivened the hope expressed by Constantine's biographer in his version of Rastislav's letter, "that also other nations, seeing it, imitate us."

So it happened that, in spite of the setback suffered by Rastislav in 864, the Byzantine mission was able to work in Moravia for three years and four months, according to Constantine's biographer. Having laid the foundation for a Moravian Church with its own Slavic liturgy and religious literature, and having formed a new school of disciples, the brothers could plan the fulfillment of the second stage of their missionary operations, which was the ordination of their disciples to the priesthood and the establishment of a hierarchy.

*   *   *

After leaving Moravia with some of their disciples, they stopped in Pannonia where they were well received by its ruler Kocel, the successor of Pribina, who certainly knew of their presence and work in Moravia. Their hopes of spreading the faith among other Slavic nations using the new medium of Slavic literature, as expressed by Constantine's biographer, found their first fulfillment here. Kocel was so much interested in Slavic letters that he himself learned them and entrusted about fifty disciples to the brothers for instruction in Slavic letters. We are well informed about the religious situation in Kocel's land thanks to the document called *Conversio* of the Bavarians and Carantanians. Pribina had been very active in founding churches and Kocel continued his work. The *Conversio* enumerates thirty churches and priests in Kocel's land.[78] The missions were directed by an archpriest who resided at Mosaburg, near Lake Balaton, the administrative center of the Mark. The Archbishop of Salzburg was a frequent guest at Mosaburg. He probably increased his activity after 863 when he learned about the Byzantine mission in Moravia. It was, thus, rather a daring gesture on the part of Kocel, a subject of Louis the German, to manifest such an interest in Slavic liturgy and letters.

The Frankish missionaries who worked in his lands must also have spoken the Slavic language and had certainly educated a considerable number of native clerics. The fifty disciples entrusted to the brothers were without doubt Slavs. The first attempts at the translation of some liturgical prayers into Slavic were done in Pannonia by the Frankish, or perhaps also the Irish missionaries, before the arrival of the Byzantine missionaries. As we have seen, the so-called *Fragments of Freisingen* have preserved some of these first attempts, mostly prayers connected with confession.

One of these documents, a kind of sermon for which no Latin or Greek original has so far been found, and called by the specialists *adhortatio*, seems to testify to the activity of the brothers in Pannonia. It presupposes an original connected with the preaching of the Byzantine missionaries in Moravia.[79]

The two brothers, with their companions, must have spent several months in Kocel's lands [80] and their activity must have been very successful, as later events were to show. The biographer stresses that Constantine did not accept any material compensation for his work from Rastislav and Kocel. He asked in exchange nine hundred prisoners, whom he freed.

Then, without any explanation as to why the brothers took this course, the biographer presents them in Venice facing an assembly of bishops (*jepiskopi* in the text), priests, and monks who attacked their liturgical innovations, maintaining that the liturgy should be performed only in three languages. None of the great Fathers had dared to invent an alphabet for the Slavs.

Constantine is said first to have pointed out how many other nations, besides the Hebrews, Greeks, and Latins, had their own alphabet. He enumerates the Armenians, Persians, Basques, Iberians, Suzdalians, Goths, Avars, Turks, Khazars, Arabs, Egyptians, Syrians, and many others (chapter sixteen).[81]

Constantine also used many quotations from Holy Writ in order to defend the right of every people to glorify God in its own language. The longest quotation is from chapter fourteen of the First Letter to the Corinthians. The biographer quoted it from the Old Slavonic translation made by the two brothers.[82]

When reading this chapter one has the impression that Constantine has already composed, in Moravia, a short apology for his innovation, choosing from the Bible some passages which could be used by his disciples against the attacks of the Trilinguists. He probably used this apology in Venice and later on also in Rome.

It is interesting to compare the fourteen scriptural quotations used, according to the biographer, by Constantine in defense of his innovation in Venice with the quotations used later in the bulls of Hadrian II and John VIII, approving the Slavonic liturgy. One has the impression that both popes knew of Constantine's apology and used some of his scriptural quotations in their bulls.[83] It is probable that Constantine wrote his apology in Greek and that it was translated into Slavonic by Methodius before the departure from Moravia. The Greek text was probably presented in Rome to Anastasius the Librarian, who was a fervent supporter of the brothers. The latter was able, in his capacity as director of the papal chancery, to instruct the popes and to insert into the bulls some of Constantine's scriptural arguments.

The disputation in Venice, if there was one, could have been held in Greek with Latin interpreters. The biographer, when describing it, was using the Slavonic translation of the apology which, probably, was much longer than the excerpt given by him.

V. Rome and the Moravian Mission

The brothers, returning to Constantinople, are invited to stop in Rome—Pope Hadrian II and the Slavic liturgy—Anastasius the Librarian and Constantine; Gauderich and the Legenda italica; *reversal in Constantinople—Constantine becomes a monk (Cyril); his death—Was Constantine-Cyril ordained bishop or priest?— Intervention of Kocel of Pannonia. Methodius abandons plans of returning to Constantinople—Papal bull approving Slavic liturgy— Methodius ordained archbishop of Sirmium with jurisdiction over Pannonia and Moravia—Political upheaval in Moravia; Methodius condemned and imprisoned by the Frankish hierarchy— Methodius, freed by papal intervention; his stay in Pannonia— Methodius received by Svatopluk in Moravia—Agathon "of the Moravians" ordained by Ignatius to replace Methodius?*

Constantine's biographer, after describing how his hero had overwhelmed his adversaries with his eloquent arguments, states simply that "the Pope of Rome heard about him and sent for him." When he arrived in Rome, Constantine was received by the "apostolic" Hadrian II who came with the citizens to meet him, as they learned that he was bringing the relics of St. Clement, Pope and Martyr (chapter seventeen).

Methodius' *Vita* (chapter six), and the Italian Legend, attribute this invitation to Pope Nicholas. The latter died November 11, 867, and Hadrian II was enthroned on December 14 of the same year. This gives us a reliable starting point for dating the movement of the brothers. The *Life of Constantine* suggests that the papal invitation reached the brothers in Venice. It must have been in the late autumn or early winter of 867 and they must have reached Rome in December 867 or, at the latest, in January 868.

The question now arises whether the brothers intended to go to Rome when leaving Moravia, or whether they stopped in Venice in order to embark there for Constantinople. The historians and Slavic philologists who dealt with the problems concerning the activities of the two brothers, are still trying to find a satisfactory answer to this question. We can ask ourselves with reason if a definite and generally acceptable answer will ever be given, because the journey of the brothers coincided with events in Rome and in Constantinople which cast an ominous shadow over relations between the two Churches.[1]

The Bulgarians separated themselves from the patriarchate of Byzantium and, in the first half of 866, Boris turned once more toward Louis the German and asked Rome for Latin missionaries. Nicholas I welcomed the opportunity and his priests, led by Formosus, Bishop of Porto, and Paul, Bishop of Populonia, were welcomed so enthusiastically by Boris that he even dismissed the Frankish clerics led by Hermanrich (Ermenrich), Bishop of Passau. Boris also found the pastoral letter sent to him by the pope on November 13, 866—in which all his naïve questions were fully answered—much more useful than the learned exhortation which the Patriarch Photius had addressed to him in 865.

The result of this Roman "invasion" of Byzantine missionary territory was the convocation of a council by Photius in 867, which condemned some Latin usages introduced into Bulgaria, especially the addition to the Nicaean Creed of the *Filioque*, condemned the pope's action and decided to ask the Western Emperor Louis II to depose Nicholas. The *Acts* of the Council, however, did not reach Louis II, because on September 24th of the same year, Basil I—who had been made co-emperor by Michael III—murdered his benefactor, became emperor, and, in order to win the support of Michael's opponents and of Rome, deposed Photius and reinstated Ignatius as patriarch.[2] These events influenced many students of the history of Constantine and Methodius who, because of religious prejudice, were anxious to separate the brothers from Photius, who had been condemned by Nicholas, and to connect them as closely as possible to the papacy.

However, at the time when the brothers were leaving Moravia and even during their stay in Venice, they could hardly have

known about events in Byzantium and Rome. They may have
learned about the hostility of Pope Nicholas I to their Patriarch
Photius and also about the change of attitude on the part of
Boris of Bulgaria. But the news of the council of 867, and of the
change in the political and religious situation in Byzantium, did
not reach Rome until 868. Thus, when leaving Moravia, they still
regarded Photius as the legitimate patriarch of Constantinople.
It was he who, with Michael III and Bardas, had organized the
Moravian mission.

One thing seems certain, namely, that the two brothers regarded their mission in Moravia and Pannonia as accomplished
and considered they were leaving the country for good.[3] This is
also indicated by the desire of Rastislav and Kocel to reward
them for what they had achieved in their countries. Constantine,
refusing gold and silver, as his biographer states, asked for the
release of 900 prisoners. The biographer described in a similar
way the brothers' leavetaking at the end of their Khazarian mission (chapter eleven).

In chapter seven, Methodius' biographer reports how Constantine, before dying, asked his brother to abandon his intention of
returning to his monastery at Mount Olympus and instead to
continue the missionary work. Thus, the biographer confirms that
Methodius did want to return to his monastery. Constantine's
request may only be imagination on the part of Methodius' biographer. The author of Constantine's *Vita* would appear better
entitled to report the last words of his hero, and he does not say
anything of this kind. On the contrary, he reports that Methodius,
after the death of his brother, asked the pope for permission to
bring the body back to Byzantium for burial in his monastery.
Such had been the desire of their mother. This again shows that
Methodius had decided to return to his monastery.

It is thus most probable that the brothers stopped in Venice in
order to return to Constantinople by sea. Constantine's health
must already have been frail at that time, a circumstance which
may have persuaded them to choose a sea voyage. They may have
thought that they could continue their activity as teachers of the
Slavs in Constantinople.

The choice of the sea route from Venice to Dyrrhachium can
also be explained by the desire to avoid travelling through
Bulgaria.[4] The account already given of relations between Mora-

via, Bulgaria, and the Franks indicates why it was desirable to avoid going through a territory whose rulers were never very friendly toward their Moravian neighbors. The news that the Bulgarians had turned again to Louis the German, and that the latter had chosen Hermanrich, Bishop of Passau, as leader of a Frankish missionary expedition to Bulgaria had certainly reached Moravia in 866 before the brothers left the country.

But what about the disciples who were accompanying them? Is it possible that they wished to have them ordained in Constantinople? One circumstance indeed favors such an explanation. Rastislav had certainly informed them that he had asked Nicholas I to arrange the ecclesiastical organization of his country, and that his request had been refused. They were aware of the hostility of the Frankish bishops to any ecclesiastical independence on the part of the Moravians. Rastislav's political position was stronger, and he could afford a new approach to Constantinople repeating his request for a bishop, independent of the Frankish hierarchy. The brothers had certainly chosen one or more candidates for bishoprics.

There is, however, one objection to this interpretation. The brothers carried with them the relics believed to be those of St. Clement, Bishop of Rome. Does this not indicate their intention to go to Rome and deposit the relics there?[5] Then there was the desire shared by many pious Byzantines to make a pilgrimage to Rome, the burial place of SS. Peter and Paul and the seat of the first patriarch. Contrary to what is still sometimes believed, there was no hostility to Rome in the Byzantine religious world of that time. We know of many Byzantine pilgrims who went to Rome, and there were several Greek monasteries with Byzantine monks in the center of Rome.[6] On the other hand, it must not be forgotten that the whole of southern Italy was still under Byzantine sovereignty. All this could indicate that the brothers desired to make a pilgrimage to Rome and return to Constantinople via Rome and southern Italy. If the pope refused to fulfill Rastislav's request for a bishop and would not accept their liturgical innovations, they could still obtain what they wanted in Constantinople.

But if the brothers really intended to go to Rome why should the pope invite them to visit him? Nicholas must have learned of their activity in Moravia and Pannonia long before. He must have realized that a Byzantine mission would never have reached

Moravia if he had responded favorably to Rastislav's request in 861 or 862. He was in competition with Byzantium in Bulgaria, and also with the Franks in Croatia, where he founded the bishopric of Nin, probably in 860, and subjected it directly to his own jurisdiction. If the brothers had intended to go to Rome, he would have learned about it and it would not have been necessary to invite them to visit him. It seems much more logical to suppose that he heard of their intention to return to Constantinople while they were waiting for a boat in Venice. In the autumn of 867 Nicholas was a very sick man and the invitation was one of his last acts. He must have regarded it as very important, as it was made almost on his deathbed.

With regard to the relics believed to be those of St. Clement, the brothers could very well have carried them back to Constantinople. A part of them was left by Constantine in Cherson. We learn from the *Russian Primary Chronicle* that Vladimir, the first Russian Christian Prince, transferred them to Kiev after his baptism in 988, together with the relics of St. Clement's disciple Phoebus, several priests, sacred vessels, and icons.[7] This was to be expected. The local Christians were entitled to a share in this marvelous discovery. Moreover, Constantine was leaving Cherson for good. We do not learn, however, that part of the relics were left in Constantinople, most probably because Constantine intended to bring them back after he had accomplished his mission to Moravia.[8] St. Clement was regarded by him as the patron saint of his mission.

An understanding with Rome would have been necessary if the brothers had already intended at that time to join Pannonia to the Moravian diocese soon to be organized. Kocel's territory was administered by the Archbishop of Salzburg through the medium of archpriests sent by him. This was evidently within the sphere of the Roman patriarchate and any change in the ecclesiastical organization of this country could be made only by the pope.

But the mission of the brothers was originally limited to Moravia. It was a pleasant surprise for them to find such an interest in their innovation in Kocel's land, but the idea of an independent diocese for his land was not theirs, but Kocel's, and it was realized later in quite different circumstances.

This, however, does not exclude the probability that Kocel,

who had shown such an interest in the innovations of the brothers, had expressed to them the desire to have a bishop, independent from the Bavarian hierarchy, also for his land. Of course, he meant that the bishop would be sent by the patriarch of Constantinople to whom the brothers were about to give an account of their work in Slavic lands. He knew as well as Rastislav that he could never obtain such a privilege from the Frankish hierarchy and that the latter were powerful enough to prevent the pope from giving an independent hierarchy to his land. It is also possible that Rastislav was informed about Kocel's desire and was supporting him. Both thought that their political situation was strong enough to resist any attempt on the side of the Franks to interfere with their plans. Both princes were aware of the fact that the brothers were leaving their countries for good and both were expecting bishops from Constantinople after the return of the brothers to their home.

The suggestion that the brothers wanted to obtain recognition from the Patriarch of Aquileia of their liturgical innovations, as well as the consecration of a bishop for Moravia and Pannonia,[9] must be rejected. According to the decision of Charlemagne of 811 the jurisdiction of Aquileia extended in the northeast only to the Drava river. The Bavarian bishops would never have allowed the patriarch to interfere in religious affairs outside this boundary. It is true that Patriarch Vitalus, who resided in Venice, could claim more freedom in his relations with the Frankish Empire than his colleague Lupus, who resided in Forumiulii. But Carniola, Carinthia, and Pannonian Croatia, over which he exercised his jurisdiction, were firmly in the hands of the Franks, who would certainly react if he dared to trespass beyond the limits of his jurisdiction. Rastislav and Kocel knew this and, although they accepted Latin priests from the territory of the patriarchate, they could never hope to obtain an independent bishopric from Aquileia. Only the Franks, Rome, or Byzantium could offer that.

Consideration of all these facts inclines one to the interpretation that the brothers were on their way back to Constantinople and waited in Venice for an opportunity to sail. It was not a good season for sea travel in the Adriatic. It may have been their intention to reach Venice earlier, but they stayed too long in Pannonia, where they had been so well received.[10]

The fact that the season was too far advanced for safe travel by sea may also have influenced them to accept the pope's invitation to go to Rome. They could continue their voyage in the early spring when sea travel was safer. Although they were Byzantine patriots, they felt no animosity toward Rome. It should be stressed once more that such sentiments were not yet general in Byzantium in the first half of the ninth century.

✳ ✳ ✳

The solemn reception of the brothers in Rome is ascribed by Constantine's biographer to the fact that they carried the relics of St. Clement. They were met outside the gates of Rome by the pope and a group of Roman citizens carrying lighted candles, and were conducted probably to the church of St. Clement, where the relics were deposited for public veneration. The biographer even enumerates some of the miraculous recoveries of those who invoked the saint's name.

There may be one more reason why the pope's invitation was welcome to them. It offered them an opportunity to explain their missionary system to him and to complain about the attitude of the Bavarian clergy towards them. If they could obtain from Rome an approval of their methods, the hostile clergy would be disarmed and their disciples freer to continue their work in Moravia. It seems that the Byzantines did not like to travel by sea during the winter. Instead of continuing their voyage from Cherson to the Khazar Khagan, the two brothers stopped in Cherson and, after spending the winter there, continued their journey in the early spring. They may have intended to do the same in Rome after obtaining the invitation. They were carrying the relics believed to be of St. Clement, third successor to St. Peter, and author of the famous letter to the Corinthians. The acceptance of these relics could become a precious guarantee of the pope's approval of their innovations in missionary methods, and of his determination to put an end to the opposition of the Bavarian clergy.

The brothers arrived in Rome at a time when the new pope's attitude to the Byzantine problem was still not clear. There were signs which indicated that Hadrian II might adopt a more conciliatory attitude toward Photius who, it was supposed, still occupied the patriarchal throne.[11] There was some dissatisfaction in

Rome with Nicholas' oriental policy, as is indicated by Anastasius, Nicholas' Bibliothecarius, in his letter to Addo, Bishop of Vienne.[12]

The Greek refugees in Rome, who were responsible for Nicholas' uncompromising attitude toward Photius, were alarmed at the prospect of a change in papal policy. Hadrian II thought it necessary to ease the tension, and he invited them to a banquet in February 868.[13]

All this must have influenced the pope's attitude to the brothers and their missionary work. Constantine's biographer says that "the Pope received the Slavic books, blessed them, and deposited them in the church of Holy Mary which is called *Phatne* [*ad Praesepe*, now called S. Maria Maggiore] and they sang the liturgy over them. After that he ordered two bishops, Formosus and Gondrichus [Gauderich of Velletri], to ordain the Slavic disciples, after which they sang the liturgy in the Slavic tongue in the church of St. Peter, and the following day in that of St. Petronilla, and on the third day in the church of St. Andrew.[14] After this they sang again through the whole night in the church of the great teacher of the world, the Apostle St. Paul, glorifying him, in Slavic, and in the morning again they sang the liturgy over his holy tomb, having as assistants Bishop Arsenius, one of the seven bishops, and Anastasius the Librarian."

The *Life of Methodius* (chapter six) attributes all this to Pope Nicholas—this is certainly a lapse of memory on the part of the biographer. He mentions also that the innovation was criticized by some of the clergy. However, the pope defended it, calling its opponents disciples of Pilate—this is certainly an addition by the biographer—and ordered a bishop, who was one of these opponents, to ordain the Slavic disciples. This bishop was Formosus, the former papal legate and missionary in Bulgaria. This *Vita* also supplies further details about the ordination. The biographer says that Methodius was ordained priest with three others, and that two of them received the minor order of lectors.

This, however, does not mean that these were the only ones who had been ordained in Rome. The *Life* of Methodius stresses that the pope had ordered Formosus, one of the bishops who was critical of Constantine's innovations, to carry out this ordination. The *Life of Constantine* (chapter seven, ed. Lavrov, pp. 34, 65) says simply that the pope ordered Bishops Formosus and Gauderich of Velletri to ordain their disciples. For the ordination of a priest only one bishop was needed. It can be concluded from this that Gauderich had also ordained some other disciples of the brothers, whose number is not given. Gauderich was not opposed to the innovations of the brothers.[15]

All the personalities mentioned in the Legends as being connected with the ordination and liturgical performances of the Slavic disciples were well known in contemporary Rome. The mention of Arsenius is particularly important for dating the approval of the Slavic liturgy by the pope and for the ordination of the Slavic disciples. Arsenius, Bishop of Orte, was married before his ordination and had a son, Eleutherius. He supported the Emperor Louis II, and because Nicholas I owed his election to the imperial party, the pope used his services as envoy to the Frankish kings and bishops. Because Arsenius had the interests of his family rather than those of the pope in view, he lost the confidence of Nicholas I, but, as one of the seven suburbicarian bishops, he became an influential mentor of the papal court under Hadrian II. But, in supporting his son Eleutherius, who wished to marry the daughter of the pope—Hadrian had also been married before his ordination—he lost Hadrian's favor when his son, exasperated by the refusal of the pope to give him his daughter in marriage, abducted her and her mother, on March 10, 868. Arsenius saw himself forced to leave Rome. He wanted to join the emperor in Southern Italy, but died soon after his arrival in Acerenia.[16]

This allows us to date the approval of the Slavic clergy and the ordination of the disciples as being prior to March 868, at a time when Hadrian II was inclined to develop a more lenient policy toward the Patriarch Photius. The pope must have known of the relations of the two brothers with the patriach, without whose cooperation the Moravian mission could not have been realized. And Photius was still regarded as the head of the Byzantine Church.

✤ ✤ ✤

Arsenius' nephew Anastasius, ordained in 847 or 848, was also a zealous member of the imperial party.[17] Because of his intrigues against Pope Leo IV (847–855), he was excommunicated in 850 and in 853. After the death of Leo IV, the imperial party elected him as anti-pope against Benedict III, but he lost all his supporters because of his arrogant attitude. Benedict III accepted his submission and admitted him to lay communion. His mastery of the Greek language, which he had probably learned in one of the Greek monasteries in Rome, opened the way for him to the chancery of Nicholas I. As his secretary (*bibliothecarius*) Anastasius had an important share in the composition of Nicholas' correspondence with Byzantium. Hadrian II continued to use his services.

Arsenius and Anastasius were chosen by Hadrian as protectors of both the brothers and their disciples. Anastasius became Constantine's friend and admirer as can be gathered from remarks about him in his correspondence. In a letter to Bishop Gauderich, probably written in 875, he calls him a man of apostolic life, a great and true philosopher, the wisest man. In his missive to Charles the Bald, written in 875, he also exalts him as a great teacher and a man of apostolic life. In his preface to his translation of the *Acts* of the Council of 869–870 he praises him as a man of great holiness.[18]

He must also have known of Constantine's relations with Photius, because in the same document he characterizes Constantine as Photius' strongest friend (*fortissimus amicus*). These are strong words, and indicate that what Anastasius says about Constantine's rebuke of Photius should be interpreted as an exchange of views on a subject on which the two friends differed. The subject of this rebuke—namely, Photius' teaching that man had two souls— is suspicious, because not even the council which condemned him reproached him for propounding such an heretical doctrine. Anastasius may have heard these slanderous rumors in Constantinople, among the circle of Photius' bitterest enemies.[19]

We learn also from Anastasius' letter to Gauderich, Bishop of Velletri, of the latter's interest in the history of Constantine's discovery of St. Clement's relics. Because his cathedral church was dedicated to St. Clement, Gauderich asked the deacon John to describe the *Life of St. Clement* and the transfer of his relics. In order to find the necessary documentation he addressed himself to Anastasius, knowing of the intimate relationship between him and Constantine. Anastasius informed Gauderich that he had translated two of the short works of Constantine describing the discovery, but that he did not dare to translate the hymn composed by Constantine. In his letter he gives great praise to Constantine's style.[20]

The brothers certainly found sympathizers and supporters also among the monks of the Greek monasteries in Rome. They took up their abode in one of them, probably that of St. Praxedis in the vicinity of Santa Maria Maggiore. Instead of calling the church S. *Maria ad praesepe*, as it was then called in Rome, the biographer uses the Greek word *phatne* (praesepe), which is an indication that the brothers lived with Greek monks in Rome.[21]

The disappearance of Arsenius deprived the brothers of one influential protector. Unfortunately, Eleutherius' affair was to cause even more inconvenience to them. The pope asked the Emperor Louis II to proceed against the rapist according to the stipulations of Roman law. Eleutherius, seeing that he could not find any support, became enraged, and killed not only the pope's daughter but also Hadrian's former wife. This seems to have happened in June. The emperor then acted and Eleutherius was condemned and executed.

Although Anastasius does not seem to have been involved in this crime, his influence declined, the more so as his enemies were using this regrettable incident to weaken his position. Anastasius was accused by one of his relatives of having sent a messenger to his cousin before the latter committed his crime. Thereupon the pope, believing that his secretary was partly responsible for what had happened, in his exasperation ordered Anastasius to appear before him in the church of St. Praxedis on the twelfth of October, 868. After enumerating his earlier misbehavior, the pope renewed all the penalties pronounced by Leo IV against him and forbade him to absent himself more than forty miles from Rome.

It is possible that the two brothers witnessed this sad scene. As we have seen, they probably lived in the Greek monastery which Pope Paschal (817–824) had founded and richly endowed near the church under the name of that saint.[22] Anastasius may have had some relations with this monastery. It may have been there that he learned his Greek. He may even have been living there when he lost favor with the pope.

The loss of another influential supporter must have been a heavy blow to both brothers, and especially to Constantine, who had often conversed with Anastasius. Their position in Rome was also affected by the unexpected news reaching them from the

East. At the beginning of the summer of 868, the spathar Euthymius arrived in Rome as envoy of the new Emperor Basil I, and reported the death of Michael III, the deposition of the Patriarch Photius and the reinstallation of Ignatius on the patriarchal throne. In the name of the emperor he asked the pope to pronounce final sentence in the affair of Ignatius and Photius.

This unexpected turn of events in Constantinople would seem to justify the strict attitude of Nicholas against Photius and, under this impression, Hadrian decided to follow the same line in his dealings with Byzantium. He sent back the Greek refugee, Abbot Theognostus, who was most responsible for Nicholas' hostile attitude to Photius, with the returning imperial envoys bearing letters of congratulation to the emperor and to Ignatius. The envoy and Theognostus can only have reached Constantinople after the eleventh of December, 868, because the letter dispatched by the emperor that day to the pope expressed anxiety about their fate. A new imperial embassy, with representatives of both parties, only reached Rome at the end of the winter of 869, in February or early March. The main representative of Photius perished at sea, a regrettable incident which shows, at the same time, the dangers of the Adriatic sea voyage in winter.[23]

✣ ✣ ✣

It can be imagined how this tragic news affected the two brothers and their disciples. These were the "numerous afflictions" which beset Constantine in Rome, as his biographer expressed it (chapter eighteen). These events also explain why the brothers stayed so long in Rome and hesitated to continue their voyage to Constantinople. They did not wish to be mixed up in new intrigues, nor in political and religious rivalries. The best way out was to wait for the definitive decision of the pope for which the emperor had asked.

These unexpected handicaps undermined the delicate health of Constantine, already weakened by his missionary labors, his travels, and the Roman climate. He became seriously ill and, realizing that he would not recover, he desired to die as a monk. According to Byzantine practice, on taking the solemn vows, a monk must choose a new name with the same initial letter as his former name. Constantine therefore chose the name of Cyril.

The words with which the biographer lets Constantine announce his decision are particularly interesting: "From now on I am the servant neither of the emperor nor of anyone else on earth, but only of God the Almighty." These words confirm the supposition that Constantine's mission to Moravia was not only in the interests of religion, but also in those of the Empire. Here Constantine and his biographer manifest once more their patriotism.[24]

This declaration enables us to decide the question often debated by Constantine's biographers, as to whether he had already become a monk during his stay in Methodius' monastery on Mount Olympus.[25] It appears that there were in Byzantium two degrees of monastic vows, a simple acceptance of the monk's black cloth and tonsure, and the highest degree called *schema*, entailing solemn vows and a change of name. Because Constantine regarded himself, prior to his taking the solemn vows, as being in the service of the emperor, this status would hardly be compatible with the life of a monk. As professor of philosophy at the university he was in the imperial service, and he does not seem to have resigned this post when taking refuge in the monastery of his brother. When appointed by the patriarch as professor of philosophy at the Academy near the church of the Holy Apostles, he did not reside in a monastery. This indicates that he did not become a monk until shortly before his death in Rome.

This interpretation is also confirmed by the *Vita*. We read in chapter eighteen: "He took the venerable monacal habit and he stayed the whole day, full of joy and saying: 'From now on I am the servant neither of the emperor nor of anyone else on earth, but only of God Almighty. I was not and I became and I remain for ever, Amen.' The next day he put on the holy monacal dress and adding counsel to counsel he accepted the name of Cyril."

Hitherto the last phrase has been translated "adding light to light" and was interpreted as meaning that Cyril had added to the baptismal vows—often called by the Byzantines "light" (phos) —the monacal vows which would be regarded as a new baptism. Such an interpretation seems somewhat awkward. It should rather be read in the original not as *svjet'* which means light, but as *s'vjet'* which means counsel (consilium, pactum). In this way the passage becomes perfectly clear and shows that Constantine took the two monacal vows in Rome.[26] This is also indicated by the biographer, who speaks of two monastic dresses, meaning naturally the small and the great degree (schema) of monacal status.

Constantine lived only fifty days as a monk. He died on February 14, 869. The biographer lets the dying man utter a touching prayer in which he implored God's blessing for his work, for the protection of his disciples against the Trilinguists, and for unity in the Church. The plea for unity may have been inspired also by the sad events which happened in Constantinople and which augured disunity in the church of Constantinople, and in its relations with Rome.

During his stay in Rome Constantine must have found many admirers, and also great sympathy on the part of the pope. Hadrian is said to have ordered all monks, Greek and Latin, to take part in his funeral. When, however, Methodius approached him with the request to transfer his brother's body to his monastery, the pope only agreed reluctantly. Preparations were made for the transfer, but after seven days a delegation of Roman clergy asked the pope not to deprive Rome of the remains of so holy a man. Hadrian then offered Methodius burial of his brother in the papal tomb at St. Peter's, but, on the insistence of Methodius, he gave permission for his burial in the church of St. Clement. The fresco depicting Constantine facing the Lord's judgment, placed by contemporaries over his grave, still exists, although considerably damaged.[27]

* * *

Some historians think that Constantine was consecrated as bishop together with his brother Methodius, for this would seem to be indicated by the *Legenda Italica,* which was known only from one manuscript in the Vatican Library. The crucial passage concerning Constantine's ordination was scarcely legible and was wrongly interpreted. The discovery of another manuscript in Prague, in much better condition, solved this problem for good. There is no question of the episcopal ordination of Constantine, and the Latin legend confirms the information given by the *Vita Methodii* that Methodius was only ordained in Rome as a priest before Constantine's death.[28]

There is not even a certainty that Constantine himself was ever ordained as a priest. When he was appointed chartophylax during the patriarchate of Ignatius, he could only have been a deacon, because this dignity, like most similar dignities at the patriarcheion, could not be held by a priest. Moreover, at that time he was not yet thirty years old, the minimum age for priestly ordination. There was no reason why he should be ordained a priest when he started his career at the imperial university. In Byzantium priests had occupations other than teaching and preparing young men for the imperial service. It is thus quite possible that Constantine died as a deacon.

There is, however, one passage in this *Vita* which suggests that perhaps he was ordained a priest before coming to Rome. In chapter seventeen, the biographer describes how the newly ordained Slavic priests celebrated the liturgy in Roman churches. He quotes five churches, which would suggest that one of the Slavic priests led the liturgical celebration in each. This would refer to Methodius and three disciples. The fifth could have been Constantine. Of course, the fifth could also have been another disciple who came with them and who was already a priest, or who had been ordained by Gauderich. Constantine could have been ordained a priest on two previous occasions—before the Khazarian mission, or before his departure for Moravia. In this case, however, we would have to admit that he was ordained by Photius, and this would not be palatable to many who like to separate him as far as possible from that patriarch.

* * *

Constantine's premature death—he was only 42 years old— amounted almost to a catastrophe for the Byzantine mission in Moravia and Pannonia. The situation was made even more desperate for Methodius and his disciples by their uncertainty as to the degree to which the unexpected changes in Byzantium would influence the attitude of the pope, or of the new patriarch, to their mission. All decisions seem to have been postponed. Constantine probably died before the arrival of the new imperial embassy, which was also to bring the representatives of the rival patriarchs, who were to appear before the pope for his final decision. They did not come until early spring. Methodius postponed his departure, waiting for further developments. There were only two circumstances which favored the mission: the sincere veneration of the Romans for the memory of the deceased Constantine, who was regarded by them as a saint, and the previous acceptance by the pope of their liturgical innovations.

The situation was saved by the direct intervention of Kocel, the Pannonian prince. The brothers were most probably in touch with him, and one or two of their disciples may have been sent back to him by them to inform him of what was happening in Rome. He seems to have learned about the death of Constantine, because the biographer of Methodius says (chapter eight) that Kocel dispatched an embassy to the "apostolicus" asking him to send back Methodius, "our teacher."[29] He does not mention Constantine, possibly because Kocel knew what had happened.

Kocel's initiative clarified the tense atmosphere of uncertainty which oppressed Methodius, who was aggrieved by the death of his beloved younger brother. Hadrian decided to act. He saw in Kocel's readiness to accept Methodius as spiritual head of his country a welcome opportunity of further advancing the realization of Nicholas' lofty plan, namely, the subordination to direct papal jurisdiction of all the lands which had been lost through barbarian invasion or imperial intervention. Nicholas won over the western part of Illyricum by founding the bishopric of Nin for the Croats, and a great part of Eastern Illyricum was occupied by the Bulgars. The opportunity to regain Pannonia was beckoning and Hadrian did not hesitate to exploit it.

Methodius, seeing that the pope was willing to save and even to promote the results of his brother's work, and abhorring the prospect of being involved in religious and political machinations upon his return to Constantinople, abandoned the idea of returning home and placed himself at the disposal of the pope.

The whole plan was discussed, and it was decided that Methodius should return to the lands where he had worked with his brother and disclose to the Slavic princes—Kocel of Pannonia, Rastislav of Moravia, and Rastislav's nephew Svatopluk, who was administering Pribina's former territory of Nitra—the pope's plan to renew direct papal jurisdiction over their countries by erecting a new hierarchical organization for them.

The bond which would link their countries to each other, and to Rome, was the approval of the Slavic liturgy and letters by the Holy See. Therefore Methodius, sent as a papal legate to the

Slavic princes, was the bearer of a papal letter approving the liturgical innovations of the Greek brothers.

✳ ✳ ✳

This letter is only preserved in Old Slavonic in Methodius' biography. The Latin original is lost, and this circumstance has led numerous specialists to hesitate to accept its authenticity. This is understandable, but not warranted. The document is, of course, not a literal translation; but a comparison with other papal documents shows that the biographer used the original letter.[30] It is addressed to the three princes from Hadrian "the servant of God." This is evidently the biographer's rendering of the papal attribute "servant of God's servants." It starts with the words "Glory to God in the Highest" (Luke 2:14), and praises the desire of the addressees to seek for God. They have asked for help not only in Rome, but also from the "pious emperor Michael." The emperor had sent them the departed philosopher and his brother. "When these, however, learned that your lands belong to the apostolic see, they did nothing against the canonical prescriptions, but came to us bringing the relics of St. Clement." Rejoicing over this, the pope decided to send to them Methodius, "our son,"—this is generally regarded as an indication that Methodius was not yet a bishop, otherwise the Pope would have called him "our brother"— that he might preach to them and continue to translate the books into their language, as did Constantine, aided by the grace of God, on the intercession of St. Clement.[31] During the service the Epistle and Gospel only should be read first in Latin and then in Slavic. The letter quotes two passages from Holy Writ in favor of the use of the vernacular in God's service (Psalm 116:1; Acts 2:4,11). It ends with a threat of excommunication to anyone who expressed contempt for books written in the Slavic language.

The fact that the passage which contains the privilege of using the Slavic language in the liturgy is almost identical with the approval of the Slavic liturgy in John VIII's letter, whose authenticity cannot be doubted, is puzzling, and has made certain specialists hesitate to accept the authenticity of Hadrian's letter. This hesitation, however, is not substantiated. The Slavic liturgy, and the translation of the holy books into Slavic had already been approved by Hadrian when Constantine was still alive. The pope must have known how much the Slavic princes, especially Kocel, appreciated this. In order to induce them to accept his plan, he had to offer them some privilege that they would appreciate, and which would also bind their peoples more closely to Rome. This was the concession of the Slavic liturgy.

There was also another motive which prompted the pope to take this initiative. As we have seen, Moravia and most probably also Pannonia would have been lost to Roman jurisdiction if the two brothers had been able to realize their original plan and if, after reaching Constantinople and reporting to the patriarch, they had recommended that some of their disciples be consecrated bishops in Constantinople for the new Slavic churches of Moravia and Pannonia. In order to save these countries for the Roman patriarchate the pope had to act promptly, offering their princes an independent hierarchy and giving his approval to the celebration of the liturgy in their language.

On the other hand, the project of restoring the metropolis of old Sirmium made it easier for Methodius to offer his services to the pope without becoming unfaithful to his mother Church of Constantinople. Sirmium had always been a part of the Roman patriarchate and the restoration of its metropolitan rights could in no way be regarded as hurting the interests of the patriarchate of Constantinople. The extension of its jurisdiction over Moravia could not be disputed by Constantinople, because Moravia was a missionary land which had not yet been incorporated into the Eastern patriarchate.

It is quite possible that Hadrian II also had the Bulgarians in mind. The extension of such a privilege to them was, perhaps, thought likely to put an end to their wavering between Constantinople, the Franks, and Rome, and to tie them to Rome for good. Given more time this might have worked. Of course in 869 the pope could not foresee that in 870 Bulgaria would replace his priests with Greek clergy.

We may also assume that Anastasius the Librarian had something to do with the decision of the pope, and with the composition of the papal letter. The reversal of the religious situation in Byzantium, and the pope's decision to continue the uncompromisingly strict policy of his predecessor, had probably brought Anastasius to the surface again from the depths into which the crime of his cousin had thrown him. The pope needed a "specialist" in Byzantine affairs, the more so as the reversal seems to have shown that Nicholas' Byzantine policy, in the severity of which Anastasius had his share, was justified by events. The responsible charge of being Papal Librarian was probably restored to Anastasius in June. He appears to have taken an active part in the Roman synod convoked by the pope, and to have composed the papal letters which the legates were asked to carry to Constantinople, to the emperor and to the Council, which was to assemble there. It was most probably in June that Methodius was sent to the Slavic princes.

✻ ✻ ✻

Methodius was well received in Pannonia. Although the Franks had twice attacked Rastislav in the spring of 869, it is possible that Methodius himself, or one of his disciples, was able to get in touch with the Moravian princes. The main expedition against Rastislav and Svatopluk was organized in August by Louis the German. Because of his illness, his youngest son Charles led the troops against Rastislav, and Carloman led those against Svatopluk. They penetrated as far as the "formidable fortress" of the Moravians, and although they claimed a victory, Rastislav's main forces were left almost intact and his submission to the Empire was ended.[32] This, and the circumstance that Louis the German soon became involved in complications in the West concerning the inheritance of his nephew Lothair II, had encouraged the Slavic princes, especially Kocel, to accept the pope's plan. Of course, they also counted on the prestige and authority of the papacy throughout the Christian West.

The weight of papal authority was soon to be felt in Pannonia. The archpriest Rihpald, who represented the Archbishop of Salzburg in Kocel's territory, left the country and returned to Salzburg. He was unwilling to accept either the liturgical innovation approved by the pope, or Hadrian II's evident intention to erect an independent metropolitan see in Pannonia.[33]

Kocel sent Methodius back to Rome with an honorary escort of twenty Slavic nobles, to ask the "apostolic Father" to consecrate him Archbishop of Pannonia, "the throne of Saint Andronicus, one of the seventy Apostles."

The idea of Methodius' becoming a successor of Saint Andronicus, the legendary founder of the metropolis of Sirmium, was not
Kocel's but Hadrian's. Determined to recover direct jurisdiction
over Pannonia, the pope was, at the same time, anxious to endow
his creation with a solid historical and juridical basis. Until its
occupation by the barbarians, Pannonia was part of Illyricum
and was governed by a prefect whose residence was at Sirmium.
The bishop of that city was metropolitan of all the bishops of
Illyricum and Pannonia. His prestige was enhanced by the legendary tradition that its first bishop had been Saint Andronicus, one
of the seventy disciples of the Apostles. Sirmium thus claimed a
quasi-apostolic origin. Andronicus was regarded as a disciple of
St. Paul because the Apostle mentioned him in his letter to the
Romans (16,7).

The names of the seventy disciples chosen by Christ (Luke
10,1) are unknown, but their list was compiled by the early
Christians from names mentioned in the Epistles and in the Acts
of the Apostles. Legendary tradition has made some of them
founders of important episcopal sees—Andronicus for Sirmium,
Stachys for Byzantium, Trophimus for Arles—but the legends
were firmly believed to be genuine.[34] Such also was the conviction
of Methodius' contemporaries, and this helps to explain the great
veneration for St. Paul in the old Slavonic Church.

The city of Sirmium, devastated in 448 by the Huns, was destroyed in 582 by the Avars. After the destruction of the Avars by
Charlemagne, the popes should have renewed their claims. However, they left the initiative in the hands of the emperor, and the
inheritance of Sirmium was taken over by Aquileia and Salzburg.
Hadrian II wanted to recapture what had been allowed to fall
into the hands of the Frankish clergy.

The revival of the metropolis of Sirmium, and the ordination of
Methodius as Archbishop of Pannonia and Moravia, was a very
bold stroke. It can be explained as being one aspect of the continuation of papal policy inaugurated by Nicholas I. Seeing how
dangerous the formation of territorial Churches, formed by the
alliance of the hierarchies with the rulers, could be for the position of the papacy in the Church Universal, Nicholas ended deci-
sively the attempts of John of Ravenna, who was supported by
the emperor, to create a territorial ecclesiastical formation in Italy
which would rival Rome. He broke such an alliance in Frankish

territory, where he condemned Lothair II and the bishops who sanctioned his divorce. He forced Hincmar of Rheims, who was becoming a dangerous rival in the Western Frankish kingdom, to submit, and prevented him from gaining the support of King Charles the Bald.[35]

The first blow against the Eastern Frankish clergy, which was supported by their able king Louis the German, was the foundation of an independent Croat bishopric. The second blow was the elimination of Frankish influence from Bulgaria. Hadrian, determined to continue Nicholas' policy, prepared the third blow, which was to eliminate Frankish influence from Pannonia and Moravia.

❊ ❊ ❊

Toward the end of 869, Methodius returned to Pannonia as Archbishop of Sirmium and papal legate. Even though the Archbishop of Salzburg's representative had left Kocel's land without a fight, it was not to be expected that the Frankish hierarchy would yield without making an attempt to reverse the situation. They were not only opposed to the liturgical innovations introduced by the Byzantine mission, but were particularly hurt by the papal decision taking the contested territories, especially Pannonia, from their jurisdiction. They must have had priests who spoke the Slavic language, and the first attempts to translate Latin liturgical prayers into Slavic were made by Frankish or Irish missionaries.[36] They thought that this was what should be done for the new Christians. In any event, the celebrations of the liturgy in Slavic became one of the main targets of their attacks.

In spite of this Methodius seems to have assumed the ecclesiastical administration of Kocel's Pannonia without opposition. There is no evidence to suppose that the change had been announced officially by the pope to the Archbishop of Salzburg, who might regard himself as especially affected by a papal decision. The unexpected tragic events in Moravia, however, emboldened the Bavarian hierarchy to take drastic measures against Methodius and to ignore the papal decision.

Svatopluk, who had hitherto supported his uncle but was anxious to become sole ruler over the whole of Moravia, submitted to Carloman, Louis the German's son, in the winter of 869–70. After

capturing Rastislav, Svatopluk delivered him, in bonds, to Carloman in May 870. The latter sent Rastislav to Bavaria, giving his
father at the same time an account of what had happened. This
reversal of the situation in Moravia consolidated the position of
Louis the German in his negotiations in the West for Lothair's
inheritance. Later Rastislav was condemned by Louis as a traitor,
deprived of his eyesight, and left to finish his life miserably in a
Bavarian monastery.[37]

Carloman invaded Moravia, probably in company with Svatopluk, and without difficulty forced the whole country to submit.
This reversal of fortune had fatal consequences for Methodius. He
went to Moravia after making the necessary arrangements in Pannonia. It was in Moravia, and not in Bavaria, as has been thought
by some, that he was arrested by Hermanrich, Bishop of Passau,
who entered the country with Carloman and his military forces in
order to reaffirm his claim that Moravia was a part of his diocese.[38]
The biographer's account of what happened to Methodius is very
short. He attributes (chapter nine) Methodius' misfortune to the
"old foe, the envious of good and adversary of truth" who "instigated against him the heart of the hostile (Moravian) king with
all bishops" who said: "You are teaching in our territory." However, he answered: "I would have avoided it, had I known that it
is yours, but it belongs to Saint Peter. Really you proceed against
canonical prescription to the old boundary, prompted by jealousy
and avarice and, thus you are impeding the teaching of God's
word. Be on guard that you do not shed your brain when trying
to pierce the iron mountain with a skull of bone."

Specialists are still debating as to where and when Methodius
was arrested, where he was judged, how he was treated, and
where he was finally imprisoned. The letters sent by Pope John
VIII to Louis the German and his bishops in 873, when he had
learned what had happened, help us to reconstruct events.[39]

The displeasure of the Frankish bishops with the new arrangements can be readily understood. They had worked for seventy-
five years in Pannonia and Moravia at the conversion of the Slavs,
and now they were asked to abandon the fruits of their labor to a
Greek who had introduced unheard-of innovations into their territory. Moreover, they were also deprived of the benefices in
Pannonia which had been given previously to the Archbishop of
Salzburg, and other bishops, by Pribina. The biographer seems to

have known about it, because he reproaches them for their avarice. However, the means by which they defended their interests were unjust and brutal.

The most violent of them was Hermanrich, Bishop of Passau. He had certainly not forgotten how the papal legates had barred him and his missionaries from Bulgaria and he could not tolerate the idea that another papal legate—a Greek to boot—should deprive him of yet another territory, which he considered belonged to his diocese. He arrested Methodius, treated him tyrannically, according to the papal letter, cast him into jail, allowed him to suffer cold and rain—probably while transporting him to Bavaria where he was to be judged—and even attacked him with his horsewhip at the assembly of the Frankish bishops.

Anno of Freisingen's behavior was also characterized by the pope as tyrannical, rather than canonical. He acted alone, without consulting his priests and canons, rejected all appeals by Methodius, and condemned him. The Archbishop of Salzburg seems to have behaved less despotically, although he was deeply hurt by the new ecclesiastical arrangement. The papal letter addressed to him, which is preserved fragmentarily, only contains the order to reinstate Methodius in his rights.

The bishops, assembled in November 870 at the Reichstag in Regensburg, formed a kind of synod which condemned Methodius as an intruder, completely ignoring the papal orders. Although discussion still continues as to the city where the synod was held, the most likely place was Regensburg. This is indicated also by the biographer who notes the presence of the king,[40] and his remark that Methodius was sweating as if he were near an oven. Methodius' riposte was that he was sweating like a philosopher who had had a discussion with stupid men, is probably a gloss of the biographer.

The bishops decided to get rid of Methodius for good and to imprison him, not in Bavaria but in distant Swabia. It is now generally accepted that the place where he was kept prisoner was the monastery of Ellwangen.[41] The place, and the whole affair, were kept secret. Even when Anno of Freisingen, who administered the papal patrimonies in Germany, was asked in Rome about the whereabouts of Methodius, he declared insolently that he did not know the man.

The Frankish bishops also defended their cause in writing. Most probably we owe to the initiative of Adalwin of Salzburg the important document *Conversio Bagoariorum et Carentanorum,* already often quoted and the only written source on the Christianization of the Slovenes in Carinthia and Pannonia. In spite of its bias the document gives us information which is of great value. It was most probably written at the beginning of 871, after the condemnation and imprisonment of Methodius.[42] It was destined to substantiate the pretensions of Salzburg over Pannonia, in enumerating the churches consecrated by the archbishops of Salzburg, and of the missionaries sent there.[43] It was intended to justify the action taken against Methodius in the eyes of Louis the German and of contemporaries. It is interesting to note that the use of the Slavic language in the liturgy, although blamed for degrading the Latin language, is not the main target of the attack. The main purpose of the document is to defend the ecclesiastical and material interests of the Bavarian hierarchy.

Methodius was imprisoned for two and a half years. Only in the spring of 873 did the new Pope John VIII learn what had happened and he acted energetically. Not only did he order the three bishops to release Methodius from prison and suspend them from the exercise of their episcopal functions until he should be released, but he also ordered them to restore the unfortunate prelate to the enjoyment of his functions. The pope sent Paul, Bishop of Ancona, to Pannonia with strict instructions to see that the papal prescriptions were fulfilled. He should explain to Louis the German that the rights of the Holy See could never be regarded as having expired. The legate was to conduct Methodius safely to the Moravian Prince Svatopluk.[44]

It seems that, during the imprisonment of Methodius, Kocel's territory was administered ecclesiastically by Methodius' disciples. We do not learn anything about the activity of the See of Salzburg there down to 873.[45] Kocel appears to have continued to be in direct touch with Rome, without the mediation of the Archbishop of Salzburg. The fragments of two letters sent to Kocel by Pope John VIII in May 873 are preserved.[46] Both give advice in matrimonial affairs, which must have been forwarded to the pope for a decision. Such cases were usually treated by the bishops in whose dioceses they had occurred, and the bishops addressed themselves to the Holy See in cases of doubt.

This should indicate that Kocel's position was quite strong. It may even have been strengthened by new events in Moravia. Svatopluk soon had good reason to regret his treachery. As early as 871 he was accused unjustly of infidelity to Carloman and imprisoned. His country was put under the administration of the margraves William and Engelschalk. The Moravians, thinking that their prince had been killed, revolted and forced the priest Slavomir, a relative of Svatopluk, to assume the leadership. A new expedition against the Moravians became necessary and Svatopluk, cleared of the accusations, volunteered to lead the Frankish army and subdue the revolt. When the Bavarians had reached the main fortress of the Moravians, Svatopluk, under the pretext of negotiating for its surrender, entered the city, made an alliance with the rebels and annihilated the Bavarian army. Its leaders William and Engelschalk perished. Svatopluk was master of the new situation. The quarrels among the sons of Louis the German helped to strengthen his independent position and to defeat Carloman in 872. His offer of a peaceful agreement (made through his envoy John, a priest from Venice) was accepted, and peace was concluded at Forchheim in 874. This left Svatopluk in possession of Moravia after he had accepted formal submission to the Empire.[47]

After his release Methodius could thus be introduced into Pannonia. The Bavarian bishops had warned Kocel not to accept Methodius. This was often interpreted in the sense that the Franks got rid of Kocel in 873 or 874 because of his "revolt." The only argument put forward in favor of this thesis is the mention, in two short annals, that in 874 the new Archbishop of Salzburg, Theotmar, consecrated a church near Ptuj (Petovia) in the land of count Gozwin.[48] The latter could not, however, have been the successor of Kocel, because he is only called count (*comes*), and in official Frankish documents, Pribina and Kocel were generally called *dux*—duke—and their land *ducatus*—duchy.[49] Nor does this statement indicate that Kocel's *ducatus* was divided after his disappearance, or that Gozwin administered a part of it. He could also have administered a part of Kocel's territory under the latter's supremacy.

The incident only shows that Methodius was not in Kocel's territory in 874, and that Salzburg profited from the new situation by reaffirming its rights in at least a part of his territory. Kocel could not oppose this, especially if his subordinate count had pro-

Frankish sentiments, but it does not mean that Kocel was already dead. In 873 and 874 the pope's support of Kocel was still respected, and Louis the German could hardly punish Kocel because of his fidelity to the Holy See.

Kocel lived most probably until 876, the year when the Dalmatian Croats revolted against the Franks. As a vassal of the Empire he was charged with suppressing the revolt, and he lost his life in battle. It is in this sense that a passage in Constantine Porphyrogenetos' *De administrando imperio* (chapter thirty)[50] should be interpreted, which speaks of a Kotzilis who led the Frankish army and perished. Kocel most probably also administered Pannonian Croatia and was, thus, a neighbor of the Dalmatian Croats. It was natural that he should be charged with the suppression of the revolt. He is mentioned as being dead only in a document issued between 876 and 887.

The disappearance of Kocel in 873 would have indicated also the end of papal plans in Pannonia. We must, however, hesitate to accept this as a fact because Pope John VIII clearly continued to believe in the importance of Pannonia for the further progress of Rome among the other Slavs of former Illyricum. In his letter of May 873,[51] John asked the Serbian Prince Mutimir to follow his predecessors and return to the obedience of the Archbishop of Pannonia, meaning Methodius, metropolitan of Sirmium.

The same reasons prompt us to reject the information given in a short extract from the *Conversio,* with some additions,[52] dating from the twelfth century, which indicates that Methodius was expelled from Pannonia in 873 and was forced to go to Moravia. The extract dates from a much later period and has other additions which are untrue. This report reflects events which happened after Kocel's death. Thereafter Methodius had not much authority left in Pannonia before its conquest by Svatopluk.

We learn also from the *Life of Methodius* (chapter ten) that the Moravians had expelled all the German priests. This could have happened during the revolt led by Slavomir,[53] before the arrival of Svatopluk. The biographer then speaks of another Moravian embassy to Rome which requested that Methodius be sent as "archbishop and teacher."[54] This indicates that after their revolt in 871, the Moravians had really addressed themselves to Rome with the request that Methodius be sent to them, that he had disappeared in 870, and that they were uncertain about his whereabouts. This could have happened after they had expelled the Frankish priests, as we read in the same chapter of the Legend. The biographer thus indicated by his words that the Moravians also made an attempt to free Methodius from the hands of the Frankish hierarchy.[55] This interpretation would make more comprehensible the biographer's reason for depicting Methodius' reception after the "apostolic"[56] had sent him to Moravia: "And the Prince Svatopluk received him together with all Moravians and he entrusted to him all churches and clerics in all castles." From that time on the number of clerics grew, and many more pagans were converted.[57]

* * *

Methodius, freed by the intervention of the pope, was definitively won over to the obedience of Rome. He was thus also saved from the complications in which he would certainly have been involved if he had returned to Constantinople, where Ignatius had been reinstated as patriarch. In this connection, an attempt should be mentioned which was made to connect the name of Methodius with the ecclesiastical upheaval which followed on the fall of Photius.

In the *Acts* of the Council of 879–880,[58] which rehabilitated Photius after Ignatius' death, we find in the list of participating bishops the name of "Agathon of the Moravians." In the *Annals* of Fulda[59] we read that in 873 a Byzantine embassy, headed by the Archbishop Agathon, had been dispatched to Louis the German in order to confirm friendly relations. It has been suggested that the two Agathons are identical, and it was concluded that the Patriarch Ignatius, who knew the pro-Photian sympathies of Methodius, had, after 870, ordained another archbishop for Moravia, namely Agathon, one of his followers. The embassy of Agathon to Regensburg in 873 was also connected with this ordination, as Agathon is supposed to have made an attempt to secure recognition with the consent of the Frankish bishops as the true Archbishop of Moravia.[60]

This theory has too many weak points to deserve serious consideration. First, the identification of the two Agathons is in no way proved. The list of the bishops present at the Photian council is very confused. Agathon is mentioned among the metropoli-

tans and archbishops, but, because bishops are also listed among
them, and metropolitans are named with bishops, this cannot be
taken as a proof of Agathon's higher ecclesiastical rank. In this
respect the list is unreliable and cannot be compared with similar
lists of bishops present at other councils, where the ranks are
carefully distinguished.[61]

The embassy of 873 had quite a different object. Basil I wished
to come to an agreement with Louis the German concerning
Byzantine claims in Italy, in case of the death of Louis II.[62] As
far as Ignatius is concerned, he was forced to accept the collaboration of the Photian clergy in Bulgaria after the Council of 869–870
had decided that this country formed a part of the Byzantine
patriarchate.[63] He could hardly "spare" a bishop for distant Moravia. Why then would he risk a conflict with the pope, who had
recognized him as the legitimate patriarch? Moreover, at the
Council of 869–870, Anastasius the Librarian was also present as
a member of an embassy sent to Basil I by Louis II. He would
certainly have protested strongly against any such intervention,
as indeed he did concerning Bulgaria, and all the more so as he
was a friend of Methodius.

How could it be imagined that the Bavarian bishops would
have consented to recognize another Greek as archbishop in
Moravia? They regarded this country as under their jurisdiction
and had gone very far in order to get rid of Methodius. In 870
and 871 they were masters of the situation in Moravia and were
able to prevent any possible appeal by the Moravians to Constantinople for help, or for another archbishop. In the following years
they were helpless because of the reversal of the political situation in Moravia.

The Agathon mentioned in the list of bishops at the Council of
879–880 could only have been the Bishop of Morava, a locality
at the confluence of the Serbian river Morava with the Danube.
Such a see existed and was united with that of Braničevo, perhaps as early as the tenth century.[64]

In the ninth century this region was part of Boris' Bulgaria,
together with Belgrade, which also had its own bishop. Agathon
was thus one of the bishops consecrated by Ignatius for Bulgaria.
If he was an archbishop, which is not proved, he could have been
the archbishop sent by Ignatius to Bulgaria. We do not know the
name of this man. According to a later tradition it was Joseph.[65]

Agathon could have been his successor. However, this and his identification with the Archbishop Agathon who was sent to Louis the German in 873 present difficulties. We learn from a letter sent by John VIII to Boris in 878,[66] that there was a bishop in Belgrade, called Sergius. The pope, regarding Bulgaria as being still subject to Rome, deposed him because of his scandalous life. He complained to Boris that Sergius had been appointed bishop of Belgrade by George "who falsely called himself bishop." It would thus be logical to regard this George as the Archbishop of Bulgaria appointed by Ignatius. The pope, of course, questioned the validity and legality of this appointment. If George was the successor of Joseph, as can be accepted, then the Agathon of 873 could not be a Bulgarian archbishop. The Agathon of 879–880 could hardly have this distinction unless we suppose that he succeeded George in 879 or that the territory of the river Morava was regarded as being very important for the advance of Christianity, and that the titulary of Morava was promoted to an archbishop independent of the Bulgarian archbishop, and subject directly to the Patriarch of Constantinople. This would perhaps have been in the interests of Byzantium, but there is no evidence that this was so. The safest solution is to regard the Agathon of 879–880 as a Greek bishop of Morava, then in Bulgaria. He may have represented the Archbishop George, if the latter was still alive in 879. If George was already dead, then Agathon, as archbishop, represented the Bulgarian Church at the Council. This supposition would be the most logical. In any event, the Agathon mentioned in the list of the Photian Council is in no way connected with the religious history of Great Moravia.[67]

VI. Methodius in Moravia

Svatopluk and Methodius. Prelude to investiture contest in Moravia?—The Filioque, the Franks, and the Slavic clergy—Methodius vindicated by Rome—Wiching's duplicity—Svatopluk's expansion in Pannonia, Bohemia, White Serbia, and Poland. His ambitions in Francia—Historicity of Methodius' journey to Constantinople—Basil and Methodius, Boris and the Byzantine embassy to Svatopluk—Methodius' translation of the Old Testament—Methodius' Nomocanon and John VIII's Latin collection of Canon Law; First Slavic Code of Laws—Paterikon and homilies, translations of Constantine's compositions—Encounter with the "Hungarian King"—Excommunication of Wiching?—Gorazd recommended as successor—Methodius' death and burial—Wiching's intrigues in Rome, falsification of Stephen V's letter—Expulsion of Methodius' prominent disciples.

In spite of the enthusiastic reception of Methodius in Moravia, his position had been considerably weakened by the recent political events. After the conclusion of the peace of Forchheim in 874, Moravia was again open to the Frankish clergy. Many of them, who had worked there during the absence of Methodius and who had been expelled in 871, returned and continued their pastoral work. Svatopluk himself did not show the same enthusiasm for the Slavic liturgy as had his late uncle. Among his principal counsellors were two Latin priests—John of Venice and Wiching. The latter may have befriended him during his stay in Bavaria. His new policy of friendship with the Empire led Svatopluk to favor the Frankish clergy. Because the sympathies of the great majority of his subjects lay with Methodius and his Slavic

160

liturgy, the Prince had to accept Methodius, who was supported by the Holy See, and to tolerate his liturgical innovations. He himself gave preference to the Latin liturgy.

It is not easy to find the reasons which prompted Svatopluk to favor the Frankish clergy and to give only half-hearted support to Methodius. Some scholars have tried to explain Svatopluk's attitude by Methodius' severe criticism of the prince's private life. This is possible, but it does not explain everything. Methodius, as a Byzantine, knew well the practice of "oeconomy" of his own Church, which meant the toleration of certain behavior on the part of the mighty ones without openly betraying Church principles.[1] Some think that the Frankish clergy were more tolerant of Svatopluk's moral lapses than was Methodius. But even if this were so, it would not provide a sufficient reason for Svatopluk's animosity. After all, he owed to Methodius the ecclesiastical independence of his realm.

The predilection of Svatopluk for the Latin rite can be explained to some extent by the fact that he was used to it from his boyhood. The rite introduced by Methodius, although basically Latin and Roman, presented some Byzantine features to which he was unaccustomed.

Such may also have been the case with some of his nobles who had been converted by the Frankish missionaries. Attempts were made to show that the higher social classes in Great Moravia advocated the Latin liturgy, while the lower classes preferred the Slavonic liturgy and the missionary methods of Methodius.[2] There is some truth in this assertion. The Christianization of the Moravians started with the conversion of the nobles, who may also have been attracted by the privileged position which the nobles enjoyed in the feudal system of the Frankish Empire. It would, however, be an exaggeration to see in this conflict a clash between two social classes in Great Moravia. The Slavonic liturgy and letters appealed not only to the masses but also to some of the nobles.[3] Gorazd, for example, was the scion of a noble family.

However, this attitude on the part of Svatopluk and of many of his nobles may be explained, to some degree, by their predilection for some of the feudal privileges enjoyed by the Frankish nobles. There was, moreover, a considerable variation in the rights of rulers over churches they had built, as these rights were defined variously in Rome, in Byzantium, or among the Franks.

On the basis of Germanic conceptions of proprietary rights, very different from the principles of Roman law, a new system of so-called proprietary churches was introduced in all Germanic lands. According to this system, kings and noblemen claimed not only the ownership of sanctuaries they had established, but also the right to appoint both higher and lower clergy in ecclesiastical institutions endowed by them. This was a dangerous breach with the old Roman conception and with the Roman canon law, admitting that the *persona moralis* also had proprietary rights.

The system of proprietary churches, already developed in Bavaria, was also introduced by Salzburg missionaries into Pannonia and Carinthia. The priests from Passau who had worked in Moravia before the arrival of the Greek mission certainly introduced the same system, even if only in an embryonic way, in the new missionary land. Svatopluk became further acquainted with this system during his stay in Bavaria. It naturally appealed to him because it gave him increased control over the churches and the ministers, in whose appointment he could claim a decisive voice.

It can be imagined that Methodius objected to this Germanic practice, so alien to Byzantine and Roman canon law, and defended the right of the Church—as a *persona moralis*—to possess and to administer churches even when they had been founded by feudal lords. Svatopluk was supported in this matter by some of his nobles and by the Frankish clergy. But the contest between Svatopluk and Methodius in Moravia provided a prelude to the gigantic investiture contest initiated by Gregory VII in the eleventh century, which shook the basis of the German Empire of Henry IV. Its consequences were to become as disastrous for Moravia as was the great contest of the following centuries for the unity of Western Christianity. The roots of the Reformation which disrupted this unity lay in this contest and its consequences.[4]

* * *

Rome certainly supported Methodius in this respect, but John VIII weakened his position by the concession he thought necessary to make to the Frankish clergy. We learn from a letter the pope sent to Methodius in 879[5] that he had forbidden the use of the Slavic liturgy, allowing Methodius to celebrate only in Greek or in Latin. This injunction was probably contained in a letter which the papal legate was ordered to deliver to Methodius. The letter is not preserved and there is no mention of this prohibition in the instruction given to the legate. The order seems to have been intended rather as a recommendation. Methodius most probably explained to the legate the reasons why he could not abandon a practice which formed the basis of the success of his mission in Moravia and which was the main instrument for converting the rest of the population and consolidating the new Church.

His enemies, however, must have learned of the letter, and this gave them new reasons for attacking Methodius. Their accusation that he was propagating heretical teaching was more serious. By this can only be meant the controversy concerning the procession of the Holy Ghost from the Father and the Son.

The Creed promulgated by the first Oecumenical Council of Nicaea (325), which was accepted by all Christians, defined the Holy Ghost as proceeding from the Father (*qui ex Patre procedit*), thus stressing the single principle of spiration. At the end of the sixth century the Spanish Church added to the Nicaean Creed the word *Filioque* (*qui ex Patre Filioque procedit*). This addition did not deny the single principle of the spiration, but was intended to express the participation of the Second Person in the spiration from the Father, on the ground that, being of the same divine nature, the Son participated in the activity of the Father.

It would not have been thought that the Greeks would have objected so passionately to the Latin interpretation of the mystery, since some of their own Fathers admitted spiration from the Father through the Son. However, the addition of the word *Filioque* to the Creed, without its authorization by a new council, was regarded by them as inadmissible and heretical.

The popes, although accepting the Latin interpretation of the mystery, did not sanction this addition, and until the eleventh century Rome maintained the Nicaean Creed intact, without the addition of the *Filioque*. In spite of Roman opposition, the Spanish practice spread to the Franks, and in the ninth century it was also generally accepted in Germany.

Methodius naturally followed the Byzantine and Roman custom, and his disciples recited the Creed without the addition of

Filioque. The Frankish clergy accused Methodius of spreading heretical teaching on the Holy Trinity by his refusal to follow their practice. The Frankish clergy may have interpreted the Latin doctrine too radically, because the disciples of Methodius accused them of professing the "hyiopateric" heresy.

The author of the *Vita* (chapter twelve) showed in this a surprising familiarity with Greek theological terminology. This word was used in the East to designate teachings which identified or unified the first divine Person, the Father, with the Second. This indicates that the followers of Methodius saw in the Frankish definition of the Trinity an identification of the Father with the Son.

On the other hand the Frankish priests, stressing their own interpretation of the mystery, gave the Greek disciples of Methodius the impression that they believed in two principles of spiration, both by the Father and the Son. This seems to be indicated by the reproach which, according to the author of the Greek *Life of Clement* (chapter eight),[6] Methodius' disciples addressed the Frankish priests in Moravia thus: "When admitting two principles, the Father for the Son and the Son for the Spirit, you fell into a new Manichaean heresy. We recognize only one God and one principle—the Father—for they who are from Him (the Son and the Spirit)."

This shows, at the same time, that the Greek priests of Slavic extraction who had come with the two brothers to Moravia professed, in this respect, the beliefs of the Greek Church. They seem, however, to admit the spiration of the Spirit through the Son, as taught by some Greek Fathers, especially Maximus and John of Damascus. We find in the same passage of the *Life of St. Clement* an allusion to such an interpretation. The author compares the Father to a mighty king who gives away a great treasure. His son profits by this generosity and distributes the treasure. Then the author continues: "The son of the king is the Son of the Father to whom the Spirit [the mentioned treasure] belongs and through whom it is imparted. You see, the Spirit, as we know it, is not proceeding from the Son, but imparted through him."

Methodius, accused by the Frankish clergy of heretical teaching, was summoned by Pope John VIII to appear in Rome to justify himself. With him came also Wiching, the leader of the Frankish clergy and the chief accuser. We learn from the letter addressed to Svatopluk in June or July 879,[7] that the complaint against Methodius was voiced in Rome by another of Svatopluk's councillors, John of Venice, and that the accusation was endorsed by Svatopluk himself. In letters to Svatopluk and to Methodius the pope expressed his astonishment at this accusation. From the letter to Methodius [8] we learn also that John of Venice had presented a further complaint, namely, that Methodius was celebrating the Mass in Slavonic, a "barbaric" language, although he had been advised not to do so.

However, another missive to Svatopluk, sent in June 880 and starting with the words *Industriae tuae*,[9] provides evidence that Methodius justified himself by explaining to a local synod, presided over by Pope John VIII, what he and his disciples believed. The pope, after commending Svatopluk for his fidelity to St. Peter, stressed in the letter that Methodius professed the same Creed as Rome. This was natural, because in Rome, as in Byzantium, the Nicaean Creed was still recited without the addition *Filioque*, of which the popes did not approve. The pope, however, stated in the letter that Methodius was found orthodox even in other articles of faith, including the doctrine on the Procession of the Spirit. Methodius most probably followed the Greek Fathers, who taught that the Holy Ghost proceeded from the Father through the Son. Such an explanation seemed satisfactory to the pope and his bishops.

The pope confirmed Methodius in his rank of Archbishop of Moravia, and in his other privileges, probably meaning the rank of apostolic legate in Slavic lands. He also approved very solemnly the liturgical innovation of celebrating the Mass and holy offices in the Slavic language. In a solemn Mass, however, the Gospel should be read first in Latin and then in Slavic. Against the assertion that the liturgy should be celebrated only in Latin, Greek, and Hebrew, he quoted several passages of Holy Writ (Ps. 116:1; Acts 2:11; Phil. 2:11; 1 Cor. 14:4). Svatopluk himself could, of course, choose priests who used the Latin liturgy for his worship. All priests, whether using the Slavic or the Latin liturgy, would be subject to Methodius under threat of being excommunicated in the event of disobedience. This was a noteworthy victory for Methodius, but it was dimmed by the fact that on Svatopluk's demand the pope had ordained Wiching as Bishop of Nitra. The pope, moreover, had invited Svatopluk and the two bishops to choose another priest to be consecrated bishop in Rome, in order that there would be the required number of three bishops to ordain others, should it be necessary.

* * *

According to the account of the author of the *Life* (chapter twelve), the Frankish clergy were almost certain of victory. All the Moravians who assembled to hear the papal decision together with the Franks, were dismayed when they heard that John VIII had rejected their accusations and had confirmed Methodius in his rank.

This short report of the biographer is completed by what we learn from another papal letter addressed to Methodius on March 23, 881.[10] It is in answer to a letter sent to John VIII by Methodius in 880, almost immediately after his return to Moravia. His letter is not preserved, but we learn from the papal missive that Wiching had presented to Svatopluk a document allegedly given to him by the pope, in which the papal decisions were presented in a manner unfavorable to Methodius.[11] At the same time, he pretended that the pope had given him instructions to supervise Methodius' actions, while the latter was placed secretly under oath to accept this.

The pope denied vigorously that any other letter than the one which Methodius had carried to Svatopluk had been dispatched by him, and asserted that he had given no other instructions to Wiching than those mentioned in the genuine letter. He again expressed his great satisfaction at having found Methodius' teaching to be in conformity with the doctrine of the Church, and assured him of his sympathies in the troubling experiences he had had to endure after his return.

When the information given in this letter is compared with the short report of the biographer, we come to the conclusion that Wiching returned to Moravia before Methodius and presented his version of the papal decisions to Svatopluk. Counting on his new episcopal status and the favor which Svatopluk had hitherto manifested to him, he hoped that he would convince the prince of the genuineness of his report, and thus induce Svatopluk to reject Methodius when he appeared. This seems to be indicated by the words of the Franks, according to the *Legend*: "the Pope had given the power to us, and he orders us to expel him [Methodius] with his doctrine." Svatopluk, however, preferred to await the arrival of Methodius. Even if the reading of the genuine letter did not convince him of Wiching's falsehood, he did not dare to repudiate Methodius because of the sympathies which the great majority of his subjects manifested for the archbishop. At the same time he did not wish to alienate the pope who, in the letter addressed to him, had praised so highly his fidelity to St. Peter and his vicar in Rome.[12]

Methodius, knowing his master well, decided to dispatch a letter to the pope immediately, asking him to clarify the situation and to confirm the authenticity of the letter he himself had presented to Svatopluk in the pope's name. The short report of the biographer should be completed in this way.

It is interesting to read in the biographer's report words which recall the letter sent by Hadrian II to Kocel, and quoted by Constantine's biographer, namely, "in his hands are from God and the apostolic See all Slavic lands." These words are not contained in the letter "*Industriae tuae.*" It could, however, be supposed that the words, "we have confirmed through the precept of our apostolic authority the privilege of this archbishopric," are indicative of the papal confirmation of Methodius' rank as legate to all the Slavic nations. It cannot mean the privilege to use the Slavic liturgy, because the pope spoke about this in another passage of the same letter.[13]

❖ ❖ ❖

Svatopluk's choice of the Frankish Wiching as second bishop of his realm is very puzzling. Nitra, the See of the new bishop, was an important political center in that part of Great Moravia which is now Slovakia. We have seen already that Frankish influence must have been very strong there. Because Nitra was also a prominent commercial center, the Franks seem to have established a colony there in the first half of the ninth century and built a church which was consecrated by Adalwin, Archbishop of Salzburg. This would indicate that Nitra was a stronghold of both Franks and Moravians who favored the Latin liturgy and letters. This could explain the choice of a bishop of the Latin rite for Nitra.

The fact that Svatopluk favored the Latin liturgy and that he chose his main advisers from among the Latin clergy—John of Venice and Wiching—suggests, however, that he was motivated by other reasons. One may wonder whether Svatopluk did not cherish far-reaching political ambitions concerning the inheritance of the Carolingian dynasty in East Francia, or the expansion of his power into the Latin West.

Svatopluk's political power had grown to unexpected proportions. Until the year 882 he remained on good terms with the Empire and even intervened in the Ost Mark in order to restore the margrave Arib who had been expelled by the sons of the late margraves William and Engelschalk. His friendly relations with Arnulf, Duke of Carinthia and Pannonia (from 876 to 887), came to an end, however, in the same year. In 881, or 882, the Bulgarians invaded the territory of Great Moravia and seem to have plotted against Svatopluk himself.[14] The latter suspected that this invasion was made in connivance with Arnulf. He asked the Duke to deliver to him the men responsible for the plot and to declare on oath that he had no part in it.

Arnulf refused both demands. Svatopluk invaded Pannonia with a strong army in 883 and devastated a great part of the country. He repeated the invasion in 884 and occupied the whole of Pannonia as far as the river Drava. The Emperor Charles III was forced to accept the *fait accompli* in 884 when he met Svatopluk, who was willing to recognize the emperor's supremacy over the newly-conquered province. Arnulf was forced to conclude a peace treaty with Svatopluk on the same conditions.

Pannonia was now once again open to Methodius and his disciples. Another political and religious conquest was realized in Bohemia, probably after 880. Although the *Life of Methodius* does not mention the Christianization of the Czech Duke Bořivoj, this fact is attested by the *Short Word on SS. Cyril and Methodius and on the Christianization of the Moravian and Bohemian lands,* a document which was composed in Latin in Bohemia between 950 and 975.[15]

This conversion seems to have been achieved thanks to the friendly relations of Bořivoj with the court of Svatopluk. The Bohemian Duke is supposed to have recognized the political suzerainty of Svatopluk. This relationship was strengthened when Bořivoj, under pressure from his opponents, who objected to his religious policy, took refuge at Svatopluk's court. Bořivoj himself may have been baptized by Methodius in Moravia, but the arch-bishop sent some of his disciples to Bohemia—the *"Short Word"* mentions a priest, Kaich—to baptize Bořivoj's wife Ludmila and to continue the Christianization of the country.

The German chronicler Thietmar [16] indicates that, after the submission of Bohemia, Svatopluk's power extended also over the Serbs in modern Saxony as far as the rivers Oder and Saale. It is not known when this extension was realized, but there is no reason to reject the report of the German chronicler.

Another interesting report, contained in the *Life of Methodius*, testifies to the extent of Svatopluk's power toward the East. In order to show that his hero possessed a prophetic spirit, the hagi-ographer speaks of a mighty prince on the Vistula river who opposed the preaching of Christian faith. Methodius is said to have sent him the following message (chapter eleven): "It would be better for you, son, if you would accept baptism voluntarily in your land, instead of being baptized in captivity and against your will in a foreign country. You will remember me." And so it happened.

We are entitled to deduce from this report that Methodius' disciples had extended their missionary work beyond the bound-aries of Moravia and were working among the Poles on the Vistula. This biographer can have had in mind only the territory of Cra-cow. It was evidently annexed by Svatopluk, and the Duke, taken prisoner, was baptized. This is also the first indication of the spread of Christianity among the Poles. We shall see later that this success was not as ephemeral as is still often believed.

Perhaps it is during Svatopluk's expedition against the Vistulan-ians that an event mentioned by Methodius' biographer should be dated. In chapter eleven, when exalting the prophetic spirit of the saint, the biographer reports: "Another time, when Svato-pluk battled with pagans and could not achieve anything but delayed, then Methodius, when the Mass of Saint Peter, it is the liturgy, was approaching, sent to him saying: 'If you promise me that you will spend the day of Saint Peter with your soldiers with me, I am confident in God, that he will deliver them soon to you.' And so it happened."[17]

Svatopluk thus succeeded in building up an imposing empire. It was hardly to be expected that he would stop there. His mind

was definitely oriented toward the West. He was fully aware of
the declining power of the Carolingian Empire and of its eastern
part, Germany, after the death of Louis the German. He may have
hoped one day to replace the Carolingians or, at least, to be
accepted in Bavaria. Charles the Fat's position was not very
strong, as was later demonstrated by his deposition by the mag-
nates of Franconia, Saxony, Bavaria, Thuringia, and Swabia (887).
Arnulf was an illegitimate son of Carloman, the son of Louis the
German. If Svatopluk nourished such plans, it would be understandable that he would prefer the Latin liturgy. In this case he
may have thought that Wiching could help him pave the way for
the further extension of his power in the West. It is also possible
that he favored Wiching because the latter was Arnulf's confi-
dant. He needed to be on good terms with the Empire as long
as he had not secured the new additions to his realm, such as
Bohemia and the lands of the Sorbs and the Polish Vistulanians.

* * *

However, after the success won in Rome, Methodius' situation
must have improved and Wiching's influence decreased. This
enabled Methodius to realize his plan to visit his native country.

The motives which had prompted Methodius to undertake such
a long voyage are still debated by specialists. The way in which
the biographer introduces his report (chapter thirteen) is rather
puzzling. After recounting the dismay of the Frankish priests on
learning of the pope's approval of Methodius' teaching and innovations, the biographer continues:

"But their malice did not stop even there, and they calumniated
him saying: 'The Emperor is cross with him, and if he seizes him,
he will not escape alive.' But the Lord in His Mercy, Who did
not want His servant to be outraged even in this, inspired the
heart of the Emperor, as the heart of the Emperor is constantly
in God's hand (Prov. 21:1), so that he sent Methodius a letter:
'Reverend Father, I desire very much to see you. Be so good and
set out on a journey to us, in order that we may see you while
you are in this world, and that we may receive your blessing'."

It seems at first sight rather strange that the Frankish priests
should agitate against Methodius, spreading rumors that the
Byzantine emperor was hostile to the archbishop. Of course, when

Methodius accepted the appointment as archbishop of Pannonia and Moravia from the pope, he became definitely a member of the hierarchy of the Roman patriarchate. This could have been regarded in Byzantium as an act of treachery if the Eastern and Western churches had been in a state of hostility. However, this was not the case in 880 and 881 when these rumors are supposed to have been spread. On the other hand, what kind of interest could the Frankish clergy have in the relations of Methodius with Byzantium?

Such rumors could have spread in a part of Methodius' diocese which affected the interests of Byzantium.[18] This might have been the case if Methodius had extended his activity to the territory of the Serbian Prince Mutimir, whom John VIII had invited to accept Methodius as his archbishop. All this is a possibility, but the author attributes such malevolent rumors to the Frankish priests in Moravia, not to Byzantine priests who may have been working in Mutimir's land.

It seems therefore more logical to see in these words only a means by which the writer sought to introduce another incident to enhance the honor of his hero. This new honor would be all the more impressive if it came from an unexpected quarter which might have been imagined to be hostile to Methodius.

There is, however, one important fact which should be stressed. The initiative for Methodius' visit to Constantinople came from the Emperor Basil I himself and from the Patriarch Photius. This seems clear. We can even fix the exact date of this invitation. It most probably occurred in 880 before Methodius' trip to Rome. It is in this sense that we must interpret the enigmatic passage in the pope's letter of 881: "when you have returned, with God's help." Then the pope promises to investigate according to canonical rules all the acts which Wiching had committed against Methodius, and, after hearing both sides, to punish the guilty.

The words, "when you have returned with God's help," cannot mean Methodius' return to Rome. The only interpretation can be that the pope postponed the hearing of both parties in Rome until after the return of Methodius from a long journey which he was planning and of which the pope knew. Clearly, Methodius had informed the pope of the invitation from the emperor and the patriarch to visit them in Constantinople.

Such an interpretation used to be rejected by many specialists, because it was thought that Pope John VIII had again broken with the Patriarch Photius in 881. It has been shown that this was not so.[19] After his rehabilitation by the Union Council of 879–880, a rehabilitation which was confirmed by the pope, Photius remained on good terms with Rome. The story of his excommunication by John VIII in 881 is legend and is now generally rejected. Because Rome and Constantinople were reconciled, there was no reason why Methodius should not disclose to the pope his intention of accepting the imperial and patriarchal invitation. It was, on the contrary, in the pope's interest to strengthen good relationships through the visit of a native Greek who was well acquainted with the patriarch and was, at the same time, a legate of the Holy See in Slavic lands.

It should not be forgotten that Photius, after his rehabilitation, did all he could to let bygones be bygones and offered his hand in reconciliation, even to Bishop Marinus, his most outspoken adversary in Rome.[20] This shows that he could not have borne any grudge against Methodius, who was on good terms with Rome. On the contrary, Methodius could become a new link to strengthen his relations with Rome.

As regards Basil I, he was very much interested in the conversion of the Slavs. It was in his reign that the second conversion of the Serbians took place. The Bulgarians had Byzantine bishops, but the Patriarch Photius, in agreement with the emperor, had consented to their being placed under the jurisdiction of the Roman patriarchate.[21] John VIII continued vainly to exhort Boris to send his delegates to Rome, but the Khagan preferred to have an autonomous Church. The Byzantines must have heard about the success which the Greek mission had enjoyed in Moravia and it is quite natural that the emperor and the patriarch should have wished to learn more details about Methodius' missionary methods among the Slavs. On the other hand, it was also in the interests of Rome to attract the Bulgarians, perhaps through the intermediary of a Slavic teacher who was a Roman archbishop of Byzantine extraction.

It can be imagined that all this was discussed in Rome in 880 by Pope John VIII and Methodius. The pope welcomed the voyage and was certainly eager to learn of its outcome. He was dismayed to learn about the intrigues against Methodius in Moravia, all the more so as this incident could delay the execution of

Methodius' plan. He postponed the definitive arraignment of Wiching until after Methodius' return from Constantinople. Possibly it was agreed that Methodius would visit the pope in Rome in order to report on the success of his interview with the emperor and the patriarch, and perhaps also to report on the situation in Bulgaria.

Methodius probably left Moravia for Constantinople before the winter of 881 and returned in the spring of 882. His visit proved very successful. The biographer describes it thus: "The Emperor received the Moravian Archbishop with great honor and joy, he praised his doctrine [this means his missionary method and the Slavic liturgy] and kept of his disciples a priest and a deacon with books. He fulfilled all his desires whatsoever he wanted, without refusing him anything, he embraced him, presented him with numerous gifts and accompanied him to his see. The Patriarch also."

This shows that even in Byzantium there was a lively interest in Slavic liturgy and literature which could be used as a means to attract the converted Slavs to the Byzantine obedience. The conversion of the Serbians, and the Bulgarian problem, must have enlivened this interest considerably. We have seen that there were a number of priests of Slavic extraction who were interested in the mission of Constantine and Methodius. Not all of them were sent to Moravia, as they were needed for other Slavic missions.[22] Their center in Constantinople was now strengthened by two members of Methodius' circle who could teach them Slavic letters. It was most probably agreed that this center should provide the Moravian mission with Greek works for translation into Slavonic.

This friendly reception of Methodius in Byzantium was to prove beneficial to those disciples of Methodius who were expelled from Moravia after his death and who found refuge in Constantinople.[23] This proves that the interest which the emperor and the patriarch manifested in Methodius' missionary methods was genuine.

But the friendly reception of some of Methodius' other disciples in Bulgaria[24] after they were exiled by Wiching also indicates that Boris must have been informed of Methodius' activities. It was in the interests of Byzantium to acquaint Boris with Methodius' missionary methods. But this does not mean that Methodius met Boris on his return from Constantinople. What makes us hesitate to accept the historicity of such an encounter is the fact, that, according to the *Vita*, the Emperor Basil caused Methodius to be escorted to his metropolitan see. This indicates that Basil profited by this occasion to send an embassy to Svatopluk, the aim of which could only have been a renewal of friendly relations with Svatopluk's country.

Because of the suspicion with which the Bulgarians had always regarded the Moravians, a Byzantine embassy to Svatopluk's court would not have dared to cross Boris' land. The ambassadors, together with Methodius, most probably traversed Mutimir's land, which bordered on Byzantine territory, and continued their journey through Pannonian Croatia, which was governed by the Croatian Prince Zbraslav under Arnulf's overlordship, but with whom Svatopluk enjoyed friendly relations down to 883.[25]

The fact that the emperor's envoys accompanied Methodius to Moravia and brought an imperial message to the Moravian ruler must have impressed Svatopluk. Friendly relations with Byzantium could help Svatopluk to eliminate a possible danger emanating from Bulgaria, especially if he had ambitions to extend his power in the West.[26]

The renewal of a kind of alliance, or, at least friendship between Moravia and Byzantium could not please the Bulgarians. There may be a connection between this new diplomatic move and the Bulgarian invasion of Moravian territory in 881, or, more probably, in 882. Svatopluk's suspicion that this was done in connivance with Arnulf also becomes more understandable when we recall the Franco-Bulgarian alliance under Louis the German, aimed against the Moravia of Rastislav, which had induced the latter to turn toward Byzantium. It is quite possible that this renewal of Moravo-Byzantine friendship, in order to restrain the Bulgarians, accelerated Svatopluk's plans of expansion toward the West.

✻ ✻ ✻

The success which Methodius won in Constantinople undoubtedly enhanced his prestige at the court of Svatopluk. The enmity toward the Franks which began after 882 certainly led to a decline of Wiching's influence. At last Methodius enjoyed some years of peace; he profited by them to complete his literary works and to leave to his disciples the translations of all the liturgical and canonical books necessary for the normal functioning of the young Slavic Church. The biographer describes Methodius' activity in the following way in chapter fifteen:

"Afterwards, when he had liberated himself from all tumult and placed all his confidence in God, after placing before himself two priests from among his disciples, able stenographers, he soon translated from the Greek into Slavonic all the books of the Holy Writ completely, with the exception of the Books of the Macabees, in eight months, commencing in the month of March, until the twenty-sixth of October. After finishing, he rendered due thanks and praise to God who gives such grace and success, and offering with his clergy the holy and mysterious sacrifice, he celebrated the memory of Saint Demetrius. Because, before that, he had translated with the Philosopher only the Psalter, the Gospels, and the Apostolos with selected ecclesiastical formulars. Then he translated also the Nomocanon, that is the rule of the law, and the Books of the Fathers."

The biographer's description of Methodius' literary activity is explained differently by the specialists. Many hesitate to attribute to Methodius the translation of all the books of the Old Testament because such a translation is not preserved. The biographer's report is confirmed, however, by the affirmation of a Bulgarian ecclesiastical writer of the tenth century, John Exarchus. In the introduction to his translation of John of Damascus' main work on theology, he says that Methodius had translated all sixty books of the Old Testament.[27] Although he does not say that he had used or even seen this translation, it is quite possible that the tradition to which he refers is reliable. It is true that this translation is not preserved; it could have been destroyed during the persecution of Methodius' disciples after his death.

The skepticism of the older generation of specialists concerning Methodius' translation of all the books of the Old Testament is not shared by modern scholars. J. Vajs' thorough study of lessons from the Old Testament contained in the glagolitic breviaries used in Dalmatia strengthened the opinion that there existed a translation of the Old Testament from the Greek made during the Moravian period.[28] Of course, none of the copyists of the glagolitic breviaries had a complete copy of this translation, but this can be explained, as already mentioned, by the fact that the original translation was only partly saved during the upheaval after Methodius' death. Most modern scholars accept the veracity of the biographer's report contained in chapter fifteen.

In the same chapter, the biographer completes the information given in the *Life of Constantine* about the literary activity of Methodius' brother (chapters fourteen and fifteen). He says that Methodius collaborated with his brother on the translation of the Gospels and of the *Apostolos*—liturgical readings from the letters of the Apostles. He is also more precise when describing the translation of the liturgical books. According to him, the brothers did not translate all the liturgical books, as is said in the *Life of Constantine*, but only those indispensable to the religious services of the young Slavic Church. As already mentioned, the breviary was translated from the Greek Office. The liturgical books for the Moravian Church presented a mixture of the Roman liturgy and the Byzantine rite.

✣ ✣ ✣

The translation of the Nomocanon could have been made earlier, perhaps before the voyage of Methodius to Constantinople. It is now established that Methodius translated the Byzantine collection of John Scholasticus, called *Synagogê of Fifty Titles*. Scholasticus was Patriarch of Constantinople from 565 to 577. On the basis of philological evidence, many scholars attributed to Methodius the authorship of this translation, and this was definitely proved by H. F. Schmid.[29] His argumentation was recently strengthened by the discovery of some glosses in Slavonic found in a Latin manuscript of canon law which once belonged to the Monastery of St. Emmeram in Ratisbon, and is now kept in the Bavarian National Library in Munich (Cod. lat. Monas. 14008). The glosses are on folio 28[v] of the manuscript over some Latin words of the pseudo-apostolic canon 35, one of the canons dealing with the hierarchic organization. The glosses, however, are not a translation of Latin, but of Greek words from the same canon, which is contained with a slightly different wording in the *Synagogê* of John Scholasticus. The words are evidently taken from a Slavonic translation of the *Synagogê*, and betray a Cyrilo-Methodian origin.[30]

This Latin collection with the Slavic glosses seems to have had a very interesting history. It is not the collection called *Dionysiana Hadriana*, which was exclusively used in the Frankish Empire from 774 on, when it was presented to Charlemagne by Hadrian I, but a collection called by the specialists *Dionysiana adaucta*.[31] Some of these changes betray the fact that it was compiled in a Byzantine part of Italy. Originally it contained, besides the list of the popes, another one of the Byzantine patriarchs. These lists are left out of the manuscript in Munich, although they are indicated in the Table of Contents.

A copy of this collection was given by Pope John VIII to Methodius in 880, and it is this copy which is now in Munich. It is important to note that canon 35 of the pseudo-apostolic canons is quoted in the letter which Methodius transmitted to Svatopluk in 880. After ordering that all priests and clerics, Slavs or Franks, should be subject to Archbishop Methodius, the pope quoted verbally the words of the canon *ut nihil omnino praeter eius conscientiam agant* (that they may not do anything without his knowledge). These words, together with two others which occur in the same canon, are glossed in Slavonic. It is evident that the glossator wished to coordinate these words with the Slavonic translation of the same canon in the *Synagogê*.[32]

This shows that the wording of the canon was discussed at the court of Svatopluk and that an examination was made of all three documents—the pope's letter, Methodius' translation of the canon in question, and the wording of the canon in the collection that the pope had given to Methodius. All the documents were equally eloquent concerning the subordination of the clergy to the archbishop.[33]

It should also be stressed that the pope did not give Methodius the same collection of canon law which was in use in the Frankish Church. This can be interpreted in the sense that the pope desired to stress the direct subordination of Moravia to Rome. The fact that the collection presented to Methodius betrayed sympathies for Byzantium is also of some significance. It points to the fact that in 880 a friendly atmosphere prevailed in Rome concerning relations with Byzantium. By this gesture the pope evinced respect for the Byzantine origin of Methodius, who had been on friendly terms with Photius, then reconciled with Rome, whom Methodius was about to visit in Constantinople.

The Byzantine collections of canon law also contained a selection of imperial laws (nomoi). They were therefore called nomo-canons. In his translation of the *Synagogê* Methodius omitted the imperial laws which were regarded as superseded, even in Byzantium. It would have been pointless to present them to the Moravians.

Methodius also excluded from his translation all canons which did not fit a Western Christian community. Of the 377 canons in the original collection, 142 were, in this way, omitted. The Slavic translation discloses that its author was well versed in canon law and knew what was necessary for the development of the young Church in Moravia.

In the light of new research by Weingart we must now reject the thesis that Methodius was also the translator of two short scholia refuting the arguments of canon twenty-eight of the Council of Chalcedon. This canon defined that the second place after the Patriarch of Rome should be given to the Patriarch of Constantinople, whose jurisdiction should extend over Thrace and the whole of Asia Minor.

These scholia are translated from the Greek. Most probably they originated in one of the Greek monasteries in Rome, but the translation is very awkward and the language lacks the characteristic expressions used by Methodius. They could only have been translated after the death of Methodius.[34] Another document of Byzantine jurisprudence, adapted into Slavonic, is the first Slavonic law collection called *Zakon sudnyi ljudem* (Judicial Code for Laymen). The origin of this Code is still controversial. It has been thought that Rastislav asked the Emperor Michael III for a Code, that he was given a copy of the *Ecloga*, a juridical handbook used at that time by the Byzantine courts, and that Constantine translated parts of the *Ecloga* and adapted it to the needs of Moravian primitive jurisprudence.[35] Bulgarian specialists pretended to have discovered in it Bulgarian elements and claimed that it was composed in Bulgaria by St. Methodius' disciples. The possibility of a Russian or Pannonian origin was also debated.

Now it seems that the question is definitely answered. The Moravian origin, proved already by J. Vašica, cannot be doubted, but the author of the Code was not Constantine. It should be regarded as the work of the circle of clerics grouped around Methodius. It served as a directory for clergy, indicating how to proceed in certain cases. It was also meant as an appeal to official judicial institutions, recommending that they proceed in the spirit of Christian moderation when judging certain transgressions of the law. But it was not at all in the mind of its authors to introduce it as an official handbook for judicial courts in Moravia.[36]

The initiator of this composition could have been Methodius himself. He was familiar with judicial matters because he had been archon of a Slavic province under Byzantine supremacy. It is quite possible that his disciples, if not Methodius himself, added this compilation to the translation of the *Synagogê*. At least the oldest Slavonic manuscript of the *Zakon* is contained in the Russian collection of canon law, called *Kormčaja Kniga* (Pilot's book) of Ustjug. It contains the *Zakon*, and Methodius' translation of the *Synagogê*. This seems to indicate that a combination of both documents may already have been made in Methodius' time.

✳ ✳ ✳

The specialists are still discussing the question of what should be understood by the words "the Books of the Fathers" (*ot'c'skyja k'nigy*), the translation of which is also attributed to Methodius. The question cannot yet be definitely answered. The indication of the biographer can mean works, biographies, sentences or homilies of the Fathers. The problem of the numerous Greek *Paterica* is also far from clear, and many of them are unpublished. So far, W. van Wijk, who has devoted much study to this problem, seems to have indicated the way to its solution by showing that Methodius had translated a Greek *Paterikon*, called *andron hagion biblos*.[37] An Old Slavonic translation of a Greek *Paterikon* exists, preserved in a manuscript in the Austrian National Library in Vienna (no. 152). It may contain the translation made by Methodius. However, this problem is far from solved.

Methodius certainly composed a number of homilies during his stay in Moravia. Only one of them is preserved in the so-called *Glagolita Clozianus*, a collection of homilies of the Fathers, translated into Old Slavonic and written in the glagolitic alphabet.[38] Only a minor part of the originally very large collection is preserved. The homily contains an exhortation to the princes to watch over the strict observation of Church rules concerning the conclusion of marriages by Christians. The homily is anonymous, but the textual comparison with Methodius' works betrays a great similarity to his vocabulary. Moreover, as can be seen from chapter eleven of the *Vita*, Methodius was very much preoccupied with this problem. The biographer reports that Methodius admonished one of Svatopluk's counsellors to separate himself from his wife, because, according to the Church precepts of this time, a man's marriage with his godchild was invalid. When the counsellor refused to listen to Methodius' admonition, the archbishop excommunicated him. We have seen that similar matrimonial problems occurred even in Kocel's land.[39] This is understandable in countries which had only recently been converted. Therefore the homily in question can be ascribed rightly to Methodius.

On the other hand, we can hardly see in the long introduction to the *Life of Methodius* another of his homilies. The introduction is really based on a treatise on the Oecumenical Councils. Such treatises were very numerous in Byzantium and formed parts of a Byzantine catechism. It is preceded by a short description of the creation of the world by God, and of the history of the Old Testament which prepared the new revelation. This was expanded by the Apostles and further defined by the Fathers of the first Six Oecumenical Councils. The fact that the popes are mentioned in first place in the listing of the main personalities of the councils is not surprising. This tradition is followed in most of the Byzantine anonymous treatises.[40] The introduction reflects the doctrine of the two brothers, and the Byzantine tradition of stressing the importance of the councils in defining the Faith.[41]

It is also quite natural that only six Councils should be enumerated. The Seventh Council against iconoclasm was officially included in the Byzantine treatises only after the second patriarchate of Photius, although its oecumenicity was accepted from the end of the eighth century. A similar tradition was followed in the West where the oecumenicity of the Seventh Council was definitely recognized after Rome's reconciliation with Photius.[42] In the description of the *Acts* of the Sixth Council, the condemnation of Pope Honorius is also noted. This was done not only in the Eastern Church but also in Rome.

As we have seen, it is also largely accepted by specialists that the translation of the Gospels made by Constantine and Methodius was preceded by an introduction in verse composed by Constantine.[43]

More uncertainty enshrouds the authorship of another theological work, *On the True Faith*. F. Grivec[44] is inclined to attribute its composition to Constantine, but the specialists are divided when discussing this problem. There is also a possibility that this discourse is simply a translation from the Greek made at a much later period.

Also of Moravian origin is an old Slavonic penitentiary called *Zapovĕdi sventych ot'c'* (Prescriptions of the Holy Fathers).[45] It was translated from a Latin penitentiary book used by Latin missionaries in Moravia. The translator must have used a penitentiary which was very similar to that contained in a codex preserved in the library of the Cathedral church in Merseburg.[46] The adaptation was made by one of the clerics of Methodius who was familiar with the Latin language.

Methodius seems also to have translated into Slavonic some writings of his late brother: The author of the *Life of Constantine* (chapter ten) mentions that Methodius translated Constantine's writings, arranging them into eight *besĕdy* (treatises). It is difficult to say what the author of the *Life* meant by the *besĕdy*. Constantine described in Greek the manner in which he had found the relics of St. Clement, in Cherson. His description was translated into Latin by Anastasius Bibliothecarius in Rome, and into Slavonic by Methodius. This might have been one of the eight *besĕdy*. The defense of the Slavonic liturgy was probably another one, although it may have been outlined by Constantine himself before leaving Moravia. The discussion with the Jews and Moslems at the court of the Khazar Khagan was most probably yet another one. It is a long and interesting theological treatise, and we can presume that Constantine wrote it in Greek after returning from the Khazar mission. We have seen that the embassy to the Arabs, of which Constantine was a member, can be accepted as an historical fact. Thus we can imagine that Constantine summarized his experiences from discussions with the Arabs in a short treatise against Islam.

We have seen that Constantine's disputation with the iconoclastic ex-Patriarch Joannicius cannot be accepted in the way the biographer reports it. Although Constantine might have met Joanicius, a public disputation between the two could not have taken place. There is, however, the possibility that Constantine had written a short treatise against iconoclasm when staying in

Constantinople, and that this short treatise, translated by Methodius, was the basis of the biographer's description. These might have been the *besědy* translated by Methodius. Of course, this conclusion is highly hypothetical (cf. above, Ch. II, note 30). The text is not clear. One could also deduce from it that Methodius arranged in eight chapters the description of Constantine's disputation at the Khazar court.

The finest products of the literary circle grouped around Methodius are the *Lives* of the two brothers. The *Life of Constantine* must have been written between 874 and 880 by one of his disciples, possibly Clement, under the inspiration of Methodius himself and on the basis of some of Constantine's writings, translated by Methodius into Slavonic, as we have seen. The *Life of Methodius* was written soon after his death before the expulsion of his disciples from Moravia. In order to show the reliability of the two writings, I compared them and their data with contemporary Byzantine historical facts and hagiographical literature in my book *Les légendes de Constantin et de Méthode vues de Byzance* (Prague, 1933). This comparison has shown that both *Lives* are not ordinary legendary compositions, but important historical documents reflecting the Byzantine mentality of this time, and completing in many ways our knowledge of the history of Byzantium and of Central Europe in the ninth century. Thanks to this research and that of other scholars, the literary and historical importance of the two *Lives* is now recognized by all specialists.

Although composed by a writer who was well acquainted with Byzantine mentality and the theology and literary achievements of that period, they were not meant for the Byzantine reader, but for the Slavic Christians of Moravia and Pannonia. This is shown by the general tendency which we can detect in them. The author of the *Life of Constantine* intended to give the young Slavonic Church of Moravia a firm ideological basis. He was anxious to portray its founder, the Philosopher, as an orthodox theologian well versed in divine lore. Constantine's literary and liturgical innovations were willed by God and were the best means for the propagation of His word among the newly-converted people. His innovation was approved by the pope, and the hostility of the Frankish clergy toward him and his work was unjust. Numerous protestations from Holy Writ gave his disciples reliable weapons for the defense of the Slavonic liturgy. Not only the historical and the theological, but also the literary value of this composition is very high, and it can be regarded as one of the best literary achievements of this period in Byzantium and in the West.

An apologetic tendency can be traced also in the *Life of Methodius* even to a higher degree.[47] The hostility of the Latins to the Slavonic liturgy impelled the writer to stress even more the orthodoxy of the late archbishop. This is shown especially in the introduction, which is a kind of confession of faith of both brothers. The approval by the popes of the innovation is also put forward, against the suspicion of the Frankish clergy. Methodius' devotion to St. Peter is emphasized. His work was approved, not only by the popes, but also by the Byzantine emperor, and even the Frankish king showed his favor to Methodius. Anxiety for the survival of the new Church after the loss of its head, and in the face of intense hostility, is especially evident in the last chapter of his work. The author of the *Life* remains anonymous, but it could also have been composed by Clement.

Apart from his literary activities, Methodius also accomplished missionary work; this involved considerable travel through his vast archdiocese. The biographer describes these travels in chapter fourteen, comparing them with the travels of St. Paul and stressing that Methodius had to undergo all the troubles and support all the sufferings described by the Apostle in his Second Letter to the Corinthians (2 Cor. II: 26–27). Because of this narrative by the biographer, some historians believed that Methodius also visited Bohemia and Poland in the course of his missionary wanderings. This appears very hypothetical. Methodius already had a sufficient number of disciples; being himself an archbishop, he was able to consecrate his own priests and send them to the newly-converted countries under Svatopluk's suzerainty. We do not know if he revisted Pannonia after its conquest by Svatopluk. His disciples probably worked there too, because the Frankish clergy were certainly reduced in numbers after Svatopluk's conquest. The main preoccupation of Methodius after his return from Rome and Constantinople was to provide his Slavic Church with liturgical books and religious literature in Slavonic.

During one of his journeys, probably in modern Slovakia, Methodius is said to have encountered "the Hungarian King."

The biographer says that Methodius' entourage had warned the archbishop not to go to see the king, although the latter had expressed his desire to meet him. They did not trust the king, fearing that he would maltreat Methodius. However, the king received Methodius with great honor, talking with him "as such men should talk"; after honoring him with many gifts, he asked Methodius to remember him in his prayers.

The description of this encounter seems to suggest that the "king" in question was a Christian ruler. In this case it might be supposed that the ruler whom Methodius encountered was the Emperor Charles III, the third son and successor of Louis the German (882–888). This encounter could have taken place in the autumn of 884, when Svatopluk met Charles III to conclude the peace, in the Wiener Wald near Tuln.

This, however, does not quite correspond with the description given by the biographer. If Svatopluk was present, Methodius had nothing to fear. On the other hand, all existing manuscripts read that the encounter was with the Hungarian king.

It seemed difficult, therefore, to most specialists to accept the suggestion that the word Hungarian (ug'r'skyi) was added to the word king (korol') by a later copyist, as was suggested by A. Brückner.[48] It was pointed out that, at that time, the Hungarians were already in Bessarabia. They may have been making inroads into that part of the Danube basin which was under Bulgarian overlordship, and one of the bands of Hungarians could have approached the boundary of Great Moravia somewhere near the Danube.

Perhaps this problem can now be regarded as solved in a study published by V. Vavřínek.[49] He has approached the problem of the title "korol" found in this chapter of the *Vita Methodii* from the Byzantine point of view, showing what kind of titles were given by the Byzantine protocol to other Christian rulers who were regarded as forming a spiritual family of which the Roman emperor—the Basileus—was the head, appointed by God as His representative. The Frankish ruler was regarded as the spiritual brother of the Basileus and was normally given the title *"rex."* Vavřínek has shown that this Byzantine custom also inspired the authors of the two biographies. The Slavic name "korol" is of West Slavic origin, derived etymologically from the name Charlemagne. The title was already used in Moravia before the arrival of the Byzantine mission and was accepted also by the disciples of the two brothers. In the Moravian dialect the title took a different form, probably "kral'." The form "korol'," as found in the *Vita*, corresponds to the Russian dialect. This shows that a Russian copyist of the *Vita* who did not understand the meaning of the title "kral," replaced it with the Russian, "korol" and added to it the word "ug'r'skyi," because he knew that in his time a Hungarian king reigned over Pannonia and Moravia.

The king in question could only have been Charles III, and the encounter of Methodius with the Western emperor should be dated in 884. Methodius, with other prominent Moravians, accompanied Svatopluk to his meeting with Charles III to conclude the peace.

V. Vavřínek rightly sees in the description of how the "King" received Methodius an apologetic trait in favor of Methodius' work in Moravia. The archbishop was well received, not only by the Basileus, but also by the Frankish emperor—King Charles III. This should have strengthened the position of Methodius' disciples in Moravia in the face of opposition from the Frankish clergy, because as interpreted by the biographer—who wrote after Methodius' death—the person and the work of his master was honored also by both the Frankish king and the emperor.

※ ※ ※

The last chapter of the *Life of Methodius* opens with the enigmatic words: "In this way, after having hewn off all the guilty on all sides, and closed the mouths of the loquacious, he finished the course of life, preserved his faith, waiting for the crown of justice."

The Slavonic word for "hewn off"—"ot'sěšti"—is often used to mean excommunication from the Church.[50] Therefore these words are explained by most specialists as implying that, toward the end of his life, Methodius excommunicated his adversaries, using the power conferred by his status and also strictly defined in the papal letter,[51] in order to terminate their constant enmity.

If these words should be explained in this way, it is to be regretted that the author of the *Life* was so reticent on this special occasion. The *Life of Clement*, Methodius' disciple, is more explicit in this respect, and affirms that Methodius excommuni-

cated Wiching and his adherents.[52] He naturally attributed heretical teaching to Wiching which, however, he did not specify. He
probably had in mind the procession of the Holy Ghost, because
he lived in the atmosphere of the Eastern Church. If there was
an excommunication—I would rather say suspension—we need
not suppose that it was motivated by any particular heretical
teaching. Wiching's disobedience and constant hostility to his
metropolitan provided a sufficient reason.

The so-called *Moravian Legend,* composed during the eleventh
century, reports expressly that Methodius excommunicated Svatopluk himself (chapter two).[53] This report is certainly an exaggeration. Methodius was a Byzantine, and the Byzantines professed great reverence for their rulers. It was unthinkable that
the patriarch should excommunicate the emperor. The principle
of "oeconomy" was applied to the utmost every time a conflict arose
between the Church and the emperor. The report of the *Legend*
is animated by the dislike which the Slavic priests in Bohemia held
for the memory of Svatopluk. His lack of support of Methodius,
and his preference for Frankish priests, had speeded the ruin of
Methodius' work in Moravia and caused the destruction of his
own empire.

The letter of Pope Stephen V to Svatopluk after Methodius'
death contains a passage [54] which could be interpreted to mean
that Methodius had used his right to proceed against his adversaries according to the canons. The words are, however, not quite
clear. They can also be interpreted to mean that Methodius had
threatened his opponents with excommunication if they continued to oppose him. Thus we can admit the possibility of the
excommunication of Wiching or, at least, of a threat to use this
radical measure against him and his followers, but we must
exclude the possibility of any kind of hostile action against Svatopluk by Methodius. Whenever his biographer mentions Svatopluk, he does so in a friendly way.

※ ※ ※

The last days of Methodius are described in a short but extremely touching way by his biographer. When the day of his
demise was clearly approaching, his disciples asked him to designate a successor to continue his work. The ailing archbishop

pointed to Gorazd, one of his most devoted disciples, saying: "This man is free and of your country, well versed in Latin books, and orthodox."

The choice of Gorazd as his successor reveals the strained situation in Moravia. Methodius had probably chosen Gorazd as the third bishop some time before, but was unable to consecrate him, as the rubrics require the presence of three bishops. He could hardly obtain the collaboration of Wiching. He probably planned a new trip to Rome, after his return from Constantinople. But the news of the death of John VIII on December 16, 882, followed soon after by the demise of his two successors Marinus II (882–May 884), and Hadrian III (884–September 885), most probably forced him to postpone his plan. He also thought it of paramount importance for the instruction of his flock to provide his disciples with Slavic liturgical and ecclesiastical books. His illness may have interfered also with his plan to consecrate Gorazd, perhaps together with another disciple, in Rome.

The choice was wise. Gorazd was of noble origin [55]—Methodius stressed that he was a free man—and a Moravian by birth. It was to be expected that he would find the necessary support among the Moravian nobles, being one of them himself. On the other hand, although a supporter of Slavic liturgy and literature, he was well versed in Latin letters. Gorazd could only have obtained his Latin education from Frankish priests in Moravia or perhaps even in Bavaria. This circumstance may have gained him sympathy from the Latin and Frankish clergy and perhaps from Svatopluk, who favored the Latin culture.

* * *

Methodius performed his last episcopal function on Palm Sunday. Although ill, the archbishop assembled the people in the church and blessed the emperor, the prince, and all the faithful, foretelling that he would die on the third day. So it happened. He died in the early morning of the sixth of April, 885.

His disciples performed the funeral rites in the Latin, Greek, and Slavic liturgies, and he was buried in his metropolitan church. This description also illustrates well Methodius' mentality and the situation in Moravia. Even at the end of his life, far from his native country, Methodius remained faithful to Byzantine traditions. His first blessing was for the Byzantine emperor, who was regarded by his subjects as the representative of God on earth and leader of the Christians. The second blessing reflects the sentiments of loyalty which the Byzantine Church always cherished for the rulers instituted by God. This simple statement shows, at the same time, that Methodius had always paid the respect due to the ruler, in spite of his differences with him.

The performance of the funeral rites in the three liturgies again shows the multilingual character of the Church in Moravia. The Greek liturgy was performed by Methodius' Greek disciples who had accompanied him to Moravia, the Latin by Slavic and Frankish priests under his jurisdiction who had preferred it to the Slavic liturgy. The manner in which the biographer describes the funeral rites seems to indicate that a peaceful coexistence of the three liturgies in Moravia was possible if it were not disturbed by adverse events.

Interest also attaches to the report that Methodius was buried in his cathedral church. The Prologue—a short Breviary lesson—on SS. Cyril and Methodius [56] completes this information, specifying that his tomb lay on the left side beyond the main altar of Our Lady. It has so far proved impossible to identify Methodius' cathedral church and to find his tomb. The fact that he had a cathedral church testifies to the fact that the religious situation in Moravia was well stabilized. His residence was, naturally, near the cathedral.

An old tradition locates this church in the region of Staré Město (Old City), a part of the modern city of Uherské Hradiště (Ungarisch Gradisch),[57] so called because in the Middle Ages it was an outpost near the frontier of Hungary. Numerous archaeological finds dating from the ninth and tenth centuries, and the discovery of the foundations of three stone churches dating from the ninth century, show, as we have seen, that this region was an important political and religious center in the days of Great Moravia. This, however, does not mean that Methodius' residence was located there. The name of a locality in this region, called Velehrad (Great Castle), induced many Czech historians to place the political center of Rastislav's and Svatopluk's realm in this region. Excavations have not confirmed this supposition to date.

The ruins of an even more imposing center were recently discovered at Mikulčice, 45 kilometers from Velehrad and Staré Město. Besides the foundations of nine other churches, parts of a basilica, the largest church so far known in Great Moravia, were excavated there, but the grave of the Moravian archbishop was not found.[58] The archaeologists have not yet finished their work and there is still hope that the remains of Methodius' cathedral church and his tomb may be found.

The last chapter of the *Life of Methodius* ends with a prayer addressed to the holy man: "And you, holy and venerable head, look from on high with your intercessions at us who are full of desire for you, and deliver your disciples from all danger, spread your doctrine and disperse heresies, in order that we may live in dignity according to our vocation and, afterwards, that we may stand with you, your flock, at the right side of Christ, our God, and receive from him eternal life."

The words are written in the original in verses of fifteen and thirteen syllables,[59] and echo invocations addressed to the saint in Byzantine hagiography.[60] At the same time they betray the anxiety which filled the hearts of Methodius' disciples concerning their own fate and that of their leader's work after his death.

❖ ❖ ❖

Their anxiety was well founded. Immediately after Methodius' departure Wiching hastened to Rome in order to win over Pope Stephen V to his own plans. From the letter which the pope addressed to Svatopluk at the end of 885, we gather that Wiching accused Methodius of heretical teaching concerning the procession of the Holy Ghost, of disobedience to the injunction of the Holy See, which had forbidden him to use the vernacular language in the liturgy, and of transgressing the ecclesiastical canons because he named his own successor—Gorazd. He also accused Methodius of having introduced into Moravia the Byzantine prescriptions for fasting.[61]

Wiching must have left Moravia with the consent of Svatopluk because, at the beginning of his letter, the pope is very outspoken in his praise of Svatopluk's loyalty to the Holy See and of his desire to follow its teaching. This praise of the most powerful ruler in Central Europe is understandable, as the pope's position was shaky at the beginning of his reign, and the support of such an influential prince was desirable. It was not surprising that the pope addressed Svatopluk as "Slavic King." [62] It is evident that Wiching well knew how to exploit the unstable position of the papacy to his own aims, in stressing the loyalty of the mighty prince and of himself to St. Peter.

The pope first gives a long explanation of the Roman doctrine on the procession of the Holy Ghost remarking, however, that this mystery is not fit for discussion by those who are not well versed in theology. He then gives Svatopluk information on the character of fasting. It is interesting to note that, although he speaks of Methodius without giving him his title, the pope is very reticent concerning the accusation that Methodius had taught heretical doctrine. He expresses his astonishment at hearing such an accusation, and condemns Methodius' doctrine conditionally, "if it be true." Then he forbids the use of the Slavonic language in the liturgy.

The genuineness of the letter must be examined, together with the instructions which the pope gave to his legates—Bishop Dominicus and two priests—when he sent them to Moravia to regulate the situation. The legates are first told how to address Svatopluk in the name of the pope and the Roman clergy. Then come instructions concerning the *Filioque*.[63] "The Holy Ghost is neither said to be begotten by the Father and the Son lest this imply two Fathers, nor begotten, lest this imply two Sons, but He is said to proceed. If they should say: 'It is forbidden by the Holy Fathers to add or subtract anything from the Symbol,' say: 'The Holy Roman Church is the guardian of the holy dogmas and confirms them, because, representing the prince of the Apostles, she does not vacillate in anything concerning the catholic faith' as the Lord himself said: 'Simon, Simon, behold, Satan has desired to have you, that he may sift you as wheat. But I have prayed for thee, that thy faith may not fail; and do thou when once thou hast turned again, strengthen thy brethren (Luke 22:31, 32).' This Church guided to the faith all erring churches and confirmed the vacillation, not by changing the holy dogmas, but by explaining them to people who did not understand them or were interpreting them wrongly."

From the words of the pope it is clear that Methodius and his disciples reproached their adversaries with having added the *Filioque* to the Nicaean Creed, affirming that the Holy Fathers had forbidden any addition to, or detraction from, this Symbol. This had already been enacted by the Council of Ephesus.[64] But a very recent council, that of 879–880, called by the Greeks the Union Synod, had made such a decision in a most telling way, by rehabilitating Photius. The Nicaean Creed was solemnly recited during the sixth session of the Council, held in the imperial palace under the presidency of the Emperor Basil and, after the recital, the Fathers very solemnly forbade not only the use of any other Symbol—this used also to be stressed in other oecumenical councils—but equally any addition to or detraction from it. The same injunction was repeated during the last session, held in the church of the Holy Wisdom, where the Fathers who had attended the previous session reported what had happened and presented the signature of the emperor.[65]

It is probable that Methodius and his disciples knew about the decision of the Union Synod and recognized it the more willingly, as this decision was also signed by the legates of John VIII. Evidently Methodius learned about this during his stay in Constantinople, if not before. Methodius' disciples regarded themselves as being perfectly entitled to ask their opponents to respect the decision of synods which also had been accepted by Rome.

Pope Stephen V avoided sanctioning this addition to the Creed, but approved the Western interpretation of the mystery in stressing that the Roman Church had the privilege not only of defending the dogmas but also of interpreting them.

The prohibition of the Slavic liturgy is listed in the instruction together with the injunction that only preaching in the vernacular is recommended. Regarding fasting, the instructions contain only a short recapitulation of what the pope said in the letter.[66]

All this was therefore in the letter. But the last point of the instruction contradicts the letter as we know it. The pope blames Methodius for having chosen a successor, against the canonical rules. Gorazd is forbidden to exercise these functions until he appears in person in Rome and himself states his case.[67]

This seems to indicate that the pope did not make a definite decision concerning the succession to Methodius. In the papal letter there is no mention of Gorazd. We read there, however, a long passage concerning Wiching, who is recommended to Svatopluk as being orthodox and devoted to him, and that the pope is sending him back "to direct his Church commissioned to him by God." What is even more puzzling is that the words of this recommendation are almost identical with the words in which John VIII had recommended Methodius to Svatopluk. These words are regarded by editors of this letter as having been interpolated by Wiching himself. Another interpolation is found in the passage in which the pope forbade the use of the vernacular in the liturgy. We read there that when in Rome Methodius had taken an oath in the name of St. Peter that he would never do such a thing.[68] We know that this is untrue and that such an assertion could hardly have been written in Rome.

There is no doubt that the papal decision was taken rather hastily and without giving a hearing to the accused party. Nevertheless, the pope does not seem to have made a definite decision concerning the succession to Methodius. This decision was probably intended to be made after the return of the legates, and after hearing Gorazd.

* * *

If the pope intended to appoint Wiching only as administrator of the archdiocese *ad interim*, before he made a definite decision, he did not know Wiching. The papal letter, cleverly interpolated, gave Wiching sufficient pretext to appoint himself as sole administrator of the archdiocese, charged with the power to execute the order of the pope forbidding the Slavic liturgy, and to intervene against Methodius' disciples as being suspect of heresy.

We have no genuine information concerning the manner in which Wiching proceeded. Only the Greek *Life of St. Clement*, Methodius' disciple, which is an eleventh century adaptation of a Slavic *Life* of the saint, gives us some information which, although somewhat biased, is trustworthy.

From this source [69] we gather that, after the arrival of the legates, a discussion was held at Svatopluk's court between Wiching's adherents and Methodius' Slavic disciples. The main subject seems to have been the *Filioque*. Svatopluk is said to have confessed his ignorance in theological matters, and to have declared that he intended to support the party which was ready to swear that their doctrine was the true one. The Franks took the oath immediately and Svatopluk declared their teaching obligatory.

Then the persecution of Methodius' disciples began. The leaders—Gorazd, Clement, Naum, Laurentius, and Angelarius—were imprisoned and maltreated. The author notes that Svatopluk was not present when the persecution started. Was he on a military expedition, or did he simply absent himself in order not to be blamed for what Wiching did? It seems that this persecution did not occur without arousing opposition on the part of the Slavic population. We can explain in this way the miracles which are said to have happened during the imprisonment of the disciples. When they were singing the liturgical prayers in prison an earthquake took place and their chains fell off.

It is probable that all this happened in Nitra, the residence of Wiching.[70] The Frankish element seems to have been strongest in this center, and most of his adherents were there. This may help to explain the absence of Svatopluk during the trial of the disciples. It was also in Nitra that a garrison of Svatopluk's German soldiers—the writer calls them in Slavic *Nemitzoi*—were ordered to expel the prisoners. They were deprived of their clothes in very cold weather and expelled from the city toward the Danube. There the soldiers left them. Other priests and deacons are even said to have been sold into slavery and brought to Venice.

The unfortunate disciples separated in groups in order to escape more easily from their possible pursuers, and some of them, after following the Danube, at last reached Belgrade, then in Bulgarian hands. They were received by the commander of the fortress, who sent them to Boris himself. So it came about that Methodius' legacy, ruined in Moravia, was saved by the Bulgarians.[71]

VII. The Cyrilo-Methodian Heritage in Poland and Bohemia

*Moravian hierarchy reestablished, end of Great Moravia—
Gorazd and Slavonic bishops in Poland?—Slavonic liturgy and
hierarchy in Poland?—The problem of two metropolitan sees in
Poland—Wiślica a metropolitan see?—Casimir the Restorer, Boleslas II, disappearance of the Slavonic hierarchy and liturgy in
Poland—Archaeological evidence for cultural influence of Great
Moravia on Bohemia—Bořivoj and Ludmila; churches at Levý
Hradec and Prague—The chronicler Christian on Slavic liturgy
—his sources—*Privilegium moraviensis ecclesiae: *Latin defense
of Slavonic liturgy, written in Moravia—*Epilogus terrae Moraviae *composed in Latin by Moravian refugee priest—First Slavonic compositions in Bohemia—Tolerance of Slavonic liturgy and
letters—St. Adalbert and Slavonic liturgy—Foundation of Slavonic
Abbey Sázava by St. Procopius—Cult of Cyril and Methodius in
Bohemia?—Translation of Latin Legends into Slavonic; Czech
Benedictins and Slavonic letters—Invocation of Western Saints
in Slavonic translations of Latin prayers—Relation between Kiev
and Bohemia through Sázava—King Vratislav II, Gregory VII
and Slavonic liturgy—End of Slavonic center in Sázava, disappearance of the Slavonic liturgy, memory of the Slavonic past
under Přemysl II and Charles IV.*

Although Wiching's persecution inflicted a serious setback
to the Slavonic liturgy in Moravia, it did not mean that all Methodius' disciples were expelled from the country. The main blow was
dealt to those priests who were Byzantine subjects—Clement,
Angelarius, Naum, and Laurentius—and to the native Gorazd who
194

was particularly dangerous to Wiching, because he had been chosen as Methodius' successor and had been summoned to Rome to justify himself. There were other disciples who failed to escape from Wiching's clutches, but many must have found refuge in the castles of Slavic nobles who favored the Slavonic liturgy.

We can hardly accept the idea that Svatopluk gave permission for the expulsion of all his Slavic clergy. Even the author of Clement's *Vita* excuses him, saying that such things would not have happened had Svatopluk been present. Although he favored the Franks, he "respected the virtue of such men." [1] We may also suppose that Slavonic literature was not entirely destroyed. A complete elimination of the Slavonic liturgy may be thought to have been achieved only in the diocese of Nitra, where Wiching was in absolute control.

Svatopluk continued his pro-Western policy even after Arnulf had revolted against Charles III in 887, and had become emperor and ruler of Germany. He met Arnulf in 890 and presented him with Stephen V's invitation to come to Italy as protector of the Church in order to help the pope in a difficult situation. On that occasion, Arnulf seems to have confirmed Svatopluk in possession of Bohemia, but the situation soon changed, and in 892 Arnulf made an unsuccessful, although devastating, invasion of Moravia. [2]

In order to break Svatopluk's resistance, Arnulf renewed his alliance with the Bulgarians in the same year. He sent a special embassy to the Bulgarian ruler Vladimir, who had succeeded Boris, especially requesting his ally to cut off the export of salt to Moravia. Because Pannonia was still in Svatopluk's possession, the embassy had to cross lower Pannonia and reach Bulgaria by travelling along the river Sava. In spite of the renewal of the Franko-Bulgarian alliance, Svatopluk in 893 was able to defend his possessions and independence against Arnulf.

In the same year, however, Svatopluk realized that the hopes he had entertained concerning the usefulness of Wiching in his plans for expansion in the West were vain. For Wiching, seeing that Germany again had an energetic ruler, thought it more profitable for himself to change sides, and he fled to Arnulf, who appointed him as his chancellor. In 894 Svatopluk died.

His son and successor Mojmír II made peace with Arnulf in the same year. A fresh danger emanating from the new invaders of the Danubian basin forced him to cease hostilities with the

Franks. In 892 the Magyars had already made a devastating invasion of Pannonia, then still in the hands of Svatopluk. There was
the danger that they might invade the territory of Moravia proper.
In order to avoid a war on two fronts, Mojmír II ceded Pannonia
to Arnulf. He suffered another loss in 895. The Bohemian princes,.
led by Bořivoj's successor Spytihněv, appeared at Regensburg
and became Arnulf's vassals. In 896 Arnulf was crowned emperor,
and in 897 even the Sorbs of modern Saxony became his subjects.

In spite of these losses, Mojmír's Great Moravia was still a
powerful state. The young ruler even tried to restore his rule
over Bohemia, and, in spite of the hostility of his brother Svatopluk, who allied himself with the Bavarians, he was able to withstand Arnulf's attacks in 898 and in 899. His defeated brother
Svatopluk left Moravia with the enemy.[3] Arnulf died in the same
year, leaving one illegitimate son, Louis the Child.

This gave Mojmír II the opportunity of reorganizing his state
and of renewing its ecclesiastical independence. We learn that he
sent an embassy to Rome, probably in 899, asking for bishops.
Because Great Moravia had once had an archbishop, it was not
difficult for John IX to fulfill his request. Archbishop John, and
the Bishops Benedict and Daniel, were sent to Moravia with the
task of ordaining bishops for Mojmír's realm. We learn this from
a letter which the Bavarian higher clergy, led by Theotmar, Archbishop of Salzburg, addressed to John IX in 900.[4] It is an astonishing document, which reveals that the Bavarian episcopate of
this time was not so much interested in the progress of Christianity in the newly-converted lands as in the extension of their
power and material profit.

There is no mention of Archbishop Methodius. Moravia is presented as having always belonged to the diocese of Passau. Not
even Wiching's consecration by John VIII had reduced Passau's
rights.[5] The Moravians are presented as barbarians, allying themselves with the pagan Magyars. When the latter invaded Italy
in 898, the Moravians are said to have refused to conclude peace
with the Empire and thus to have prevented the king from helping Italy. All this is false, and one can only marvel how such a
complaint, which ignored the former decisions of the Holy See
and was so full of bias and false assertions, could ever have been
written. It throws a sharp light on the manners of the period.

One assertion, however, can be accepted without hesitation.
The bishops complained that the legates had consecrated an arch-

bishop and three suffragan bishops. This was the main object of their intervention in Rome. The pope had sent three bishops to Moravia, as, according to canon law, such a consecration must be performed by three bishops.

The new Moravian hierarchy was able to function for a short time. Mojmír II, who had repulsed a Bavarian attack in 900, concluded a solemn peace treaty with the Empire in 901, in order to face his new invaders, the Magyars. He defeated them in 902, but their repeated assaults increasingly weakened his people. The peace with the Empire seems to have been kept, since the Bavarian chronicles do not report any armed conflict with Mojmír II. Finally the Moravians proved unable to stop the waves of invaders and their empire was finally destroyed, probably between 905 and 908.[6]

Even this destruction does not seem to have stopped all religious life in the invaded country. Some of the churches and cemeteries, the existence of which have recently been discovered, appear to have continued to serve their purpose during the first half of the tenth century. There must thus have been some priests who survived the catastrophe. But all cultural and political activity was stopped.

There are no reports extant on the work, or the fate, of the archbishop and bishops ordained by the papal legates. Their presence in Moravia before the catastrophe was, however, not forgotten. As late as 973, Pilgrim, the Bishop of Passau, recalls their existence in the document addressed by him to Pope Benedict VII.[7] He renewed the pretensions of the see of Passau over Moravia, pretending in the forged bull that the pope had raised his see to an archbishopric with jurisdiction over both Moravia and Pannonia.

It is quite probable that the archbishop in question, who was ordained by the legates, was in fact Gorazd himself. Mojmír II had plenty of opportunity to inform the legates of the duplicity of Wiching, and the wish of St. Methodius that Gorazd should succeed him was still well remembered. Wiching imprisoned Gorazd, but he could hardly expel Gorazd because he was a native and of noble origin. The *Life of Clement* does not include him with those other disciples who had found refuge in Bulgaria. Most probably Gorazd sought refuge in the castle of a Moravian noble after being released from prison.

Because Nitra was already a bishopric, one of the suffragans was certainly ordained for that see. Another suffragan may have been installed in Olomouc or in southeastern Slovakia,[8] and the third was sent to the Polish Vistulanians. We do not hear of this part of Great Moravia seceding from Mojmír II, as did the Czechs of Bohemia and the Sorbs. This part of Great Moravia seems to have retained a certain independence after the catastrophe, probably as a Magyar tributary.[9]

* * *

The discovery of a Polish calendar dating from the fourteenth century has thrown more light on the fate of Gorazd.[10] According to this, his feast was celebrated in southern Poland on the seventeenth of July. The calendar was in use at Wiślica, in Little Poland, and was a copy of an older manuscript. This is the only evidence for the veneration of Gorazd in the Western Church.[11] This discovery entitles us to suppose that Gorazd had found refuge in the territory of the Vistulanians. He does not seem to have been alone. The catalogue of the bishops of Cracow contains the names of two bishops who are said to have occupied the see before the year 1000, namely, Prohorius and Proculphus. The names are unfamiliar in the Latin West, but were common in the Greek Church. This circumstance suggests the possibility that they were bishops from Great Moravia who had found refuge with Gorazd in this part of modern Poland. An annalist of the thirteenth century suggested specific dates for both of them—970 for Prohorius, and 986 for Proculphus—and he adds to them a third bishop, Lampertus (995).[12] These dates may not be exact, but the annalist must have based his testament on an old local tradition.

There is sufficient evidence to show that the Slavonic influences penetrating from Moravia into southern Poland were considerable, and were felt during the tenth and eleventh centuries. Both the Polish and the Czech religious terminology betray Old-Slavonic roots.[13] The oldest Polish composition, a hymn in honor of Our Lady—also shows clearly that its original version was composed in Slavonic.[14]

There are certain other indications, such as the Slavonic inscriptions on the denarii of Boleslas the Great, and the testimony of the first Polish chronicler, called Anonymus Gallus, stating that

Boleslas was mourned by the whole Polish population—both Latins and the Slavs—meaning Poles of both the Latin and the Slavonic rites. There is, moreover, the letter of Matilda of Swabia to Mieszko II praising him for his worship of God in Slavic, Latin, and Greek.[15]

The most recent archaeological discoveries in Moravia add new evidence. The small, round churches which were so popular in Bohemia in the tenth and eleventh centuries had their prototype in Moravia, as is shown by the discovery there of round churches dating from the ninth century. This style was also popular in Poland in the eleventh century, as is evidenced by a church built on the Wawel, in Cracow, and another at Teschen in Silesia. In Polish Wišlica the foundations of a small church were discovered, which seems to have had its prototype in ninth-century churches with a semi-circle apse in Moravia.[16] Possibly, further evidence of this kind will be found by Polish archaeologists. It should also be noted that many churches in the region of Cracow were dedicated to St. Clement. Although of later origin, they show that the cult of the favorite saint of Great Moravia, which was introduced into Poland by Slavonic priests from Moravia, had struck root there.[17]

All this makes more plausible the recently suggested thesis that the Slavonic hierarchy continued to exist in Poland from the beginning of the tenth down to the end of the eleventh century. Southern Poland, or the lands of the Vistulanians, was a part of Great Moravia, and it was thus natural that the bishops who had been ordained by the papal legates and had survived the catastrophe should take refuge in this part of Great Moravia and continue their work there. One of them was most probably already there after being ordained in 900, and was joined by Archbishop Gorazd and one or two other bishops. It is less probable that one of the bishops fled to Bohemia, since that country ceased to form part of Great Moravia, and had not enjoyed friendly relations with Mojmír II before the Moravian catastrophe, but it is not absolutely impossible.

※ ※ ※

The existence of the Slavonic liturgy in Poland is also confirmed by other testimony. The first Polish chronicler, Anonymus Gallus, probably a Walloon priest, affirms that under Boleslas the Great (992–1025) Poland possessed two metropolitans. This can only mean the one in Gniezno (Gnesen), of the Latin rite, whose see was founded in 1000, and the other in southern Poland, a successor of Gorazd. The hierarchy of the Slavonic liturgy could have been continued, if as many as three bishops escaped to Poland, as they could ordain their successors. This information given by the first Polish chronicler is confirmed in some ways by the thirteenth-century writer Vincent Kadlubek, Bishop of Cracow.[18] Speaking of Boleslas the Great, he praises his tender concern for the infant Polish Church, and the maturity of his judgment when he created twin metropolitan sees, providing each with suffragans and clearly establishing the boundaries of their dioceses.

The existence of two metropolitan sees in Poland in the twelfth century would also seem to be indicated by two entries in the Year-book of the Chapter of Cracow,[19] which disclose that during the years 1027–1028 three Metropolitans held office—Hippolitus, Bossuta, and Stephen. It is hardly possible that three archbishops held office in one year in Gniezno alone. One or two of them must have held another metropolitan see. It seems logical to admit that the other see must have been the heir to the Moravian archbishopric transferred to the land of the Vistulanians. The name of Hippolitus recalls those of Prohorius and Proculphus because his namesake—martyr, theologian, anti-pope—was more popular in the East than in the West at that time. These names were all current in the East, but not in the West. Bossuta is certainly a Polish name. It is also noteworthy that the province of Gniezno, founded in 1000, comprised only the western part of Poland together with the bishoprics of Cracow, Wroclaw (Breslau) in Silesia, and Kolobrzeg in Pomerania. The bishopric of Poznań was directly subject to Rome.[20] It is highly improbable that the eastern part of Poland remained pagan at the time of the ecclesiastical organization of the country. Pomerania was barely touched by Christian influences and yet a bishopric was founded in that province. Would it not have been expected that bishoprics would be founded also for the expansion of Christianity in the eastern half of Poland?

In order to answer this question, S. Kętrzynski[21] advanced the theory that Boleslas the Great intended to reserve the foundation of the second metropolitan see for the time when Bruno of

Querfurt, the great admirer of St. Adalbert, over whose tomb the metropolitan see of Gniezno was erected, should reach Poland. He thought that the second metropolitan see was erected, or was intended to be erected, in Sandomierz with bishoprics in Plock, Kruszwica, Lęczyca, and perhaps also in the province of Chelm. He did not touch upon the question of rites, thinking that both metropolitan sees would be of the Latin rite.

This proposition, however, does not offer a solution to all problems. First, Bruno of Querfurt did not desire to become a diocesan bishop or archbishop. His idea was to spread the faith among the pagans and to die as a martyr. Even in this he followed his ideal—St. Adalbert. There is no clear evidence that he really resided in Poland as archbishop. On the other hand, the supposition that both metropolitan sees were to be of the Latin rite leaves unanswered the question of how to explain the many traces of the existence of a Slavonic rite in southeastern Poland.

The solution proposed by H. Paszkiewicz, namely, that Poland had two metropolitan sees, one of the Latin and the other of the Slavonic rite, seems more adequate.[22] The Slavonic metropolitan see may have embraced the regions of Sandomierz, Przemysl, Halicz, Lublin, Mazovia, and later the land of the Buzhians. The seat of the Slavonic archbishop is placed by him in Sandomierz. The author takes at face value the information given by the annalist Vincent, and attributes the foundation of the Slavonic metropolitan see to Boleslas the Great, who endowed it with a political aim. This was to counterbalance the Slavonic influence emanating from Kiev, where a bishopric was established about the year 988. There was competition between the Poles and the Russians for the possession of the Red Cities (modern Eastern Galicia). This part of Galicia was occupied by Mieszko after the final defeat of the Magyars by the Emperor Otto I in 955. In 981, however, Vladimir of Kiev regained the Red Cities. There seems to have been another clash between the two nations in 992.[23] All this could have inspired Boleslas to create a Slavonic metropolis for that part of his realm which might be attacked by Kiev.

Even this proposed solution does not explain everything. Anonymus Gallus does not attribute the foundation of the Slavonic metropolitan sees. His and Vincent's statements indicate only that Boleslas had something to do with the Slavic see.

It is more natural to accept the existence of a kind of Slavonic

ecclesiastical organization in eastern and southern Poland from
the beginning of the tenth century which was a continuation of
the Moravian metropolis re-established in 900, as has recently been
suggested.[24] In this case, Prohorius and Proculphus, who are listed
as among the first bishops of Cracow, may have been successors
of another Moravian bishop. Prohorius may also have been ordained by a Slavonic metropolitan, who had succeeded Gorazd.

✷ ✷ ✷

It has been suggested that the Slavonic metropolis was established in Cracow. Both the above-mentioned bishops are called
archbishops in the catalogues and listed by the editor as IV and V,
but these catalogues give this title to all the bishops of Cracow
down to Lampertus Zula, predecessor of St. Stanislas, who was
executed in 1079. Three shorter catalogues, which also start with
Prohorius and Proculphus, list only bishops in Cracow. It would
thus be too daring to place the see of the Slavonic metropolis in
Cracow on this basis only.[25]

If Cracow was only the see of a Slavonic bishop, the metropolitan must have resided elsewhere. The most logical place would
be Sandomierz, although in 1030 only a bishop seems to have
been mentioned as having died in this city.[26] These data are not
quite reliable, but they must be founded on some facts.

If there was a metropolitan see, the heir of the Moravian archbishopric, it must have possessed several suffragans. Wiślica would
appear a logical choice for a Slavonic episcopal if not metropolitan
see, and perhaps Zawichost, and one see in Mazovia. Łęczyca,
Sieradz, and perhaps also Przemysl are other possibilities.[27] As
long as no further evidence is available (the archaeologists may
discover some as they did in Moravia), this is only guesswork
resting on fairly reliable suppositions.

One thing is certain. A Slavonic metropolis with several episcopal sees did exist in Poland, in continuation of the Moravian hierarchic order established in 900 by Pope John IX. We are unable
to learn anything of the attitude of Rome toward Slavonic liturgy
on that occasion. However, we may suppose that after the departure of Wiching from Moravia, and after the disclosures made by
the remaining Slavonic clergy and by Mojmír II to the legates,

the native clergy were allowed to proceed as they did during the lifetime of St. Methodius.

The existence of the Slavonic rite in southeastern Poland was not affected by the conquest of this country by Boleslas I of Bohemia, which occurred after the defeat of the Magyars in 955 by Otto I, whom he had supported in his campaign.[28] The Slavonic liturgy had spread also into Bohemia, as will be described later. This country was bi-liturgical down to the end of the eleventh century, and the two dynasties which existed in Bohemia at that time, the Přemyslides and the Slavníks, were not hostile to the Slavonic liturgy. Although the episcopal see founded in Prague in 973 was of the Latin rite, many native priests continued to celebrate the liturgy in Slavonic. The foundation of a Polish bishopric in 968 in Poznań[29] did not alter the situation, because Mieszko I, the first Christian Polish Duke, was not yet master of Cracow. He seems, however, to have occupied the region of Sandomierz and the rest of modern Galicia and the Red Cities.

Even the transfer of this former part of Great Moravia to the rule of the Polish Duke did not affect the existence of the Slavonic liturgy and hierarchy there. Like his father-in-law, Boleslas I of Bohemia, Mieszko had to deal with the Empire and to accept the Latin influences emanating from there. Because the Czech dynasties, as we will see, were not hostile to the existence of the Slavonic rite in Bohemia, we can suppose that even Boleslas' daughter Dubravka knew about it. It is thus quite possible that Mieszko was also acquainted, through his Czech wife, with the Slavonic liturgy, and tolerated and favored both Latin and Slavonic priests.[30] After he had taken Silesia and Cracow from Boleslas, between 987 and 990, he became master of all the territories where the Slavonic hierarchy continued as the spiritual heirs of Great Moravia. He probably recognized the necessity for reform of the ecclesiastical situation in his vast realm. However, this was done, not by Mieszko, but by his son and successor, Boleslas the Great. He obtained from Otto III permission to found an independent metropolitan see in Gniezno, the site of the tomb of St. Adalbert.[31] St. Adalbert, with whom the emperor had been friendly, was the second bishop of Prague, and was martyred while preaching to the Prussians. The western part of Poland, still more or less pagan, was given over to the care of Latin bishops

and priests, but Boleslas the Great must also have intervened in
the eastern and southern part of his realm, and reorganized the
Slavonic metropolis and bishoprics. In this way we can explain
why Vincent attributed to him the foundation of two metropolitan
sees and the delimitation of the dioceses which were placed under
the two metropolitans.

* * *

The disappearance of the Slavonic hierarchy and liturgy from
Poland should be attributed to the reorganization of Polish religious life by Casimir the Restorer after 1038. This was preceded by
the pagan protest in western Poland after the death of Mieszko II
(1035). There is some evidence showing that this protest was confined only to the western part of Poland, and was followed by a
struggle between the partisans of the Latin rite and those of the
Slavonic rite. Casimir, who returned to Poland with the help of
Germany, wished to impose the Latin rite in the eastern part of
his realm also. The defender of the Slavonic rite, Maslow, Prince
of Mazovia, was defeated by Casimir, who was supported by the
Germans, and the sons of Vladimir the Great of Kiev, to whom
Casimir had to cede the Red Cities. Casimir regained possession
of the whole country and imposed the Latin liturgy in the eastern
and southern part of the country. Cracow's Latin bishop extended
his jurisdiction over most of the territory which had belonged to
the Slavonic metropolitan see.[32]

The question arises whether Casimir's successor, Boleslas II the
Bold (1058–1079), changed the religious policy of his father.
There is a letter sent by Pope Gregory VII to Boleslas the Bold
which seems to indicate that the latter had asked for the creation
of more bishoprics.[33] The Cracow Capitular Calendar[34] attributes
to Boleslas the Bold the raising of new bishoprics in Poland. Lambert of Hersfeld[35] says that fifteen bishops took part in the ceremony of Boleslas' coronation in 1076. This could mean that the
king had reversed his father's policy and renewed the Slavonic
metropolis with its suffragan sees. If this is so, the conflict between
the king and Stanislas, Bishop of Cracow, which ended so tragically for the prelate and resulted in the expulsion and death of
Boleslas, could have been provoked by the opposition of Stanislas
to the curtailment of his jurisdiction and to the reintroduction of

the Slavonic liturgy. Of course, there must also have been other reasons which compelled the king to impose on Stanislas the punishment of dismemberment, a sentence generally pronounced against traitors.[36] In any event, the end of Boleslas' rule in Poland also marked the end of the Slavonic hierarchy, if it really was reinstated by the energetic and unfortunate king.[37]

❖ ❖ ❖

It seems logical to suppose that a few Slavonic priests also found refuge in Bohemia during the persecution by Wiching, and especially after the destruction of Great Moravia. Recent archaeological discoveries in Bohemia show that this country was under the direct cultural influence of Great Moravia. It appears that the Bohemian tribe of the Zličans in northeastern Bohemia was most open to these influences. The excavations made in the residence of their chief, Kouřim, and in cemeteries in its neighborhood revealed that this region was in lively commercial contact with the industrial centers of Great Moravia.[38] Numerous decorative objects—earrings, buttons, and other objects—were imported from Moravian workshops. Also, battle axes, so characteristic of Moravain warriors,[39] were found with other objects which are definitely of Moravian origin. Other finds testify that Kouřim had become an important industrial center producing its own wares on Moravian models. Some of these workshops may have been erected by Moravian artisans who were looking for more business or who had escaped the catastrophe which had befallen their country.

These workshops were active also after Bohemia had separated itself from Moravia and when Moravia had been destroyed. Bohemian artisans had even improved on the technique and the decorative types which they had learned from their Moravian colleagues. We find proof of it in the tomb of a princess of Kouřim from the tenth century, with such objects as a silver reliquary, silver harnesses for three horses, large silver buttons, and a splendid silver earring with a lamb (or horse).[40] The workshops of Kouřim seem also to have provided silver ornaments for neighboring communities. The Moravian cultural influence also reached the central region of Bohemia, which was settled by another Bohemian tribe—the Czechs—who, toward the end of the ninth century, had already assumed a dominating position over several other Bohemian tribes.[41]

* * *

The first prince known in central Bohemia was Bořivoj, whose Christianization is mentioned in the *Life of St. Wenceslas* attributed to Christian.[42] He reports that Bořivoj was baptized in Moravia in the residence of Svatopluk. He returned to Bohemia accompanied by a priest called Kaich. Although only Kaich is mentioned at this occasion, it would be preposterous to suppose that, because his is the only name mentioned, he was the only Slavic priest who joined Bořivoj and his wife Ludmila at their residence at Levý Hradec.[43] It was an official mission in which even Svatopluk, the ruler of Moravia, was interested, because the spread of Moravian Christianity in Bohemia would have strengthened his sovereignty over Bohemia. Let us recall that, for example, the author of the *Life of Constantine* mentions his hero as chosen by the Emperor Michael III for the Khazarian and Moravian mission. We learn that Methodius had accompanied his brother on both missions, but only from a casual reference to Methodius in chapter twelve and in the last chapter, when the writer describes how Methodius wanted to take his brother's body back to Constantinople. If the *Vita Methodii* and the papal documents had not been preserved, our knowledge of Methodius' life and activities would have been very slight indeed. Sometimes we expect too much from the biographers of saints. They often leave out in their descriptions circumstances and facts which they regard as self-evident or which were known to their contemporaries—this may be applied in the case of Christian mentioning only Kaich— and omit things which we wish they had mentioned, but which they regarded as unimportant in the lives of their heroes. We are forced to condone their inaccuracies; for they were not historians trained in seminars at modern universities. With regard to the Kaich case, let us remember that the description of St. Ludmila's martyrdom speaks of another priest from Ludmila's court at Tetín —Paul.[44] Another priest, Krastej, is said by the author of the first Slavonic *Legend of St. Wenceslas*[45] to have taken the body of the murdered Wenceslas, put it in front of the church in Stará Boleslav, and covered it with a white sheet. This priest must have been friendly with the priests from the circle around Ludmila and Wenceslas, although this does not show that he was favorable to the Slavonic liturgy. Anyhow, he cannot be identified with another priest of Stará Boleslav who, according to the second Slavonic *Legend of St. Wenceslas*,[46] had started the bell ringing in the church earlier, as was the custom, in order to confound Wenceslas' companions and prevent them from helping their master when he was about to be attacked by the conspirators.

The fact that a church dedicated to St. Clement was built at Levý Hradec indicates clearly that the Moravian mission had worked there. It is true that St. Clement was venerated in the whole Western Church long before Constantine had discovered the relics which he believed to be those of Clement, thanks to the legend composed by an anonymous author in the fourth century, which had become very popular. It was this legend which inspired Constantine to look for the saint's relics. Churches dedicated to St. Clement in western Europe cannot be regarded, therefore, as pointing to a Cyrilo-Methodian tradition in the lands which were not touched by the work of the two brothers or of their disciples.[47] But this is different for the Slavic lands, where the echo of their activity had sounded. St. Clement was a patron saint of the Cyrilo-Methodian mission. Bohemia was touched by this mission; thus the building of a church dedicated to St. Clement at Levý Hradec testifies that this church became a small center of Slavic liturgy in Bohemia. Christian informs us further that this first introduction of Christianity into Bohemia had provoked a pagan revolt, and Bořivoj was forced to take refuge in Moravia.[48] This report is quite plausible. A similar reaction took place in Bulgaria and in Kievan Russia, first when Kiev was conquered by Oleg, and again in the reign of Svjatoslav and also under Vladimir, whose Christian policy was opposed in Novgorod.

Bořivoj, while staying in Moravia, is said to have made a promise to build a church to "the blessed mother of God, the immaculate Virgin Mary," after his return to the throne. When his supporters had overcome the pagan reaction and had brought him back, Bořivoj fulfilled his promise and built a church at his castle in Prague. The reinstallation of Bořivoj in Bohemia could not have been achieved without the help of Svatopluk. This again means that more Slavic priests had come with Bořivoj in order to strengthen Christianity in his dukedom. The choice of Prague as his residence does not mean that Levý Hradec had lost its importance;[49] on the contrary, another small Slavic center was created around the new church in Prague. This is logical, and there is no reason to deny the Slavic character of these two first Christian centers built by Bořivoj.[50]

These Slavic centers found a zealous protectress in Ludmila, the wife of Bořivoj, who is said by the anonymous author of the first Slavonic *Legend of St. Wenceslas* to have instructed her grandson in Slavonic letters.[51]

✣ ✣ ✣

These are direct arguments pointing out that Slavonic liturgy and letters were introduced into Bohemia. Christian also offers an indirect argument when speaking about the christianization of Moravia. He has a hazy knowledge of the origins of Christianity in that land, dating its origins to the time of St. Augustine and believing that the Bulgarians were converted before the Moravians.[52] But when describing the activity of Cyril in Moravia, he relates in an unbiased way that Cyril had invented an alphabet for the Moravians and that he had translated the Holy Writ and other texts from Greek and Latin. Then he says, "Besides that he ordered that the Mass and other canonical hours should be sung in churches in vernacular language, as it is done till today often in Slavic lands, especially in Bulgaria, and many souls are gained for Christ in this way."

These words are significant. The fact that Christian omits to mention Bohemia does not mean that, in his time, the Slavonic liturgy was unknown in that land. After all, Bohemia was a Slavic land. It is also to be stressed that, after this passage, Christian describes in detail how Cyril had defended his liturgical innovation in Rome. He quotes also two scriptural arguments in favor of the innovation, used by Constantine-Cyril in Venice, namely, the Psalm 150:6, "Let everything that has breath praise the Lord," and I Cor. 14:39, "Do not hinder the gift of speaking in tongues." "Convinced by Cyril's argumentation, the director of the Church decided and confirmed by letters that in those lands it was allowable to sing the Mass ceremonies and other canonical hours in the aforementioned tongue." It is generally accepted that Christian used in his description a Latin document.[53] It is important to note that this Latin defense of Slavonic liturgy existed in Bohemia and that Christian had used this in his work. The quotations given above point out that the author of this defense was inspired by the *Vita Constantini,* even though some of the inaccuracies contained in it reveal that Christian was unfamiliar with the original *Vita.*

❖ ❖ ❖

What was the Latin source used by Christian? Was it the *Privilegium moraviensis ecclesiae* or *Epilogus Moraviae et Bohemiae,* two writings known to the first Czech chronicler Cosmas? [54] The chronicle quotes them as the two main sources of Czech religious history, together with the *Life and Martyrdom of St. Wenceslas.* The *Privilegium* is regarded as a defense of Slavonic liturgy and letters which, according to V. Chaloupecký,[55] began to be in danger after the establishment of the bishopric in Prague in 973. Chaloupecký tried to reconstruct this document by analyzing four Latin legends on the conversion of the Czechs. In his analysis he made a basic error when dating the *Legend of St. Ludmila,* starting with the words *Diffundente sole* before Christian's composition. The contrary is true. The Ludmila *Legend* is based on the narrative contained in Christian's work. Because of this error his reconstruction of the document is faulty.

R. Jakobson proposed another solution. He supposes the existence of a Slavonic prototype of the *Privilegium* which originated in Moravia during the reign of Mojmír II.[56] If this were true, then a Latin translation could have been made in Moravia, or in Bohemia. In spite of all attempts at its reconstruction and dating, it has not yet been established what it contained or when it was composed. I would rather be inclined to see in this document a work compiled in Moravia on the basis of the two papal bulls permitting the use of the Slavonic language in the liturgy, the bull issued by Hadrian II starting with the words *Gloria in excelsis,* and especially that issued by John VIII starting with the words *Industriae tuae,* addressed to Svatopluk.[57] This latter contained not only the confirmation of the Slavonic liturgy but also an authentic declaration that Methodius' teaching had been examined in Rome and found to conform to the Creed accepted by the Roman Church. This was the *Privilegium* of the Moravian

Church confirmed by Rome and it would be quite logical to suppose that on this basis a work was composed in Moravia after the death of Methodius. It was intended to dispel all doubts being spread in Moravia by Wiching and the German priests about the orthodoxy of Methodius and his disciples and the legitimacy of the use of Slavonic in the liturgy. It was vitally important for Methodius' disciples to show that their practice had been sanctioned by the pope, that they professed the same Creed as Rome, and were not hostile to Roman liturgical practices. This tendency is shown also by the author of Methodius' *Life*. He stressed the fact that Methodius recommended Gorazd as his successor because he was a native, a free man, orthodox, and well versed in Latin books. He emphasized also that the funeral service for Methodius was celebrated not only in Slavonic and Greek, but also in Latin rite. The Latin rite is mentioned first; therefore I think that the *Privilegium* was written only in Latin soon after Methodius' death and was destined rather for the Latin enemies of the Slavonic liturgy. Its defense in Slavonic was contained in the *Lives* of both brothers. The refugee priests brought this Latin document into Bohemia, and so it happened that it became known also to Cosmas.

As the two Latin bulls which formed the basis of the document contained a papal approval of the Slavonic liturgy, this fact would explain why Cosmas did not give any details of the contents of the *Privilegium*, because of his hostile attitude to the Slavonic liturgy.

However, the fact that Cosmas knew it and regarded it as a source for the early history of Christianity in Moravia is important. It is most probable that Christian got his information on Cyril and his defense of the Slavonic liturgy from this document.

❖ ❖ ❖

The contents and the composition of the *Epilogus terrae Moraviae et Bohemiae* is still debated. R. Jakobson[58] thinks that it was an Old Slavonic composition made in Bohemia at the beginning of the tenth century. The original is lost. Christian, however, knew of a Latin translation of that document and incorporated most of it into his history of the end of Moravia, and on the Christianization of Bohemia.

I do not think that the *Epilogus* was written first in Slavonic. I would like to attribute its composition perhaps to some refugee priests who had found asylum in Bohemia after the destruction of their native country. It was in their interest to win the sympathies of their hosts and to show the merits of their master Methodius in the introduction of the Christian faith into the country which had become their second fatherland. They had good reason to include detailed descriptions of how Bořivoj became a Christian and what Methodius had done for him, because in the *Life of Methodius* the baptism of Bořivoj was not even mentioned.

This circumstance can be perhaps explained in the following way. We would expect the description or at least a mention of it in chapter eleven of the *Life,* where the author speaks of the defeat of the Vislanian prince, and of his baptism in the land of his victor. The author speaks of this incident in order to show that Methodius had a prophetic gift. This and the two other cases are, of course, prophecies *post eventum.* Such utterances are characteristic of hagiographical writings, but in Bořivoj's case there was no basis for a prophesying of the event because Bořivoj was baptized voluntarily in Moravia, after submitting to Svatopluk. It is also no wonder that the author of the *Life* is silent about the expulsion of Bořivoj from Bohemia by his enemies, on his flight to Svatopluk's court, and on his return to Prague. These were political events and had no connection with Methodius. Mentioning them would be rather harmful to his hero's prestige.

The author of the *Epilogus* had first to explain why his country, Moravia, encountered such a tragic end, and who was responsible for it. Of course it was Svatopluk, and in this respect the author again completes and almost corrects the *Life of Methodius,* which treats Svatopluk with respect and a certain sympathy. To show how things had happened he first describes the usurpation of power by Svatopluk from his uncle (Rastislav), "Consumed with arrogance, Svatopluk scorned, together with the courtiers devoted to him, the mellifluous preaching of Archbishop Methodius, nor did he follow fully his most revered admonitions, but let his members, namely his subjects, and his folk to serve partly Christ and partly the devil." We perceive in these words the great disappointment of Methodius' disciples with Svatopluk's religious policy favoring Wiching and the Latins. The lives of Naum and of Clement contain even more violent outbursts condemning Svatopluk. Christian, following the author of the *Epilogus,* continues: "Because of that his land and country, with its inhabitants, were anathematized by the above mentioned pontife of blessed memory, were crushed by different disasters on field and their produce, and are suffering to our days. For it was given to plunder and bond, to booty and derision, desert and mockery to all bodies travelling through it, because there cannot be communion of light with darkness, nor peace between Belial and Christ." To these descriptions, taken from the *Epilogus,* Christian adds his own reflections and warning to his compatriots: "And these examples concern also those of us who are trying to follow in the same paths, because the man who sees the house of his neighbor burn has to take care of his own."

The second part of the *Epilogus* was devoted to the description of Bořivoj's baptism at the court of Svatopluk. Invited to a banquet by the latter, Bořivoj is said to have been seated not with the nobles but outside the hall, because he was still a pagan and unworthy to be in the company of Christian nobles. Methodius, regretting that such a great prince was so humbly treated, exhorted him to become a Christian, and promised him in a prophecy that he would become master of all masters, and victorious over all his enemies.[59] Then follows the description of his instruction in the faith, his baptism, return to Bohemia, the pagan revolt under Strojmir, Bořivoj's return to Moravia, and his victorious reinstatement in Prague. In describing these events, Christian may have used other sources, or oral tradition, but the role of Methodius in the history of Bořivoj's baptism must have been taken from the *Epilogus,* and reveals the tendency of its author to enhance the memory of Methodius and the connection of Bohemian Christianity with Moravia. Let us point out that the author of the *Epilogus* stresses also Methodius' prophecies concerning Bořivoj's victories over all his adversaries—again prophecies *post eventum*—but also faithfully copied by Christian.

* * *

We have seen that Slavonic priests were active in Bohemia, at least, in two places—at Levý Hradec and in Prague. In this milieu originated the first Slavonic writings in Bohemia—the *Legend of St. Ludmila,* who was murdered at the instigation of her daughter-in-law Drahomíra and was venerated as a martyr. The Slavonic legend is lost, but a part of it survived in a Russian liturgical prologue read in the office of her feast.[60]

The Slavonic priests of these two "centers" are authors also of the Slavonic *Life of St. Wenceslas;*[61] he was murdered at the instigation of his brother Boleslas in 929.[62] Weingart's edition is, at the same time, a reconstruction which seems reliable, in spite of some criticism by Slavic philogolists. It should be stressed that Wenceslas' mother, Drahomíra, is placed in a much more favorable light by the author, as is done in a later Latin *Vita* of Wenceslas. Boleslas is not presented as a cruel murderer, the responsibility for the crime being put on Boleslas' companions. We learn also from this *Vita* that Wenceslas had to contract a marriage—other legends stress his virginity—but lived separated from his wife after she had borne him a son. All these details show that the *Vita* must have been composed soon after the death of Wenceslas, during the reign of his brother Boleslas, whose responsibility for Wenceslas' tragic end is downgraded on purpose.

This might, however, also signify that the small group of Slavonic priests was afraid that their situation would be endangered after the loss of their two protectors—St. Ludmila and St. Wenceslas. It was the position of the Slavonic priests which in reality was in danger. Bohemia had become a part of the bishopric of Regensburg and, as the Slavonic *Vita* has it, Wenceslas invited a great number of Latin priests from the neighboring German lands to strengthen and spread the Christian faith in Bohemia.

This report of the *Vita* confirms also that, at the beginning of the tenth century, the number of priests in ecclesiastical administration in Bohemia was rather small. This scarcity of priests explains why the Slavonic priests brought by Bořivoj and the refugees from Moravia were welcomed. The question of liturgy had lost its importance after the disappearance of Moravia. The devastated land was no longer considered important for Passau's jurisdiction. On the other hand, Regensburg was firmly established in Bohemia and no one, the Slavonic priests not excepted, opposed its claims to jurisdiction over the land. The German priests had to acquire the native language if they wished to be successful in their pastoral activities. It was not in the interest of the princes and the bishop to discard priests who spoke the language, were loyal to both authorities, and were liked by the people. Although no

Slavonic school is known to have existed—only a Latin school at Budeč, where Wenceslas was educated, is mentioned in the old Slavonic *Legend*—we should not exclude the possibility of the Slavonic priests having occasion to instruct the young Czechs in Slavonic letters and liturgy. As for the ordination of priests,[63] the decision was in the hands of the prince, who presented the candidates to the bishop in Regensburg or when the bishop was on visit in Bohemia. Thus it could happen that new Slavonic priests were ordained. We do not hear of any opposition to the Slavonic practice from Regensburg. When Boleslas had succeeded in obtaining a bishopric in Prague (973), the first bishop was naturally a German named Thietmar, who spoke the Slavic language. I have explained on another occasion that, at the same time, a bishopric for Moravia was founded.[64] Moravia was a land of missions, and any priests, Latin or Slavic, were welcomed by the new bishop, whose name we do not know. Both bishoprics were subordinated to the Archbishop of Mainz. This again was favorable to the prince and the bishops, as it assured them of greater freedom in the administration than if the new bishoprics had been subjected to Salzburg, or to Magdeburg.

The foundation charter of the bishopric of Prague, preserved in Cosmas' chronicle,[65] offers another indirect argument for the survival of Slavonic liturgy in Bohemia. Pope John XIII, after giving his approval to the erection of a bishopric in Prague, at the church of St. Vitus and St. Wenceslas, and of a Benedictine Abbey at the church of St. George, under the Abbess Mlada-Mary, is supposed to have added: "However, not according to the rite or sect of the Bulgarian or Russian nation, or of Slavonic language, but, following rather the institution and decrees of the apostles, you should choose rather, according to your will, for this work a cleric who would be well trained in Latin letters."

If these words are genuine, they show that Slavonic liturgical practice still prevailed in Bohemia in 973. Otherwise why should the pope be so outspoken concerning the danger of introducing Slavonic liturgy in the new see? We know that this charter was interpolated by Cosmas himself. He was very hostile to the Slavonic liturgy. If there had been no traces of the Slavonic liturgy in Bohemia at his time (1045–1125), why should he have taken so much trouble to insert these words into the charter?

※ ※ ※

The second bishop of Prague was St. Vojtěch-Adalbert.[66] He was not a scion of the Přemyslide ruling house in Prague, but of the Slavník dynasty which ruled over northeastern Bohemia from its center of Libice. Vojtěch studied in Magdeburg and was, of course, of the Latin rite. There is a late tradition preserved in a Russian manuscript that Vojtěch was a forceful enemy of the Slavonic liturgy, which he exterminated.[67] This tradition is biased, and originated in the atmosphere of enmity of the Russian orthodox against the Latins, which increased after the rupture between Rome and Byzantium in 1054. There is, however, another and earlier tradition which counts Vojtěch among those saints whose names are invoked in two prayers preserved in Russian manuscripts, but probably translated into Slavonic in Bohemia.[68] On the other hand, Adalbert was fully conscious of his Slavic origin, and when he left Prague because of political tension between the two dynasties, he went to Italy and visited the great Greek ascetic, the Abbot Nilus. He was so impressed by him and by Greek religiosity that he wanted to become a monk in Nilus' monastery. On the advice of his hero he went to Monte Cassino.[69] Such an experienced man cannot be thought of as fiercely opposed to the Slavonic liturgy and its priests.

It was to him that Christian, his uncle, dedicated his Latin *Life of St. Wenceslas*. We have already seen that Christian regarded the Slavonic liturgy as permissible. Adalbert certainly read this passage. Although faithful to the use of Latin in liturgy, he had, at least, an appreciation of the use of the vernacular in worship. He is supposed, with good reason, to have played a part in the composition of the first Czech hymn—*Hospodine pomiluj ny* (Lord have mercy on us), which is a version of the *Kyrie eleison*. Some Slavic philologists see in the first and oldest strophe of this hymn Church Slavonic elements.[70] He is also supposed by many to have initiated the first Polish religious song "Bogurodzica," as we have already seen.[71] Let us remember that Libice had become heir to the castle of Kouřim, the former center of the Bohemian tribe of Zličans. We have seen that this region was under a strong cultural influence of Moravia, especially toward the end of the ninth and the beginning of the tenth century. If Moravian artisans had reached this territory, one can also suppose that some Moravian priests had found refuge in the territory ruled by the Slavníks.

So it is possible that Slavonic liturgy did survive in Bohemia in the tenth century, tolerated by ecclesiastical leaders for pastoral reasons. There was no Slavonic center at this time in Bohemia, in the proper sense of the word, but we cannot exclude the possibility that the Slavic priests who came from Moravia may have formed small circles of religious men to whom the Slavonic liturgy and letters appealed. In such circles were preserved remnants of the Moravian missal such as the *Leaflets of Kiev* and *Prague*. Of course, we have no documentary evidence for the existence of or copies of such liturgical books in Bohemia, but how will an historian determined to admit only direct evidence explain the Bohemianisms which have been detected in the *Leaflets of Kiev?*

* * *

How can an historian who is too selective in his evidence explain the appearance of a Benedictine Abbey of the Slavonic liturgy founded around 1032 in Sázava by St. Procopius, and generously endowed by Břetislav I, Duke of Bohemia?It is easy to say that Procopius became acquainted with the Slavic liturgy somewhere outside Bohemia, but where?[72] The specialists who reject the possibility of the existence of Slavonic liturgy in Bohemia agree that the Moravian religious centers were all destroyed by the Hungarian invaders. Should we thus admit that at least one of them had survived? Where? Perhaps one could think about Visegrad in Hungary, which had been a part of Moravia, but again we have no "documentary" evidence for it. There existed a monastery in Visegrad. It was founded by the Hungarian King Andrew I (Endre) (1047–1061). He had taken refuge in Kiev where he was baptized. The Grand Duke Jaroslav (1036–1054) gave him his daughter Anastasia as wife. When he returned to Hungary Andrew founded two monasteries, one at Tihany in honor of St. Anianus, the other at Visegrad in honor of St. Andrew.[73] This monastery was, however, settled with Russian monks who practiced not the Moravo-Slavonic but Byzantine liturgy in Slavonic.[74] Could Procopius have learned there about the Slavonic liturgy of Roman rite? Or did there exist another center which had survived in Hungary? Where?

Supposing Procopius learned about Slavonic liturgy somewhere outside Bohemia, where did he find monks for his Slavonic monastery if there was no continuation of Moravian liturgical practice in Bohemia? And why would Břetislav I have given his permission for this foundation if all his predecessors on the Bohemian throne had been unfavorable to the Slavonic liturgy, as is supposed? No religious foundation could have been put into existence without the consent of the prince. He must have obtained also the consent of the bishop, who had to consecrate the abbey and the abbot. How could he have obtained it if there was declared hostility to anything Slavonic in leading religious centers in Bohemia? Or should we admit that a Slavonic religious center had survived in the land of the Vislans where Procopius had stayed and had become acquainted with the Slavonic liturgy and letters? Such an occurrence should not be completely out of the question when we take into consideration that Boleslas I had occupied this region as far as the rivers Styr and Bug, together with Moravia and Silesia, after the defeat of the Magyars in 955 by Otto the Great.[75] We have seen that some of the Moravian bishops ordained in 900 had taken refuge in the land of the Vislans, which had not been touched by the Magyar invasion.[76] However, if we accept this possibility, we have to admit that contacts between Bohemia and the land of the Vislans could have existed even during the tenth century, and that priests of Slavonic liturgy could have been ordained and sent to Bohemia by the refugee Moravian bishops. These are the complicated problems which face the historians who reject the continuation of the Slavonic liturgy in Bohemia after the collapse of Moravia.

✳ ✳ ✳

It is said that the continuation of Slavonic liturgy and letters in Bohemia should have been based on the cult of their originators—Constantine-Cyril and Methodius. This need not necessarily be so. The cult of a saintly person is based on official sanction by an ecclesiastical authority, and the veneration of his contemporaries who were convinced that the person had led a saintly life. The cult was promoted if there were relics of that person available. We do not know of any official canonization of the two brothers. As concerns Constantine-Cyril, his burial in the basilica of St. Clement in Rome could be regarded as a *translatio* or canonization, but it should be noted that the author of his *Life* never calls him saint, and the so-called Italian Legend gives him the epithet *vir sanctus* only once. His relics remained in Rome. His brother visited his tomb during his stay in Rome, but no part of his relics was brought to Moravia. He was certainly venerated by his disciples in Moravia, but Rome was far away from Bohemia and the main incentives for the spread of his cult were missing. Was Methodius canonized by the bishops who went to Moravia in 900? We do not know anything about such an act. His disciples certainly venerated him as a saint, but the catastrophe which had befallen Moravia soon after his death put an end to the spread of his cult. The church in which he was buried was destroyed, his relics disappeared and have never been found. Even the place of his burial remains unknown.

Thus was left only the veneration by his contemporaries, who were soon scattered to the four parts of the world. In spite of the unfavorable circumstances hampering the spread of his devotion, Christian is again witness to a cult of the two brothers in Bohemia.[77] He gives Cyril the epithet *beatus* and Methodius *pontifex beatae memoriae*. It is true that the epithets *beatus* and *sanctus* were often given, at that time, to persons who were not regarded as canonized saints,[78] but I would not make light of this attitude of Christian's to the memory of the brothers as insignificant. Christian probably found this designation of the brothers in the Latin documents which were his main source for his account of their activities.

This can be regarded, at least, as a proof that the brothers were venerated by their disciples as saints. As concerns the spread of their cult in Bohemia, this is another question. Let us not forget that only success is most successful. The Moravian period was not a permanent success. Moravia disappeared from the horizon of contemporary Europe and of the Church too suddenly and too early. Regensburg was more successful in Bohemian religious life than Moravia. When Regensburg had taken over, new cults penetrated Bohemia, especially that of St. Imram and Saint Vitus. Soon Bohemia had its own saints—Ludmila and Wenceslas. They are called by Christian "our only saints"[79]—they really were the only Czech saints—and his work was written to celebrate their memory, not that of Cyril and Methodius, or of Imram and Vitus.

This introduction of new cults explains, for example, why even Procopius—this name heralds eastern influences from Moravia—had called his son Imram, why Wenceslas had dedicated the church built by him in Prague to St. Vitus, and why the successor of Abbot Procopius was called Vitus. This does not mean that the memory of SS. Cyril and Methodius was forgotten in the Abbey of Sázava. One would rather expect that Procopius would give to his son the name of Wenceslas, or that his successor would have adopted the name of this Czech saint. Can this be regarded as a proof that the cult of Wenceslas did not exist in Sázava? This simply means that Procopius and his successor followed the new vogue introduced by the German Church through Regensburg and Saxony. One can also deduce from these two examples that the Slavonic priests were not hostile to the Latin liturgy and the cult of Latin saints. As they themselves adhered to the Slavonic liturgy, this shows that a kind of symbiosis of the Latin and Slavonic liturgies and traditions existed in tenth- and eleventh-century Bohemia.

Were the *Lives* of Constantine and Methodius known in Bohemia? R. Večerka pretends to have discovered in the Old Slavonic offices to the honor of Cyril and Methodius and to St. Wenceslas, preserved in two glagolitic breviaries—one from the fourteenth and the second from the fifteenth centuries [80]—numerous Bohemianisms which seem to show that the offices were composed in Bohemia, and that the *Life of Constantine* and perhaps also that of Methodius were known in Bohemia.[81] It is for the Slavic philologists to decide if these deductions can be accepted. But, if the *Lives* were unknown in Bohemia, how can we explain that the *Life of Methodius* is preserved only in Russian manuscripts? The philological examination of these manuscripts shows that the *Life* did not reach Kiev from Bulgaria, but from Bohemia. As we have seen, the report on the origin of Slavonic letters continued in *The Russian Primary Chronicle* is based on the *Vita* of Methodius and perhaps on one Russian liturgical prologue on Methodius. The author of the *Chronicle* does not seem to have known the *Vita Constantini*. Could this indicate that this *Vita* had reached Kiev, not from Bohemia, but from Bulgaria, only after the composition of this part of the *Primary Chronicle*?

❖ ❖ ❖

What about the continuation of Slavonic literature in Bohemia during these two centuries? The Russian scholar Sobolevskij had discovered a certain number of Slavonic translations from Latin literary documents in Russian manuscripts. The style of these translations suggests that they were translated in Bohemia, whence they reached Kiev.

The most particular of these translations is that of the *Life of St. Benedict.*[82] It was in the interest of the Benedictines to have this document translated into Slavonic. This could have been done by the monks of Sázava, but it could also have been done by a monk from the first Benedictine Abbey in Bohemia, which had been founded by Bishop Adalbert and the Duke Boleslav in 992 at Břevnov, near Prague. The *Life of St. Stephen* was also translated into Old Slavonic from a Latin original. It should be noticed that St. Stephen was especially venerated in Czech Benedictine oracles. An altar was dedicated to him at Břevnov, and the Benedictine Abbey of Hradiště in Moravia, founded in 1078, had St. Stephen as its patron. This translation could also have been done in Sázava, but if Procopius had lived for some time at the Abbey of Břevnov, he may have educated some of the monks of this abbey in Slavonic letters.

Procopius must have become acquainted somewhere with the rule of St. Benedict. In his oldest Latin *Vita* (*Vita antiqua*) which appears to have been composed in Sázava between 1061 and 1067 and which was dedicated to the Bishop of Prague Šebíř, we read[83] that Procopius, after constructing a church to the honor of the Mother of God and of John the Baptist, and after gathering around some brothers, had chosen to observe with them the rule of St. Benedict. This information is repeated in the *Vita Minor,*[84] based on the oldest legend, and is amplified in the *Vita Maior* composed in the fourteenth century. There we read that when Procopius decided to embrace the monastic life, "he accepted the rule of St. Benedict from a certain monk, and, after being well instructed by him, he returned to his homeland" looking for a place where he could live as a hermit. He is said to have presented himself to Prince Oldřich (Udalrich), who had discovered his cavern, as "God's servant," living according to the rule of St. Benedict.[85]

The author of this late legend was convinced that Procopius had been instructed in the monastic rule by an experienced monk, although the author of the oldest *Vita* limits himself to saying that the rule of St. Benedict was accepted by Procopius and his disciples. This information presupposes that Procopius must have become acquainted with the rule of St. Benedict somewhere where it was practiced. This could have been at the monastery of Břevnov, or of Ostrov, founded in 999. Although this monastery was of Latin rite—the monks came from Altaich in Bavaria—some glosses in Slavonic were found in Latin manuscripts deposited in its library.[86] Even if the monk who wrote these glosses was one of the Slavonic monks who had found a refuge in this monastery after they had been expelled from Sázava in 1094, this would show that in the Benedictine circles in Bohemia a kind of symbiosis of the Slavonic rite and literature with Latin uses was tolerated. Such a situation may have existed also in the monastery of Veliš, erected in 1003 as a dependency of the Abbey of Ostrov. Slavonic glosses were also found in the Abbey of Rajhrad in Moravia, which was founded about 1045.[87]

It should be stressed also that, according to the first *Life of Procopius*, the Abbey of Hradiště, near Olomouc, was founded in 1078 by Prince Otto, brother of the first Czech King Vratislav, who is known to have favored the Slavonic liturgy.[88] Otto's wife was Euphemia, daughter of the Hungarian King Andrew and of his Russian wife Anastasia, who was the daughter of Jaroslav the Wise of Kiev. With regard to the mentality of the founders, one can scarcely imagine that this new foundation was hostile to the Slavonic liturgy and letters, although the monks were of Latin rite. This symbiosis of the Slavonic and Latin rite is indicated also by the report that Bishop John of Olomouc, of course of the Latin rite, and Abbot Vitus of Sázava, of the Slavonic rite, were present at the dedication of the Abbey.[89] This attitude of the Czech Benedictines has, so far, not been brought out. This, of course, does not mean that the Benedictine foundations had become centers of Slavonic liturgy, but it does show that monks favoring Slavonic liturgy and letters were not excluded from the Latin Benedictine communities. We can conclude from these observations that Sázava was not necessarily the only place where Slavonic letters were cultivated and where new translations into Slavonic from Latin originals were made.

We must look also to these Latin circles for the continuation of Slavonic literary activity in Bohemia in the tenth and eleventh centuries. Let us review some of the works which could have been produced in these circles. There must have existed in Bohemia a Slavonic translation of the Latin *Life of St. Vitus*. It is preserved in a Russian manuscript from the twelfth century.[90] It could have been made only in Bohemia, probably by a priest from the Ludmila-Wenceslas circle after Wenceslas had obtained a part of Vitus' relics from the monastery of Corvey, a center of the Vitus cult in western Europe; this occurred after Wenceslas had decided to dedicate the church to St. Vitus, although he had first intended to dedicate it to St. Emmeram. This change illustrated also a change in Bohemia's political relations with Saxony.[91] The dating of the translation from the tenth century would seem logical. But Vitus was venerated also in Sázava. Procopius' nephew and his successor in the direction of the Abbey was called Vitus, as already mentioned. Anyhow, the Bohemian origin of this translation cannot be doubted. It is true that Olga and her son Jaropolk had approached Otto I, but this contact with the Saxon dynasty of which Vitus was the patron saint was minimal and without any consequence for Russia's conversion.[92] There could hardly have been any interest in Russia in St. Vitus and his Latin Legend.

The cult of St. Apollinaris of Ravenna, of Saint Anastasia of Sirmium, and of St. Chrysogonus, who was believed to have been Anastasia's teacher and who was martyred under Diocletian in Aquileia, might already have been introduced into Moravia by priests from Dalmatia and Aquileia. Their cult was well established in the Western Church—the names of Anastasia and Chrysogonus are mentioned in the Mass canon; it could thus have penetrated into Bohemia without the intermediary of Moravia. Their Latin legends must also have been translated in Bohemia, probably in the eleventh century, and are preserved in late manuscripts in Russia.[93]

An important work was the translation of the Latin homilies of St. Gregory the Great, again preserved in a Russian manuscript.[94] The Bohemian origin of this translation was recently demonstrated beyond any doubt.[95] A similar case is presented by the translation of the Pseudo-gospel of Nicodemus from the Latin.[96] Among other translations, two are particularly interesting, that of the martyrdom of Pope Stephen I and of St. George. Both saints were venerated in the Western and Eastern Churches, and there exist legends describing their martyrdom in Greek and in Latin. The Slavonic translations which are preserved, again in Russia, were made from Latin texts.[97] This shows that such translations must have originated in Bohemia, since a Russian translator would have chosen a Greek original.

❖ ❖ ❖

Even more important are two documents, preserved in Russian manuscripts, which are certainly of Western origin and translated from Latin into Slavonic, namely, the prayers to the Holy Trinity and for protection against the devil.[98] I have dealt with these documents on other occasions,[99] and therefore I will limit myself to some general observations. What makes these prayers interesting are the lists of saints invoked in them. Besides saints venerated in the Eastern Church, many names of Western saints are mentioned. The prayer to the Holy Trinity invoked St. Magnus, founder of the Swabian monastery of Fuess; St. Canute of Danemark; St. Olaf, King of Norway; St. Alban, patron saint of Mainz; St. Botulf, the Anglo-Saxon Abbot of Ikanhoe; St. Martin of Tours; St. Victor, a martyr venerated in Switzerland; the Popes Linus, Anacletus, Clement, and Leo; the brothers Cyril and Methodius; St. Wenceslas; and St. Adalbert (Vojtěch). The prayer could have been composed and translated at the end of the eleventh century, since St. Canute and St. Olaf died in 1086 and 1070 respectively. The cult of Scandinavian saints could have penetrated into Russia independently, but when we bear in mind Bohemia's relations with Saxony, Mainz, and Regensburg—where these saints were also venerated—we may conclude that such a selection of Germanic and Slavonic saints could have been made only in eleventh-century Bohemia where this prayer was translated because, as A. I. Sobolevskij points out, it has retained words betraying its lineage from the Old Slavonic period.

It should be pointed out that the list contains several saints of the Benedictine order—Magnus, Botulf, and two Benedicts. The first is listed between Canute and Alban. Probably he should be identified with St. Benedict of Aniane (750–821), the abbot who worked for the reform of Frankish monachism under Charlemagne and Louis the Pious. One also might think that the author of the prayer had in mind St. Benedict Biscop (628–689). This Benedictine was an Anglo-Saxon, became a monk in the Abbey of Lerins, and accompanied Archbishop Theodor of Canterbury in England, where he had founded the Abbeys of Wearmouth and Yarrow. The second Benedictine is listed at the end of the series of oriental monks and ascetics—Paul the Hermit, Anthony, Macarius, Ephrem the Syrian, Sava, Hilarion, Euthymius the Great, Pachomius, Arsenius, Simeon the Stylite, Andrew the fool for Christ, Achatius of Sinaj, Cyril, and Methodius. This Benedictine can only be the founder of Western monachism. The mention of his name fits well with the monks and ascetics venerated in the East. The list of holy women also contains names of saints venerated in the West—Anastasia, Christina, Agriffina, Victoria, and Lucia. Others mentioned in the prayer were venerated in both Churches (Thecla, Barbara, Marina, and Matrona).

The other Old Slavonic prayer, for protection against the devil, also has a list of Western saints, some of them taken from the prayer to the Holy Trinity. The list contains the names of St. Vitus, St. Florian (who is still popular in Austria and in the Czech lands), the Popes Clement and Sylvester, St. Ambrose, St. Martin of Tours, St. Emmeram, and St. Cyprian. St. Benedict is also listed among the monks venerated in the East. Among the holy women one finds Lucia, Agatha, Cecilia, and the famous Abbess Walburga of Heidenheim. Other saints were venerated by both Churches.

The manner in which the popes are listed in the prayer to the Holy Trinity—they are placed immediately after the Apostles and Evangelists as "the holy order of the popes"—seems to indicate that the prayer and its translation must have originated in a land of Roman obedience. One also reads there a Latin homage to the popes—*ave papa*—written in Cyrillic letters. The same can be said concerning a prayer book (*molitvenik*) from the thirteenth century found by Sobolevskij in a monastery of Jaroslavl.[100] Some prayers are taken from the homilies of St. Gregory the Great, one attributed to St. Ambrose. The invocation of St. Peter could hardly have been composed by a member of the orthodox faithful of that period.

All this tells us is that the translations of these prayers were made in Bohemia in the eleventh century, probably in Benedictine circles. It is, of course, possible that some names, especially of the oriental saints, were added later in Russia by the copyists, but the names of Slavic saints—Cyril, Methodius, and Vojtěch— and of other Western saints—especially St. Vitus—were already there in the original.

Let us recall, moreover, that some of the saints whose names are invoked in those prayers are mentioned in the canon of the Latin Mass: Chrysogonus, Agatha, Lucia, Cecilia, Anastasia, Linus, Cletus, Clement, Xystus, Leo. This points out that the origin of the prayers and their translations should be sought in a Slavic land using the Latin rite.

On the other hand, if the prayers in question had been composed and translated at the end of the eleventh century, the invocation to Cyril and Methodius in those prayers would show that some traces of the cult of the brothers must have existed in Bohemia at that time.

Again it will be the duty of Slavic philologists to determine which part of these documents originated in Bohemia and what, if anything, was added to them in Russia.

❖ ❖ ❖

In order to reduce the amount of literary activity credited to Bohemia, it has been suggested that Slavonic priests may have accompanied the two Czech wives of Vladimir to Kiev (as well as other princesses who married Russian princes), have learned Slavonic in Kiev, and thus have written the works mentioned.[101] But even if this theory could be accepted, it presupposes that there must have been priests in Bohemia in the tenth and eleventh centuries who were familiar with Slavonic letters. Moreover, there were not many intermarriages between the Ruriks and the Přemyslides during the tenth and eleventh centuries, as far as we know.[102]

More frequent relations between Kiev and Bohemia began after 981, when Vladimir[103] conquered the Red Cities as well as Přemysl in modern Galicia, and when his realm became a neighbor of the Přemyslide State, which at that time contained not only Bohemia but also Moravia, Silesia, and the region of Cracow as far as the rivers Bug and Styr. The main channels of intellectual intercourse were the Slavonic monks, especially from the Abbey at Sázava. We do not know when and how these relations had begun. It is quite possible that the year 1057 had stabilized their contacts. When the monks of Sázava were expelled from their abbey by the Czech Duke Spytihněv, with their Abbot Vitus, they found refuge in Hungary, as is attested by the *Chroni-*

cle of Sázava.[104] It seems most probable that they were received by the russophile King Andrew, and that for six years they were guests of the Russian monks from Kiev for whom Andrew had built a monastery at Visegrad. As we have seen, evidence from the thirteenth century shows that, up to 1214, this monastery was occupied from its foundation by Russian monks of the Byzantine rite. We do not know of any other place in Hungary using the Slavonic rite where the monks from Sázava could have taken refuge. If they stayed for six years with Russian monks, who certainly were in touch with their monastic centers in Kiev, the intellectual contact between Bohemia and Kiev must have been strengthened.

The most eloquent proof of lively communication by the Slavonic monks of Sázava with Kiev is the deposition of the relics of two Russian saints, the Princes Boris and Gleb, who were canonized by the Russian Church in 1072, to one of the altars of the abbey in 1093.[105] The relics were most probably brought by Slavonic monks from Kiev. This contact of Sázava, under Latin obedience of the Bishop of Prague, with the orthodox monks of Kiev is the more important as it continued after 1054, the year which is regarded as the beginning of the schism between Rome and Constantinople. The cult of the two Russian saints may have been quite lively in Bohemia, and a short biography of the saints may have been composed at Sázava. There exists, at least, a short account of their life and death which, in the opinion of Sobolevskij,[106] reveals certain Western hagiographical features. At least, the name of Boris appears quite frequently in Czech medieval documents. The same could be supposed concerning the cult of Olga, the first Russian Christian princess.[107] Her name was frequently given at baptism to girls in Bohemia during the twelfth and thirteenth centuries. All this indicates how certain Slavonic writings, which had originated in the tenth and eleventh centuries in Bohemia, were so readily accepted in Kievan ecclesiastical circles and have been preserved to our time.

* * *

These contacts must have been looked upon with favor by the first Czech King Vratislav II (1061–1092), who had also taken refuge in Hungary at the same time as the monks from Sázava.

After he returned to the ducal throne following the death of his brother Spytihněv, he called back the exiled monks and settled them once again in their monastery. He became a zealous supporter of the Slavonic Abbey and of the Slavonic liturgy. He went even further, and tried to obtain permission for the use of the Slavonic liturgy in his kingdom. He addressed himself some time before 1080 to Pope Gregory VII (1073–1085) with such a demand. We can reconstruct the main points of his request only from the pope's letter to the king in 1080;[108] the pope rebuked him sharply for his support of the Emperor Henry IV, whom the pope had excommunicated in the famous struggle for investiture, and to whom the Czech king had remained faithful. After this reproof the pope continued:

> While, however, your grace demanded our permission to celebrate the divine office in your country in the Slavic language, be informed that we can in no way favor such a petition. It is truly clear . . . that it pleased the omnipotent God to keep the holy scripture in darkness in some places, since, if all were clear to everyone, it might become villainous and be despised, or, if misunderstood by men of little ability, could induce them into error. Nor can you resort to the excuse that this is the demand of simple people and that certain religious men had patiently tolerated this use and left it uncorrected, since the primitive Church left in darkness many things which, after Christianity had been firmly established and the religion was growing, were corrected after a profound examination by the holy fathers. Therefore, by the authority of St. Peter, we forbid the accomplishment of your unwise demands, and we order you to resist, in honor of the omnipotent God, this vain temerity with all your strength.

This sharp refusal and rebuke, of course, was a mortal blow to the Slavonic liturgy in Bohemia. Some think that the king had in mind only the continuation of the Slavonic liturgy at Sázava. His demand, however, cannot be explained in this way. Sázava had practiced the Slavonic liturgy for many years and, because the king favored it, did not need further confirmation of its practice. It seems that the king really had in mind the authorization of its use in his kingdom, without, of course, excluding the Latin liturgy.

He hoped that such a symbiosis would continue as it was done in the past. The words pointing out that "religious men [this can only mean the bishops] had patiently tolerated [the Slavonic liturgy] and left [this use] uncorrected," are very important, as they reveal that the Czech religious authorities in the past had admitted or tolerated this practice.

*** ** **

The pope's refusal might have been expected. Hostility against the Slavonic liturgy was growing among the reformers, who were not only opposed to the practice of royal investiture, but anxious to eradicate every liturgical practice which did not correspond to the Roman and Latin tradition. This movement had gained solid ground in Bohemia under Spytihněv; the first expulsion of the Slavonic monks from Sázava, which abbey had been given to Latin monks, must be attributed to the pressure that these reformers exercised on the prince. It may be also that the special character of the abbey contributed to it, for it was not only founded by the Duke Břetislav, but also by the family of Procopius. His family seems to have claimed certain rights which were regarded unfavorably by both the prince and the bishop. This would explain why Procopius' successor was his nephew Vitus, who was followed by Procopius' son Emmeram.

In spite of all this, Vratislav II continued to support the abbey and the Slavonic liturgy. His successor Břetislav II yielded at last to the growing pressure from the reformers and enemies of the Slavonic liturgy—the first Czech chronicler Cosmas, dean of the chapter at St. Vitus Cathedral, was one of them—and in 1096 drove the Slavonic monks from Sázava, and settled Latin monks in the abbey. The Slavic monks were scattered and their Slavonic books destroyed. It is possible that some of them found refuge in other Czech abbeys and that others emigrated to Kiev. Most of them later returned to Sázava and were accepted by the new Latin abbots. This was a mortal blow to Slavonic liturgy and letters in Bohemia. At the beginning of the twelfth century the last vestiges of the Slavonic practice disappeared definitely from Bohemia.

The Slavonic past was not forgotten, however. The memory of St. Procopius and of his work was revived in 1204 when King Přemysl Otakar I obtained from the pope the canonization of the founder of Sázava. In 1268 King Přemysl Otakar II asked Pope

Clement IV to elevate the bishopric of Olomouc to archepiscopal rank, arguing that Moravia had once been honored with this distinction. The memory of St. Methodius was evidently recalled. Although the pope was not unfavorable to this request, the creation of an archbishopric for Bohemia and Moravia was only realized by Charles IV in 1344.

The memory of the Slavonic past was revived during his reign and new compositions celebrating the Czech national saints were written. The Emperor Charles was so enthusiastic about the Slavonic liturgy that he asked Pope Clement VI to renew this privilege for the Czech lands. In 1346 the pope gave permission for the erection of one abbey where the Slavonic liturgy should be celebrated. Charles IV built the Abbey of Emaus in Prague, and invited thither Benedictine priests and brothers from Dalmatia, where the Slavonic liturgy was still celebrated and the glagolitic alphabet, invented by St. Cyril, was still used.[109]

The Hussites also recalled the old privilege and introduced the national language into their liturgy.

VIII. Byzantium, Rome, and the Cyrilo-Methodian Heritage in Croatia, Bulgaria, and Serbia

Slavonic liturgy in Croatia; Methodius in Dalmatia?—Byzantine intervention in Croatia—Existence of the Slavonic liturgy in Dalmatia at an early date—Its tolerance during the tenth century—Spalato against Nin; the synods of Spalato (925) did not forbid Slavonic liturgy—The Roman reformist movement and the Slavonic liturgy; the synod of 1060—Revolt of the Slavonic clergy against the synodal decree of 1060—Tolerance of the Slavonic liturgy in spite of its prohibition—St. Jerome "promoted" as the inventor of glagolitic letters and liturgy; approval of his invention by Rome in 1247—Arrival of Methodius' disciples in Bulgaria—Boris creates a Slavonic center in Macedonia; Clement's activity—Clement established bishop by Symeon; Slavonic schools of Ochrida and Preslav—Byzantine attitude to the Slavonic liturgy and letters; formation of the Cyrillic alphabet; Chrabr's defense of the glagolitic alphabet—Slavonic school in Constantinople and Bulgaria—The priest Constantine; literary activity of the Preslav school under Symeon's inspiration—Latin and Greek missions among the Serbians—First Serbian bishopric of Rasa founded by Symeon—Dyrrhachium's and Ochrida's rivalry over Serbia—Latin influence in the first Serbian state of Dioclea—Stephen Nemanja becomes orthodox and master of Rascia and Dioclea; Rome, mistaken policy—Stephen I obtains the royal crown from Innocent III; Sava consecrated by the Patriarch of Nicaea as first Archbishop of Serbia; Rome's failure to win over the Serbians.

T he connection of Slavonic Christianity among the Czechs with the Cyrilo-Methodian mission in Moravia is evident, although

230

the Slavonic liturgy did not find a general acceptance in Bohemia and was suppressed in the twelfth century. The origin and development of the Slavonic liturgy in Croatia is more problematical. Was it introduced into that country during the life of Constantine-Cyril and Methodius? Were those disciples of the two brothers who were expelled from Moravia responsible for its spread? What were the reactions of Rome, of the Latin bishoprics in Dalmatia, and of the Croatian bishop of Nin to this innovation?

The Slavonic liturgy first appeared in Croatia between the years 866 and 876 when Kocel of Pannonia opened his country to it. Some of the fifty young men who had been instructed by the two brothers in Slavic letters may have reached Pannonian Croatia, especially if we accept the fact that this part of the Frankish Empire was governed by Kocel himself, and that he died in 876 when leading the Frankish army against Iljko, son of Domagoj of Croatian Pannonia, who had revolted against the Franks. Kocel enjoyed a strong position until at least 873, and the fifty young Slavic clerics did not disappear without having attempted to implant the new liturgical practice in Kocel's lands. Pannonian Croatia had been converted from Aquileia and belonged to the jurisdiction of its patriarchs.[1] The hostility against their liturgical innovation may not have been as pronounced in this country as it was in Upper Pannonia, which was under the jurisdiction of the Bavarian clergy. Even when the country was administered after Kocel's death by Prince Brasla,[2] who was a Slav, the Slavonic liturgy could well have persisted in this land which was remote from the control of the Frankish clergy.

The fact that Methodius was Archbishop of Sirmium and Apostolic Legate to the Slavic lands makes the penetration of the Slavonic liturgy into Pannonian Croatia more probable. Even in 873, after freeing Methodius from his captivity, Pope John VIII confirmed him in his rank as Bishop of Sirmium and Apostolic Legate. The letter to Mutimir, inviting the Serbian prince to submit his land to the metropolis of Sirmium, confirms this.[3] After the death of Kocel all traces of Slavonic liturgy and letters may well have disappeared from Upper Pannonia, but a sporadic survival in Pannonian Croatia under a Slavic prince is quite admissible.

Dalmatian Croatia was not placed under Methodius' jurisdiction because the country already had a bishopric, that of Nin, founded most probably in 860 by Nicholas I,[4] and there were also Latin bishoprics in the coastal cities. It has not yet been satisfactorily explained how and by which means the Slavonic liturgy had penetrated into Dalmatian Croatia, where it has survived down to our own days.

Dalmatian Croats could have become acquainted with the Slavonic liturgy through the intermediary of Slavic priests from the dominions of Kocel. Some of them may have reached that country after Kocel's death. It is admissible to imagine that St. Methodius made a short stay in that country when returning from Rome after his rehabilitation by John VIII in 880. We have seen that he seems to have reached Moravia some time after Wiching, who had accompanied him to Rome. This delay was used by Wiching to spread false rumors about Methodius and his own mission in Moravia. This is a possibility which needs more detailed examination.

* * *

Before Methodius had got as far as Rome in 880, a very important event took place in Dalmatian Croatia. The dynasty of Trpimir which ruled there was dethroned about 864 by Domagoj, who refused to recognize Frankish supremacy and ruled until 876. He was followed by his son Iljko (876–878). Trpimir's son Zdeslav, who had found refuge in Byzantium, returned with Byzantine help in 878, dethroned Iljko's sons and became ruler of the country. There was a danger that Dalmatia might come under the political influence of Byzantium; this would also have had repercussions in the ecclesiastical field if the Byzantines had been able to consolidate their position in that country.[5]

It seems, however, that this new orientation of Croatian foreign policy was not welcome to certain influential members of the Croat aristocracy and to the Croat clergy. They revolted against Zdeslav, who was killed, and Branimir assumed power.

Pope John VIII does not seem to have been aware of the danger, because in 879 he sent a letter to Zdeslav,[6] asking for a safe conduct for the legates he was sending to Boris of Bulgaria requesting him to return to the Roman jurisdiction. The pope was informed of the dangers and of the new situation by an embassy sent to Rome by Branimir and Bishop Theodosius. The letters addressed to the new Croat leaders are dated June 7, 879,[7] about the same time as those sent to Svatopluk and to Methodius summoning the latter to Rome for his justification.[8] The pope expressed his lively satisfaction at the pledge of fidelity to St. Peter given by the Croat bishop and the prince. Methodius must have reached Rome in the late spring of the following year. The letter to Svatopluk announcing the rehabilitation of Methodius and the approval of the Slavonic liturgy is dated June 880.[9]

The anxiety of the pope to attach Croatia as intimately as possible to the Roman See must not be forgotten, nor the fact that he also invited the bishops of the coastal cities to return to the Roman obedience.[10] Bearing these facts in mind, we are entitled to suppose that he also tried to employ Methodius to visit the Croatian ruler and bishop on his return to Moravia. This visit could have initiated the penetration of the Slavonic liturgy into Dalmatia.

We can perhaps detect an echo of these events, and of the role played by Methodius in Croatia, in a short *Prolog Vita* of Methodius.[11] When speaking about the victory of Methodius over his calumniators in Moravia—Wiching and his followers are naturally meant—the author is inspired by the account given in chapter twelve of the *Vita Methodii*, where a clear allusion is made to the sedition of Dathan and Abiram against Moses (Num. 16). It is, however, curious to note that besides Zambrii (Abiram) he also mentions Sedislav "whom the earth had swallowed up" (Num. 16:32). Only Zdeslav of Croatia, called also Sedeslav, can be meant in this connection. The *Prolog* is, of course, of later origin—it is preserved in copies dating from the fourteenth to sixteenth centuries—but it may reflect events which happened in Croatia in 879 and the role which Methodius played in that country in 880 at the request of the pope.

✤ ✤ ✤

There are other indications which suggest the existence of the Slavonic liturgy in Dalmatian Croatia at an early date. We have seen that lessons contained in the glagolitic breviaries copied and used in Dalmatia contained a translation of the Old Testament of Moravian origin. This fact is used as an argument that St. Methodius had really translated all the books of the Old Testament, with the exception of the Books of the Maccabees.[12] How did parts of this translation reach Dalmatian Croatia? Methodius most probably finished it after his return from Constantinople. This could indicate that copies of it could have reached Croatian Dalmatia between 882 and 885.

Because, however, it seems certain that the Croatian copyists did not possess a complete copy of this translation, we should conclude that it was partly destroyed after Methodius' death during the persecution of Slavonic letters initiated by Wiching. Fragments of this translation may have been saved by some of the disciples of Methodius who had found refuge in Dalmatian Croatia after 885.

There is still another possibility. We learn from a Slavonic *Life of St. Naum*[13] that many disciples of Methodius were sold to the Jews as slaves, and the Jewish slave merchants brought them to Venice for sale. Fortunately, a high imperial officer, who was at that time in Venice on official business, learned about them. He bought and freed them all. Some of them were brought by him to Constantinople, where Basil I granted them all the clerical rank which they had previously held. Not all of them seem to have been brought to the capital. It is probable that some of them went to Dalmatian Croatia and continued to exercise their clerical functions there, celebrating the Office in Slavonic. This may have happened in the spring of 886, because Basil I, who is said to have reinstated in their offices the clerics brought to Constantinople, died in August of the same year.

There is still one circumstance which deserves to be stressed. It is remarkable to note that the Byzantines failed to support their protégé Zdeslav against his enemies, although he appears to have recognized Byzantine supremacy over Croatia when staying in Constantinople. This puzzling lack of interest on the part of the Byzantines over the fate of Zdeslav seems to find its explanation in the events happening in the capital in 878 and 879. The Patriarch Ignatius died October 23, 877, and Photius, who had become reconciled with his antagonist before the latter's death, was reinstalled on the patriarchal throne. Ignatius and the Emperor Basil had already asked John VIII to send legates to Constantinople to make peace with the Church.[14] The legates arrived after Ignatius' death, in 878, and were in a dilemma at finding Photius, who had been condemned by Nicholas I and Hadrian II, on the patriarchal

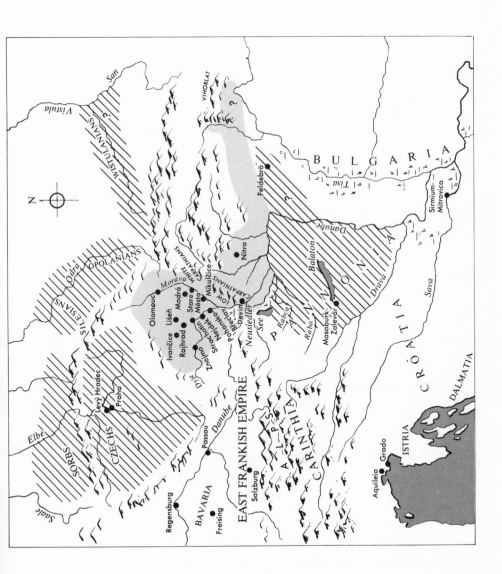

GREAT MORAVIAN EMPIRE

Original territory

Territory under
Great Moravian
Sovereignty

Areas of
Questionable
Sovereignty

Marsh Lands

150 KILOMETERS

150 MILES

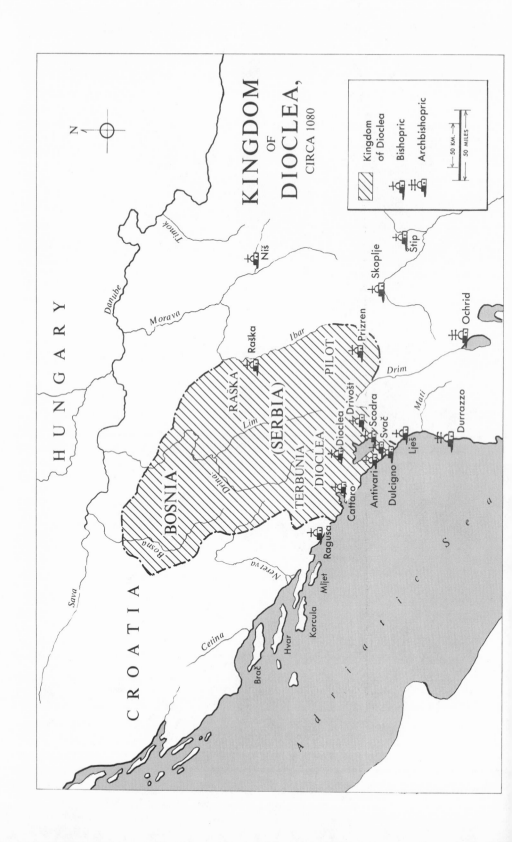

KINGDOM
OF
DIOCLEA,
CIRCA 1080

Kingdom of Dioclea
Bishopric
Archbishopric

50 KM.
50 MILES

HUNGARY

CROATIA

BOSNIA

RAŠKA

(SERBIA)

TERBUNIA

DIOCLEA

PILOT

Timok

Danube

Morava

Niš

Skoplje

Štip

Ochrid

Raška

Ibar

Prizren

Drim

Drivošt

Dioclea

Scodra

Svač

Lim

Drina

Mati

Durrazzo

Lješ

Antivari

Dulcigno

Cattaro

Ragusa

Mljet

Korcula

Hvar

Brač

Nerelva

Cetina

Bosna

Sava

Adriatic Sea

N

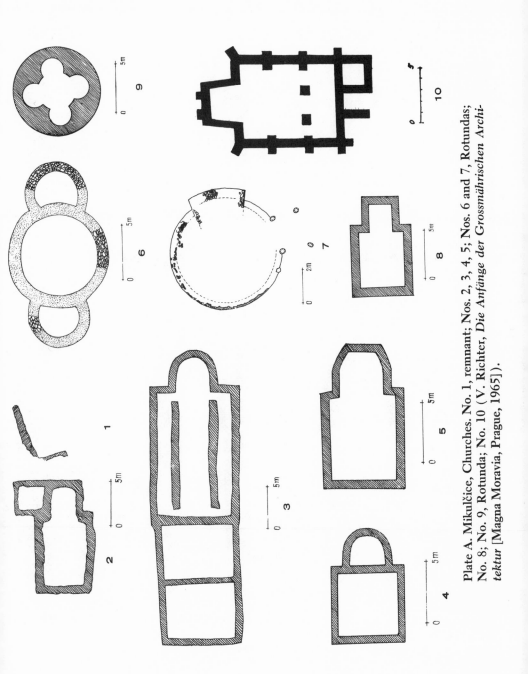

Plate A. Mikulčice, Churches. No. 1, remnant; Nos. 2, 3, 4, 5; Nos. 6 and 7, Rotundas; No. 8; No. 9, Rotunda; No. 10 (V. Richter, *Die Anfänge der Grossmährischen Architektur* [Magna Moravia, Prague, 1965]).

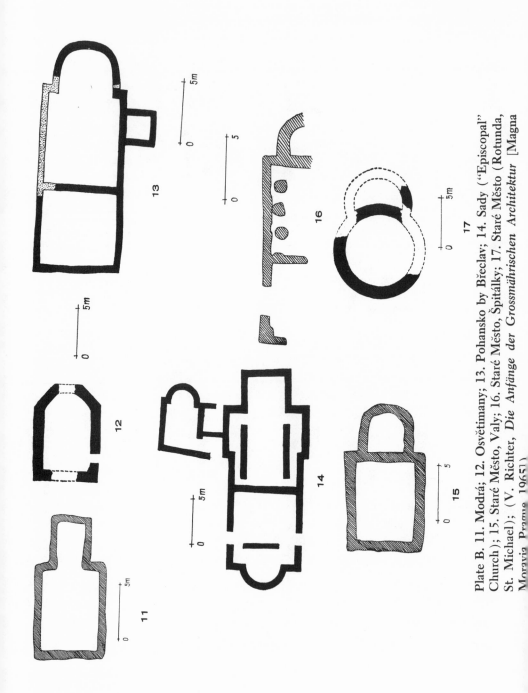

Plate B. 11. Modrá; 12. Osvětimany; 13. Pohansko by Břeclav; 14. Sady ("Episcopal" Church); 15. Staré Město, Valy; 16. Staré Město, Špitálky; 17. Staré Město (Rotunda, St. Michael); (V. Richter, *Die Anfänge der Grossmährischen Architektur* [Magna Moravia. Prague. 1965).

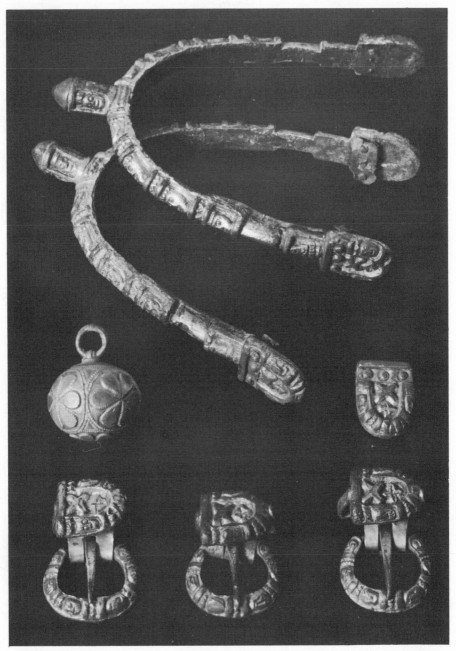

Figure 1. Mikulčice. Gilded Bronze Ornaments. From the Tomb of a Nobleman (No. 44).

Figures 2 and 3. Mikulčice. Silver Belt-ends. Found near Church #3 (Plate A).

Figure 4. Mikulčice. Silver Gilt Belt-end. Found near Church #2 (Plate A).

Figure 5. Mikulčice. Silver Belt-end, with the Figure of a Nobleman Orant.

Figure 6. Mikulčice. Gold Earrings, Buttons, and Pendant. Found near Church #3 (Plate A).

Figure 7. Mikulčice. Bone Medallion, with an Archer. From Tomb 251, near Church #3 (Plate A).

Figure 8. Mikulčice. Gilded Bronze Reliquary. From Tomb 505, near Church #3 (Plate A).

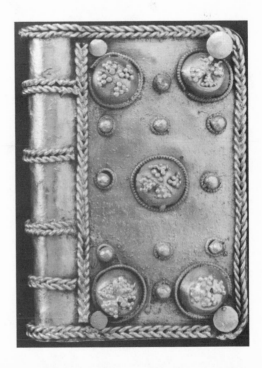

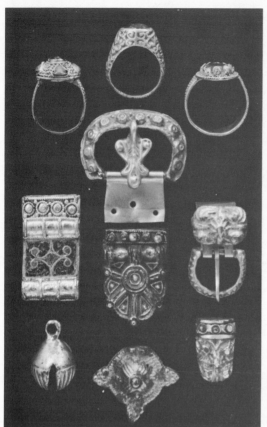

Figure 9. Pohansko. Rings, Buckles, and Ornaments. From Tombs near the Church (Plate B, No. 13).

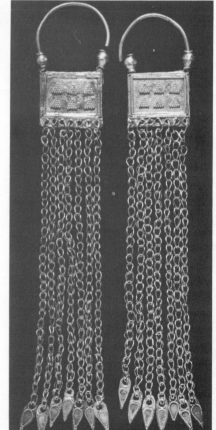

Figure 10. Pohansko. Unique Silver Earrings.

Figure 11. Kouřim (Bohemia). Earrings and Reliquary. From the Tomb of a Noblewoman.

Figure 12. Sady. Necklace with Shell, Glass Paste Beads, and Topaz.

Figure 13. Staré Město, Špitálky. Silver Plaque, with a Falconer.

Figure 14. Staré Mesto, Valy.
Gold Earring.

Figure 15. Staré Město, Valy.
Gilded Copper Button.

Figure 18. Zlaté Moravce (Slovekia). Gold Cross, with Christ Crucified.

Figure 16. Trnovec (Slovekia). *Top*, Cross. *Bottom*, Cross Reliquaries.

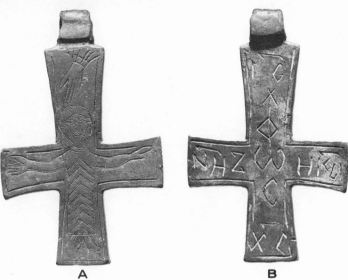

A   B

Figure 17. Sady. Cross with the Figure of Christ Crucified and the Hand of God on the obverse; Greek Inscription on the reverse. A. *Obverse.* B. *Reverse.*

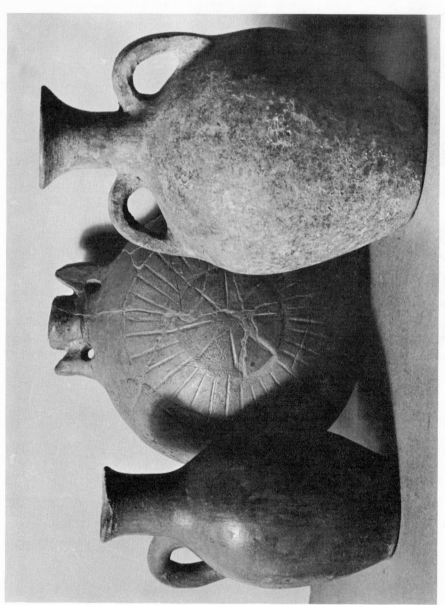

Figure 19. Staré Město. Ceramic Vases of Antique Character.

throne. Both the emperor and the new patriarch were anxious to effect a complete reconciliation with Rome. The legates reported to the pope at their reception, and their report was completed by a letter from the emperor asking for recognition of Photius as patriarch.[15] In August 879, the pope sent Cardinal Peter with new instructions to them, and these contained recognition of the legitimacy of Photius' elevation.[16]

One can understand that, in those circumstances, the Byzantines did not wish to antagonize the papacy. A political and religious offensive in Croatia would certainly have alienated John VIII, who would be reluctant to accept the proffered reconciliation. It is thus most probably for these reasons that the Byzantines abandoned their plans for the political and religious conquest of Dalmatian Croatia. They left Zdeslav to his fate, esteeming more highly a peaceful solution of the Ignatian and Photian controversy.

In this light the attitude of John VIII toward Methodius, during the stay of the latter in Rome, becomes more understandable. In the peaceful atmosphere prevailing in the relations between East and West, the affairs of Methodius, a Byzantine, could be examined more sympathetically. Methodius was also pleased to learn that Constantinople and Rome were about to be definitely reconciled and that Photius, who had initiated the Moravian mission, was again recognized as a legitimate patriarch. In this situation, he would be able to accept the suggestion of the pope to visit Dalmatian Croatia, because his compatriots had withdrawn from that country, recognizing its allegiance to Rome. Also an eventual visit by Methodius to Constantinople may well have been discussed. This appears the more probable if we accept the possibility, already mentioned, that the invitation of the Emperor Basil I, suggested in all likelihood by the patriarch, had reached Methodius before his journey to Rome, in 878, or rather in 879. Such a move on the part of the emperor and the patriarch would be perfectly understandable as a reflection of the peaceful and conciliatory atmosphere which enveloped Constantinople before the opening of the Union Council in 879.

Although we cannot give an exact date for the introduction of the Slavonic liturgy into Dalmatian Croatia, there were, as we have seen, many opportunities which show that it could have been introduced there in the ninth century.

It appears that the Dalmatian priests who used the Slavonic liturgy were, during the tenth and eleventh centuries, in lively contact with the Slavonic priests of Bohemia. This seems to be illustrated by the fact that the Slavonic *Life of St. Wenceslas,* which was written in glagolitic letters in Bohemia in the tenth century, was preserved, not in Bohemia, but in the glagolitic breviaries of Dalmatian Croatia. It has been shown that its text contains not only some bohemisms but also archaic expressions, which betray the fact that it was composed, not in Croatia, but in Bohemia by an author familiar with the language in which the Cyrilo-Methodian literature was composed.[17]

The *Life of Constantine* must also have been known in Croatia very early. The glagolitic breviaries of Croatian origin from the thirteenth to the sixteenth century contain readings on St. Cyril, which, according to specialists, were excerpts from an original written in the ninth or tenth century in glagolitic letters.[18]

* * *

Although there can be no doubt about the existence of the Slavonic liturgy in Dalmatian Croatia from the ninth century on, information is lacking about its extension and development in the following centuries.[19] The Magyar danger forced the Pannonian Croats to enter into a political union with Dalmatian Croats during the reign of Tomislav (910–928), who had assumed the title of King of the Croats.[20] There is no mention of any hostile attitude to the Slavonic liturgy on the part of Croatian rulers or of the Bishop of Nin. This is the more interesting as it was the ambition of the Croatian rulers to gain control over the Latin cities of the littoral. The Latin bishops of these cities were under the jurisdiction of Rome, and until the middle of the tenth century we do not hear of any animosity on their part to the Slavonic liturgy.

The bishops of Nin would have liked to extend their jurisdiction over the bishoprics of the coastal cities, and, about 886, Theodosius of Nin also occupied the bishopric of Spalato. Stephen VI reproached Theodosius for doing so without the authorization of Rome. He also reproached him for having been consecrated bishop by the Patriarch of Aquileia, although he should have asked for consecration in Rome.[21] The Patriarch Walpertus of

Aquileia was also admonished by Stephen VI for having usurped a right which belonged to the Holy See when he ordained Theodosius.[22]

This case is not quite clear. It seems certain that Theodosius was ordained in Aquileia, but it must have been done with the approval, tacit or expressed, of Pope John VIII. The latter was evidently pleased with Theodosius' loyalty to him, as has been mentioned before. After his consecration Theodosius must have visited the pope, because he was charged by him with a mission to Boris of Bulgaria which he seems to have accomplished with some success.[23] Stephen VI was displeased with the fact that Theodosius took over the administration of the diocese of Spalato without his consent, and also recalled the other incident—the consecration by the Patriarch of Aquileia—but without going into details, and this omission would alleviate the "transgression." In any event, he saw how important it was that Spalato should be in the hands of a bishop who had always been loyal to Rome and, therefore, sent Theodosius the pallium which he had requested.

* * *

Soon, however, a counter-offensive from Spalato against Nin arose. The ecclesiastical reorganization of the whole of Croatia was effected at the Synod of Spalato in 925. Pope John X sent two bishops as his legates. King Tomislav and Michael, Prince of Hum, were also present. The reorganization of the Croat Church seemed to be necessary because of the new political situation in Croatia and Dalmatia. The Emperor Romanus I Lecapenus (919–944), anxious to assure the neutrality of the Croats in his conflict with the Bulgarian Tsar Symeon, bestowed on Tomislav the title of proconsul and entrusted to him the administration of the Byzantine "thema of Dalmatia," together with the coastal cities and islands. Tomislav was supposed to rule over this territory as the representative of the emperor, but actually this arrangement meant the subjection of the last Byzantine possessions in Dalmatia to Croatia.[24]

The Bishop of Nin, naturally, defended his position, claiming the ecclesiastical primacy of Croatia for the first Croat national see. However, it was in the interest of the king to bring the coastal cities, whose possession he had coveted for so long, closer to the rest of his realm. Tomislav was, therefore, ready to subordinate all Croatia to the archbishops of Spalato. The bishops of the coastal cities, of course, supported the king and the Archbishop of Spalato. In spite of the protests of the Bishop of Nin, the Synod confirmed the Archbishop of Spalato in his position as Metropolitan of all Croatia, subordinating to his jurisdiction all the bishoprics from Istria to Cattaro.

In the *Acts* of this Synod[25] there are two passages in the letters sent by the pope to the fathers, and to the king, which prohibited the use of the Slavonic language in the liturgy. This prohibition is also stressed in Canon Ten of the Synod. The genuineness of this Synod is frequently disputed. If the *Acts* are original, then they contain the first confirmation of the existence of a Slavonic liturgy in Croatia. At the same time the hostility of Rome, and of the Latin bishops in Dalmatia, to the continuation of this custom in the tenth century would be documented.

We know that Gregory, Bishop of Nin, protested to the pope. It was thought that he protested not only against the degradation of his see but also against the prohibition of the Slavonic liturgy and that, thanks to his protest, the existence of this liturgy was saved.[26]

This interpretation does not seem to correspond to facts. The report sent by the Synod to the pope, and his letter confirming the Canons, show that Gregory of Nin protested only against the decision which subjected his see to Spalato. The pope declared that he was ratifying all decisions except that which provoked Gregory's protest. Archbishop John of Spalato and Gregory of Nin were invited to come to Rome so that the affair could be definitely decided.[27] There is no mention of a protest against Canon Ten forbidding the ordination to the priesthood of candidates devoted to the Slavonic liturgy. Moreover, neither Gregory nor John of Spalato went to Rome, and a final decision was made at the Second Synod of Spalato, which took place at the beginning of the year 928, under the direction of the papal legate, Bishop Madalbertus.[28]

The decisions of this Synod were again directed toward the definitive organization of the Croatian Church. The Archbishop of Spalato was confirmed in his metropolitan function, the bishopric of Nin was suppressed and its territory divided between other

Dalmatian bishoprics. Again, there is no mention of the Slavonic liturgy.

The *Acts* of the two Synods must be regarded as basically genuine, although they are preserved only in two seventeenth-century Vatican manuscripts of the history of Spalato by Archdeacon Thomas. However, the manner in which the Slavonic liturgy is forbidden does not accord with the spirit of the first half of the tenth century. The price which the Latin bishops of Dalmatia, led by Spalato, asked for their integration into the Croatian political and ecclesiastical framework was the suppression, not of the Slavonic liturgy, but of the bishopric of Nin. This sacrifice was heavy enough for the Croats, and it would not have been prudent to show hostility as well to the custom which was so dear to the Croat people.

It would be more logical to imagine such hostility to the Slavonic liturgy in the eleventh century when Roman reformists had initiated their campaign against national liturgies. It seems probable that the genuine *Acts* of the First Synod of Spalato of 925 were interpolated in order to give the anti-Slavonic propaganda more authority.[29]

❖ ❖ ❖

The reformist movement in Rome was inaugurated by Clement II (1046–1047) and continued by Leo X (1049–1054) and his successors Victor II, Stephen X, and Nicholas II. It reached its peak under Gregory VII (1073–1085). The abuses which the reformists tried to eradicate—simony and the marriage of priests—existed also in Croatia. This is illustrated especially by the case of Dabral, Archbishop of Spalato (circa 1040 to circa 1059), who is said to have lived with his wife and children even after his promotion to episcopal rank.[30] The Synod of the Lateran (April 13, 1059) voted a series of canons condemning the main abuses, and in December of the same year Pope Nicholas II (1059–1061) sent Abbot Mainard to Croatia to initiate the reform of the Croatian Church. In March 1060 a new Synod was convened in Spalato which declared the decisions of the Lateran obligatory in Croatia and Dalmatia. An additional canon was directed against the use of the Slavonic liturgy.

This canon started with the same words as the canon believed to have been accepted in Spalato in 928: "We forbid, under the threat of excommunication, the ordaining of Slavs if they do not know the Latin language."[31] This identical stylization makes it more probable that Canon Ten of the Synod of 928 is a later interpolation.

The *Acts* of this Synod are preserved only fragmentarily. The Archdeacon Thomas, when reporting in his *Historia Salonitana*[32] on this Synod and its decision against the use of the Slavonic liturgy, completes the synodal decision as it is preserved, adding: "They said, namely, that the gothic [glagolitic] letters were invented by some heretic, Methodius, who had written many false things in the same Slavonic language against the rules of the Catholic faith. Because of that he is said to have been condemned through divine judgment to a sudden death."

These words are interesting, because they show that hostility to the Slavonic liturgy was being justified by dogmatic reasons. Methodius is compared with Ulphila, who invented an alphabet for the Goths, and the Croats using the glagolitic alphabet are identified with the Goths, who were Arianists. The memory of Methodius was becoming more and more obscured.

The Synod shows also that, although the Croats had been for many centuries under Roman obedience, they were still influenced by some usages of the Byzantine Church.

When Archbishop Dabral was asked by the Apostolic Legate how he could dare to live with a wife and produce a family, he is said to have answered that he was living in legitimate matrimony according to the usage of the Eastern Church. The Croat clergy using the Slavonic liturgy also grew beards and let their hair grow long, as did the Orthodox clergy. The wearing of beards and long hair was also forbidden by the Synod.

The new synodal intervention against the Slavonic liturgy shows clearly that it was in use down to the middle of the eleventh century and was tolerated by the bishops and the rulers. It can hardly be thought that the Latin bishops were ordaining Slavonic priests, but a national Croat episcopal see was erected in Knin about the year 1040.[33] After the suppression of the bishopric of Nin, the titulary of this See, who was at the same time a royal secretary, most probably ordained Slavonic priests.

* * *

Pope Honorius II confirmed the decisions of the Synod of 1060 in Rome in 1063. But it was not easy to put them into practice. The Slavonic clergy protested and was supported by the laity. The introduction of the tithe, hitherto unknown in Croatia, was very unpopular. This was a new instance of Byzantine influence on the organization of the Croat Church. The extension of the prohibition on marriage to minor degrees of relationship also provoked sharp criticism. The discontent was so great that a schism arose in the Croatian Church.

The originator of the new development was a certain priest, called Vuk (Ulfus).[34] He advised the Slavic priests to send a delegation to the pope asking for the reopening of the churches using the Slavonic liturgy, and for the ordination of Slavonic priests. The nobles who favored the Slavonic liturgy and their priests assembled, and they sent Vuk to Rome in their name with presents for the pope. Vuk asked the pope to rescind the decision of the Synod and to re-establish in the Croatian Church the *status quo* prior to the Synod. The pope answered that he could not rescind so lightly the decision of bishops confirmed by his legates. He asked Vuk to present to the king, the archbishop, and the other prelates a papal letter requesting the presence of two bishops in Rome to explain the case.

Vuk, however, did not present the papal letter to the king and the prelates, but assured the Slavonic clergy and the nobles that the pope was favorably disposed to their demand and had invited them to send a priest whom he would ordain bishop. The assembly of Slavonic priests chose Zdeda, an old priest who did not know Latin, and sent him to Rome with Abbot Potepa and Vuk. The pope asked why there were no bishops in the delegation and after expressing his surprise that Zdeda wore a beard, he cut a piece of it off, ordered him to be shorn and his beard cut off according to the Latin custom. The pope then repeated to Vuk what he had said before, namely that he could not grant this concession to the "Goths." The memory of the Arianist Goths was again invoked, according to the report given by the Archpriest Thomas.

Vuk is said to have convinced the ignorant Zdeda that the pope, when cutting off his beard, had consecrated him as a bishop. The latter believed the story, and, with his followers, expelled the Bishop of Veglia (Krk) from his throne, and himself acted as bishop, ordaining priests and consecrating churches. This caused great confusion in Croatia; the pope sent Cardinal John as legate to the country, who explained to the "Goths" that Zdeda had not been consecrated a bishop. He was excommunicated, and Vuk, condemned by a synod in Spalato, was punished for his treachery by imprisonment.

The account given by Thomas is certainly biased. This serious incident indicates that the Croat national party, favoring the Slavonic liturgy, was endeavoring to obtain a national bishopric such as Nin had been, which would be subordinate, not to Spalato, but directly to the Holy See. All this shows that the Slavonic liturgy had many adherents, and that even the strictest synodal decrees could not uproot it, but only increased the enmity between the Latin and Slavonic clergy and the animosity against the reformists.[35]

The influence of Byzantine customs on the Slavonic clergy can also be explained by the fact that Byzantium's prestige had increased considerably in the Balkans after the destruction of the Bulgarian Empire. In 1018, even the Croat King Gojslav had to recognize Byzantine supremacy. In 1024 Dalmatia again came under direct imperial administration. Only in 1069 were the Dalmatian cities again placed under the protection of the Croat King Kresimir IV by the Emperor Romanus IV.[36]

These influences came not only directly from the Byzantine Empire, but also, especially in the tenth century, from Bulgaria where, as will be seen, Slavonic letters flourished. It is admitted by Slavic philologists that some Slavonic texts may have been brought to Croatia from the centers of Slavonic letters in Bulgarian Macedonia in the tenth century, and at the beginning of the eleventh. A thorough study of some of the glagolitic texts originating in Croatia has shown certain linguistic peculiarities pointing to their Bulgarian origin.[37] This shows that the Bulgarian priests of the Eastern Slavonic rite were in contact with the Croat priests of the Roman Slavonic rite.

The violent reaction against the decision of the Spalatan synod concerning the use of the Slavonic liturgy illustrates its popularity among the people and some of the nobility. It seems also to have slowed down the anti-Slavonic campaign. Another synod held at Spalato in 1075, under the chairmanship of Gerard, Archbishop of Siponto,[38] legate of Gregory VII, confirmed the restoration of the bishopric of Nin,[39] but did not renew the decree prohibiting the

Slavonic liturgy.[40] The Slavonic liturgy continued to exist through the eleventh and twelfth centuries, despite the animosity of a great part of the Latin clergy. Thomas, a thirteenth-century writer, testifies in his Salonitan history not only to this animosity, but also to the liturgy's continued existence.

Even the Latin bishops seem to have tolerated the Slavonic liturgy, because it has survived down to our own days, mostly on the Dalmatian islands and in the neighborhood of the coastal cities. These were of course losing their Latin character as the Croat population replaced the natives. The existence of the Slavonic liturgy can even be traced in former Pannonian Croatia. After the extinction of the national dynasty, the Hungarian King St. Ladislas was elected King of Croatia. He founded a new Croat diocese in Zagreb[41] about the year 1093. The first bishop was Duh, a Czech. It was thought that the new bishop was a Benedictine monk who had been expelled from the Abbey of Sázava in Bohemia when the Slavonic monks were replaced by Germans. This supposition cannot be substantiated, although traces of the existence of the Slavonic liturgy in the new diocese seem to have been found.[42]

✳ ✳ ✳

In the meantime a legend was developing in Croatia which was destined to save the Slavonic liturgy. The memory of St. Methodius and his brother was fading away increasingly in the minds of the Slavonic clergy. They remembered, however, that the great Latin father, St. Jerome, was a native of Dalmatia. The invention of the glagolitic letters and the translation of the Latin Mass into Slavonic was therefore ascribed to him. He was a better patron saint than Methodius, who was compared with Ulphila, the Arian bishop of the Goths, by the enemies of the Slavonic liturgy. In spite of the apparent clumsiness of such a switch in tradition, the legend took firm roots in the twelfth century and was also accepted in Rome as an historical fact.

This is shown by the rescript which Pope Innocent IV addressed to Philip, Bishop of Senj. He was sent in 1247 by Ugrin, Archbishop of Spalato, to Lyons, where the pope was staying, in order to receive the pallium for his metropolitan. The bishop profited by the occasion to obtain from the pope confirmation for the Slavonic liturgy which was used in his diocese. The confirmation was granted in the following words:[43]

> In the petition you presented to us, it is said that in Sclavonia there existed a special alphabet which the clerics of that land were using in the celebration of the divine office, affirming that they had it from St. Jerome. Therefore you asked and prayed our permission to celebrate the divine office in the said letters, in order to conform to these priests and to the custom of the land where you are acting as bishop. Thus, we give you through the authority of this letter the permission asked for, well aware of the principle that the letter is subject to the matter and not the matter to the letter, but only in those parts where, according to the above-mentioned custom, it is observed, on condition that the meaning shall not be disturbed because of the use of different letters.

This rescript is still regarded as the *Magna Carta* of the Slavonic liturgy in Croatia. The contact during the Crusades of Western Christians with Eastern Christians using different liturgies in different languages helped to change the rigid mentality of the Roman Curia. Canon Nine[44] of the Fourth Lateran Council of 1215 ordered that all the different rites, languages, and customs in countries where they exist side by side should be respected, and invited the bishops to provide priests who would serve the faithful according to the liturgies and languages to which they were accustomed. This was the great achievement which saved the Slavonic liturgy inherited by the Croats from SS. Constantine-Cyril and Methodius. The Slavonic liturgy, originally permissible only for the diocese of Senj, soon spread also to the ecclesiastical districts of Spalato and Aquileia.[45]

✢ ✢ ✢

The cultural innovations of the two Greek brothers constituted a generous present to the Slavic nations. Rome endeavored to use this gift in order to bring the newly-converted Slavs in Central Europe closer to herself. The attempt, boldly initiated by Hadrian II and John VIII, was abandoned, and the Slavic letters and liturgy were rejected as a means of propagating the Catholic faith among the Slavs by using their language.

This was, however, not the end. The work of Constantine-Cyril and Methodius, rejected by the West, was saved by the Bulgarians, and became a medium by which Byzantium was to tie the majority of the Slavic nations to its culture and Church. The disciples of the two brothers, exiled from Moravia, were instrumental in this operation.

The *Life of Clement,* the most prominent among these disciples, is the most important source allowing us to follow this transformation in its first stages. The work is attributed to Theophylactus, Archbishop of Bulgaria, and was written in Greek in the eleventh century. It is, however, based on an earlier Slavonic *Vita,* composed in the tenth century in Bulgaria by a disciple of Clement.[46]

The *Vita* is also often called *Bulgarica,* because from the beginning of his writing, even when describing the activity of the two brothers, its author only has Bulgarian interests in mind. Cyril and Methodius had invented the alphabet and translated the Holy Writ and the liturgical books only for the Bulgarians. Although the *Lives* of Constantine-Cyril and Methodius—which are also used by the author—do not say anything about their activities in Bulgaria, the author of Clement's *Vita* attributes the conversion of the first Christian ruler of Bulgaria, Boris-Michael, to Methodius (chapter four).

We learn from the author (chapter fifteen) that one group of the refugees, consisting of Clement and his companions Naum and Angelarius, after having been expelled and deprived of everything, even of their clothing, found a temporary refuge in the house of a Moravian noble somewhere between Nitra and the Danube river. They are said to have resuscitated the dead son of their host by their prayers. The fact that they were well received by a wealthy Moravian indicates that other disciples of Methodius could also have found shelter with Moravian nobles who favored the Slavonic liturgy.

Provided with the necessary means, the three disciples continued on their way and reached the banks of the Danube. After constructing a raft, they gained the other side and were on territory which belonged to Bulgaria. Following the river, they came to Belgrade and were well received by the commander of this fortress, called Boritakan[47] by the author. When he learned of their fate and of their condition, the governor sent them to Boris, "knowing that Boris thirsted after such men."

The welcome the three refugees received in Bulgaria does not

necessarily mean that Boris had met Methodius when the latter
was returning from Constantinople. When the strained relationship between Great Moravia and Bulgaria is borne in mind, we
can understand that any refugees from Moravia were welcome in
Bulgaria.

Boritakan is said to have despatched the disciples to Boris because he knew that the latter "had very much desired to have
such men" (chapter sixteen). If this report is interpreted in a
strict sense, it could indicate that Boris knew about the work of
the two Greeks in Moravia, and that he was well aware of the
advantages which such men could bring to his country. His hesitation between Byzantium, the Franks, and Rome seems to indicate that he did not feel happy with the presence of Greek, Latin,
and Frankish priests in his country. Although he must have
known of the "bargain"[48] concluded between the Byzantines and
Rome, he not only continued to retain Greek clergy, but limited
himself to answering the papal exhortations to return to the
Roman obedience by sending cordial greetings and assurances
that he was well and hoped that the pope was too.[49]

❉ ❉ ❉

In any event, the presence of three learned priests celebrating
the liturgy in Slavonic must have given him the idea that they
might provide the right solution for his problem: the formation of
a Slavic clergy with a national liturgy. It appears that this idea
also found sympathy with some of his nobles. The hagiographer
reports that one of the nobles, called Eschatzes,[50] asked Boris to
allow Clement and Naum to stay in his house. Angelarius found a
home in the house of another noble, Caslav, but only for a short
time, because he died exhausted by the sufferings he endured in
Moravia and on the long journeys.

We do not learn from the *Vita* how long Clement and Naum
spent in the neighborhood of Boris' residence. We are also ignorant of the fate of Laurentius and some of the other disciples of
Methodius, who must also have reached Bulgaria by another
route. The refugees separated after reaching the Danube and
travelled in groups. The chronicler is interested primarily in the
life of Clement.

It appears that Boris soon realized that it would be better if the Slavic nucleus for the formation of a native clergy were created, not in the center of his country, but in distant Macedonia. We know that Boris still encountered opposition to his policy among his Bulgar nobles of Turkic origin. They defended their rights to a share in the government of the country. In order to strengthen his own position, Boris favored the new nobles of Slavic origin. However, he did not want to antagonize the Turkic nobles, who would be suspicious of a Slavic literary circle established in their midst. On the other hand, the Greek clergy in Bulgaria would naturally see in such activity near the residence of the ruler a threat to diminish their influence in the country. Even among the Greek clergy in Bulgaria there may have been clerics who pretended that the liturgy should not be celebrated in the vernacular. Moreover, Christianity was not yet as solidly established in Macedonia as in the center of the country. Boris could only hope that the preaching of the faith in the native language would speed up the Christianization of these remote regions.

Boris provided well for Clement in this task. The hagiographer says that he established Clement in Kutmičevitsa, which he separated from the whole district of Kotokion, and that he put Dobeta[51] in charge of it. The latter was most probably asked to relieve Clement of material and administrative preoccupations. Clement was given three large houses in Devol and two places at Ochrida and Glavinitsa. Devol and Glavinitsa no longer exist, a circumstance which makes difficult a more precise delimitation of the region which was entrusted to Clement's missionary activity.[52]

From the description of Clement's evangelizing missions it is clear that the region was still pagan to a great extent, and that Boris was well inspired in sending there a missionary who could preach and teach in the language of the natives. Besides preaching, Clement devoted himself to the formation of a Slavic school for native candidates to the priesthood. He started teaching at the level of primary schools, choosing more advanced students for preparatory schools for the priesthood, and encouraged the most advanced and talented to indulge in independent writing and speculation. In this way he trained about 3,500 disciples, whom he sent in groups of about three hundred into the twelve regions which were entrusted to him to instruct.

Priests, deacons, and lectors were ordained from their numbers, and many of them most probably went to other regions also. Even if the number of disciples seems to be exaggerated by the chronicler, Clement's activity and his success were outstanding. The author also discloses that Clement had chosen from among his most advanced disciples those who became his intimate collaborators and teachers. The author of the Slavonic *Life of Clement* was one of them. So also was the author of the *Life of Naum* and Bishop Marko, the fourth Bulgarian bishop of the Slavonic liturgy. Boris exempted Clement's disciples from all obligations to the state in order that they might devote all their energies and time to preaching and teaching.

This work lasted for seven years. According to the Greek author of the *Legend*, Boris died in the eighth year of Clement's work (893) and was succeeded by his son Vladimir. After four years Vladimir was replaced by his brother Symeon. It is difficult to explain how the author could have made such an erroneous statement. Boris resigned his throne in 888–889 and became a monk. His older son Vladimir was, however, less favorable to Christianity and looked for support for his policy among the Turkic boyars who were still pagans. Boris, seeing that his son was ruining his work, left his monastery, gathered his faithful boyars around him, deposed his son, blinded him, and put him in prison. After defeating Vladimir's supporters, Boris convoked an assembly of boyars from the whole kingdom and proclaimed his younger son Symeon as ruler over Bulgaria.[53] This happened in 892–893. Boris retired again to the monastery which he had built near Preslav, and there he died on May 2, 907. We can attribute this error to the Greek author of the *Vita* who, writing in the eleventh century, had no clear picture of the history of the Bulgarian empire before its destruction by the Byzantines.

* * *

We do not know whether the activity of Clement and of his disciples was affected during the short reign of Vladimir. In any event Symeon, the new ruler, appreciating Clement's ability to Christianize the remote regions of Macedonia, established him as Bishop of Drembitsa and Velitsa (chapter twenty). Clement thus became the first Slavonic bishop in Bulgaria. The two localities no longer exist, but it seems certain that the newly-established diocese comprised most of the territory of southwest Macedonia where Clement had worked.[54]

His see must have been at an easy distance from Ochrida, where Clement had already built a monastery during the reign of Boris and where he often stayed with his disciples, who were members of the literary school he had founded. The biographer praises Clement's literary and pastoral activities in Ochrida, where three churches were built, and in the rest of his diocese. Anxious to help his people in their material welfare, Clement taught them how to improve their arboriculture by grafting on to their wild fruit trees good shoots brought from Greece (chapter twenty-three). Symeon refused to give him permission to retire from his episcopal office. Clement obeyed, but died soon after in his monastery in Ochrida in 916.

Clement was the most prominent among the disciples of Methodius who had sown the seed of the Gospel in Bulgaria. Another zealous worker was Naum. His short Slavonic *Vita* says very little of Naum's activity before 893. It seems that he was charged by Boris to collect young Slavic men and instruct them in the monastery of Panteleimon, which he had founded. Symeon, who had been educated in Constantinople, seems also to have been a member of the academic circle formed there. Two other prominent members were Bishop Constantine and the monk Tudor. Naum himself did not develop any literary activity. He limited himself to teaching and to encouraging others to write. Until 893 his interest was limited to northeastern Bulgaria.

A change in his activity was inaugurated by Symeon. His biographer says that after Symeon had appointed Clement bishop, he sent Naum from Preslav to southwest Macedonia to replace Clement as a teacher to the natives. He taught for seven years and built a monastery of the Holy Archangels on Lake Ochrida, which is called White Lake. After these seven years he entered the monastery, where he lived for ten years, taking monastic vows at the end of his life. He died there on December 23, 906. He was buried by Clement, who died in 916. Naum was soon venerated as a saint, and the name of the monastery which he had built, and which still exists, was changed to that of its founder.

In this way two important Slavic literary schools had been formed in Bulgaria, in Ochrida and in Preslav. That of Ochrida, founded by Clement, was the first and he was its foremost writer. He was most probably the author of the *Life of St. Methodius*, which he had written when still in Moravia. From this school there also emanated three original writings, the *Life of Clement*, now lost, the short *Life of Naum*, and the *Defense of Slavic Letters* composed by the monk Chrabr. Clement himself was anxious to provide his disciples with homiletic literature which they needed for their pastoral work. He adapted from the Greek numerous sermons for the liturgical year, in honor of the Virgin Mary, of St. John the Baptist, the Prophets, the Apostles, and the Martyrs. He also composed *Lives* of the Holy Fathers, translated their homilies, and wrote liturgical hymns for the divine service held in Slavonic.[55] The other school at Preslav, initiated by Naum, only became more productive after 893.

❖ ❖ ❖

The question arises as to the attitude of the Byzantine Church to the massive introduction of the Slavic language into the liturgy. It is very often thought that the Greek clergy was hostile to these innovations. As an argument for this hostility the *Defense of Slavic Letters* by the monk Chrabr is still quoted. It seems, however, that this *Defense* was not addressed directly to the Greek opponents of the Slavonic liturgy. This composition appears to be connected with a great innovation which was introduced into Bulgaria in 893, namely, the replacement of the glagolitic alphabet by the Cyrillic, which is still used by the Eastern Slavs.

Before the arrival of Methodius' disciples in Bulgaria, Greek was the official language at court and in the Church. Greek letters were used in the transcription of Slavic names. Greek letters were, however, inadequate to express all the sounds of the Slavic language. The glagolitic alphabet expressed all the particularities of the Slavic spoken language, but its letters were unfamiliar to the Bulgarian Slavs. So it came about that the Greek uncial letters were used by some Slavic writers, and the adapted Greek alphabet was augmented by new letters in order to express all the Slavic sounds, under the inspiration of the glagolitic alphabet. This transformation was worked out in the school of Preslav and found wide reception in the center of the Bulgarian Empire. It can be assumed that it was also favored by the Greeks because it presented a kind of compromise in the revolutionary development which was going on in Bulgaria.

Clement and his school with Naum defended, however, the traditions of SS. Cyril and Methodius and insisted that the glagolitic alphabet should be kept in Bulgaria also. If this is so, then we can, perhaps, explain why Clement did not become a trusted counsellor of the new ruler Symeon, who had obtained his entire education in Constantinople and was a great promoter of Slavic letters. Because of his opposition to this innovation, Clement preferred to work in the remote part of Velika in Macedonia, where he was also joined by Naum.[56]

The *Defense of Slavic Letters* composed in Clement's school should therefore be regarded as a defense of the glagolitic alphabet against the new alphabet which is called Cyrillic,[57] although Constantine-Cyril had nothing to do with its composition. It is logical to suppose that this innovation was sanctioned by Boris and the assembly convoked by him in 893. Some think that the Slavonic liturgy was imposed at the same time, throughout the Bulgarian Church. This seems, however, hardly possible. In 893 the Greek clergy was still needed in many parts of Bulgaria because the number of native clergy, although considerable thanks to the work of Clement, Naum, and the school of Preslav, was not yet large enough to replace the Greek clergy. The introduction of the Slavonic liturgy in all the Bulgarian churches could only have been realized gradually during the reign of Symeon as the number of Slavic priests increased.

❖ ❖ ❖

This kind of compromise could be accepted by the Greeks. Seeing that it was not possible to preserve the dominant position of the Greek language in the State and the Church, the Byzantines seem to have contented themselves by attaching the Bulgars to their culture.[58] In this respect the Slavic school in Constantinople, initiated by Methodius and Photius in 882, most probably played an important role. The priest and deacon left in Constantinople by Methodius were most probably joined by other clerics working among the Slavs. Their number increased considerably in 886 when the imperial envoy brought from Venice other Slavic clerics freed from slavery. One can suppose that Symeon, while studying in Constantinople, also frequented this circle. The Byzantine civil and religious authorities were determined to use in Bulgaria the members of this school who were impregnated with Byzantine culture.

There were certainly some clerics who were sent to Bulgaria soon after 886. The most prominent among them was the priest Constantine who probably came to Bulgaria in 887 with Symeon himself.[59] He lived in the monastery of St. Panteleimon, where he had met Naum. He confessed in the introduction to his explanation of the Gospels[60] that he started his literary career at the exhortation of Naum. Constantine seems to have been the main promoter of the replacement of the glagolitic letters by the Cyrillic alphabet. He most probably did so at the invitation of Symeon. The latter was thoroughly permeated with Greek culture and letters, and it was natural that he should prefer a Slavonic alphabet similar to the Greek, which was so familiar to him, and that he found the glagolitic letters too strange and difficult. Constantine also had occasion, during his stay in Constantinople, to see the advantage of inventing an alphabet similar to the Greek uncial letters. Clement and Naum lacked this experience, and they preferred to use the letters to which they were accustomed and which were invented by their beloved master Constantine-Cyril.

So it came about that both alphabets were used in Bulgaria in the ninth and tenth centuries. The priest Constantine manifested his respect for the glagolitsa when using the acrostichon of glagolitic letters in his *Alphabetic Prayer*.[61]

❖ ❖ ❖

Constantine, who later became a bishop, was one of the most prominent writers of the school of Preslav. Besides the writings already mentioned, he translated the catechesis of Cyril of Jerusalem and the apologetic treatises against the Arians of St. Athanasius. He most probably also translated the homilies of St. Gregory the Theologian (of Nazianzus). It was perhaps in deference to the memory of his master Constantine-Cyril, who greatly venerated this saint and who is said to have memorized his writings, that Constantine chose the works of St. Gregory for his translation.

His contemporary, John the Exarch, representative of the patriarch, translated a part of the Byzantine handbook of dogmatic theology, the *Source of Knowledge* of St. John the Damascene. His *Hexameron* reveals more originality, but even in this work he follows the composition of similar works by John Chrysostom, St. Basil, and other Greek fathers.

The priest Gregory prepared a new translation of the five books of Moses, Joshua, Judges, and Ruth. It was a kind of revision of Methodius' translation, characterized by a Bulgarization of the Macedonian and Moravian words used in the original translation which Gregory corrected according to the Greek text.

The inspiration for this activity at Preslav was Symeon. He himself translated extracts from the homilies of St. John Chrysostom. This collection is called *Zlatostruj* (Gold Flow). On his orders members of the school of Preslav composed a *Sbornik*, a very rich collection of sayings and writings of Greek and Latin fathers and other writers, with a short chronicle.

The translation of the *Chronicle of Malalas* by the priest Gregory became a handbook of history for the new Bulgarian intelligentsia. The same author also translated for Symeon a romantic tale of Troy. These works of more secular taste were followed by the translation of a collection called *Hellenic and Roman Chronograph*, the *Palaia*, an abridged version of the Bible with many extracts from Apocryphal literature which was very popular in Bulgaria, and by the translation of the *Physiologus*, which became a popular handbook of natural science in Bulgaria, as it was also in the West during the Middle Ages.

It can be supposed with good reason that the two Slavic schools in Bulgaria, especially that of Preslav, were in touch with the kind of school which continued to exist in Constantinople. It was this center which provided the Bulgarian translators with Greek originals.

So it came about that Christianity in Bulgaria was byzantinized. It preserved its Byzantine character in spite of the introduction of the Slavonic language into the liturgy. Even in other cultural aspects Bulgaria remained in the sphere of Byzantine intellectual development. Not even the wars with Byzantium victoriously conducted by Symeon, and later by Samuel, could change this. Bulgaria was a Slavic counterpart of the Greek Byzantium, and Byzantium profited greatly from the toleration of Slavic letters and liturgy during the first stage of the Bulgarian Christianity.

❄ ❄ ❄

As we have seen, the Serbian Slavs were converted to Christianity under initiatives coming from Byzantium. The conversion of the Slavs of the ancient Roman province of Praevalis was initiated by priests from the Latin coastal cities. Their activity extended even to Raška—Serbia proper. The Greek metropolitan of Dyrrhachium worked, on the other side, on the conversion of the Slavs in the ancient province of Epirus Vetus.[62] There were also two Bulgarian bishoprics which were nearest to Serbian territory—Belgrad and Morava-Braničevo. Some Christian influence might have come to the Serbians also from this side. However, among the Bulgarian bishoprics erected by the Patriarch Ignatius after 870, there was no see for the Serbians.[63]

The situation in Serbia proper was clarified when, after the dynastic troubles between the sons of Vlastimir—Mutimir, Strojnik, and Gojnik—Peter (892–917), son of Gojnik, had become ruler. He extended Serbian domination over the Narentans.

During the Bulgaro-Byzantine wars under Symeon the sympathies of the Serbs were rather with Byzantium. A result of this was the occupation of Serbia by Symeon. The latter, who called himself Tsar of Bulgaria and Byzantium, created the Bulgarian Patriarchate in about 925 [64] and introduced profound changes into the ecclesiastical organization of the countries under his sway. Probably about the same time he founded for the Serbs the special bishopric of Rasa (Ras, Raška, modern Novi Pazar). It was at this time, at the latest, that the Serbs were acquainted with the Byzantine liturgy in the Slavonic language. Rasa and Braničevo remained under the jurisdiction of Ochrida even after the suppression of the Bulgarian patriarchate by Basil II and the erection of an autonomous archbishopric of Ochrida, only nominally subject to the Patriarch of Constantinople. In spite of the attempts at the Hellenization of the Bulgarian Church by the victorious Byzantines, the Slavonic liturgy could not be eliminated.

* * *

During the eleventh century the bishoprics of Dioclea, Scutari (Skadar), Drivasto, and Pulati were restored, and—as we have seen—Dyrrhachium claimed jurisdiction over them. Dyrrhachium must also have claimed jurisdiction over some of the bishoprics in the part of Bulgaria which later became a Byzantine province after the subjection of the Macedonian Tsardom of Samuel. The Chrysobull of Basil II of 1020[65] confirmed the autonomous status of the Archbishopric of Ochrida, and subordinated to it all the bishoprics previously under the Bulgarian patriarchate since the reign of Symeon, Peter, and Samuel. This document contains the following "admonitions" addressed to the Metropolitan of Dyrrhachium:

"We command the Metropolitan of Dyrrhachium to be quiescent only on his throne, to be satisfied with his property and goods and not to trespass into the bishoprics of Bulgaria." This indicates clearly that the metropolitan of Dyrrhachium wanted to "annex" to his metropolitan jurisdiction some of the bishoprics from the suppressed Bulgarian patriarchate which the emperor subordinated in this Chrysobull to the Archbishop of Ochrida.

This admonition follows the enumeration of four bishoprics subordinated to Ochrida by the emperor: Ras, Oreja, Černik, and Chimara. It seems reasonable to suppose that Dyrrhachium claimed jurisdiction over the Serbian bishopric at Ras, and the three others which should be situated in what is today Central Albania.[66] The claims of the metropolis of Dyrrhachium over the whole coastal region were challenged by Latin foundations on the Adriatic coast. The Latin offensive started as early as 928 when the second synod of Spalato decided to erect a new bishopric, that of Stagno. At the same time, besides the bishoprics of Iader, Arbo, Veglia, and Apsaron, those of Stagno, Ragusa, and Cattaro were also subordinated to Spalato. However, the jurisdiction of Spalato could not be extended further down the coast and into the interior of the future Serbia, because it was soon arrested by two other growing Latin Sees—those of Antibari and of Ragusa.

❖ ❖ ❖

Dioclea, Scodra, and Dulcigno, although claimed by Dyrrhachium, were also Latin foundations, but under Byzantine supremacy. Just as, farther north, Spalato and Zara with their Latin culture attracted the Croats, so, in the South, the Latin coastal cities were an attraction for the Slavic tribes of the future Serbia and their rulers. Their importance increased when these Slavs won their independence from Byzantium.

The first attempt at the creation of a Serbian state was made not in the interior of the future Serbia, where Serbian Župans ruled under Byzantine supremacy with their religious center in Ras, but in the south, in the land of Dioclea, Tribunje, and Zachlumja. The Župan Vojislav revolted against the Byzantines and gained independence for his lands in 1042. The Latin coastal cities were included in his new state. His successor, Michael, stabilized the situation, and Michael's son Constantine Bodin added new territories to his realm, thus extending his sway over Rascia with its center in Ras, over Bosnia and, in the south, as far as the river Drin. Michael already called himself King of Dioclea.[67]

This, of course, also meant a change in the ecclesiastical policy of the new rulers. The ecclesiastical supremacy of Dyrrhachium was ended, and this situation was exploited by Antibari, the most important Latin religious center in the kingdom of Dioclea. Its Bishop Peter obtained from Pope Alexander II the promotion of his see to a Metropolis (1067) with supremacy over the bishoprics of Dioclea, Cattaro, Dulcigno, Suacia (Svač), founded about 1030, Scodra, Drivasto, Pulati, Serbia (Ras), Bosnia, and Trebinje.

The list of bishoprics enumerated in the papal bull is interesting. It reveals the progress of the Christianization of the Slavs for whom two new bishoprics were erected, those of Bosnia and of Trebinje. This was the work of Latin priests. On the other hand, the list shows that the bishopric of Ras which, according to Byzantine canon law, was subject to the archbishopric of Ochrida and was of the Eastern rite, was put under the jurisdiction of a Latin metropolitan. The Slavonic liturgy of the Eastern rite was practiced in Rascia. It may also have penetrated into the interior of the kingdom of Dioclea, because the pope made special mention in his bull that the Metropolitan of Antibari should administer all Latin and Greek and Slavic ecclesiastical institutions.

The first Serbian state was thus tri-liturgical. The Latin element, although numerically inferior to the Slavic population, predominated. It was in the interest of the Serbian rulers to support the Latins. Michael obtained his royal title from Pope Gregory VII. Michael and Bodin supported the claim of the Metropolitan of Antibari to possess jurisdiction over the coastal cities against the claims of Ragusa, which became a metropolis in 1022. Bodin obtained a new bull from the anti-pope Clement III in 1088 which confirmed the rights of Antibari.

The kingdom of Dioclea did not enjoy its freedom for long. Bodin was defeated and captured by the Emperor Alexius I (1081–1118). Bodin's dynasty continued to govern the land, but under Byzantine sovereignty. Alexius and his second successor, Manuel Comnenus (1143–1180), also frustrated the attempts of the Župans of Rascia to lead the Serbians to independence.

* * *

However, this setback did not change considerably the religious situation in Rascia and Dioclea. This is illustrated by the fact that Stephen Nemanja (ca. 1166–1196), who became the real founder of the medieval Serbian kingdom, was baptized by a Latin priest in the former Dioclean kingdom. When he was a young man, he returned to Rascia, and the Bishop of Ras introduced him to Orthodoxy by anointing him according to the rite of the Orthodox Church.[68] After becoming Župan of Rascia, Nemanja occupied the territory of the kingdom of Dioclea with Ulcinium (Dulcigno), Antibari, Cattaro, and other Latin cities, with the exception of Ragusa, which resisted him successfully.[69]

During his struggle for freedom against the Byzantines, Nemanja needed help from the West. The Latin bishoprics could serve as useful intermediaries between his realm and the papacy, which was the leading power in the West. Unfortunately Rome failed to appreciate the new situation. The growth of Ragusa impressed the Roman See and, instead of restoring the prestige of Antibari which was in Nemanja's realm, Popes Alexander III (1167) and Clement III (1188) confirmed the claims of Ragusa to primacy over the coastal cities, including Antibari. Clement IV introduced the Archbishop of Ragusa as Metropolitan over all bishoprics in Dioclea, Serbia, and Hum. Even the bishopric of Ras was intended to be included in this jurisdiction.

This was a gross misinterpretation of the new situation. The new rulers would have preferred the promotion of Antibari, which was incorporated in their realm, as Metropolitan over the Latin coastal bishoprics. On the other hand, the center of the Serbian state was then not Dioclea, but Rascia, where the bishopric of Ras was the national religious center.

* * *

This mistake was corrected by Innocent III at the request of Stephen's brother Vlkan, to whom the successor of Nemanja had entrusted the administration of the former kingdom of Dioclea. Vlkan even tried, with the help of the Hungarian king Emmerich, to depose his brother and to become king over the whole of Serbia. In order to win over Rome he promised to submit his country to the Roman obedience.

With the help of the Bulgarians, Stephen forced Vlkan to submit, and Sava succeeded in reconciling his two brothers. Roman prestige was, however, also very high in Stephen's eyes. This is documented by his request to the pope to send him a royal crown; in 1218 Innocent III sent a cardinal to Serbia to perform the coronation.

In spite of this promising development, Rome lost Serbia when, in the year after the coronation, the Byzantine patriarch residing in Nicaea consecrated Sava as first Archbishop of Serbia, and the Serbian Church became autonomous. One of the main reasons for the new development was Stephen's desire to free Ras from the jurisdiction of Ochrida, under which Ras was still placed, according to the canon law of the Eastern Church. Ochrida was, at that time, in the hands of Theodore, who established himself as Despot of Epirus after the destruction of the Byzantine Empire by the crusaders in 1204, and was on hostile terms with Stephen.

Another very important reason which explains the failure of the papacy in Serbia, despite promising developments and its prestige, was the fact that Ras was able to transmit to the Serbians Slavonic liturgy and letters inherited from Ochrida. This proved more attractive to Nemanja, Stephen, Sava, and the Serbians than the cultural influence which emanated from the Latin cities and from Rome. On this basis the Serbs were able to create in the thirteenth and fourteenth centuries a flourishing national literature inaugurated by St. Sava.[70]

So it happened that the Byzantine Church also profited from the Cyrilo-Methodian inheritance in Serbia. Rome had rejected it, and was therefore at a great disadvantage when trying to win over other Slavic nations. If Rome had been able to offer the Serbians what SS. Cyril and Methodius had invented for the Slavic nations, it is possible that Serbia would have developed in a Western religious and cultural atmosphere.

IX. Byzantium and the Cyrilo-Methodian Heritage in Kievan Russia

Eastern Slavic tribes among the last to be Christianized; Armenian and Georgian claim to apostolic origin of their Churches— St. Andrew and Scythia—Future Russia—Slavic tribes approaching the Crimea; the Byzantines and the Slavs on the Dnieper— influence of the Khazars on the Slavs—Christianity among the Slavs around Don river?; Byzantine mission in Kuban—First contact of Byzantium with the Rhos—Attack on Constantinople; first Christianization of Kiev; its ruin and survival—Baptism of Olga; her message to Otto the Great—Vladimir's conversion; introduction of Slavonic liturgy—Main features of Kievan literary school— Characteristic traits of Kievan Christianity—St. Vladimir a new Constantine, isoapostolos—Byzantine impact on Russian art— Russian and Byzantine jurisprudence—Byzantine political ideas and Russia; Moscow a Third Rome.

The Slavic tribes, which were to become the nucleus from which the immense political unit known as modern Russia was formed, were among the last of the Slavic family to be introduced into the orbit of Christian influence. This seems rather strange when we take into consideration the fact that the southern lands which are now part of the modern Russian state were the nearest to that most important Christian center in the East, Constantinople, which had Christian outposts, not only in the Crimea, but also in the Caucasus. The Transcaucasian lands of Georgia and Armenia were the intermediaries between Asia Minor, where Christianity predominated in its early history, and the cradle of

259

Christianity in Palestine. Both lands claimed that Christianity had been implanted in the midst of their populations in the time of the Apostles. The Armenians appropriated the Apostles Bartholomew, Judas Thaddaeus, and Simon as their first teachers and patrons,[1] but they had competitors in Edessa, Syria, Mesopotamia, Phoenicia, and Persia who made the same claims. It is, however, possible that Christianity had already penetrated into Armenia during the first century A.D. Traces of Christianity are reported in the second century, and the christianization was brought to an end by Gregory the Illuminator (240–320), who had also won over King Tiridat I to the new faith. Armenia was also the first land which declared Christianity to be the official religion of the state (about 280). Gregory also became the head of the Armenian Church, as *Catholicos* with twelve suffragan bishops. The Catholicos Sahak, with the help of Mezrob, invented, in about the year 396, a special alphabet for their language, a deed which became the source of a flourishing Armenian literature.

Georgia[2] possessed numerous Jewish Diaspora which seems to have been strengthened by refugees after the destruction of Jerusalem. Lively contacts with Palestine and Syria opened the land for Christian missionaries as early as the first century. During the reign of Constantine the Great the country was Christian, and the Christian religion was declared the official religion of the state between 297 and 356. Its religious center in Mzchet was in touch with all the important eastern Christian centers, and Georgian monachism developed lively missionary activities.

Justinian the Great supported Christian missionaries in the Caucasian region, especially among Ossetes, Alans, and Abasques, and even the Huns are said to have been touched by Christian propaganda.[3]

❈ ❈ ❈

The claims of the Armenians to the apostolic origins of their conversion are doubtful, as is well known. However, the claim of the Russians that their land had been at least touched upon by an apostle before the Slavs came there may have more solid basis. There is a tradition codified by the first Church historian, Eusebius of Caesarea, and based on the report given by Origen (died 253) that the Apostle Andrew had preached the new faith in

Scythia.⁴ There were two Scythias, one between Thrace and the Danube which had become a Roman province (modern Dobrudsha), and another Scythia, called "cold," which lies between the rivers Danube and Don in modern southern Russia. We are entitled to suppose that Origen had in mind the "cold Scythia," and this seems to be suggested also by the apocryphal *Acts of Andrew.* According to them, Andrew preached first in Asia Minor with his brother Peter. This could be so because the cities of Asia Minor possessed strong Jewish colonies. Jewish propaganda was successful even among the pagans. The synagogues were the first places from which the apostles began to preach about Christ. These cities, and their Jewish Diaspora, were in lively contact with the Greek cities and Jewish Diasporas in the Crimea and in the ancient Greek colonies around the Azov sea. The legendary *Acts of Andrew* allow him to come as far as Sinope, the important port of Asia Minor whence it was easy to reach the Crimea and its main port, Cherson. Andrew may have used this maritime commercial way to reach the Crimea; it is quite possible that he also touched upon the land of the Scythians, and it seems that he may even have died somewhere in these parts. There is a tradition that he returned from Cherson to Asia Minor, passed through Byzantium and travelled on to Greece, where he died as a martyr at Patras. But this should be considered as legendary. The only reliable information we have concerning Andrew's travels is that transmitted to us from Origen by the first Church historian, Eusebius, who tells us that Andrew preached the new faith in Scythia.

This tradition appears to be much more trustworthy than that of the Armenians concerning Bartholomew, Judas Thaddaeus, and Simon. Therefore, the claim made by the Russians that Andrew did visit the lands which were to become Slavic has some solid basis. The author of the *Russian Primary Chronicle* tried to make the most of this tradition about the apostle, which was increased by legend, for the glory of his nation which, when he wrote his *Chronicle* at the beginning of the eleventh century, was already Christian. There we read that "when Andrew was teaching in Sinope and came to Cherson, he observed that the mouth of the Dnieper was nearby. Conceiving a desire to go to Rome, he proceeded therefore to the mouth of the Dnieper and thence journeyed up the river and, by chance, halted upon the shore beneath the hills. He prophesied to his disciples that on that spot a great city with many churches would arise. He blessed the spot, erecting there a cross, then continued his journey to Novgorod, and, after a stay with the Varangians, reached Rome. Leaving Rome, he returned to Sinope." [5]

This last passage shows us that in the eleventh century the Russians were well acquainted with the legendary *Acts of Andrew*, which tell of his travels from Sinope to Thrace and Achaia, where he is said to have died. The chronicler had to allow Andrew to leave from Rome for Sinope in order to fit his account to that of the legendary *Acts*.

* * *

At the time the Apostle was supposed to have reached the Dnieper and travelled this river, the Slavs had not yet arrived. Some of their tribes had already left their original home between the Vistula, Oder, and Bug, and were expanding toward the territory of the Scythians, from whom they borrowed many pagan beliefs. The movement to the south was accelerated by the migration of the Germanic Goths. The first knowledge of Christianity reached the Eastern Goths (Ostrogoths) after they penetrated the Crimea, from reports of prisoners taken by them in Trebizond (between 256 and 267).[6] The Gothic Church in the Crimea maintained relations with Palestine and stayed independent of the Byzantine Church up to 451. The Western Goths (Visigoths) had already sent a bishop to the First Oecumenical Council of Nicaea (325), and Ulphila (311–381) translated the Gospels into Gothic. They adhered to the heretical doctrine of Arius, but those Goths who had remained in the Crimea professed the orthodox faith, although using Ulfila's translation. Thanks to John Chrysostom (398–404), Byzantium, for the first time, was able to play a direct role in the conversion of the peoples in the Crimea and in former Scythia. Georgian and Armenian monks brought the Christian faith to the peoples in the northern Caucasus; these missions were supported by the Emperor Justinian (527–565) who, at the same time, defended the Crimea against the Huns.

It is doubtful if any of these attempts to Christianize the lands of modern southern Russia influenced the Slavic tribes which, in the seventh century, were already firmly established on the middle Dnieper. Perhaps after the Goths had become Christian and had extended their sway over them, certain Christian elements did penetrate. On the other hand, Byzantine cultural influences did reach those Slavic tribes living in the middle Dnieper in the seventh century. Archaeological finds made in this region present very important discoveries. Hidden treasures found in Martinovka, Sjenkov, Chacki, and especially in Malaja Peresčepina and in the cemetery of Pastyrskoje, included Byzantine silver ware, ornaments, and coins in large numbers. These finds show us that trade with Byzantium existed in the sixth and seventh centuries. Broken pieces of silver and semi-manufactured objects testify that some of these pieces must have been produced on the spot by foreign or native artisans, who also made a special kind of *fibulae* (brooches) characteristic of the Dnieper region. The imported objects could have reached this area from Byzantine possessions in the Crimea, or from the cities on the Black Sea. It is of interest that some of the objects produced in the Dnieper workshops were found in the Crimea where the Goths lived. This would seem to indicate that commerce between the Slavs on the Dnieper and the Goths of the Crimea must have existed.

None of the objects discovered bears a religious character, but it is quite possible that the Slavic tribes on the Dnieper had acquired a slight knowledge of Christianity from the Christian Goths in the Crimea, and from the Byzantines living in Cherson. The finds reveal that the Slavic tribes of this region had reached a certain level of culture and had acquired a certain amount of wealth.[7] These tribes were the predecessors of that Slavic group which was to build, on the middle Dnieper, that important Slavic settlement called Kiev.

It is to be noted that the coins found in that region are of the reign of Constans II (641–668). The treasures I have described must have been buried during the second half of the seventh century, which indicates the threat of invasion, possibly from the Khazars.

� � �

This Turkic nation, whose people lived between the Don and the Caspian Sea and near the delta of the Volga, extended their domination in the sixth century toward the West.[8] They cut off the Slavic tribes on the Dnieper from the cultural Christian centers in the Crimea and succeeded in taking the city of Kerch in 576 for a short time. They extended their dominion over the Slavic tribes on the Dnieper and occupied the growing commercial and cultural region in the middle Dnieper which had developed into the flourishing city of Kiev.

Perhaps some knowledge of Christianity reached the Slavic tribes during the Khazar occupation, for the latter were in touch with the Christian Transcaucasian countries of Georgia and Armenia, and Christian merchants traded in Khazaria. From the seventh century on, the Khazars maintained friendly relations with the Byzantines as a protection from their common danger threatening from the Persians and later from the Arabs. The *Life* of St. Abo, a converted Arab who travelled in Khazaria and who died in Georgia in 786, testifies that Christian communities existed in many Khazarian cities and villages. He himself was baptized in Khazaria. The presence of Christian communities among the Khazars is confirmed also by the reports of Arab historians, especially by Idrisi and Ibn-Hauqual. But Moslem propaganda also had some success among the Khazars.[9] The Jewish Diaspora in the Crimea and in Transcaucasian cities was also very active among the Khazars, and in about the year 740 the Jews succeeded in winning over the Khagan of the Khazars to Judaism. Political reasons were behind this strange decision of the Khagan. Fearing that if he accepted either the Christian or the Islamic faith, his country would become dependent on Byzantium or on the Arabs, he chose Judaism, which also offered a higher degree of civilization than did paganism. In spite of this, the Khazars maintained a tolerant religious policy toward both Christians and Mussulmans.

❖ ❖ ❖

There are indications that Christianity in the Crimea and in the Caucasian lands flourished during the eighth century. We have but to recall the *Notitia* of bishoprics from this time, in which a number of new sees is noted in the Crimea and its neighborhood. Although these listings are unreliable, the document seems to suggest that this region was thoroughly Christianized and quite capable of launching a Christian offensive among the population on the Don and the Dnieper.[10] Unfortunately, we have no direct reports of the spread of Christianity in these lands which, at that time, were inhabited by Slavic tribes, and archaeological research has produced only vague indications of Christian life on the Don. One of them deserves a special mention. Near the confluence of the river Tichaja Sosna and the Don stands an old castle called Majackoe gorodišče. It was built on a high rock, and on one side of the rock was discovered a catacomb with two stories, connected on the interior by a corridor. The lower part of the catacomb seems to have served as a church, while the upper story revealed several cells. This may mean that the place was a monastery with a church. On the top of the rock remnants of stone buildings and fortifications were also discovered, and a cemetery with an inscription which, however, is not yet deciphered. The tombs of the cemetery can be dated from the eighth to the tenth centuries.[11]

This region was inhabited from the sixth to the ninth centuries by Slavic tribes called Antes, probably because their governing class was of non-Slavic, perhaps of Alanic or Sarmatic, origin. It is thus quite possible that in the eighth and ninth centuries the Slavic tribes on the Don came under the direct influence of Christian elements. The missionaries came probably from the Crimea. Perhaps further excavations will throw more light on this problem.

Further missionary activity from the Crimea, on the initiative of the Patriarch Photius, in the territory which was to become part of the Russian Empire, can be traced in the ninth century in the region of Kuban, among the Indo-European people of the Alans. We have seen that this mission had introduced into that territory a new type of ecclesiastical architecture which had developed in Greek provinces on the basis of early Christian church architecture.[12] But even this attempt, although very interesting and lasting over almost a century among the Alans, did not get as far as the Slavic tribes of modern southern Russia.

* * *

A direct contact with the center of Eastern Christianity was necessary in order to win over these new peoples to the faith. This was effected by another pagan nation from Scandinavia, the Varyags from Sweden, who for some time had been trading with the Khazars by means of the river Volga. These adventurers crossed even the Caspian Sea in order to reach the Arab capital of Baghdad. During their piratical and commercial expeditions they must have learned of the splendors of Constantinople and of the riches which had accumulated within her walls. The opportunity of reaching this marvellous city was offered to them after they discovered the river way to the Black Šea—the Dnieper. The discovery of this new highway was not made by Rurik (probably Roerek), the founder of the first Varyag colony in Slavic lands, later called Novgorod, but by another group of Varyags led by Askold and Dir. Together with their retinue, they subdued the Slavic tribes on the upper Dnieper and got as far as Kiev, then under Khazar rule. The Slavs welcomed the newcomers, believing them to be better protectors against the invasions of the nomadic tribes than their present rulers, and Kiev became a center of Varyag political formation on the Dnieper. The Finns called the new invaders the "Ruotsi," and the Byzantines, when they got in touch with them, adapted this word to the nature of their own language and called them the "Rhôs." [13] This name is given to the new rulers of the Slavic tribes on the Dnieper for the first time by the Byzantines in 839, as is attested in the *Annales Bertiniani.*[14] The Emperor Theophilus sent an embassy to Louis the Pious asking him to give free passage through his lands to the Rhôs, whose Khagan had sent them to Constantinople to affirm the state of peace existing between himself and the emperor. They were unable to return to their own country by the same route as it was in danger from hostile invaders. Louis the Pious, after enquiring about their homeland, found that they were from Sweden.

If this report is reliable, we can see in it the first attempt by the Rhôs to enter into peaceful relations with Byzantium. It is also possible that these envoys were in the service of the Khazar Khagan who had sent them to Constantinople. However, the title of Khagan, as given to the chief of the Rhôs, could also have been used by Askold of Kiev, although borrowed from the Khazars.

Nevertheless, the Rhôs of Kiev got as far as the delta of the Dnieper river by the beginning of the ninth century, at the latest. There are reports of their attempting to attack the Byzantine cities in the Black Sea basin. The *Life of St. Stephen of Surož*

(Sugdaea) tells of an attack against Sugdaea in the Crimea during the early part of the ninth century, and in the *Life of St. George of Amastris* is a description of the Rhôs plundering the city in 835. Both reports are legendary, especially the description of the miraculous intervention of the saints, who stopped or punished the attackers.[15]

* * *

The only historical expedition against Byzantium is that in June of 860. However, it could not have been organized by the Rhôs who, according to some scholars, lived on the peninsula of Taman opposite Kerch. The existence of a Russian settlement in this region is an invention of some patriotic Russian scholars who would not accept the fact that the founders of the Kievan State were Germanic Swedes, and who saw its origin in the south where the Rhôs, united with the Indo-European Alans, had founded a colony.[16]

The consequence of this incident was the sending of an embassy to the Khazars in order to renew the alliance against the new danger which threatened both Byzantium and the Khazars.[17]

Their defeat, under the walls of Constantinople, was a sharp lesson for the Rhôs and their Slavic tribes. Being pressed by the Khazars and the Byzantines, they began to entertain friendly relations with Byzantium. The Patriarch Photius, taking advantage of this change in disposition, sent missionaries to the Russians and to the peoples of the Caucasus, and the Indo-European Alans on the Kuban river appear to have been partly converted as a result. Photius' disciple, Patriarch Nicholas Mysticus, completed the work in the same area in the tenth century.[18] The missions to the Rhôs and the Slavs on the Dnieper were successful. In a letter to the Eastern patriarchs written in 867, Photius announced that the Rhôs, who were renowned for their cruelty and among the worst enemies of Byzantium, were now their friends, had accepted bishop and priest, and were showing great zeal for the Christian teaching.[19]

The bishop in question could only have resided in Kiev, where a Christian church was built and probably dedicated to the Prophet Elias. At least, such a church is mentioned in the *Russian Primary Chronicle* on another occasion. But, unfortunately, this first attempt to Christianize the Rhôs and the Slavs did not last. Jealous of the success of the Rhôs in Kiev, the Rhôs from Novgorod-Ladoga led by Oleg, a kinsman of Rurik, invaded Kiev about 882. Askold and Dir were killed, and later were venerated as martyrs by the Russians.[20] It seems that Christianity was not completely eradicated from Kiev. Constantinople attracted even the new ruler of Kiev, and we learn from the *Primary Chronicle* that Oleg concluded a treaty of friendship with Byzantium in 911, which contained stipulations regulating commercial relations between Byzantium and Kiev favorable to the Russians. On this occasion the Emperor Leo VI (886–912) is said to have presented precious gifts and relics to Oleg's envoys, and ordered that they should be instructed in the Christian faith.[21]

Commerce with Byzantium could only strengthen the remnants of Christianity in Kiev. The most zealous converts to the new faith were the Varyags, who, while trading with Byzantium, now had occasion to discover the attractions of the capital and to visit its beautiful churches.

The spread of Christianity in Kiev is illustrated by yet another trade agreement with Byzantium in 943. It was concluded after the disastrous expedition against Constantinople in 941, led by Oleg's successor, Igor. We read in the *Chronicle*[22] that the pagan Rhos were obliged to confirm the treaty on oath in Kiev, in the temple of Perun, but that the Christian Varyags took their oath in the church of St. Elias and in the Christian manner.

The growth of Christianity in Kiev explains the decision of Olga, the widow of Igor, to become a convert. She was instructed in the faith in Kiev, and in 957 went to Constantinople, where she was baptized. In his *Book of Ceremonies* Constantine Porphyrogenitus describes the honors with which she was received at court, but he does not mention her baptism. Because of this omission many scholars are of the opinion that her reception into the Church took place in Kiev, and that she was baptized by the priest Gregory, who had accompanied her on her journey to Constantinople. The imperial author described her solemn reception at the court in order to make known the manner in which a Byzantine court would receive a Russian prince, but he did not speak of her baptism, for it would be assumed that such a visitor would already be a Christian.[23]

It appears that her conversion and visit to Constantinople displeased the influential Varyags in Kiev, who feared the possibility of Byzantine political influence in their country. In order to dispel these fears and to make Christianity more acceptable to them, Olga asked the Western Emperor Otto I to send a bishop to Kiev. Here, for the first time, we notice the attraction which the West held for the Kievan State, and the oscillation of the Russians between East and West. It is possible that some of the Varyags were aware of the Western brand of Christianity. Two bishops from Hamburg-Bremen, St. Ansgar (died 865)[24] and St. Unni (died 936), were zealous missionaries who worked in Denmark, in Sweden, and especially in Roslagen in Sweden. Many of the Varyags came from that part of Sweden called Roslagen, and it is thus quite possible that they suggested to Olga that she approach the Western emperor, in order to prevent the Byzantines from becoming too powerful in Kiev.

Olga's messengers were well received at the court of Otto the Great. It had been his desire to extend his influence as far as the Slavonic lands, and he founded the metropolis of Magdeburg which, in his dreams, was destined to embrace all the Slavonic nations from the Elbe to the East, as far as his ambition would carry him. In answer to Olga's request, he sent her Bishop Adalbert, who, in company with some German priests, went to Kiev.[25]

* * *

But Olga was deposed as regent before Bishop Adalbert arrived, and her son Svjatoslav was the new master of Kiev. He was unsympathetic to Christianity in either form, East or West. He was a true Varyag, only interested in military display. He extended the Kievan State in the East on the middle Volga by defeating the Khazars and the Turkic Bulgars who had settled there. The Bulgars had become Mussulmans, and the Arab splendor which Svjatoslav found in the city of Bolgar made such an impression on him that he dreamed of transferring his capital to the Volga. This was just one more example of the attraction which Eastern civilization held for him, and there was a danger that the Russians might embrace the religion of the Prophet, should Svjatoslav reject the request of the Byzantines to help them defeat a division of the Bulgars living south of the Danube in former Byzantine territory. But Svjatoslav accepted their invitation, and was at first so successful that once more he had dreams of founding an empire, this time on the Danube. This, of course, did not suit the Byzantines, who turned against him. Defeated by them, he died on his return to Kiev.[26]

Christianity continued to exist in Kievan Russia even during the reign of Svjatoslav. There are traditions which cannot be completely substantiated, such as that Olga had built a church in Pskov,[27] a chapel over the remains of Askold and Dir,[28] and that even in Novgorod a church had been built in her lifetime.[29]

The existence of Varyag Christians in Kiev before Vladimir's conversion is attested also by the *Primary Chronicle*. We read there that, in 983[30] when Vladimir had conquered the Yatwigians, a Lithuanian tribe, he offered sacrifices to the gods for the victory. The boyars thought that the sacrifice of a maiden or a youth would be more appropriate on such an occasion. There was a certain Varangian who had emigrated from Greece and lived with his son in a house where later the church of the Holy Virgin was built. The boyars chose the boy by lot to be the object of the sacrifice. Both were Christians. When the father refused to surrender his son, the crowd invaded his house; when the father again refused, they destroyed the house and killed both of them, "and no one knows where they are buried," adds the chronicler.

The story tells of a genuine event and shows, at the same time, that Christianity attracted the Varangians and that Christian influences were coming directly from Constantinople. The martyred Varangian was evidently a merchant who, after becoming a Christian in Constantinople, had returned to Kiev for business reasons.

The definite conversion of the Russians is due to the intervention of the Byzantines. The Emperor Basil II (976–1025) was endangered by the rebellion of Bardas Phocas, a pretender to the imperial throne, and he asked Vladimir, Olga's grandson and Svjatoslav's successor, to send auxiliaries to help him crush the revolt, according to the stipulations of the treaties concluded with Oleg in 943, and with Svjatoslav in 971, after his defeat. Vladimir was willing to oblige but, as a condition, he demanded to be given in marriage an imperial princess "born in purple." The prestige of Byzantium was so great in Kiev that its ruler regarded it as the greatest honor to be related to the imperial house.

Vladimir sent six thousand Varyags to Byzantine territory in the spring of 988, where, led by the emperor, they defeated the rebels in a crushing victory. They remained in the service of the emperor to the great satisfaction of Vladimir, who did not know what to do with them. This Varangian contingent, reinforced by new arrivals from Scandinavia, became an important factor in the Byzantine army.

When, after the defeat of the insurgents, the emperor hesitated to send an imperial bride to Vladimir, the latter invaded the Byzantine territory of Crimea and occupied Cherson. Finally, the emperor yielded and sent his own sister,. Anne, daughter of the Emperor Romanus II, to Cherson. As she was "born in the purple" and the daughter of an emperor, Vladimir was satisfied. In 988 or 989 he was baptized in Cherson by its bishop, flanked by Greek priests who had accompanied the princess. Marriage followed, and Vladimir gave back the city of Cherson to his brother-in-law, the emperor, as a present.

The *Russian Primary Chronicle* reports that before deciding to abandon paganism Vladimir sent envoys to the Mussulman Bulgars, to the Jewish Khazars, to the Germans, and to Byzantium, asking them to investigate the relative merits of the religions practiced by these peoples. The envoys are said to have given a glowing description of the splendor and beauty of the liturgy they had seen and admired in the Byzantine churches. On the strength of their report, Vladimir decided to accept the eastern version of Christianity. Of course, this account is legendary, but it shows that cultural and political influences both of East and West were to be found in Kiev during the tenth century.

Western Christianity is also represented by the Germans in this account, and this recalls the hesitation of Olga between the East and the West. If we are to believe the report of the German *Annals of Lambert,* another Russian embassy went to Germany in 973 and was present at the last diet held by Otto I. This would indicate that Vladimir's brother, Jaropolk, who occupied the throne after the death of Svjatoslav, and whom Vladimir had defeated, had again reopened negotiations with Otto I, which would lead us to believe that the attraction of the Germanic West was still quite strong in Kiev.[31]

Because the *Russian Primary Chronicle* speaks of an embassy sent from Rome to Vladimir after his baptism, some scholars have assumed that Rome played a leading part in the organization of the new Kievan Church. This theory is completely unfounded. Vladimir did receive an embassy from Rome, not from the pope, but from his wife's cousin, the Empress Theophano, widow of Otto II. The sister of Basil II had not fancied her union with a barbarian. Her cousin sympathized, for she, too, had had to marry a barbarian, the son of Otto I, for political reasons. Hence she sent her relics of some saints, together with a few words of consolation. At that time, she resided in Rome with her son Otto III; if the pope had anything to do with her embassy, it was simply to send his blessing to the Russian princess and her husband.[32]

The poor imperial princess, although so disinclined to union with a barbarian, at least found consolation in the knowledge that, for her sake, her husband had dismissed his five wives and his eight hundred concubines. But this seems to be too great a number even for a pagan Varyag. Surely the chronicler must have added to these figures, perhaps to demonstrate what a miraculous transformation holy baptism could make in a pagan soul. Vladimir endeavored to console his new wife by showing her how sincerely he appreciated his new faith. First, he ordered that the statue of the Slavic supreme god Perun "should be bound to a horse's tail and dragged to the stream." He appointed twelve men to beat the idol with sticks, in order to "affront the demon who had deceived man in this guise, that he might receive chastisement at the hands of men" as the chronicler has it. After they had dragged along the idol, they cast it into the Dnieper. Vladimir then organized another exhibition in an effort to console his new wife. All the inhabitants of Kiev, rich or poor, were ordered to gather on the banks of the Dnieper. Standing beside the princess, and with the bishop and priests from Cherson, he commanded the assembled multitude to go into the water to be baptized. The chronicler describes this remarkable scene with great relish.[33]

As concerns the ecclesiastical organization of the Kievan Church, it seems that a compromise was reached by establishing the Archbishop of Cherson as a kind of supervisor of the young Russian Church. This state of affairs lasted until the reign of Jaroslav the Wise (1036–1054), on whose initiative Kiev was raised to metropolitan status. As Dimitri Obolensky suggested, it is possible that, according to an agreement concluded by the Russians with the Byzantines—probably under Jaroslav the Wise—

the metropolitan see of Kiev was to be held alternately by Greek and Russian prelates. Should a native be elected, he must be consecrated by the Patriarch of Constantinople.[34]

Although the methods adopted by Vladimir to implant Christianity were forceful, he encountered serious opposition only in Novgorod. It seems that the introduction of the Slavonic liturgy helped considerably in spreading the new faith across the Russian lands. It is not yet quite clear how and by whom Slavonic liturgy and Slavic letters were brought to Kievan Russia. In any case, Bulgarian priests were probably the most zealous propagators of Slavic letters, but we do not know when the first Slavic priests reached Kiev from Bulgaria. It was probably before the destruction of the first Bulgarian Empire by Basil II (1018). It is possible that priests from Bulgaria accompanied Svjatoslav's army on its return to Kiev from Bulgaria in 972, after its defeat by the Byzantines.

Following the destruction of the first Bulgarian Empire, the exodus to Kiev of Slavic priests from their cultural centers must have increased considerably. The refugees brought with them not only Slavic liturgical books, but all the literary achievements of Slavic schools under Tsar Symeon (893–927), and Tsar Peter (927–989). It was a great contribution to the cultural development of the Kievan State. The Byzantines appear to have favored this exodus because, in this way, they were rid of a discontented element liable to threaten their rule in the Bulgarian provinces. The Patriarchs of Constantinople, though trying to reintroduce the Greek liturgy into Bulgaria, permitted the spread of Slavonic liturgy in Kiev, which was such a great distance from Byzantium.

These works brought by the Bulgarian refugees were written in a language based on a Macedonian dialect which, however, thanks to the philological genius of Constantine-Cyril and also of Methodius, became the official language of the Bulgarian Church and of the Bulgarian intellectual elite.[35] This language imported from the Balkans also became the language of the Russian Church, and the literary language of the Russian intellectuals.

* * *

On the basis of the Old Slavonic literary treasures which had reached Kiev from Bulgaria, as well as from Bohemia, literary activity was developing. Many translations from the Greek were made in Kiev especially by the literary school of Jaroslav the Wise. They are mostly of a religious character. It is true that the Russian language developed an excellent philosophical terminology. This, however, is based not on translations of Greek philosophical works, but on Old Slavic translations of the works of the Greek Holy Fathers so familiar with classical philosophers. What a difference there is between the Russian and Arabic translations from the Greek! Before St. Thomas Aquinas, the works of Aristotle were known in the West only in Arabic translations, for the Arabs rivalled the Byzantines, not only in philosophy, but also in mathematics, geometry, and other sciences. Even the Armenians possessed translations of the works of some of the classical and Hellenistic philosophers, because they were converted to Christianity when interest in classical philosophy was very much alive in Byzantium.

In the tenth century the Byzantines were more interested in encyclopedic works, as illustrated, for example, by the literary activity of Constantine Porphyrogenitus and his circle. Because of this the Eastern Slavs became acquainted with certain sayings of Greek philosophers only from translations of encyclopedic works, particularly the Greek *Melissa* (Bee), and other similar writings. Only in historical compositions were the Kievan clergy able to develop a literature, based on the Byzantine model, and sometimes surpassing them, as we see particularly in the *Russian Primary Chronicle*. This is based on many sources, even including Scandinavian Sagas and the *Life of St. Methodius*, which had reached Kiev from Bohemia; the erudition of the compilers is genuine. It is rightly regarded as one of the best chronicles written during the Middle Ages in East and West. It became the basis of numerous local annalist compilations. Almost all Russian principalities and great cities had their own annalists. Very few Western nations possessed so many mediaeval chronicles.

Other original works were composed in Kiev or the Byzantine model—Duke Vladimir Monomach's book of instruction for his children; Abbot Daniel's description of his pilgrimage to the Holy Land; *Pecherski Paterik*, a collection of translated and original biographies; the sermons of Cyril of Turov (1185), who was compared to St. John Chrysostom; Clement Smoljatič, Metropolitan of Kiev (1147–1155), who was accused of quoting Homer, Plato, and Aristotle in his sermons. Kievan literary products show, in general, more originality than works produced by the Bulgarian literary schools.

Russian epic literature was also influenced by the translation of the great Greek epic of Digenis Akritas, describing the fight of Byzantine frontiersmen with the Arabs. The most original Kievan epic poem is the Lay of Igor's Campaign of the twelfth century.[36]

✻ ✻ ✻

We should stress yet another character of Kievan Christianity. Although the Byzantine impact on its development is incontestable and very profound, the Kievan Christians were conscious that their Church was a sister to all older Churches, and wanted to stay in union with them. This seems attested by the embassies which Vladimir is said to have sent to all famous Christian centers and shrines—to Jerusalem, Egypt (probably Alexandria), Babylon, and Rome, informing the old Christian centers that his country had entered into the Christian commonwealth.[37]

This is also indicated by the lively contact with the Bohemian Old Slavonic clergy, by the popularity which some Western saints enjoyed in the Kievan Church, by the ready acceptance of translations of Western saints,[38] and by the contact with Western Catholic courts.[39]

Another interesting and characteristic trait of Kievan Christianity is the tendency to connect its Christian origin with an apostle and with that of other Slavic nations. In this respect we find in the *Primary Chronicle* a very curious passage.[40] The author describes the requests addressed to Michael III by Rastislav, Svatopluk, and Kotsel (sic!) to send them a teacher who would reveal to them the words of the Scriptures, and how the emperor prevailed upon the sons of Leo of Thessalonica, Constantine and Methodius, to undertake the mission. He relates the discovery of the Slavic alphabet, the first translations of the Holy Book into the Slavic language, the defense of the Slavic books by Constantine, and the approval of the innovation by the pope. He even goes on: "Prince Kotsel appointed Methodius Bishop of Pannonia in the see of St. Andronicus, one of the Seventy, a disciple of the holy Apostle Paul. Methodius chose two priests who were very rapid writers, and translated the whole of the Scriptures in full from Greek into Slavic in six months between March and the twenty-sixth day of October. After completing the task, he appropriately rendered praise and honor to God, who had bestowed such a blessing upon Bishop Methodius, the successor of Andronicus. Now Andronicus is the apostle of the Slavic race. He travelled among the Moravians, and the Apostle Paul taught there likewise. For in that region is Illyricum, whither Paul first repaired and where the Slavs originally lived. Since Paul is the teacher of the Slavic race, from which the Russians too are sprung, even so the Apostle Paul is the teacher of us Russians, for he preached to the Slavic nation, and appointed Andronicus as Bishop and successor to himself among them. But the Slavs and the Russians are one people, for it is because of the Varangians that they latterly became known as Rus', though originally they were Slavs."

These passages mostly interested only Slavic historians and specialists in Old Slavonic literature, who tried to discover the probable sources used by the author of the *Primary Chronicle*. As already said, the main source of this passage is the *Life of St. Methodius*, with modifications of later Bulgarian origin to which the many inaccuracies in the recital are due. What interests us here is the insistence on the apostolic origin of the Slavic Church, on the fact that Methodius was a successor of St. Andronicus, "one of the Seventy, a disciple of the holy Apostle Paul." In his desire to bring Andronicus and his master Paul as near to the Slavs and the Russians as possible, the author invents the story that the Slavs lived primitively in Illyricum "whither Paul first repaired." Therefore St. Paul is the teacher of the Slavs and also of the Russians who are Slavs. This insistence on an apostolic origin of the Slavic Church is explained by the desire of the young Kievan Church to show that the Russians are no "poor relations" of other Christian nations, because they are entitled to claim both St. Andronicus and St. Paul as their patron saints. This is certainly an improvement on the legend about the Apostle Andrew, who is said to have travelled in Russia, but before the country was Christian.

*   *   *

This was, however, not enough. The young Kievan Church needed also to exalt its first Christian ruler who was, on his merits, not inferior to the first Byzantine Christian ruler, St. Constantine the Great.

This idea inspired the Metropolitan of Kiev Ilarion (Hilarion) who, about the middle of the eleventh century, composed the famous *Treatise on Law and Grace,* one of the most remarkable writings of the Kievan period. After discussing God's plan of human salvation—first the Mosaic Law and Jewish history, then its realization through the Savior, the source of grace—Ilarion enumerates the main nations and their Christian teachers in the following way:[41]

> With grateful voices the Roman land praises Peter and Paul, through whom it was induced to believe in Jesus Christ, the Son of God; Asia and Ephesus, John the Theologian of Patmos; India, Thomas; Egypt, Mark—all these countries, cities, and peoples, venerate and praise the teachers who instructed each of them in the orthodox faith. Let even us thus praise with modest paeans our great miraculous [man] who became our teacher and instructor, the great Khagan of our land—Vladimir.

Then Ilarion describes the virtues of the first Russian Christian ruler in the spirit of treatises on kingship, preserved from the Hellenistic and Byzantine periods, which praised the king as benefactor of his people. Byzantine inspiration is even more perceptible in the following passage:

> How much you should be praised, because you have not only confessed that Christ is the Son of God, but you have established the faith in this entire land. You have erected churches to Christ, and have guided his servants. You are similar to Constantine the Great, you are equally wise, and you love Christ as much, and therefore you equally deserve respect from his servants. Constantine, with the holy Fathers of the Nicaean Council, established the law for men, and you, after deliberating often with our new Fathers, the bishops, have announced with much humility how the law should be kept by men newly acquainted with it. While he established the Kingdom of God among Greeks and Romans, you [accomplished something] similar, O praiseworthy one, because Christ is recognized as Tsar among them and among us, and whilst he and his mother, Helena, brought the Cross from Jerusalem, and sending to all his empire, confirmed the faith, you again like them, brought the Cross from the new Jerusalem—the city of

> Constantinople—and after planting it in your land confirmed [the faith].

Thus Russia had a new Constantine who was similar to the first Christian emperor—Constantine, the isoapostolos—similar to the apostles.

* * *

Byzantium's legacy to Russia was especially generous in the arts.[42] If one wants to study Byzantine architecture and the art of the eleventh century, one has to go to Kiev. A jewel of Byzantine art is the church of Holy Wisdom, begun by Jaroslav the Wise. Its mosaics and frescoes are particularly striking, and native artists soon began to imitate them. The church of Holy Wisdom in Novgorod and the Nereditsa church were imitations of the Kievan church. Its crown of thirteen cupolas appealed especially to Russian taste and became the classic feature of Russian religious architecture.

A new architectural style was introduced by the Byzantine masters at the end of the eleventh century. The church of Our Lady's Assumption in Kiev was its typical example. Its style was copied by two other churches in Kiev, and the type was introduced also to Černigov. One of these churches, that of St. Michael with the Golden Cupola (1108), was decorated by the native monk Olympus, whose work is one of the finest examples of medieval Russian religious art. Native masters were also working with the Byzantines on the frescoes in the churches of Novgorod and Vladimir. The practice of painting icons also owes its origin to Byzantine inspiration.

This development was interrupted in Kievan Russia by the Mongol invasion toward the end of the thirteenth century. Fortunately the Kievan artistic traditions were preserved in Novgorod, the only principality that survived the onslaught. There a new school of architects, formed in the thirteenth and fourteenth centuries, improved the inherited traditions under the influence of the Byzantine renaissance of art during the period of the Palaeologan dynasty. Also, the Novgorod school of icon painters was famous in the fourteenth century.

The Novgorod artistic traditions were passed on to Moscow in the fifteenth century. Contacts with the West through Venice, with Serbian and Bulgarian schools, and especially with the Italo-Cretan school famous for the Byzantine icons of a Western Renaissance character, brought about a revival of Russian painting during the Muscovite period from the fifteenth to the seventeenth century. The Greek Theophanes with his "illusionism" introduced the new fashion of icon painting. The most famous painter was Rublev (died 1430), followed by Daniel Černy and Dionysius. The latter's frescoes at the Therapontov monastery (1500–1581) in Moscow are sometimes compared with the works of Giotto. Icon painting became a Russian national art, and it is to be regretted that its further development was stopped by the westernization introduced by Peter the Great.

During the Mongol period Russian architects made good progress in the craft of wood carving. Improving on their Byzantine models, they created new types of quadrilateral, octagonal and cruciform wooden churches. These often have a great number of onion-shaped domes and curiously pointed gables. The new period of Moscow stone architecture drew its inspiration from the old Vladimir-Suzdal school. The Italian Renaissance architects were bound to conform to the old Russian tradition, by order of Ivan III. The cathedral of the Assumption in the Kremlin is the finest work of this period (1475–9). Artisans from Pskov who built the cathedral of Annunciation (1490) reverted to native tradition, which followed the architecture of the wooden churches. Italian architects replaced their Greek counterparts in Moscow, fusing the Renaissance style with Russian forms. But the Russian architects soon mastered the new technique and adapted the forms peculiar to the national craft of woodwork to stone architecture. Many buildings were constructed in this new style, the finest of them being the cathedral of St. Basil the Blessed on Red Square in Moscow. Here we see the final stage of the evolution that took its origin from Byzantium.

* * *

The Byzantine impact was also considerable in the development of Russian jurisprudence. The first Slavonic handbook of civil law was a compilation called *Zakon sudnyj ljudem,* which was composed by disciples of Constantine-Cyril and Methodius for the Moravians, and had reached Kiev from Bulgaria.[43] It was

based on the Byzantine law handbook *Ecloga,* which was in use
in Byzantium in the ninth century. But the original text of the
Ecloga, and of the new handbook *Procheiron,* translated in Bulgaria, had also become known in Kievan Russia. In addition, the
Byzantine Agrarian Law (Nomos Georgicos) was translated in
the twelfth or thirteenth century. The ecclesiastical legislation
was also Byzantine. It was a collection of Canon Law of John
Scholasticus, a heritage from Archbishop Methodius of Moravia,
and the Collection of Fourteen Titles. It is interesting to note that
all these translations of civil and canon laws were united in Russia
in the so-called Pilot's book (*Kormčaja Kniga*) used by ecclesiastical courts in the Kievan and Muscovite period.

The first Slavic Code was so popular in Russia that a second
edition was made, probably in the eleventh century. The original
contained only thirty-two titles. To these forty-five more were
added. Sixteen were adapted from the Greek "Mosaic Law," the
others were based on Byzantine law, and also on Russian customary law.[44]

In this respect, however, the Russians showed their independence from Byzantine legal practices. There had existed in Kiev a
customary law before the conversion to Christianity, and the
Kievan courts in many cases had to follow it. It was codified in
the eleventh century in the legal collection called *Russkaja Pravda*
(Russian law). This handbook continued to be used in Russian
courts to the end of the Muscovite period. The language in which
this codification was composed is not Old Slavonic, which is
based on a Macedonian dialect and was promoted by Cyril,
Methodius, and their disciples, to become the language in which
most literary works were written. The *Russkaja Pravda* was written in the idiom spoken by the native Russian, which was probably also used in the courts.[45]

* * *

Some independence from Byzantine political ideas was manifested in Kievan Russia, such as in political philosophy and government. Together with the Byzantine version of Christianity,
Russia also accepted the main principle of Byzantine political
theory, based on the Hellenistic notion of the divinized king and
adapted to Christian principles. According to this theory, the

Emperor of Constantinople was appointed by God as His representative on earth, and was therefore supreme legislator, even in ecclesiastical matters, for all Christians.[46] This kind of subordination to the Emperor of Constantinople, successor of Constantine the Great, in which Russia was held during the first four centuries of its existence, was perfectly compatible with the political independence of the Grand Prince of Kiev and other princes.

The other main principle of the Byzantine political theory was, namely, that the emperor, being instituted by God, was an autocrat wielding absolute power, was not applied to the political organization of the Kievan State. The Rurik dynasty preferred the old native system of division of the state into principalities governed by its members, the eldest of them becoming the Grand Prince of Kiev. The system of the večes—city councils which participated in the government of principalities or city states—was maintained, although it limited considerably the powers of the princes.

But, as concerns the relations between state and church, Kievan Russia accepted the Byzantine principle expressed by Justinian in his Novel VI on the *Imperium* and *Sacerdotium,* stressing the divine origin of both, the necessity of intimate relations between these two main factors in human society, the ruler's role in establishing harmony between the spiritual and temporal powers, and his right, or rather his duty, to watch over the church.[47] The Kievan clergy willingly transferred these prerogatives to the Grand Prince of Kiev. The willing acceptance of this Justinian principle helps us to understand why the Russian hierarchy had made it its first task to be on good terms with the ruling princes. The preservation of a harmonious relationship between the *Sacerdotium* and *Imperium*—one of the leading principles of Byzantine political philosophy—became also the guiding star for political and religious development in Russia for many centuries.

The Byzantine system of absolute monarchy was applied for the first time in Russia by Andrew Bogoliubsky in the new principality of Vladimir-Suzdal established between the rivers Volga and Oka. His attitude seemed to be so strange and hateful that in 1174 he paid with his life for his despotic policy.[48]

It was only under the Mongol rule that the Russians learned to appreciate absolutism. The first attempts at strengthening the

power of the princes were made again in the principality of
Vladimir-Suzdal, where the princes of Moscow had succeeded in
subduing the princes of the territory. They found little difficulty
in establishing gradually absolute power among the Russians. All
the Byzantine notions of monarchism and absolutism were contained in the legal writings inherited from Byzantium, and needed
only local adaptation.[49] In this the Russian Church, imbued with
Byzantine principles as outlined in Byzantine writings, favored
monarchism, as did her Byzantine confrères; when the Metropolitan of Kiev, the head of the Russian Church, eventually settled
in Moscow (1326), the city rose to power uncontested. Dimitri
Donskoy's victory over the Tatars confirmed its supremacy and
inaugurated the liberation from the Mongol yoke which the genius
of Ivan III the Great completed in 1480. Russian absolutism was
firmly established by Basil II and Ivan III. The latter declared in
a Byzantine fashion that by God's grace he was hereditary sovereign of the state, having received the investiture from God
Himself, as had his ancestors. But it was not enough. The disciple wanted to replace his master—Byzantium.

When the Byzantines had concluded the union of their Church
with the West after the Council of Florence (1439), the Grand
Prince Basil II and the Russian clergy denounced Byzantium's
betrayal of Orthodoxy. When Constantinople fell in 1453—which
was God's punishment for its betrayal—Ivan III was the legitimate successor of the Greek Basileus, and Moscow was hence-
forth to be known as the Third Rome.

In 1547 Ivan IV lent concrete and final expression to this general feeling by accepting the imperial crown and officially assuming the title of Tsar. The court of Moscow was organized on the
Byzantine model, and the Tsar defined his absolute powers in
words which not even a Byzantine emperor would have dared to
use. The creation of the Móscow patriarchate in 1589 finally
sealed the transition.[50]

So it happened that the barbaric Slavic tribes which were converted and educated by Byzantium had developed into a mighty
nation, which outgrew its former teacher and took its place of
precedence over all Eastern Christians, jealously guarding and
developing the cultural, religious, and political ideas inherited
from Byzantium, a unique example in the history of the Slavs
and of Christianity.

APPENDICES

I. The Embassies of Constantine-Cyril and Photius to the Arabs

II. The Survival of Roman Provincial Culture in Pannonia and Noricum Reaching Moravia

III. By Which Route Did the Byzantine Embassy Reach Moravia?

Notes to the Appendices will be found following each Appendix.

NOTES

Chapter I—Chapter IX

BIBLIOGRAPHY

INDEX

I. The Embassies of Constantine-Cyril and Photius to the Arabs

Among the problems concerning the career of Constantine-Cyril in Byzantium, the question of his participation in an embassy to the Arabs has not yet been answered satisfactorily. It is related in chapter six of the *Vita Constantini*,[1] in which the author speaks of an invitation being sent by the Arabs to Constantinople to hold a religious disputation, with particular reference to the Holy Trinity and belief in one God. The emperor thereupon is said to have convoked the Senate in order to deliberate as to what should be done. He asked Constantine, at that time only twenty-four years old, to go to the Arabs and to take part in the religious discussion.

What are we to think of this? Is this a story invented by the biographer anxious to extol the scholarship of his hero as being superior to that of his opponents? There are so many details which cannot be substantiated. First of all, it is unlikely that the Arabs would have requested the emperor to arrange a dispute on the subjects of Islam and Christianity. Also, the biographer's affirmation that Constantine headed the embassy sent to the Caliph is unacceptable, and his pretension that the Arabs intended to poison Constantine when the council ended, during which he had shown his superiority over the Arab theologians, is hardly tenable.

These are all inventions of the author for the glorification of his hero.[2] On the other hand, they correspond to the spirit of Byzantine hagiographical writings. Nevertheless, the story does have an historical background. We do not know of an embassy sent to the Arabs in 851, when Constantine was twenty-four years old. However, it is not absolutely impossible that there was a series of *pourparlers* between Byzantium and the Arab Caliph Mutawakkil (847–861) in that year.

The most recent exchange of prisoners made between Byzantium and the Arabs took place in the year 845–846.[3] From this time on we do not hear of any military action taking place on the Arab frontier up to the year 851, for during this period the Byzantines were heavily engaged in fighting the Arabs in Sicily.[4] It is possible that in 851 the Byzantines attempted to renew the truce with the Caliph so as to leave their hands free for their operations in Sicily, which were not going well.

There are details in the account of the disputation which favor the assumption that such an event as a religious discussion really did take place in 851. First, the biographer's description of the city in which the conference was held corresponds to what was known at the time of the residence of the Caliphs, which, from 836 to 889, was in Samarra, near Baghdad. Another point mentioned in the recital could be regarded as confirmation of the hypothesis that some kind of *pourparlers* had taken place between the Arabs and the Byzantines in 851, for Constantine was asked by them why it was that the Byzantines refused to pay tribute to them.

Constantine replied that Christ had paid tribute only to the Roman Empire, and that therefore tribute should be paid only to the Romans. It could be deduced from this that the Arab request for tribute was a condition for continuance of the truce, and that the ambassadors had refused. Another detail referred to by the author of the *Vita* points out that such an incident could have taken place in the first years of the reign of the Caliph Mutawakkil.

The Caliph manifested a keen interest in religious matters, and showed his hostility to the Christians by promulgating, in 849–850, several edicts restricting the free movement of his Christian subjects. One of these anti-Christian measures is mentioned in the *Vita*. The Arabs are said to have pointed out that a figure of the devil "adorned" the doors of all Christian houses, and· to have asked Constantine what this meant. He is said to have answered cleverly that the devil, being expelled from the interior of the houses of Christians, was hanging onto their doors, while he was not to be seen on the doors of the Mussulmans because he was inside their houses. It was to be expected that the religious disputes would take place at the court, and therefore the philosopher Constantine was asked to accompany the ambassador.

Constantine's replies to certain objections made by the Arabs, preserved or imagined by the biographer, disclose a clever mind. Christian doctrine is compared to a large, deep sea. Only strong souls are able to penetrate its depths and sail to its coasts. The feeble spirits fail and become heretics, because they master only a small part of the sea. The doctrine of Mohammed is a small, shallow lake which anyone can subdue. In defending Christian doctrine on the Trinity, Constantine is said to have quoted Sura 19, 17 of the Koran, where the incarnation of the Word through the Spirit of God is described. This passage was often quoted in Byzantine polemic literature.

If such an embassy took place in 851, Constantine certainly did not lead it. We are told by the hagiographer that the emperor sent with him the *asecrete* George, who was probably the senior envoy. Since it was expected that religious problems would be discussed at the Caliph's court in view of Mutawakkil's great interest in these matters, Constantine, as a young cleric and scholar, was present.

If this embassy did take place, it did not fulfill the hopes of the Byzantines. This would seem to be indicated by the biographer's report of the Arabs wanting to poison Constantine. According to Tabari, the Arab historian, hostilities between the Byzantines and the Caliph were initiated in the summer of 851, by an incursion into Byzantine territory, a move which was repeated in 852, and again in 853.[5] It is thus quite possible that diplomatic negotiations were opened between the Byzantines and the Caliph in 851, and that a religious dispute did take place at the Caliph's court, during which Constantine defended the Christian faith.

Because Constantine was a disciple of Photius, one is tempted to associate him with an embassy to the Arabs in which Photius participated. Unfortunately, the manuscript tradition of the passage in the *Vita* referring to his participation in such an embassy is rather confused. I was tempted to follow another manuscript which seems to suggest that a personage with the title of *palata* (*palatine*) who was perhaps Photius, took part in this embassy. Such a reading, however, is problematic. It is safer to read simply: "They attached to him the asecrete George and sent them" (*asikrita Georgia i poslaše ja*).[6]

It is an established fact that Photius was a member of a Byzantine embassy sent to the Arabs. He himself says so in the introductory letter addressed to his brother Tarasius, to whom he dedi-

cated his *Bibliotheca,* composed at his brother's request before
his departure on a mission to the "Assyrians."[7] Photius excuses
himself from not describing in more exhaustive fashion the books
read by the members of his circle, during Tarasius' absence, and
he promises to continue the work after his return. It is evident
from the contents of the *Bibliotheca* that the work is incomplete.
If the embassy, of which Photius was a member, did occur in 851,
he would have had enough time to finish his promised continuation before his elevation to the patriarchate in 858. If we accept
Photius' testimony as genuine, then the embassy to which he was
attached must have taken place between the years 851 and 858.

However, because to some scholars it seems impossible that he
could have accomplished such a literary achievement in the short
time before leaving Constantinople on a diplomatic mission, they
have advanced the hypothesis that the letter to Tarasius, which
opens and closes the *Bibliotheca,* is fictitious. Krumbacher[8] himself was of such an opinion. A similar view was ventured recently
by F. Halkin in his paper, "La date de composition de la '*Bibliothèque*' de Photius remise en question."[9] He bases his conclusions
of the Greek *Life* of St. Gregory the Great, from which Photius
quotes certain passages in his *Bibliotheca* (codex 252). Since it
has been shown that the Greek *Life* of St. Gregory was based on
the Latin *Life* of the saint, composed between 873 and 875 by the
Roman deacon John Hymnonides, at the invitation of Pope John
VIII,[10] Photius could not have known of the Greek *Life* before
877, and therefore the composition of the *Bibliotheca* should be
dated somewhere between 877 and 886.

This argument, however, is unconvincing. We are not certain
that the passages quoted by Photius are extracted from the Βίος
ἐνσυντόμῳ which a Greek monk had taken in shorter form from
the Latin *Life,* which contained four books. St. Gregory the Great
was popular also in Byzantium, and it is not improbable that the
authors of both the Greek *Life* (known to Photius) and the Latin
Life used an older source which has not been preserved.[11]

The author affirms that Photius added the fictitious letter to his
work, written during his second patriarchate (877–886), in order
to escape the criticism of his enemies[12] who would attack him
because, as patriarch, he was reading and propagating works of a
profane, and even heretical, nature. In order to protect himself

from this accusation, Photius is said to have fabricated a letter to his brother, Tarasius, in which he gives the impression that it was in his youth, and before he entered holy orders, that he read the books about which he was writing.

Such an interpretation is preposterous. On the other hand, it has been shown that Photius' opponents were not numerous, consisting mostly of intransigent monks and bishops.[13] After his reconciliation with Ignatius, which took place before the death of the latter,[14] and after his rehabilitation by the synod of 879–880, Photius was almost unanimously reinstated. He was therefore able to ignore the small number of fanatics whose attitude continued hostile.

The fact that Photius had reviewed the writings of certain heretics induced M. Hemmerdinger[15] to state that it would have been impossible for Photius to have found such books in Constantinople, since the works of heretics were condemned. But such books could have been found in Baghdad, where, in the ninth century, lived many Greeks, famous scribes and translators. These works were kept in the Caliph's library (which was destroyed in 1258) and Photius had access to what he could not find in Constantinople, while staying in Baghdad during the negotiations with the Caliph. This explanation may be ingenious, but cannot be accepted. The writings of heretics were obtainable in Constantinople, and from 836 to 889 the residence of the Caliphs was not in Baghdad, but in Samarra, which is some distance from Baghdad. It is difficult to understand how members of the embassy, who were there to negotiate with the Arab authorities, could absent themselves for so many days in Baghdad.

The theory that Photius had taken his library with him and that he finished his *Bibliotheca* while travelling to Samarra, or that he took some of his students with him, cannot be accepted.[16] Ziegler, in his study on Photius, has already rejected this fantastic explanation.[17] All these difficulties can be explained if we suppose that Photius, after reading or studying a work with his friends, made notes as to the content, author, and style, to which he added his own criticism. It would then be easy to assemble his notes in a reasonably short time before his departure with the embassy.

Thus it remains established that Photius wrote his *Bibliotheca* before leaving with the embassy to the Arabs, and that both parts of his letter to his brother Tarasius, the introduction and the postscript, are genuine.

However, we still have the problem of when the embassy, to which he was attached, took place. H. Ahrweiler, in her recently published paper, thinks that it occurred in 838, before the capture of Amorion by the Arabs, during the first half of August, or soon after the disastrous defeat of the Byzantine army. Her main argument is to be found in her interpretation of Photius' letter to Tarasius. She quotes Photius' words describing to Tarasius the difficulty of such an enterprise, and she deduces from them that Photius was afraid, even for his survival. This would, so she thinks, fit in very well with the embassy sent by Emperor Theophilus to the Caliph after the loss of Amorion.[18] In reality, this embassy was badly received, and suffered mistreatment from the victorious Arab ruler.[19] On the other hand, the fact that Photius does not give his brother the title of *patricius,* which he had done in previous letters, indicates, according to H. Ahrweiler, that Tarasius was too young at that time, and that Photius was not very far along in his career in the imperial service. But she thinks that he was already an *asecretos,* or, perhaps, *decanos* in the imperial chancellery. In this function he would accompany the emperor on military expeditions, and he would be in charge of the official papers which were transported in a special vehicle. The young Photius would thus be able to hide his own notes on the books he had read among the official documents, and he would be able to find time during the expedition to finish the work he sent to his brother in Constantinople. This interpretation is believed to explain why it was so difficult for Photius to find a scribe to whom he could dictate his comments. Although there would be no difficulty in finding one in Constantinople, it was not easy to do so in a military camp in Asia Minor.

Although very plausible, this interpretation cannot be accepted. Photius may have had difficulty in finding a good scribe even in Constantinople. He may have tried out several, and, at last, found one who was qualified for the task for which he was hired. Photius was in a hurry and wanted to finish up his domestic affairs while he was still in Constantinople, and he was anxious to send his composition to his "dear" brother as early as possible. It is not easy to find a good secretary for an urgent task.

The fact that Photius does not give his brother the title of *patricius* should not be exaggerated. It was his last letter to Tarasius; it could have been his very last, since travelling to an enemy country, at that time, was dangerous and might have ended tragically. Photius was well aware of this and preferred to write to his brother quite simply as "my beloved brother." There is a tenderness in this address felt by all of us when leaving our families for some time, and when the future is uncertain. Photius writes to Tarasius, "You who are dearest to me of all who were born from the womb of the same mother as myself." These words are very indicative.

But again, H. Ahrweiler is faced with the difficulty of explaining how a work of such dimensions as the *Bibliotheca* could have been written in the tents of military camps. The supposition that Photius was only twenty-five years old at that time, and that neither he nor his brother held a prominent place in Byzantine society, is unwarranted and hangs in the air. However, the author is right when she affirms that Photius was not at the head of that embassy. She is also correct in saying that it is necessary to distinguish between simple exchanges of prisoners between the Arabs and the Byzantines on the frontier, on the one hand, and between embassies which represented the emperors at the Arab court, on the other.

Because of this, she rejects the possibility that Photius was attached to an embassy in 855–856, since the Byzantine authors speak only of an exchange of prisoners during that time. However, may we not suppose that such exchanges were sometimes prepared by negotiations conducted by an embassy? Such seems to be the case in 855. Photius says, when speaking of his participation in the embassy, that not only was he encouraged to join it by the members already selected, but that the emperor himself chose him, as he had chosen the others. Such ceremonial practice was unnecessary when an exchange of prisoners took place, as this function was carried out by the *strategos* and the officers of the Asiatic theme. In reality, the exchange of prisoners which took place on the River Lamos was directed—according to Tabari—by one such officer called George, but it was effected after the embassy had finished its negotiations with the Arabs in Samarra. Arab sources, in particular Tabari and Yaqūbī,[20] speak of embassies sent by Theodora to the Caliph, and of the Arab envoy Ibn

Farag whose task it was to discover how many Arab prisoners were held captive by the Byzantines. Both sources—especially that of Yaqūbī [21]—mention an exchange of gifts by the embassies to both courts. It is thus established that an exchange of prisoners in 855–856 was arranged by a solemn embassy sent by the Empress Theodora and her prime minister, Theoctistos, to the Caliph Mutawakkil. It was to this embassy that Photius was attached.

There is yet one more fact which supports the dating of Photius' embassy in 855–856. At this time an important political upheaval occurred in the capital in 856. The logothete Theoctistos, Theodora's prime minister, was murdered by the supporters of Theodora's brother, the ambitious Bardas, with the consent of the young Emperor Michael III, who was distrustful both of his mother and of Theoctistos. Other events followed. The Senate put an end to the regency of Theodora in the same year and, to prevent a counter-revolution by her partisans, she was expelled from the palace at the end of the summer of 857. Patriarch Ignatius, a supporter of Theodora, became embroiled with the new regent, Bardas, and, in order to avoid an open clash between the Church and the new government, the bishops advised Ignatius to resign his patriarchate. This he did in 858. The local synod elected as his successor Photius, the chancellor of the Empire.[22] The consent of all the bishops was given to the election of the new patriarch, even by those who most fervently supported Ignatius, their attitude having been influenced by the fact that Photius was not involved in any way in the upheaval of 856, since he was absent from the city and on his way back from the embassy to the Arabs. He may not have returned until the early part of 857, thus giving the followers of Theodora time to become reconciled to the idea of Photius as the successor of Ignatius. Had he been present in Constantinople at the time of the disturbance, it is possible that the reactionary members of the clergy would have refused to accept Bardas' proposal to elevate him to the patriarchate, for it was Bardas who was responsible for the changes in the government, and who was favorably inclined to the intellectual circle of which Photius was the center.

Let me recall two other Byzantine embassies to the Arabs which show that discussions of a religious character really used to take place at the courts of the caliphs with members of the Byzantine embassies. In 905 Leo Choerosphactes was sent as

ambassador to the Caliph Al-Muqtafi (902–908) and was charged
to negotiate an exchange of prisoners. His mission was successful,
but the Byzantines saw themselves forced to stop the exchange
because of the revolt of Ducas against the emperor. The ambassador had to return to Constantinople. It appears that during the
winter of 905–906, the Vizir of the Caliph—not the Emir of
Damascus—addressed a letter to Choerosphactes reproaching him
for interrupting the exchange of prisoners, and also criticizing
certain articles of the Christian faith. This would seem to indicate
that the vizir, and the ambassador, had discussed at Bagdad not
only political matters but also religious beliefs.

Leo sent the vizir a long missive in which he defended the
Christian teaching and attacked some of the beliefs of the Mussulman religion. This letter is preserved among the writings attributed to Arethas of Caesarea and has been dated by specialists
from 918 to 923.

Recently A. Canard discussed the whole problem in the Appendix to his *Byzance et les Arabes*.[23] He gives a résumé of the
letter and compares the different opinions concerning its authorship and date. Canard seems to have shown definitely that the
author of this letter was Leo Choerosphactes, who may have
written it, probably in Constantinople, before his second embassy
to the Arabs in the spring of 906, during which the agreement to
continue the exchange of prisoners was concluded, or after his
return from the second embassy. Both missives should be regarded
as the echo of religious discussions which took place at the
Caliph's court during the first embassy of Choerosphactes. The
exchange of prisoners took place in 908 on the river Lamos.

Let us recall in this connection the report on an embassy sent
by Constantine Porphyrogenitus in 957–58 to the Fatimid Caliph
al-Mu'izz proposing a perpetual truce between the Caliph of
Ifrigiya and Byzantium.[24] The reply given by the caliph to the
ambassador contains several quotations from the Koran forbidding
perpetual peace with unbelievers. The caliph refused to send an
embassy to the emperor because "he was not in need of him,
neither was he in any way obliged to him. . . . It would be, of
course, quite a different thing if we had to correspond with him
in a matter touching religion. Now, although such a correspondence is permitted to him by his religion, we think he [the em-
peror] would dislike it. If we knew that he would accede to our

demand if we sent an envoy in that matter, we would find it possible to send an ambassador as he [the emperor], and you [the envoy], have asked. We would not do that, were it not for the sake of Almighty God and His religion. . . ."

The editor of this document, S. M. Stern, remarks that the last sentence is not clear. It may mean that the caliph invited the emperor to accept Islam or, perhaps—and this seems more probable—to take an active part in the religious disputation conducted by letter.

This discussion was written by a contemporary Arab writer called al-Nu'man, and the information should be complemented with that given by a fifteenth-century author, Imad al-din-Idris. He mentions the Byzantine embassy to al-Mu'izz and gives information about the curious attempts of al-Mu'izz to convert the emperor. He says, "The Commander of the faithful al-Mu'izz composed a book and sent it to him [the emperor]. It contains an exposition of the errors of the Christians and proves the prophecy of Mohammed which they deny. . . . This book composed by the Commander of the faithful al-Mu'izz for the ruler of the Byzantines is well known and is still in existence." The editor, S. M. Stern, has at last discovered some traces of this book composed by al-Mu'izz, in an Arabic manuscript at the Bibliothèque Nationale in Paris.

All this is instructive and shows us that the presence of Byzantine ambassadors at the Arabic courts very often led to the discussion of religious matters. This also indicates that among the members of these Byzantine embassies there must have been some attachés well versed in theology, like Constantine-Cyril called the Philosopher. It is quite probable that the choice of Photius to participate at the embassy of 855 was motivated by the same need.

Notes

1. P. A. Lavrov, *Materialy po istorii vozniknovenija drevnejšej slavjanskoj pismennosti* (Leningrad, 1930), p. 7 ff., p. 45 ff.

2. H. H. Schaeder, "Geschichte und Legende im Werk der Slavenmissionare Konstantin und Method," *Historische Zeitschrift*, CLII (1935), p. 232 ff., thinks that the whole story was invented by the hagiographer who wanted to ascribe three disputations to the hero, because of his predilection for the sacred number three. This, however, cannot be the case. Not three, but four disputations are attributed to Constan-

tine, one with the ex-Patriarch John, the second with the Arabs, the third with the Khazars, and the fourth with the Venetians, as described in chapter 14 of the *Vita*.

3. A. A. Vasiliev, H. Grégoire, M. Canard, *Byzance et les Arabes* (Bruxelles, 1935), I, p. 198 ff.

4. *Ibid.,* p. 204 ff.

5. *Ibid.,* p. 214 ff.

6. F. Dvornik, *Les Légendes de Constantin et de Méthode vues de Byzance* (Prague, 1933), pp. 93, 94. See *ibid.*, pp. 104–111, on theological controversies between the Arabs and the Byzantines. Cf. also A. Abel, "La lettre polémique d'Aréthas à l'émir de Damas," *Byzantion*, XXIV (1954), pp. 344–370; J. Meyendorff, "Byzantine views of Islam," *Dumbarton Oaks Papers*, XVIII (1964); pp. 115–132.

7. The letter is written as an introduction and conclusion of the *Bibliotheca, PG* 103, cols. 41, 44; 104, cols. 353, 356. Cf. J. Hergenröther, *Photius, Patriarch von Konstantinopel* (Regensburg, 1867–69), III, p. 14. The latter is not to be found in the manuscripts used by the modern edition. Hergenröther found it in Codex Vallicellanus graecus 125 (R 2 6) which contains only the letter to Tarasius on folio 50. It is known that the letter is found only in a few manuscripts of the *Bibliotheca*. It is quite possible that the manuscript of the Vallicellanus contains an authentic version which was abridged in other manuscripts. On the manuscripts of the *Bibliotheca*, see E. Martini, *Textgeschichte der Bibliotheke* (= *Abhandlungen der sächsischen Akademie*, phil. hist. Cl., vol. 28, no. 6) (Leipzig, 1911). On the Vallicellanus, see *ibid.*, p. 46. A new edition with a German translation is to be found in K. Ziegler, "Photios," *Paulys Real Encyclopädie*, XXXIX (Stuttgart, 1941), cols. 685–688; R. Henry, *Photius Bibliothèque* (Paris, 1959). (Collection byzantine de l'Association Guillaume Budé), vol. I, p. XIX ff., p. 1 ff.

8. *Geschichte der byzantinischen Litteratur* (Munich, 1896), p. 519.

9. *Analecta Bollandiana*, LXXXIII (1963), pp. 414–417.

10. *PL,* 75, cols. 59–242; H. Delehaye, "S. Grégoire le Grand dans l'hagiographie grecque." *Analecta Bollandiana*, XXIII (1904), pp. 449–454.

11. This was rightly pointed out by H. Ahrweiler, "Sur la carrière de Photios avant son Patriarcat," *Byzantinische Zeitschrift,* LVIII (1965), p. 538.

12. F. Halkin, "La date," p. 417.

13. See my book *The Photian Schism. History and Legend* (Cambridge, 1948), p. 39 ff., p. 159 ff.

14. See F. Dvornik, "The Patriarch Photius in the Light of Recent Research," in *Berichte zum XI. Internat. Byzantinisten-Kongress* (Munich, 1958), pp. 34, 35. According to the *Sinaiticus graecus*, no. 482 (1117) fols. 357^r–365^v, Photius did not only reconcile himself with

Ignatius, but even canonized him after the latter's death. The manuscript contains another version of the *Synodicon Vetus* published by J. Pappe in J. A. Fabricius and G. C. Harles, *Bibliotheca graeca*, XII (Hamburg, 1809). Another manuscript containing the same information as the manuscript of Sinai has been found. The document will be published by Dumbarton Oaks.

15. "Les 'notices et extraits' des bibliothèques grecques de Bagdad par Photius," *Révue des études grecques*, LXIX (1956), pp. 101–103. Cf. R. Henry, *Photius Bibliothèque*, LI, LII.

16. Put forward especially by E. Orth, *Photiana* (Leipzig, 1929).

17. "Photios," cols. 689, 690.

18. "Sur la carrièrede Photios," p. 360.

19. The Byzantine sources are unanimous in describing the humiliating reception of the embassy by the Caliph. See Genesios, Bonn, pp. 64, 65; Cedrenus, Bonn, II, pp. 531, 532; Theophanes continuatus, Bonn, pp. 129, 130.

20. A. A. Vasiliev, H. Grégoire, M. Canard, *Byzance et les Arabes,* I, p. 224. It is not certain that this George is the same person as the official mentioned in the *Life of Constantine,* but it is possible.

21. See *ibid.,* p. 224 ff., pp. 276, 277. An exchange of prisoners during the reign of Leo the Wise was also prepared by solemn embassies, as is described by George the Monk (Bonn), p. 868.

22. For details, see F. Dvornik, *The Photian Schism,* p. 39 ff. Cf. also, *idem,* "Patriarch Ignatius and Caesar Bardas," *Byzantinoslavica,* XXVII (1966), pp. 7–22.

23. Vasiliev, A. A., Canard, M., *Byzance et les Arabes,* vol. II, 1 (Bruxelles, 1968), p. 399 ff.

24. Stern, S. M., "An Embassy of the Byzantine Emperor to the Fatimid Caliph Al-Mu'izz," *Byzantion* 20 (1950), pp. 239–258. Cf. also M. Canard, *Byzance et les Arabes,* p. 420 ff.

II. The Survival of Roman Provincial Culture in Pannonia and Noricum Reaching Moravia

So far it has generally been believed that the Slavs northeast of the Danube were barely touched by the Roman provincial culture which flourished in Pannonia and Noricum. It is thought that only the Teutonic tribes, which had preceded the Slavs in Noricum, were in direct contact with the antique culture. Many of them became Roman *feoderati*, were romanized and played a prominent role as Roman provincial citizens. When the Romans were forced to evacuate the province, the romanized Teutons left Noricum with them. When the Slavs settled in this country in the fifth and sixth century, there was no one left to transmit the cultural traditions and technical knowledge of the antique world.[1] It is often pointed out that the Slavs were unable to acquaint themselves with the benefits of Roman provincial culture which flourished in Pannonia because of the invasions by the Huns and later by Lombards and the Avars into this province. The blows inflicted by these invasions had forced the Romans to evacuate Pannonia.

It is true that the Roman garrisons and functionaries with their dependents had to leave Noricum on the order of Odoacer (488), but most of the romanized natives stayed on in village formations, and especially in the woodlands where they continued to live according to the old Roman custom.[2] The existence of a Roman population is mentioned often in documents originating in Salzburg.[3] They were Christians and they may have played a certain role in the Christianization of the Bavarian newcomers. It is characteristic that in the eighth century many priests and monks in

297

the Alpine lands, judging from their names, were of Roman
origin. The Slavs who from the fifth century on were pushing into
these territories also came into touch with the few remaining
Romans, and thus had the opportunity of learning about some
aspects of antique traditions.

We must not forget that Moravia was crossed by a most important road, in use from neolithic times. This was the famous Amber
Road, which started in Aquileia, passed through Noricum, crossed
the Danube at Carnuntum, followed the rivers Morava and Bečva,
joined the river Oder which led it through the Moravian Gates
into Poland, and ended up on the Baltic sea.[4] This road was used
in Roman times not only by the Legions, but also by Italian merchants who traded with the native populations settled north of the
Danube river. Although this commercial road crossed the fortified
Roman *limes* on the Danube, Roman guard garrisons were established even outside the *limes* to protect this important trade route.
Such a garrison was established in Moravia at Mušov south of
the city of Brno and at Stupava in Slovakia.[5] Roman buildings,
probably of a similar kind, must have existed near the Slavic
settlement of Staré Město, because Roman bricks with the imprint
of Legions XIV and XVI were turned up in the foundation of the
rotunda discovered there.[6] This route was used even after the
evacuation of Noricum by the Romans, by merchants from Italy
acquainting the Slavic tribes with more refined products from
Italy and Greece.

Even an exchange of products between former Noricum and
Moravia can be supposed. Perhaps the problem could be solved
as to where the ninth century's Moravian goldsmiths got their
precious material, if we could substantiate the theory that it came
from ancient Noricum in exchange for the grain which was abun-
dant in the valleys of Moravia.[7] Already in the time of the Roman
Republic Noricum was famous for its gold and iron mines. Strabo[8]
mentions particularly the city of Noreia as a center of gold wash-
ing and of flourishing metallurgy. The question deserves further
investigation.

The territory of modern Slovakia was also touched by Roman
culture from Pannonia. The most important center on the middle
Danube was Brigetio, near modern Komárno. A bridge-head in
the territory of modern Leányvár opened the way to the valley
of Vag. The route following the Vag river was probably con-

nected with the Amber route of Moravia through the pass of Vlára
and the Roman garrison at Leugaricio, the modern Trenčín, was
supposed to guard this important passage.[9] In 179 a legion of
Marcus Aurelius hibernated at this place, as is witnessed by a
Latin inscription on the rock of Trenčín.[10] The emperor did not
succeed in extending the Roman *limes* to the Carpathian Mountains—he died in Vienna the year after.

The last emperor to be interested in strengthening the fortifications of the *limes* on the Danube was Valentinian I (364–375),
who hoped to launch his conquest of the Germanic tribes in modern Slovakia from there. He made some effort to protect Roman
merchants trading with the barbarians north of the Danube. During his reign a kind of octagonal fort was erected at Milanovce
on the river Nitra, about fifty kilometers from the Roman station
at Leányvár, near Komárno, which was to protect Roman merchants trading with the barbarians north of the Danube. In its
construction bricks taken from the ruins of another Roman castle,
which had been built nearby in the second century perhaps for
the same purpose, appear to have been used. It was probably
destroyed during the Marcomanic wars.[11]

As a matter of fact, the lands north of the Danube were frequently visited by Roman merchants before they were occupied
by the Slavs. This is demonstrated by numerous finds of Roman
coins, jewelry, iron products, and other implements.[12] All this,
however, could only have indirectly influenced those Slavs who
replaced the Celtic and Germanic tribes. After the third century
Bohemia was completely cut off from the western part of the
Roman Empire, but not Moravia. The Roman cultural traditions
did not disappear completely from Pannonia even after the gradual collapse of the *limes* and the evacuation of the Roman garrisons. During the occupation by the Huns of the main part of
Pannonia, especially between the Danube and Tisza, the Roman
and romanized population continued to exist, concentrating its
limited artistic and economic activity in fortified cities in the
interior of the province, and in estates of wealthy families that
had survived the invasion or perhaps had profited from the
turmoil which the new situation had caused. Roman trade with
the country continued, as is illustrated by many discoveries of
Roman products and coins dating from as late as the fifth century
in this land. Some archaeological discoveries show that Roman

artistic traditions in the production of jewelry were still alive in the first half of the fifth century, but they had been adapted to the taste of the new inhabitants.[13]

During the occupation by the Lombards, the decline of the fortified places continued. The wealthier of the Roman population took refuge in Italy and Gaul, and only the lower classes, colons, small peasants, and artisans remained in smaller fortified centers, continuing to produce their agricultural and other implements, using Roman methods. Even Roman artistic traditions were not completely forgotten, as we see in the production of Roman *fibulae*, again accommodated to the costume of the new inhabitants.[14]

The old cities continued here and there to be inhabited in spite of their dilapidated status. Two old centers, which survived all the troubles of the migration of nations up to the arrival of the Avars in 568, were Valcum, before called Mogentianae, in Fenekpuszta near Lake Balaton, and Sopianae, modern Pecz in Hungary. The excavations in Valcum have shown that the romanized inhabitants continued to live and work according to the old Roman tradition up to the arrival of the Avars. The latter lived for some time in peaceful relations with the citizens. In this way the Avars became acquainted by means of trade with goods made in the old Roman fashion of the fourth century. The settlement existed even when the Avars had incorporated it into their empire, and its workshops continued to produce artifacts for the Avars, to suit the taste of the new masters but which were often imitations of Byzantine and other imports.[15]

A similar situation seems to have existed in Sopianae. There appear to be serious indications that in Sopianae the inhabitants continued to practice the Christian religion during the whole Avar period down to the eighth century.[16] Anyhow, the old Roman traditions in the workshops which had survived in the old Roman settlements and environments continued to be preserved, the artisans trying to accommodate them to new technical and iconographic elements brought by the new masters who were their customers. In many cases the surviving artisans moved themselves and their workshops into Avar settlements.

During the occupation of Pannonia by the Avars, lively contact with Byzantium is documented by the finds of numerous Byzantine coins in Avar graves,[17] from the coins of Anastasius I (491–518) to those of Constantine IV Pogonatus (668–685), but after Constantine IV the influx of Byzantine coins to the Avars ceased almost completely. The finds of coins presuppose also the importation of Byzantine products, especially jewelry. The finds of Byzantine weights, exagia, point moreover to the presence of Byzantine artisans or, at least, of craftsmen who were familiar with the techniques used in Byzantine workshops.

This is confirmed by the discovery of a treasure at Zemiansky Vrbovok in Slovakia[18] in 1937 and 1951, containing a silver chalice, a bracelet, earrings, a necklace, two silver dishes, eight half silver globules with some silver pieces, and eighteen coins from 654 to 669, which allow the treasure to be dated to the seventh century. The objects belonged to a Byzantine artisan who intended to settle in the seat of a prominent Avar chieftain and there produce jewelry in the Byzantine fashion, but suited to the taste of the new rulers. He hoped to profit from the peaceful relations existing between the Avars and the Byzantines which prevailed in the second half of the seventh century and which were strengthened by Constantine IV Pogonatus in 677. Avar power was considerably diminished by their defeat in 626 under the walls of Constantinople, by the wars with the Croats and Serbs in Dalmatia and Pannonia, and by the insurrection of the Moravians and other Slavs led by Samo. After the death of Bojan the tribal chiefs were more independent and established their own courts.

The unfortunate silversmith, however, did not enjoy his stay among the Avars for long. Fresh danger threatened his new customers, when in 681 the Bulgars invaded Avar territory, and, after crossing the Danube, established their new state among the Slavic tribes in Moesia, Thrace, and Macedonia. The artisan hoped most probably to cross the pass in the Carpathian mountains and to try his chances among the barbarian, mostly Slavic tribes, north of them. He did not succeed in accomplishing his purpose and hid his treasure at the foot of the hills, hoping to recover it when peace was made. He never returned to his cache.

The silversmith whose treasure was found at Zemiansky Vrbovok was not alone. Other artisans of Byzantine origin or trained in Byzantine techniques had settled among the Avars and con-

tinued to produce jewelry, using Byzantine motifs. The tombs of
several artisans have been found by Hungarian archaeologists,
mostly in the neighborhood of important political or economic
centers.[19] Although the Avars in former Pannonia were completely
cut off from the Byzantine Empire by the new Bulgarian political
formation, which was hostile to Byzantium, the new incentives
brought to them by Byzantine influences in the seventh century
did not disappear from Pannonia. The foreign masters who had
established their workshops before 681 continued their production. The native artisans learned from them new techniques and
added new designs to their traditional motifs. Moreover, the fact
that after 681 the Byzantines stopped the distribution of their
coins to the Avar chiefs, and even to the Bulgars in the Danube
region, does not mean that all trade between the Avars and
Byzantium had ceased. It was natural that the Slavs who remained under Avar domination in Pannonia, and their tribesmen
north of the Danube, were affected by all this, and that their
artisans improved their own primitive methods of production by
using Roman and Byzantine techniques, which the remnants of
the Roman and romanized population in Pannonia had preserved
from the times when the country was a flourishing Roman
province.

As concerns Moravia, there are indications that Byzantine, or
byzantinized, artisans and merchants did reach that country.
This seems to be indicated by the finds of Byzantine coins in this
territory, which are not numerous but are significant.[20] They are
from the reigns of the Emperor Zeno (476–491), Anastasius I
(491–518), Justinian (527–565) (four coins), Justin II (565–
578), Phocas (602–610), Heraclius (610–641), and Constans II
(641–668). During the sixth and seventh centuries the Slavic
tribes in Moravia, freed from the Avars, were slowly being formed
into a kind of political group, a process which ended in the
eighth century.

From that time on this new political formation began to grow
in importance benefitting from the decline of Avar power in
Pannonia. It is logical to suppose that the new opportunities
opening up in Moravia attracted artisans working for the Avars
at the courts of their chieftains, and that they began a kind of
exodus to the new country, an exodus accelerated by rivalries
among the Avar chieftains and by the blows dealt them by the

Franks under Charlemagne, which were undermining Avar domination in the lands which are now modern Hungary.

Byzantine influences in the seventh century had reached not only the Avars but also the Slavic tribes beyond the Carpathian mountains.[21] We can, however, hardly suppose that these same traditions could also find their way into Moravia.[22]

Notes

1. Cf. A. Schober, *Die Römerzeit in Österreich* (Vienna, 1935), p. 12.

2. For general information on Romans and Bavarians in Noricum see I. Zibermayr, *Noricum, Baiern, und Österreich* (München, Berlin, 1944), pp. 1–78. On the evacuation see *ibid.*, p. 56. In 565 Venantius Fortunatus made a pilgrimage from Ravenna to the grave of St. Afra in Augsburg, although the city was already occupied by the Bavarians, *ibid.*, p. 76.

3. There seem to have been fewer "Romans" left in Raetia among the Alemani than in Noricum among the Rugians and Bavarians. In the *Breves Notitiae* of Salzburg we find several references to *Romani* who probably were regarded as *colons* but also as *tributales*. The Bavarian duke had the right to dispose of them at his will. In the *Notitia Arnonis* we learn that when Bishop Rutpert decided to restore some of the buildings, probably from the Roman period, in the territory of Glanhofen, Duke Thodo (c. 700) richly endowed the church constructed by the bishop, adding to the endowment "de Romanis tributales homines LXXX cum coloniis suis in diversis locis." See W. Hauthaler, *Salzburger Urkundenbuch*, vol. 1, *Traditionscodices* (Salzburg, 1910), pp. 19, 20. Other dispositions of *Romani*, *ibid.*, p. 5 (Theodo: *Romanos et eorum tributales mansos LXXX*), p. 7; (Tassilo: *Romanos cum mansos tributales XXX*), p. 14; (Theodbertus: *Tributarios Romanos CXVI*), p. 15, (*idem dux Romanos at eorum mansos tributales LXXX*), p. 23, (*Romanos . . . in diversis locis colonos CXVI*), p. 24 (*Romanos tributales LXXX*), p. 50 (Romani); cf. J. Kudrna, *Studie k barbarským zákoníkům Lex Baiuvariorum a Lex Alamanorum* (Brno, 1959), *Opera universit. Brunensis, Facultas philosophica*, vol. 60, pp. 114, 121, 122, 125; J. Cibulka, *Velkomoravský kostel*, p. 117.

4. J. Dobiáš, *Dějiny československého území před vystoupením Slovanů* (The History of the Czechoslovak Territory before the Arrival of the Slavs) (Prague, 1964), pp. 154, 169, 175, 325–329.

5. R. Hošek, "Antique Traditions in Great Moravia," *Magna Moravia*, p. 74. The garrison at Mušov had probably to defend a detour from the Amber Road to the valley of the river Svitava, and the road following it into Bohemia: Mušov seems to have been a very important crossroad;

cf. J. Dobiáš, *Dějiny československého území*, p. 327; cf. *ibid.* on Stillfried (in Austria), a Roman fort protecting the Amber Road on the right of the Danube, and on other Roman fortifications, pp. 215, 280, 328.

6. V. Hochmanová-Vávrová, "Nálezy římských cihel u Starého Města a Uherského Hradiště" (Finds of Roman Bricks at Staré Město near Uherské Hradiště), *Spisy Purkyňovy university*, E 3 (Brno, 1957), pp. 23–26.

7. R. Hošek, "Antique Traditions," p. 76.

8. The *Geography* of Strabo, V, 1, 8, C214, ed. H. L. Jones (Loeb Library, 1923), vol. 2, p. 318. On the important road-net in Noricum see E. Polaschek, "Noricum," *Real-Encyklopädie*, vol. XVII, p. 968. On relations of Aquileia with Noricum and Noreia, *ibid.*, p. 1039 ff.

9. See J. Dobiáš, *Dějiny československého území*, p. 328. On Leugaricio, *ibid.*, pp. 13, 227, 257, 332.

10. On the inscription, see J. Dobiáš, *Dějiny československého území*, pp. 213, 257, 258.

11. T. Kolnik, "Ausgrabungen auf der römischen Station in Milanovice in den Jahren 1956–1957," *Limes Romanus Konferenz Nitra* (Bratislava, 1959), pp. 27–61; cf. also B. Svoboda, "Über das Nachleben der röm. Kultur im mittleren Donaubecken," *ibid.*, p. 110. On Roman fortifications in the territory of modern Slovakia see O. Pelikán, *Slovensko a rímské imperium* (Slovakia and the Roman Empire) (Bratislava, 1960), pp. 101–135; cf. also T. Kolnik, "Zu neuen römisch-barbarischen Funden in der Slowakei und ihrer Chronologie," *Studia historica slovaca*, 2 (1964), pp. 7–51.

12. For details see K. Majewski, *Importy rzymskie na zemiach slowianskich* (Roman Imports in Slavic Lands) (Wroclaw, 1949); *idem, Importy rzymskie w Polsce* (Roman Imports in Poland) (Warsaw, 1960); V. Ondrouch, *Bohaté hroby z doby rímskej na Slovensku* (Rich Tomb Found in Slovakia from the Roman period) (Bratislava, 1957); *idem, Limes Romanus na Slovensku* (Limes Romanus in Slovakia) (Bratislava, 1938); O. Pelikán, *Slovensko a rímské Imperium*, pp. 135–156; cf. also J. Dobiáš, *Le strade romane nel territorio cecoslovacco* (Rome, 1938) and B. Svoboda, *Čechy a římské Imperium* (Bohemia and the Roman Empire), *Acta musei nationalis Pragae*, vol. 2, A, Historia (Prague, 1948); with a résumé in English.

13. Cf. the short but well-written study by B. Svoboda, "Über das Nachleben," *Limes Romanus Konferenz Nitra*, pp. 107–116, especially pp. 110, 111; J. Dekan, "Die Beziehungen unserer Länder mit dem spätantiken und byzantinischen Gebiet in der Zeit vor Cyrill und Method," *Das Grossmährische Reich* (Prague, 1966), pp. 45–52.

14. B. Svoboda, "Über das Nachleben," p. 112.

15. For details see A. Alföldi, *Der Untergang der Römerherrschaft in Pannonia*, vol. 2 (Berlin, Leipzig, 1926), Ungarische Bibliothek, vol. 12, pp. 36–56.

16. Alföldi puts forward the theory that the *cella trichora* discovered in Sopianae was repainted in the eighth century in the style of Santa Maria Antiqua. Alföldi's papers were unavailable to me. See the quotations in B. Svoboda, "Poklad byzantského kovotepce v Zemianském Vrbovku" (The Treasure of a Byzantine Metalsmith Found in Zemianský Vrbovok), *Památky archeologické*, 44 (1953), 79, 80.

17. See D. Csallány, "Vizantijskie monety v avarskich nachodkach," résumé in French: "L'importance de la circulation monétaire byzantine pour les legs archéologiques des Avares," *Acta archaeologica Academiae scientiarum Hungaricae*, 2 (1952), p. 235 ff., 245 ff. J. Kovačević, "Avari i zlato," *Starinar*, XIII–XIV (1963–1964), pp. 125–135, attributes the lack of gold coins in Avar archaeological finds after the seventh century to the general monetary crisis in the Byzantine Empire which developed rapidly after the reign of Justinian I.

18. B. Svoboda, "Poklad," pp. 33–108. The eighteen silver coins were described and evaluated by P. Radoměrský in his study "Byzantské mince z pokladu v Zemianském Vrbovku" in *Památky archeologické*, 45 (1953), pp. 109–122. Both studies have a résumé in German. The author rightly states that the coins had not been in circulation. They represent a store of precious metal. They were minted in Constantinople and were most probably part of a tribute paid to an Avar chief, or a present offered to him by the Byzantine government. It would have been difficult for the artisan to gather so many new coins for his purpose. This may indicate that the Avar chief who possessed the coins commissioned them to the Byzantine artisan who was in his service and who had to produce jewels for him.

19. B. Svoboda, *Poklad,* pp. 79–85 with bibliographical notices of publications by Hungarian archaeologists. Cf. J. Eisner, *Devínská Nová Ves*, pp. 312, 313.

20. R. Hošek, *Antique Traditions*, p. 75. E. Pochitonov, "Nálezy antických mincí" (Finds of Antique Coins), in *Nálezy mincí v Čecháh na Moravě a ve Slezsku* (Finds of Coins in Bohemia, Moravia, and Silisia), ed. by E. Nohejlová-Prátová, 1 (Prague, 1955), pp. 85–134. Cf. V. Ondrouch, *Nálezy keltských, antických a byzantských mincí na Slovensku* (Finds of Celtic, Antique, and Byzantine Coins in Slovakia) (Bratislava, 1964), nos. 564, 565, 566, 577 (Theodosius II), no. 573 (Justinian I?), nos. 574, 575 (Justin II), no. 576 (Constans II, Constantine IV Pogonatus).

21. J. Werner, "Slawische Bügelfibeln des 7. Jahrhunderts," *Reinecke Festschrift,* ed. G. Behrens, J. Werner (Mainz, 1950), pp. 150–177, especially pp. 170, 171.

22. *Ibid.,* p. 168. Only one miniature fibula has been found, so far, in Moravia in Určice, and this is regarded by J. Werner as coming rather from Hungary. This fact seems to weaken the theory that many objects could have reached Moravia from the Pontus region. This influence was strong among the Slavs on Dnieper, but the supposition that they could have been an intercourse between these Slavs and the Moravians seems, so far, very doubtful. In this connection cf. also the study by B. Szöke, "Über die Beziehungen Moraviens zu dem Donaugebiet in der Spätavarenzeit," *Studia Slavica,* 6 (1960), pp. 75–112. The author tries to show that the material culture of Moravia was influenced more by Avar art than by Byzantium, and thinks that this art was introduced into the Carpathian basin from the region of Pontus and the Caucasus. His study contains some interesting and stimulating points, but his arguments, especially concerning the Caucasian influences on cultural development in the Carpathian basin in the ninth and tenth centuries, are not convincing. Even the regions of Pontus and the Caucasus could not escape Byzantine cultural influences. He recognizes, however, that Moravia became the heir of this civilization and developed it to a very high degree, as is shown by the results of recent excavations. But even Szöke admits some Byzantine influences on the products of Moravian artisans. However, J. Dekan, in his penetrating study "Les motifs figuraux humains sur les bronzes moulés de la zone danubienne centrale à l'epoque précédant l'empire de la Grande Moravie," *Studia historica slovaca,* 2 (1966), pp. 52–102, has shown that the motifs of human figures on the objects of bronze which were popular among the Avars in the eighth century were not inspired by ancient Avar mythology, which is unknown, nor brought into Avar Pannonia by another Avar wave from the interior of Asia, but were created under the influence of Byzantine artifacts reproducing old Hellenic, Hellenistic, and other mythological subjects. These traditions were revived in Byzantium during the iconoclastic period. The artists, not allowed to produce images of saints and of Christ, went back to Hellenic profane traditions and decorated the churches with motifs taken from Hellenic and Hellenistic art, with scenes from animal life, reproductions of trees, plants, and other profane objects. He shows that even some Sassanid and other Oriental motifs on those objects had reached the Avars through Byzantium.

III. By Which Route Did the Byzantine Embassy Reach Moravia?

The authors of the *Lives* of Constantine and Methodius do not reveal how and when the Byzantine embassy had reached Moravia. It is generally believed that after crossing Bulgaria the brothers travelled to Moravia by following the river Danube. This belief seems to be confirmed by the *Life of St. Wenceslas* written by the monk Christian (10th century), by the description of the Christianization of Bohemia and Moravia called *Diffundente sole* (12th century), the legend *Tempore Michaelis imperatoris* (13th century), and the legend *Beatus Cirillus* (12th century).[1] All these legends attribute the Christianization of the Bulgarians to Constantine when he crossed their country on his way to Moravia. These recitals deserve, however, no credit. We have more reliable information as to the Christianization of Bulgaria, and Constantine had no part in it. These legends cannot even be quoted as an indication of the fact that the brothers did reach Moravia by going through Bulgarian territory. Their narration reflects the situation in the tenth century when the disciples of Constantine and Methodius, expelled from Moravia, found refuge in Bulgaria, where the Slavonic liturgy introduced by the two brothers was in use.

Recently an attempt has been made by J. Cibulka[2] to give more precise information about the route taken by the two brothers. The basis of his ideas is to follow the old Roman roads which crossed the former Roman provinces of Thrace and Macedonia to Singidunum (modern Belgrade), and from there led through Pannonia along the river Danube to Brigetium, or Carnuntum. On the basis of the indications given by the famous map of

Peutinger,[3] he enumerates the resting places and relays which the brothers are supposed to have used, and the distances separating them. Assuming that the travellers covered forty kilometers daily, he comes to the conclusion that the brothers could have reached the Moravian boundary in 38 days, or in three weeks, perhaps even more rapidly.

It is an interesting attempt which gives valuable information about travels in the early Middle Ages, but it has many weaknesses. First, the author's account is rather arbitrary, and is influenced by the tendency to disprove the old tradition, so far generally accepted, that the brothers got to Moravia in the autumn of 863. To support his own original thesis he prolongs the stay of the Moravian embassy in Constantinople, assuming that the composition of the new alphabet, the choice of the Greek texts necessary for the mission, their translation into a language which had no literary tradition, together with other preparations, must have lasted at least one year. Therefore, the Byzantine mission could have left Constantinople only in the spring of 864.

There is, however, no reason to suppose that the preparations for the Moravian mission took so long. As has been already shown, the conversion of the Slavs on Greek soil had been in progress for some decades and was a very urgent matter for the Byzantine Church and for the consolidation of what was left of former Illyricum. It was necessary that not only Frankish but also Byzantine missionaries translated into Slavonic the most important prayers and beliefs in order to instruct the new converts. The brothers and their companions could make profitable use of these first attempts, and compare the adaptations with what they were able to learn from the members of the Moravian embassy, who were certainly Christians and must have had some instruction. We have seen that efforts had been made to transliterate Slavic words with Greek letters. It is generally accepted that the main basis of the glagolitic alphabet is the Greek minuscule. It was therefore natural for the Greek missionaries to use this current writing in their works. Constantine may have been helped in his composition by these first essays. On the other hand, the envoys were anxious to return to their country with the new missionaries as early as possible. There is no reason to suppose that the Moravian envoys got to Constantinople only in 863. Everything indicates that Rastislav had addressed himself to Rome in 862 and, after the refusal of his request by Rome, was anxious to get help from Byzantium at the earliest date.

Moreover, there is no documentary evidence that the mission had chosen the route described by J. Cibulka. He does not pay sufficient attention to the fact that in 863 the old Roman roads must have been in rather bad shape after so many invasions into Pannonia, and after the bitter fighting between the Bulgars and the Byzantines in the first half of the ninth century. We have seen that Pannonia had been cut off from Byzantium at the end of the seventh century. Almost all contact of the Avars with the Byzantines ceased for more than a century. The Bulgars were fighting for their existence in the eighth century, and more peaceful conditions and better commercial relations between Bulgaria and Byzantium were possible only after 839. We can imagine how all this contributed to the destruction of old Roman roads in Thrace and Macedonia. The Bulgars do not seem to have repaired roads which followed the Danube into Moravia. They were more interested in intercourse with the Franks, and had better links with them through the valleys of Drava and Sava. The author quotes a few instances of travels from the eleventh century through Hungary to Constantinople. However, this does not show that this route was in frequent use in the ninth century.

It is true that commercial relations between Bulgaria and Byzantium existed for about twenty years before 863, but how frequent were they? We have noticed that direct Byzantine imports into Moravia were rather insignificant during the first half of the ninth century. Then, was it safe to send a Christian mission with so many important persons through pagan Bulgaria? The Byzantine intelligence service was certainly well aware of Boris' sympathy for the Franks. As we have seen, even before 853 Boris seems to have intrigued with Charles the Bald against Louis the German, when he attacked the Pannonian Croats living under Louis' sovereignty, and his improved relations with Louis would have been known in Byzantium. In such circumstances a Byzantine embassy crossing Bulgaria to its other neighbor could hardly expect to find a warm welcome in Boris' territory. There was, however, an old Roman road with relays which had remained in better condition, the Via Egnatia,[4] which crossed Byzantine territory from Constantinople through Saloniki to Dyrrhachium, from where there was easy access by boat to another Byzantine possession—Venice. From there the Amber Road, used by Aquileian and Venetian merchants, and probably in better condition than the old Roman roads in Pannonia, led to former Carnuntum, near the confluence of the river Morava with the Danube. The Via Egnatia was also the artery which connected Constantinople with Rome, through Dyrrhachium, the Adriatic, and the old Roman roads leading to the capital. Travel from Constantinople to Rome, in the imperial period, took twenty-four days.[5] The Via Egnatia and Dyrrhachium connected Constantinople also with the remains of Byzantine possessions in Dalmatia and their capital Zara. This was, for the Byzantines of this time, the safest way to the West, and it would seem normal that the Byzantine government should choose this route to send its embassy to Moravia.

Cibulka thinks that the brothers took the route through Bulgaria and ancient Pannonia rather than the route by water in order to avoid danger of piratical attacks at sea. However, they travelled by sea from Constantinople to Cherson and back in 861. There was also the danger of hostile action on the part of the Russians settled in the Delta of Dnieper, from where they had attacked Constantinople the previous year. The ships carrying the envoys probably sailed not far from the coast, as the navigators of those times usually did. This shows that the brothers were familiar with this kind of travel and were probably escorted by imperial war vessels.

As concerns the Adriatic sea, it is known that the Slavic Narentans were dangerous pirates. The Venetians had tried to put a stop to this activity and had even tried to convert them to Christianity, but with little success. However, we do not hear of any hostile action by the Narentans against Byzantine Dalmatia. Probably the reorganization of the *Thema* of Dyrrhachium and of the naval *Thema* of Cephalonia was responsible for this restriction on their piratical activities.

On the other hand, there is the famous affair of the papal legates returning from Constantinople after the completion of the Ignatian council of 869–870. They reached Dyrrhachium safely, together with Anastasius Bibliothecarius, the envoy of Louis II to Basil I. The latter discloses[6] that the emperor gave them a military escort led by a *drungarios* on the Via Egnatia. This reveals, at the same time, that this old Roman road was again in good repair and under military protection, although it touched or passed through Bulgarian territory on Lake Ochrida. The legates took a ship bound for Ancona, but fell into the hands of the Narentans, who deprived them of everything, including the volumes containing the *Acts* of the Council, as well as the documents signed by the assisting bishops who professed their submission to Rome. Pope Hadrian II complained to Basil that he had not given sufficient protection to the legates on their return journey.[7] The Emperor Louis II also sent a letter to Basil with the same complaint,[8] putting most of the blame on the imperial navy in the Adriatic sea which, instead of turning against the Narentans, raided the camps of the Croats who were helping Louis to conquer Bari from the Arabs.

This episode is often quoted in order to show how risky navigation was in the Adriatic at that time. The complaints voiced by the pope and by Louis II show, however, that the incident would not have taken place if the emperor had given to the legates the protection they expected and deserved. This neglect seems to have been intentional. We know that Basil was dissatisfied with the attitude of the legates at the Council. He disliked especially their insistence that the bishops sign a declaration in which they accepted the decision made at the Roman synod condemning Photius. He even made an attempt to get hold of this document with the signatures to destroy it.[9] One is thus tempted to suspect that the Byzantines were in some way responsible for this incident. If the emperor had really wanted to destroy these documents he should have created a similar incident for Anastasius. The latter had copied the *Acts* of the Council in Constantinople and had accompanied the legates on their return journey as far as Dyrrhachium. There he took a boat for Siponto. This part of the Adriatic was too far from the land of the Narentans, and so it happened that Anastasius arrived safely in Siponto, and reached Rome via Benevento. Had hé not saved the *Acts*, together with the other documents, Rome would never have learned what had really happened in Constantinople.

Anyhow, the bitter complaints voiced by the pope and Louis II indicate that such incidents could be prevented by the imperial administration if certain protective measures were taken. Such measures were certainly taken to safeguard the imperial embassy to the Moravians. There is thus no reason to suppose that the two brothers had no choice but to take the route through Bulgaria.

They could reach Moravia via Dyrrhachium and Venice. Even by this road, they could have arrived at the Court of Rastislav in the autumn of 863.[10]

Notes

1. Christian's *Legend* was published by J. Pekař, *Die Wenzels- und Ludmila-Legenden und die Echtheit Christians* (Prague, 1906). The other three legends were republished by V. Chaloupecký in the supplement of his work *Prameny X. století* (Sources of the Tenth Century) (Prague, 1939), Svatováclavský Sborník (Symposium on St. Wenceslas), vol. II, 2, p. 459 ff. Cf. the bibliographical notices given by A. Salajka in the symposium *Soluňští bratři* (The Brothers of Thessalonica) (Prague, 1962), p. 217 ff.

2. "Der Zeitpunkt der Ankunft der Brüder Konstantin-Cyrillus und Methodius in Mähren," *Byzantinoslavica*, 26 (1965), pp. 318–364.

3. Published with commentary and some old *Itineraria* by K. Miller, *Itineraria romana, römische Reisewege an der Hand der Tabula Peutingeriana dargestellt* (Stuttgart, 1926).

4. K. Miller, *Itineraria romana*, p. 516 ff. Itinerarium Antonini, *ibid.*, pp. LXII, LXIII; Th. L. F. Tafel, *Via Egnatia* (Tübingen, 1837–1842).

5. Cf. the map in M. P. Charlesworth, *Trade Routes and Commerce of the Roman Empire* (Cambridge, 1926), and p. 118. L. Duchesne gives convincing documentary evidence that in the sixth century Constantinople could be reached from Rome in a month's time. Favorable conditions on sea travel could help to shorten the duration of the trip. See his study "Liber diurnus et les élections pontificales au VIIe siècle," *Bibliothèque de l'Ecole des Chartes*, vol. 52 (Paris, 1891), p. 17.

6. In his introduction to his translation of the *Acts* of this synod, *PL*, 129, col. 39; *MGH Ep* 7, p. 410. Cf. especially *Vita Hadriani II* in L. Duchesne, *Liber pontificalis* (Paris, 1892), vol. 2, pp. 180, 184, the description of how the legates had travelled on the road from Dyrrhachium to Constantinople and back. The emperor sent the spatharius Eusebius to Thessalonica to greet them. The official reception was in Selymbria, where the protospatharius Sisinius had put forty horses from imperial stables at their disposal, as well as silver ware and a number of servants. The legates must have travelled rather leisurely. They left Rome in June and arrived in Constantinople only on September 15, but this can also be an indication of how the old Roman roads had deteriorated since imperial times.

7. *MGH Ep* 6, p. 759: "Apocrisiarios quoque nostros . . . licet sero"— they had left Constantinople in March 870 and, after being released by the pirates, had reached Rome only on December 22, 870—"post multa

tamen pericula, depredationesque atque propriorum hominum trucida-
tionem, nudos tamen recepimus.... Unde audientes haec universi
gemunt... quod ita dispositionis vestrae constitutio improvide prodire
potuerit ut in barbarorum gladios, nullo imperii vestri fulti praesidio,
miseriter inciderint...."

8. The letter is quoted by the author of the *Chronicon Salernitanum,*
MGH Ss 3, p. 525.

9. See for details F. Dvornik, *The Photian Schism* (Cambridge, 1948),
p. 144 ff.

10. According to the *Itinerarium Antonii* the distance from Constantinople to Dyrrhachium is 754 miles. When we add to this the distance
from Venice-Aquileia to Carnuntum, indicated by J. Cibulka, according
to the same *Itinerarium* and the sea passage, the route through Bulgaria and Pannonia appears shorter. We can, however, presume that
the travel on the Via Egnatia was more comfortable and speedier because of numerous imperial relay stations where fresh horses were
available. It may be that the Moravian envoys had reached Constantinople by the same route. It is possible that they were identical with
Rastislav's envoys to Rome. The old Amber Road was the only direct
connection of Moravia with the Adriatic and must have been used by
merchants, because the disciples of St. Methodius, sold as slaves in
Moravia by Wiching, appeared on the slave market in Venice and were
redeemed by an envoy of Basil I (see above, p. 251). It is difficult to
compare the traveling on the Roman roads in the ninth century with
traveling on the same roads in imperial days. We have seen that the
legates sent to the Ignatian council left Rome in June 869—at least the
papal letters which they carried were dated June 10—and arrived in
Constantinople on September 15. The envoys of Louis II to Basil I—
Anastasius and two nobles—reached Constantinople in February 870,
because they were present at the tenth and last session of the council,
which took place on February 28. It is not known when they left Italy,
but presumably it was in November 869. Unfortunately, Anastasius,
who had left Constantinople with the legates in March 870, does not
say when they reached Dyrrhachium. He does not say either when he
arrived at Benevento, where he had to report to Louis II on the result
of his embassy. He must have stayed there for some time but was active in Rome in his old position in July. Cf. A. Lapôtre, *De Anastasio
bibliothecario* (Paris, 1885), pp. 244–252; E. Perels, *Papst Nikolaus I
und Anastasius bibliothecarius* (Berlin, 1920), pp. 235–239. In imperial
days the journey from Rome to Constantinople could be made in
twenty-four days. Basil's envoy to Hadrian II, the spathar Euthymius,
who probably had left Constantinople in the spring of 868, was in Rome
in the early summer of the same year. Another embassy with the repre-

sentatives of the two patriarchs travelled during the winter of 868 and seems to have reached Rome at the end of February or the beginning of March. See. F. Dvornik, *The Photian Schism* (Cambridge, 1948), pp. 139–141.

Notes

CHAPTER I

1. For details see L. Niederle, *Slovanské starožitnosti,* vol. 2 (Prague, 1906–1910), devoted to the Southern Slavs; F. Dvornik, *Les Slaves, Byzance et Rome au IXᵉ siècle* (Paris, 1926), p. 3 ff.; *idem, The Slavs, their Early History and Civilization* (Boston, 1956), pp. 3–45; on the Antes, cf. *idem, The Making of Central and Eastern Europe* (London, 1949), pp. 279–286, 309–311. A thorough review of the problems connected with the earliest history of the Slavs, with bibliographical references, is given by B. Zástěrová, "Hlavní problémy z počátku dějin Slovanskych národů" (Main Problems Concerning the Primitive History of the Slavic Nations), *Vznik a počátky Slovanů,* ed. J. Eisner (Prague, 1956), vol. 1, pp. 28–83. For complete bibliography on the origins and migration of the Slavs, see J. Eisner, *Rukověť slovanské archeologie* (Handbook of Slavic Archaeology) (Prague, 1965), and H. Lowmianski, *Początki Polski* (Origins of Poland) (Warsaw, 1963), vol. 1, pp. 31–97; (Origin of the Slavs), vol. 2, p. 7 ff. (Migration, Origin of Croats, Huns, Avars, and the Slavs.

2. For details, cf. L. Hauptmann, "Les rapports des Byzantins avec les Slaves et les Avars pendant la seconde moitié du VIᵉ siècle," *Byzantion,* 4 (1927–1928), pp. 137–170; H. Preidel, "Avaren und Slaven," *Südostdeutsche Forschungen,* 11 (1946–1952), pp. 33–45; P. Lemerle, "Invasions et migrations dans les Balkans depuis la fin de l'époque romaine jusqu'au VIIIᵉ siècle," *Revue historique,* 78 (1954), pp. 265–308; G. Labuda, "Chronologie des guerres de Byzance contre les Avars et les Slaves à la fin du VIᵉ siècle," *Byzantinoslavica,* 11 (1950), pp. 167–173; A. Kollautz, "Die Awaren," *Saeculum,* 5 (1954), pp. 129–178; B. Zástěrová, "Avaři a Slované," *Vznik a počátky Slovanů,* ed. J. Eisner, 2 (Prague, 1958), pp. 19–54 (review of modern works on Avars).

3. A. Alföldi, *Der Untergang der Römerherrschaft in Pannonien* (Berlin-Leipzig, 1924–1926), 2 vols.

4. See A. Bon, *Le Péloponnèse byzantin jusqu'en 1204* (Paris, 1951), p. 15 ff., 48, 63, 71, 80, 102, 163.

5. M. Vasmer, *Die Slaven in Griechenland* (Berlin, 1941). Cf. also P. Charanis, "The Chronicle of Monemvasia and the Question of the Slavonic Settlements in Greece," *Dumbarton Oaks Papers,* 5 (1950), pp. 139–166, with a more recent bibliography; P. Lemerle, "La Chronique improprement dite de Monemvasie: le contexte historique et légendaire," *Revue des études byzantines,* 21 (1963), pp. 5–49.

6. Cf. Nicephorus, *Historia syntomos,* ed. C. de Boor (Teubner ed., 1880), pp. 12, 24; see S. Runciman, *A History of the First Bulgarian Empire* (London, 1930), pp. 11–16.

7. This is suggested by G. Vernadsky in his study, "The Beginning of the Czech State," *Byzantion,* 17 (1944–1945), p. 321.

8. The only reliable information on the revolt is given by Fredegar's Chronicle, book IV, chs. 48, 68, 75, ed. B. Krusch, *MGH Ss Rer. Merov.,* 2 (Hanover, 1888), pp. 144, 154, 158. Cf. J. M. Wallace-Hadrill, *The Fourth Book of the Chronicle of Fredegar* (London-New York, 1960), pp. 39, 56, 63. Fredegar dates the assumption of the leadership by Samo as 623. For details, see G. Labuda, *Pierwsze państwo Slowian-śkie, państwo Samona* (Poznań, 1949), p. 30 ff. A summary in French with critical remarks on Labuda's work is given by V. Chaloupecký in *Byzantinoslavica,* 11 (1952), pp. 223–239. Cf. also F. Dvornik, *The Slavs,* p. 60 ff. It is not impossible that Heraclius approached the Franks in this respect, although we have no evidence for it. Fredegar (ch. 62, ed. B. Krusch, p. 152; J. M. Wallace-Hadrill, p. 51) reports that in 629 "Servatus and Paternus, the ambassadors whom Dagobert had sent to the Emperor Heraclius, returned home with the news that they had made with him a treaty of perpetual peace." It was the first year of Dagobert's reign over the whole of Francia—from 623 to 629 he was king of Austrasia—and it could be assumed that the ambassadors were announcing the beginning of Dagobert's reign, but the mention of the conclusion of a treaty of friendship seems to indicate that there was something more in this sending of an embassy. The Avars were common enemies of the Franks and the Byzantines. It is not impossible that this was an answer to a previous move of Byzantine diplomacy. R. Barroux has little to say on this problem in his book, *Dagobert, roi des Francs* (Paris, 1938), p. 155 ff. Cf. also below, Ch. III, p. 74.

9. For details, see F. Dvornik, *The Making of Central and Eastern Europe,* p. 268 ff. G. Moravcsik, R. J. H. Jenkins, *Constantine Porphyrogenitus, De Administrando Imperio* (Budapest, 1949), chs. 29, 30 (Croats), 32 (Serbs), p. 129 ff., 153 ff. I have given a new review of the problem in *Constantine Porphyrogenitus, De Administrando Imperio,* 2, *Commentary,* ed. R. J. H. Jenkins (London, 1962), pp. 93–100, 114–118 (Croats), 131–134 (Serbs).

10. *De admin, imperio,* ed. G. Moravcsik, R. J. H. Jenkins, ch. 131, p. 149.

11. *Geschichte der Serben* (Gotha, 1911), 1, p. 104.

12. On Illyricum, see F. Dvornik, *Les Légendes de Constantin et de Méthode vues de Byzance* (Prague, 1933), pp. 249–256.

13. See M. V. Anastos, "The Transfer of Illyricum, Calabria, and Sicily to the Jurisdiction of Constantinople in 732–33," *Silloge Byzan-*

tina in onore de S. G. Mercati (Rome, 1957), pp. 14–36, with more recent bibliography on Illyricum. On the early history of Illyricum see R. Rogošić, *Veliki Ilirik* (*284–395*) *i njegova konečna dioba* (*396–437*) (Zagreb, 1962), with a summary in Latin, pp. 209–217: De Illyrico toto (284–395) deque eius divisione (396–437).

14. I have discussed these problems in detail in my commentary on Constantine's report in *Constantine Porphyrogenitus, De Administrando Imperio, 2, Commentary,* p. 124 ff.

15. *Historia Salonitana,* publ. by F. Rački in *Documenta spectantia ad historiam Slavorum meridionalium,* 26 (Zagreb, 1894), ch. 11, p. 33.

16. For details see F. Balić, J. Bervaldi, *Kronotaksa Solinskih biskupa, Kronotaksa spljetskih nadbiskupa* (Zagreb, 1912–13), p. 116 ff.; F. Šišić, *Povijest Hrvata* (Zagreb, 1926), p. 290 ff.

17. Ch. Diehl, *Etudes sur l'administration byzantine dans l'exarchat de Ravenne* (Paris, 1888), pp. 3–23, 31–40, 81–92; L. M. Hartmann, *Untersuchungen zur Geschichte der byzantinischen Verwaltung in Italien* (*590–750*) (Leipzig, 1889), pp. 1–28; F. Šišić, *Povijest Hrvata,* pp. 166–174.

18. *Gregorii I papae Registrum epistolarum,* ed. L. M. Hartmann, *Registrum,* II, ep. 23 (*MGH Ep* 1, p. 121).

19. *Registrum,* IV, ep. 20, *MGH Ep* 1, p. 254 ff.

20. *Registrum,* V, ep. 6, *ibid.,* p. 286.

21. *Registrum,* VI, ep. 25, *ibid.,* pp. 402–404.

22. *Registrum,* VIII, ep. 24, *ibid.,* 2, p. 26.

23. *Registrum,* IX, ep. 157, *ibid.,* 2, p. 155; *Registrum,* IX, ch. 158, *ibid.,* 2, p. 159.

24. *Registrum,* IX, ep. 149, 151, 177, *ibid.,* 2, pp. 150, 155, 156, 171 ff.

25. *Registrum,* IX, ep. 176, *ibid.,* 2, p. 172.

26. Procopius, *De bello gothico,* III, 33, 40, ed. Bonn (1833), pp. 418, 450 (for years 549, 550); Menander, *Historia,* ed. Bonn (1829), ch. 31, p. 340 (for the year 519).

27. The Ostrogothic king Odoacer, after having conquered Dalmatia (482) detached it from the Italian prefecture, but incorporated it into his kingdom of Italy. Cf. E. Stein, *Histoire du Bas-Empire,* 2 (Bruges, 1949), pp. 50, 51. Cf. also B. Saria, "Dalmatien als spätantike Provinz," *Pauly's Realencyclopedie,* Supplement Band 8 (1956), p. 24 ff.

28. *Ibid.,* p. 801.

29. Ph. Jaffé, *Regesta pontificum romanorum,* 2d edition by W. Wattenbach (Leipzig, 1885), vol. 1, no. 1052, p. 138.

30. E. Stein, *Histoire du Bas-Empire,* pp. 424, 802. It is to be regretted that Stein did not pay any attention to the correspondence of Gregory the Great concerning Archbishop Maximus of Salona. He would probably have seen that Gregory's letter to Jobinus of Illyricum

does not prove his opinion. J. Ferluga, *Vizantiska uprava u Dalmaciji* (Beograd, 1957), p. 27 ff., followed Stein in dating the creation of the proconsulate of Dalmatia from the period of Justinian I. D. Mandić in his *Rasprave i prilozi iz stare hrvatske povjesti* (Essays and Annexes Concerning Old Croat History) (Rome, 1963), does not know Stein's and Ferluga's works, but shows convincingly (pp. 32–50) that Dalmatia was part of the exarchate of Ravenna. See the English translation of his arguments in *Byzantion,* 34 (1964), pp. 347–374 under the title "Dalmatia in the Exarchate of Ravenna from the Middle of the VI until the Middle of the VII Century." Cf. also my remark in the paper "Byzantium, Rome, the Franks, and the Christianization of the Southern Slavs," *Cyrillo-Methodiana* (Cologne, Graz, 1964), pp. 89, 93.

31. J. Ferluga, *Vizantiska uprava,* p. 36.

32. See the excerpt from his writing in Constantine Porphyrogenitus' *De Ceremoniis,* I, ed. Bonn, p. 388.

33. There is yet another letter of Gregory of March 591, addressed to Malchus, bishop of Dalmatia, which seems to attest this interest (*Registrum,* I, ep. 36, *MGH Ep* 1, p. 49). The pope discloses to Malchus that John, the "consularius" of the exarch George, has some controversies with Stephen, bishop of Scodra. Malchus is invited to investigate the complaints of John and to execute the decisions of the council of bishops.

34. Book 2, ed. Bonn (1840), p. 57; ed. A. Pertusi, *Costantino Porfirogenito De Thematibus,* Studi e Testi, 160 (1952), pp. 40–44, 94.

35. Justinian's *Novella 131* of March 18, 545, ed. R. Scholl, W. Kroll (Corpus Iuriscivilis, vol. 3) (Berlin, 1928), p. 655.

36. E. Schwartz, *Vigiliusbriefe. Zur Kirchenpolitik Justinians,* Sitzungsberichte der bayer. Akademie, Phil. hist. Kl. (1940), pp. 19, 21, perhaps also p. 11, if we accept Schwartz' reading *Dalmatarum* instead of *aliarum.*

37. *Liber contra Mocianum, PL,* 67, col. 864.

38. *Liber Pontificalis,* ed. L. Duchesne (Paris, 1886, 1892), 1, pp. 279, 323, 325.

39. *Historia Salonitana Maior,* ch. 10, ed. F. Rački, p. 33, ed. N. Klaić (Beograd, Serbian Academy, 1967), p. 93.

40. Cf. G. Ostrogorsky, *History of the Byzantine Empire* (New Brunswick, 1969, rev. ed.), p. 106.

41. D. Mandić, *Rasprave i prilozi,* p. 178 ff., would like to date this rescript in the reign of Constans II and his son, the Emperor Constantine IV, who reigned between 654 and 668. This can hardly be accepted. These incidents seem to have happened soon after the refugees had settled in Diocletian's palace.

42. *Liber Pontificalis,* vol. 1, p. 330.

43. L. Karaman, "Sarkofag Ivana Ravenjanina," *Starinar*, ser. III 3 (Beograd, 1925), p. 43: *Hic requiescit fragilis et inutilis Iohannis pecator harchi episcopus.* Cf. also G. Novak, *Povijest Splital* (The History of Split) (Split, 1957), 1, pp. 43–46.

44. "O počecima srednjevjekovnog Splita do godina 800" (The Early Period of Medieval Spalato to the Year 800), *Serta Hoffilleriana*, Vjesnik hrvatsko-archeol. društva (Zagreb, 1940), pp. 419–436, with a résumé in German.

45. M. Barada, "Nadvratnik VII stoletia iz kaštel Sućurca" (A Church Portal of the VIIth Century in the Castle of Sućurac), *ibid.*, pp. 401–418. The inscription is only partly preserved: *aspice hunc opus miro quo decore facto, quo Domino iubante pre* . . . Barada's dating is more reliable than Karaman's. The latter seems to have been influenced by the opinion of modern Croat historians who dated the Christianization of the Croats in the eighth and ninth centuries.

46. *Historia Salonitana*, ch. 11, p. 33, ed. N. Klaić, p. 94.

47. The discovery was made on February 24, 1958, and was announced in *Slobodna Dalmacija* (Spalato, February 26, 1958), p. 5. I am using the photos and the description given by D. Mandić in *Rasprave i prilozi*, p. 8 ff., 16–18. The exterior sarcophagus dates from the fourth century, and is adorned with a relief of the Good Shepherd. It bears an inscription from 1103 stating that in this year Archbishop Crescentius had ordered the inspection of the relics of St. Domnius which were contained therein. The relics are in a small leaden container of early Christian character. The container lay in another sarcophagus of white marble shaped from the pedestal of a monument in honor of the Emperor Trajan in Spalato. It was probably used in the transfer of the relics to Spalato. It bears the following inscription: "Hic requiescit corpus beati Domnii Salonitani archiepiscopi discipuli sancti Petri apostolorum principis translatum ab Salona in Spalatum a Joanne eiusdem sedis archipresule."

48. This was also my opinion in my commentary on Porphyrogenitus' work, *Const. Porphyrogen. De admin, imp.*, 2, ed. R. J. H. Jenkins, *Commentary*, p. 109. The Commentary was written before 1958. Of course, Domnius was not a disciple of St. Peter. See the bibliography on this legend in my *Commentary*, p. 109.

49. Cf. V. Laffarini, "Un'iscrizione Torcellana del sec. VII," *Atti Istituto Veneto sc. lett. e arti*, 73 (1914), p. 2 ff.

50. Paulus Diaconus, *Historia Langobardorum*, IV, 44, *MGH*, ser. Lang., p. 134 ff. Cf. D. Mandić, *Razprave i prilozi*, p. 11.

51. *De admin. imp.*, ch. 30, ed. G. Moravcsik, R. J. H. Jenkins, p. 142.

52. *Mansi*, II, col. 294; *PL*, 87, cols. 1224 ff. Cf. my commentary to *De admin. imp.*, p. 126.

53. S. Sakać, "Ugovor pape Agatona i Hrvata proti navalnom ratu," *Crotia sacra,* 1 (1931), pp. 1–84, dates this "pact" in the years 679–680, but he exaggerates its importance.

54. This observation has already been made by J. Markwart, *Osteuropäische und ostasiatische Streifzüge* (Leipzig, 1903), p. XVII.

55. It is true that the old catalogue of the bishops of Zara does not mention any name after Sabinianus (598) until that of Donatus (802). See N. Brunelli, *Storia di Zara* (Venice, 1913), 1, pp. 162, 163. But even F. Šišić, *Povijest Hrvata,* p. 286, admits that they are not reliable. However, C. F. Bianchi, *Zara christiana* (Zara, 1877–1879), 1, pp. 33, 34, traced the existence of certain bishops in the seventh and eighth centuries. M. Barada, "Episcopus Chroatensis," *Croatia sacra,* 1 (1931), pp. 164–172, thinks that the reorganization of the ecclesiastical situation in Dalmatia was carried out by Byzantium in the second half of the eighth century, after the loss of Ravenna to the Lombards.

56. F. Šišić, *Priručnik izvora hrvatske historije (Enchiridion fontium historiae croaticae)* (Zagreb, 1914), pp. 157–164.

57. *Chronicon gradense, MGH Ss* 7, pp. 44–45. Rački, *Documenta,* p. 235. Cf. also *Chronicon Venetum (Altinate), MGH Ss* 14, p. 13 ff. The patriarch of Aquileia took refuge in Grado after the occupation of northern Italy and of Aquileia by the Lombards. The patriarchal title for Aquileia first appears in 558–560 in a letter of Pope Pelagius I, *Regesta pontificum Romanorum, Italia pontificia,* ed. P. F. Kehr, 7 (Berlin, 1923), p. 20.

58. The metropolitan of old Aquileia refused to join his colleague of Grado, and also assumed the title of patriarch. In recognition of his submission, the Pope granted this title to the bishop of Grado. The patriarch of Aquileia, residing in Cividale, submitted to Rome about 700. From that time on the titularies of both seats were in constant dispute about the right of using the patriarchal title and the extent of their jurisdiction (see above, pp. 20, 21). Only in 1180 was a compromise reached according to which the titularies of both sees were permitted to use the title. Grado–Nova Aquileia–became the metropolis for the bishoprics of the Adriatic islands. From 1156 the patriarch of Grado resided in Venice, and in 1451 the patriarchate of Grado was abolished and the title given to the archbishop of Venice. The patriarchate of Aquileia was abolished in 1751. On the history of the patriarchate see W. Lenel, *Venezianischistrische Studien* (Strassburg, 1911); F. Heiler, *Altkirchliche Autonomie und päpstlicher Zentralismus* (Munich, 1941), pp. 108–112; H. Schmidinger, *Patriarch und Landesherr* (Graz, Cologne, 1954), pp. 1–11.

59. *Ljetopis popa Dukljanina,* ch. 9, ed. F. Šišić (Beograd, Zagreb, 1928), p. 302, ed. V. Mošin (Zagreb, 1950), p. 50.

60. G. Marini, *I papiri diplomatici* (Rome, 1805), p. 121. Cf. D.

Mandić, *Razprave i prilogi,* p. 90. The document is not clear. However, the donation of money for the redemption of captives seems to authorize its dating from this period. D. Mandić seems to exaggerate the importance of some of the documents published by Marini.

61. *Historia Salonitana,* ch. 13, ed. F. Rački, pp. 39, 40, ed. N. Klaić, p. 10.

62. I also expressed such an opinion in my book, *Les Légendes de Constantin et Méthode vues de Byzance* (Prague, 1933), p. 262 ff.

63. *MGH Ep* 6, pp. 438, 439. Cf. F. Dvornik, *Les Légendes,* p. 265 ff.

64. See G. Parthey, *Hieroclis Synecdemus et Notitiae graecae episcopatuum* (Berlin, 1866); H. Gelzer, "Ungedruckte und wenig bekannte Bistümerverzeichnisse der orientalischen Kirche," *Byzant. Zeitschrift,* I (1892), pp. 245–282; 2 (1893), pp. 22–72; *idem,* "Ungedruckte und ungenügend veröffentlichte Texte der Notitiae episcopatuum," Abhandlungen der bayer. Akad., phil. hist. Kl., 21 (1901), pp. 529–641.

65. This is confirmed by the *Tacticon* of the ninth century, published by Th. I. Uspenskij, *Vizantijskaja tabel' o rangach,* Mémoires de l'Institut archéologique russe de Constantinople, 3 (Sofia, 1898), pp. 99–137; p. 124: Ὁ ἄρχων Δαλματίας. We know the name of the governor of Byzantine Dalmatia from about 820. Einhard, in his *Annals,* calls him *Joannes praefectus provinciae illius, MGH Ss* 1, pp. 207–208. The patriarch of Grado, Fortunatus, accused of having encouraged the revolt of Ljudevit and of sending him artisans and masons for the construction of fortresses, took refuge in Zara. After disclosing the reasons for his flight from Grado to the governor, John put him straight away on a boat sailing for Constantinople.

66. *De admin, imp.,* chap. 30, ed. G. Moravcsik and R. J. H. Jenkins, p. 142. Cf. F. Dvornik, *Commentary to De admin. imp.,* ed. R. J. H. Jenkins, pp. 116, 117.

67. Cf. B. Grafenauer, "Prilog kritici izvještaja Konst. Porfirogeneta," Historicki Zbornik, 5 (1952), p. 31. In any event Constantine's Illyricum cannot be identified with Noricum.

68. Cf. Mandić, *Rasprave,* pp. 70–73.

69. See F. Dvornik, *Les Slaves, Byzance et Rome au IX's.* (Paris, 1926), p. 85 ff. We lack more precise information on the bishopric of Dyrrhachium.

70. *Ljetopis popa Dukljanina,* ch. 9, ed. Mošin, pp. 39–105, ed. F. Šišić, p. 30 ff. The meeting should have happened in the reign of a Pope called Stephen, and the representatives of the emperor are called John and Leo.

71. Mandić, *Rasprave,* p. 145 ff. He would like to date it under the reigns of the Croat Chief Budimir, Pope Stephen II (752–757), and the Emperor Constantine V. The report is, however, very confused. The Croat Chief is called Svetopelek, and there is talk of the activity of

St. Cyril in Croatia. This is certainly a reminder of the Moravian ruler
Svatopluk and of the Cyrilo-Methodian mission in Moravia. Even the
law book—*Methodos* or *Methodius*—which is said to have resulted
from this meeting, reminds us strangely of the *Nomocanon* which St.
Methodius had translated in Moravia, and which may have been
known in Dalmatia after 880. The Croat historians date this meeting,
if it really took place, at different periods. The safest date could be
the year 882, proposed by F. Šišić, *Povijest Hrvata*, p. 387 ff. Cf. also
V. Štefanić, "Tisuću i sto godina od moravske misije," *Slovo*, 13
(Zagreb, 1963), pp. 1–42, especially pp. 37, 38.

72. F. Šišić, *Povijest*, pp. 308, 309.

73. Cf. P. Skok, *Dolazak Slovena na Mediteran* (Split, 1934), p. 143
ff.: *koludar, koludrica* (Monk, nun) from the Greek *kalogeros* meaning venerable (monk), used in northern Dalmatia; *duvna* (nun), from
domina, used in the south; *žežinjati* (fast), from *jejunium*, used as far
as Tuzla in Bosnia; *oltar* (altar); *kum* (godfather) from *compater;*
koleda (Christmas songs) from *calendas*. The cult of the patron saints
of the coastal cities must also have spread very early to the Slavic
population, as we see from the slavicization of their names by the
people: Tripun (Triphon in Split), Dujam (Domnius in Trogir),
Lovrec (Laurentius in Zadar), St. Krševan (Chrysogorus), St. Stošija
(Anastasia). Cf. also P. Skok, "La terminologie chrétienne en slave: le
parrain, la marraine et le filleul," *Revue eds études slaves,* 10 (1930),
pp. 186–204.

74. C. Jireček, "Die Romanen in den Städten Dalmatiens während
des Mittelalters," *Denkschriften der Akademie der Wissenschaften,*
Phil. hist. Kl., vol. 28 (Vienna, 1902), pp. 51–58. Cf. also J. Šetka,
Hrvatska kričanska terminologia (Zagreb, 1940, 1964, 1965).

75. *Idem,* "Das christliche Element in der topographischen Nomenclatur der Balkanländer," Sitzungsberichte der Akad. Phil. hist. Kl.
(Vienna, 1897), p. 20 ff. A similar development can be found in the
former Epirus. The Albanians changed the word *sanctus* into *sin, ibid.,*
p. 18 ff. P. Skok, *Slavenstvo i romanstvo na jadranskim otocima* (Zagreb, 1950), p. 179, stresses that the prefix *sut* attached to combinations
of the names of saints can be found mostly in the toponymy near the
Adriatic sea where the Slavs were under the direct influence of the
Latin Christian population. V. Putanec, in his study "Refleksi starodalmato-romanskog prodjeva *sanctus* u onomastici obalne Hrvatske,"
Slovo, 13 (Zagreb, 1963), pp. 137–175, gives an index of names of
saints with the prefix *sut, sud, st, su,* etc., derived from the word *sanctus*. He shows convincingly (pp. 156, 157) that the names with the
prefix *sut* could have been formed only during the first period of the
Christianization of the Croats, from the seventh century to the tenth.
The slavic word *sveti* which was, in the prechristian period, an at-

tribute of pagan divinities, replaced the prefix *sut* only from the fifteenth century on. For the later period, see G. Novak, "The Slavonic-Latin Symbiosis in Dalmatia during the Middle Ages," *The Slavonic and East European Review*, 32 (1953), pp. 1–28.

76. Annales Laurissenses, *MGH Ss* 1, p. 186, Einhardi Annales, *ibid.*, p. 187. See F. Dvornik, *Les Slaves, Byzance et Rome au IXe siècle* (Paris, 1926), p. 46 ff.

77. Einhardi Annales, *ibid.*, p. 193, Rački, *Documenta,* p. 310.

78. Cf. Šišić, *Povijest,* p. 308.

79. See Alcuin's letters, *MGH Ep* 4, pp. 104 (ep. 60), 139 (ep. 95), 140 (ep. 96), 142 (ep. 98). Paulinus also participated in the synod of 796, held by the Bavarian hierarchy "somewhere on the border of the river Danube" where questions concerning a rapid Christianization of the conquered territory after the defeat of Avars were discussed. *MGH Conc II/1*, no. 20, pp. 173–176.

80. Cf. A. Kuhar, *The Conversion of the Slovenes* (New York, Washington, 1959), p. 101 ff.

81. For details, see F. Dvornik, *Les Slaves, Byzance et Rome,* p. 47 ff.

82. P. Skok, *Dolazak,* p. 143, quotes two words of Christian terminology which were derived from Aquileian Latin—*korizma* (holy fast), an expression used in western Dalmatia, and *sutli, sutla* (godfather, godmother), from the Aquileian term *sanctulus.* This latter word is used instead of *kum* in the Quarnero Islands which were nearest to Aquileian influence. The patron saint of Aquileia, St. Hermagoras, was also venerated by the Slovenes as St. Mohor, and by the Croats as St. Mogor. Moreover, the cult of SS. Asellus, Martin, Martha, Marcella, and Lazarus, popular among the Franks, may have been introduced into western Croatia from Aquileia. It should, however, be pointed out that even Zara was in lively contact with Aquileia. Bishop Donatus is said to have transferred from Aquileia to Zara the relics of St. Chrysogonus and St. Zoilus. See C. Jireček, *Die Romanen,* p. 52. The cult of some of these saints can be traced also in the Byzantine coastal cities. In Spalato, for example, was a church dedicated to St. Martin, built in the ninth century. A *margo S. Martini* is mentioned as being on a Venetian island by John the Deacon in his *Chronicon Venetum,* (*MGH Ss* 7), p. 16. A *curtis S. Martini* is also spoken of, *ibid.,* p. 17. In 839 the Doge Peter concluded a peace treaty with the Croat Prince Mislav at this place, the location of which is unknown. Since the Duke sailed from there to the country of the Narentans, it must have been situated near the sea, not in Byzantine but in Croat territory. We can conclude from this that at the beginning of the ninth century the cult of St. Martin had penetrated also to the Croats. However, this cannot be quoted as an indication of Frankish influence since the place is far from the Frankish border, but rather Venetian or Dalmatian influence

should be admitted. This should make us more cautious in evaluating the influence of Aquileia in Croatia. Cf. also Barada, "Episcopus Croatensis," *Croatia sacra,* 1 (1931), p. 173, and Mandić, *Rasprave,* pp. 116, 117.

83. Rački, *Documenta,* pp. 3–6. Mislav accorded to Justin a tithe from his property in Klis. The donation v;as made on the occasion of the consecration of the Church in Putalj, and certainly by Justin.

84. Rački, *ibid.,* p. 4: "ac deinde ut in fatam matrem ecclesiasm, quae est metropolis usque ad ripam Danubii et pene per totum regnum Chroatorum."

85. F. Šišić, *Priručnik,* p. 183 ff.

86. "Crkva sv. Krsta u Ninu," *Strena Buliciana* (Zagreb-Split, 1921), pp. 449–456; *idem, Architektura i skulptura u Dalmaciji* (Belgrade, 1922), p. 7 ff. L. Jelić, who devoted a special study to this church in Nin, *Dvorska kapela sv. Križa u Ninu,* Djela Jugosl. Akad., vol. 29 (Zagreb, 1911), came to the conclusion that if the churches of Nin and Zara were not built by the same architect, they certainly belong to the same period, and their architects were of the same school. He found similar architectural features on the Adriatic Islands. He thinks that the Church of the Holy Cross was a kind of mausoleum of Godeslav and his family. The baptismal font, which according to its inscription was built by the priest John under the reign of Višeslav, testifies that the Christianization of the Croats was speeded up under the first known Croat Christian prince. The font, now in Venice, was used until 1746 in the episcopal church of Nin. See the inscriptions in F. Šišić, *Priručnik,* pp. 118–120.

87. Jelić, *Dvorska kapela,* p. 15, found that the inscription of Godeslav was made in the Franco-Gallic Latin alphabet. However, one cannot deduce from this that Nin was already at that time under the direct influence of Aquileia. A similar script may also have been used in Zara. The coastal cities, including Zara, were in active contact with Istria, especially during the period when Istria was under Byzantine supremacy. Latin was spoken and written in Istria as well as in Zara and other Byzantine coastal cities. Jelić himself stresses that the writing of the inscription on the baptismal font in Nin is very similar to that of an inscription of this period found in Zara.

88. *Povijest Hrvata,* p. 394 ff.

89. F. Rački, *Documenta,* No. 12, p. 15: Cum magnae inter salonitanum et nonensem praesulibus verterentur de quadam facta donatione a Tirpimiro piisimo duce, in iuris sanctae matris ecclesiae Domnii et Anastasii beatorum martyrum quandam mancipando ecclesiam sancti Georgii, quae sita est in Putalo videtur, contentiones dicente Petro spalatensium episcopo: "Hanc, quam dicitis ecclesiam donatam a praefato duce et privilegii statuto roboratam, in nostrae iuris ecclesiae sub

testimoniorum notitia mancipatam habemus." Respondens Aldefreda nonensis ecclesiae praesul dicebat: "Non ita habetur, sed nostrae potius ecclesiae dominio detinetur, quoniam non in ecclesia sanctorum Domini et Anastasii, ut dicitur possidenda sed ipsius praesuli fruenda ad tempus tradita est."

90. This suggestion has already been made by M. Barada in his study, "Episcopus Chroatensis," *Croatia sacra*, 1 (1931), p. 173.

91. *MGH Ep* 6, p. 659: "Nicolaus episcopus clero et plebi Nonensis ecclesiae. Ecclesia, id est catholicorum collectio, quomodo sine apostolicae sedis instituetur nutu, quando iuxta sacra decreta nec ipsae debent absque praeceptione papae basilicae noviter construi, quae ipsam catholicorum intra semet amplecti catervam dinoscuntur?"

92. *MGH Ep* 6, pp. 433–439.

93. In my book, *Les Légendes,* p. 264 ff., I connected Nicholas' letter to the clergy of Nin with his struggle for Illyricum. Impressed by Šišić's arguments concerning the existence of the bishopric of Nin before 852, I admitted that it could have been founded by Aquileia, but placed under the direct jurisdiction of Rome by Nicholas. M. Barada, "Episcopus Croatensis," pp. 180–181, advanced the idea that the bishopric was founded by Nicholas between 866 and 867 when the hierarchy of Byzantine Dalmatia sided with Photius. This is not warranted. The Photian affair could hardly have had repercussions in Dalmatia. The importance of the schism is often exaggerated. The year 860 appears to be much more logical. From 860 to 879, the see of Nin could have been occupied by at least two bishops. John VIII in his letter of 879 to Theodosius of Nin (*MGH Ep* 7, p. 153) mentions the fidelity of his predecessors to Rome. This letter may also be quoted in favor of our thesis that the see of Nin was founded by Rome; "Ad gremium sedis apostolicae unde antecessores tui divinae legis dogmata melliflua cum sacrae institutionis forma summique sacerdotis honorem sumpserunt...."

94. As is stated by L. Karaman in his study, *O počecima,* p. 428, quoted above.

95. L. Karaman, *O počecima,* p. 430, assumed that Dalmatia had been made a Byzantine *thema* by the middle of the eighth century, because Zara was the residence of a Byzantine *dux.* However, *dux* is not a Latin translation of *strategos,* the head of a *thema* who had in his hand all administrative and military power, but of *archon.* This was a special title given to governors of certain territories called *archontiai.* The *thema* of Dalmatia was not founded before 842 and most probably only by Basil I. Cf. J. Ferluga, *Vizantiska uprava u Dalmaciji,* p. 47 ff. See my commentary in *Constantine Porphyrogenitus, De adm. imp.,* vol. 2 (commentary), ed. Jenkins, p. 123.

96. We read in the Acts of the Synod of Spalato of 926 that before

the foundation of the bishopric, Nin was administered by an archi-presbyter; F. Rački, *Documenta*, p. 195: "Nonnensis vero ecclesia non episcopum antiguitus sed archipraesbyterum sub (iuris) dictione episcopi habuisse dignoscitur." Archpriests used to be sent to mission-ary lands by the Frankish hierarchy. The first known archpriest in Pannonia, Domenicus, who was instituted by Liupram of Salzburg, died about 859. He was succeeded by Swarnagal, Altfrid, and Rihpald. (Cf. A. Kuhar, *The Conversion of the Slovenes*, p. 73.) It is quite pos-sible that the archpriest mentioned above was instituted by Aquileia which may have followed the same practice. If this were so, then we could understand better the intervention of Nicholas I in erecting a bishopric and putting it under his own direct jurisdiction. An archi-presbyter could have been sent to Nin before 852. At least Peter I, Archbishop of Spalato, when declaring that his jurisdiction extended over territories as far as the Danube, added cautiously "et *pene* per totum regnum Chroatorum" (F. Rački, *Documenta*, p. 4). Was he con-scious of the fact that Aquileia was claiming jurisdiction over the west-ern part of Dalmatia? It appears that Aquileia did not relish the papal intervention. The Patriarch Walpertus is accused by Stephen V of hav-ing tried to recover his jurisdiction over Nin, when ordaining Theo-dosius, Bishop of Nin. Theodosius was sharply reprimanded for having been ordained by the patriarch (*MGH Ep* 7, p. 338). The pope was wrong in his accusation. John VIII said clearly in his letter of 881 or 882 to the Croatian Prince Branimir that he was sending Bishop Theodosius from Rome back to Croatia (*ibid.*, p. 258). This could only mean that Theodosius, only a deacon and newly chosen as a bishop, went to Rome as the pope exhorted him (*ibid.*, p. 153) in a letter sent June 7, 879, and was consecrated bishop by John VIII. It is, however, possible that Walpertus had ordained an archbishop of Spalato, per-haps Marinus, who seems to have died in 886. In any case Stephen V reprimanded Walpertus for this transgression (*ibid.*, p. 346). This seems, at least, to show that Aquileia did not lose all interest in Dal-matia. Cf. F. Dvornik, *Les Slaves*, p. 307 ff.; F. Balić, J. Bervaldi, *Kronotaksa*, p. 155 ff.

97. See the letters of John VIII in *MGH Ep* 7, pp. 153, 158, 258, the letters of Stephen V, *ibid.*, pp. 338, 346. Cf. F. Dvornik, *Les Slaves*, pp. 223, 229 ff.

98. *Const. Porphyr., De admin. imp.*, ch. 34, ed. G. Moravcsik, R. J. H. Jenkins, pp. 153–155.

99. Cf. my commentary in *Const. Porph., De admin. Imper.*, vol. 2, p. 137 ff.

100. J. v. Pflugk-Hartung, *Acta pontificum Romanorum inedita*, 3 vols. (Stuttgart, 1881–1886), vol. 2, pp. 21, 22.

101. Rački, *Documenta,* pp. 191, 195. Cf. F. Dvornik, *Les Slaves,* pp. 76, 77.

102. *MGH Ss* 7, p. 16 (John the Deacon); Dandolo, *Chronicon Venetum,* ed. Muratori, *Scriptores rerum italicarum,* vol. 12, p. 172; Rački, *Documenta,* pp. 334, 335.

103. On Justinian II, cf. F. Dvornik, *Les Slaves, ibid.,* p. 13. On the foundation of the European *themas; idem, Les Légendes,* p. 4 ff. For further details on the establishment of the themas of Thrace, Macedonia, and Hellas, see P. Lemerle, *Philippes et la Macédoine orientale à l'époque chrétienne et byzantine* (Paris, 1945), Bibliothèque des Ecoles françaises d'Athènes et de Rome, vol. 158, p. 118 ff.

104. He was represented at the first session by the monk John, but assisted personally at other sessions. *Mansi,* XII, cols. 994, 1090; ZIII, cols. 61, 136, 366, 381.

105. *PG,* 99, cols. 1490, 1492, 1493 (Epistolae, lib., II, 157).

106. *PG,* 99, col. 1632A.

107. Arsenij, *Žitie i podvigi sv Theodory Solunskoj* (Jurjev, 1899), p. 5. On the Life of Theodora, cf. *Bibliotheca hagiographica graeca,* ed. F. Halkin (Brussels, 1953), vol. 2, p. 273; H. G. Beck, *Kirche und theologische Literatur im byzantinischen Reiche* (Munich, 1959), pp. 563, 564.

108. *PG,* 99, col. 1492C.

109. J. B. Bury, *The Imperial Administrative System in the Ninth Century* (London, 1911), pp. 44, 45.

110. *PG,* 99, col. 1632A.

111. *Mansi,* XIII, col. 136.

112. Th. Uspenskij, *Vizantijskaja tabel' o rangach,* p. 124. These *archontes* are, however, local governors who also existed in the *themata.* Cf. J. Ferluga, "Niže vojno-administrativne jedinitsa tematskog uredjenja" (Military and Administrative Thematic Units of an Inferior Rank), *Zbornik radova* of the Serbian Academy, vol. 22 (1953), p. 88 ff. According to G. Ostrogorsky, "Taktikon Uspenskog i Taktikon Beneševića," *ibid.,* pp. 39–59, the Uspenski Tacticon was composed during the regency of Theodora (842–856), after the year 845 and before 856. The *archontes* of Dyrrhachium governed certainly also the Slavic tribes incorporated into the *thema.*

113. *Theophanes,* 6275, ed. Bonn, 1, p. 707, de Boor, 1, p. 456. Cf. F. Dvornik, *Les Slaves, Byzance et Rome* (Paris, 1926), pp. 42, 99.

114. On the establishment of the Macedonian *thema,* see P. Lemerle, *Philippes et la Macédoine orientale,* p. 122 ff. It was believed that the *thema* of Peloponnesus was established by the Emperor Nicephorus (802–811) after the defeat of the Slavs who attacked the city of Patras (805), and that the emperor detached the peninsula from the *thema*

of Hellas. Cf. F. Dvornik, *Les Légendes*, p. 8. G. Ostrogorsky, *History of the Byzantine State* (New Brunswick, 1969), p. 193, has shown, however, that the *thema* of Peloponnesus had already existed before 805, although a *strategos* of this *thema* is mentioned only in 812. Cf. also P. Charanis, "The Chronicle of Monemvasia and the Question of the Slavic Settlement in Greece," *DOP*, 5 (1950), p. 147. See, for details, G. Ostrogorsky, "Postanak tema Helada i Peloponez" (Foundation of the *Thema* of Hellas and Peloponnesus), *Zbornik radova* of the Serbian Academy, vol. 21 (1952), pp. 64–77. On Hellas cf. also P. Charanis, "Hellas in the Greek Sources of the Sixth, Seventh, and Eighth Centuries," *Late Classical and Medieval Studies in Honor of A. M. Friend*, ed. K. Weitzmann (Princeton, 1955), pp. 161–177.

115. On the controversy concerning the introduction of the thematic system in Byzantium, see A. Pertusi, *Costantino Porfirogenito de Thematibus* (Città del Vaticano, 1952), Studi e Testi, vol. 160); G. Ostrogorsky, "Sur la date de la composition du livre des Thèmes en Asie Mineure," *Byzantion*, 23 (1953), pp. 31–66; A. Pertusi, "Nuova ipotesi sull origine dei temi bizantini," *Aevum*, 28 (1954), pp. 126–150; J. Karygannopulos, *Die Entstehung der byzantinischen Themenordnung* (Munich, 1959, Byzantinisches Archiv, vol. 10). Even if this system was already introduced by Heraclius, it is to be stressed that the existence of the four great *themas* of Asia Minor can be traced with certainty only during the reign of Constantine IV.

116. See A. Pertusi, *Costantino Porfirogenito*, pp. 93, 177, 178. See especially J. Ferluga, "Sur la date de la création du thème de Dyrrhachium," *Actes du XIIe Congrès international d'études byzantines* (Ochrid, 1964), vol. 2, pp. 83–92.

117. I was inclined to date the foundation of the *thema* of Cephalonia from the end of the eighth century, in my book *Les Légendes*, p. 12, on the basis of a lead seal published by B. A. Pančenko, "Katalog molivdovulov" (Catalogue of Lead Seals), in *Izvjestija* of the Russian Archaeological Institute in Constantinople, 13 (1908), p. 117. However, it seems that the reading and the date of this seal is not reliable, as was noted by G. Ostrogorsky, *History of the Byzantine State*, p. 193. The Emperor Theophilus seems to have strengthened the position of the Empire in the Peloponnesus and in Cephalonia, in order to prevent the Arabs from establishing themselves in the Peloponnesus where they would be able to win the support of the Slavs. But both *themas* were already in existence during his reign. Cf. Dvornik, *Les Légendes*, pp. 88, 89. Cf. also G. Ostrogorsky, "The Byzantine Background of the Moravian Mission," *DOP*, 19 (1965), pp. 6–8.

118. *Einhardi Annales*, *MGH Ss*. 1, pp. 197, 198; Rački, *Documenta*, p. 312.

119. *Gregorii M. Registrum,* vol. 1, p. 132 ff., vol. 2, p. 358; cf. F. Dvornik, *Les Slaves,* pp. 85, 238.

120. Chapter 29, ed. Moravcsik, Jenkins, p. 124.

121. Cf. Šišić, *Povijest Hrvata,* pp. 152, 171; *idem, Priručnik,* vol. 1, p. 160.

122. See the most recent detailed description of these discoveries in the publication *Istorija Crne Gore* (History of Montenegro) written by Serbian specialists (Titograd, 1967), especially chapters four and five, pp. 281–482: *Od dolazka Slovena do kraja XII vjeka* (From the Arrival of the Slavs to the Twelfth Century), by Jovan Kovačević. The author mastered well many archaeological, historical, and epigraphical problems connected with the new discoveries. Cf. also *idem,* "Srednjovekovni epigrafski spomenici Boka Kotorska" (Epigraphical Medieval Monuments of Boka Kotorska), *Spomenik* of the Serbian Akademy, 15 (1956), pp. 1–13; *idem,* "Na tragu književnosti južnog Primorja i Dukle" (Traces of Literary Activity—during the Tenth and Eleventh Centuries—in Dioclea and on Southern Adriatic Littoral), *ibid.,* pp. 93–98.

123. H. Gelzer, "Ungedruckte und ungenugend veröffentlichte Texte der Notitiae episcopatuum," Abhandlungen der K. Akademie der Wissenschaften, 1, Cl., vol. 21 (Munich, 1901), pp. 557, 558.

124. G. Parthey, *Hieroclis Synecdemus et Notitiae graecae episcopatuum* (Berlin, 1866), *Notitia* 3, pp. 124, 125. On the names of the sees, cf. C. Jireček's remarks in the study, L. v. Thallóczy, C. Jireček, "Zwei Urkunden aus Nordalbanien," *Archiv für slavische Philologie,* 21 (1899), p. 80. He found the bishopric of Polati in a *Notitia* of 877. *Notitia* 10, Parthey, *Hieroclis,* has about the same order as *Notitia* 3. I was unable to verify what Jireček says about a *Notitia* from 877. He seems to have been mistaken. See below, Chapter VI, p. 256, on the controversy between Dyrrhachium, Antibari, and Ragusa, concerning the jurisdiction over these bishoprics in the eleventh and twelfth centuries.

125. Cf. F. Dvornik, *The Slavs, Their Early History and Civilization* (Boston, 1958), pp. 165, 279, 280. Some scholars think that Bar-Antibari had become a bishopric in the ninth century because it is listed in a *Notitia* of this period. See "Antivaris" in *Enciclopedia italiana,* vol. 3 (1929), p. 538, and "Bar" in *Enciklopedija Yugoslavie,* vol. 1 (Zagreb, 1955), p. 359. In *Enciclopedia catolica,* vol. 1 (Città del Vaticano, 1948), p. 1510, the bishopric of Bar is dated from the eighth century, and is said to have been a suffragan see of Dyrrhachium. We have seen, however, that under Leo the Wise Dyrrhachium possessed only four suffragan sees and Bar was not among them. There may be some kind of misunderstanding. There is a bishopric of Baris in the

Byzantine *Notitia* composed by a certain Basil in the ninth century, but it is a bishopric of the eparchy of Hellespont with a metropolis in Cyzicus. Another bishopric of the same name is listed in the same catalogue under the metropolis of Antioch in Pisidia, in Asia Minor. See. H. Gelzer, *Georgii Cyprii Descriptio orbis romani* (Teubner, 1890), pp. 9, 22. The bishopric of Baris is listed also in the *Notitia* of Epiphanius from the seventh century, but only under the metropolis of Pisidian Antioch, not under the metropolis of Cyzicus. A bishopric of Baris reappears, however, under both metropolitans in the *Notitia* composed under the Emperor Leo the Wise (886–912). See H. Gelzer, *Georgii Cypris*, pp. 537, 541, 552.

126. *De Administrando imperio,* ch. 29, ed. Moravcsik, Jenkins, p. 129 ff.

127. J. Kovačević, in *Istorija Crne Gore,* pp. 354, 355.

128. Cf. Šišić, *Povijest Hrvata,* pp. 397, 398.

129. *MGH Ep* 7, p. 282.

130. Already G. Millet, in *L'ancien art serbe, les églises* (Paris, 1919), p. 16, stressed the cultural and economic influence of the Latin coastal cities on the interior of future Serbia. He admitted Latin influence in the Christianization of the Serbs. He attributed the cult of SS. Peter and Paul, popular in ancient Serbia, to the influence of Latin missionaries, and mentioned also a Latin inscription in the ruins of the small church, near Prepolje on the river Lim.

131. For details, see D. Bosković, *Architektura Srednjeg veka* (Beograd, 1957), p. 178 ff., pp. 273–275. On the old churches of Raška from the earliest times, before the appearance of the Nemanja's dynasty, see also A. Deroko, *Monumentalna i dekorativna arhitektura u sredn jevekovnoj Srbiji* (Beograd, 1953), pp. 49–57.

132. *PL,* 77, col. 799.

133. *Mansi,* XIII, col. 137, 146.

134. *Mansi,* XVI, col. 194.

135. H. Gelzer, *Ungedruckte Texte,* pp. 557, 558.

136. Cf. F. Dvornik, *Les Légendes,* pp. 88, 89. Cf. J. B. Bury, *A History of the Eastern Roman Empire* (London, 1912), p. 378.

137. B. A. Pančenko, "Katalog Molevdovulov," pp. 203, 204, nos. 3, 4. Cf. Pertusi, *Costantino Porfirogenito,* p. 176. The catepano Petronas of the Boilas family, mentioned by Porphyrogenitus in his *De administrando imperio,* ch. 45, was most probably the chief of an Armenian force stationed at Nikopolis in the *thema* of Koloneia in Asia Minor, not in the *thema* of Nicopolis. See R. J. H. Jenkins, *De admin. imperio,* vol. 2, *Commentary,* p. 177.

138. See F. Dvornik, *La vie de SS. Grégoire le Décopolite* (Paris, 1926), pp. 36, 62, 63; Pertusi, *Costantino Porfirogenito,* p. 168.

139. The region of Strymon became, most probably, after the victory

of Justinian II, a *kleisura,* comprising the passes of the river Strymon. Its commander, with his Slavic contingent, was responsible for the defense of these important passages against the Bulgars. Before the creation of the Macedonian *thema,* he was under the orders of the *strategos* of Thrace, and later of the *strategos* of Macedonia. The region might have become an *archontia* at the beginning of the ninth century, but we lack documentary evidence for this. Cf. P. Lemerle, *Philippes,* p. 124 ff.

140. For details, see S. K. Kyriakides, Βυζαντιναὶ μελέται, part 4 (Thessalonica, 1933), Τὸ Βόλερον. Cf. P. Lemerle, *Philippes,* pp. 129, 130.

141. H. Gelzer, *Georgii Cyprii Descriptio orbis romani,* p. 3 ff.: Basilii Notitia.

142. *Mansi,* XVII, cols. 373, 376. For details, see F. Dvornik, *Les Slaves,* pp. 234–239.

143. Cf. F. Dvornik, *The Slavs,* pp. 97, 163, 164. Cf. below, Ch. V, p. 158.

144. Published by H. Gelzer, *Ungedruckte und ungenügend veröffentlichte Texte der Notitiae episcopatuum,* p. 554 ff. The same names are found also in the *Nova tactica* from the time of Constantine Porphyrogenitus, published by H. Gelzer, *Georgii Cyprii Descriptio,* pp. 67, 68, 80.

145. The mention of a *strategos* of Belgrade by Constantine in ch. 32, *Const. Porph.,* ed. Moravcsik, Jenkins, p. 152, is important. It shows that the Byzantines had most probably reconquered the city after the Avar defeat of 626. See my commentary, *Const. Porph., De Admin. Imperio,* vol. 2, ed. Jenkins, p. 133, and above, p. 4.

146. See my book, *Les Slaves,* p. 239 ff.

147. Cf. *ibid.,* p. 246. The description given there on pp. 240–248 on the ecclesiastical reorganization of the Peloponnesus is completed by A. Bon, *Le Péloponnèse byzantin,* pp. 103–113. Cf. also S. K. Kyriakides, Οἱ Σλάβοι ἐν Πελοποννήσῳ (Saloniki, 1939). See also P. Lemerle, "Une province byzantine: le Péloponnèse," *Byzantion,* 21 (1951), pp. 341–353.

148. H. Gelzer, *Georgii Cyprii descriptio,* p. 12. We can regard as Slavic also the see called Modrine. See F. Dvornik, *Les Slaves,* p. 103. The *Vita S. Ioannicii Magni* (754–846) seems to give us an example of how quickly the Slavs in Bithynia were Byzantinized. The saint was born in the village of Marykatos in Bithynia. At the age of nineteen (in 773) he was enrolled in the eighteenth *bandon* of the imperial *excubitores.* He served in the army for more than twenty-five years and distinguished himself particularly when, under Constantine II, the Bulgars invaded Byzantine Thrace. His exploits attracted the attention of the emperor and, in an interview with him. Joannicius said that his

family's name was Boilas. This is a Bulgar name designating boyars of special rank. It is quite possible that among the prisoners transferred to Asia Minor, there were also some Bulgar boyars who had commanded their Slavic warriors, and that the family of Joannicius descended from one of them. His parents were Christians with Byzantine names—Anastaso and Myritzikos. See the *Vita*, written by Sabas in *Acta Sanctorum Novembris II* (Brussels, 1894), pp. 337, 338. Around 795 Joannicius left the army and became a monk at Mount Olympus. The father of St. Paul the Younger, one of Joannicius' relatives, was an officer in the fleet. See the *Vita Pauli* in *Analecta Bollandiana*, 11 (1892), pp. 20, 21. See Speros Vryonis, "St. Joannicius the Great (754–846) and the Slavs of Bithynia," *Byzantion*, 31 (1961), pp. 245–248. The author rightly points out that the army and the Church were the main instruments in this Byzantinization.

149. F. Dvornik, *Les Slaves*, pp. 72, 73.

150. G. Ostrogorsky, *History of the Byzantine State*, p. 204.

151. See F. Dvornik, *Les Slaves*, p. 73; G. Hopf, *Geschichte Griechenlands* (Leipzig, 1867), p. 97.

152. Cf. G. S. Radojčić, "La date de la conversion des Serbes," *Byzantion*, 22 (1952), pp. 253–256.

153. For the early history of Bulgaria, see S. Runciman, *A History of the First Bulgarian Empire* (London, 1930), p. 3 ff.; W. Swoboda, "Powstanie państwa bulgarskiego v Dolnej Mezji" (Foundation of the Bulgarian State in Lower Moesia), *Slavia occidentalis*, 22 (1962), pp. 50–66.

154. Cf. G. Ostrogorsky, *History of the Byzantine State*, p. 194 ff., pp. 199, 200.

155. *Propylaeum ad Acta Sanctorum Novembris—Synaxarium*, ed. by H. Delehaye (Brussels, 1902), cols. 414–416. Besides Manuel, four bishops are especially mentioned: George, Leo, Marinus, Pardo, two *strateges* Leo, John and Gabriel with Sionios.

156. *Menologium Basilii imperatoris*, PG, 117, cols. 276, 277.

157. See K. M. Loparev, "Dve zametki po drevnej bolgarskoj istorii," in *Zapiski russkago arkheologičeskago obsčestva*, vol. 3 (St. Petersburg, 1888), pp. 341–362, esp. 348. Cf. also V. N. Zlatarski, *Istorija na bŭlgarskata dŭržava*, vol. 1 (Sofia, 1918), p. 292 ff.

158. *Theophanes Continuatus* (Bonn, 1838), p. 217.

159. It was published by Enrica Follieri and commented on by I. Dujčev, "Acolutia inedita per i martiri di Bulgaria dell'auno 813," *Byzantion*, 33 (1963), pp. 71–106.

160. See what H. G. Beck says on the two authors in his work *Kirche und theologische Literatur im byzantinischen Reich* (Munich, 1959), pp. 505, 601, 602; E. Follieri, "Acolutia inedita," p. 73, with more bibliography.

161. *Chronographia*, ed. de Boor, vol. 1, p. 498.

162. Cf. N. Adontz, "L'âge et l'origine de l'empereur Basil I," *Byzantion,* 9 (1934), p. 238 ff.

163. Cf. G. Moravcsik, Berliner byzantinishsche Arbeiten, vol. 10 (Berlin, 1958), *Byzantinoturcica,* vol. 2, pp. 75, 76, 165.

164. The veneration of the 377 martyrs was very popular in Byzantium. A later legendary tradition had tried to connect the Emperor Basil I in some way with the martyrs. It was said that he had been one of those deported from Adrianopolis and that some of his relatives were among the martyrs slain by Omortag. It is quite possible that Basil's parents were among the prisoners transferred by Krum, and that he was born in captivity, but shortly before the prisoners had escaped from the Bulgarians (see below, footnote 169). See, for details, G. Moravcsik, "Sagen und Legenden über Kaiser Basileios I," *Dumbarton Oaks Papers,* 15 (1961), pp. 61–126, especially p. 70 ff.

165. *The Little Catechesis,* ed. E. Auvray (Paris, 1891), p. 220 ff.; *PG,* 99, col. 591.

166. See V. Beševliev, "Souveränitätsansprüche eines bulgarischen Herrschers im 9. Jahrhundert," *BZ,* 55 (1962), pp. 11–20; cf. also *idem,* "Protobuglarische Inschrift auf einer Silberschale," *Byzantion,* 35 (1965), pp. 1–9.

167. Cf. S. Runciman, *A History of the First Bulgarian Empire,* pp. 71–84. The results of the excavations, renewed in 1945, have been published in the *Izvestija* of the Bulgarian Archaeological Institute, vols. 13 (1939), 14 (1940–42), 20 (1945), 22 (1959). Cf. R. Krautheimer, *Early Christian and Byzantine Architecture* (Baltimore, 1965), pp. 224–226, 346.

168. *Historia martyrii XV martyrum, PG,* 126, cols. 192 ff.

169. The suspicion of disloyalty among the Greeks in Bulgaria was not unfounded. The ten thousand prisoners brought by Krum from Adrianople in 813—their number had grown to twelve thousand—were concentrated beyond the Danube. They were given the privilege of a kind of self-government, and the khagans appreciated their services. It was natural, however, that they wished to return to their own country. At last their chief, Cordyles, succeeded in reaching Constantinople, and in persuading the Emperor Theophilus to help them to escape by sending ships to the Danube, which he did in 836. The Greeks were stopped by the local Bulgarian commander, but they defeated not only him, but also the Magyars, from whom he had askèd help, and escaped safely, landing on Byzantine soil. Cf. *Leo Grammaticus* (Bonn), p. 232; *Theophanes Contin.* (Bonn), p. 216; Zlatarski, *Istorija,* vol. 1, pt. 1, pp. 339, 340; Runciman, *First Bulgarian Empire,* p. 86.

170. *Einhardi Annales, MGH Ss* 1, pp. 212, 213.

171. *Ibid.,* p. 216, *Annales Fuldenses, ibid.,* 1, pp. 359, 360; ed. F. Kurz, p. 25.

172. *Annales Fuldenses, ibid.,* p. 364, ed. F. Kurz, p. 35. On Srěm,

see Zlatarski, *Istorija,* vol. I, p. 316, vol. I, 2, p. 787; Bury, *A History,* pp. 363, 365. Already J. Šafařík, *Slawische Altertümer* (Prague, 1844), vol. 2, pp. 291, 292, 301, 302, had established that the territory of Srěm, former Sirmium, from Osek and Brod as far as Semlin, remained under Bulgarian rule from the reign of Omortag through the rest of the ninth and during the whole of the tenth century. The Frankish territory in Pannonian Croatia went only as far as the rivers Sutla and Kulpa. The Bulgarians seem to have entrusted the ruling over the territory of Sirmium to native Croat governors under their sovereignty. The last of these governors was Sermon who resided in Srěm. When the Byzantines had made an end to the first Bulgarian empire, Sermon refused to accept Byzantine supremacy, trying to rule this territory as his own independent domain. The Byzantine governor Diogenes, unable to break his resistance, had Sermon treacherously assassinated (1019). See Cedrenus (Bonn, 1839), vol. 2, p. 476. After the assassination of her husband, his widow surrendered Sirmium to the Byzantines. She was brought to Constantinople where she was given in matrimony to a nobleman. Zonaras (Bonn, 1897), vol. 3, p. 667, mentions also that Sirmium surrendered to the Byzantines only after the destruction of Bulgaria and the submission of the Croats. Both authors regarded the territory of Sirmium as a particular province of the first Bulgarian Empire. The importance of Sirmium and the fact that it was part of the Bulgarian Empire is also illustrated by the erection of a Bulgarian bishopric in the city. This is attested by the list of bishoprics under Tsar Samuel in the tenth century; however, Sirmium seems to have been the see of one of the seven bishops sent to Bulgária after 870 by the Patriarch Ignatius. We know the sees of two others—Belgrad and Morava. See J. Jireček, *Geschichte der Serben* (Gotha, 1917), vol. 1, p. 194, and especially H. Gelzer, "Ungedruckte und wenig bekannte Bistümer der Orientalischen Kirche," *BZ,* 1 (1892), p. 257: ʹΟ Σιρμίου ἤτοι Στριάμου under the sees of ancient Justinana Prima, *BZ,* 2 (1893), p. 53.

173. The existence of Khagan Presiam, or Peresian, has been the object of discussion among specialists of Bulgarian history. V. N. Zlatarski, *Istorija na bŭlgarskata dŭržava,* vol. 1 (Sofia, 1918), pp. 447–459, thinks that Presiam was the son of Svinitse and that he reigned from 836 to 852. S. Runciman, *First Bulgarian Empire,* pp. 86, 88, 292–297, saw in Presiam a general, a scion of the reigning house, whom the Serbs took for the Khagan himself. He thought that Malamir was Khagan from 831 to 852. However, he overlooked two inscriptions rediscovered in Philippi, and published by F. Dvornik, "Deux inscriptions gréco-bulgares de Philippes," *Bulletin de correspondence hellénique,* 52 (1928), pp. 125–143. In one of these Presiam, the Khagan, is said to have sent the Khagan Isboulos with an army against the

Slavic tribe of the Smoljans. This inscription, studied anew by V. Beševljev, "Inscriptions protobulgares," *Byzantion*, 29–30 (1959–1960), pp. 485–488, proves that Malamir, who had succeeded Omortag, reigned only to 836 and was followed by Presiam, or Peresian, son of Omortag's son Svinitse. P. Lemerle, *Philippes*, pp. 135–139, rejecting the thesis of H. Grégoire, "Les sources épigraphiques de l'histoire bulgare," *Byzantion*, 9 (1934), p. 773 ff., who thought, as did J. Bury, *A History of the Eastern Roman Empire* (London, 1912), pp. 481 ff., that Presiam was another name for Malamir, combines the episode described in the inscription with the escape of Byzantine prisoners, aided by the emperor, in 836. The Bulgars saw in this the violation of the peace treaty which should have lasted for thirty years, and invaded the territory of the Smoljans, who occupied the land near Philippi. The Bulgars were victorious and took possession of that city as is indicated in the second inscription from Philippi. The Byzantines confined themselves to guarding the coast, thus assuring communications between Thessalonica and Constantinople. The Byzantine army was commanded by the Caesar Mosélé, as is attested in the biography of St. Gregory the Decapolite, published by F. Dvornik, *La vie de Saint Grégoire le Décapolite et les Slaves Macédoniens au IXe siècle* (Paris, 1926), pp. 36–40, 62, 63. Mosélé's expedition has to be dated in the year 837 (cf. Lemerle, *Philippes*, pp. 132–134). G. Ostrogorsky, "Byzantine Background of Moravian Mission," *DOP,* 19 (1965), p. 10, when discussing the problem of Malamir and Presiam, overlooked the publication of the inscriptions of Philippi, by F. Dvornik and V. Beševljev. Ivan Dujčev discovered in the name Presiam an Iranian root pers-, admitting Iranian cultural influence on the proto-Bulgarians in their early history. See his study "Presiam-Persian," *Ezikovedsko-etnografski izsledvanija v pamet an akademik Stojan Romanski* (Bulgarian Academy, Sophia, 1960), pp. 478–482.

174. *Const. Porph. De Adm. Imp.,* ed. Moravcsik, Jenkins, ch. 32, p. 154; see *Const. Porph. De Adm. Imp.,* vol. 2, ed. Jenkins, p. 134, for commentary by F. Dvornik.

175. *Annales Fuldenses,* p. 376, ed. F. Kurz, p. 42.

176. *MGH Ss* 1, p. 448.

177. *Istorija,* vol. 1, pt. 2 (1927), p. 6 ff.

178. *A History of the Eastern Roman Empire* (London, 1912), p. 383.

179. Cf. S. Runciman, *First Bulgarian Empire,* p. 92.

180. *Historia Martyrii,* col. 197. He combines the Frankish cloud with the famine which had forced Boris to come to an agreement with the Byzantines, and to accept their form of Christianity. This could also indicate that he had in mind the pact with Louis the German, and Boris' preparations to join him in an attack against the Moravians.

181. S. Runciman, *First Bulgarian Empire,* p. 92, discards the pos-

sibility of Boris' attack on Dalmatian Croatia, arguing that Boris could have reached Trpimir's territory only through Pannonia or Serbia. However, the territory of Sirmium, under Bulgarian rule, also touched on Dalmatian Croatia. Constantine (ch. 31, ed. Moravcsik, Jenkins, p. 150) seems to be speaking in this chapter only of the Dalmatian Croats, stressing that "never yet have these Croats paid tribute to the Bulgarians." See my book, *The Slavs*, p. 54, and my commentary to *Const. Porph. De Adm. Imp.*, vol. 2, ed. Jenkins, pp. 128, 129. Cf. also F. Šišić, *Geschichte der Kroaten* (Zagreb, 1917), p. 81. Zlatarski in *Istorija*, 1, 2, p. 8 ff.; *idem*, "Velká Morava a Bulharsko v IX st.," *Říša Velkomoravská*, ed. J. Stanislav (Prague, 1933), p. 247 ff., thinks that Louis had instigated the conflict between the Croats and Boris in order to prevent Boris from helping the Moravians. He dates the conflict in the year 854. However, we have no evidence for a Moravo-Bulgarian alliance as he supposes. I have discussed the problem in my book, *Les Légendes*, p. 226 ff., and have expressed certain doubts about the existence of such an alliance. It is safer to attribute Boris' attack on Frankish Pannonian Croatia in 853 to the instigation of Charles the Bald, and to see the Slavs who had sided with Boris as the Slavs from Pannonian Croatia.

182. *Const. Porph. De Adm. Imp.*, ch. 32, ed. Moravcsik, Jenkins, p. 154.

CHAPTER II

1. This highly debated event seems to have been definitely clarified. For details, see A. Vasiliev, *The Russian Attack on Constantinople in 860* (Cambridge, Mass., 1946) with full bibliography. A clear, succinct review of problems concerning this event was given by C. Mango, *The Homilies of Photius, Patriarch of Constantinople* (Cambridge, Mass., 1958), pp. 74–82.

2. C. Mango, *Photius,* p. 98.

3. Some Russian scholars still believe that the first attack was made by the Russians in 842. This is based on the misinterpretation of a passage in the *Life of St. George of Amastris,* as has been shown by G. Da Costa-Louillet, "Y eut-il des invasions russes dans l'Empire byzantin avant 860," *Byzantion,* 15 (1940–41), pp. 231–248. On the origin of the name "Russians," "Rhôs," see F. Dvornik, *The Making of Central and Eastern Europe* (London, 1949), pp. 62, 305–314. The Scandinavian origin (from the old Swedish word *rodi, rodhsi,* "rowing") is still much more plausible than the Sarmatian origin defended by G. Vernadski, *Ancient Russia* (New Haven, 1943), pp. 280, 343; *idem, The Origins of Russia* (Oxford, 1959), p. 198 ff. The Finns still call the Swedes "Ruotsi." See below, Chapter VII, p. 266, for details.

4. For details, see F. Dvornik, *Les Légendes de Constantin et de Méthode vues de Byzance* (Prague, 1933), p. 148 ff.

5. For more details, see F. Dvornik, *Les Légendes,* pp. 148–176, with complete bibliography to 1933. In 1939 the Slavic division of the New York Public Library compiled a bibliography of all the sources and works on the Khazars published up to 1939 (*The Khazars, a Bibliography,* New York, 1939). On Khazar history from the fifth to the seventh century, see M. I. Artamonov, *Očerki rdevnejšej istorii Chazar* (*Studies on the Ancient History of the Khazars* [Leningrad, 1936]). On St. Abo, see P. Peeters, "Les Khazars dans la Passion de S. Abo de Tiflis," *Analecta Bollandiana,* 52 (1934), pp. 21–56. H. Grégoire rejected the authenticity of the Jewish documents in his study, "Le Glozel' Khazare," *Byzantion,* 12 (1937), pp. 225–266. A. Zajączkowski, in his study *Ze studiów nad zagadnieniem Chazarskim* (*Studies on the Khazar Problem* [Cracow, 1947]), admits the apocryphal character of the Jewish letters on Khazar history—he dates them from the twelfth century—but shows that they are based upon a national Jewish tradition and should not be neglected. D. M. Dunlop, in his *The History of the Jewish Khazars* (Princeton, 1954), pp. 89–170, after examining the

Arabic and Judaic sources, comes to the conclusion that about the year 740 the khagan accepted a modified form of Judaism, and at around 800 his descendant accepted Rabbinic Judaism. S. Szyszman, "Le roi Balan et le problème de la conversion des Khazars," *Actes du X. Congrès international d'études byzantines* (Istanbul, 1957), pp. 249–252, thinks that the first missionaries—Karaites—came from Khorezm in the eighth century, but that the final conversion should be attributed to the Karaites coming from Byzantium through the Crimea or the Caucasus region. Cf. also his study, "Les Khazars, problèmes et controverses," *Revue de l'Histoire des religions*, 152 (1957), pp. 174–221. The most recent history of the Khazars was written by M. I. Artamonov, *Istorija Chazar* (Leningrad, 1962). S. P. Tolstov, *Po sledam drevnochorezmijskoi tsivilizatsii* (Moscow, 1948), brings also the judaization of the Khazars into connection with the expulsion of Jewish scholars from Khorezm by Kutaiba after the defeat of Khurzad's insurrection. I used the Czech translation of his work by P. Poucha, *Po stopách dávného Chórezmu* (Prague, 1952), p. 226 ff.

6. This was the aim of my book *Les Légendes*. It was challenged only by the Polish philologist A. Brückner, in his review in *Archiv für slavische Philologie*. Their genuineness, disputed since the time of their discovery, is now accepted by all specialists.

7. See the introduction to, and French translation of, these *Lives* in my *Les Légendes*, pp. 339–392. There is a German translation with a commentary, by J. Bujnoch, *Zwischen Rom und Byzanz.* (Graz, Vienna, Cologne, 1958), pp. 19–100.

8. For details, see F. Dvornik, *La Vie de St. Grégoire le Décapolite et les Slaves macédoniens au IXe s.* (Paris, 1926), p. 32 ff., 35 ff., 54, 62 ff., Cf. *idem,* "Deux inscriptions gréco-bulgares de Philippi," *Bulletin de correspondance hellénique*, 52 (1928), p. 138 ff. Cf. above, Ch. I, p. 40.

9. Cf. H. Schaeder, "Geschichte und Legende im Werk der Slavenmissionare Konstantin und Method," *Historische Zeitschrift*, 152 (1935), p. 232 ff.

10. F. Dvornik, *Les Légendes*, p. 19 ff. Cf. also G. Hunger, "Die Schönheitskonkurenz in Belthandros und Chryzantza und die Brautschau am Byzantinischen Kaiserhof," *Byzantion*, 55 (1965), pp. 150–158

11. A. Benoit, *Saint Grégoire de Nazianze* (Paris, 1876), p. 22 ff.

12. *PG,* 37, cols. 1369 ff.; V. Vavřínek in his study *Staroslovenské životy Konstantina a Metoděje* (*Old Slavonic Lives of Constantine and Methodius*), *Rozpravy* of the Czech Academy, vol. 73, 7 (Prague, 1963), acknowledged that the author of the *Life* of Constantine was inspired, on several points, by Gregory's panegyric on Basil the Great, especially in the description of his hero's studies in Athens, but he manifested a certain originality in his description. A. Dostál has devoted a short

study to the scholarly education of Constantine: "Konstantin der Philosoph und das Ausmass seiner geistigen Bildung," *Byzantinische Forschungen,* 1 (1966), pp. 76–91; on pp. 80–82 he tries to show the metrical form of Constantine's prayer to Gregorius of Nazianzus. In his paper, "Staroslovenské životy Konstantina a Metoděje a panegyriky Nazianzu" ("The Old Slavonic Lives of Constantine and Methodius and the Panegyrics of Gregory of Nazianzus"), *Listy filologické,* 85 (1962), pp. 96–122. The author shows convincingly that the *Lives* were not written according to the models of these panegyrics as was stated by F. Gnidovec, *Vpliv sv. Gregorija Nazianskega na sv. Cirila u Metodija* (*Influence of St. Gregory of Nazianzus on Ss. Cyril and Methodius*), Dissertation XX (Ljubljana, 1942). Gnidovec followed F. Grivec who had expressed this thesis on many occasions, lately in his book *Konstantin und Method.* See R. Keydell, "Die Literarhistorische Stellung der Gedichte Gregors von Nazianz," *Studi bizantini e neoellenici,* 7 (1953), pp. 134–143, for literary appreciation of Gregory's poetical work.

13. It was written in Greek and in verse on the wall of Constantine's room. See, for details, I. Dujčev, "Costantino Filosofo nella storia della litteratura bizantina," *Studi in onore di Ettore Lo Gatto e Giovanni Mayer* (Rome, 1961), pp. 205–222, esp. pp. 211–214. This kind of writing on the wall of religious items seems to have been customary in Byzantium, as is shown by a passage in the *Vita Euthymii, PG,* 86, col. 2321.

14. *De admin. imperio,* ch. 50, ed. Moravcsik and R. J. H. Jenkins, p. 233. Cf. also the *Commentary,* ed. R. J. H. Jenkins, vol. 2 (1962), pp. 185, 186.

15. The invitation to go to Constantinople should not be regarded as a mere commonplace of hagiographers in order to exalt their hero, as H. Schaeder, "Konstantin und Method," thinks. The government seemed to have accepted responsibility for the orphans of high functionaries.

16. G. Ostrogorsky, *History of the Byzantine State,* p. 219. C. Mango has proved definitely that Michael III was born, not in 836 or 839 as has been thought, but in January 840. See his paper, "When Was Michael III Born?" *DOP,* 21 (1967), pp. 184–193.

17. A detailed study of Leo, the former iconoclastic metropolitan of Thessalonica, and professor at the University, who was very highly thought of for his learning, was published by E. E. Lipšič, "Vizantijskij učenyj Lev Matematik," in *Vizant. Vremmenik,* 2 (1949), New series, pp. 106–149. More recently, V. Laurent, "Jean VII Grammarien (837–843)," *Catholicisme,* vol. 6 (Paris, 1964), cols. 513–515.

18. See F. Dvornik, *Les Légendes,* pp. 49–66, on the ecclesiastical commentary on chaps. 37–42 in *De administrando imperio* (ed. Jenkins), vol. 2, p. 142 ff.

charges in Constantinople. No other treatise on this problem has appeared since 1933.

19. On the organization of the *themata,* see above, Ch. I, p. 30 ff.

20. It was published by P. A. Lavrov, *Materialy po istorii vozniko-venija drevn. slav.´pismennosti* (Leningrad, 1930), p. 122 ff.

21. For details, see F. Dvornik, *Les Légendes,* p. 25 ff.

22. Cf. F. Dvornik, "Patriarch Photius Scholar and Statesman," *Classical Folia,* 13 (1959), pp. 3–18; 14 (1960), pp. 3–22.

23. The main Latin source for the history of Constantine—the *Legenda italica*—seems to indicate that this title was given to Constantine for his great learning: "Constantine who, because of his admirable talent for which he was wonderfully illustrious from his youth on, was rightly given the name of philosopher." Ed. F. Méyvaert and P. Devos, "Trois énigmes cyrillo-méthodiennes de la 'Légende Italique,'" *Analecta Bollandiana,* 73 (1955), p. 455. On this Legend, see pp. 144, 380.

24. F. Grivec, "Vitae Constantini et Methodii," *Acta Academiae Velehradensis,* 17 (1941), pp. 10, 12, 17, 55.

25. It is to the credit of I. Ševčenko to have drawn the attention of specialists to these sources in his well-documented study, "The Definition of Philosophy in the Life of Saint Constantine," *For Roman Jakobson* (The Hague, 1956), pp. 449–457. His interpretation is also accepted by I. Dujčev, *Costantino Filosofo,* p. 209.

26. *Commentaria in Aristotelem graeca,* vol. 18, 2. p. 18, ed. A. Busse (Berlin, 1904). On the interest of Byzantium in the Greek classics at this time, see the notes by B. Hemmerdinger, "La culture grècque classique du VIIᵉ au IXᵉ siècle," *Byzantion,* 34 (1964), pp. 127–133. On Byzantine schools and teachers useful comments will be found in the paper by Robert Browning, "Byzantinische Schulen und Schulmeister," *Das Altertum,* 9 (1963), pp. 105–118. His other study, "The Correspondence of a Tenth Century Byzantine Scholar," *Byzantion,* 24 (1954), pp. 397–452, gives an interesting insight into the private life of the teachers and of their relations with their students, and that of the students with their parents. See the edition of such letters by R. Browning and B. Laourdas in 'Επετηρὶς τῆς 'Εταιρείας τῶν Βυζαντινῶν Σπουδῶν, 27 (1957), p. 185 ff.

27. F. Grivec, who rightly praised this interpretation, is exaggerating when he continues with his definition of philosophy, seeing in it a poetic spirit and an ascetic character. He is pushed to this exaggeration in his frantic effort to separate Saint Constantine from the "wicked" Photius. See his study, "Constantinus philosophus amicus Photii," *Orientalia Christ. Periodica,* 23 (1957), pp. 415–422, and his book *Konstantin und Method, Lehrer der Slaven* (Wiesbaden, 1960), p. 28 ff.

28. Until now, one of the replies of the ex-Patriarch used to be

translated as follows: "One should not look for flowers in the autumn nor chase an old man, one Nestor, into a fight as a young man." It has been suggested, however, that the Nestor mentioned in this passage is not the figure from Classical mythology, but a young Christian called Nestor who, in the presence of the Emperor Maximian in Thessalonica, had defeated in single combat a famous gladiator named Lyacus who enjoyed great favor with the emperor because of his prowess and strength. Because he confessed to being a Christian, Nestor died a martyr's death. This story is told in the *Life of Demetrius,* patron saint of Thessalonica, preserved by Metaphrastes (*Acta Sanctorum,* October IV, cols. 99 ff.). It is said that Nestor owed his strength to the prayers of St. Demetrius. This story seems to have been quite popular in Byzantium. The Old Slavonic glagolitic calendar of Assemani lists the feast of St. Nestor on October 25, which indicates that this story must have been known also to Constantine's Slavic disciples. However, the Nestor mentioned in this passage is the well-known figure who was hailed in classical literature as an archetype of a wise old man.

29. The situation is described by F. Dvornik, "The Patriarch Photius and Iconoclasm," *DOP,* 7 (1953), pp. 69–97, especially p. 81.

30. For details, see F. Dvornik, *Les Légendes,* p. 73 ff. I. Dujčev, *Costantino Filosofo,* p. 221, includes among the Greek writings of Constantine the description of his disputation with the ex-patriarch, although this is not vouched for by the author of the *Vita.* If it could be proved that Constantine had composed a short treatise against iconoclasm this would show once more what the religious situation in Byzantium was about 850. In this case, we should suppose that the author of the *Life* used the short treatise of Constantine as a base for his narration. He presented it as a disputation with the iconoclastic ex-patriarch, following here a pattern with which he was familiar from other hagiographical works of his time.

31. The best account of the events from 856 to 859 is still that given by J. B. Bury, *A History of the Eastern Roman Empire* (London, 1912), p. 157 ff., p. 469. Cf. also F. Dvornik, *The Photian Schism, History and Legend* (Cambridge, 1948), p. 36 ff.

32. The main reason for the break between Ignatius and Bardas was the rumor spread by his enemies in the city that Caesar Bardas was living with his daughter-in-law, the wife of his deceased son. The Patriarch, taking these rumors seriously, is said to have refused the Holy Communion to Bardas during a solemn Mass. However, there does not seem to be any direct evidence to confirm these rumors. A contemporary and partisan of Ignatius, the Metropolitan Metrophanes, when informing the logothete Manuel about Photius' case, does not say a word about Bardas or his misbehavior. Both should have known

what had really happened (*Mansi*, 16, col. 416). Theognostus (*ibid.*, col. 296C), who acted as Ignatius' representative in Rome, and Nicetas, Ignatius' biographer (*ibid.*, cols. 224, 225), speak only of rumors which had spread in the city and had reached Ignatius. The encomium on Ignatius by Michael (*ibid.*, col. 292) is very vague. Even Stylianus, the great enemy of Photius (*ibid.*, col. 428), speaks only of news which had reached Ignatius of Bardas' incest. The biographer of Nicholas of Studios (*PG*, 105, col. 905) is more explicit, but does not say more than Nicetas. The historians, Leo the Grammarian (Bonn, p. 240), the Continuator of George (Bonn, p. 826) and Symeon Magister (Bonn, p. 667) who represent the same tradition, also speak only of rumor which had reached the patriarch. Only the Continuator of Theophanes (Bonn, p. 193), Cedrenus (Bonn, vol. 2, p. 172) and Zonaras, XVI, 4 (Bonn, vol. III, p. 403, ed. Dindorf, vol. 4, p. 15) report in almost identical words, that Bardas had divorced his wife and taken home his daughter-in-law. There is a detail not given in earlier sources—namely his divorce—and not even in the chronicles of the circle around Constantine Porphyrogenitus, the chief aim of which was to discredit Michael III and his reign as much as possible. One has the impression, from reading these reports, that Bardas' elder son, husband of Eudocia, was not alive when these rumors spread. V. Grumel (*Diskussionbeiträge zum XI. Internat. Byzantinisten-Kongress* [Munich, 1958]), pp. 49, 50, tried to show the veracity of these reports without revealing their biased background. It is a repetition of his earlier statement, rather hastily compiled, as is shown by mistakes in his quotations (Nicetas is left out; Michael's encomium should be col. 292, not 192; Stylianus, col. 428, not 272; and Metrophanes is not mentioned). On the behavior of Ignatius and of his partisans towards Basil (who had killed both Bardas and Michael III) cf. J. B. Bury, *Eastern Roman Empire*, p. 188 ff. With regard to Bardas, I have been able to discover more evidence about him in the Life of St. Eustratius, abbot of the monastery of Agauron. It was published by A. Papadopoulos-Kerameus in Ἀνάλεκτα ἱεροσολ. σταχυολογίας (St. Petersburg), vol. 4 (1897), pp. 367–400. On p. 389 the biographer speaks of the veneration which Bardas' wife, Theodosia—this is the only text which gives us her name—had for the saint, and he describes a miracle the saint had performed in her house where he had been a frequent guest. When speaking of Theodosia, the biographer says only that she "had been injured by her husband . . . and has been banished from cohabitation with him." There is no mention of Bardas' misbehavior with his daughter-in-law. Neither does the biographer of Theodosia's sister, St. Irene, say anything of this kind, although when speaking of Theodosia's husband, Bardas, he calls him "an unworthy man, consumed with ill will, enjoying robbery and killing." He may have had in mind the murder of Theoctistos (*Acta Sanc-*

torum, July 28, vol. 6, p. 604). See F. Dvornik, "Patriarch St. Ignatius and Caesar Bardas," *Byzantinoslavica,* 27 (1966), pp. 7–22.

33. In my book *Les Légendes,* p. 146 ff., I suggested that perhaps Constantine was already in the capital when the Khazar embassy was discussed. It is safer, however, to follow the text of the Legend literally and admit that he stayed at Olympus until that time.

34. In spite of some critics (M. Weingart, *Byzantinoslavica,* 5 [1933–34], p. 537) I maintain that basically the mission had both a political and diplomatic character. The fact that the Legends do not mention it cannot be used as an argument against this interpretation. The hagiographers were interested only in the religious aspect and they often omitted details which did not contribute to the glorification of their hero. To say that the mission also had another object, and that it was led by high imperial officials who were the chief personalities, would have diminished the importance of the role which Constantine had to play in Khazaria. Constantine's biographer also speaks of the presence of Methodius in the mission only in passing in chapter 12. The words which are put into the mouths of the Khazarian envoys, "you are a great nation and you have your imperium from God," would hardly have been spoken by the Khazars. But they reveal the Byzantine patriotism of the hagiographer and the main thesis of Byzantine political philosophy.

35. A. Vaillant, "Les lettres russes de la vie de Constantin," *Revue des études slaves,* 15 (1935), pp. 75–77; R. Jakobson, "Saint Constantin et la langue Syriaque," *Annuaire de l'Institut de philologie et d'histoires orient. et slave,* 1 (1939–44), pp. 181–186; *idem,* "Sources for Early History of the Slavic Church," *Harvard Slavic Studies,* 2 (1954), p. 68 ff.; D. Gerhard, "Goten, Slaven oder Syrer im alten Cherson," Beiträge zur Namenforschung, 4 (1953), pp. 78–88; K. Horálek, "St. Kirill i semitskie jazyki," *For Roman Jakobson* (The Hague, 1956), pp. 230–234.

36. See the Old Slavonic text of the transfer with Latin translation, historical commentary, and bibliographical indication, in J. Vašica's study "Slovo na perenesenie moštem preslavnago Klimenta neboli Legenda Chersonská," *Acta Academiae Velehradensis,* 19 (1948), pp. 38–80. Cf. also A. P. Péchayre, "Les écrits de Constantin le Philosophe sur les réliques de St. Clément de Rome," *Echos d'Orient,* 35 (1936), pp. 465–472. Cf. also A. Essen, "Wo fand der hl. Konstantin-Kyril die Gebeine des hl. Clemens von Rom?" *Cyrillo-Methodiana* (Cologne, Graz, 1964), Slavische Forschungen, ed. R. Olesch, vol. 6, pp. 126–147.

37. On Anastasius and his account of Constantine, see pp. 139–142.

38. Cf. the most recent study by G. Vernadsky-M. de Ferdinándy, *Studien zur ungarischen Frühgeschichte, I. Lebedia, II. Almos, Südeuropäische Arbeiten,* 47 (Munich, 1957). Cf. also G. Moravcsik's

39. In my book *Les Légendes,* I accepted the interpretation suggested by some manuscripts that the embassy went to Semender (Samander), near Derbend, on the Caspian Sea. In his review of my book (*Byzantinoslavica,* 5, 1933–34, p. 239) Weingart pointed out that instead of *Kaspiskaja vrata* one should read *Kapiskaja.* This would mean the Strait of Panticapaeum (Kerč). On the history of this city, see Pauly Wissowa, *Realanzyklopädie* (1949), vol. 18, 2, cols. 780 ff. On col. 791 is a history of the Byzantine and Khazar period. From the eighth to the tenth century the city belonged to the Khazars. Weingart's interpretation was discarded by another eminent Slavic philologist J. Vašica, *Na úsvitu Křestanství* (Prague, 1942), p. 246, on philological grounds. Therefore I maintain my interpretation which corresponds to our knowledge of the summer residence of the khagans.

40. G. Vernadsky, *Ancient Russia* (New Haven, 1943), p. 350, thinks that Constantine could not have used the Strait of Kerč because of the presence of the Russians at Tmutorakan and he would have had to board a boat on the north coast of the Crimea. He places the encounter with the Magyars somewhere there. However, the presence of the Russians in these places at that time is unwarranted. Vernadsky, too, thinks that Constantine met the Khagan at his residence at Samander. F. Grivec, *Konstantin und Method* (Wiesbaden, 1960), p. 50, places the encounter at Derbend.

41. This is stressed by A. Zajączkowski, *Ze studiów nad zagadnieniem Chazarskim,* p. 18.

42. Cf. I. Dujčev, *Costantino Filosofo,* pp. 214, 215. Cf. also, below, Ch. VI, p. 181.

43. Cf. I. Dujčev, "Zur literarischen Tätigkeit Konstantins des Philosophen," *BZ,* 44 (1951), pp. 105–110. He explains the confusion over the name "alexandros" given to the oak tree and meaning "protecting the men" and which is not the proper name of the tree. Cf. also *idem, Costantino Filosofo,* p. 216. It seems that the author of the Legend misunderstood this passage, interpreting the name as that of Alexander the Great.

44. "S. Cyril really knew Hebrew," *Mélanges P. Boyer* (Paris, 1925), pp. 94, 95: "this means that Cyril was so familiar with the Hebrew text as to use its insignificant variants for his own purposes."

45. Cf. the text published by P. A. Lavrov, *Materialy,* p. 26, text in the *Fontes Rerum Bohemicarum* (Prague, 1865), vol. 1, p. 26: v tsrkvi svetikh apostolov siede. Ed. T. Lehr-Splawinski, *Żywoty Konstantyna i Metodego* (Poznan, 1959), p. 63.

46. For details on this council, see F. Dvornik, *The Photian Schism, History and Legend,* pp. 69–90.

47. For details, see F. Dvornik, "Photius et la réorganisation de l'Académie patriarcale," *Analecta Bollandiana,* 68 (1950), cols. 108–125.

48. G. Downey, *Nikolaus Mesarites, Description of the Church of the Holy Apostles* (Philadelphia, 1957. Transactions of the Amer. Philosoph. Soc., vol. 47), pp. 865–867, 898, 899 (text).

49. G. Downey, *Nikolaus Mesarites*, pp. 894–896, 916–918 (text).

50. The Byzantines seem to follow an old practice when establishing schools in or near churches. The sophists also often held their classes in temples. Libanius' *Oratio* I, 102 (ed. R. Foerster, Teubner, 1903), vol. 1, p. 133 is advised to establish his school in a temple. Cf. J. W. H. Walden, *The Universities of Ancient Greece* (New York, 1909), p. 366.

51. See, for example, Libanius' *Oratio* I, 102, pp. 132, 133: an old man came to Libanius in Antioch and told him that it was no wonder that, as Libanius says, "I did not succeed when I lay at my ease in my own house, for, of course, those (teachers) who *sat* in public had the advantage." Libanius followed his advice, hired rooms in the city and *sat down* near the agora. His class soon increased threefold.

52. G. Kittel, *Theologisches Wörterbuch zum Neuen Testament* (Stuttgart, 1938, reprint 1950), vol. 3, p. 446, notes fourteen passages in the Gospels having this meaning. It seems to have been a rabbinic custom which was accepted by Christ.

53. For details, see J. Kollwitz, "Christus als Lehrer und die Gesetzübergabe an Petrus in der konstantinischen Kunst Roms," *Römische Quartalschrift*, 44 (1936), pp. 45–66.

54. F. Dvornik, *Photius et la réorganisation*, pp. 114, 115. It is not clear if the school in which Constantine was appointed as teacher of philosophy was established in the Church of the Twelve Apostles, described by Mesarites, or in the Church of SS. Peter and Paul which was also often called by the Byzantines the Church of the Holy Apostles, or the Church of St. Paul. This school had been reorganized by the Emperor Alexis I (Anna Comnena, *Alexiad*, XIV, i, ed. Leib, vol. 3, p. 217 ff.). We have information about the functioning of this school from the eleventh century on. There is no doubt that it was a part of the Patriarchal Academy. It is possible that the school at the Church of the Twelve Apostles was organized only during the patriarchate of John XI Kamateros (1198–1206) who may have transferred there some sections from other churches. See, for more details, R. Browning, "The Patriarchal School of Constantinople," *Byzantion*, 32 (1962), p. 167 ff., especially pp. 175–179.

55. Thanks to the discovery made by I. Ševčenko of Dumbarton Oaks, the problem of this inscription is at least partly solved. He found a Greek text of a part of this inscription in a Greek manuscript in the Escurial (Esc. Ψ. III, 7). Cf. I. Ševčenko, "The Greek Source of the Inscription on Solomon's Chalice in the *Vita Constantini*," *To Honor Roman Jakobson* (The Hague, 1967), III, pp. 1806–1817.

CHAPTER III

1. See especially J. Poulík, "Kultura moravských Slovanů a Avaři" (The Civilization of the Moravian Slavs and the Avars), *Slavia antiqua*, 1 (1948), pp. 325–348; *idem, Staroslovanská Morava*, Monumenta Archaeologica, 1 (Prague, 1948), pp. 103–117. Most of the new archaeological evidence concerning the Avars and Slavs will be found in his book *Jižní Morava, země dávných Slovanů* (Southern Moravia, the Land of Ancient Slavs) (Brno, 1948–50), pp. 53–126. H. Preidel in his book *Die Anfänge der slawischen Besiedlung Böhmens und Mährens* (Munich, 1954), 1, pp. 82–106 (König Samo und sein Reich), still places the center of Samo's realm in Bohemia. His appreciations of the new discoveries are hypercritical. K. Oettinger, in his book *Das Werden Wiens* (Vienna, 1951), pp. 52–71, thinks that even the region of Vienna belonged to the empire of Samo and that he may have resided in its *Berghof*, a medieval fortress the ruins of which have been recently discovered. He argues that even the Slovenes with their prince Valak had joined the empire of Samo which he characterizes as a *Fürstenbund*, union of princes. Vienna—hitherto called by the Slovenes *Dunaj* —was again occupied by the Avars after 568. Cf. a good review of different ideas concerning the empire of Samo by F. Tiso, "The Empire of Samo (623–658)," *Slovac Studies*, 1; *Historica*, 1 (Rome, 1961), pp. 1–21. On Fredegar's Chronicle and the work by Labuda, see above, ch. I, fn. 2, 8.

2. Fredegar's Chronicle, *MGH Ss rer Merov* II, bk. 4, chs. 48, 68, pp. 144–145, 154. The battle took place near a fortified place called Wogastisburg. See the more recent bibliography on this place in A. Frinta's remarks "Wogastisburg," *Slavia*, 32 (1963), pp. 528–531. He locates Wogastisburg on the river Mainz near Staffelberg. Cf. also E. Herrmann, *Slawisch-germanische Beziehungen im südostdeutschen Raum* (Munich, 1965), pp. 40–46. The author gives extracts from Fredegar's Chronicle with commentary and recent bibliography. In the following pages he reprints all the reports on the Slavs and their relations with the Germans from Frankish chronicles and other documents to the end of the tenth century, with useful critical and bibliographical comments. The problem of the location of Wogastisburg is not yet solved. It must have existed somewhere near the border between the Frankish territory and Bohemia. It is, however, possible that the insurrection against the Avars had started in Moravia, because the Avar domination must have provoked a reaction in the neighborhood of the

Avar empire. This would indicate that Moravia became an important part of Samo's empire.

3. (ad a. 791) *MGH Ss* 1, p. 177; ed. F. Kurze (1895), p. 120; V. Novotný, *České dějiny* Prague, (1912), 1, p. 269, allows convincingly that Einhard had in mind Bohemia proper.

4. (ad a. 805) *MGH Ss* 1, p. 192; ed. F. Kurze, p. 120.

5. *MGH Ss* 1, p. 307; 2, p. 258.

6. *MGH Ss* 13, p. 33.

7. (ad a. 822) *MGH Ss* 1, p. 209; ed. F. Kurze, p. 159.

8. *An. Fuld.* (ad a. 845), *ibid.*, p. 364; ed. F. Kurze, p. 159.

9. *Annales Regum Francorum* (ad a. 822), *MGH Ss* 1, ed. F. Kurze, p. 159.

10. *Annales Laurissenses* (ad a. 803), *MGH Ss* 1, p. 191.

11. *Annales Lobienses* (ad a. 803), *MGH Ss* 2, p. 195.

12. *Annales Regum Francorum* (ad a. 811), *MGH Ss* 1, p. 199, ed. F. Kurze, p. 135.

13. Latest edition by B. Horák, D. Trávníček, *Descriptio civitatum ad septentrionalem plagam Danubii, Rozpravy* of the Czechoslovak Academy, 66 (1956), with bibliography and commentary. L. Havlík, "Moravané v údajích franko-bavorského Descriptia" (The Moravians in the Reports of the Franko-Bavarian Descriptio), *Historický časopis*, 7 (Bratislava, 1959), pp. 282–289, with more recent bibliography, and by H. Bulín, "Z diskuse o počátcích velkomoravské říše" (On the Discussions of the Origins of the Great Moravian Empire), *Slavia occidentalis*, 22 (1962), pp. 67–111, with a summary in English.

14. "Moravané," pp. 282–289.

15. See H. Bulín, "Staré Slovensko v datech Bavorského geografa" (Old Slovakia in the Description of the Bavarian Geographer), *Historický časopis*, 6 (1958), pp. 405–433; *idem, Z diskuse*, pp. 85–88.

16. *MGH Leges* 1, p. 198.

17. J. Poulík, *Staří Moravané budují svůj stát* (The Ancient Moravians Build Their State) (Gottwaldov, 1963), pp. 116–138. See also the more detailed description of Moravian fortified settlements in V. Richter's study, "Die Anfänge der Grossmährischen Architektur," *Magna Moravia*, Opera Universitatis Purkynianae Brunensis, Facultas philosophica, 102 (Brno, 1965), pp. 175–182.

18. M. Hellmann, in his study "Grundlagen slavischer Verfassungsgeschichte des frühen Mittelalters," *Jahrbücher für Geschichte Osteuropas*, 2 (1954), p. 391, rightly stresses the economical and commercial importance of Pribina's Nitra. It was a prominent center of communications, dominating the way from the Danube through the valley of Vag (Waag) to the upper Oder and Vistula, through the pass of Jablunka. It was not surprising that foreign, mostly Bavarian, merchants established a permanent commercial center there.

19. *Conversio Bogoariorum et Carantanorum,* ed. M. Kos (Ljubljana, 1936), ch. 11, p. 136; *MGH Ss* 11, p. 12.

20. Cf. Zagiba, "Die bairische Slavenmission," *JGOE,* 9 (1964), p. 13. Z. R. Dittrich, *Christianity in Great Moravia* (Groningen, 1962), p. 69, rejects this date because it "finds no support in the sources." But neither does his or any other dating. The date 828 fits better with Dittrich's interpretation (*ibid.,* p. 70) of the decision made by Louis the German in November 829, extending the boundary of the diocese of Passau almost as far as the river Raab (*MGH Dipl Lud. Germ,* I, 1, nr. 173, p. 244 ff.). The decision was made because Reginhar of Passau had accused Adalram of Salzburg of interference in the area which he regarded as belonging to his diocese. If Dittrich's interpretation, namely that this area included the Slavic lands north of the Danube, is right, then it would seem natural that the complaint of Reginhar, made in 829, should have been motivated by a recent act of the archbishop which was interpreted by Reginhar as interference in his "parochia"; this could be the consecration of the church in Nitra in 828. Salzburg was the metropolis of Passau. It is not certain if the new delimitation of the two dioceses was made by Louis, or if it was the result of a mutual agreement between Salzburg and Passau. The document attributed to Louis may not be genuine. Cf. J. Cibulka, *Velkomoravský kostel v Modré u Velehradu a začátky křesťanství na Moravě* (The Church of the Great Moravian Period in Modrá and the Beginning of Christianity in Moravia) (Prague, 1958), p. 260 ff. The date of 828 was first proposed by Cibulka, p. 266 ff.

21. J. Cibulka in his interesting although most controversial book noted above, p. 252 ff., thinks that Iro-Scottish monks from St. Peter's monastery in Salzburg may have spread Christianity in Nitra. Because they had no bishop in their Abbey, having been induced to accept the Benedictine rule which did not admit monastic bishops subordinated to abbots, as was the custom in Iro-Scottish monasteries, they had to invite the Archbishop of Salzburg to perform the consecration. Unfortunately there is no evidence to show that the Iro-Scottish missionaries who had worked in Bavaria and in Carinthia in the eighth century had spread their activity so far and so late. It is more logical to admit that there was in Nitra an important German colony for which the church was built. This seems to be confirmed by the fact that Nitra later became a center of opposition against the Slavic liturgy. Cf. my book *Les Slaves, Byzance et Rome au IXᵉ siècle* (Paris, 1926), p. 263. In 1933 J. Cibulka expressed a similar opinion quite opposed to his present contention in his study "Pribina a jeho kostol v Nitre" (Pribina and his Church in Nitra), *Ríša Velkomoravská* (The Empire of Great Moravia), ed. by J. Stanislav (Bratislava, 1933), p. 46 ff.

22. We learn of this event from the author of the *Conversio* quoted above.

23. Z. R. Dittrich, *Christianity*, p. 67 ff., rejects the generally accepted view that Pribina was an independent tribal ruler and puts forward the theory that his territory had been "long since an integral part of the Moravian state," an appanage of the ruling dynasty, and that Pribina ruled there as "a kinsman, probably a cousin or even a brother of Mojmír." A similar opinion was voiced by J. Sieklicki, "Quidam Priwina," *Slavia occidentalis*, 22 (1962), pp. 116–145. If this could be substantiated it would be more understandable that the Franks should have rejected Pribina's request to reinstate him in his princedom. There is, however, one serious objection to this interpretation. Mojmír and his house were already Christians. If Pribina was a member of the ruling dynasty he should have accepted Christianity with its other members. One can hardly imagine that Mojmír, who had done so much for the Christianization of his country, would have entrusted its eastern part to a pagan. It is safer to accept J. Cibulka's explanation (*Velkomoravský*, p. 265 ff.) that the Franks favored Mojmír because he was not only friendly to them, but also a Christian, while Pribina was a pagan. But the fact that not even the Archbishop of Salzburg could induce Pribina to become a Christian shows that, contrary to Cibulka's pretension, Christianity could hardly have made notable progress in Pribina's lands. The philological arguments brought forward by M. Weingart in his study "Pribina, Kocel a Nitra," *Říša velkomoravská*, ed. J. Stanislav (Bratislava, 1933), p. 319 ff., to show that Pribina's name indicates that he was ruling over a different Slavic tribe akin to the Moravian tribes, should not be dismissed as lightly as Z. R. Dittrich does. The other gives also on p. 58 ff. a good account of the activity of Frankish missionaries in Moravia. He rightly attributes the main merit for the Christianization of the Moravians to Bishop Reginhar.

24. J. Cibulka, *Velkomoravský*, p. 199 ff. Cf. also his study in German "Zur Frühgeschichte der Architektur im Mähren," *Festschrift K. M. Swoboda* (Vienna, 1959), pp. 55–74.

25. A. L. Kuhar, *The Conversion of the Slovenes* (New York, Washington, 1959), pp. 29–52. More complete bibliography in F. Zagiba, "Bairische Slavenmission und ihre Fortsetzung durch Kyrill und Method," *JGOE*, 9 (1961), p. 4 ff. Cf. also the study by W. H. Fritze, "Slaven und Avaren im angelsächsischen Missionsprogram," *Zeitschrift für slavische Philologie*, 21 (1963), pp. 316–338; 22 (1965), pp. 231–251.

26. J. Cibulka's theories on Iro-Scottish missions in Moravia were rejected by almost all Czech archaeologists and historians. See especially F. Graus, "K počátkům křesťanství na Moravě" (On the Introduction of Christianity into Moravia), *Český časopis historický* (Czech Historical Review), 7 (1959), pp. 478–483; V. Vavřínek, "K otázce počátků christianisace Velké Moravy" (The Question of the Christian-

ization of Great Moravia), *Listy filologické,* 7 (1959), pp. 217–224; J. Poulík, *Staří Moravané budují svůj stát* (The Ancient Moravians Build Their State) (Gottwaldov, 1963), p. 77 ff. Cf. also H. Preidel, "Archäologische Denkmäler und Funde zur Christianisierung des östlichen Mitteleuropas," *Die Welt der Slaven,* 5 (1960), p. 62 ff., who is very skeptical about Cibulka's conclusions. Z. R. Dittrich (*Christianity,* p. 40 ff.) wanted to "prove beyond all doubt" that the first missionaries in Moravia to enjoy lasting success were the Iro-Scottish monks. But he had to admit that he could explain their activity only "hypothetically," because he could gather only "circumstantial evidence" (!). He thinks that the Irish monks had built the church in Modrá and (p. 43 ff.) that their mission facilitated the conversion of the Moravians near the Moravian political center in Staré Město-Veligrad. But, on p. 66, he had to agree that the Staré Město-Veligrad cemeteries near Modrá, the supposed center of Irish missions in the period before 825 when they are believed to have thrived, "still show a predominantly pagan character." One should be rather cautious when making striking conclusions. Dittrich found "a new argument" for the important role of the Irish missionaries in the conversion of Moravia in *Vita Methodii,* ch. 10. The Moravians, having asked Pope Hadrian II to send Methodius back to them, are supposed to have said: "Our fathers had in the past received baptism from St. Peter." The Irish missionaries had a special veneration for St. Peter, and the Moravians are said to have recalled their activities before that of the Franks (p. 47). This is a somewhat hasty conclusion. The *Life* was written after Methodius' death, and his disciples defended his liturgical innovation by stressing its approval by the See of St. Peter. This explains also the popularity of St. Peter in Old Slavonic documents. Nor can one see an "Irish influence" in the defense of St. Methodius at his trial (ch. 9), when he affirms that Pannonia belongs not to Salzburg but to St. Peter. It was subordinated by the recent decision of the Pope to the Petrine See of Rome. As concerns the "Irish" doctrine on antipodes, see below, pp. 177, 370.

27. *Bernardi Cremifanensis Historiae, MGH Ss* 25, p. 655: "Item Renharius episcopus baptizat omnes Moravos"; *Notae de episcopis Pataviensibus, ibid.,* p. 623: "Anno Domini 831 Regenharius episcopus Patavorum baptizat omnes Moravos." The authors of both documents were monks from the monastery of Kremsmünster. Cf. J. Cibulka, *Velkomoravský,* p. 272 ff.

28. *PL,* 131, cols. 3–38.

29. See below, p. 115.

30. In my book *Les Slaves,* p. 155, I mentioned this as a possibility without drawing any conclusions from it. J. Cibulka, in his paper "Zur

Frühgeschrichte der Architektur in Mähren (800–900)," Swoboda Festschrift (1959), followed this suggestion without quoting my book (p. 73). He, however, attributed to these refugees the introduction into Moravia of a new church architecture, of which the excavated church of Saint Sofia in Sofia (believed to have been built in the fourth century) served as a model, and which was revived in Bulgaria at the end of the ninth and in the beginning of the tenth century after the Christianization of Bulgaria by a Byzantine mission. These refugees are supposed to have worked in Moravia in the first half of the ninth century. These claims cannot be accepted. There is, as we show here, a better explanation for the presence of priests from Greece in Moravia and also for the appearance of this type of church architecture in that country. Cf. below, p. 86 ff.

31. *PL*, 131, col. 35: synodalem cum suis, et etiam ibi inventis conventum frequentavit.

32. The reader will find short descriptions of archaeological discoveries in Moravia in the following works written in non-Slavic languages: F. Dvornik, *The Slavs, Their Early History and Civilization* (Boston, 1956), pp. 148–153; H. Preidel, "Die altslavischen Funde von Altstadt in Mähren und ihre Bedeutung," *Stifter Jahrbuch*, 4 (1955), pp. 254–277; *idem, Slavische Altertumskunde des östlichen Mitteleuropas im 9. und 10. Jahrhundert* (Graefeling, 1961), pp. 117–142; J. Böhm, "Deux églises datantes de l'Empire de Grande Moravie découvertes en Tchécoslovaquie," *Byzantinoslavica*, 11 (1950), pp. 207–222; J. Poulík, "The Latest Archaeological Discoveries from the Period of the Great Moravian Empire," *Historica*, 1 (Prague, 1959), pp. 7–70; V. Vavřínek, "Die Christianisierung und Kirchenorganisation Grossmährens," *Historica*, 7 (1963), pp. 5–56; *idem*, "Study of the Church Architecture from the Period of the Great Moravian Empire," *Byzantinoslavica*, 25 (1964), pp. 288–301.

33. See the first publication of these finds in V. Hrubý, V. Hochmanová, J. Pavelčík, "Kostel a pohřebiště z doby velkomoravské na Modré u Velehradu" (The Church and the Cemetery from the Great Moravian Period in Modrá near Velehrad), *Časopis Moravského Musea*, 40 (1955), pp. 42–126. See also the study by V. Richter, *Die Anfänge der Grossmährischen Architektur*, pp. 144–162. The author dates this structure from the second half of the ninth century. This dating does not seem to be sufficiently founded, but even this date could be placed before the arrival of the Byzantine mission. V. Hrubý, in his critical publication of the discoveries made so far at Staré Město, after discussing all that has been published on this church, rejects the Iro-Scottish origin of this church and dates its construction, on the base of the archaeological material found in the graves near the

church to around 840, perhaps between 830–840. V. Hrubý, *Staré Město–Velkomoravský Velehrad* (Prague, 1965). Monumenta archaeologica no. 14, pp. 198–201.

34. First published by J. Poulík, "Výsledky výzkumu na velkomoravském hradišti 'Valy' u Mikulčic" (The First Results of the Investigations Made on the Great Moravian Settlement "Valy" near Mikulčice), *Památky archeologické*, 48 (1957), pp. 241–388. See also *idem, Staří Moravané*, p. 90 ff.; and *idem, The Latest Archaeological Discoveries*, pp. 27–41.

35. Discovered by J. Poulík. The details of these discoveries are not yet published. Cf. the description in his book *Pevnost v lužním lese* (A Forthill in a Wooded Meadow) (Prague, 1967), p. 151 ff., 182 ff., 194 ff.

36. J. Cibulka, "První tři velkomoravské kostely nalezené na hradišti u Mikulčic" (The First Three Churches Discovered on the Settlement near Mikulčice), Symposium *Soluňští bratři* (Prague, 1962), pp. 87–159. Another study was published by him in German in the Symposium under the title *Sancti Cyrillus et Methodius* (Prague, 1963), pp. 49–117, esp. pp. 50–59, under the title "Grossmährische Kirchenbauten." Cibulka recently summarized his ideas on the origins of Moravian church architecture in *L'information de l'histoire de l'art*, under the title "L'architecture de la Grande-Moravie au IXᵉ siècle à la lumière des récentes découvertes," ii (Paris, 1966), pp. 1–34. It should be stressed that in these two last publications he does not attribute the construction of churches with rectangular presbyteries to Iro-Saxon missionaries. He speaks only of the Celtic type of church architecture introduced into Moravia by Bavarian missionaries who were acquainted with it from the time when Iro-Scottish monks had worked in Bavaria. Such a thesis would appear quite plausible if there could be found in Bavaria a number of churches constructed in this style. Unfortunately, the excavations made in German lands from 1938 to 1953 have discovered about 130 unknown foundations of churches, many of them with rectangular presbyteries, but mostly in Westphalia, the Rhineland, and in neighboring lands—Holland, Belgium, and Luxemburg—not in Bavaria. See "Übersicht über die wichtigsten Grabungen in einzelnen Ländern," in *Kunstchronik*, 8 (1955), pp. 117–124, by F. Bellmann, especially the sketches on pp. 118, 119. Cibulka himself was able to point out only one Bavarian sanctuary, that in Mühltal-Elpolding, as a proof that the type of Celtic church architecture had taken roots also in Bavaria. Similar constructions in Carinthia cannot be quoted as an indication that such a style was exported from Bavaria into Moravia as well.

37. The small dimensions of the church at Modrá and of four other churches discovered in Moravia suggested to J. G. Cincík ("Early

Slovak Oratories, a Study in Slavic-Iranian Architectural Tradition," *Most,* 7 [Cleveland, 1960], pp. 135–147) the idea that they had perhaps served individual clans, and that old Slavic customs were followed in their construction. Pagan Slavic shrines used also to be of small dimensions, because the people assembled around them beneath the open skies to participate in the sacrifices offered by the priests inside the shrines. He thinks that it could perhaps be assumed that the churches were destined only for the clergy and that the faithful assisted at the liturgy by assembling around the churches. The separation of the presbytery from the narrow apse in those churches indicates, according to him, a blending of old pagan customs with the Roman Christian architectural tradition. More archaeological evidence is needed to test this theory. They seem rather to have served as burial churches. V. Richter, *"Die Anfänge . . . ,"* pp. 202–205, has also tried to find a connection between the Slavic pagan sanctuaries and the first Christian churches, but with little success.

38. See V. Vavřínek, "Study of the Church Architecture," pp. 290–291. Latest criticism by V. Richter, "Die Anfänge," pp. 156–165.

39. E. Dyggwe, *History of Salonitian Christianity* (Oslo, 1951), p. 125 ff., especially p. 131, fig. VI, 34: comparison between early Christian and early Croatian church forms; also fig. VI, 35: early Croatian church forms with buttresses.

40. Cf. E. Dyggwe, "Das Mausoleum von Marušinac und sein Fortleben," *Actes du VIe Congrès international des études byzantines,* Bulletin de l'Institut archéologique bulgare, 10 (Sofia, 1936), pp. 228–237.

41. E. Dyggwe, *History of Salonitian Christianity,* p. 134, fig. VI, 25, 26.

42. To 1966 only preliminary findings reports have been published by the excavator V. Hrubý in local publications unobtainable in the United States. See V. Vavřínek, *Study of the Church Architecture,* p. 209; J. Poulík, *Staří Moravané,* pp. 80–82. A definite publication of the finds was made by V. Hrubý in his book *Staré Město-Velkomoravský Velehrad,* pp. 202–206, tables XLV, XLVI. On the other two parts of the complex, see below, p. 125.

43. See the detailed report on the two rotundas in J. Poulík's study, *Dvě velkomoravské rotundy v Mikulčicích* (Prague, 1963), Monumenta archaeologica, vol. 12. A detailed résumé in German (pp. 197-233) accompanies this edition. Cf. also J. Cibulka, *Sancti Cyrillus et Methodius,* pp. 93–100 (in German).

44. The remains of the rotunda were discovered by V. Hrubý in 1958, and 1962 under the presbytery of St. Michael's church in Staré Město in the terrain where a Slavic settlement, called the fourth, was previously located by Hrubý. The archaeological finds in the graves inside and outside the building permit us to date the construction of

the rotunda to the beginning of the second half of the ninth century (V. Hrubý, *Staré Město-Velkomoravský Velehrad,* pp. 184–190, tables XLII, XLIII). Cf. V. Richter, "Die Anfänge," p. 192, who agrees with the excavator concerning the date of the rotundas. The rotunda was dedicated to St. Michael and had survived the destruction of Great Moravia. It was rebuilt in the first half of the thirteenth century, and the new church was reconstructed in 1734. Many fragments of Roman bricks with the mark of the Legion XIV are to be seen in its foundations, which are preserved.

45. J. Cibulka, "První tři velkomoravské kostely," pp. 154–156.

46. *Ibid.,* pp. 156, 157.

47. For a short review of pre-romanesque sacral buildings in Zadar, with bibliographical indications, see *Enciklopedia likovnih umjetnosti* (Encyclopedia of Visual Arts) (Zagreb, 1959– 1966), four vols., vol. 4, p. 592. For more details, see I. Petricioli, "Neki preromanički spomenici Zadra i okolice u svjetla najnovijih istraživanja" (Some Pre-Romanesque Monuments in Zadar and Its Surroundings in the Light of Most Recent Research), *Zbornik Instituta za histor. nauke v Zadru,* 2 (1956–57) (Zadar, 1956), p. 56; *idem,* "Maketa Zadra u pomorskom muzju Venecije" (Scale Model of Zadar in the Maritime Museum in Venice), *ibid.,* p. 101. On this old model Petricioli discovered the remnants of another church with six apses in Zadar, north of the renaissance fountain. Cf. also Lj. Karaman, "Spomenici umjetnosti u Zadru u vrijeme hrvatskih narodnih vladara" (Art Monuments in Zadar During the Period of National Rulers), *Zbornik Instituta za histor. nauke u Zadru* (Zagreb, 1964), publ. by Matice Hrvatska. Cf. also Lj. Karaman, *Pregled umjetnosti u Dalmaciji* (Review of Dalmatian Art) (Zagreb, 1952), p. 17.

48. See *Enciklopedia,* Nin, Krk.

49. Gj. Bosković, *Architektura sredneg veka* (Medieval Architecture) (Beograd, 1957), p. 178 ff., fig. 236.

50. See *Enciklopedia,* Vis; J. Strzygowski, *Die altslavische Kunst* (Augsburg, 1929), pp. 66, 69.

51. See the remarks given by Gj. Bosković, *Architektura,* p. 180, fn. 17. The small chapel in Drivasto near Skadar also has several apses (*ibid.,* fn. 5.) For details of Gunjača's excavations see: "Kratak osvrt na rad i prilike muzeja u Kninu" (Short Survey of the Work and Condition of the Museum in Knin), *Starohrvatska prosvjeta,* 3d series, 3 (Zagreb, 1953), pp. 189–191; *idem,* "Trogodišnji rad Museja hrvatskih archeoloskih spomenika" (The Three Years of Work of the Museum of Croatian Archaeological Monuments), *ibid.,* 7 (Zagreb, 1960), pp. 207–271; *idem,* "Starohrvatska crkva i kasnosredovjekovno groblje u Brnazima kod Sinja" (The Old-Croatian Church and the Late Medieval Cemetery at Brnazi near Senj), *ibid.,* 4 (Zagreb, 1955), pp. 85–134,

with a résumé in French. The author dates this church from the ninth to tenth century. It was destroyed in the 13th century. His re-excavation and description of a church near Knin with an apse, oblong nave, and a narthex deserve a special study. See for details S. Gunjača, "Starohrvatska crkva i groblje na Lopuskoj Glavici u Biskupijo kod Knina" (The Old-Croatian Church and Cemetery in Lopuska Glanica in Biskupia near Knin), *ibid.*, 3 (Zagreb, 1954), pp. 7–30. The excavator dates the construction of this church to the ninth century. Cf. also his answer to Karaman's criticism, *ibid.*, 5 (Zagreb, 1956): "Oko revizije iskopina u Biskupije" (Concerning the Revision of the Excavations in Biskupije), pp. 21–32.

52. See T. Marasović, "Iskapanje ranosrednjovjekovne crkve sv. Marije u Trogiru" (The Excavation of the Early Medieval Church of Our Lady in Trogir), *ibid.*, 8–9 (Zagreb, 1963), pp. 83–100, with a résumé in French. The excavator does not give an exact date for its construction, but, taking into account other analogies of this kind of church architecture, it should be dated to about the ninth century.

53. For details see *Istoria Crne Gore* study by Kovačević, pp. 289, 369, 376, 374–377, 378; I. Nikolajević, "Rapport préliminaire sur la recherche des monuments chrétiens à Doclea," *Actes du Ve Congrès international d'archéologie Chrétienne* (Paris, 1957), pp. 567–572 (The Church of Our Lady in Dukla); P. Mijović, "Acruvium-Decatera-Kotor u svetlu novich archeoloskich otkrića" (Acruvium-Decatera-Kotor in the Light of New Archeological Discoveries), *Starinar*, New Series, vols. XIII–XIV (1962–1963), p. 27 ff., with a résumé in French (date of the construction of the basilica in Kotor).

54. Kovačević, *Crna Gora*, p. 374, sees in Porphyrogenitus' description of the church of St. Triphun an indication that it was a rotunda.

55. On the church in Ošlje see Gj. Bosković, *Architektura*, p. 180, fig. 237; T. Marasović, "Ranosrjednjevekovna crkvica u Ošlju kad Stona" (The Early Medieval Little Church of Ošlje near Ston), *Peristil*, 2 (1957), pp. 85–91. Cf. also A. Deroko, *Monumentalna i dekorativna architectura u srednjevkovnoj Serbii* (Monumental and Decorative Architecture in Medieval Serbia) (Beograd, 2nd ed., 1962), fig. 31 (Ošlje), fig. 32 (Church with three apses in Zaton on Lim), fig. 50 (Stara Pavlica). Cf. in this connection the study by A. Mohorovičić, "Problem tipoloske klasifikacije objekata srednjovjekovne architekture na području Istre i Kvarnera" (The Problem of a Typological Classification of Medieval Architectural Monuments in the Territory of Istria and Quarnero), *Ljetopis* of the Yugoslav Academy, kniga 62 (Zagreb, 1957), pp. 487–541. On the origin of basilicas in Istria, see the remarks made by B. Marušić describing the three basilicas with three naves at Guran, "Dva spomenika ranosrednjovjekove architekture u Guranu kod Vodnjana" (Two Examples of Early Medie-

val Architecture at Guran near Vodnjan), *Starohrvatska prosvjeta,* 3d series, 8–9 (Zagreb, 1963), pp. 121–149 (with a résumé in French), esp. pp. 139–145, 149.

56. V. Vavřínek was the first who discussed the possibility of the presence of Aquileian missionaries in Moravia in his study "Předcyrilometodějské missie na Veliké Moravě" (Missionary activity in Moravia before Cyril and Methodius), *Slavia,* 32 (1963), pp. 465–480.

57. We shall see that it was a Venetian priest John who had later played an important role at the Moravian court. See below, p. 155.

58. V. Richter, "Die Anfänge," pp. 138–140, rightly stresses that this point is often overlooked by art historians.

59. The first specialist who has pointed out that the prototypes of some Moravian churches should be looked for in the sphere of the Adriatic sea, especially in Dalmatia, was J. Pošmourný in his paper "Stavební umění Velkomoravské říše" (The Architectural Art of Great Moravia), *Architektura ČSSR,* 20 (1961), pp. 129–135; *idem,* "Církevní architektura Velkomoravské říše" (Church Architecture in Great Moravia), *Umění,* 12 (1964), pp. 187–202, with a résumé in German. Cf. also the remarks made by T. Marasović, "Evidence of Byzantine Art in Preromanesque Architecture in Dalmatia," XII Congrès international des études byzantines (Belgrad, Ochrid, 1961), résumé des communications, p. 65. See also V. Vavřínek, "Study of the Church Architecture from the Period of the Great Moravian Empire," *Byzantinoslavica,* 25 (1964), pp. 288–301; recently J. Poulík, *Dvě velkomoravské rotundy,* p. 88 ff.; M. Šolle, "Die Bedeutung des dalmatinischen altkroatischen Gebietes in der Frage nach dem Ursprung der Grossmährischen Kultur," *Das Grossmährische Reich,* ed. F. Graus, J. Filip, A. Dostál (Prague, 1966), pp. 105–107.

60. See V. Hrubý, *Staré Město. Velkomoravské pohřebiště "Na Valách"* (Old City. The Great Moravian Cemetery "On the Ramparts"), Monumenta archaeologica, 3 (Prague, 1965). *Idem, Staré Město. Velkomoravský Velehrad,* gives more detailed descriptions of the results of his discoveries. He describes first the eight settlements which had existed around Staré Město with the localities in Uh. Hradiště-Sady and Osvětimany (pp. 32–104), the fortifications (pp. 215–236), and gives interesting details on the agricultural and industrial achievements of the inhabitants (pp. 237–336). Cf. also J. Poulík, *Staří Moravané,* pp. 60–84.

61. J. Poulík, "Výsledky výzkumu na velkomoravském hradišti 'Valy' u Mikulčic" (Result of the Search Survey on the Great Moravian Stronghold 'Valy' near Mikulčice), *Památky archeologické,* 48 (1957), pp. 241–388, with a résumé in German; *idem, Staří Moravané,* p. 84 ff.

62. *MGH Ss* 1, pp. 381, 383 (ad a. 869, 871), ed. F. Kurze, pp. 69, 74.

63. B. Dostál, "Výzkum velkomoravského hradiska Pohansko u

Břeclavi" (Archaeological Exploration of the Great Moravian Castle Pohansko near Břeclav), *Slovácko* (1961), pp. 16–31; F. Kalousek, "Velkomoravské Pohansko u Břeclavě," *Archeologické rozhledy*, 12 (1960), pp. 498–530, figs. 121–198. *Idem*, "Die grossmährische Burgwaldstadt Břeclav-Pohansko," *Sborník prací filos. fakulty University J. E. Purkyně*, 9 E 5 (1960), pp. 5–22; J. Poulík, *Staří Moravané*, p. 116 ff. A detailed description of the discoveries is not yet published. On the other stronghold, Pohansko near Nejdek, cf. B. Novotný, "The Survey of a Great Moravian Stronghold 'Pohansko' near Nejdek," *Památky archeologické*, 54 (1963), pp. 3–40, with a résumé in German.

64. The results of the archaeological research in Děvín were published by J. Dekan in *Archeologické rozhledy*, 3 (1951), pp. 164–168; cf. *idem*, "Mosaika," *Sborník* of the philosophical faculty of Komenský University in Bratislava, 12 (1961), pp. 51–55.

65. So far there have been found in the territory around Nitra five strongholds, eighteen cemeteries, fifteen settlements with pottery kilns, glass works, and iron workshops. For more details, see B. Chropovský, "The Situation of Nitra in the Light of Archaeological Finds," *Historica*, 8 (Prague, 1964), pp. 5–33. Most of the discovered material is not yet published. In the *Sborník O počiatkoch slovenských dejín* (On the Beginning of Slovak History), ed. P. Ratkoš (Bratislava, 1965), three studies give more details on the economic situation of Slovakia in this period: that by A. Habovštiak on agriculture in the ninth to the eleventh centuries (pp. 55–80), that by D. Bialeková on the development of artisanry in Slovakia during the same period (pp. 81–96), and that by R. Pleiner on the technology of smithery trade and iron production. The significance of the latest archaeological discoveries in Slovakia for early Slavic history and that of Great Moravia was discussed by A. Točík in *Historický Časopis*, 3 (Bratislava, 1955), pp. 410–421.

66. A lively discussion on the social differentiation of the Moravians at this early period is taking place among Czech and Slovak historians. We cannot go into details here. An extensive bibliography of this problem will be found in the study by P. Ratkoš, "Počiatki feudalizmu na Slovensku" (Beginnings of Feudalism in Slovakia), *Historický Časopis*, 2 (Bratislava, 1954), pp. 252–275. See also F. Graus, *Dějiny venkovského lidu v Čechách v době předhusitské* (A History of the Peasantry in Bohemia Before the Hussite Period) (Prague, 1953), vol. 1; *idem*, "L'origine de l'état et de la noblesse en Moravie et en Bohême," *Revue des études slaves*, 39 (1961); *idem*, "L'Empire de Grande Moravie, sa situation dans l'Europe de l'époque et sa structure intérieure," *Das Grossmährische Reich*, pp. 133–219.

67. The findings in the cemetery *Na Valách*, published with reproductions by V. Hrubý, *Staré Město*, give quite a clear picture of the material culture in Great Moravia. See also J. Poulík, *Staroslovanská*

Morava (Prague, 1948), Monumenta archaeologica, 1, reproduction of Moravian pottery, corals, earrings, axes, agricultural implements, buttons, etc. on 78 plates. On the production of iron in Great Moravia see R. Pleiner, *Základy slovanského železářského hutnictví v českých zemích* (Foundations of Slavic Metallurgy in Czech Lands) (Prague, 1958). Cf. *idem, Staré evropské kovářství* (The Smith's Trade in Old Europe) (Prague, 1962). The finds of numerous iron bars of different length in the form of axes indicate that this kind of iron product served as means of payment on the interior market. They were described by R. Pleiner, "Slovanské sekerovité hřivny" (Slavic Ax Iron Bars), *Slovanská archeologie*, 9 (1961), pp. 405–450; *idem*, "Velkomoravské železné hřivny jako platidlo" (Moravian Ax Iron Bars as Means of Payment), *Numismatické listy*, 18 (Prague, 1963), p. 134 ff. See also J. Pošvář, "Die byzantinische Währung und das Grossmährische Reich," *Byzantinoslavica*, 26 (1965), pp. 308–317. The author comes to the conclusion that in international commercial transactions Moravian merchants used the Byzantine monetary system as a basis to which also the Frankish and other monetary standards of that time were related. In the cemetery at Staré Město a small lead weight was found which corresponded to an eighth of a Roman pound. This seems to indicate that in commercial transactions Roman-Byzantine weights were used (V. Hrubý, *Staré Město*, pp. 114, 115). Probably most of the commercial transactions were by barter.

68. For example, the decision of the Reichstag held in Thionville at the end of 805. See *Capitularia regum Francorum, MGH Leg* 2, part 1; ed. A. Boretius (Berlin, 1881), pp. 122–126, no. 44.

69. Reproduction in J. Poulík's book, *Dvě velkomoravské rotundy*, table 18. Cf. tables 16, 20; *idem*, "Výsledky výzkumu," p. 325.

70. See especially the Slavic cemetery in Devínská Nová Ves, near Bratislava, published by J. Eisner, *Devínská Nová Ves, slovanské pohřebiště* (Bratislava, 1952). The cemetery was in use from about 625 to about 800. It is one of the oldest and largest burial grounds within the period of the Avar cultural development. It shows that the Slavic population lived in intimate relations with the Avars. One could even speak of a beginning of Slavization of some Avar groups. The buried men were mostly free warriors, and their equipment discloses Avar, Bavarian, Alamanic, and Slavic features. The ceramic and iron products especially reveal a great similarity with products current in Moravia between 800 and 950. This points out a continuity in craftsmanship and in population. On 114 plates J. Eisner gives illustrations of Avar and Slavic products found in the graves. There is a detailed résumé in German.

71 J. Poulík, *Dvě velkomoravské rotundy*, plate 26; *idem, Staří Moravané*, plate 20.

72. L. Havlík, *Velká Morava* (Prague, 1964), p. 136 (Great Moravia and the Slavs of Central Europe).

73. Remnants of such a workshop were discovered near Staré Město. See V. Hrubý, *Staré Město-Velkomoravský Velehrad,* pp. 258, 259.

74. K. Benda, "Stříbrný terč se sokolníkem ze Starého Města" (Silver Disc with a Falconer from Staré Město), *Památky archeologické,* 54 (1963), pp. 41–66, with a résumé in German.

75. On the Slavic ceramics of this period see especially J. Eisner, *Devínská Nová Ves,* pp. 248–278, plates 55 ff.; V. Hrubý, *Staré Město,* pp. 125–163, plates 38–68. Wooden buckets circled with iron bands were also numerous in Moravian graves. Cf. *ibid.,* plates 49–51. For the development of the Slavic ceramics see J. Eisner, *Rukovět slovanské archeologie* (Handbook of Slavic Archaeology) (Prague, 1966), pp. 137–312.

76. J. Poulík, *Výsledky výzkumu,* p. 333 ff.; V. Hrubý, *Staré Město,* pp. 203–214. Hrubý's description is completed by B. Dostál, *Slovanská pohřebiště ze střední doby hradištné* (Slavic Cemeteries from the So-called Middle Castle Period) (Prague, 1966), pp. 60–64. On p. 62 he rightly calls to the attention of archaeologists that some of the decorative motifs on the button are common in monuments in Croatia and Dalmatia from the eighth to the eleventh century.

77. V. Hrubý, *Staré Město,* pp. 246-261, color plates nos. 85, 86; B. Dostál, *Slovanská pohřebiště,* pp. 45–54, plates 85, 86.

78. Published by V. Hrubý, "Archeologický výzkum v Sadech u Uh. Hradiště r. 1959" (Archaeological Research in Sady near Uh. Hradisté in 1959), *Našim krajem-Sborník OPS v Uh. Hradišti,* 1 (1960), p. 14. The necklace is composed of 130 glass corals of different colors with a large bluish topaz. Czech archaeologists will have to compare the jewelry and decorative objects discovered by them with similar objects found in Yugoslavia, especially in Dalmatia. There is a good account of earrings found in Yugoslavia by Dušan Jelovina, "Statisticki tipolosko-topografsko pregled starohrvatskih naušnica na podračju SR Hrvatske" (A Statistic, Typologic and Topographic Review of Old-Croatian Earrings found on the Soil of the Socialist Croat Republic), *Starohrvatska prosvjeta,* 3rd ser., 8–9 (Zagreb, 1963), pp. 101–120.

79. V. Hrubý, *Staré Město,* pp. 266–271; B. Dostál, *Slovanská pohřebiště,* pp. 56–58.

80. The best description of Moravian earrings, so far, is by V. Hrubý, *Staré Město,* pp. 228–245; cf. also B. Dostál, *Slovanská pohřebiště,* pp. 30–44, plate 34.

81. L. Karaman, *Pregled umjetnosti u Dalmaciji* (Survey of Dalmatian Art) (Zagreb, 1952), p. 14, plate 3. The treasure is kept in the Archaeological Museum in Split; cf. also M. Šolle, *Die Bedeutung des dalmatinischen altkroatischen Gebietes,* p. 106.

82. J. Korošec, *Staroslovansko grobišče na ptujskem gradu* (Old Slavonic Cemetery at the Castle of Ptuj) (Ljubljana, 1950), plates 14–16, 110; cf. V. Hrubý, *Staré Město*, p. 239. The findings in Slavic cemeteries in Moravia, Bohemia and Slovakia are classified by B. Dostál, *Slovanská pohřebiště*. On pp. 108–196 the author gives a description of all Moravian burial grounds of this period with the indication of objects found in the tombs. Most of the objects are illustrated on 86 plates.

83. Let us remember that Samo himself was the head of a group of Frankish merchants who were visiting the Slavic lands to do business with their inhabitants in revolt against the Avars. Dagobert's hostile action against Samo was provoked by the robbery and murder of Frankish traders by Samo's Slavic subjects. Fredegar's Chronicle, *MGH Ss rer Merov* 2, book IV, ch. 48, pp. 144, 154.

84. *Conversio,* ch. 10, ed. M. Kos, p. 135.

85. *Annales Iuvavenses maximi, MGH Ss* 30, p. 740; *Annales S. Rudberti Salisburgenses, ibid.,* 9, p. 770; *Auctarium Garstense, ibid.,* p. 564.

86. *Conversio,* chs. 11, 12, ed. M. Kos, pp. 136–138.

87. *An. Fuld.* (ad a. 846), *MGH Ss* 1, p. 364; ed. F. Kurze, p. 36. Cf. V. Novotný, *České dějiny,* 1 (Prague, 1912), p. 294. These troubles could also be explained simply by a struggle for the succession between certain members of the dynasty. There is, however, no evidence for the assertion (Z. R. Dittrich, *Christianity,* p. 83 ff.) that Louis the German wanted to install Pribina as Mojmír's successor, but abandoned his plan when he saw that Rastislav had strong support in the country. In such a case Pribina should have accompanied him on his expedition and Louis would have taken a stronger military contingent with him.

88. *Annales Bertiniani, MGH Ss* 1, p. 444; *An. Fuld., ibid.,* pp. 365, 366, ed. F. Kurze, pp. 38, 39; *Annales Xantenses, MGH Ss* 2, p. 229.

89. *An. Fuld., MGH Ss* 1, p. 367; ed. F. Kurze, p. 41. *An. Bertiniani, ibid.,* p. 446.

90. *An. Fuld., MGH Ss* 1, p. 369; ed. F. Kurze, p. 45. We learn from the letter addressed by the Archbishop of Mainz, Hatto, to Pope John IX in 900 in which he protested in the name of the Frankish clergy against the expulsion of Bavarian priests from Moravia (*PL,* 131, col. 1180). This must have happened between 850 and 855 when Rastislav had broken his relations with the Empire.

91. *Conversio,* ch. 13, ed. H. Kos, p. 139.

92. *An. Fuld., MGH Ss* 1, p. 369; ed. F. Kurze, p. 46; *An. Bertiniani, ibid.,* pp. 459, 490.

93. P. Ratkoš, "K otázce hranice Velkej Moravy a Bulharska" (Concerning the Problem of the Boundaries between Great Moravia and Bulgaria), *Historický Časopis,* 3 (Bratislava, 1955), pp. 206–218, with a résumé in German. A protobulgarian inscription from the reign of

Omortag (814–831) mentions a warlike expedition on the Tisza river. Omortag's Greek inscription commemorates the commander of this expedition, the zera-tarkan Onegavon, who met his death by drowning in the river. One could be tempted to think of a clash of the Bulgars with the Moravians as expanding their sovereignty to the middle Tisza. However, it is more logical to date this incident to the year 829 and see in the presence of a Bulgarian army on the Tisza a measure taken against Louis the German who in 828 moved against Omortag, whose troops penetrated into Frankish Pannonia. This incident confirms other reports of the Frankish expedition and makes more probable the presence of the archbishop of Salzburg in Nitra where, in 828, he had consecrated a church in the territory of Pribina (see above, p. 77). See the latest publication of the inscription by V. Beševliev, "Inscriptions protobulgares," *Byzantion*, 28 (1958), pp. 270–272: "The Khan Omortag did: The zera-tarkan Onegavon . . . was my man, supported by me, and, when he joined the army he was drowned in the river Tisza. He was from the tribe Kouviar." N. Zlatarski, *Istorija na bŭlgarskata dŭržava* (Sofia, 1918), vol. 1, part 1, pp. 315, 316. In my book *Les Légendes*, p. 223, I mentioned this inscription as an indication of the possibility of commercial relation between Moravia and Bulgaria exaggerating its importance in this respect. The Moravians were never Bulgarian allies against the Franks, as I have shown above, p. 100.

94. *An. Fuld., MGH Ss* 1, pars. IV, p. 400; ed. F. Kurze, p. 112.

95. Recently Z. R. Dittrich, *Christianity,* pp. 98, 99, following A. Brückner, *Die Wahrheit über die Slavenapostel* (Tübingen, 1913), pp. 40, 41, whose fantastic misinterpretations of the two *Vitae* are now rejected by all specialists. Naturally Rastislav did not expect any help from the Byzantines against the Franks—he knew the geography as well as the modern critics—but it was in his interest to secure himself against any unfriendly action from the Bulgars by a kind of alliance with Byzantium, which was trying to bring Bulgaria into the sphere of its political and cultural interest. A linking of the Bulgars with the Franks, either in political or cultural fields, presented a threat to Rastislav and the Byzantines. The author brings also forward an argument, *ex silentio* of the *Vitae,* affirming that the authors of the *Vitae* "would not have failed to report political support on the part of the Empire of Moravia." This shows the author's ignorance of the mentality of Byzantine hagiographers. They generally avoided any allusion to politics, confining themselves to describing only the pious activities of their heroes. Lack of knowledge of Byzantine history and of Byzantine mentality led Z. R. Dittrich to many other misinterpretations.

96. *Annales Fuldenses, MGH Ss* 1, p. 374; ed. F. Kurze, p. 56.

97. *Annales Bertiniani (Hincmar), MGH Ss* 1, p. 465.

98. *MGH Ep* 6, p. 293.

99. See the indications of editions of this letter and bibliography in *MGH Ep* 6, p. 763, together with a Latin translation of the Slavonic document: The Pope writes: "Non enim ab hac tantum sede magistrum petistis, verum etiam a pio imperatore Michaele." On the genuineness of the letter, cf. below, p. 147.

100.There are still some defenders of the priority of the Cyrillic letters, especially E. Georgiev, *Načaloto na slavjanskata pismenost v Bŭlgarija* (Beginning of Slavic Literature in Bulgaria) (Sofia, 1942); *idem, Kiril i Metodij* (Sofia, 1956). The Czech philologist H. Horálek refuted this argument in *Slavia,* 24 (1955), pp. 169–178, in *Byzantinoslavica,* 19 (1958), p. 320 and in *Welt der Slaven,* 3 (1958), pp. 232–235. The attempt by M. Hocij in his study "Die wörtlichen Grundlagen des Glagolitischen Alphabets," *Südost-deutsche Forschungen,* 4 (1940), pp. 509–600, to derive the origin of glagolitic letters from the Latin cursive writing, is also rejected. Cf. also W. Lettenbauer, "Zur Entstehung des glagolitischen Alphabets," *Slovo,* 3 (Zagreb, 1953), pp. 35–48. See also J. Vašica, *Literární památky* (Prague, 1966), pp. 11–14, on the controversy, and V. Kiparski, "Tschernochvostoffs Theorie über den Ursprung des glagolitischen Alphabets," *Cyrillo-Methodiana. Zur Frühgeschichte des Christentums bei den Slaven 863–1963* (Cologne, Gratz, 1964), Slavische Forschungen, ed. R. Olesch, vol. 6, pp. 392–400, and W. Lettenbauer, "Bemerkungen zur Entstehung der Glagolica," *ibid.,* pp. 401–410. Cf. also O. Nedeljković, "Još jednom o hronološkom primatu glagoljice" (Once More on the Chronologic Primacy of the Glagolitic Alphabet), *Slovo,* 15–16 (1965), pp. 19–38.

101. The Bulgarian specialist J. Dujčev also thinks that the new alphabet was not created in such a short time as seems to be indicated by the *Legends.* Its origin had a longer history; when we take into consideration the importance of Christian missions among the Slavs and the intimate relations which the brothers had with the Slavs—Thessalonica was surrounded by them, and Methodius was an *archon* of a Slavic province—it is possible that both brothers had made some attempts at a true transliteration of Slavic sounds into an alphabet before the arrival of the Moravian embassy. Cf. J. Dujčev, "V'pros't za vizantiijsko-slavjanskite otnošenija i vizantijskite opity za s'zdavane na slavjanska azbuka prez p'rvata polovina na IX veek" (The Question of Byzantino-Slavonic Relations and Byzantine Attempts at the Creation of a Slavonic Alphabet during the First Half of the Ninth Century), in *Izvestije na Instituta za b'lgarska istorija,* 7 (1957), pp. 241–267.

102. *PG,* 126, col. 1216. New editions by N. I. Tunickij, *Materialy dlja istorii žizni i delatel'nosti učenikov sv. Kirilla i Methodia* (Documents for the Lives and Works of the Disciples of SS. Cyril and Methodius) (Sergiev Posad', 1918), p. 104.

CHAPTER IV

1. It is true that the Frankish bishops assembled in 852 at a Synod at Mainz spoke about the "rudis adhuc christianitas gentis Maraeensium" (*Capitularia regum Francorum*, ed. V. Krause, *MGH Leges*, 2, no. 249, p. 189), but this does not mean that Christianity in Moravia was in its very beginnings. The bishops were prejudiced against Rastislav of Moravia because of an incident very embarrassing to them. The Count Albgis had abducted the wife of another lord and had taken refuge in Moravia. The bishops condemned the action, but Albgis was safe at the court of Rastislav, who refused to extradite the culprit.

2. Cf. P. A. Lavrov, *Materialy*, pp. 61, 134. The reading *prělož* is also to be found in the glagolitic Office to the memory of the brothers, which is older than the manuscripts of the *Life* written in the Cyrillic alphabet. See I. Berčić, *Dvie službe rimskoga obreda za svetkovinu sv. Cirila i Metoda* (Two Offices of the Roman Rite to the Honor of Saints Cyril and Methodius) (Zagreb, 1870), p. 59.

3. It was edited first by L. Geitler, *Euchologium. Glagolski spomenik monastira Sinai brda.* (Euchologium. A Glagolitic Document from a Monastery on Mount Sinai) (Zagreb, 1882). It was re-edited in the Cyrillic alphabet with a French translation, and a Greek text and commentary by J. Frček, *Euchologium Sinaiticum, Patrologia Orientalis,* vol. 24, fasc. 5 (Paris, 1933) and vol. 25, fasc. 3 (Paris, 1939). A new edition, with a photographic reproduction of the original and a commentary was published by R. Nachtigal, *Euchologium Sinaiticum,* 2 vols. (Ljubljana, 1941, 1942).

4. Ed. by J. Frček, *Euchologium Sinaiticum,* vol. 25 (1939), pp. 602–611; ed. by R. Nachtigal, *Euchologium Sinaiticum,* vol. 2, pp. 337–345. Nachtigal's edition is reproduced by M. Weingart, J. Kurz, *Texty ke studiu jazyka a písemnictví staroslověnského* (Texts on the Study of Old Slavonic Language and Literature) (Prague, 1949), pp. 142–145.

5. On the origin of the liturgy of John Chrysostom, see A. Baumstark, "Zur Urgeschichte der Chrysostomusliturgie," *Theologie und Glaube,* 5 (1913), pp. 299–313 and 394–395; Pl. de Meester, "Les origines et les développements du texte grec de la liturgie de St. Jean Chrysostom," *Chrysostomica: studi e ricerche intorno a S. Giovanni Crisostomo* (Rome, 1908), pp. 254–357. On the symbolism of the Byzantine Liturgy, see Hans-Joachim Schulz, *Die byzantinische Liturgie. Vom Werden ihrer Symbolgestalt* (Freiburg i.B., 1964), Sophia, vol. 5.

6. R. Jakobson, "The Slavic response to Byzantine poetry," *XII*ᵉ *Congrès international des études byzantines.* Rapports III (Ochrida, 1961). See also J. Vašica, *Literární památky epochy velkomoravské* (Literary Monuments of the Great Moravian Epoch) (Prague, 1966), pp. 33–37.

7. A short prayer in verse form to St. Gregory of Nazianzus is preserved in Slavic in the third chapter of his *Life.* The hymn composed by Constantine in Greek in honor of St. Clement seemed to Anastasius the Librarian to be of such high poetical quality that he did not dare to translate it into Latin. See Anastasius' letter to Gauderich, *MGH Ep* 7, pp. 437, 438. It seems that the author of the *Vita Constantini* was also an admirer of St. Gregory of Nazianzus. He seems to have used some parts of the panegyric composed by Gregory on Basil the Great. This has been shown by V. Vavřínek in his study *"Staroslověnské životy Konstantina a Metoděje,"* *Rozpravy* Čsl. Akademie věd, vol. 73 (1963), p. 57 ff. However, he stresses that the author of the *Vita Constantini* uses his source very independently. Gregory's panegyric on Basil was used also by the author of the *Vita Methodii* who, however, translated verbally and slightly adapted some passages to his pattern. See V. Vavřínek, *ibid.*, p. 93 ff. For details, cf. *idem,* "Staroslověnské životy Konstantina a Metoděje a panegyriky Řehoře z Nazianzu" (The Old Slavonic Lives of Constantine and Methodius and the Panegyrics by Gregory of Nazianzus), *Listy filologické,* 85 (Prague, 1962), pp. 96–122.

8. See the study by I. Gošev, "Svetite bratja Kiril i Metodij" (The Holy Brothers Cyril and Methodius), *Godišnik na Sofij. univ. VI, Bogoslov. fak.,* 15 (1937–38), pp. 56–69. The author gives useful indications as to the development of the Greek *Euchologia* which contained both the holy liturgy (*služebnik*) and the ritual (*trebnik*) and of other liturgical books.

9. Edited first by V. Jagić in his *Glagolitica* (Vienna, 1890). See especially the edition by C. Mohlberg, *Il messale glagolitico di Kiew* (*sec. IX*) *ed il suo prototypo Romano del sec. VI-VII,* published in Atti della Pontificia Academia Romana di archeologia (serie III). Memorie, vol. 2 (Rome, 1928), pp. 207–320. The text in Cyrillic alphabet and the Latin formulary was reproduced by M. Weingart, J. Kurz, *Texty,* pp. 114–138.

10. Cf. H. W. Codrington, *The Liturgy of Saint Peter* (Münster i.W., 1936), Liturgiegeschichtliche Quellen und Forschungen, vol. 30, p. 101. L. Pokorný, "Liturgie pěje slovansky" (The Liturgy Chanted in Slavic), *Soluňští bratři* (Prague, 1962), pp. 131–166; *idem,* "Die slavische Cyrillo-Methodianische Liturgie" in the symposium *Sancti Cyrillus and Methodius* (Prague, 1963), pp. 118–126.

11. J. Vašica, "Slovanská liturgie nově osvětlená kyjevskými listy"

(The Slavonic Liturgy Newly Clarified by the *Kievan Leaflets*), *Slovo a slovesnost,* 6 (Prague, 1940), pp. 65–77; *idem, Literární památky,* p. 45.

12. J. Vajs, "Kyjevské listy a jejich latinský (římský) originál, stol. VI–VII," *Bratislava,* 4 (1930), pp. 521–527.

13. Cf. R. Jakobson, "Český verš před tisíci lety," *Slovo a slovesnost,* 1 (1935), pp. 50–53; *idem, The Slavic Response,* pp. 258–259; *idem,* "Tajnaja služba Konstantina Filosofa i daľnejšie razvitie staroslavjanskoj poezii" (The Holy Office of Constantine the Philosopher and the Further Development of Old Slavonic Poetry), *Zbornik radova Vizantološkog Instituta,* 8 (Beograd, 1963), pp. 161–166.

14. Cf. A. Dostál, "Origins of the Slavonic Liturgy," *Dumbarton Oaks Papers,* 19 (1965), pp. 76, 77; see also *idem,* "L'Eucologe Slave du Sinaï," *Byzantion,* 36 (1966), pp. 41–50.

15. Already A. I. Sobolevskij had pointed it out in his *Materialy i izsledovanija v oblasti filologii i archeologii* (Material and Studies in Philological and Archaeological Fields) (St. Petersburg, 1910), p. 92 ff.

16. "Das glagolitische Sakramentar der Slavenapostel Cyrill und Method und seine lateinische Vorlage," *Ostkirchliche Studien,* 6 (Würzburg, 1957), 165–173.

17. It is preserved in manuscripts Munich Clm. 15815a; Vienna, Cod. Vind. Ser. nov. 4225; Salzburg Studienbibliothek, Cod. MII, 296. The latter manuscript was published by A. Dold, "Neue Blätter des Salzburger Kurzsakramentar," *Texte und Arbeiten,* 25 (Beuron, 1934), pp. 35–48; *idem,* "Abermals neue Fragmente des Salzburger Sakramentars," *ibid.,* pp. 26–28 (Beuron, 1936), 71–98. A new edition is being prepared by K. Gamber.

18. J. Vajs, "Kanon charvatsko-hlaholského misálu Illir. 4. Protějšek hlaholských listů Kijevských" (The Canon of the Croato-Glagolitic Missal Illir. 4. Counterpart of the Glagolitic *Leaflets of Kiev*), *Časopis pro moderní filologii,* 25 (Prague, 1939), pp. 113–134; *idem,* "Mešní řád charvatsko-hlaholského vatikánského misálu Illir. 4 a jeho poměr k moravsko-pannonskému sakramentáři stol. IX" (The Mass Order of the Croatian Glagolitic Missal of Vatican Ill. 4 and Its Relation to the Moravo-Pannonian Sacramentary of the Ninth Century), *Acta Academiae Velehradensis,* 15 (1939), pp. 89–156. A résumé in Italian of Vajs' discoveries will be found in his paper "Il canone del più antico Messale croatoglagolitico sec. XIV (Codice Vaticano, Sign. Illir. 4)," *Studi e testi,* 125 (Città del Vaticano, 1946), Miscellanea Giovanni Mercati, vol. 5, pp. 356–362.

19. Especially in his study "Slovanská liturgie sv. Petra" (The Slavonic Liturgy of St. Peter), *Byzantinoslavica,* 8 (1939–1946), pp. 1–54.

20. Published by H. W. Codrington, *The Liturgy of St. Peter;* see also J. M. Hanssens, "La liturgie romano-byzantine de Saint Pierre,"

Orientalia christiana periodica, 4 (Rome, 1938), pp. 234-258; vol. 5 (1939), pp. 103-150.

21. M. Tarchnisvili, "Geschichte der kirchlichen georgischen Literatur," *Studi e testi,* 185 (Citta di Vaticano, 1955), pp. 39, 176, 445; *idem, Liturgiae ibericae antiquiores,* Corpus scriptorum christianorum orientalium, vol. 123. Scriptores iberici, series I, tome I (Louvain, 1950); pp. 64-83, Latin translation; pp. 84-92, original text.

22. H. W. Codrington, *The Liturgy of St. Peter,* p. 28. It should be noted that two so-called bilingual fragments of the Liturgy, presenting the Greek text and the Latin original, but written in Greek letters, reveal very little of a Byzantinization which is prominent in other manuscripts. Cf. H. W. Codrington, pp. 116-129.

23. It was republished by P. A. Syrku, *K istorii ispravlenijа knig v Bolgarii,* vol. I, *Liturgičeskie trudy patriarcha Evthimija Tarnovskago, vol. 2 Teksty* (Regarding a Revised Edition of Books in Bulgaria. The Liturgical Works of the Patriarch Euthymius of Trnovo) (St. Petersburg, 1890). The editor wrongly attributed the work to the Bulgarian Patriarch Euthymius.

24. Cf. M. Weingart, "Hlaholské listy vídeňské. K dějinám staroslověnského misálu" (The Glagolitic *Leaflets of Vienna.* Contribution to the History of the Old Slavonic Missal), *Časopis pro moderní filologii,* 24 (1938), pp. 105-129, 233-245, reprint of the *Leaflets* on pp. 111-114. First published by V. Jagić in his *Glagolitica,* pp. 10-14. Reprinted also by M. Weingart, J. Kurz, *Texty,* pp. 139-141.

25. Published by V. Vondrák, *O původu kijevských listů a pražských zlomků* (On the Origin of the Leaflets of Kiev and of the Fragments of Prague) (Prague, 1904), pp. 87-90. Reprinted by M. Weingart, J. Kurz, *Texty,* pp. 146-149.

26. L. Pokorný, "Liturgie pěje slovansky" (see note 10 above), disagreeing with J. Vajs and J. Vašica, thinks that the *Fragments of Prague* are older than the *Leaflets of Kiev* and *of Vienna.* He thinks that the *Fragments* presuppose the existence of a western liturgy which was used between Milan and Constantinople (sic!) and which the Iro-Scottish missionaries had brought to Moravia. The *Fragments* should be a part of the translation of this liturgy made by the two brothers. There is no evidence for such a daring conclusion. See A. Dostál, *Origins of the Slavonic Liturgy,* pp. 79, 80, who gives decisive arguments for rejecting this attempt at the reconstruction of the Slavonic liturgy.

27. F. Zagiba, "Neue Probleme in der Kyrillomethodianischen Forschung," *Ostkirchliche Studien,* 11 (1962), pp. 103, 119. The author thinks that the translation of the Latin sacramentary and of the "Missa graeca" was made by the brothers during their stay in Rome in

869–870, although he admits that they knew the "Missa graeca" from their homeland.

28. *Annales Fuldenses, MGH Ss* 1, p. 378; ed. F. Kurze, p. 62.

29. On the origin of the theory that the liturgy could be celebrated only in these three languages, cf. F. Grivec, *Konstantin und Method* (Wiesbaden, 1960), pp. 76, 77. It was based on misinterpretations of expressions used by some Holy Fathers in the West, especially that of Isidor of Sevilla. It should be noticed that in their anti-Latin controversies some Greek polemicists counted among their objections to Latin usages also the trilinguistic theory. See the anonymous writing *Contra Francos* which dates most probably from the second half of the eleventh, or of the twelfth century, published by J. Hergenröther, *Monumenta graeca ad Photium eiusque historiam pertinentia* (Regensburg, 1869), pp. 62–71, ch. 19, p. 68. The same author wrongly attributes the writing to Photius. He goes so far as to suppose that Photius could have learned about the opposition of the Frankish clergy to the Slavonic liturgy in Moravia. J. Hergenröther, *Photius, Patriarch von Constantinopel* (Regensburg, 1869), pp. 206–208. It should be stressed, however, that the Synod of Frankfurt of the year 794 in Canon 52 protested against similar teaching: "Ut nullus credat quod nonnisi in tribus linguis Deus adorandus sit. Quia in omni lingua Deus adoratur et homo exauditur si justa petierit." *Concilia aevi Carolini* 2 *MGH Leg* sectio 3, p. 71. Even if the bishops had in mind only private prayers in the vernacular, such a stressing of the vernacular when addressing God, made by a Frankish Synod, is important.

30. *Conversio, MGH Ss* 2, p. 12; ed. M. Kos, p. 138; archpriests Altfridus and Rihpaldus, in Kocel's Pannonia. The word *archierjei* (ed. P. A. Lavrov, p. 28) is translated by F. Grivec and J. Bujnoch as *bishops*. J. Vašica, T. Lehr-Splawiński, and J. Stanislav translate it correctly as *archpriests*. This word is found only once in this connection, in the Legends. Whenever they speak about bishops, the authors of the Legends use the word *episkop'* (*Vita Const.,* ch. 23), *episkup'* (*ibid.,* chs. 14, 16, 17, 18; *Vita Meth.,* chs. 6, 8, 9, 10; *ibid., episkop' stvo,* ch. 8). Three times in each *Vita* we read the word *archiepiskup'* for *archbishop* (*Vita Const.,* chs. 8, 10, 12; *Vita Meth.,* chs. 1, 4, 10). It is evident that the author of Constantine's *Life* did not on this occasion have bishops in mind. He certainly knew of the institution of archpriests, if not from Moravia, then from Pannonia. The brothers did not meet bishops in Moravia, but Bavarian archpriests, and that after 864. Cf. also my paper, *Die Bedeutung der Brüder Cyrill und Methodius für die Slaven und Kirchengeschichte,* Prolegomena ad Acta Congressus historiae Slavicae Salisburgensis (Wiesbaden, 1964), p. 18. The ecclesiastical organization of Moravia before the arrival of the

Byzantine mission is well outlined by V. Vavřínek in his study, "Die Christianisierung und Kirchen-organisation Grossmährens," *Historica*, 7 (Prague, 1963), pp. 5–56.

31. The first Slavonic *Life of St. Wenceslas* reports that his father invited a bishop called Notarius, with his clergy, to perform the ceremony; M. Weingart, *První česká církevně-slovanská legenda o sv. Václavu*, Svatováclavský Sborník, vol. 1 (Prague, 1934), pp. 974, 975. The prayer recited by the bishop is translated into Latin by Weingart: "Domine Deus, Jesu Christe, benedic puero huic, sicuti benedixisti omnibus iustis tuis." In the *Euchologium Sinaiticum* there are three different prayers which the priest must recite during this ceremony. The above would seem to be an abbreviation of the second prayer of the *Euchologium*; cf. J. Frček, *Euchologium Sinaiticum*, vol. 24, pp. 654, 656. On the problem, cf. V. Chaloupecký, *Prameny X. století legendy Kristianovy o sv. Václavu a sv. Ludmile* (The Tenth Century's Sources on Christian's Legend on St. Wenceslas and St. Ludmila), Svatováclavský Sborník (Prague, 1939), pp. 414, 415. It is possible that the bishop in question was one of the three ordained for Moravia after 900; see below, p. 196. Cf. also J. Dostál, *Origins of the Slavonic Liturgy*, p. 80 and especially J. Frček, "Byl sv. Václav postřižen podle ritu východního či západního?" (Was the Ceremony of Hair Cutting Performed on St. Wenceslas According to Eastern or Western Rite?), *Slovanské Studie, Vajs' Festschrift*, ed. J. Kurz, M. Murko, J. Vašica (Prague, 1948), pp. 144–158. On p. 153, J. Frček quotes some other echoes of the prayer contained in the *Euchologium of Sinai* in this first Slavonic legend on St. Wenceslas, especially in the prayer for the soul of the murdered prince.

32. It is contained on folios 66b–80a. In Frček's edition, *Euchologium Sinaiticum*, vol. 25, pp. 490–523. Cf. J. Vašica, *Literární památky*, pp. 48–51.

33. It is reprinted in the original language in Frček's *Euchologium Sinaiticum*, vol. 25, pp. 499–501 with indications of other editions. The original is preserved in a manuscript retained at the monastery of Teplá in Bohemia, written between 828–876, and in two manuscripts, one in Munich, the other in Orléans, from the tenth or eleventh century. It was the Czech philologist V. Vondrák who, in his study, *Studie z oboru církevně-slovanského písemnictví* (Studies from the Field of Old Slavonic Literature) (Prague, 1903), pp. 23 ff., 153 ff., discovered this old Germanic element in the formular.

34. Published by F. Ramovš and M. Kos, *Brizinski spomeniki* (The Documents of Freisingen) (Ljubljana, 1937), reprinted in M. Weingart, J. Kurz, *Texty*, pp. 150–160. Cf. also F. Grivec, *Zarja Stare Slovenske književnosti* (Dawn of the Old Slovene Literature) (Ljubljana, 1942); A. V. Isačenko, *Jazyk a povod frizinských pamiatok* (The Lan-

guage and the Origin of the Documents of Freisingen) (Bratislava, 1943). The first and third texts are related to the so-called prayer of St. Emmeram, the second is a fragment of an exhortation which has no connection with an old German prototype and which should be ascribed to Constantine or Methodius.

35. The brothers also seem to have accepted some religious terminology formed under the influence of the Old German language used by the Frankish missionaries. This seems to be shown by the translation of the prayer Our Father (Matt. 6). Although the Gospel was translated by Constantine from the Greek original, the translation of the prayer differs from the Greek text. This does not mean that Constantine followed here the text of the Latin Vulgate. He simply accepted the translation of this prayer made by Frankish missionaries with which the Moravians were already familiar. Cf. J. Cibulka, "Epiusios," *Slavia*, 25 (1956), pp. 406–415. Other words, really of old German origin—for example, *pop'* (priest), *post'* (fasting), *oltar'* (altar), *neprijazn'* (devil)—were accepted by the brothers in their translations of ecclesiastical texts because they were already in use in the language of the Moravians.

36. Cf. K. Kalajdovič, *Ioann, eksarch bolgarskij* (Moscow, 1924), pp. 129–132.

37. A. Vaillant, "La préface de l'Evangeliaire vieux-slave," *Revue des études slaves*, 24 (1948), pp. 5–20. Cf. M. Weingart, J. Kurz, *Texty*, pp. 108–110, the reprint of the text from the first edition by A. Iljinskij, *Makedonskij listok* (St. Petersburg, 1906), pp. 7, 8.

38. F. Grivec, in his book *Konstantin und Method*, pp. 197–209, gives some interesting examples which characterize very well the ingenious techniques of the translators.

39. Such is the result of the research made by the leading specialist in this field, J. Vajs, who edited the translation of the four Gospels, with the parallel Greek text adding to his edition a rich critical material. J. Vajs, *Kritické studie staroslovanského textu biblického* (Critical Studies of the Old Slavonic Biblical Text) (Prague, 1935, 1936). Cf. also two studies published in Vajs' *Festschrift Slovanské studie:* F. Pechuška, "Řecká předloha staroslovenského textu skutků apoštolských" (The Greek Prototype of the Old Slavonic Text of the Acts of the Apostles), pp. 60–65; J. Laurenčík, "Nelukianovská čtení v Sinajském žaltáři" (Readings in the Slavonic Psalter of Sinai not Corresponding to Lucian's Redaction), pp. 66–83.

40. The best edition is given by R. Nachtigal, "Rekonstrukcija treh starocerkvenoslov izvirnih pesnilev" (Reconstruction of Three Old Church Slavonic Original Poems), *Razprave Akademije znanosti i umetnosti v Ljubljane* (Ljubljana, 1943), pp. 43–156, esp. p. 89 ff. The *Proglas* contains 110 verses and is preserved in three manuscripts of

the Gospels of Serbian origin dating from the thirteenth and fourteenth centuries. It is also partly preserved in a manuscript composed
in Russia in the sixteenth century.

41. Cf. A. Vaillant, "Une poésie vieux-slave: la préface de l'Evangile," *Revue des études slaves,* 33 (1956), pp. 7–25.

42. E. Georgiev, *Dve proizvedenija na sv. Cirila* (Two Works on
St. Cyril) (Sofia, 1938); the review of this work by J. Vajs in *Slavia,*
17 (1939–1940), pp. 602–611. Cf. F. Grivec, "Vitae Constantini et
Methodii," *Acta Academiae Velehradensis,* 17 (1941), pp. 1–127, 161–
277, esp. pp. 272–275; R. Jakobson, *Moudrost starých Čechů* (The
Wisdom of the Ancient Czechs) (New York, 1943), pp. 14–18; *idem,*
"St. Constantin's Prologue to the Gospels," *St. Vladimir's Seminary
Quarterly,* 1954, pp. 19–23, with an English translation; *idem,* "The
Slavic Response to Byzantine Poetry," *XIIᵉ Congrès international des
études byzantines,* VIII (Belgrad-Ochrid, 1961), p. 264.

43. It is quite possible that the famous Otfrid von Weissenburg,
who had composed a versified epical harmony of the Gospels in south-
Rhine-Frankish idiom, was inspired by the example of Constantine in
Moravia. At least he says in the introduction to his compilation: "In
our time many are trying to do so, writing in their own language,
endeavoring to glorify their nation. Why should the Franks neglect
such things and not start to chant God's glory in the language of the
Franks?" The editor of this work, E. Schröder, thinks that Otfrid had
in mind the work of the Byzantine mission in Moravia, as he was a
contemporary of Constantine. He wrote his work between 863–871.
See *Evangelienbuch,* ed. O. Erdmann (1882), 2nd ed. E. Schröder,
3d ed. L. Wolff (Tübingen, 1957), *Altdeutsche Textbibliothek,* vol. 49.

44. See the letter of Pope Zacharias (741–752) to St. Boniface, in
which this doctrine of which Virgil was accused by Boniface, is condemned by the pope, *PL,* 89, cols. 946, 947.

45. See F. Repp, "Zur Erklärung von Kap. XV der Legende von
Konstantin," *Zeitschrift für slavische Philologie,* 26 (1958), pp. 114–
118. I. Dujčev treated this problem more thoroughly in his study, "Un
episodio dell' attivita di Costantino Filosofo in Moravia," *Ricerche
Slavistiche,* 3 (1954), pp. 90–96. Cf. also his review of F. Repp's study
in *Byzantinoslavica,* 19 (1958), p. 323 ff. He rejects Repp's suggestion
concerning the old Germanic pagan belief without any valid reason.
The combination of those two beliefs would explain better Boniface's
reaction. See also J. Vašica's review of Dujčev's study in *Byzantinoslavica,* 20 (1959), p. 97. In my book *Les Slaves,* p. 167, I saw in this
doctrine a superstition of Latin priests. It should be concluded from
this that the two brothers did not share the belief in the doctrine, not
uncommon in the classical period, on the spherical shape of the earth.
When commenting on the studies by Repp, Dujčev, and Vašica on

this problem, V. Vavřínek rightly points out that Virgil's idea of the antipodes could have been introduced into Moravia by Bavarian missionaries who had no connection with the Iro-Scottish monks, because even other ideas contained in Virgil's cosmographical work were accepted in Bavaria. "Christianisierung und Kirchenorganisation Grossmährens," *Historia*, 7 (Prague, 1963), p. 30. On the authorship of this work, see H. Löwe, "Ein literarischer Widersacher des Bonifatius Virgil von Salzburg und die Kosmographie des Aethicus Ister," *Abhandlungen der Akademie zu Mainz*, no. 11 (1951). On Virgil's cosmological doctrine, see *ibid.*, p. 40 ff.

46. The results of the excavation were published by V. Hrubý, "Základy kostela na staroslovanském pohřebišti ve Starém Městě 'Na Valách,'" (The Foundation of a Church on the Old-Slavonic Cemetery in Staré Město "Na Valách"), *Památky archeologické*, 46 (1955), pp. 265–308; *idem*, Staré Město, pp. 280–290.

47. Published by J. Poulík, "Nález kostela z doby velkomoravské v trati 'Špitálky' ve Starém Městě" (The Discovery of a Church from the Great Moravian Period in the Zone of "Špitálky" in Staré Město), *Památky archeologické*, 46 (1955), pp. 307–351.

48. J. Poulík, "The Latest Discoveries from the Period of the Great Moravian Empire," *Historica*, 1 (1959), pp. 7–70; *idem*, *Staří Moravané*, pp. 97–102. In his later publication *Staří Moravané*, pp. 101 and 149, however, he dates the construction of the eastern part of this church from the first half of the ninth century, but the construction of both the narthexes from the last third of the same century. Neither report can be regarded as definitive because no detailed description of the exploration of this object or of the archaeological material found around it has yet been published. Cf. also the critical remarks by V. Vavřínek, *Study of the Church Architecture*, p. 296. In the mouth of the corpse of a lord buried near that church was found a gold coin of the reign of Emperor Michael III. This find cannot, naturally, be regarded as proof that Church Number Three was built after the year 863. We should, however, bear in mind that the Byzantine emperors often used to present gold coins to prominent persons. On the finding of this coin see J. Poulík, *The Latest Archeological Discoveries*, p. 39, table IX. Cf. also V. Vavřínek, "A Byzantine 'Charon's Obol' in a Great-Moravian Grave," *The Numismatic Review of the Coin Galleries*, VIII (New York, 1967), pp. 50–53. The objects found in the tombs near that church, which should be credited to Moravian workmanship, reveal a very advanced artistic performance that was attained only in the second half of the ninth century. Cf. J. Poulík, *Staří Moravané*, pp. 100–103, tables 27, 28.

49. Cf. J. Poulík, *Staří Moravané*, p. 103. The details concerning this discovery are not yet published.

50. See especially F. Kalousek, *Velkomoravské hradištní město Břeclav-Pohansko* (Břeclav-Pohansko, a Townlike Hill-fort from the Great Moravian Period) (Břeclav, 1961). The author gave the preliminary information of his discovery in the Czech archaeological review, *Archeologické rozhledy*, 12 (1960), pp. 496–530. Cf. above, Ch. III, p. 120. Cf. also J. Poulík, *Staří Moravané*, pp. 116–120; V. Richter, *Die Anfänge der grossmährischen Architektur*, pp. 193–195.

51. Its Great Moravian origin was shown by excavations made by V. Hrubý in 1958 and 1961. He describes his findings in his book *Staré Město, Velkomoravský Velehrad* (Prague, 1965), pp. 206–209. For more details see his study "Velkomoravské hradisko sv. Klimenta u Osvětiman," *Časopis moravského musea* (Review of the Moravian Museum), 44 (1959), pp. 19–70, with a résumé in German. On pp. 63 and 64 he describes the find of a Byzantine coin from the reign of Theophilus (829–842) at Osvětimany.

52. J. Cibulka, "Grossmährische Kirchenbauten," in the Symposium *Sancti Cyrillus et Methodius, Leben und Wirken* (Prague, 1963), pp. 107–111.

53. *Ibid.*, p. 107.

54. See J. Cibulka, "Zur Frühgeschichte der Architektur in Mähren (800–900)," *Festschrift Karl M. Swoboda* (Wiesbaden, 1959), pp. 69–73.

55. See above, p. 121. V. Vavřínek, "Study of Church Architecture from the Period of the Great Moravian Empire," *Byzantinoslavica*, 25 (1964), pp. 293–301 is rightly discarding Cibulka's theory. "It is not possible to accept Cibulka's claim of autonomous architectonic development in this area. For Cibulka does not take into account the great disparity of time between the early Christian buildings and the later Bulgarian churches which he refers to. These were all built at the end of the ninth or at the beginning of the tenth century, i.e. during the time when Bulgaria had already been Christianized by an official Byzantine mission." See also the critique of Cibulka's theory by V. Richter in his study, *Die Anfänge . . .*, pp. 198–223.

56. "Stavební umění Velkomoravské říše" (The Architectural Art of the Great Moravian Empire), *Architektura ČSSR*, 20 (1961), pp. 129–135, esp. p. 134; cf. also his previous study, "Chrámy cyrilometodějské na Velké Moravě" (Churches of the Time of Cyril and Methodius in Great Moravia), *Umění*, 1 (1953), pp. 42–60.

57. Cf. V. Vavřínek, "Study of Church Architecture," p. 294.

58. C. de Boor, "Nachträge zu den Notitiae episcopatuum," *Zeitschrift für Kirchengeschichte*, 12 (1891), p. 533. Cf. F. Dvornik, *Les Slaves, Byzance et Rome*, p. 241.

59. P. Kabbadia, "Ἀνασκαφαὶ ἐν Ἐπιδαύρῳ (1918, 1919)," Ἀρχεολογικὴ Ἐφήμερις (Athens, 1918, part 4), pp. 115–154, esp.

G. A. Soteriou, Αί παλαιοχριστιανικαὶ Βασιλικαὶ τῆς Ἑλλάδος (Early Christian Basilicas in Hellas), *ibid.* (Athens, 1929), pp. 198–201. I express my thanks to my colleague Professor Ernst Kitzinger who called my attention to this problem.

60. G. A. Soteriou, Αί παλαιοχριστιανικαὶ Βασιλικαὶ ..., pp. 183, 184.

61. *Ibid.*, p. 194.

62. *Ibid.*, p. 195.

63. *Ibid.*, p. 9, planche 17. Cf. also J. Werner, "Slawische Bügelfiebeln des 7. Jahrhunderts," P. Reinecke Festschrift (Mainz, 1950), pp. 150–172, esp. p. 171. The presence of Slavs in this environment is attested also by archaeological finds.

64. See France Mesesnel, "Die Ausgrabung einer altchristlichen Basilika in Suvodol," *Bulletin de l'Institut archéologique bulgare*, 10 (1936), Actes du IVᵉ Congrès international des études byzantines, pp. 184–194. A. H. S. Megaw in his paper, "The Skripou Screen," *The Annals of the British School of Archaeology at Athens*, 61 (1967), pp. 20–25, when describing the historical setting of the construction of the church of Skripou, built in 873–874 by the Protospatharius Leo, rightly connects its foundation with Basil I's policy of re-christianizing and re-hellenizing Hellas.

65. T. M. Minajeva, "Archeologičeskie pamjatniki na r. Giljac v verchovijach Kubani" (Archaeological Monuments on the River Giljac on the Riverhead of Kuban), *Materially i issledovanijapo archeologii SSSR*, 23 (1951), pp. 273–301. The plan of the church is on p. 293. On p. 300 the author enumerates ruins of several other churches of the same type in the region of Kuban. Cf. V. Hrubý, *Staré Město* (1955), p. 288.

66. Cf. F. Dvornik, *Les Slaves*, p. 288.

67. J. Kulakovskij, "Christianstvo u Alan" (Christianity among the Alans), *Vizantijskij Vremennik*, 5 (1898), pp. 1–18, esp. p. 7.

68. J. Cibulka, "První tři velkomoravské kostely" in the symposium *Soluňští bratři*, p. 153. He quotes as another example the church of Mesembria, meaning the old cathedral church whose construction is generally dated from the tenth century. This dating is questioned, however, by several specialists. Some date its construction from the beginning of the sixth century. See for details and bibliography, Dj. Stričević, "La rénovation du type basilical dans l'architecture ecclésiastique des pays centraux des Balkans au IXᵉ–XIᵉ siècles," *XIIᵉ Congrès international des études byzantines, Ochride 1961* (Belgrade-Ochrid, 1961), rapports VII, p. 179. Mesembria was taken by Krum and, if the church was already standing, it was probably greatly damaged by the victor. On the Panaghia of Skripou, see also R. Krautheimer, *Early Christian and Byzantine Architecture* (Baltimore, 1965),

pp. 223, 224. He compares this church to the cathedral of St. Sophia in Ochrid. On the dating of the construction of the Third Church in Mikulčice, see above, footnote 48.

69. See above, p. 84.

70. Cf. what was said above, p. 71, concerning the church of the Holy Apostles in Constantinople.

71. V. Hrubý, who is leading the excavations made at Osvětimany, favors this supposition.

72. See F. Dvornik, *Les Slaves, Byzance et Rome,* p. 186 ff., and *Les Légendes,* p. 228 ff.

73. A. Vaillant, M. Lascaris, "La date de la conversion des Bulgares," *Revue des études slaves,* 13 (1933), pp. 5–15. The victory of the able general Petronas over the army of Omar, the emir of Melitene, made the rapid move possible. It was not only the invasion of Byzantine territory calling for revenge, but rather the alliance of Boris with the Franks which initiated this intervention. The mild conditions imposed by the Byzantines on the defeated Boris show that the prevention of a Bulgaro-Frankish political and cultural alliance was the main reason for this intervention. Cf. G. Ostrogorsky, *History of the Byzantine State* (1969), p. 227, on the Arab defeat; cf. also Christian Gerard, *Les Bulgares de la Volga et les Slaves du Danube* (Paris, 1939), p. 199 ff.

74. The surrender of the territory of Zagorja, including the ruins of Anchialus and Develtus, should be attributed to Theodora in 852. Theophanes Continuatus (Bonn, pp. 162–165) attributes it to the empress, but connects it wrongly with Boris' conversion. Cf. V. N. Zlatarski, *Istorija,* I, p. 2 ff., and S. Runciman, *A History,* pp. 90, 91.

75. See the bibliography in my book, *Les Slaves,* p. 186. ff.

76. Theoph. Contin., pp. 162, 163.

77. *PG,* vol. 102, cols. 736, 737. For details, see below, Ch. VII, p. 267.

78. *Conversio,* ed. M. Kos, p. 136 ff.; cf. also the report by T. Bogyay on the excavations made at Mosaburg, "Mosapurc und Zalavár," *Südost-Forschungen,* 14 (1955), pp. 349–405. For more details, see A. Sós, *Die Ausgrabungen Geiza Féhers in Zalavar,* Archeologia Hungarica, series nova, vol. 41 (Budapest, 1963).

79. See the important monograph by A. V. Isačenko, *Jazyk a povod Frizinských pamiatok* (The Language and the Origin of the Documents of Freisingen) (Bratislava, 1943, with a long résumé in German); *idem,* "Nachträgliche Bemerkungen zur Frage der älteren deutsch-slavischen literarischen Beziehungen," *Zeitschrift für slavische Philologie,* 19 (1944–1947), pp. 303–311. Cf. also F. Zagiba, "Zur Geschichte Kyrills und Methods und der bairischen Ostmission," *JGOE,* 9 (1960), p. 268 ff., for other references.

80. The Italian Legend estimates their stay in Moravia, Pannonia, and Venice at four years. The *Life of Constantine* (ch. 15) let them

stay in Moravia forty months, and the *Life of Methodius* (ch. 5) three years.

81. See the explanation of these names in my book, *Les Légendes,* p. 207. The list of nations is rather arbitrary. Some of them had had only a few books of the Holy Writ translated into their language. The Basques and Iberians should be Georgians, the Suzdalians were probably an Alanic tribe in the Crimea, the Khazars may have used the Hebrew Old Testament. The Avars could hardly have any religious literature. The Tursi in the original are unknown, perhaps a Turkic tribe, or Huns and Magyars.

82. F. Grivec, *Žitja Konstantina in Metodija* (Ljubljana, 1951), p. 101, rightly thinks that Constantine did not quote the whole passage as we read it in the Legend. The biographer copied it without regard to whether it fitted the occasion or not. Other quotations were taken from Ps. 95:1; 97:4; 65:4; 116:1; 150:6; John 1:12; 17:20–21; Matt. 28:18–20; 23:13; Mark 16:15–17; Luke 11:52.

83. It was done by V. Vavřínek, *Staroslověnské životy,* p. 76 ff. He gives also a short review of works in which some specialists have discussed the historicity and reliability of the disputation and of the reports given by the biographers.

CHAPTER V

1. The explanation given by M. Lacko, "Prvá cesta sv. Cyrila a Metoda do Ríma" (The First Trip of SS. Cyril and Methodius to Rome), *Studi in onore di Ettore Lo Gatto e Giovanni Maver* (Florence, 1962), pp. 375–380, is not satisfying. He thinks that at the end of 866, after leaving Bulgaria, Hermanrich, Bishop of Passau (866–874), stopped in Moravia, where he met the two brothers. He is said to have notified them that, if they wished to do missionary work in Moravia, which belonged to the Roman patriarchate, they must have permission from the pope. The brothers therefore decided to go to Rome to obtain the necessary permission. There is absolutely no evidence for such a supposition. Why then did Hermanrich react so violently against Methodius at the Frankish synod which had condemned him? Methodius came to Pannonia with the full approval of the pope and as his legate. The quotation of later cyrilo-methodian sources which speak only of the trip from Moravia to Rome (p. 379) does not mean anything. These sources do not even mention their stay in Pannonia and in Venice and limit themselves simply to mentioning Rome.

2. For details see F. Dvornik, *The Photian Schism. History and Legend* (Cambridge, 1948), pp. 91–131.

3. This also seems to be indicated by Methodius' biographer, when he says (ch. 5): "and after the passage of three years, they returned from Moravia, after having instructed disciples." He omits to mention their stay in Pannonia, which probably lasted four months, as seems indicated by Constantine's biographer (ch. 15). See the French translation of both *Lives* in my book, *Les Légendes de Constantin et de Méthode vues de Byzance* (Prague, 1933), p. 349 ff.

4. This is also admitted by J. Dekan, *Slovenské dejiny*, vol. 2, *Začiatky slovenských dejín* (Slovak History, the Beginning of Slovak History) (Bratislava, 1915), p. 58.

5. Such is the opinion of F. Grivec, "Vitae Constantini et Methodii," *Acta Academiae Velehradensis*, 17 (1941), p. 270 ff.

6. My book, *Les Légendes*, pp. 292, 293, lists Roman pilgrims from Byzantium. *Ibid.*, pp. 286–290, gives the names of eleven Greek monasteries in Rome. Cf. also A. Michel, "Die griechischen Klostersiedlungen zu Rom bis zur Mitte des 11. Jahrhunderts," *Ostkirchliche Studien*, 1 (1952), pp. 32–45.

7. *Povesť Vremennych let*, ed. D. C. Lichačev (Moscow, 1950),

p. 80. Cf. J. Bujnoch, *Zwischen Rom und Byzanz* (Graz, 1958), p. 150 (German translation of the *Povest'*). Clement's disciple Phoebus is mentioned in the legendary *Martyrium, S. Clementis, PG,* 2, col. 631. English translation of *Povest'* by S. H. Cross, O. P. Sherbowitz-Watzor, *The Russian Primary Chronicle* (Cambridge, Mass., 1953), p. 116.

8. There is no clear evidence that any relics of St. Clement were preserved in Constantinople. Rostangnus, a monk from the Abbey of Cluny, reports that, after the conquest of Constantinople by the Latins (1204), some French crusaders stole the head of St. Clement from the monastery of Our Lady Periblepte, called also Trentafolia, and donated this precious relic to the Abbey in 1206. In the report, published in the *Bibliotheca Cluniacensis,* ed. M. Marrier (Matiscome, reprint 1915, pp. 1481–1490), col. 1485, the saint is called *"ho hagios Clementios quod Latine dicitur sanctus Clemens."* In *PL,* vol. 209, col. 911, the Greek name of the saint *ho hagios Klemtopos.* P. E. D. Riant, in his *Excuviae Sacrae Constantinopolitanae* (Genève, 1877) and in his reprint of Rostangnus' report, reads also *ho hagios Clementios* (p. 135). He mentions Rostangnus' report also in his *Depouilles religieuses enlevées à Constantinople* (Paris, 1875) on pp. 9, 27, 67, 68, 121–123, 202. On p. 188 he reports that Warin, Latin archbishop of Thessalonica, brought a part of St. Clement's skull from Constantinople in 1239 to the Belgian Abbey of Anchin, as testified by Arnoldus de Raisse in his *Hierogazophylacium Belgicum, sive Thesaurus Sacrarum Reliquiarum Belgii* (Douai, 1628). These relics could not have been those believed to derive from Pope Clement. The Greeks always called Pope Clement *Klemes.* Cf. the synaxaria in *Acta Sanctorum, Propylaeum Novembris,* ed. H. Delehaye (Brussels, 1902), cols. 249, 255, 256. His memory was especially celebrated in Constantinople in the Church of the Holy Wisdom on November 25. Cf. also the inscriptions on his images at a later period, for example in V. I. Lazarev, *Mozaiki Sofii Kievskoj* (Moscow, 1960), p. 171: *Klemis;* R. Weir Schutz, S. H. Barnsley, *The Monastery of Saint Luke of Stiris* (London, 1901), p. 55; P. Kalenić, *Staro Nagoričino* (Belgrade, 1933), pp. 39, 43: *Klemes.* Besides, the monastery of Periblepte did not exist in Constantine's time. It was founded in 1030 by the Emperor Romanus III Argyrus (Scylitses-Cedrenus, ed. Bonn, p. 497). A local Greek saint called Klementios may have existed. We find such a name in one of the synaxaria published by H. Delehaye, *Acta Sanctorum,* col. 657: Klementios, a warden of a pagan temple in Asia Minor under Domitian. The relics of St. Klementios are said in the report to have been brought by an unknown emperor. But how could a part of his skull have been found in Constantinople in 1239 if the whole skull was transferred in 1206? On the monastery of Periblepte see Ch. Du Cange, *Constantinopolis Christiana* (Paris, 1680), pp. 94, 95.

9. Recently renewed by Z. R. Dittrich, *Christianity in Great Moravia*, p. 150 ff. On p. 152 he rejects the interpretation of some scholars that the brothers waited in Venice for a ship in order to reach Byzantine territory by sea. He uses the words: "Here we have an elementary example of how not to make hypotheses." These words could be applied with better justification to his Aquileian hypothesis.

10. The biographer of Constantine—more reliable in this detail than the composer of the *Vita Methodii*—says clearly that the two brothers had spent forty months in Moravia. If we accept the thesis that they arrived in Moravia in the late autumn of 863, they left the country in the early spring of 866. The biographer does not include in the forty months of their stay in Pannonia. Their stay in Kocel's domain must have lasted several months. They could not give instruction in Slavic letters to so many young men in one or two months. This explains why they could only reach Venice in the late autumn of 866. All this fits in well with the known facts. There are no reasons why we should date the arrival of the brothers in Moravia in 864 as is done by Dekan, *Slov. dejiny*, 2, p. 76 ff. Z. R. Dittrich, *Christianity*, p. 106, rightly rejects this interpretation. See, however, pp. 306–312 (Appendix III), on their journey to Moravia.

11. For details see F. Dvornik, *The Photian Schism*, p. 130 ff. Zachary of Agnani, papal legate at the synod of 861, condemned by Nicholas, was reconciled with Hadrian II, together with other bishops also dismissed by Nicholas. *Liber Pontificalis*, ed. Duchesne, vol. 2, p. 175.

12. *MGH Ep* 7, p. 400 ff.

13. *Liber Pontif.*, vol. 2, p. 176.

14. Both churches were near the church of St. Peter. The basilica of St. Andrew was built by Pope Symmachus (498–514); cf. F. Dvornik, *The Idea of Apostolocity in Byzantium and the Legend of the Apostle Andrew* (Cambridge, Mass., 1958), pp. 153, 158. The basilica of St. Petronilla, an unknown Roman martyr, wrongly regarded as St. Peter's daughter, was dedicated by Pope Stephen II (752–757). Cf. on both churches *Liber Pontif.*, ed. L. Duchesne, vol. 1, pp. 261, 455, 461, 464.

15. Cf. my paper, "The Significance of the Missions of Cyril and Methodius," *The Slavic Review*, 23 (1964), p. 205.

16. The main sources are the Annals of Hincmar, *MGH Ss* 1, p. 477. See also L. Duchesne, *Les premiers temps de l'Etat pontifical* (Paris, 1911), pp. 244–248.

17. See A. Lapôtre, *De Anastasio bibliothecario* (Paris, 1885) and E. Perels, *Papst Nikolaus I und Anastasius Bibliothecarius* (Berlin, 1920). On p. 188 ff., Perels has shown that Arsenius was not the father of Anastasius as Lapôtre supposed, but his uncle.

18. The letters in *MGH Ep* 7, p. 433, 436 ff. (letter to Gauderich).

The preface, *ibid.*, p. 407 and *Mansi*, vol. XVI, col. 6.

19. In his book, *Konstantin und Method, Lehrer der Slaven* (Wiesbaden, 1962), p. 235 ff., F. Grivec tries to water down Anastasius' words "fortissimus amicus" in a frantic desire to separate the brothers as much as possible from Photius. This is useless. There is enough evidence showing that the brothers recognized the legitimacy of Photius' patriarchate. Of course, they did not like to be involved in the intrigues which provoked the opposition to him in Constantinople and in Rome. Cf. E. Amann's remarks on this "incident" in his study "Photius," *Dict. de théol. cath.* (Paris, 1935), vol. 12, col. 1560: "Quant à l'histoire racontée par Anastase sur l'hérésie de deux âmes, ballon d'essai lancé par Photius pour démontrer l'incapacité théologique d'Ignace, on aimerait à en avoir de plus sérieux garants."

20. The work on St. Clement was continued and finished by Gauderich after the death of John. The bishop dedicated it to Pope John VIII. The work is only partly preserved. It was, however, extensively used by Leo Marcicanus (of Ostia, died 1115) in his history of St. Clement. The third part of this work on St. Clement is identical with the so-called *Legenda italica*, the most important Latin source for the history of the two brothers, which goes back to Gauderich and John. The original work must have been composed after the death of Constantine (869) and before the death of Methodius (885). For details see P. Meyvaert, P. Devos, "Trois énigmes cyrillo-méthodiennes de la légende italique," *Analecta Bollandiana*, 73 (1955), pp. 374–454. On pp. 455–461 is a new edition of the Legend preserved in a manuscript in Prague, which was discovered by the authors. As he says in his letter to Gauderich, Anastasius learned the details of the discovery of the relics, not from Constantine, but from Metrophanes, Metropolitan of Smyrna, one of the leaders of the opposition against Photius. On account of this he was exiled by the emperor to Cherson and there witnessed the discovery. Anastasius met him in Constantinople in 869–870, where he was sent by the Emperor Louis. In Constantinople Anastasius learned also that the written reports of the discovery were published anonymously by the humble Constantine.

21. J. Vajs, J. Dobrovský, *Cyril a Metod* (Prague, 1948), p. 178, thinks that the brothers stayed in the Greek monastery near the church of S. Maria in Cosmedin where a hospice for Greek pilgrims used to be. Another hospice seems to have existed near the Greek monastery of St. Gregory "ad Clivum Scauri." It is impossible to be more precise, but the circumstance that the Slavic liturgical books were blessed by the pope at the Church of Our Lady *ad praesepe* suggests the possibility that the brothers stayed in the neighborhood.

22. *Liber Pontif.*, vol. 2, p. 54. Hincmar copied the papal documents against Anastasius in his Annals (*MGH Ss* 1, pp. 477–479).

23. For details, see F. Dvornik, *The Photian Schism*, p. 138 ff. It is very important for the understanding of events in Rome during the stay of the brothers there to bear in mind the exact chronology of events in Constantinople, and the dates when news of them reached Rome. Cf. my paper, "SS. Cyril and Methodius in Rome," *St. Vladimir's Seminary Quarterly*, 7 (1963), pp. 20–30.

24. On political ideas of the two brothers see M. V. Anastos, "Political Theory in the Lives of the Slavic Saints Constantine and Methodius," *Harvard Slavic Studies*, 2 (1954), pp. 11–38.

25. Cf. J. Vaj's commentary to the new edition of Dobrovský's *Life of Cyril and Methodius* (Prague, 1948), pp. 171, 172. See the ritual for taking simple and solemn monacal vows in Byzantium in J. Goar, *Euchologium* (Venice, 1730, 2nd ed.), pp. 378–421. Cf. also the Old Slavonic Euchologium from Mount Sinai (fols. 80b–102a), ed. L. Geitler, *Euchologium* (Zagreb, 1882), pp. 147 ff. for the first degree, p. 150 ff. for the highest degree.

26. I accept this interpretation given for the first time by J. Vašica in his Czech translation of the Legend, published in the symposium *Na úsvitu Křesťanství* (On the Dawn of Christianity), ed. by V. Chaloupecký (Prague, 1942), pp. 42, 249.

27. The basilica was seriously damaged in the eleventh century during the invasion of the Normans. The fresco and the tomb were rediscovered in the nineteenth century. The relics, however, disappeared during the occupation of Rome by the French in 1798. A part of the relics was discovered in 1963 by L. Boyle in a reliquary in the possession of the Antici-Mattei family and was deposited in the Church of St. Clement. Cf. Leonard Boyle, "The Fate of the Remains of St. Cyril," in *Cirillo et Metodio. I santi Apostoli degli Slavi* (Rome, Pontif. Istituto Orientale, 1963), pp. 159–194.

28. For details, see P. Meyvaert, P. Devos, "Autour de Léon d'Ostie et de sa Translatio s. Clementis," *Analecta Bollandiana*, 74 (1956), pp. 189–240, esp. pp. 196–211. The last echoes of this controversy are the article by S. Sakač, "Novissima de Legenda Italica," in *Orientalia Christ. Periodica*, 22 (1956), pp. 198–213, defending the thesis of Constantine's episcopacy, and that by M. Lacko, "L'épiscopat de S. Cyrille dans le Codex Vatic.," *ibid.*, pp. 385–388, showing that the new palaeographical examination of the Vatican Ms. confirms the reading of the Ms. of Prague.

29. Z. R. Dittrich, *Christianity*, p. 171 ff., thinks that Kocel did not know about the death of Constantine and asked for him, not for Methodius. There is, however, no reason why we should not accept the report of our only source, which has proved reliable in other details.

30. This comparison was made by M. Kos in his study, "O pismu papeža Hadriana II. knezom Rastislavu, Svetopulku in Koclju" (The

Letter of the Pope Hadrian II to the Princes Rastislav, Svatopluk, and Kocel), *Razprave* of the Slovene Academy, philos., philol., histor. Class, 2 (Ljubljana, 1944), pp. 271–301. A complete bibliography concerning this problem will be found there. Cf. also F. Grivec, *Konstantin und Method*, pp. 257–261.

31. The passage is not clear. The author of the *Vita* says: "But we, filled with threefold joy, have decided, after scrutiny, to send Methodius, after ordaining him and the disciples, our beloved son." The words could also be understood as indicating the ordination of Methodius to the episcopal dignity. A strict scrutiny concerning the doctrine and morals of a candidate to the episcopacy was ordered by canon law. Besides, the priestly ordination of Methodius was already mentioned in the *Vita*, ch. VI. Could it be understood that the pope wanted to say "we decided, after examining our son Methodius and ordaining him as a bishop"? If this interpretation is accepted, then Methodius was sent to the princes as a legate and missionary bishop. The extent and name of his diocese was to be decided after his consultations with the princes.

32. The main sources for these invasions are the *Annals* of Fulda, *MGH Ss* 1, pp. 380–382, ed. F. Kurze, p. 69.

33. *Conversio*, ed. M. Kos, ch. 12, p. 139. If we can assume that Methodius appeared in Pannonia not only as a papal legate but also as a missionary bishop, then the departure of Rihpald can be better understood and dated by this first appearance of Methodius in Kocel's land.

34. On the history of the compilation of such lists see F. Dvornik, *The Idea of Apostolicity in Byzantium*, p. 175 ff. On Andronicus, *ibid.*, p. 47.

35. P. J. Alexander in his study, "The Papacy, the Bavarian Clergy, and Slavonic Apostles," *The Slavonic and East European Review*, 20 (1941), pp. 266–293, rightly stressed this aspect of Nicholas' policy. If we study it from the perspective of a future clash between the emperor and the papacy, his policy was something like a preamble to the investiture contest of the eleventh century.

36. Cf. on these translations A. V. Isačenko, *Jazyk a povod frizinskych pamiatok* (The Language and the Origin of the Records of Freising) (Bratislava, 1943); *idem, Začiatky vzdelanosti vo velkomoravskej ríši* (Origins of Civilization in the Empire of Great Moravia) (Turčiansky sv. Martin, 1948).

37. *Annales Fuldenses, MGH Ss* 1, p. 382, 383; ed. F. Kurze, p. 72. The annalist reports that Rastislav, angered by the treason of his nephew, tried to get rid of him. Svatopluk, however, escaped his trap and when Rastislav pursued him, he himself fell into an ambush and was captured by Svatopluk. *Annales Bertiniani* (*ibid.*, p. 487) and

Xantenses (ibid., vol. 2, pp. 234) do not speak of the attempt by Rastislav. This report seems more plausible. Cf. J. Dekan, *Slov. dejiny,* 2, p. 119.

38. Z. R. Dittrich, *Christianity,* pp. 189 ff., thinks that Methodius, abandoned by Kocel, who had to appease the victorious Franks, went to Bavaria in order to defend his rights before the Bavarian bishops and was captured by them. On this theory we can only use his own words with which he rejects all other interpretations: "There is not a single valid ground for this view."

39. *MGH Ep* 7, pp. 280, 281, letters to Louis the German and Carloman; pp. 283–285 to Adalwin of Salzburg and to his legate Paul of Ancona; pp. 285–287 to Hermanrich of Passau and Anno of Freisingen.

40. It is now generally agreed that the king mentioned in the *Vita* was not Svatopluk, but Louis the German. The word Moravian (king) is now regarded as the addition of a copyist.

41. This is the result of investigations made mainly by A. W. Ziegler in his studies, "Der Slavenapostel Methodius im Schwabenland," *Festschrift, Dillingen und Schwaben* (1949), pp. 169–189; *idem,* "Methodius auf dem Weg in die schwäbische Verbannung," *Jahrbücher für Geschichte Osteuropas,* 1 (1953), pp. 369–382, and by F. Grivec, in several articles. See especially his study "Questiones Cyrillo-Methodianae," *Orientalia Christiana periodica,* 18 (1952), pp. 113–134 and three short studies in Slovene in *Zgodovinski časopis,* 6–7 (1952–53), pp. 159–170; 8 (1954), pp. 139–143; 10–11 (1956–1957), pp. 282–284. Cf. also his *Konstantin und Method* (Wiesbaden, 1960), 12, 13, 96 ff. It is possible that Methodius was also imprisoned temporarily in Niederaltar and Freisingen.

42. Cf. M. Kos, *Conversio,* p. 101 ff. Kos dates its composition from the last quarter of 871. This does not seem to be warranted.

43. The commentary by M. Kos, in his edition of the *Conversio* on the localities mentioned there, was completed by Th. von Bogyay in his study, "Die Kirchenorte der Conversio," *Südostforschungen,* 19 (1960), pp. 52–70. He also gives a more recent bibliography.

44. Methodius' biographer interprets the death of four prelates who had maltreated Methodius as God's punishment. In reality, Adalwin of Salzburg died May 14, 873, Hermanrich in 874, and Anno in 875. The fourth bishop is unknown; it was perhaps the titulary of Brixen.

45. Cf. F. Grivec, "Prepir o Metodovih ječah" (The Controversy on Methodius' Prisons), *Zgodovinski Časopis,* 6–7 (1952–53), p. 158 ff.; *idem, Konstantin und Method,* p. 94 ff. Z. R. Dittrich, *Christianity,* p. 181 ff., rejects this interpretation of Grivec as being "completely unfounded." Unfortunately these words could be said about his own "original" thesis. It must not be forgotten that, according to the *Life of Methodius* (ch. 10), the Frankish bishop only warned Kocel not to

support Methodius after the latter's release in 873.

46. *MGH Ep* 7, pp. 282, 283.

47. *An. Fuld., MGH Ss* 1, pp. 383, 384, 388; ed. F. Kurze, pp. 73, 74, 83.

48. *Auctorium Garstense* and *Annals of St. Ruppert of Salzburg, MGH Ss* 9, pp. 565, 770.

49. See M. Kos, *Gradivo za zgodovinu Slovencev* (Ljubljana, 1906), vol. 2, document no. 169, from the year 860 (*Pribina fidelis dux, ducatus suus*), issued by Louis the German; Kocel: document 276, donation by the deacon Gundbaton between the years 876 and 887. Kocel *dux* is mentioned as departed: document 297 issued by King Arnulf in 891: *Chocil dux*. The *Life of Constantine* calls Kocel Knjaz (*Dux*) in ch. 15. John VIII in his two letters calls him *Comes*.

50. See my interpretation of this passage in *Constantine Porphyrogenitus, Commentary,* vol. 2, ed. Jenkins, p. 119. The Slovene historians defend the thesis that Kocel died in 873 or 874, but the Croatian specialists follow Šišić's thesis that he died in 876. This latter thesis seems more logical.

51. *MGH Ep* 7, p. 282.

52. M. Kos's edition of the *Conversio,* pp. 109, 140.

53. The facts that Slavomir was ordained by a German bishop and that he was a member of the dynasty do not necessarily mean that he was hostile to the Slavic liturgy (Z. R. Dittrich, *Christianity,* p. 194). Gorazd was also educated if not ordained by the Franks, and Rastislav, the head of the dynasty, was a warm supporter of the work of the two brothers.

54. Cf. above, p. 157, the interpretation of the words, "Our fathers had in the past received baptism from St. Peter, send us therefore Methodius as archbishop and teacher." The biographer probably wanted to stress the fact that Methodius has been appointed by the successor of St. Peter as archbishop of Moravia.

55. We do not know how the pope learned of what had happened to Methodius. If the Moravian embassy to the pope should be dated from 871, one can hardly suppose that its members knew the details mentioned in John's letters. Z. R. Dittrich, *Christianity,* p. 196 (cf. also p. 209), attributes this embassy to Svatopluk and dates it from 873. This is possible, although the suggestion that Svatopluk asked the pope at the same time to mediate between him and the East Frankish Empire, cannot be substantiated. John of Venice, who was present at the peace negotiations at Forchheim, in June 874, was not a papal legate, but the Latin priest who was Svatopluk's counsellor. It appears that he must be distinguished from another John (of Venice?) who acted as papal legate in Croatia in 874 and 880 (see F. Dvornik, *Les Slaves,* p. 223). The man who had the best opportunity to gather all the infor-

mation on Methodius' condemnation and imprisonment was Prince Kocel of Pannonia. The letter addressed to him by John VIII in 873 shows that he was in touch with Rome independently of the archbishop of Salzburg. It was Kocel who, most probably, disclosed to the pope all the infamous details concerning the treatment of Methodius by the Bavarian prelates.

56. On this title see my book *Les Légendes,* pp. 295–300. It was given to the popes in the West from the sixth century. When using it the biographers of the brothers simply followed the customary habit in speaking of the pope. This title was also used by the Franks in documents issued by Charlemagne and in ninth-century Frankish chronicles. It is an exaggeration to see any more in its use by the Legends, as does F. Grivec, "Vitae Constantini et Methodii," *Acta Academiae Velehradensis,* 17 (1941), pp. 194, 195. On the origin of the title *apostolica sedes* and on the idea of apostolicity in the East, see my book, *The Idea of Apostolicity,* p. 39 ff.

57. From that time on, Methodius resided in Moravia. This does not mean, however, that he ceased to be archbishop of Sirmium and legate to the Slavic people. This is confirmed by the letter of May 873 sent by John VIII to the Serbian prince Mutimir inviting him to join the metropolis of Pannonia for which an archbishop (Methodius) had been ordained (*MGH Ep* 7, p. 282). Moravia was added to the resuscitated metropolis of Sirmium, and the archbishop could choose his residence in the part of this metropolis which was best fitted for his apostolic work. He could not take up residence in Sirmium because its territory was under Bulgarian sovereignty, as we have shown (see above, pp. 46, 47). To identify Sirmium-civitas Pannonia with Moravia, as is done by I. Boba ("The Episcopacy of St. Methodius," *Slavic Review,* 26 [1967], pp. 85–93) is too fantastic to be earnestly considered as a possibility. We do not know the name of Methodius' see. It was most probably in the residence of the prince, the name of which is also not known. It could have been called Morava. This would explain why John VIII speaks of him (880) in another letter (cf. *MGH Ep* 7, p. 222), as Methodius *archiepiscopus sanctae ecclesiae Marabensis.* On the other side, the custom of giving to a bishop the title of the city of his residence, does not seem to have been general at this period. The first archbishop of Hungary signed the *Acts* of the Synod of Frankfurt (1007) simply *Anastasius Ungrorum archiepiscopus* (*MGH Ss* 4, p. 796 [Adalberti Vita Henrici II Imperatoris]). As I have explained ("The Making," pp. 159–165), the first Hungarian archbishop had not yet a special see and resided at the court of the Hungarian king. A national bishop of Croatia (*episcopus Chroatensis*), who existed from 1024 or 1030 to 1185, had no special residence, and lived at the royal court. See M. Barada, "Episcopus Chroatensis," *Croatia Sacra,* 1 (1931),

pp. 161–215, esp. pp. 102–208. J. Cincik in his paper, "A Note on the Official See and the Burial Place of Saint Methodius," *Most* 10 (Cleveland, 1963), pp. 198–206, appears to have discovered a Great Moravian major church in Debrev (Fel-Debri) in Slovakia, in the foothills of the Matra, and places Methodius' residence there. The discovery has not yet been published. It would be interesting to add a new building to Great Moravian architecture, but any conclusion before the evidence is shown is, at least, premature. R. Jakobson in his paper "Velikaja Morava ili Velikaja nad Moravoj," *Festschrift for Stojan Romanski* (Sofia, 1960), pp. 483–486, proposed an ingenious but very hypothetical solution of Methodius' see. It could be Velikaja on the river Morava. The problem of Methodius' episcopal residence remains unsolved.

58. *Mansi*, 17, col. 373.

59. *MGH Ss* 1, p. 387; ed. F. Kurze, pp. 75, 81. On p. 384 the annalist speaks about a previous embassy sent by Basil to Louis the German in 872 without giving the name of its leader.

60. See E. Honigmann, "Studies in Slavic Church History," *Byzantion,* 17 (1944–1945), pp. 163–182.

61. One has the impression that the prelates were listed in the order of their appearance at the first session of the Council. The list of signatures of bishops confirming the decisions is missing. When confirming the decisions, the bishops used to sign according to protocol, strictly indicating their rank.

62. See E. Dümmler, *Geschichte des Ostfränkischen Reiches*, vol. 2, 2d ed. (Leipzig, 1887), p. 371; B. A. Mystakidis, *Byzantinisch-Deutsche Beziehungen zur Zeit der Ottonen* (Stuttgart, 1891), p. 75.

63. Cf. F. Dvornik, *The Photian Schism*, p. 160.

64. Cf. my book, *The Slavs*, pp. 97, 164.

65. E. Golubinskij, *Kratkij očerk pravoslavnych tserkvej* (Moscow, 1871), giving a short history of the Bulgarian, Serbian, and Rumanian churches, on pp. 34, 256, recalls the old tradition according to which the first Bulgarian archbishop was Joseph.

66. *MGH Ep* 7, p. 62.

67. Honigmann's theories were also rightly rejected, by Z. Dittrich, *Christianity*, pp. 243, 244, and by F. M. Rossejkíj, "Buržuaznaja istoriografija o vizantino-moravskich otnošenijàch," v seredine IX. 5., "*Vizantijskij Vremenik*," 3 (1950), pp. 245–257. Cf. V. Vavřínek, *Životy*, pp. 45, 46.

CHAPTER VI

1. Svatopluk's betrayal of Rastislav could not have been the reason for the estrangement. Similar cases were frequent in Byzantine political history. The two men were certainly very different in character: Svatopluk was an astute ruler and an impetuous man, not averse to cruel measures; Methodius was a highly cultured man and a devout monk, although not the stiff rigorist he is sometimes portrayed. It should be stressed that Methodius' biographer does not mention any of the cruel actions attributed to Svatopluk by the Frankish annalists. He speaks about him with respect. Only later sources—*Vita Clementis* and the *Bohemian Legend*—describe Svatopluk as an immoral and cruel man. See V. Chaloupecký, *Prameny X. století*, Svatováclavský Sborník, II, 2 (Prague, 1939), pp. 503–505, Bohemian Legend (Beatus Cyrillus).

2. I. P. Gracianskij, "Dejateľnost Konstantina i Metodija v Velkomoravskom knjažestve" (The Activity of Constantine and Methodius in the Great Moravian Empire), *Voprosy Istorii*, 1 (1945), p. 92 ff., esp. J. Dekan, Slovenski dejiny, 2, Začiatky, p. 124 ff.

3. Z. R. Dittrich, *Christianity*, p. 218 ff., rightly stresses this.

4. Cf. my book *The Slavs*, p. 95, where I was the first to draw the attention of specialists to this problem.

5. *MGH Ep* 7, p. 161.

6. *Vita S. Clementis*, attributed to Theophylactus, Archbishop of Ochrida, *PG*, 126, col. 1209. Ed. N. L. Tunickij, *Materialy dlja istorii žizni i delateľnosti učenikov sv. Kirilla i Methodii* (Documents for the History of the Lives and Works of the Disciples of SS. Cyril and Methodius) (Sergiev Posad, 1918), p. 96.

7. *MGH Ep* 7, p. 160.

8. *Ibid.*, p. 161.

9. *Ibid.*, pp. 222–224.

10. *MGH Ep* 7, pp. 243, 244.

11. That Wiching must have presented to Svatopluk a document unfavorable to Methodius, pretending that it had been handed to him by the pope, is clearly indicated by the pope when he said in his letter of 881: "Neither has any other letter been presented to him by us, nor have we ordered that bishop publicly or secretly to do anything different, nor commanded you (to do) something different." Cf. F. Grivec, *Konstantin und Methodius*, p. 124 ff. Z. Dittrich's doubt, *Christianity*,

p. 239, about it is unfounded.

12. Z. R. Dittrich, *Christianity*, p. 233, rightly rejects the idea that Svatopluk had put his lands under the protection of the pope. John VIII used similar words to Branimir, the Croat prince, in 879 (*MGH Ep* 7, pp. 152, 258). We can see in such papal claims the tendency to tie the Slavic peoples closer to the papacy, as indicated in my book, *Les Légendes,* pp. 278–281.

13. Cf. F. Grivec's suggestion in his *Konstantin und Method*, p. 114.

14. *An. Fuldenses, MGH Ss*, pp. 399–401; ed. F. Kurze, p. 112.

15. The latest edition is that by V. Chaloupecký in *Sborník svatováclavský* (Prague, 1939), 2, pp. 481–493. See below, p. 206 ff., for details.

16. Chronicon, *MGH Ss Nova Ser.* 9, p. 392.

17. This is the only passage indicating that the Mass of Saint Peter was celebrated in Moravia. J. Vašica sees in this passage an indication that the Mass formulary was rendered into Slavonic by the brothers from the Greek translation of the Latin Missal. It is true that in the passage the feast of Saint Peter is also mentioned, but this does not weaken Vašica's thesis. The Greek version of the Latin Missal was called the Mass or Liturgy of Saint Peter, and the feast of the Apostle would have been especially suited to the celebration of such a liturgy. The passage shows at the same time that Svatopluk was invited to assist, with his army, at a Mass celebrated in Slavonic, although he personally preferred the Latin liturgy. In the passage the words "it is the liturgy" are an addition by an Eastern copyist to whom the Western term Mass (*missa*) was not familiar. Cf. J. Vašica, *Slovanská liturgie sv. Petra,* pp. 1–54; *idem,* in V. Chaloupecký's edition, *Na úsvitu Křesťanství,* p. 251 (commentary to Vašica's Czech translation of the *Vita Methodii*).

18. I suggested this possibility in my book, *Les Légendes,* p. 276.

19. See F. Dvornik, *The Photian Schism* (Cambridge, 1948), pp. 202–236.

20. Cf. F. Dvornik, *The Patriarch Photius in the Light of Recent Research* (Munich, 1958, Berichte zum XI. int. Byz. Kongress), p. 40.

21. F. Dvornik, *The Photian Schism,* p. 209 ff.

22. See above, pp. 103, 104.

23. See below, pp. 193, 234, 251.

24. See below, p. 246. However, it must not be forgotten that the jealous mistrust with which the Bulgarians had always followed the growth of Great Moravia could also have been a sufficient reason for the friendly reception of the Moravian exiles.

25. Methodius must also have followed the same itinerary on his way from Moravia to Constantinople.

26. Z. R. Dittrich, *Christianity*, pp. 240–255, interprets the events after 881 erroneously. Methodius, so he says, disappointed with Pope

John VIII, who did not give him the support he had expected, turned to Constantinople, expecting more support from the emperor and the patriarch. The stay in Constantinople is supposed to have influenced Methodius also in the matter of the doctrine of the procession of the Holy Spirit. He accepted Photius' radical view. This is one of the weakest parts of the book. The author lacks a thorough knowledge of the situation in Byzantium at this period, ignores the results of recent researches on Photius and the Union Council of 879–80, and exaggerates the tension between East and West in the years 880–882. He even pretends (p. 255) that Photius had written his *Mystagogia* against *Filioque,* after having discussed this problem with Methodius. His views must be rejected.

27. See P. A. Lavrov, *Materialy po istorii vosniknovedenija drevnejšej slavjanskoj pis'mennosti* (Documents on the History of the Origins of Early Slavic Literature) (Leningrad, 1930), p. 160.

28. J. Vajs, in J. Dobrovský, *Cyril a Metod,* pp. 143–153, describes in detail the different interpretation by Slavic scholars of the report contained in ch. 15 of the *Vita.* See the résumé of his own research on the glagolitic breviaries, *ibid.,* pp. 151–153.

29. H. F. Schmid, *Die Nomokanonübersetzung des Methodius* (Leipzig, 1922), Veröffentlichungen des balt. und slav. Instituts an der Univ. Leipzig, no. 1, esp. p. 47 ff., 89, 114. See also J. Vašica, *Literární památky,* pp. 63–70.

30. See the convincing study by W. Lettenbauer, "Eine lateinische Kanonensammlung in Mähren im 9. Jahrhundert," *Orientalia christiana periodica,* 18 (1952), pp. 246–269.

31. Cf. F. Maassen, *Geschichte der Quellen und der Literatur des canonischen Rechts im Abendlande bis zum Ausgang des Mittelalters* (Graz, 1870), pp. 454 ff. However, Maassen called it wrongly *Dionysiana Hadriana adaucta.* The collection called *Hadriana* is another derivation from the primitive Dionysiana.

32. W. Lettenbauer, "Eine lateinische Kanonensammlung," p. 265 ff. Cf. also F. Zagiba, *Bairische Slavenmission,* pp. 28–31.

33. It is puzzling that the glosses are written, not in glagolitic, but in Latin letters. This could, perhaps, be explained if we imagine a discussion of the three documents by the Slavic and Latin clergy. The glosses were to show the Latin clergy that the Slavonic translation of the Nomocanon affirmed the same thing as the Latin collection, as far as the obedience of the clergy to the bishop is concerned. This was the object of the discussion. The Latin clergy did not know the glagolitic alphabet; therefore Latin letters were used.

34. See M. Weingart's review of my *Les Légendes,* in *Byzantinoslavica,* 5 (1933–34), p. 448 ff. The last edition of the *scholia* by N. P. Rutkovskij was published in the *Seminarium Kondakovianum,* 3 (1929),

"Latinskija scholii," pp. 149–168. Cf. also F. Grivec, *Doctrina Byzantina de primatu et unitate ecclesiae* (Ljubljana, 1928), p. 24 ff. My statement on this problem in *Les Légendes,* p. 303 ff., should be completed and corrected in this sense. See also V. Beneševič, "Zur slavischen Scholia angeblich aus der Zeit der Slavenapostel," *BZ,* 36 (1936), pp. 101–105. The author gives a Greek translation of the document, showing that there is only one *scholion* wrongly divided by the editors into two.

35. J. Vašica, "Origine Cyrillo Methodienne du plus ancien code slave 'Zakon sudnyj,'" *Byzantinoslavica,* 12 (1951), pp. 154–174; *idem,* "Jazyková povaha Zakona sudného (Linguistic Character of Zakon sudnyj), *Slavia,* 27 (1958), pp. 521–537; *idem,* "Právní odkaz cyrilometodějský" (Cyrilomethodian Juridical Legacy), *Slavia,* 32 (1963), pp. 327–339. In his recent book, *Literární památky epochy velkomoravské* (Literary Legacies from the Time of Great Moravia) (Prague, 1966), pp. 149–169, J. Vašica gives a Czech translation of the document with a very valuable commentary. Most of the paragraphs of the Slavic document are excerpted from the seventeenth title of the *Ecloga* containing penal sanctions. From title eighteen, the part on the division of war booty is translated; from title fourteen, the part dealing with the testimony of parents and their children against themselves and on hearsay witness; for title eight, the part dealing with the ransom of a war prisoner; from title two the part dealing with the law suits between husbands and wives. Some cruel penalties ordered in the *Ecloga* are mitigated or replaced by Christian penance. Three original paragraphs were added by the translator. Cf. E. H. Freshfield, *A Manual of Roman Law, The Ecloga* (Cambridge, 1926), and *idem, A Revised Manual of Roman Law, Ecloga privata aucta* (Cambridge, 1927), with an English translation.

36. See Vl. Procházka, "Le Zakon Sudnyj Ljudem et la Grande Moravie," *Byzantinoslavica,* 28 (1967), pp. 376–430; 29 (1968), pp. 112–150. On the Russian collection of canon law, called *Kormčaja Kniga* (Pilot's Book) which contains the *Zakon,* see F. Dvornik, "Byzantine Political Ideas in Kievan Russia," *Dumbarton Oaks Papers,* 9–10 (1956), pp. 76–94. Cf. also Ivan Žužek, "Kormčaja Kniga," *Orientalia Christiana Analecta,* 168 (Rome, 1964), p. 14 ff.

37. N. van Wijk, *Studien zu den altkirchenslavischen Paterika* (Amsterdam, 1931); *idem,* "Dva slavjanskich' paterika," *Byzantinoslavica,* 4 (1932), pp. 22–35; *idem,* "Die älteste kirchenslavische Übersetzung," *ibid.,* 7 (1937–38), pp. 108–123. See M. Weingart's review of van Wijk's studies in *Byzantinoslavica,* 5 (1933–34), pp. 461–463. F. Grivec, *Konstantin und Metod,* pp. 135–137, agrees with R. Nachtigal, "Ot'česky knigy," *Razprave* of the Slovene Acad. (Ljubljana, 1950), pp. 7–24, that the Slavic "Books of the Holy Fathers" contained

translations of homilies of the Fathers, and that the homilies preserved in the *Glagolita Clozianus* were parts of such a Slavic book.

38. The newest edition is given by A. Dostál, *Clozianus Codex Palaeoslovenicus Glagoliticus* (Prague, 1959). In his introduction, pp. 1–16, he discusses all previous editions and studies. The homily is attributed to Methodius, *ibid.*, pp. 127–144. He refers also to the previous studies and editions of this homily by Grivec, A. Vaillant, and Vašica. See also J. Vašica, *Literární památky,* pp. 70–73.

39. See above, p. 154.

40. On the Byzantine treatises, see my book *The Photian Schism,* pp. 452–456. See also P. A. Lavrov, *Materialy,* p. XLVII ff.

41. It has been suggested that the introduction may have been written by another anonymous author and then included in the *Vita.* Cf. M. Weingart in *Byzantinoslavica,* "K dnešnímu stavu bádání," 5 (1933–34), p. 448. I would prefer to this suggestion the theory proposed by V. Vavřínek in his book, *Staroslovenské životy,* pp. 88–92, that the author of the *Vita* used here a profession of faith which the brothers, especially Methodius, had composed in Rome in order to show that their teaching was orthodox, conforming to that of Rome and Constantinople. He points out rightly that a *professio fidei,* often written, was asked from all candidates for ordination. It was probably composed in Greek, and Methodius may have translated it into Slavonic for the instruction and use of his disciples. The author of the *Vita* used this confession in order to show to the enemies of Slavic letters that Methodius' orthodoxy had been confirmed by two popes—Hadrian II and John VIII.

42. Cf. F. Dvornik, *The Photian Schism,* pp. 435–447.

43. See above, p. 180.

44. *Konstantin und Method,* pp. 225–227.

45. J. Vašica, *Literární památky,* pp. 80–84.

46. Latest publication by H. J. Schmitz, *Die Bussbücher und das kanonische Bussverfahren* (Graz, 1958, reprint of Cologne, 1898), vol. 2, pp. 356–368.

47. This tendency was rightly pointed out by V. Vavřínek in his *Staroslov. životy,* pp. 77–113.

48. H. Brückner, "Thesen zur Cyrillo-Methodianischen Frage," *Archiv für slavische Philologie,* 28 (1906), p. 202 ff.; *idem, Die Wahrheit über die Slavenapostel* (Tübingen, 1913), p. 94 ff.

49. V. Vavřínek, "Ug'r'skyj Korol' dans la vie vieux-slave de Méthode," *Byzantinoslavica,* 25 (1964), pp. 261–269. On Byzantine titles and protocol, cf. the recent studies by G. Ostrogorsky, "The Byzantine Emperor and the Hierarchic World Order," *The Slavic and East European Review,* 35 (1956), pp. 1–14, and by J. Gagé, "L'empereur romain et les rois. Politique et protocole," *Revue historique,* 83

(1959), pp. 221–260, where further bibliography will be found. P. Ratkoš in his paper "Über die Interpretation der Vita Methodii," *Byzantinoslavica,* 28 (1967), pp. 118–123, tried to show that Hungarian rulers were also called *Krales* by the Byzantines. This is true for the tenth and eleventh centuries, but it is doubtful that that title was given to the Magyar chieftains Kusal and Arpad with whom the Byzantines were in touch before their war with the Bulgarians in 895. The author of the *Vita* was a Byzantine. He could know only the titles given to different rulers by the Byzantine ceremonial in the ninth century. Constantine Porphyrogenitus gives to the rulers of Hungary only the title of *archontes.* The rulers of Saxony, Bavaria, Germany, and Gallia, however, are given the title of *reges* and called spiritual brothers. Constantine Porphyrogenitus, *De caeremoniis aulae byzantinae* (Bonn, 1839), pp. 689, 691. On the other hand, Ratkoš points out rightly that some Magyar chieftains may have occupied the territory of lower Tisza at the end of the ninth century.

50. F. Grivec, "Vita Metodii," *Acta Acad. Velehradensis,* 17 (1941), p. 124; J. Vašica, in V. Chaloupecký, *Na úsvitu,* p. 252 (commentary to Vašica's Czech translation of *Vita Cyrilli*).

51. The letter *Industriae tuae,* sent to Svatopluk in 880 by John VIII, cf. above, p. 166.

52. Ed. by N. L. Tunickij, *Materialy,* ch. 7 (24), p. 92; *PG,* 126, col. 1208.

53. Published by V. Chaloupecký, "Prameny X. století," *Svatováclavský Sborník,* pp. 505–521. Cf. also *idem, Na úsvitu křesťanství,* pp. 153–160 (Czech translation of the Moravian Legend called *Tempore Michaelis imperatoris,* by J. Ludvíkovský).

54. *MGH Ep* 7, p. 357, "Anathema vero pro contemnenda catholica fide qui indixit, in caput redundabit eius."

55. Cf. J. Stanislav, "O prehodnotenie velkomoravských prvkov v cyrilometodejsky literature" (Re-estimation of Great Moravian Elements in Cyrilo-Methodian Literature), *Sbornik A. Teodorov-Balan* (Sofia, 1955), pp. 357–363. The author thinks that Gorazd originated from the region between Bratislava and Nitra, which seems quite plausible. He also regards the priest Kaich, whom Methodius had sent to Bohemia, as Gorazd's countryman.

56. P. A. Lavrov, *Materialy,* p. 101. This source also says that the altar, probably the whole church, was devoted to Our Lady.

57. See for details concerning this tradition, R. Hurt, *Dějiny cisterciáckého kláštera na Velehradě* (The History of the Cistercian Monastery of Velehrad) (Olomouc, 1934), pp. 11–29.

58. See above, p. 188. The tomb found in one of the churches shows at least that the burial method described in the Prologue was really in use in Great Moravia.

59. See D. Kostić, "Bulgarski episkop Konstantin—pisac Službe sv. Metodiju" (The Bulgarian Bishop Constantine, Author of an Office of St. Methodius), *Byzantinoslavica*, 7 (1937–38), p. 209.

60. Cf. F. Grivec, *Vita Methodii*, p. 126. He found similar expression in the works of Gregory of Nazianzus, and in the *Lives* of the Patriarchs Nicephorus and Methodius. There is an echo of this moving prayer also in the *Life of St. Clement*, ed. N. L. Tunickij, *Materialy*, pp. 136–138; *PG*, 126, col. 1237.

61. *MGH Ep* 7, pp. 354–358.

62. *Ibid.*, pp. 352, 353. However, it would be wrong to make exaggerated conclusions from this. F. Graus, in his study, "Rex-Dux Moraviae," *Sborník prací filosofické fakulty brněnské university*, 9 (Brno, 1960), řada historická C 7, pp. 181–190, examining the western Latin sources of this period, came to the conclusion that the titles of sovereigns were not yet settled. The title of *"rex"* was often used in the old Roman manner in order to stress the political independence of the sovereign. In the high Middle Ages, however, this practice was abandoned, and this title was given to any ruler of importance. On p. 185, F. Graus, analyzing the titles given to Svatopluk in the Latin sources, comes to the conclusion that, concerning Svatopluk, this title was sometimes given to him to stress his political independence, and sometimes to designate him as a ruler of some importance.

63. *MGH Ep* 7, p. 353: "Spiritus sanctus a Patre et Filio non ingenitus dicitur, nec duo patres, nec genitus, nec duo filii, sed procedens dicitur. Si dixerint: Prohibitum est sanctis patribus symbole addere aliquid vel minuere, dicite...."

64. *Mansi*, IV, cols. 1341 ff., 1348 ff., 1361, 1364.

65. *Mansi*, XVII, cols. 516, 520. Cf. my book, *The Photian Schism*, p. 194 ff., on the authenticity of these last two sessions.

66. *MGH Ep* 7, pp. 352, 353.

67. Z. R. Dittrich, *Christianity*, p. 271 ff., supposes that after the death of Methodius, Gorazd was ordained archbishop by Bulgarian bishops in Belgrade or Preslav. There is absolutely no evidence for this. If Methodius had really broken completely with Rome, as the author wrongly supposes, he would have taken Gorazd with him to Constantinople and had him ordained there as one of his suffragans. The words of the papal instructions to the legates, "ne ministret, nostra apostolica auctoritate interdicite," do not necessarily mean that Gorazd was exercising episcopal functions. They can be interpreted as meaning that he was forbidden to administer the archdiocese as an appointed archbishop. Methodius did not break with Rome, and it was most probably his intention to bring Gorazd with him to Rome, as was agreed and indicated in John VIII's letter of 881, but the death of John and other events in Rome, explained above, prevented the realization of

the plan. Gorazd was most probably ordained archbishop by the papal legates in about 900, as is explained below, p. 196.

68. Z. Dittrich, *Christianity,* p. 279, simply attributes this lie to the pope. The decadence of the papacy during the reign of Stephen was not as pronounced, however, as the author pretends, in order to justify a false statement absolutely contrary to the letter *Industriae tuae,* approving the use of the Slavic liturgical language. We know that Wiching had some experience in fabricating papal letters, and it seems more logical to suppose that Wiching had presented to the pope the letter of John VIII which he had falsified and presented to Svatopluk in 880. The pope regarded this letter as genuine and composed his missive on the basis of Wiching's false document. It is really difficult to imagine how Wiching could have falsified a letter which was in the hands of legates. This suggestion has been made already by A. Lapôtre, *L'Europe et le Saint-Siège* (Paris, 1895), p. 168.

69. Ed. N. L. Tunickij, *Materialy,* pp. 98–114, *PG,* 126, cols. 1212–1224.

70. Z. R. Dittrich, *Christianity,* p. 272, asserts that Svatopluk had transferred his court to Nitra. There is, however, no evidence for this supposition. On p. 183, the author states that, during the reign of Rastislav, Svatopluk had some area of his own over which he had power. This area was "not in Slovakia, however, but ... in what is now Western Moravia, or Southern Bohemia." He considers the view that Nitra was an appanage of Svatopluk as "a fable." The evidence with which he tries to support this theory cannot be accepted, however. His thesis (p. 284) that Wiching left Rome before the legates, hastened to Moravia, and liquidated the whole affair before their arrival in Moravia deserves more attention. This would also explain why he could convince Svatopluk with his own interpretation of the papal letter. In the presence of the legates it would have been more difficult.

71. For details, see below, p. 246 ff.

CHAPTER VII

1. *PG,* vol. 126, col. 1217; Tunickij, *Materialy,* p. 108.

2. The main source for Svatopluk's relations with Arnulf is the *Annals of Fulda, MGH Ss* 1, p. 399 ff., years 884, 885, 890–895. Cf. also *Regino's Chronicle, ibid.,* p. 601.

3. *Annals of Fulda, ibid.,* pp. 413–415.

4. The most accessible edition is in *PL,* vol. 131, cols. 34–38.

5. J. Widajewicz in his study *Państwo Wiślan* (The State of the Vistulanians) (Cracow, 1947), p. 46 ff., deduces wrongly from this passage that Wiching was sent by the pope to the Vistulanians. The Bavarian bishops wished to stress that even John IX's predecessor had respected Passau's rights and, in order to protect Wiching, said that he was sent to a newly converted nation, subjected and Christianized.

6. The destruction of Moravia by the Magyars is reported especially by *Regino's Chronicle, MGH Ss* 1, p. 611 (*ad annum* 894), and by Constantine Porphyrogenitus in his *De administrando imperio,* ed. G. Moravcsik, R. Jenkins, p. 180. Cf. F. Dvornik, *The Making,* pp. 19–22, 292 ff. Recently, P. Ratkoš, "Die grossmährischen Slawen und die Altmagyaren," *Das Grossmährische Reich* (Prague, Academy, 1966), pp. 227–255.

7. See the most accessible edition in *PL,* vol. 137, cols. 315–317. On Pilgrim's pretensions, see F. Dvornik, *The Making,* p. 150 ff., and recently I. Zibermayr, *Noricum, Baiern und Österreich,* 2nd ed. (Horn, 1956), pp. 378–404. In his letter to the pope, Pilgrim says "during the time of the Romans and the Gepides Eastern Pannonia and Moesia had their own seven bishops who were subjected to my holy Church of Lauriacum of which I am now an unworthy servant. Of these remained also four in Moravia, as it is known in present time, before the Hungarians had invaded the land of Bavaria." See for details E. L. Dümmler, *Piligrim von Passau und das Erzbistum Lorch* (Leipzig, 1854), pp. 38–43, with a German translation of this passage on p. 41. In the bull of Benedict VII falsified by Pilgrim we read: "Sancta autem Lauriacensis ecclesia in inferioris Pannoniae atque Moravia, in quibus septem episcoporum antiquis temporibus continebantur, suique antistites archiepiscopalem deinceps habeant potestatem." *Ibid.,* p. 125. It should be stressed that Pilgrim distinguishes the seven bishoprics of the time of the Romans from the four in Moravia. Cf. *PL,* 137, cols. 315–318.

8. It has been shown that the Sloveni, modern Slovaks, spread not only as far as the Middle Danube, but also east beyond the river. See J. Stanislav, *Bolo južné Slovensko bulharské?* (Was Southern Slovakia Bulgarian?) (Bratislava, 1944).

9. Cf. F. Dvornik, *The Making*, pp. 251, 296, 297.

10. It was found by J. Zathey on the binding of a manuscript and published by him in *Studia z dziejow kultury polskiej* (Warsaw, 1949), pp. 73–86, under the title "O kilku przepadlych zabytkach rękopismiennych Biblioteki Narodowej w Warszawie" (Remnant of Some Lost Manuscripts in the National Library in Warsaw). Cf. also F. Dvornik, *The Slavs*, p. 172 ff.

11. Gorazd was venerated in Bulgaria as one of the seven Bulgarian Patron Saints, together with Cyril, Methodius, Clement, Naum, Boris, Angelar. The tradition is, however, not well established and is of later date.

12. *Annals of Traska, Monumenta Poloniae Historica*, vol. 2, p. 828 ff.

13. Cf. B. Havránek, "Otázka existence církevní slovanštiny v Polsku" (The Problem Concerning the Existence of Old Slavonic in Poland), *Slavia*, 25 (1956), pp. 300–305 with bibliography.

14. See the bibliography in the new work, *Bogurodzica*, by J. Woronczak, E. Ostrowska, H. Feicht (Warsaw, 1962). Cf. especially R. Jakobson, "Český podíl na církevněslovanské kultuře (The Czech Contribution to Slavonic Church Culture) in the Symposium *Co daly české země Evropě a lidstvu* (What Had the Czech Lands Given to Europe and Humanity) (Prague, 1940), p. 18.

15. For the details see F. Dvornik, *The Making*, pp. 249–253.

16. K. Lanckoronska, *Studies on the Roman-Slavonic Rite in Poland* (Orientalia christiana periodica, vol. 161 [Rome, 1961]), p. 168 ff. See Z. Wartolowska, "Osada i gród w Wiślicy w swietle badań wykopaliskowych do 1962 r." (The City and Castle of Wiślica in the Light of Excavations Made to the Year 1962), in the Symposium *Odkrycia w Wiślicy* (Discoveries in Wiślica), published by the Polish Academy (Warsaw, 1963), pp. 33–45. Although nothing has been found in or near the foundations of the church which would point to the date of its establishment, the church can be dated from the tenth century. The west side of the foundation is an *opus spiccatum* construction made from fragments of quarry stones, as in the rotunda discovered at Staré Město (see above, p. 84). On one side of the little church are foundations of a quadrangular building, the use of which is not known. The foundations have been excavated on the main street of the city. On the same street was found also a baptismal font 4 m., 20 cm. in diameter, made of limestone, which must have served for mass baptism. The reproduction in Wartolowska, p. 34, the little church on table II. Cf. also J. Golos, "Traces of Byzantino-Slavonic Influence in Polish

Medieval Hymnology," *The Polish Review,* 9 (1963), pp. 73–81.

17. It is also remarkable that the *Calendar* of the *Chapter of Cracow* which was recopied in the thirteenth century, when any trace of the Slavonic liturgical past had been eliminated, should still register the feast of St. Demetrius on the eighth of October. The veneration of Demetrius, Patron Saint of Thessalonica, the favorite Saint of Cyril and Methodius, could have penetrated into Poland only from Great Moravia.

18. *Monumenta Poloniae Historica,* vol. 2, p. 276. Anonymus Gallus, *Chronicon, ibid.,* vol. 1, p. 407.

19. *Ibid.,* vol. 2, p. 794.

20. See F. Dvornik, *The Making,* p. 147 ff.

21. S. Kętrzynski, *O zaginionej metropoli czasów Boleslawa Chrobrego* (On the Metropolitan See of the Time of Boleslas the Great, which had Disappeared) (Warsaw, 1947). Cf. also my review of this study in *Teki historyczne,* no. 2 (London, 1947), pp. 140–144.

22. H. Paszkiewicz, *The Origin of Russia* (London, 1954), pp. 381–404.

23. See for details, F. Dvornik, *The Making,* pp. 88 ff., 298 ff.

24. Karolina Lanckoronska, "Studies on the Roman-Slavonic Rite in Poland," *Orientalia Christiana Analecta,* no. 161 (Rome, 1961), pp. 21–29.

25. See the catalogues with commentary by W. Kętrzynski in *Monumenta Poloniae Historica* (Lwów, 1878), vol. 3, pp. 313–376. See the editor's commentary (p. 324 ff.) on the false bull of Benedict IX promoting Aaron of Cracow as archbishop in 1046, and on the request to Rome in 1229 by Ivo to promote Cracow to a metropolis, as it had lost this status because of the negligence of his predecessors. One can see in this claim an echo of the fact that there had been a metropolitan see in this part of Poland. This see, however, cannot have been in Cracow, because the first bishop Prohorius is said to have been ordained in 969 only, and was succeeded by Proculphus in 986. The Moravian archbishop was in this part of Poland from about 908 on.

26. K. Lanckoronska, "Roman-Slavonic Rite," p. 46. The name of this bishop seems to have been Romanus, according to the reading in one manuscript of Dlugosius' Polish history. The author identifies him with Bishop Romanus who died in 1030, according to the entry in Rocznik Kapitulny (*Monumenta Poloniae Historica,* vol. 2, p. 794). He is associated there with Lampertus, also called a bishop, and identified by the author with Lampertus of Cracow. In accordance with Lanckoronska's theory that Cracow was a metropolis, Lampertus should have been an archbishop.

27. *Ibid.,* p. 44 ff. The author has tried to find some traces of this bishopric in the history of archdeaconries in Poland (p. 71 ff.). This is

a new and interesting attempt which deserves attention by Polish historians.

28. See F. Dvornik, *The Making*, p. 71 ff.

29. K. Lanckoronska, "Roman-Slavonic Rite," p. 31, misunderstood my statement in *The Slavs*, p. 112, that there was a close connection between the foundations of bishoprics in Prague and Poznań. I explained the moves of Mieszko I and of Boleslas I in Rome in my book *The Making*, p. 75 ff., showing that both princes turned to Rome in 967. Boleslas I sent his daughter Mlada to Rome, and Mieszko's wife Dubravka was Mlada's sister. A common intervention by the two closely related princes is, if not certain, at least very likely. Mieszko's position was much stronger, because his land was not a part of the Empire. The pope could therefore proceed more freely, and subordinated the new Polish bishopric directly to Rome. However, the pope's consent to the foundation of the bishopric of Prague was brought there by Mlada in 968, after the death of her father in the previous year. Lanckoronska also overlooked my explanation of the political reasons why the erection of the bishopric of Prague could only be effected in 973. A more extensive study of my book *The Making* would have helped her to see some problems more clearly. She probably quotes it only indirectly from Paszkiewicz. It was published in 1949 and not in 1947.

30. K. Lanckoronska, "Roman-Slavonic Rite," pp. 25, 171, would like to have some documentary evidence showing that Dubravka brought priests of the Slavonic rite to Poland. There is no direct evidence, but everybody who knows the cultural and political situation in Bohemia in the tenth century, and the attitude of the reigning dynasties to Slavonic culture, will admit the possibility that, thanks to the friendly relations between Mieszko and Boleslas I, some Slavonic cultural influences inherited by Bohemia from Moravia could have reached the court of Mieszko through the intermediary of Dubravka.

31. K. Lanckoronska, "Roman-Slavonic Rite," pp. 55, 56, 111, expressed unreasonable doubts about Adalbert's favorable attitude to the Slavonic rite. Cf. F. Dvornik, *The Making*, pp. 124–126, 250. R. Jakobson found in the first Polish hymn *Bogurodzica* an old Slavonic linguistic shift, and he even attributed this oldest part of the hymn to St. Adalbert. Cf. his study in *Slovo a Slovesnost* (Prague, 1935). Cf. also F. Dvornik, *Sv. Vojtěch* (Chicago, 1950; 2nd ed., Rome, 1967).

32. For details and documentary evidence which seems sound, see H. Paszkiewicz, *The Origin of Russia*, p. 390 ff. However, the Slavonic metropolitan see was not founded by Boleslas the Great against Kiev. Cf. K. Lanckoronska, "Roman-Slavonic Rite," pp. 113–132.

33. *Gregorii VII Registrum, MGH Ep selectae*, pp. 233–235. There is, of course, a serious objection to the interpretation of this letter

which reads into it the consent of the pope to the reintroduction of the Slavonic liturgy. This is contradictory with the centralization and latinization tendency of Gregory's policy. It might, however, be thought that Gregory made an exception here in order to find favor in Kiev. Here Duke Izjaslav, expelled from the city, turned to Rome and was supported by Boleslas the Bold. Cf. F. Dvornik, *The Slavs,* p. 213 ff.

34. *Monumenta Poloniae Historica,* 2, p. 918.

35. *MGH Ss* 5, p. 255.

36. On the relations of Boleslas the Bold with Gregory VII see F. Dvornik, *The Slavs,* p. 271 ff.

37. See for details H. Paszkiewicz, *The Origin of Russia,* p. 396 ff. and K. Lanckoronska, "Roman-Slavonic Rite," p. 62 ff. On pp. 132–145 the author gives some interesting details on the survival of the Slavonic past in Poland.

38. Published by M. Šolle, *Stará Kouřim a projevy velkomoravské hmotné kultury v Čechách* (Ancient Castle of Kouřim and the Influence of Great Moravian Material Culture in Bohemia) (Prague, Academy, 1966).

39. *Ibid.,* p. 35 ff., 126 ff., 147 ff.

40. *Ibid.,* tables 46–50 and no. 116, p. 156 ff.

41. For example, Levý Hradec, Žalov, Budeč, castle of Prague, its neighborhood, Libice, Kolín, and several other places. See a complete list and documentary evidence in Šolle, *ibid.,* p. 166 ff. Cf. also a short account of archaeological evidence of Moravian influence on Bohemian cultural development in R. Turek's paper, "Die grossmährische Epoche in Böhmen," *Das grossmährische Reich* (Prague, Academy, 1966), pp. 85–87. Cf. also *idem,* "Velkomoravský horizont v českých mohylách" (Great Moravian Horizon in Bohemian Tombs), *Památky archeologické,* 54 (1963), pp. 224–233; *idem, Čechy na úsvitu dějin* (Bohemia at the Dawn of History) (Prague, 1963), p. 149 ff.

42. See the edition by J. Pekař, *Die Wenzels- und Ludmila-Legenden und die Echtheit Christians* (Prague, 1096), ch. 2, p. 93: "tribuens ei [Bořivoj and to his companions] venerabilis vitae sacerdotem Caich. Quique reversi in sua, in castello, cui vocabulum inerat Gradic supradictum sacerdotem statuunt, fundantes ecclesiam in honorem beati Clementis papae et martyris..." The first Czech chronicler Cosmas states that Bořivoj was baptized "a venerabili Metudio episcopo in Moravia sub temporibus Arnolfi imperatoris et Zuatopluk eiusdem Moraviae regis..." *MGH Ns* 2 (Berlin, 1923, ed. B. Bretholz), book 1, ch. 10, p. 22. In the same book, ch. 14, p. 32, Cosmas dates the baptism of Bořivoj "primus dux sanctae fidei catholicae" in 894. This dating is erroneous, because at that time Methodius was already dead. The chronicler confuses with this date the disappearance of Svatopluk,

repeating the legendary tradition that the prince had that year disappeared and had later joined the hermits on the mountain of Zobor. It is evident that the first tradition concerning Bořivoj's baptism by Methodius during Svatopluk's life is correct.

43. F. Graus, in his paper "Slovanská liturgie a písemnictví v přemyslovských Čechách 10. století" (Slavonic Liturgy and Literature in Bohemia under the Dynasty of the Pzemyslides in the Tenth Century), *Československý časopis historický* (The Czechoslovak Historical Review), 14 (1966), pp. 473–495, esp. p. 484.

44. It is the first Latin *Legend of St. Ludmila* based on the old Slavonic original, preserved only partly in a Russian Prologue. The *Legend* starts with the words "Fuit in provincia Boemorum." See the edition by V. Chaloupecký in *Svatováclavský Sborník*, II, 2, *Prameny x. Století* (Sources of the Tenth Century), pp. 459–481, ch. 6, p. 474. The *Legend* was written during the first half of the tenth century. The priest Paul is mentioned also by Christian, ed. J. Pekař, *Die Wenzels- und Ludmila-Legenden,* pp. 97, 98, 105. Cf. also the second Slavonic *Legend of St. Wenceslas,* chs. 9, 10, ed. J. Vašica, pp. 98, 99. On this edition see footnote 46.

45. Ed. M. Weingart, "Prvni česká církevně slovanská legende o sv. Václavu" (The First Czech Church Slavonic Legend of St. Wenceslas), *Svatováclavský Sborník,* I, pp. 862–1115, ch. 8, p. 981.

46. Ed. J. Vašica, in *Sborník* of Old Slavonic literary documents on St. Wenceslas and St. Ludmila, ed. by J. Vajs (Prague, 1929), ch. 19, p. 110. This legend is a Slavonic translation, with some additions of the Latin *Legend* of St. Wenceslas, written by Bishop Gumpold of Mantua on the order of Otto II, about 980. The Slavonic adaptation was made in Bohemia around 1000. This adaptation was discovered by N. Nikolskij in 1909 in two Russian manuscripts from the fifteenth and sixteenth centuries. See for details J. Vašica, *ibid.,* pp. 72–83. The Slavonic text with a Czech translation, *ibid.,* pp. 84–124. Gumpold's *Legend* (*MGH Ss* 4, pp. 213–223) is based on the *Legend,* starting with the words *Crescente fide,* dated from the second half of the tenth century. Gumpold used a Bavarian copy from the end of the tenth century. For details, see J. Pekař, *Die Wenzels- und Ludmila-Legenden,* pp. 24–38 and V. Chaloupecký, *Svatováclavský Sborník,* p. 27 ff.

47. This is rightly pointed out by F. Graus, *Slovanská liturgie,* p. 481. I. Kniezsa, "Kyril und Method-Traditionen in Ungarn," *Cyrillomethodiana* (Köln, Graz, 1964), pp. 199–209, also rightly rejects some suggestions made by J. Stanislav, "K otázce učinkovania Cyrila a Metoda na Slovensku" (The Question of the Activity of Cyril and Methodius in Slovakia), *Kultura,* 15 (Bratislava, 1943), pp. 449–466, 520–539, concerning the cult of Clement and Demetrius in Hungary.

48. Ed. J. Pekař, *Die Wenzels- und Ludmila-Legenden,* ch. 2, pp. 93, 94.

49. As suggested by F. Graus, *Slovanská liturgie,* p. 481.

50. The remnants of the church of Our Lady built by Bořivoj in Prague were excavated by I. Borkovský in 1950: "Kostel Panny Marie na Pražskem hradě" (The Church of the Virgin Mary in the Castle of Prague), *Památky archeologické,* 43 (1953), pp. 129–200. Another tradition quotes his son Spytihněv as builder of this church. The excavator found an older construction with an apse, which seems to have been destroyed and replaced by another construction of similar style, and with the tomb of Spytihněv and his wife. He thinks that the sanctuary built by Bořivoj was destroyed during a further pagan revolt after Bořivoj's death, with the intention of removing anything that reminded them of Bořivoj's acceptance of Christianity. Borkovský admits that this church had been built by architects brought by Bořivoj from Moravia. Spytihněv built another sanctuary on the ruins of the first one, and a tomb in which he was later buried. However, we know of only one pagan reaction which chased Bořivoj from Bohemia to Moravia after his conversion. A further efflorescence of such a protest after his death could hardly be expected. The church could have been destroyed or damaged by a natural incident. The other explanation by the excavator for the existence of the two constructions—that the church built by Bořivoj was for priests of the Slavonic rite, but that Spytihněv's construction was meant for priests of the Latin rite (I. Borkovský, "Kostel Panny Marie," pp. 177, 178)—cannot be accepted. It is true that Spytihněv is regarded by Bavarian tradition, as expressed in a manuscript of the legend *Crescente fide,* as the first Christian prince of Bohemia, but this can be explained by the anxious efforts of Regensburg to affirm its right of jurisdiction over Bohemia. Bořivoj had accepted the jurisdiction of the Moravian archbishop, and therefore his name had to be omitted. Spytihněv definitely accepted Regensburg's claims. As we shall see further, hostility against the Slavonic rite in Bohemia does not seem to have existed that early. Regensburg was satisfied with the recognition of its rights over all ecclesiastical foundations in Bohemia. It should also be stressed that the architecture of both buildings recalls that of Moravia introduced by the Byzantine mission. Also, the ornaments found in the graves around the church are similar to those found in Moravia. Cf. also V. Richter, "Die Anfänge der grossmährischen Architektur," *Magna Moravia* (Brno, 1965), pp. 173–175.

51. Ed. Weingart, *Svatováclavský Sborník,* p. 975. The author of the legend says that Wenceslas was also instructed in Latin. Wenceslas learned Latin at the Latin school in Budeč. This is confirmed by the second Slavonic legend of Wenceslas (ed. J. Vašica, in J. Vajs, *Sborník,*

p. 90), but the same author attributes a knowledge of Latin and Greek writings to Wenceslas (*ibid.*, p. 94). This affirmation is characterized by F. Graus ("Slovanská liturgie," p. 485) as a hagiographical topos. I would not go that far, the less so, as the examples of this kind quoted by him do not fit well this case. If we admit that in the circle of Ludmila were priests from Moravia, the declaration of both legends may have some solid basis. Wenceslas may have obtained from them a certain basic knowledge of Greek. However, the authors have magnified the extent of his knowledge, which could hardly have been profound. This exaggeration can be characterized as a hagiographical topos, and in this respect F. Graus is right.

52. Ed. J. Pekař, *Die Wenzels- und Ludmila-Legenden,* ch. I, pp. 89–91. As concerns Christian's dating the Christianization of Moravia from the time of St. Augustine, F. Graus sees in this exaggeration a hagiographical topos found in many works of early medieval writers anxious to date the Christianization of their lands or the foundation of their dioceses from the earliest period. F. Graus, "Velkomoravská říše v české středověké tradici" (The Great Moravian Empire in the Czech Medieval Tradition), *Československý časopis historický,* 11 (1963), p. 292.

53. This is rightly admitted also by F. Graus, "Slovanská liturgie," p. 489.

54. Book I, ch. 15, ed. B. Bretholz, p. 35.

55. V. Chaloupecký, *Prameny X-stoleti,* 80–91. Cf. J. Ludvikovský, "Great Moravian Tradition in Tenth Century Bohemia and the Legenda Christiani," *Magna Moravia* (Brno, 1965), p. 552.

56. R. Jakobson, "Minor Native Sources for the Early History of the Slavic Church," *Harvard Slavic Studies,* 2 (1954), pp. 55–60.

57. See pp. 166, 192, 210.

58. *Ibid.,* pp. 57–60. I do not think that the last redactor of the *Russian Primary Chronicle,* when describing the origin of Slavonic letters, found it necessary to use the Slavonic originals of the *Privilegium* and of the *Epilogus.* His account is based on the *Vita Methodii* which was brought from Bohemia to Kiev. Even his insistence that Methodius was a successor of Andronicus, and that St. Paul is said to have preached in Illyricum and therefore should be regarded as the teacher of the Slavs, is based on the *Vita,* where Methodius is also compared with Paul. *The Russian Primary Chronicle,* years 6396–6406, ed. D. C. Lichačev (Moscow, 1950), pp. 21–23. English translation by O. P. Sherbowitz-Wetzor (Cambridge, Mass., 1953), pp. 62–64. Cf. below, pp. 275, 276.

59. Cf. what J. Ludvikovský, "Great Moravian Tradition," p. 541, has to say on the substantiation of the Christmas story concerning Bořivoj who, as a pagan, was not invited to sit at table with a

Christian ruler, and about the three-stage conversion of Bořivoj, which seems to agree fully with Alcuin's missionary method (750–804). Bořivoj's case finds an analogy in the episode which relates how the Carinthian Duke Ingo replaced pagan nobles at his table with Christian subjects. See *Conversio Bagoariorum at Carantanorum*, ch. 7, ed. Kos, pp. 132, 133. Cf. V. Vavřínek, "Die Christianisierung und Kirchenorganisation Grossmährens," *Historica*, 7 (1963), pp. 11, 12. On the different stories concerning the end of Svatopluk and on the different interpretations of the history of Svatopluk in Medieval Czech chronicles, see the paper by F. Graus, *Velkomoravská říše*, pp. 299–303. The author is right when rejecting the so-called theory of translation of the kingship from Moravia to Bohemia. Neither the *Privilegium* nor the *Epilogus* authorizes such an interpretation. Both authors were only anxious to show the connection of Bohemian Christianity with Moravian and with St. Methodius.

60. Published by J. Vašica, in J. Vajs, *Sborník*, pp. 64, 65.

61. Published by M. Weingart, *Svatováclavský Sborník*.

62. The date 929 is generally accepted on the basis of Christian's indication. Cf. F. Dvornik, *The Making of Central and Eastern Europe* (London, 1949), p. 28 ff. There is, however, a statement by Widukind in his *Saxon Chronicle* (*MGH Ss in us schol*), p. 50, which could be interpreted in the sense that Wenceslas, not Boleslas, had remained faithful to the German king Henry I up to his death (936). If this reading is accepted, Wenceslas' death should be dated in 936 and Boleslas' reign should begin at that date. This interpretation is favored recently by Z. Fiala in his study "Dva kritické příspěvky ke starým dějinám českým" (Two Critical Contributions to the Ancient History of Bohemia), *Sborník Historický*, 9 (1962), pp. 5–40. If this later date should be accepted, then the Slavonic priests favored by Wenceslas had a longer period of quiet activity.

63. F. Graus, *Slovanská liturgie*, p. 491, rightly pointed out this difficulty. We may recall here the practice followed in Dalmatia, at the same time (see below, p. 242 ff). The Latin bishops were allowed to ordain priests on the condition that they knew Latin. A similar situation could have developed in Bohemia. It is quite possible that among the refugee priests from Moravia were some who were educated by Latin missionaries.

64. F. Dvornik, *The Making*, p. 77 ff.

65. *Chronica Bohemorum*, book 1, ch. 21, ed. B. Bretholz, *MGH Ns* II (Berlin, 1923), p. 43.

66. On Adalbert, see F. Dvornik, *The Making*, pp. 95–135.

67. See A. V. Florovskij, *Čechi i vostočnyje Slavjane* (The Czechs and the Eastern Slavs) (Prague, 1935), p. 147. We find this information in a late chronicle written in 1494 in Pskov.

68. See below, p. 223.

69. See for details, J. Canaparius, *Vita et Passio St. Adalberti, Fontes rerum Bohemicarum*, vol. 1, pp. 235–265; cf. ch. 15, p. 248, the praise of Adalbert by St. Nilus. F. Dvornik, *The Making*, pp. 104, 105, 120, 125.

70. Cf. *The Making*, p. 125. See especially the recent study by J. Racek, "Sur la question de la genèse du plus ancient chant liturgique tchèque *Hospodine pomily ny*," *Magna Moravia* (Brno, 1965), pp. 435–460. He dates the origin of the chant to the end of the tenth, or the first half of the eleventh centuries in Bohemia. This chant is attributed to Adalbert in 1260 by the continuator of Cosmas. A complete bibliography of the problem will be found in J. Racek's study. Cf. also J. Fukáč, "Über den musikalischen Charakter der Epoche von Grossmähren," *Magna Moravia* (Brno, 1965), pp. 417–434.

71. See pp. 198, 215.

72. F. Graus, *Slovanská liturgie*, p. 492. The earliest *Lives* of Procopius, *Vita antiqua* and *Vita minor,* say simply: "Procopius, nacione Boemus, slavonicis apicibus a sancto Cyrillo, episcopo [Willegradensi] quondam inventis at statutis canonice, admodum imbutus. . . ." See V. Chaloupecký, B. Ryba, *Středověké legendy prokopské* (Medieval Legends on Procopius) (Prague, 1953), pp. 112, 132. Cf. also the Latin translation of the older Czech Legend, *ibid.,* p. 171. The so-called *Vita Maior,* p. 247, pretends wrongly that Procopius had learned his Slavonic in Vyšehrad (near Prague), which is said—again wrongly—to have been a center of Slavonic letters. Let us remember that Procopius was a native of Chotun, a locality near the castle of Kouřim (B. Ryba, *Středověké legendy prokopské,* p. 176, according to the chronicle of Sázava). All *Lives* stress that the hermitage of Procopius was not far from the castle of Kouřim. We have seen (see above, p. 205) that Kouřim was an important transmitter of Moravian material culture to Bohemia. It is most probably in this region, where Slavonic liturgy was preserved, that Procopius—ordained priest for Slavonic liturgy—had found novices for his monastery. Cf. Šolle, *Stará Kouřim,* p. 229.

73. I. Kniezsa, "Kyril und Method-Traditionen in Ungarn," p. 206.

74. Cf. the letter of Honorius III from 1221 where we read: "abbatia de Wissegrade . . . graecos habet monachos et habuit ab antiquo," in A. Theiner, *Vetera monumenta historica Hungariam sacram illustrantia,* vol. 1 (Rome, 1859), p. 29.

75. F. Dvornik, *The Making*, pp. 53, 72, 78–81, 292.

76. See above, p. 198.

77. Cf. J. Ludvikovský, *Great Moravian Tradition,* p. 550.

78. This is rightly stressed by F. Graus, *Slovanská liturgie*, p. 490.

79. Ed. J. Pekař, *Die Wenzels- und Ludmila-Legenden,* p. 89: "At nos horum carentes sanctorum nos, ut ita fatear post Deum *solos*

habentes. . . ." Besides these reservations, I share F. Graus's skepticism concerning the spread of the cult of Cyril and Methodius in Czech lands before the fourteenth century.

80. Published by P. A. Lavrov, *Materialy* (Leningrad, 1930), pp. 128–145.

81. R. Večerka, *Velkomoravská literatura v přemyslovských Čechách* (Great Moravian Literature in Bohemia under the Dynasty of the Przemyslides), *Slavia*, 32 (1963), pp. 398–416; *idem*, "Cyrilometodějský kult v české středověké tradici" (The Cult of Cyril and Methodius in the Czech Medieval Tradition), *Československý časopis historický*, 12 (1964), pp. 40–43. F. Graus rejected in a postscript (*ibid.*, p. 43) Večerka's conclusion. I do not share Graus' disesteem of certain philological arguments, but, in this case, I would like to be given more solid evidence. A historian would like to find out which kind of relations had existed between Bohemia and Dalmatia in the tenth century, where the glagolitic Slavonic rite prevailed.

82. A. Sobolevskij, *Žitie prep. Benedikta Nursijskogo po serbskomu spisku XIV. veka* (The Life of the Blessed Benedict of Nursia in a Serbian Version of the Fourteenth Century), *Izvestija Otdelenija russk. jazika i slovesnosti, Akad. Nauk*, vol. VIII, 2 (1903), pp. 121–137. So far no Russian manuscript has been discovered. Sobolevskij, however, notices (p. 122) that the name of Benedict in its Latin form —the Russian transliteration should be Venedikt—is found in some ancient Russian documents: in the canon law book (*Kormčaja*) of Rjazan of 1284; in a gloss of the fourteenth century of a Galician book of Gospels from the year 1144 and in a Russian Prologue from 1400 where Benedict is called Roman archimandrite. This seems to indicate that Benedict was popular among Russian monks and worshipped. See also *idem, Žitija svjatych v drevnem perevode na tserkovno-slavjanskij ot latinskogo jazyka* (Life of Saints Translated into Church-Slavonic from the Latin) (St. Petersburg, 1904), the same edition of the Serbian version.

83. Ed. V. Chaloupecký, B. Ryba, *Středověké legendy prokopské*, pp. 44 ff., 112, 113. The editors think (p. 42) that this *Vita* is a Latin translation of a lost Slavonic *Vita*. This may be so, but it is rather doubtful.

84. *Ibid.*, p. 135.

85. *Ibid.*, pp. 249, 250.

86. See M. Weingart, "Hlaholské listy vídeňské" (Glagolitic Leaflets of Vienna), *Časopis pro moderní filologii*, 24 (1938).

87. The Glosses, however, are written with the Cyrillic alphabet, not glagolitic. See K. Horálek, "K otázce české cyrilice (Apropos of Czech Cyrillic letters), *Listy filologické*, 66 (1939).

88. V. Chaloupecký, B. Ryba, *Středověké legendy prokopské*, p. 119.

89. G. Friedrich, *Codex diplomaticus et epistolaris regni Bohemiae* (Prague, 1904–1907), vol. 1, pp. 82–84, no. 79, the foundation charter by Otto; no. 80, confirmation of the foundation and addition of a village to Otto's donations by the King Vratislav. The first document is dated February 3, 1078, the other February 5 of the same year. John and Vitus are mentioned as witnesses in both documents.

90. A. I. Sobolevskij, *Žitija svjatych,* pp. 1–19, cf. also *idem,* in *Izvestija,* vol. VIII, 1 (1903), pp. 278–296.

91. See F. Dvornik, *The Making,* pp. 25, 26.

92. See below, p. 269.

93. A. I. Sobolevskij, *Žitija svjatych,* pp. 20–38 (Apollinaris), pp. 55–62 (Anastasia, Chrysogonus).

94. A. I. Sobolevskij, "Cerkovno-slav. texty moravskogo proischoždenija" (Church-Slavonic texts of Moravian Origin), *Russkij filologiskij vjestnik*, vol. 43 (Warsaw, 1900), pp. 153–217.

95. V. Mareš, "Česká redakce církevní slovanštiny v světle Besed Řehoře Velikého" (The Czech Redaction of Church Slavonic in the Light of Gregory the Great's Homilies), *Slavia,* 32 (1963), pp. 417–451.

96. Published by A. I. Sobolevskij in *Sbornik otdelenija russk. jazyka i slovesnosti,* vol. 88, 3 (1918), p. 36 ff.

97. Ed. by A. I. Sobolevskij in *Izvestija,* vol. X, 1 (1905), p. 113 ff. (martyrdom of St. George), *ibid.,* p. 105 ff. (martyrdom of St. Stephen I). See also Sobolevskij's edition of the *Life* of Pope Clement in *Izvestija,* vol. XVIII, 3 (1912), p. 215 ff. Let us also remind ourselves that the Slavonic redaction of the *Life of St. Wenceslas,* written by the Bishop Gumpold of Mantua, was discovered by N. Nikolskij in 1909 in two Russian manuscripts. See the edition by J. Vašica in J. Vajs' *Sborník staroslov. liter. památek,* pp. 71–135.

98. Published by A. I. Sobolevskij in *Sborník,* vol. LXXXVIII, 3 (1910), pp. 36 ff., 41–45.

99. F. Dvornik, "The Kiev State and Western Europe," *Transactions of the Royal Historical Society,* 4th series, vol. 29 (1947), pp. 38–40; *idem, The Making,* p. 242 ff., and especially in my paper "Les bénédictins et la christianisation de la Russie," *L'Eglise et les églises* (Chevetogne, 1954), pp. 326–329.

100. "Njeskoľko rjedkich' molitv' iz' russkogo sbornika XIII vjeka" (Some Rare Prayers from a Russian Collection of the Thirteenth Century), *Izvestija,* vol. X, 4 (1905), pp. 66–78. Cf. A. V. Florovskij, *Čechi i vostočnye Slavjane* (The Czechs and Eastern Slavs) (Prague, 1935), vol. 1, pp. 110–114, a review of Slavic philologists who had accepted or criticized Sobolevskij's discoveries. Cf. also R. Večerka, *Slovanské počátky české knižní vzdělanosti* (Slavonic Origins of Czech Literary Culture) (Prague, 1963).

101. J. Hamm, "Hrvatski tip cerkvenoslovenskog jezika" (Croat Type of the Church-Slavonic Language), *Slovo,* 13 (Zagreb, 1963), pp. 43–67.

102. Cf. Florovskij, *Čechi i vostočnye Slavjane,* pp. 14–21, 41–43, on the two wives of Vladimir who are supposed to have been Czech princesses, and their sons, and their influence on Vladimir. On pp. 83–92, political relations between the Czech and Russian dynasties.

103. Cf. F. Dvornik, *The Making,* pp. 90, 91.

104. *Fontes rerum bohemicarum,* 2, p. 246.

105. *Ibid.,* p. 251 ff.

106. A. I. Sobolevskij, in *Izvestija,* vol. XVII, 3 (1912), p. 222.

107. Cf. R. Jakobson, "The Kernel of Comparative Slavic Literature," *Harvard Slavic Studies,* 1 (1953), p. 48.

108. E. Caspar, *Das Register Gregors VII, MGH Ep selectae* (Berlin, 1920), vol. 2, book VII, 11, pp. 473–475.

109. F. Dvornik, *The Slavs in European History and Civilization* (New Brunswick, 1962), p. 160; cf. also pp. 204, 207.

CHAPTER VIII

1. See above, p. 136.

2. Cf. above, p. 174.

3. See above, p. 38.

4. Cf. above, Ch. I, p. 23.

5. For details see F. Dvornik, *Les Slaves*, p. 227 ff.; *idem*, in the commentary on *Const. Porph. De admin. imperio*, ed R. J. H. Jenkins, vol. 2 (London, 1962), p. 127 ff.

6. *MGH Ep* 7, p. 147.

7. *Ibid.*, pp. 151–153.

8. *Ibid.*, pp. 160, 161.

9. *Ibid.*, pp. 222–224.

10. *Ibid.*, p. 157. The Bishops Vitalis of Zara and Dominic of Absor are especially mentioned.

11. Published by P. O. Lavrov, *Materialy*, pp. 102, 103. Cf. R. Jakobson, "Minor Native Sources of the Early History of the Slavic Church," *Harvard Slavic Studies*, 2 (1954), p. 64 ff.; F. Dvornik, *The Slavs*, p. 125.

12. See above, Ch. V, p. 175.

13. P. O. Lavrov, *Materialy*, pp. 180, 181. Cf. F. Dvornik, *Les Slaves*, p. 298 ff.

14. We learn this from the papal letter sent to the emperor in 878, *MGH Ep* 7, p. 67.

15. On the reconciliation between Ignatius and Photius, see F. Dvornik, *The Patriarch Photius in the Light of Recent Research*, Berichte zum XI. internat. Byzantinischen Kongress (Munich, 1958), pp. 34, 35.

16. This is confirmed by the papal letter of August 879, *MGH Ep* 7, p. 168. For details cf. F. Dvornik, *The Photian Schism*, p. 180 ff.

17. See J. Vajs, *Charvatskohlaholská redakce původní legendy o sv. Václavu* (The Croat Glagolitic Edition of the Original Legend of St. Wenceslas), in *Sborník staroslov. liter. památek o sv. Václavu a sv. Ludmile* (Collection of Old Slavonic Literary Monuments on St. Wenceslas and Ludmila) (Prague, 1929), p. 28 ff. M. Weingart, *První česko-církevněslovanská legenda o sv. Václavu* (The First Czech Church Slavonic Legend of St. Wenceslas), in *Svatováclavský Sborník* (Collection of Documents on St. Wenceslas) (Prague, 1934), p. 863 ff.

18. J. Vajs in J. Dobrovský, *Cyril a Metod* (Prague, 1948), p. 113.

19. *Fragmenta Vindobonensia* (*The Leaflets of Vienna*). Two leaves of parchment containing a part of the liturgy of the Mass, dating from the eleventh or twelfth century, and kept in Vienna, are the oldest liturgical documents in glagolitic from Croatia. Some glagolitic fragments from the thirteenth century are also preserved. The oldest glagolitic missal dates from the fourteenth century and is kept in the Vatican Library. For details, see J. Vajs, *Najstariji hrvatskoglagolski misal* (The Oldest Glagolitic Missal) (Zagreb, 1948). The most important inscription in glagolitic letters, mentioning King Zvonimir, dates from 1100. Cf. F. Šišić, *Enchiridion fontium historiae Croaticae* (Zagreb, 1914), p. 135 ff. A complete survey of the glagolitic literature is given by V. Jagić in B. Vodnik's *Povijest hrvatske kniževnosti* (History of Croat Literature) (Zagreb, 1913). Cf. also R. Strohal, *Hrvatska glagolska kniga* (Croat Glagolitic Books) (Zagreb, 1915). On the peculiarities of glagolitic letters in Croatia, cf. J. Vajs, *Rukovět hlaholské paleografie* (Handbook of Glagolitic Paleography) (Prague, 1932).

20. Cf. F. Dvornik, *The Slavs,* p. 133.

21. *MGH Ep* 7, p. 338.

22. *Ibid.,* p. 346.

23. *Ibid.,* p. 260. On Theodosius, cf. also F. Šišić, *Povijest Hrvata* (Zagreb, 1925), pp. 377–391. The author gives more details here than in his *Geschichte der Kroaten* (Zagreb, 1917), p. 106 ff.

24. See, for details, F. Šišić, *Geschichte der Kroaten,* p. 129 ff.

25. F. Rački, *Documenta historiae Croaticae periodum antiquam illustrantia* (Zagreb, 1877), p. 187 ff. See also F. Šišić, *Enchiridion,* p. 211 ff.

26. Cf. S. Ritig, *Povijest i pravo slovenštine* (History and Justification of the Slavônic Language) (Zagreb, 1910), p. 143 ff.

27. F. Rački, *Documenta,* p. 193.

28. *Ibid.,* pp. 194–197.

29. J. Srebrnić, "Odnosaji pape Ivana X prema Byzantu i Slavenima na Balkanu" (The Relations of Pope John X with Byzantium and the Balkan Slavs), *Zbornik kralja Tomislava* (Zagreb, 1925), pp. 128–164. Cf. also F. Dvornik, *The Slavs,* p. 176.

30. Thomas Archidiaconus, *Historia Salonitana,* ch. 15, ed. F. Rački, *Monumenta spectantia histor. Slavorum meridionalium,* vol. 26, p. 46.

31. The statutes of the Synod are preserved only fragmentarily and were published in the *Starine,* published by the Yugoslav Academy, vol. 12, pp. 221–223.

32. Ch. 16, ed. Rački, p. 49. Cf. Ritig, *Povijest,* pp. 152–164.

33. Cf. Rački, *Documenta,* p. 47. The first titulary was Mark, called Croat bishop. Šišić, *Geschichte,* p. 214.

34. *Historia Salonitana,* ch. 16, ed. Rački, pp. 49–53.

35. The upheaval which the prohibition of the use of the Slavonic liturgy by the Synod of 1060 had created in Croatia also indicates that no such decision was made at the Synod of 925. If there was such a violent reaction against this prohibition after 1060, one would have expected similar protests after 925. This confirms the thesis that the *Acts* of the Synod were interpolated after 1060, perhaps in the eleventh century.

36. For details, see F. Šišić, *Geschichte*, p. 203 ff., p. 247 ff.

37. Cf. K. Horálek's study in *Slavia*, 19 (1950), pp. 285–292: "Kořeny charvatsko-hlaholského písemnictví" (Roots of Glagolitic Letters in Croatia).

38. *Historia Salonitana,* ch. 16, ed. Rački, pp. 53–54. The legate also freed Vuk from prison and took him to Rome. In this way the last vestiges of the schism disappeared.

39. F. Šišić, *Geschichte*, p. 345 ff.

40. For details, see the study by J. Srebrnić, published in *Zbornik kralja Tomislava,* cited above, footnote 29.

41. L. Jelić, *Fontes historici liturgiae glagolito-romanae* (Veglia, 1906), p. 9.

42. Cf. S. Ritig, *Povijest i pravo slovenštine* (Zagreb, 1910), p. 164.

43. See A. Potthast, *Regesta pontificum romanorum 1198–1304* (Berlin, 1874–75), vol. 2, no. 12880, p. 1082; A. Theiner, *Vetera monumenta historica Hungariam sacram illustrantia* (Rome, 1859), vol. 1, no. 386, reprinted by L. Jelić, *Fontes*, p. 9, no. 3, and by S. Ritig, *Povijest*, pp. 215–224 (with a Croat translation and commentary).

44. *Mansi,* vol. XXII, col. 998.

45. Detailed documentation of the spread of the glagolitic Mass liturgy in Dalmatia and Istria will be found in L. Jelić, *Fontes.* The popularity of the glagolitic letters and liturgy in Croatia in the sixteenth century is illustrated furthermore by the fact that the Slovene reformer Primož Trubar, in his Slavic press at Urach near Tübingen, also printed Protestant literature in glagolitic letters and propagated it in Croatia and Dalmatia. His glagolitic types were brought to Rome and were used by the press of the Propaganda Congregation. The Franciscan R. Levaković was charged with the revision of the glagolitic Missal and breviary. The Czech specialist J. Vajs made a modern edition of the Missal in 1927. I. Ostojić has given us interesting material on the use of the glagolitic liturgy and letters in Benedictine monasteries from as early as the eleventh and twelfth centuries in his study, "Benediktine i glagoljaši," *Slovo,* 9–10 (Zagreb, 1960), pp. 14–42. On Primož Trubar see F. Dvornik, *The Slavs in European History and Civilization* (New Brunswick, 1962), pp. 421–423, 427, 428.

46. The best edition of the *Life of Saint Clement* is by N. L. Tunickij in his *Materialy* (Sergiev Posad, 1918). See also *PG,* vol. 126 (*Vita*

Clementis), cols. 1194–1240. Cf. also on editions and translations Gy. Moravcsik, *Byzantinoturca* (Berlin, 1957), vol. 1, pp. 555–557; M. Kusseff, "St. Clement of Ochrida," *Slavonic and East European Review*, 27 (1948–49), p. 198 ff.; J. Stanislav, *Osudy Cyrila a Metoda a ich učenikov v živote Klimentovom* (The Fate of Cyril, Methodius and their Disciples According to the Life of Clement) (Bratislava, 1950), pp. 7–62, evaluation of the authorship and Slovak translation; P. Gautier, "Clément d'Ochria, évêque de Dragvitsa," *Revue des études byzantines*, 22 (1964), pp. 199–214; G. Soulis, "The Legacy of Cyril and Methodius to the Southern Slavs," *Dumbarton Oaks Papers*, 19 (1965), p. 22. The *Lives of St. Naum* (Nahum) were published by J. Ivanov in his *B'lgarski starini iz' Makedonija* (Sofia, 1931), pp. 305–311 (The Old *Life*); pp. 311–314, the second *Life*, discovered by him in 1906. For commentary, bibliography, and English translation, see M. Kusseff, "St. Naum," *The Slavonic and East European Review*, 29 (1950), pp. 139–152. The last critical edition of the *Vita Clementis*— Greek text with a translation into Bulgarian—was published by A. Milev (Sofia), 1955.

47. Takan, targan is a Turkic title of nobility. G. Fehér, "Der proto-bulgarische Titel kanar," *BZ*, 36 (1936), p. 58, interprets this name as Bori Teken = The Prince Bori (Wolf).

48. For details see F. Dvornik, *The Photian Schism*, p. 212 ff. At the council of 879–80 the Byzantines seem to have recognized the su-premacy of Rome over Bulgaria on condition that the Greek clergy would not be replaced by Latin clergy. Cf. the well-documented study by R. E. Sullivan, "Khan Boris and the Conversion of Bulgaria. A Case Study of the Impact of Christianity on a Barbarian Society," *Studies in Medieval and Renaissance History*, 3 (Lincoln, Nebraska, 1966), pp. 55–139. The author discusses in detail the attitude of Boris toward Pope Nicolas I, Byzantium, and the Slavic Liturgy.

49. Cf. the Letter of John VIII to Boris, sent in June or July 879. *MGH Ep* 7, p. 158.

50. The writer gives him the title of *sampses*. This old Bulgar word seems to have survived in the Bulgarian language in the word *sanovnik,* meaning a functionary.

51. The name is a Slavic form of the Greek Dometios, Dometianos.

52. See the discussion of the different theories in F. Dvornik, *Les Slaves*, p. 315. I. Snegarov, "B'lgarskiat pervoučitel sv. Kliment Ochrid-ski," *Godišnik na Bogoslovskia Fakultet* (Sofia, 1926–1927), p. 276, extended the area of Clement's activity over the whole extreme south-west of Macedonia, a territory which is today included in Yugoslavia, Greece, and Albania. On other theories, see G. Soulis, "The Legacy," *DO*, 19, pp. 23, 24. Cf. V. Vangeli, "Prilog bibliografijsta za Kliment Ohridski (Contribution to the Bibliography on Clement of Ochridi),

Istorija, III, 1 (Skopje, 1967), pp. 187–197.

53. Cf. S. Runciman, *A History of the First Bulgarian Empire* (London, 1930), p. 130 ff. Zlatarski, *Istorija,* I, 2, p. 254 ff., thinks that, on this occasion, Greek was replaced by Slavonic as the official language. This is possible. Boris always favored the Slavic boyars, and such a measure would have been directed against the Turkic boyars and contributed to the slavicisation of the country. This must, however, have happened gradually, for Greek was still spoken at the court of Symeon.

54. Velitsa must have been located somewhere on the river Velika, an affluent of the river Vardar.

55. A very useful review of the early Bulgarian literature, with a bibliography, was given by M. Weingart, *Bulhaři a Cařihrad před tisíciletím* (Bulgaria and Constantinople before a Millennium) (Prague, 1915). On the role of Boris' son Symeon in the development of old Bulgarian literature and arts, see G. Sergheraert (Christian Gérard), *Syméon le Grand (893–927)* (Paris, 1960), pp. 89–117.

56. The Czech Slavic philologist V. Vondrák already suggested this solution of the problem in his *Studie z oboru církevněslov. písemnictví* (Studies on Church Slavonic Literature), *Rozpravy* of the Czech Academy, 20 (1903), p. 124. The most important recent studies on this problem are: G. Iljinskij, "Gde, kogda, kem i s kakoju celju glagolica byla zamenena kirilicej" (Where, When, by Whom, and Why was the Glagolitic Alphabet Replaced by the Cyrillic), *Byzantinoslavica,* 3 (1931), pp. 79–88; B. Koneski, "Ohridska kniževna škola" (The Literary School of Ochrida), *Slovo,* 6–8 (Zagreb, 1957), pp. 177–194. Cf. also J. Vajs, "Chrabrova apologie o písmenech," *Byzantinoslavica,* 7 (1937–38), pp. 158–163. J. Vlášek, in his paper "Quelques notes sur l'apologie slave par Chrabr," *Byzantinoslavica,* 28 (1967), pp. 82–97, distinguishes two layers in the composition. The original, probably written in glagolitic alphabet, reflects the crisis when the Cyrillic alphabet was replacing the glagolitic. The second layer was composed by another author, who enlarged the original composition and who wrote it at a time when the Slavic writing in general had to be defended against attacks. This could have been the case during the oppression of Bulgaria by the Greeks, at any date before 1348. He praises the originality of the true Chrabr, the author of the first layer of the composition.

57. It seems to be established that the author of the *Defense,* who called himself Chrabr, was Naum. Cf. M. Weingart, *Bulhaři a Cařihrad,* p. 6 ff. Idem, *"K dnešnímu stavu bádání o jazyce a písemnictví cirkevněslovanském"* (Up-to-date Results of Studies on the Old-Slavonic Language and Letters), *Byzantinoslavica,* 5 (1933–34), p. 419 ff. Cf. also J. Vajs, in J. Dobrovský, *Cyril a Metod,* p. 197, and F. Grivec, *Konstantin und Method,* p. 169 ff. Because the author

of the *Defense* used the Moravian form Rastic instead of Rastislav, and knew Kocel and called his castle Blatensk' kostel', which is a Slavic rendering of the German Mosapurc, he must have worked with Methodius in Moravia. All this points to Naum as the author of the work. See also I. Snegarov, "Černorizets Khrabur," *Khilyada i sto godini slavyanska pismenost 863–1963. Sbornik v čest na Kiril i Metodij* (Sofia, 1963), pp. 305–319; A. Dostál, "Les origines de l'Apologie slave par Chrabr," *Byzantinoslavica,* 24 (1963), pp. 236–246; V. Tkadlčík, "Le moine Chrabr et l'origine de l'écriture slave," *Byzantinoslavica,* 25 (1964), pp. 75–92. Cf. also G. Soulis, "The Legacy," *DO,* 19, p. 34; J. Vašica, *Literární památky,* pp. 14–19.

58. The fact that the author of the *Defense* also mentions the argument against Slavic letters used by the "Trilinguists"—namely, the inscription on the cross in Hebrew, Latin, and Greek—does not necessarily mean that he had in mind "Trilinguists" among the Greek clergy opposing the liturgy in Slavonic. This can only be an allusion to the "Trilinguist heresy" against which Constantine-Cyril and Methodius were fighting in Moravia. If it is accepted that the author of this work was their disciple and had worked with them in that country this would be natural. On the other hand, the new alphabet was adapted from Greek letters and was thus akin to one of the alphabets used in the inscription on the cross, but the glagolitic letters could in no way be compared with the three alphabets used in the inscription. The whole tenor of the short work emphasizes that the author had in mind the defense of the glagolitic alphabet. See the latest edition of the *Defense,* in P. A. Lavrov, *Materialy,* pp. 162–164; P. Rankoff, "Die byzantinisch-bulgarischen Beziehungen," *Aus der byzantinischen Arbeit der deutschen demokratischen Republik,* ed. J. Irmscher, 1 (Berlin, 1957), p. 138, still thinks erroneously that this work is directed "gegen die antislavische Propaganda der Byzantiner."

59. Cf. V. N. Zlatarski, *Istorija,* I, 2, p. 347.

60. B. Angelov, M. Jenov, *Stara B'lgarska literatura* (Ancient Bulgarian Literature) (Sofia, 1922), p. 88. Bibliographical indications on Bulgarian writers and their works from the ninth century on will also be found there. See also I. Dujčev, *Iz' starata b'lgarska knižnina* (Sofia, 1943), vol. 1, p. 76.

61. See the latest edition by P. A. Lavrov, *Materialy,* pp. 199, 200. Cf. F. Dvornik, *The Slavs,* p. 178 ff., on Bulgarian literature on this period. For more detailed and more recent bibliography and editions, see G. Soulis, "The Legacy," *DO,* 19, pp. 33–37. Recently A. Vaillant discovered another homily attributed to Constantine the Priest: "Une homélie de Constantin le Prêtre," *Byzantinoslavica,* 28 (1967), pp. 68–81, with French translation and commentary.

62. See above, Ch. III, footnote 25.

63. D. S. Radojičić, "Srpske Zagorje, das spätere Raszien," *Südostforschungen,* 16 (1957), pp. 271, 272, thinks that a Serbian bishopric existed, having been established at that time. His arguments are, however, not convincing. There is also no evidence that this bishopric was under the jurisdiction of Split (Spalato). The *Serborum proceres* who were present at the council of Spalato in 952 were refugees from Serbia, then occupied by Bulgaria. Their presence at a Latin council well illustrates the religious situation in Serbia, where Latin elements were numerous.

64. The question of the founding of a Bulgarian patriarchate is not yet definitely solved. It could have happened also during the reign of Symeon's son Peter, who was on good terms with the Byzantines. The first patriarch may have been Damian, and the patriarchal see seems to have been in Dorostolon. Anyhow, the Bulgarian Church was regarded as autocephalous by the Byzantines. The Bulgarian primates had transferred their seat on the territory of Tsar Samuel, who from 976 to 1014 had reestablished the independence of the western part of Symeon's Bulgaria. But during the wars which Samuel waged with the Byzantines, the primates found it necessary to change their residence according to political and military circumstances. Their last residence was at Ochrida. Cf. the paper by P. d'Huillier, "Les relations bulgaro-byzantines aux IXᵉ et Xᵉ siècles et leurs incidences ecclésiastiques," published by the Faculty of Theology of Athens, Ἑορτίος τόμος Κυρίλλου καὶ Μεθοδίου ἐπὶ τῇ 1100 ἐτηρίᾳ (Athens, 1966), pp. 213–232.

65. For details, see H. Gelzer, "Ungedruckte und wenig bekannte Bistümerverseichnisse der orientalischen Kirche," *BZ,* 2 (1893), pp. 40–66 (text of the Chrysobull). For the passage concerning Dyrrhachium, see *ibid.,* p. 45.

66. See the study by S. Novaković, "Ochridska archiepiskopija u povetku XI veka" (The Archbishopric of Ochrida at the Beginning of the Eleventh Century), *Glas* of the Serbian Academy, vol. 76 (1908), pp. 1–62. On Ras and Basil II's Chrysobull, *ibid.,* p. 57 ff. Cf. also D. S. Radojičić, *Srpsko Zagorje,* pp. 274, 275.

67. Cf. for details, F. Dvornik, *The Slavs,* p. 279 ff.

68. We learn this from the *Life of Nemanja,* written by his son Stephen and St. Sava. See the German translation with commentary in S. Hafner, *Serbisches Mittelalter* (Graz, 1962), p. 76.

69. Cf. I. Rubarac, *Raski episkopi i metropoliti, Glas,* vol. 62 (1894), p. 12 ff. For details, see F. Dvornik, *The Slavs,* p. 89 ff.

70. For details, see F. Dvornik, *The Slavs,* p. 173 ff.

CHAPTER IX

1. Cf. F. Haase, *Apostel und Evangelisten in den orientalischen Überlieferungen* (Münster i. W., 1922), pp. 259–263, 273–275; *idem, Altchristliche Kirchengeschichte nach orientalischen Quellen* (Leipzig, 1925), p. 47 ff. For Armenia, see also J. Markwart, J. Messina, "Die Entstehung der armenischen Bistümer," *Orientalia christiana,* 27, no. 80 (1932). See the short history on the Christianization of Armenia by L. Petit in *Dictionnaire de théologie catholique* (Paris, 1931), cols. 1892–1896.

2. Cf. R. Janin, "Georgie," *Dictionnaire de théologie catholique,* 6 (1924), p. 1244 ff.

3. See a short description of Justinian's missionary efforts in these regions in F. Dvornik, *Les Slaves, Byzance et Rome au IXe siècle* (Paris, 1926), pp. 64–66, 70.

4. I discussed the problems concerning the legendary *Acts of Andrew,* his preaching in Scythia, his legendary travel from Sinope to Byzantium and Patras, where he is supposed to have died, in my book *The Idea of Apostolicity in Byzantium and the Legend of the Apostle Andrew* (Cambridge, 1958), p. 138 ff.

5. I quote from the English translation made by S. H. Cross and O. P. Sherbowitz-Wetzor, *The Russian Primary Chronicle, Laurantian Text* (Cambridge, Mass., 1953), pp. 53, 54. Original edition by A. A. Šachmatov, *Povjest vremennykh let* (Petrograd, 1966); ed. V. I. Adrianovoj-Perets (Moscow, 1950).

6. On the Christianization of the Goths in general and especially on the Goths in the Crimea, see the work by A. A. Vasiliev, *The Goths in the Crimea* (Cambridge, Mass., 1936), pp. 3–70 (The Early Period of Christianity and the Epoch of the Migrations). F. Dvornik, *Les Slaves,* p. 143 ff.

7. Cf., especially for bibliography and appreciation of the finds, J. Werner, "Slawische Bügelfibeln des 7. Jahrhunderts," *Reinecke Festschrift,* ed. by G. Behrens, J. Werner (Mainz, 1950), p. 168 ff. Especially see the publication of the treasure of Pereščěpina by A. Bobrinskoj in *Materialy po archeologii Rossii,* vol. 34 (1914), pp. 111–120, plates 1–16.

8. On the history of the Khazars from their origin to the ninth century, on Christian missions among them, and on their conversion to Judaism, see my book, *Les légendes de Constantin et de Méthode vues*

de Byzance (Prague, 1933), p. 148 ff. Cf. also above, p. 65 ff.

9. See F. Dvornik, *Les légendes,* p. 164; cf. also A. A. Vasiliev, *The Goths in the Crimea,* pp. 96–97. Recently G. von Rauch "Frühe christliche Spuren in Russland," *Saeculum,* 7 (1956), pp. 40–67, esp. p. 50. Von Rauch's study gives more details on the subject than the study by V. A. Mošin, "Christianstvo v Rossii do sv. Vladimira" (Christianity in Russia before St. Vladimir), *Vladimirskij Sbornik* (Beograd, 1938), pp. 1–19. An interesting attempt to show that the legendary founder of Kiev—Kyyě—had become Christian after an unsuccessful attack on Constantinople was made by E. Ericsson in his paper "The Earliest Conversion of the Rus' to Christianity," *The Slavonic and East European Review,* 44 (1966), pp. 98–121. The author attributes this conversion to the Emperor Theophilus and the Patriarch John the Grammarian. He identifies also the Rhôs, whom Theophilus had recommended to Louis the Pious for safeconduct to their native country, with the Slavs of Kiev. Because this first attempt was made by iconoclasts, it was obliterated by the iconodoules after the victory over iconoclasm. He thinks also that the people of Derbent to whom Constantine-Cyril was sent were the remnants of Kievan Christian Slavs under Khazar rule. This attempt is too daring and in collision with sources which are more reliable than this interpretation of Russian chronicles and Byzantine sources. Therefore this attempt cannot be accepted.

10. I made a thorough study of this *Notitia* in my book *Les légendes,* p. 160 ff., where I tried to identify the names listed there.

11. For documentation, see B. Spicyn, "Archeologija v temach načaľnoj letopisi" (Archaeology in the Time of the Early Period), *Sbornik v čest' S. F. Platonova* (St. Petersburg, 1922), pp. 1–12; cf. I. Stratonov, "Die Krim und ihre Bedeutung für die Christianisierung der Ostslaven," *Kyrios,* 1 (1936), p. 385; von Rauch, "Frühe christliche Spuren," p. 55.

12. See above, p. 121 ff.

13. I discussed the history of the Varyags and their discovery of the Volga and Dnieper routes in my book, *The Making of Central and Eastern Europe* (London, 1949), p. 61 ff., where all the most important bibliography on these problems will be found. See also the more recent discussion of the problem by H. Paszkiewicz, *The Origin of Russia* (London, 1954), pp. 109–132.

14. *MGH Ss* 1, p. 434, ed. G. Waitz (1883), pp. 19, 20; H. Paszkiewicz, *The Origin of Russia,* pp. 116, 124, 172, 414.

15. See for details, F. Dvornik, *The Making,* p. 313 ff.; G. Da Costa-Louillet, "Y eut-il des invasions russes dans l'empire byzantin avant 860?" *Byzantion,* 15 (1940, 1941), pp. 231–248. H. Paszkiewicz, *The Origin,* pp. 421, 422.

16. See above, Ch. II, p. 50. See F. Dvornik, *The Making*, pp. 312, 313, more recently H. Paszkiewicz, *The Origin*, p. 422. Cf. A. L. Jakobson, "Ranne srednevekovyj Chersones" (Chersones during the Early Middle Ages), *Materialy i issledovanija po archeologii SSSR*, vol. 63 (1959), pp. 46–66, for opinions of Russian scholars on the history of Cherson and Russians during the ninth and tenth centuries. On the Russian attack, see the English translation of Photius' two sermons on it by C. Mango, "The Homilies of Photius Patriarch of Constantinople," *Dumbarton Oaks Studies* 3 (Cambridge, 1958), pp. 74–122, with notes and complete bibliography. On editions and translations of these two Homilies see *ibid.*, pp. 34–37. The easiest accessible Greek text was reprinted by C. Müller in his *Fragmenta historicorum graecorum*, 5 (Paris, 1883), pp. 162–173. A. A. Vasiliev, *The Russian Attack on Constantinople* (Cambridge, Mass., 1946). On the duration of the attack, see H. Grégoire, P. Orgels, "Les invasions russes dans le Synaxaire de Constantinople," *Byzantion*, 24 (1954), pp. 141–145.

17. F. Dvornik, *Les légendes*, p. 172 ff. Cf. also above, p. 65. On the Khazars see above, p. 68 ff.

18. Cf. above, p. 124.

19. *Photii Epistolae, PG*, 102, col. 736 D–737 C. Cf. F. Dvornik, *Les Slaves*, pp. 143–145.

20. See for details, F. Dvornik, *The Making*, pp. 65–67. *The Russian Primary Chronicle* (English translation quoted above), p. 61.

21. It is described in detail in *The Russian Primary Chronicle*, pp. 64–69.

22. *The Russian Primary Chronicle* (English translation), pp. 71–79.

23. See for details, F. Dvornik, *The Making*, pp. 67–69.

24. Cf. *Vita Anskarii auctore Rimberto*, ed. B. Schneid in *Scriptores rerum germanicarum in usum scholarum* (Hannover, 1917). E. de Moreau, *Saint Anschaire, missionnaire en Scandinavie au IXe siècle* (Louvaine, 1930). Between 852–853 Ansgar won even King Olaf for Christianity. He seems to have left Rimbert as bishop in Sweden.

25. On Otto's religious policy concerning the Slavs, see F. Dvornik, *The Making*, pp. 60, 68–70, 73, 167.

26. On Svjatoslav, see F. Dvornik, *The Making*, pp. 89, 90; G. Ostrogorsky, *History of the Byzantine State* (New Brunswick, 1969), pp. 292, 295 ff.

27. Cf. N. F. Okunic Kazarin, *Sputnik po drevnemu Pskovu* (Guide to Ancient Pskov) (Pskov, 1913), pp. 68, 69, 89, 113, 234, 262, on traditions concerning Olga's activity in Pskov. Cf. G. v. Rauch, "Frühe christliche Spuren," p. 66.

28. Filaret of Černigov, *Istorija russkoj tserkvi* (St. Petrograd, 1862), 4th ed., vol. 1, p. 7.

29. A. M. Amann, *Abriss der ostslavischen Kirchengeschichte* (Vienna, 1950), p. 14.

30. Year 6491, English translation, pp. 95, 96, 244 (commentary) with bibliography on the names of the two martyrs.

31. Annals of Lampert, *MGH Ss* 3, p. 63. For details, see F. Dvornik, *The Making*, p. 169 ff.; G. Ostrogorsky, *History of the Byzantine State*, p. 269 ff.

32. F. Dvornik, *The Making*, p. 175. It is useless to repeat the different theories about the origins of Christianity in Kiev. They were neither Roman, nor Scandinavian, nor Bulgarian, but Byzantine. See a concise bibliography on those theories in D. Obolensky's paper, "Byzantium, Kiev, and Moscow," *Dumbarton Oaks Papers* 11 (1957), pp. 23, 24. The problem is definitely solved.

33. Read the picturesque description of the scenes in the *Primary Chronicle*, year 6496, English translation, p. 111 ff.

34. Obolensky's study, "Byzantium, Kiev, and Moscow," *DO*, 11 (1957), pp. 23–78, gives an interesting appreciation of ecclesiastical relations between the Russian Church and the patriarchate of Constantinople. Although he was not able to bring more convincing evidence for his thesis, his proposed solution of these relations can be accepted as most probable.

35. Cf. the appreciation of the Church Slavonic language, based on a Slavic dialect, rich in vocabulary, and modelled according to the Greek syntax, by F. Grivec, *Konstantin und Method*, pp. 197–209. See also the study by A. Dostál, "Sprachenprobleme in der Zeit Cyrills und Methods," *Das Grossmährische Reich* (Prague, 1966, Czechoslovak Academy), pp. 329–355. Cf. also bibliographical remarks by R. Večerka, "Grossmähren und sein Kulturerbe in den Arbeiten der tschechischen Philologie der Nachkriegszeit," *ibid.*, pp. 355–377.

36. I am limiting myself only to some general remarks in order to show the impact of Byzantium on Kievan literary production. I have treated the subject in detail in my *The Making*, p. 236 ff.; *The Slavs, their Early History and Civilization* (Boston, 1956), p. 189 ff., where the most relevant bibliography will be found. Cf. also my paper, *The Slavs Between East and West*, Marquette University Slavic Institute Papers (Milwaukee, 1964), p. 4 ff.

37. They are reported by the *Chronicle of Nikon* and the *Book of Degrees*, edited in the *Polnoe sobranie russkich letopisij*, vol. IX, p. 68 (ad a. 6509), Nikon's chronicle; vol. 21, p. 127, ch. 67, *Book of Degrees*. Cf. F. Dvornik, *The Making*, p. 175.

38. See above, p. 219 ff.

39. See F. Dvornik, "The Kiev State and its Relations with Western Europe," *Transactions of the R. Historical Society*, vol. 29 (London, 1947), pp. 27–46, reprinted in *Essays in Mediaeval History*, ed. R. W.

Southern (London, 1968), pp. 1–23. For more details, see N. de Baumgarten, "Généalogies et mariages occidentaux des Rurikides russes du Xe au XIIIe siècle," *Orientalia Christiana,* nos. 35, 94 (Rome, 1927, 1934).

40. Years 6396–6406, English transl., pp. 42, 43.

41. F. G. Kalugin, *Illarion, mitropolit Kievskij i ego tserkovnoučitel'nyja proizvedenija* (Illarion, Metropolitan of Kiev, and his Religious and Didactic Works), Pamjatniki drevne-russk učit. literatury, 1 (St. Petersburg, 1894). I am following here the translation from the original used by me in the paper, "Byzantine Political Ideas in Kievan Russia," *Dumbarton Oaks Papers,* 9, 10 (1956), pp. 103, 104.

42. I am limiting myself to giving only a general picture of Byzantine influences on the development of art in the Kievan State which was inherited by Muscovy. I treated this problem in more detail in my *The Making,* p. 239 ff.; *The Slavs, their Early History and Civilization,* p. 223 ff.; *The Slavs in European History and Civilization,* pp. 316–319, 519, 524. In both works will be found also the most important bibliography on Russian art. A precise description will be found in my contribution to *The Root of Europe,* ed. M. Huxley (London, 1952), pp. 85–95 (Byzantium and the North), pp. 95–106 (Byzantine Influences in Russia).

43. Cf. above, pp. 178–180.

44. Indications as to the editions of these works, their history, and the most important bibliography on Kievan jurisprudence, the reader will find in my paper, "Byzantine Political Ideas in Kievan Russia," *DO,* 9, 10 (1956).

45. This difference is well illustrated by R. O. Unbegaum in his paper, "L'héritage cyrillo-méthodien en Russie," in *Cyrillo-Methodiana,* ed. Görresgesellschaft (Cologne, Graz, 1964), pp. 470, 482.

' 46. On the development of this Hellenistic theory and its adaptation to the Christian teaching, see my book *Early Christian and Byzantine Political Philosophy, Origin, and Background,* Dumbarton Oaks Studies, Vol. 9 (Washington, 1966), vol. 2, ch. X, p. 611 ff.

47. See the English translation of the Novel from the Kormčaja kniga (Pilot's Book) in my paper "Byzantine Political Ideas," *DO,* 9, 10 (1956), pp. 82, 83.

48. For details see F. Dvornik, *The Slavs,* pp. 215, 251.

49. This was shown in my paper, "Byzantine Political Ideas," in all detail.

50. I have tried to outline this development in my book *The Slavs in European History,* especially in ch. XV, p. 362 ff. The history of the growth of absolute monarchism in Muscovy and the role of the Church in this development would deserve a special, more detailed study.

Bibliography

PRIMARY SOURCES

Acta Concilii Constantinopolitani IV (869–870), *Mansi,* 16, cols. 1–208 (Versio Latina Anastasii Bibl.); *Mansi,* 16, ols. 300–413 (Versio Graeca).

Acta Concilii Constantinopolitani V (879–80), *Mansi,* 17, cols. 365–525.

Acta Concilii Ephesini, Mansi, 4, cols. 567–1482.

Acta Concilii Nicaeni II, Mansi, 12, cols. 951–1154; 13, cols. 1–820.

Acta Pontificum Romanorum inedita, ed. by J. V. Pflugk-Hartung (Stuttgart, 1881–1886), 3 vols.

Acta Sanctorum, Propylaeum Novembris, ed. H. Delehaye (Brussels, 1902).

Agatho, Pope, *Letter to Constantine IV, PL* 87, cols. 1213–1230.

Alcuin, *Epistolae,* ed. E. L. Dümmler (1830–1902), *MGH Ep* 4, pp. 1–481.

Anastasius Bibliothecarius, *Epistolae sive praefationes, PL* 129, cols. 1 ff.; *Mansi,* 16, cols. 1 ff.; *MGH Ep* 7, p. 395 ff., ed. E. Perels, G. Laehr.

Anna Comnena, *Alexias,* ed. Bonn (1829–1897); ed. B. Leib (Paris, 1937–1943), 3 vols.

Annales Bertiniani, MGH Ss 1, pp. 423–515; *Ss in us schol,* 11; ed. G. Waitz (Hanover, 1883).

Annales Einhardi, MGH Ss 1, pp. 135–218; *Ss in us schol;* ed. F. Kurze (1895).

Annales Fuldenses, MGH Ss 1, pp. 343–415; *Ss in us schol,* 13; ed. F. Kurze (Hanover, 1891).

Annales Iuvavenses Maximi, MGH Ss 30, pp. 735–744 (Leipzig, 1934).

Annales Lamberti Hersfeldensis, MGH Ss 3, pp. 22–29, 33–69, 90–102 (to the year 1039).

Annales Laurissenses, MGH Ss 1, pp. 134–218.

Annales Lobienses, MGH Ss 2, pp. 194, 195, 209–211.

Annales Mettenses, MGH Ss 13, pp. 26–33, ed. G. Waitz.

Annales regum Francorum, see *Annales Einhardi.*

Annales S. Rudberti Salisburgensis, MGH Ss 9, p. 757 ff.
Annales Xantenses, MGH Ss 2, pp. 219–235.
Annals of Hincmar, see *Annales Bertiniani.*
Annals of Traska, Monumenta Poloniae Historica, 2, pp. 826–861.
Auctarium Garstense, MGH Ss 9, pp. 561–569.

Balić, F., and Bervaldi, J., *Kronotaksa Solinskih biskupa, Krono-taksa spljetskih nadbiskupa* (Zagreb, 1912–13).
Basil II, Emperor, *Menologium, PG* 117, cols. 9–613.
The Bavarian Geographer, *Descriptio,* ed. B. Horák and D. Tráv-níček, *Descriptio civitatum ad septentrionalem plagam Danubii, Rozpravy,* of the Czechoslovak Academy, 66 (1956).
Beševliev, V., "Inscriptions protobulgares," *Byzantion,* 28 (1958), pp. 270–272.
———, "Inscriptions protobulgares," *Byzantion,* 29–30 (1959–1960), pp. 485–488.
———, "Protobulgarische Inschrift auf einer Silberschale," *Byzantion,* 35 (1965), pp. 1–9.
Book of Degrees, ed. in *Polnoe sobranie russkich letopisej,* vol. 21.
Bruno, Archbishop, *Vita S. Adalberti Episcopi, MGH* Ss 4, cols. 596–612.

Canaparius, J., *Vita et Passio St. Adalberti, Fontes rerum Behemi-carum,* 1, pp. 235–265.
———, *Vita St. Adalberti episcopi, MGH* Ss 4, cols. 581–592.
Capitularia regum Francorum, MGH Leg 2, ed. A. Boretius and V. Krause (Hanover, 1897).
Caspar, E., *Das Register Gregors VII, MGH* Ep selectae 2 (Berlin, 1920).
Catalogues of Bishops of Cracow with commentary by W. Kętrzynski, *Monumenta Poloniae Historica* (Lwów, 1878), vol. 3, pp. 313–376.
Cedrenus, G. (Skylitzes), *Historiarum Compendium, PG* 121, cols. 23–1166 (Bonn, 1839).
Chaloupecký, V., *Na úsvitu Křestănství* (Prague, 1942).
———, "Prameny X. století legendy Kristiánovy o sv. Václavu a sv. Ludmile," *Svatováclavský Sborník,* 11, 2 (Praha, 1939). Latin Legends, texts: Fuit in provincia Boemorum, pp. 467–481; Diffundente sole, pp. 486–492; Crescente fide, pp. 495–501; Beatus Cyrillus (Bohemian Legend), pp. 503–505; Tempore Michaelis

imperatoris, pp. 511–521; Latin Legends on Ludmila, pp. 523–562.

———, Ryba, B., ed. *Středověké legendy prokopské* (Medieval Legends on St. Procopius) (Prague, 1953).

Chronicle of Nikon, ed. in *Polnoe sobranie russkich letopisej*, vol. 9.

Chronicon Fredegarii, ed. B. Krush, *MGH Ss rer Merov*, 2 (Hanover, 1888), pp. 18–168.

Chronicon Gradense, MGH Ss 7 (1846), pp. 39–45; *PL* 139, cols. 939–952.

Chronicon Venetum (Altimate), *MGH Ss* 14, pp. 5–69.

Chronicon Salernitanum, MGH Ss 3, pp. 467–561.

Commentaria in Aristotelem graeca, vol. 18, ed. A. Busse (Berlin, 1904).

Constantine Porphyrogenitus, *De Administrando Imperio*, ed. G. Moravcsik and R. J. H. Jenkins (Budapest, 1949); 2nd ed. Dumbarton Oaks Texts, 1 (1968).

———, *De Ceremoniis aulae Byzantinae*, ed. I. I. Reiske (Bonn, 1829, 1830), 2 vols.

———, *De thematibus* (Bonn, 1840), ed. A. Pertusi (Città del Vaticano, 1952), Studi e Testi, 160.

Contra Francos, ed. J. Hergenröther, *Monumenta graeca ad Photium eiusque historiam pertinentia* (Regensburg, 1869).

Conversio Bogoariorum et Carantanorum, MGH Ss 11, cols. 1–15, ed. M. Kos (Ljubljana, 1936).

Cosmas, *Chronica Bohemorum, MGH Ns* 2, ed. Bretholz (Berlin, 1923).

Dandolo, *Chronicon Venetum, Scriptores rerum italicarum*, ed. Muratori, XII, pp. 13–416.

Dlugossius, *Historia Polonica*, 10–14, *Opera omnia*, ed. A. Przezdiecki (Cracow, 1863–1887).

Dostál, A., *Clozianus Codex Palaeoslavenicus Glagoliticus* (Prague, 1959).

Duchesne, L., *Liber Pontificalis*, 3 (Paris, 1886, 1892, 1957), 2 vols.

Dvornik, F., *Les légendes de Constantin et de Méthode vues de Byzance* (Prague, 1933). Documentary evidence on the Legends, pp. 339–348; French translation of the Legends, pp. 349–393.

———, *La vie de St. Grégoire le Décapolite et les Slaves macédoniens au IXe siècle* (Paris, 1926).

Euchologium, see Frček, J.; Geitler, L.; Goar, J.; Nachtigal, R.

Eusebius Pamphili, Bishop of Caesarea, *Historia ecclesiastica,* *PG* 20 (Paris, 1857); ed. Kirsopp Lake (Loeb Classical Library), with English translation (1926).

Fabricius, J. A., Harles, G. C., *Bibliotheca graeca,* 12 (Hamburg, 1809).

Facundus, *Liber contra Mocianum, PL* 67, cols. 853–878.

Fontes rerum Bohemicarum, 1, ed. J. Emler (Vitae S. Cyrilli et Methodii) (Prague, 1865–1871).

Fragmenta Vindobonensia (Leaflets of Vienna), see Weingart, M.

Frček, J., *Euchologium Sinaiticum, Patrologia Orientalis,* 24, fasc. 5 (Paris, 1933), and 25, fasc. 3 (Paris, 1939).

Freshfield, E. H., *A Manual of Roman Law, The Ecloga* (Cambridge, 1926).

―――, *A Revised Manual of Roman Law, Ecloga privata aucta* (Cambridge, 1927), with an English translation.

Friedrich, G., *Codex diplomaticus et epistolaris regni Bohemiae* (Prague, 1904–1907).

Gallus Anonymus, *Chronicon, Monumenta Poloniae Historica* 1 (Lwów, 1864), ed. A. Bielowski, pp. 379–484.

Genesios, J., *Regum Libri* IV (Bonn, 1834).

George the Monk (Hamartolas), Cont., *Vitae recentiorum imperatorum* (Bonn, 1838).

Georgii Cyprii Descriptio orbis Romani (Teubner, 1890), ed. H. Gelzer.

Georgius Continuatus, *Vitae imperatorum* (Bonn, 1838).

Gregorii I Papae Registrum epistolarum, MGH Ep 1, ed. P. Ewald, L. M. Hartmann (Berlin, 1887), books 1–7; 2nd ed. L. M. Hartmann (Berlin, 1890), books 8–14.

Gregory of Nazianzus, *Poemata, PG* 37, cols. 397–1599 (Paris, 1862).

Gregorii VII Registrum, ed. E. Caspar, *Das Register Gregors VII, MGH Ep selectae* 2 (1920, 1923), 2 vols.

Gumpold, *Vita S. Venceslai, MGH Ss* 4, cols. 211–223.

Hadrian II, Pope, *Epistolae, MGH Ep* 6, pp. 691–765.

Hafner, S., *Serbisches Mittelalter; altserbische Herrscherbiographien* (Graz, 1962), vol. 1, Stefan Nemanja nach den Viten des hl. Sava und Stefans der Erstgekrönten.

Hatto, Archbishop of Mainz, *Letter to Pope John IX in 900, PL* 131, cols. 1179–1182.

Itinerarium Antonini, in K. Miller, *Itineraria romana, römische Reisewege an der Hand der Tabula Peutingeriana dargestellt,* pp. LXII, LXIII (Stuttgart, 1926).

Joannes Diaconus, *Chronicon Venetum, MGH Ss* 7, pp. 4–47.

John VIII, Pope, *Epistolae, PL* 126, cols. 651–967; *Mansi,* 17, cols. 3–242; *MGH Ep* 7 (ed. E. Caspar).

Justinian, Emperor, *Corpus Iuris Civilis,* 3: *Novellae,* ed. R. Schoell and W. Kroll (Berlin, 1928).

Kadtubek, Vincent, Bishop of Cracow, *Chronicle, Monumenta Poloniae Historica,* 2 (Lwów, 1872), pp. 249–447 (ed. A. Bielowski).

Kusseff, M., "St. Clement of Ochrida," *Slavonic and East European Review,* 27 (1948–49), p. 198 ff.

———, "St. Naum," *Slavonic and East European Review,* 29 (1950), pp. 139–152.

Lamanskij, V. I., *Slavjanskoe žitie sv. Kirilla* (Petrograd, 1915).

Lambert of Hersfeld, see *Annales Lamberti Hersfeldensis.*

Lavrov, P. A., *Materialy po istorii vozniknovenija drevnějšěj pis-'mennosti* (Documents on the History of the Origins of Early Slavic Literature) (Leningrad, 1930).

Legenda italica, ed. F. Meyvart and P. Devos, "Trois énigmes cyrillométhodiennes de la 'Légende italique,'" *Analecta Bollandiana,* 73 (1955), pp. 374–454.

Lehr-Sptawinski, T., *Żiwoty Konstantyna i Metodego* (Poznan, 1959).

Leo Grammaticus, *Chronographia, PG* 108 (Bonn, 1848).

Libanius, *Orationes,* in *Libanii opera,* ed. R. Foerster (Teubner, 1903–1908), 1–4.

Liber Pontificalis, ed. L. Duchesne (Paris, 1886, 1892), 2 vols.

Ljetopis Popa Dukljanina, ed. F. Šišić (Beograd, Zagreb, 1928); ed. V. Mošin (Zagreb, 1950).

Louis the German, *Die Urkunden des Ludwigs des Deutschen, MGH Dipl., Lud. Germ.,* 1, 1, ed. P. Kehr (Berlin, 1934).

Magnae Moraviae Fontes historici, vol. 2, *Textes biographici, hagiographici, liturgici*, Opera Universitatis Brunensis (Brno, 1967).

Martyrium S. Clementis, PG 2, cols. 617–631.

Menander, *Historia* (Bonn, 1829).

Metrophanes of Smyrna, *Letter to the Logothete Manuel, Mansi* 16, cols. 413–420.

Michael of Anchialos, *Encomium on Ignatius, Mansi* 16, cols. 291–294.

Milev, A., Last critical edition of the *Vita Clementis*, Greek text with translation into Bulgarian (Sofia, 1955).

Nachtigal, R., *Euchologium Sinaiticum* (Ljubljana, 1941, 1942), 2 vols.

Nicephorus, *Historia syntomos*, ed. C. de Boor (Teubner, 1880).

Nicetas-Davis, *Vita Ignatii, Mansi*, 16, cols. 209–292; *PG* 105, cols. 487–574.

Nicholas I, Pope, *Epistolae, MGH Ep* 6, pp. 257–690.

Notae de episcopis Pataviensibus, MGH Ss 25, pp. 623–628.

Otfrid von Weissenburg, *Evangelienbuch*, ed. O. Erdmann (1882), 2nd ed. E. Schröder, 3rd ed. L. Wolff (Tübingen, 1957), Altdeutsche Textbibliothek, vol. 49.

Parthey, G., *Hieroclis Synecdemus et Notitiae Graecae episcopatuum* (Berlin, 1866).

Pastrnek, F., *Dějiny slovanských apoštolů Cyrilla a Methoda* (Prague, 1902), ed. of *Lives*, pp. 154–215.

Paulus Diaconus, *Historia Langobardorum, MGH Ss Lang.* (Hanover, 1878), pp. 12–219.

Pekař, J., *Life of St. Wenceslas* attributed to Christian, ed. J. Pekař, *Die Wenzels- und Ludmila-Legenden und die Echtheit Christians* (Prague, 1906).

Pelagius II, Pope, *Epistola, Regesta pontificum Romanorum, Italia pontificia*, ed. P. F. Kehr (Berlin, 1923), vol. 7, p. 20.

Photius, *Bibliotheca, PG* 103, 104; ed. R. Henry (Paris, 1959).

——, *Epistolae, PG* 102, cols. 585–990.

Photius Homiliae, Mango, C., *The Homilies of Photius, Patriarch of Constantinople*, Dumbarton Oaks Studies, 3 (Cambridge, 1958).

Pilgrim, Bishop of Passau, *Document* addressed to Pope Benedict VII, *PG* 137, cols. 315–318 (Benedicti Papae VII Epistolae et privilegia).

Potthast, A., *Regesta pontificum romanorum 1198–1304* (Berlin, 1874–75), vol. 2.

Povjest Vremennykh Let (Russian Primary Chronicle), ed. D. S. Lichačev (Moscow, 1950); ed. A. A. Šachmatov (Petrograd, 1916); ed. V. I. Adrianovoj-Perets (Moscow, 1950); English translation by S. H. Gross and O. P. Sherbowitz-Wetzor (Cambridge, Mass., 1953).

Procopius, *De bello gothico* (Bonn, 1833).

Rački, F., *Documenta historiae Croaticae periodum antiquam illustrantia* (Zagreb, 1877).

——, *Historia Salonitana Maior,* published by F. Rački in *Documenta spectantia ad historiam Slavorum meridionialium,* 26 (Zagreb, 1894); ed. F. Rački and N. Klaić, Serbian Academy (Beograd, 1967), 2nd ed.

Regino, *Chronicon, MGH Ss 1; MGH in us schol,* ed. F. Kurze (1830).

Registrum Gregorii VII, see Caspar, E.

Rocznik Kapitulny Krakowski, *Monumenta Poloniae Historica,* 2 (1872), ed. A. Bielowski, pp. 783–816.

Rostangnus monachus, Tractatus de translatione capitis S. Clementis, PG 209, cols. 905–913.

The Russian Primary Chronicle, Laurentian Text, English translation by S. H. Gross and O. P. Sherbowitz-Wetzor; original edition by A. A. Šachmatov, *Povjest vremennykh let* (Petrograd, 1916); ed. V. I. Adrianovoj-Perets (Moscow, 1950).

Šišić, F., *Priručnik izvora hrvatske historije (Enchiridion fontium historiae croaticae)* (Zagreb, 1914).

Sobolevskij, A. I., "Cerkovno-slav. texty moravskogo proischoždenija" (Church Slavonic Texts of Moravian Origin), *Russkij filologiskij Vjestnik* 43 (Warsaw, 1900), pp. 153–217.

——, ed. "Glagoličeskoe žitie sv. papy Klimenta," *Izvestija,* XVIII, 3 (1912), pp. 215–222.

——, "The Martyrdom of George, Stephen I," *Izvestija,* X, 1 (1905), p. 105 ff., 113 ff.

——, *Materialy i izsledovanija v oblasti filologii i archeologii*

(Material and Studies in Philological and Archaeological Fields) (St. Petersburg, 1910).

——, "Njeskoľko rjedkich' molitv' iz' russkogo sbornika XIII vjeka" (Some Rare Prayers from a Russian Collection of the Thirteenth Century), *Izvestija*, X, 4 (1905), pp. 66–78.

——, *Pseudo-gospel of Nicodemus, Sbornik otdelenija russk. jazyka i slovesnosti*, 88, 3 (1918).

——, "Russkyje molitvy s upominaniem zapadnych svjatych" (Russian Prayers that Mention Western Saints), *Sbornik otd. russk. jazyka i slovesnosti*, 88, 3 (St. Petersburg, 1910).

——, "Žitie prep. Benedikta Nursijskogo po serbskomu spisku XIV. veka" (The Life of the Blessed Benedict of Nursia in a Serbian Version of the XIVth Century), *Izvestija otd. russk. jazyka i slovesnosti, Akad. Nauk*, 8, 2 (1903).

Tacticon of the Ninth Century, see Th. I. Uspenskij in MODERN WORKS.

Theiner, A., *Vetera monumenta historica Hungariam sacram illustrantia* (Rome, 1859).

Theodore of Studios, St., *The Little Catechesis, PG* 99; ed. E. Auvray (Paris, 1891).

Theodorus Studita (of Studios), St., *Epistolae, PG* 99, cols. 904–1670.

Theognostos, *Libellus, Mansi*, 16, cols. 804–849.

Theophanes, *Chronographia*, ed. J. Classen (Bonn, 1839, 1841), 2 vols.; ed. C. de Boor (Leipzig, 1883, 1885), 2 vols.

Theophanes Continuatus (Bonn, 1838).

Theophylactus of Ochrid, *Historia martyrii XV martyrum, PG* 126, cols. 151–222.

——, *Vita S. Clementis Ochridensis, PG* 126, cols. 1194–1240.

Thietmar, *Chronicon, MGH Ss Ns* 9; ed. R. Holtzmann (1935).

Thomas Archidiaconus, *Historia Salonitana*, ed. F. Rački, *Monumenta spectantia histor. Slavorum meridionalium*.

Tunickij, N. I., *Materialy dlja istorii žizni i dějateľnosti učenikov sv. Kirilla i Methodia* (Documents on the Lives and Works of the Disciples of SS. Cyril and Methodius) (Sergiev Posad', 1918).

Vajs, J., *Charvatskohlaholská redakce původní legendy o sv. Václavu* (The Croat Glagolitic Edition of the Original Legend on

St. Wenceslas), *Sborník staroslov. liter. památek o sv. Václavu a sv. Ludmile* (Collection of Old Slavonic Literary Monuments on St. Wenceslas and St. Ludmila) (Prague, 1929).

———, *Sborník staroslovenských literárnich památek o sv. Václavu a sv. Ludmile* (Collection of Literary Monuments on SS. Wenceslas and Ludmila) (Prague, 1929); N. J. Serebrjanskij, Russian Redactions of the Old Slavonic Legend on St. Wenceslas; J. Vajs, Croat Glagolitic Redaction; J. Vašica, The Second Old Slavonic Legend on St. Wenceslas (pp. 84–124).

Vašica, J., Czech translation of the Legends, the symposium *Na úsvitu Křesťanstvi* (On the Dawn of Christianity), ed. V. Chaloupecký (Prague, 1942), pp. 19–54.

———, ed., Old Slavonic literary documents on St. Wenceslas and St. Ludmila, see J. Vajs, *Sborník* (Prague, 1929).

———, "Slovo na perenesenie moštem preslavnago Klimenta neboli Legenda Chersonská," *Acta Academiae Velehradensis,* 19 (1948), pp. 38–80.

———, *Život a pochvala sv. Cyrila* (Prague, 1927), Czech translation.

Vita Anskarii auctore Rimberto, ed. B. Schneid, *Scriptores rerum germanicarum in usum scholarum* (Hanover, 1917).

Vita S. Adalberti, see Bruno, Canaparius.

Vita S. Clementis Ochridensis, PG 126, cols. 1194–1240; N. L. Tunickij, *Grečeskoje prostrannoje žitie sv. Klimenta slověnskago* (Sergiev-Posad, 1918), with a Russian translation; vol. 1 of his *Materialy,* pp. 1–144; ed. A. Milev (Sofia, 1955), with a Bulgarian translation.

Vita S. Demetrii, AS, October, 4, cols. 99 ff.

Vita S. Eustratii, publ. by A. Papadopoulos-Kerameus, Ἀναλέκτα ἱεροσολ. σταχιολογίας, 4 (1897), pp. 367–400 (St. Petersburg). *Vita S. Euthymii, PG* 86; ed. C. de Boor (Berlin, 1888).

Vita S. Gregori Decapolitae, see F. Dvornik.

Vita S. Joannicii Magni, auctore Sabas, *AS,* Novembris, 2 (Bruxelles, 1894).

Vita S. Naumi, publ. by J. Ivanov, *B'lgarski starini iz' Makedonija* (Sofia, 1931); for commentary, Lavrov, pp. 181–192; bibliography and English translation, M. Kusseff, "St. Naum," *The Slavonic and East European Review,* 29 (1950), pp. 139–152.

Vita S. Nicolai Studitae, by John the Deacon, *PG* 105, cols. 864–925.

Vita S. Pauli Iunioris, Anal. Bol., 11 (1892), pp. 5–74, 136–182.
Vita S. Procopii, see V. Chaloupecký and B. Ryba.
Vita S. Theodorae of Salonica, ed. Arsenij Bishop, *Žitie i podvigi sv. Theodory Solunskoj* (Jurjev, 1899).
Vita S. Wenceslai, Slavonic Legends, see M. Weingart, *První česká;* J. Vajs, *Sborník* (second Slavonic Legend publ. by J. Vašica); Latin legends, see Gumpold and Chaloupecký, *Prameny X. století.*
Vita SS. Constantini-Cyrilli et Methodii, editions, see Grivec-Tomšić, Pastrnek, Lavrov, Lehr-Splawinski; translations, see Dvornik, Vašica, Bujnoch, Stanislav, Grivec; Latin medieval legends, see Chaloupecký, *Prameny X. století.* See also *Magnae Moraviae Fontes historici,* vol. 2, *Textes bibliographici, hagiographici, liturgici,* Opera Univers. Brunensis (Brno, 1967), p. 57 ff.

Weingart, M. "Hlaholské listy víděnské K. dějinám staroslověnskeho misálu" (The Glagolitic *Leaflets of Vienna.* Contribution to the History of the Old Slavonic Missal), *Časopis pro moderní filologii,* 24 (1938), offprint, pp. 3–39, with reprint of the *Leaflets.*
———, "První česká církevně-slovanská legenda o sv. Václavu," *Svatováclavský Sborník,* 1 (Prague, 1934) (First Czech Church-Slavonic Legend on St. Wenceslas).
———, Kurz, J., *Texty ke studiu jazyka a písemnictví staroslověnského* (Texts to the Study of Old Slavonic Language and Literature) (Prague, 1949).
Widukind, *Chronica Saxonum, MGH Ss in us schol* (ed. P. Hirsch, H. E. Lohmann).

Zacharias, Pope, *Epistolae et decreta, PL* 89, cols. 917–960.
Zonaras, Ioannes, *Epitomae historiarum,* vol. 3, ed. Th. Büttner-Wobst (Bonn, 1897).

MODERN WORKS

Abel, A., "La lettre polémique d'Aréthas à l'émir de Damas," *Byzantion*, 24 (1954), pp. 344–370.

Adontz, N., "L'âge et l'origine de l'empereur Basil I," *Byzantion*, 9 (1934), p. 238 ff.

Ahrweiler, H., "Sur la carrière de Photius avant son Patriarcat," *BZ* 58 (1965), p. 538.

Alexander, P. J., "The Papacy, the Bavarian Clergy, and Slavonic Apostles," *The Slavonic and East European Review*, 20 (1941), pp. 266–293.

Alföldi, A., *Der Untergang der Römerherrschaft in Pannonia*, 2 (Berlin, Leipzig, 1926), Ungarische Bibliothek, vol. 12.

Amann, A. M., *Abriss der ostslavischen Kirchengeschichte* (Vienna, 1950).

Amann, E., "Photius," *Dict. de théol. cath.* (Paris, 1935), p. 12, cols. 1536–1604.

Anastos, M. V., "Political Theory in the Lives of the Slavic Saints Constantine and Methodius," *Harvard Slavic Studies*, 2 (1954), pp. 11–38.

———, "The Transfer of Illyricum, Calabria, and Sicily to the Jurisdiction of Constantinople in 732–33," *Silloge Bizantina in onore di S. G. Mercati* (Rome, 1957), pp. 14–36.

Angelov, B., and Jenov, M., *Stara B'lgarska literatura* (Ancient Bulgarian Literature) (Sofia, 1922).

Arnoldus de Raisse, *Hierogazophylacium Belgicum, sive Thesaurus Sacrarum Reliquiarum Belgii* (Douai, 1628).

Arsenij, *Žitie i podvigi sv. Theodory Solunskoj* (Jurjev, 1899).

Artamonov, M. E., *Istorija Chazar* (Leningrad, 1962).

———, *Očerki drevnejšej istorii Chazar* (Studies on the Ancient History of the Khazars) (Leningard, 1936).

Barada, M., "Episcopus Chroatensis," *Croatia sacra*, 1 (1931), pp. 161–215.

———, "Nadvratnik VII stoletia iz kaštel Sučurća" (A Church Portal of the VIIth Century in the Castle of Sučurać), *Serta Hoffilleriana*, Viesnik hrvatsko archeol. društva (Zagreb, 1940), pp. 401–418.

Barroux, R., *Dagobert, roi des Francs* (Paris, 1938).

Baumgarten, N., de, "Généalogies et mariages occidentaux des

Rurikides russes du Xᵉ an XIIIᵉ siècle," *Orientalia Christiana,* nos. 35, 94 (Rome, 1927, 1934).

Baumstark, A., "Zur Urgeschichte der Chrysostomusliturgie," *Theologie und Glaube,* 5 (1913), pp. 299–313 and 394–395.

Beck, H. G., *Kirche und theologische Literatur im byzantinischen Reich* (Munich, 1959).

Bellmann, F., "Übersicht über die wichtigsten Grabungen in einzelnen Ländern," *Kunstchronik,* 8 (1955), pp. 117–124.

Benda, K., "Stříbrný terč se sokolníkem ze Starého Města" (Silver Disc with a Falconer from Staré Město), *Památky archeologické,* 54 (1963), pp. 41–66, with résumé in German.

Beneševič, V., "Zur slavischen Scholia angeblich aus der Zeit der Slavenapostel," *BZ,* 36 (1936), pp. 101–105.

Benoit, A., *Saint Grégoire de Nazianze* (Paris, 1876).

Berčić, I., *Dvie službe rimskoga obreda za svetkovinu sv. Cirila i Metoda* (Two Offices of the Roman Rite to the Honor of St. Cyril and St. Methodius) (Zagreb, 1870).

Beševliev, V., "Souveränitätsansprüche eines bulgarischen Herrschers im 9. Jahrhundert," *BZ* 55 (1962), pp. 11–20.

Bianchi, C. F., *Zara Christiana* (Zara, 1877–1879).

Bogyay, Th., von, "Die Kirchenorte der Conversio," *Südostforschungen,* 19 (1960), pp. 52–70.

——, "Mosapurc und Zalavár," *Südostforschungen,* 14 (1955), pp. 349–405.

Böhm, J., "Deux églises datant de l'Empire de Grande Moravie découvertes en Tchécoslovaquie," *Byzantinoslavica,* 11 (1950), pp. 207–222.

Bökönyi, S., *Die Ausgrabungen Géza Féhers in Zalavár,* Archeologia Hungarica, series nova, vol. 41 (Budapest, 1963).

Bon, A., *Le Péloponnèse byzantin jusqu'en 1204* (Paris, 1951).

Boor, C. de, "Nachträge zu den Notitiae episcopatum," *Zeitschrift für Kirchengeschichte,* 12 (1891), pp. 303–322; 14 (1894), pp. 519–539.

Borkovský, I., "Kostel Panny Marie na Pražském hradě" (The Church of the Virgin Mary in the Castle of Prague), *Památky archeologické,* 43 (1953), pp. 129–200.

Bošković, Gj., *Architektura sredneg veka* (Medieval Architecture), (Beograd, 1957).

Boyle, L., *Cirillo et Metodio i santi apostoli degli Slavi* (Rome, Pontif. Istituto Orientale, 1963).

Browning, R., "Byzantinische Schulen und Schulmeister," *Das Altertum*, 9 (1963), pp. 105–118.

———, "The Correspondence of a Tenth Century Byzantine Scholar," *Byzantion*, 24 (1954), pp. 397–452.

———, "The Patriarchal School of Constantinople," *Byzantion*, 32 (1962), p. 167 ff.

Brückner, A., "Thesen zur Cyrillo-Methodianischen Frage," *Archiv für slavische Philologie*, 28 (1906), p. 202 ff.

———, *Die Wahrheit über die Slavenapostel* (Tübingen, 1913).

Brunelli, N., *Storia di Zara* (Venice, 1913).

Bujnoch, J., *Zwischen Rom und Byzanz* (Graz, Vienna, Cologne, 1958).

Bulín, H., "Staré Slovensko v datech Bavorského geografa" (Old Slovakia in the Description of the Bavarian Geographer), *Historický časopis*, 6 (1958).

———, "Z diskuse o počátcích velkomoravské říše" (Concerning the Discussions on the Origins of the Great Moravian Empire), *Slavia occidentalis*, 22 (1962), pp. 67–111, with a summary in English.

Bury, J. B., *A History of the Eastern Roman Empire* (London, 1912).

———, *The Imperial Administrative System in the Ninth Century* (London, 1911).

Caspar, E., *Geschichte des Papsttums* (Tübingen, 1930, 1933).

Chaloupecký, V., *Na úsvitu křesťanství* (Prague, 1942).

———, *Prameny X. století legendy Kristiánovy o sv. Václavu a sv. Ludmile* (Tenth Century Sources of Christian's Legend on St. Wenceslas and St. Ludmila) (Prague, 1939), *Svatováclavský Sborník*, vol. II, 2.

Charanis, P., "The Chronicle of Monemvasia and the Question of the Slavonic Settlements in Greece," *DO*, 5 (1950), pp. 139–166.

———, "Hellas in Greek Sources of the Sixth, Seventh, and Eighth Centuries," *Late Classical and Medieval Studies in Honor of A. M. Friend*, ed. K. Weitzmann (Princeton, 1955), pp. 161–177.

Charlesworth, M. P., *Trade Routes and Commerce of the Roman Empire* (Cambridge, 1926).

Chropovský, B., "The Situation of Nitra in the Light of Archeological Finds," *Historica*, 8 (Prague, 1964), pp. 5–33.

Cibulka, J., "L'architecture de la Grande-Moravie au IXᵉ siècle à la lumière des récentes découvertes," *L'information de l'histoire de l'art*, 2 (Paris, 1966), pp. 1–34.

——, "Epiusios," *Slavia*, 25 (1956), pp. 4–15.

——, "Grossmährische Kirchenbauten," Symposium *Sancti Cyrillus et Methodius, Leben und Wirken* (Prague, 1963), pp. 49–118.

——, "Pribina a jeho kostol v Nitře" (Pribina and His Church in Nitra), *Ríša Velkomoravská* (The Empire of Great Moravia), ed. J. Stanislav (Bratislava, 1933).

——, "První tři velkomoravské kostely nalezené na hradišti u Mikulčic" (The First Three Churches Discovered in the Settlement near Mikulčice), Symposium *Soluňští bratří* (Prague, 1962), pp. 87–159.

——, *Velkomoravský kostel v Modré u Velehradu a začátky křesťanství na Moravě* (The Church of the Great Moravian Period in Modrá and the Beginning of Christianity in Moravia) (Prague, 1958).

——, "Der Zeitpunkt der Ankunft der Brüder Konstantin-Cyrillus und Methodius in Mähren," *Byzantinoslavica*, 26 (1965), pp. 318–364.

——, "Zur Frühgeschichte der Architektur in Mähren," *Festschrift K. M. Swoboda* (Vienna, 1959), pp. 55–74.

Cincík, J. G., "Early Slovak Oratories, a Study in Slavic-Iranian Architectural Tradition," *Most*, 7 (Cleveland, 1960), pp. 135–147.

——, "A Note on the Official See and the Burial Place of St. Methodius," *Most*, 10 (1963), pp. 198–206.

Codrington, H. W., *The Liturgy of St. Peter* (Münster i.W., 1936), Liturgiegeschichtliche Quellen und Forschungen, vol. 30.

Constantine Porphyrogenitus, *De Administrando Imperio, II*, Commentary by F. Dvornik, B. Lewis, G. Moravcsik, D. Obolensky, S. Runciman; ed. R. J. H. Jenkins (London, 1962).

Costa-Louilet, G. da, "Y eut-il des invasions russes dans l'Empire byzantin avant 860?", *Byzantion*, 15 (1940–41), pp. 231–248.

Csallány, D., "Vizantijskie monety v avarskich nachodkach," *Acta archaeologica academiae scientiarum Hungaricae*, 2 (1952), p. 235 ff., with résumé in French: "L'importance de la circulation monétaire byzantine pour les legs archéologiques des Avares."

Dekan, J., "Die Beziehungen unserer Länder mit dem spätantiken und byzantinischen Gebiet in der Zeit vor Cyrill und Method," *Das Grossmährische Reich* (Prague, 1966), pp. 45–52.

——,"Les motifs figuraux humains sur les bronzes moulés de la zone danubienne centrale à l'époque précédant l'empire de la Grand Moravie," *Studia historica slovaca*, 2 (1966), pp. 52–102.

——, *Slovenské dejiny*, vol. 2, *Začiatky slovenských dejin a ríša Velkomoravská* (Slovak History, Beginning of Slovak History and the Great Moravian Empire) (Bratislava, 1951).

Delehaye, H., "S. Grégoire le Grand dans l'hagiographie grecque," *Analecta Bollandiana*, 23 (1904), pp. 449–454.

Deroko, A., *Monumentalna i dekorativna architektura u srednjevjekovnoj Srbiji* (Monumental and Decorative Architecture in Medieval Serbia) (Beograd, 1953; 2nd edition, 1962).

D'Huillier, P., "Les relations bulgaro-byzantines aux IXe et Xe siècles et leurs incidences ecclésiastiques," Ἑόρτιος Τόμος Κυρίλλου καὶ Μεθοδίου (Athens, 1966), pp. 213-232.

Diehl, Ch., *Etudes sur l'administration byzantine dans l'exarchat de Ravenne* (Paris, 1888).

Dittrich, Z. R., *Christianity in Great Moravia* (Groningen, 1962).

Dobiáš, J., *Dějiny československého území před vystoupením Slovanů* (The History of the Czechoslovak Territory Before the Arrival of the Slavs) (Prague, 1964).

——, *Le strade romane nel territorio cecoslovacco* (Rome, 1938).

Dobrovský, J., *Cyril a Metod*, new edition with commentary by J. Vajs (Prague, 1948).

Dold, A., "Abermals neue Fragmente des Salzburger Sakramentars," *Texte und Arbeiten*, 25 (Beuron, 1936), pp. 71–98.

——, "Neue Blätter des Salzburger Kurzsakramentars," *Texte und Arbeiten*, 25 (Beuron, 1934), pp. 35–48.

Dostál, A., "L'Eucologe Slave du Sinai," *Byzantion*, 36 (1966), pp. 41–50.

——, "Konstantin der Philosoph und das Ausmass seiner geistigen Bildung," *Byzantinische Forschungen*, 1 (1966), pp. 76–91.

——, "Les origines de l'Apologie slave par Chrabr," *Byzantinoslavica*, 24 (1963), pp. 236–246.

——, "Origins of the Slavonic Liturgy," *DO*, 19 (1965), pp. 67–87.

——, "Sprachenprobleme in der Zeit Cyrills und Methods," *Das*

Grossmährische Reich, Czechoslovak Academy (Prague, 1966), pp. 329–355.

Dostál, B., *Slovanská pohřebiště ze střední doby hradištní na Moravě* (Slavic Cemeteries in Moravia from the So-Called Middleburg Wall Period) (Prague, 1966).

———, "Výzkum velkomoravského hradiska Pohansko u Břeclavi" (Archeological Exploration of the Great Moravian Castle Pohansko near Břeclav), *Slovácko* (1961), pp. 16–31.

Downey, G., *Nikolaos Mesarites, Description of the Church of the Holy Apostles* (Philadelphia, 1957), Transactions of the American Philosophical Society, 47, pt. 6.

Du Cange, Ch., *Constantinopolis Christiana* (Paris, 1680).

Duchesne, L., "Liber diurnus et les élections pontificales au VIIe siècle," *Bibliothèque de l'Ecole des Chartes,* 52 (Paris, 1891).

———, *Les premiers temps de l'Etat pontifical* (Paris, 1911).

Dujčev, Ivan, see also Follieri, Enrica.

———, "Costantino Filosofo nella storia della letteratura bizantina," *Studi in onore di Ettore Lo Gatto e Giovanni Maver* (Rome, 1961), pp. 205–222.

———, "Un episodio dell' attivitá di Costantino Filosofo in Moravia," *Ricerche Slavistiche,* 3 (1954), pp. 90–96.

———, *Iz' starata b'lgarska knižnina* (Sofia, 1943).

———, "Presiam-Persian," *Ezikovedsko-etnografski izsledvanija v pamet na akademik Stojan Romanski,* Bulgarian Academy (Sofia, 1960), pp. 478–482.

———, "V'pros't za vizantiijsko-slavjanskite otnošenija i vizantijskite opity za s'zdavane na slavjanska azbuka prez p'rvata polovina na IX viek" (The Question of Byzantino-Slavonic Relations and Byzantine Attempts at a Creation of a Slavonic Alphabet during the First Half of the Ninth Century), *Izvestije na Instituta za b'lgarska istorija,* 7 (1957), pp. 241–267.

———, "Zur literarischen Tätigkeit Konstantins des Philosophen," *BZ,* 44 (1951), pp. 105–110.

Dümmler, E., *Geschichte des Ostfränkischen Reiches* (Leipzig, 1887), 2nd ed.

———, *Piligrim von Passau und das Erzbistum Lorch* (Leipzig, 1854).

Dunlop, D. M., *The History of the Jewish Khazars* (Princeton, 1954).

Dvornik, F., "Die Bedeutung der Brüder Cyrill und Methodius

für die Slaven und Kirchengeschichte," *Prolegomena ad Acta Congressus historiae Slavicae Salisburgensis* (Wiesbaden, 1964), pp. 17–32.

———, "Les Bénédictins et la christianisation de la Russie," *L'Eglise et les Eglises* (Chevetogne, 1954), pp. 326–329.

———, "Byzantine Influences in Russia," *The Root of Europe,* ed. M. Huxley (London, 1952), pp. 95–106.

———, "Byzantine Political Ideas in Kievan Russia," *DO,* 9–10 (1956), pp. 76–94.

———, "Byzantium and the North," *The Root of Europe,* ed. M. Huxley (London, 1952), pp. 85–95.

———, "Byzantium, Rome, the Franks, and the Christianization of the Southern Slavs," *Cyrillo-Methodiana* (Cologne, Graz, 1964), pp. 89–93.

———, Commentary on *Const. Porph. De admin. imperio,* ed. R. J. H. Jenkins, vol. 2 (London, 1962), pp. 93–142.

———, "Deux inscriptions gréco-bulgares de Philippes," *Bulletin de correspondance hellénique,* 52 (1928), pp. 125–143.

———, *Early Christian and Byzantine Political Philosophy, Origin, and Background,* Dumbarton Oaks Studies, 9 (Washington, 1966), vol. 2.

———, *The Idea of Apostolicity in Byzantium and the Legend of the Apostle Andrew* (Cambridge, Mass., 1958).

———, "The Kiev State and its Relations with Western Europe," *Transactions of the Royal Historical Society,* 29 (London, 1947).

———, *Les légendes de Constantin et de Méthode vues de Byzance* (Prague, 1933).

———, *The Making of Central and Eastern Europe* (London, 1949).

———, "The Patriarch Photius and Iconoclasm," *DO,* 7 (1953), pp. 69–97.

———, *The Patriarch Photius in the Light of Recent Research,* Berichte zum XI. Intern. Byz. Kongress (Munich, 1958).

———, "Patriarch Photius, Scholar and Statesman," *Classical Folia,* 13 (1959), pp. 3–18; 14 (1960), pp. 3–22.

———, *The Photian Schism, History and Legend* (Cambridge, 1948).

———, "Photius et la réorganisation de l'Académie patriarcale," *Analecta Bollandiana,* 68 (1950), pp. 108–125.

———, "Patriarch St. Ignatius and Caesar Bardas," *Byzantinoslavica,* 27 (1966), pp. 7–22.

———, "Sts. Cyril and Methodius in Rome," *St. Vladimir's Seminary Quarterly*, 7 (1963), pp. 20–30.

———, "The Significance of the Missions of Cyril and Methodius," *The Slavic Review*, 23 (1964), pp. 105–211.

———, *The Slavs Between East and West*, Marquette University Slavic Institute Papers (Milwaukee, 1964).

———, *Les Slaves, Byzance et Rome au IXᵉ siècle* (Paris, 1926).

———, *The Slavs in European History and Civilization* (New Brunswick, 1962).

———, *The Slavs, their Early History and Civilization* (Boston, 1956).

———, *Sv. Vojtěch* (Chicago, 1950; 2nd ed., Rome, 1967).

———, *La Vie de St. Grégoire le Décapolite et les Slaves macédoniens au IXe siècle* (Paris, 1926).

Dyggwe, E., *History of Salonitian Christianity* (Oslo, 1951).

———, "Das Mausoleum von Marušinac und sein Fortleben," *Actes du VIᵉ Congrès International des Etudes Byzantines, Bulletin de l'Institut archéologique bulgare*, 10 (Sofia, 1936), pp. 228–237.

Eckhardt, T., "Theorien über den Ursprung der Glagolica," *Slovo*, 13 (1963), pp. 87–118.

Eisner, J., *Devínská Nová Ves, slovanské pohřebiště* (Bratislava, 1952).

———, *Rukovět slovanské archeologie* (Handbook of Slavic Archaeology) (Prague, 1966).

Enciklopedia likovnik umjetnosti (Encyclopedia of Visual Arts) (Zagreb, 1959–1966), 4 vols.

Ericsson, E., "The Earliest Conversion of the Rus' to Christianity," *The Slavonic and East European Review*, 44 (1966), pp. 98–121.

Essen, A., "Wo fand der hl. Konstantin-Kyril die Gebeine des hl. Clemens von Rom?" *Cyrillo-Methodiana* (Cologne, Graz, 1964), Slawische Forschungen, ed. R. Olesch, vol. 6, pp. 126–147.

Feher, G., "Der protobulgarische Titel kanar," *BZ* 36 (1936), pp. 58–62.

Fergula, J., "Niže vojno-administrativne jedinetsa tematskog uredjenja" (Military and Administrative Thematic Units of an Inferior Rank), *Zbornik radova* of the Serbian Academy, 22 (1953), p. 88 ff.

———, "Sur la date de la création du thème de Dyrrhachium," *Actes du XIIᵉ Congrès International d'Etudes Byzantines,* 2 (Ochrid, 1964), pp. 83–92.

———, *Vizantiska uprava u Dalmaciji* (Beograd, 1957).

Fiala, Z., "Dva kritické příspěvky ke starým dějinám českým" (Two Critical Contributions to the Ancient History of Bohemia), *Sborník Historický,* 9 (1962), pp. 5–40.

Filaret of Černigov, *Istorija russkoj tserkvi* (St. Petrograd, 1862), 4th ed.

Florovskij, A. V., *Čechi i vostočnye Slavjane* (The Czechs and the Eastern Slavs) (Prague, 1935).

Follieri, Enrica, and I. Dujčev, "Acolutia inedita per i martiri di Bulgaria dell'anno 813," *Byzantion,* 33 (1963), pp. 71–106.

Frček, J., "Byl sv. Václav postřižen podle ritu východního či západního?" (Was the Ceremony of Hair-cutting Performed on St. Wenceslas According to Eastern or Western Rite?), *Slovanské Studie, Vajs' Festschrift,* ed. J. Kurz, M. Murko, and J. Vašica (Prague, 1948), pp. 144–158.

Frinta, A., "Wogastisburg," *Slavia,* 32 (1963), pp. 528–531.

Fritze, W. H., "Slawen und Avaren im angelsächsischen Missionsprogram," *Zeitschrift für Slawische Philologie,* 21 (1963), pp. 316–338; 22 (1965), pp. 231–251.

Fukáč, J., "Über den musikalischen Charakter der Epoche von Grossmähren," *Magna Moravia* (Brno, 1964), pp. 417–434.

Gage, J., "L'Empereur romain et les rois. Politique et protocole," *Revue historique,* 83 (1959), pp. 221–260.

Gallus Anonymus, *Chronicon. Monumenta Poloniae Historica,* 1 (Lwów, 1864), ed. A. Bielowski, pp. 379–484.

Gamber, K., "Das glagolitische Sakramentar der Slavenapostel Cyrill und Method und seine lateinische Vorlage," *Ostkirchliche Studien,* 6 (Würzburg, 1957), pp. 165–173.

Gautier, P., "Clement d'Ochrida, évêque de Dragvitsa," *Revue des études byzantines,* 22 (1964), pp. 199–214.

Geitler, L., *Euchologium. Glagolski spomenik monastira Sinai brda* (Euchologium. A Glagolitic Document from a Monastery on Mt. Sinai) (Zagreb, 1882).

Gelzer, H., "Ungedruckte und ungenügend veröffentlichte Texte der Notitiae episcopatuum," *Abhandlungen der bayer. Akad., Phil. hist. Kl.,* 21 (1901), pp. 529–641.

———, "Ungedruckte und wenig bekannte Bistümerverzeichnisse

der orientalischen Kirche," _BZ_ 1 (1892), pp. 245–282; 2 (1893), pp. 22–72.

Georgiev, E., _Dve proizvedenija na sv. Cirila_ (Two Works on St. Cyril) (Sofia, 1938).

———, _Kiril i Metodij_ (Sofia, 1956).

———, _Nacăloto na slavjanskata pismenost v Bŭlgarija_ (Beginning of Slavic Literature in Bulgaria) (Sofia, 1942).

Gerard, C., _Les Bulgares de la Volga et les Slaves du Danube_ (Paris, 1939).

Gerhard, D., "Goten, Slawen oder Syrer im alten Cherson," _Beiträge zur Namenforschung_, 4 (1953), pp. 78–88.

Gnidovec, F., _Vpliv sv. Gregorija Nazianskega na sv. Cirila i Metodija_ (Ljubljana, 1942).

Goar, J., _Euchologium_ (Venice, 1730), 2nd ed.

Goos, J., "Traces of Byzantino-Slavonic Influence in Polish Mediaeval Hymnology," _The Polish Review_, 9 (1964), pp. 73–81.

Golubinskij, E., _Kratkij očerk pravoslavnych tserkvej_ (Moscow, 1871).

Gošev, I., "Svetite bratja Kiril i Metodij" (The Holy Brothers Cyril and Methodius), _Godišnik na Sofij. Univ. VI, Bogoslov. fak._, 15 (1937–1938), pp. 56–69.

Gracianzkij, I. P., "Dejateľnost Konstantina i Metodija v Velkomoravskom knjažestve" (The Activity of Constantine and Methodius in the Great Moravian Empire), _Voprosy Istorii_, 1 (1945), p. 92 ff.

Grafenauer, B., "Prilog kritici izvještaja Konst. Porfirogeneta," _Historicki Zbornik_, 5 (1952).

Graus, F., _Dějiny venkovského lidu v Čechách v době předhusitské_ (A History of the Peasantry in Bohemia Before the Hussite Period) (Prague, 1953).

———, "L'Empire de Grande Moravie, sa situation dans l'Europe de l'époque et sa structure intérieure," _Das grossmährische Reich_, ed. F. Graus, J. Filip, and A. Dostál (Prague, Academy, 1966), pp. 133–219.

———, "K počátkům kresťanstvi na Moravě" (On the Introduction of Christianity into Moravia), _Československý časopis historický_ (The Czechoslovak Historical Review), 7 (1959), pp. 478–483.

———, "L'Origine de l'état et de la noblesse en Moravie et en Bohême," _Revue des études slaves_, 39 (1961).

―――, "Rex-dux Moraviae," *Sbornik prací filosofické fakulty brněnské university*, 9 (Brno, 1960), řada historická C 7, pp. 181–190.

―――, "Slovanská liturgie a písemnictví v přemyslovských Čechách 10. století" (Slavonic Liturgy and Literature in Bohemia Under the Dynasty of the Przemyslides in the Tenth Century), *Československý časopis historický* (The Czechoslovak Historical Review), 14 (1966), pp. 473–495.

―――, "Velkomoravská říše v české středověké tradici" (The Great Moravian Empire in the Czech Medieval Tradition), *Československý časopis historický* (The Czechoslovak Historical Review), 11 (1963), p. 292.

Gregoire, H., " Le 'Glozel' Khazare," *Byzantion*, 12 (1937), pp. 225–266.

―――, "Les sources épigraphiques de l'histoire bulgare," *Byzantion*, 9 (1934), p. 773 ff.

Gregoire, H., and Orgels, P., "Les invasions russes dans le Synaxaire de Constantinople," *Byzantion*, 24 (1954), pp. 141–145.

Gregory of Nazianzus, *Poemata, PG* 37, cols. 397–1599 (Paris, 1862).

Grivec, F., and Tomšić, F., *Constantinus et Methodius Thessalonicenses. Fontes* (Zagreb, 1960).

―――, "Constantinus philosophus amicus Photii," *Orientalia Christ. Periodica*, 23 (1957), pp. 415–422.

―――, *Doctrina Byzantina de primatu et unitate ecclesiae* (Ljubljana, 1928).

―――, *Konstantin und Method, Lehrer der Slawen* (Wiesbaden, 1960).

―――, "Prepiro Metodovih ječali" (The Controversy on Methodius' Prisons), *Zgodovinski Časopis*, 6–7 (1952–53), p. 158 ff.

―――, "Vitae Constantini et Methodii," *Acta Academiae Velehradensis*, 17 (1941), pp. 1–127, 161–277.

―――, *Zarja Stare Slovenske književnosti* (Dawn of the Old Slovene Literature) (Ljubljana, 1942).

―――, *Žitja Konstantina in Metodija* (Celj, 1936) (Slovene translation), 2nd ed. (Ljubljana, 1951).

Grumel, V., *Diskussionbeiträge zum XI. Internat. Byzantinisten-Kongress* (Munich, 1958).

Gunjača, S., "Kratak svrt na rad i prilike muzeja u Kninu" (Short

Survey of the Work and Condition of the Museum in Knin), *Starohrvatska prosvjeta*, 3rd series, 3 (Zagreb, 1953), pp. 189–191.

———, "Oko revizije iskopina u Biskupije" (Concerning the Revision of the Excavations in Biskupije), *Starohrvatska prosvjeta*, 3rd series, 5 (Zagreb, 1956), pp. 21–32.

———, "Starohrvatska crkva i groblje na Lopuskoj Glanici u Biskupijo kod Knina" (The Old Croatian Church and Cemetery in Lopuska Glanica in Biskupia near Knin), *Starohrvatska prosvjeta*, 3rd series, 3 (Zagreb, 1954), pp. 7–30.

———, "Starohrvatska crkva i kasnosredovjekovno groblje u Brnazima kod Sinja" (The Old Croatian Church and the Late Medieval Cemetery at Brnazi near Sinje), *Starohrvatska prosvjeta*, 3rd series, 4 (Zagreb, 1955), pp. 85–134, with a résumé in French.

———, "Trogodišnji rad Museja hrvatskih archeoloških spomenika" (The Three Years of Work of the Museum of Croatian Archaeological Monuments), *Starohrvatska prosvjeta*, 3rd series, 7 (Zagreb, 1960), pp. 207–271.

Haase, F., *Altchristliche Kirchengeschichte nach orientalischen Quellen* (Leipzig, 1925).

———, *Apostel und Evangelisten in den orientalischen Überlieferungen* (Münster i.W., 1922).

Halkin, F., "La date de composition de la 'Bibliothèque' de Photius remise en question," *Analecta Bollandiana*, 83 (1963), pp. 414–417.

Hamm, J., "Hrvatski tip cerkvenoslovenskog jezika" (Croat Type of the Church Slavonic Language), *Slovo*, 13 (Zagreb, 1963), pp. 43–67.

Hanssens, J. M., "La liturgie romano-byzantine de Saint Pierre," *Orientalia christiana periodica*, 4 (Rome, 1938), pp. 234–258; 5 (1939), pp. 103–150.

Hartman, L. M., *Untersuchungen zur Geschichte der byzantinischen Verwaltung in Italien (590–750)* (Leipzig, 1889).

Hauptman, L., "Les rapports des Byzantins avec les Slaves et les Avars pendant la seconde moitié du VIe siècle," *Byzantion*, 4 (1927–1928), pp. 137–170.

Hauthaler, W., *Salzburger Urkundenbuch, Traditionscodices*, 1 (Salzburg, 1910).

Havlík, L., "Moravané v údajích franko-bavorského Descriptia," (The Moravians in the Reports of the Franko-Bavarian Description), *Historický časopis*, 7 (Bratislava, 1959), pp. 282–289.

———, *Velká Morava a středoevropští Slované* (Great Moravia and the Slavs of Central Europe) (Prague, 1964).

Havránek, B., "Otázka existence církevní slovanštiny v Polsku" (The Problem Concerning the Existence of Old Slavonic in Poland), *Slavia*, 25 (1956), pp. 300–305, with bibliography.

Heiler, F., *Altkirchliche Autonomie und päpstlicher Zentralismus* (Munich, 1941).

Hellmann, M., "Grundlagen slawischer Verfassungsgeschichte des frühen Mittelalters," *JGOE*, 2 (1954), p. 391.

Hemmerdinger, B., "La culture grècque classique du VIIᵉ au IX siècle," *Byzantion*, 34 (1964), pp. 127–133.

Hergenröther, J., *Photius, Patriarch von Constantinopel* (Regensburg, 1869), 3 vols.

Herrmann, E., *Slawisch-germanische Beziehungen im südost deutschen Raum* (Munich, 1965).

Hochmanová-Vávrová, V., "Nálezy římských cihel u Starého Města u Uherského Hradište" (Finds of Roman Bricks at Staré Město near Uherské Hradiště), *Spisy Purkyňovy university*, E 3 (1957), pp. 23–26.

Hocij, M., "Die wörtlichen Grundlagen des glagolitischen Alphabets," *Südost-deutsche Forschungen*, 4 (1940), pp. 509–600.

Honigmann, E., "Studies in Slavic Church History," *Byzantion*, 17 (1944–45), pp. 163–182.

Hopf, G., *Geschichte Griechenlands* (Leipzig, 1867).

Horálek, K., "Kořeny charvatskohlaholského písemnictví" (Roots of Glagolitic Letters in Croatia), *Slavia*, 19 (1950), pp. 285–292.

———, "K otázce české cyrilice" (Apropos of Czech Cyrillic Letters), *Listy filologické*, 66 (1939).

———, "St. Kirill i semitskie jazyki," *For Roman Jakobson* (The Hague, 1956), pp. 230–234.

———, "Zum Verhältnis der Kyrillica und Glagolica," *Welt der Slaven*, 3 (1958), pp. 232–235.

Hošek, R., "Antique Traditions in Great Moravia," *Magna Moravia* (Prague, 1965), pp. 71–84.

Hrubý, V., "Archeologický výzkum v Sadech u Uh. Hradiště r. 1959" (Archeological Research in Sady near Uh. Hradiště in

1959), *Našim krajem-Sborník OPS v Uh. Hradišti,* 1 (1960).

———, *Staré Město. Velkomoravsképohřebiště "Na Valách"* (Old City. The Great Moravian Cemetery "On the Ramparts"), *Monumenta archaeologica,* 3 (Prague, 1955).

———, *Staré Město-Velkomoravský Velehrad, Monumenta archaeologica,* 14 (Prague, 1965).

———, "Velkomoravské hradisko sv. Klimenta u Osvetiman," *Časopis moravského musea* (Review of the Moravian Museum), 44 (1959), pp. 19–70, with résumé in German.

———, "Základy kostela na staroslovanském pohřebišti ve Starém Městě 'Na Valách' " (The Foundation of a Church on the Old Slavonic Cemetery in Staré Město "Na Valách"), *Památky archeologické,* 46 (1955), pp. 265–308.

Hrubý, V., Hochmanová, V., and Pavelčik, J., "Kostel a pohřebiště z doby velkomoravské na Modré u Velehradu" (The Church and the Cemetery from the Great Moravian Period in Modrá near Velehrad), *Časopis moravského musea,* 40 (1955), pp. 42–126.

Hunger, G., "Die Schönheitskonkurenz in Belthandros und Chryzantza und die Brautschau am Byzantinischen Kaiserhof," *Byzantion,* 55 (1965), pp. 150–158.

Hurt, R., *Dějiny cisterciáckého kláštera na Velehradě* (History of the Cistercian Monastery of Velehrad) (Olomouc, 1934).

Iljinskij, G. A., "Gde, kogda, kem i s kakoju celju glagolica byla zamenena kirilicej" (Where, When, by Whom and Why was the Glagolitic Alphabet Replaced by the Cyrillic), *Byzantinoslavica,* 3 (1931), pp. 79–88.

———, *Makedonskij listok* (St. Petersburg, 1906).

Isačenko, A. V., *Jazyk a povod frizinských pamiatok* (The Language and the Origin of the Documents of Freisingen) (Bratislava, 1943).

———, "Nachträgliche Bemerkungen zur Frage der älteren deutsch-slawischen literarischen Beziehungen," *Zeitschrift für slawische Philologie,* 19 (1944–1947), pp. 303–311.

———, *Začiatky vzdelanosti vo velkomoravskej říši* (Origins of Civilization in the Empire of Great Moravia) (Turčianský sv. Martin, 1948).

Jagić, V., *Glagolitica* (Vienna, 1890).

————, in Vodnik, B., *Povijest hrvatske kniževnosti* (History of Croat Literature) (Zagreb, 1913).

Jakobson, A. L., "Ranně-srednevekovyj Chersones" (Chersones During the Early Middle Ages), *Materialy i issledovanija po archeologii SSSR*, 63 (1959), pp. 46–66.

Jakobson, R., "Český podíl na církevněslovanské kultuře" (The Czech Contribution to Slavonic Church Culture), Symposium *Co daly české země Evropě a lidstvu* (What Had the Czech Lands Given to Europe and Humanity) (Prague, 1940), pp. 9–19.

————, "Český verš před tisíci lety," *Slovo a slovesnost*, 1 (1935), pp. 50–53.

————, "The Kernel of Comparative Slavic Literature," *Harvard Slavic Studies*, 1 (1953), pp. 1–71.

————, "Minor Native Sources for the Early History of the Slavic Church," *Harvard Slavic Studies*, 2 (1954), pp. 55–60.

————, *Moudrost starých Čechů* (The Wisdom of the Ancient Czechs) (New York, 1943).

————, "Saint Constantin et la langue Syriaque," *Annuaire de l'Institut de Philologie et d'histoires orientales et slaves*, 1 (1939–1944), pp. 181–186.

————, "St. Constantine's Prologue to the Gospels," *St. Vladimir's Quarterly* (1954), pp. 19–23.

————, "The Slavic Response to Byzantine Poetry," *XIIe Congrès International des Etudes Byzantines*, Rapports III (Ochrida, 1961).

————, "Sources for Early History of the Slavic Church," *Harvard Slavic Studies*, 2 (1954), p. 68 ff.

————, "Tajnaja služba Konstantina Filosofa i dal'nejšie razvitie staroslavjanskoj poezii" (The Holy Office of Constantine the Philosopher and the Further Development of Old Slavonic Poetry), *Zbornik radova Vizantoloskog Instituta*, 8 (Beograd, 1963), pp. 161–166.

————, "Velikaja Moravija ili Velikaja nad Moravoj" (Great Moravia or Velika on Morava), *Festschrift Stojan Romanski* (Sofia, 1960), pp. 483–486.

Janin, R., "Géorgie," *Dictionnaire de théologie catholique*, 6 (Paris, 1924), p. 1244 ff.

Jelić, L., *Dvorska kapela sv. Križa u Ninu*, Djela Jugosl. Akad., vol. 29 (Zagreb, 1911).

————, *Fontes historici liturgiae glagolito-Romanae a XIII ad XIX saeculum* (Veglia, 1906).

Jelovina, D., "Statisticki tipološko-topografsko pregled starohrvatskih naušnica na području SR Hrvatske" (A Statistic, Typologic, and Topographic Review of Old Croatian Earrings Found on the Soil of the Socialist Croat Republic), *Starohrvatska prosvjeta*, 3rd series, 8–9 (Zagreb, 1963), pp. 101–120.

Jireček, C., "Das christliche Element in der topographischen Nomenclatur der Balkanländer," *SB*, Phil. hist. Kl. (Vienna, 1897), p. 20 ff.

————, *Geschichte der Serben* (Gotha, 1911).

————, "Die Romanen in den Städten Dalmatiens während des Mittelalters," *Denkschriften der Akademie der Wissenschaften*, Phil. hist. Kl. 28 (Vienna, 1902), pp. 51–58.

Kabbadia, P., "Ἀνασκαφαὶ ἐν Ἐπιδαύρῳ," Ἀρχεολογικὴ Ἐφήμερις (Athens, 1918, part 4), pp. 115–154.

Kalajdović, K., *Ioann, eksarch bolgarskij* (Moscow, 1924).

Kalenić, P., *Staro Nagoričino* (Belgrade, 1933).

Kalousek, F., "Die grossmährische Burgwaldstadt Břeclav-Pohansko," *Sborník prací filos-fakulty University J. E. Purkyně*, 9 E 5 (1960), pp. 5–22.

————, *Velkomoravské hradištní město Břeclav-Pohansko* (Břeclav-Pohansko, a Townlike Hill-fort from the Great Moravian Period) (Břeclav, 1961).

————, "Velkomoravské 'Pohansko u Břeclavě,'" *Archeologické rozhledy*, 12 (1960), pp. 498–530.

Kalugin, F. G., *Illarion, mitropolit Kievskij i ego tserkovnoučitel'ny ja proizvedenija* (Illarion, Metropolitan of Kiev and His Religious and Didactic Works), *Pamjatniki drevně-russk. učit. literatury*, 1 (St. Petersburg, 1894).

Karagannopulos, J., *Die Entstehung der byzantinischen Themenordnung*, Byzantinisches Archiv, 10 (Munich, 1959).

Karaman, L., "O počecima srednjevjekovnog Splita do godina 800" (The Early Period of Medieval Spalato to the year 800), *Serta Hoffilleriana*, Viesnik hrvatsko archeol. društva (Zagreb, 1940), pp. 419–436.

————, *Pregled umjetnostiu Dalmaciji* (Survey of Dalmatian Art) (Zagreb, 1952).

————, "Sarkofag Ivana Ravenjanina," *Starinar*, ser. III, 3 (Beograd, 1925).

————, "Spomenici umjetnosti u Zadru u vrijeme hrvatskih narodnih vladara" (Art Monuments in Zadar during the Period of Croatian National Rulers), *Zbornik Instituta za histor. nauke u Zadru* (Zagreb, 1964), published by Matice Hrvatska.

Ketrzynski, S., *O zaginionej metropoli czasów Boleslawa Chrobrego* (On the Metropolitan See of the Time of Boleslas the Great, which had Disappeared) (Warsaw, 1947).

Keydell, R., "Die litteraturgeschichtliche Stellung der Gedichte Gregors von Nazianz," *Studi bizantini e neoellenici*, 7 (1953), pp. 134–143.

The Khazars, a Bibliography (by the Slavic division of the New York Public Library) (New York, 1939).

Kiparski, V., "Tschernochvostoffs Theorie über den Ursprung des glagolitischen Alphabets," *Cyrillo-Methodiana. Zur Frühgeschichte des Christentums bei den Slawen 863–1963* (Köln, Gratz, 1964), Slawische Forschungen, ed. R. Olesch, vol. 6.

Kittel, G., *Theologisches Wörterbuch zum Neuen Testament* (Stuttgart, 1938; reprint 1950).

Kniezsa, I., "Kyril und Method-Traditionen in Ungarn," *Cyrillo-Methodiana* (Köln, Graz, 1964), pp. 199–209.

Kollautz, A., "Die Awaren," *Saeculum*, 5 (1954), pp. 129–178.

Kollwitz, J., "Christus als Lehrer und die Gesetzübergabe an Petrus in der konstantinischen Kunst Roms," *Römische Quartalschrift*, 44 (1936), pp. 45–66.

Kolnik, T., "Ausgrabungen auf der römischen Station in Milanovice in den Jahren 1956–1957," *Limes Romanus Konferenz Nitra* (Bratislava, 1959), pp. 27–61.

————, "Zu neuen römisch-barbarischen Funden in der Slowakei und ihrer Chronologie," *Studia historica slovaca*, 2 (1964), pp. 7–51.

Koneski, B., "Ohridska kniževna škola" (The Literary School of Ochrida), *Slovo*, 6–8 (Zagreb, 1957), pp. 177–194.

Korošec, J., *Staroslovansko grobišče na ptujskem gradu* (Old Slavonic Cemetery at the Castle of Ptuj) (Ljubljana, 1950).

Kos, M., *Gradivo za zgodovinu Slovencev* (Ljubljana, 1906).

————, "O pismu papeža Hadriana II. knezom Rastislavu, Svetopulku in Koclju" (The Letter of Pope Hadrian II to the Princes Rastislav, Svatopluk, and Kocel), *Razprave* of the Slovene

Academy, philos., philol., histor. Class, 2 (Ljubljana, 1944), pp. 271–301.

Kostić, D., "Bulgarski episkop Konstantin- pisac glužbe sv. Metodiju" (The Bulgarian Bishop Constantine, Author of an Office of St. Methodius), _Byzantinoslavica_, 7 (1937–38), p. 189 ff.

Kovačević, J., "Avari i zlato" (The Avars and Gold), _Starinar_, XIII–XIV (1963–1964), pp. 125–135.

––––––, "Na tragu kniževnosti iužnog Primorja i Dukle" (Traces of Literary Activity in Dioclea and on the Southern Adriatic Littoral), _Spomenik_ of the Serbian Academy, 15 (1956), pp. 93–98.

––––––, _Od dolazka Slovena do kraja XII vjeka, Istorija Crne Gore_ (History of Montenegro) (Titograd, 1967).

––––––, "Srednjovekovni epigrafski spomenici Boka Kotorska" (Epigraphical Medieval Monuments of Boka Kotorska), _Spomenik_ of the Serbian Academy, 15 (1956), pp. 1–13.

Krautheimer, R., _Early Christian and Byzantine Architecture_ (Baltimore, 1965).

Krumbacher, K., _Geschichte der byzantinischen Literatur_ (Munich, 1897).

Kudrna, J., _Studie k barbarským zákonikům Lex Baiuvariorum a Lex Alamanorum_, Opera universit. Brunensis, Facultas philosophica, 60 (Brno, 1959).

Kuhar, A., _The Conversion of the Slovenes_ (New York, Washington, 1959).

Kulakovskij, J., "Christianstvo u Alan" (Christianity Among the Alans), _Vizantijskij Vremennik_, 5 (1898), pp. 1–18.

Kyriakides, S. K., Βυζαντιναὶ Μελέται, part 4 (Thessalonica, 1933).

––––––, Οἱ Σλάβοι ἐν Πελοποννήσῳ (Saloniki, 1939).

Labuda, G., "Chronologie des guerres de Byzance contre les Avars et les Slaves à la fin du VIe siècle," _Byzantinoslavica_, 11 (1950), pp. 167–173.

––––––, _Pierwsze panstwo Slowianskie, panstwo Samona_ (Poznań, 1949); French summary by V. Chaloupecký in _Byzantinoslavica_, 11 (1952).

Lacko, M., "L'épiscopat de S. Cyrille dans le Codex Vatic.," _Orientalia Christiana Periodica_, 22 (1956), pp. 385–388.

––––––, "Prvá cesta sv. Cyrila a Metoda do Ríma" (The First Trip of SS. Cyril and Methodius to Rome), *Studi in onore di Ettore Lo Gatto e Giovanni Mayer* (Florence, 1962), pp. 375–380.

Laffarini, V., "Un inscrizione Torcellana del sec. VII," *Atti Istituto Veneto Sc., Lett. e Arti,* 73 (1914), p. 2 ff.

Lanckoronska, K., "Studies on the Roman-Slavonic Rite in Poland," *Orientalia Christiana Analecta,* 161 (Rome, 1961).

Lapôtre, A., *De Anastasio bibliothecario* (Paris, 1885).

——, *L'Europe et le Saint-Siège* (Paris, 1895).

Laurenčík, J., "Nelukianovská ctení v Sinajském žaltáři" (Readings in the Slavonic Psalter of Sinai Not Corresponding to Lukian's Redaction), *Vajs' Festschrift: Slovanské Studie* (Prague, 1948), pp. 66–83.

Laurent, V., "Jean VII Grammairien (837–843)," *Catholicism,* 6 (Paris, 1964), cols. 513–515.

Lazarev, V. I., *Mozaiki Sofii Kievskoj* (Moscow, 1960).

Lemerle, P., "La Chronique improprement dite du Monemvasie: le contexte historique et légendaire," *Revue des études byzantines,* 21 (1963), pp. 5–49.

——, "Invasions et migrations dans les Balkans depuis la fin de l'époque romaine jusqu'au VIIIᵉ siècle," *Revue historique,* 78 (1954), pp. 265–308.

——, *Philippes et la Macédoine orientale à l'époque chrétienne et byzantine,* Bibliothèque des Ecoles Françaises d'Athènes et de Rome, vol. 158 (Paris, 1945).

——, "Une province byzantine: le Péloponnèse," *Byzantion,* 21 (1951), pp. 341–353.

Lenel, W., *Venezianischistrische Studien* (Strasburg, 1911).

Lettenbauer, W., "Bemerkungen zur Entstehung der Glagolica," *Cyrillo-Methodiana. Zur Frühgeschichte des Christentums bei den Slawen 863–1963* (Köln, Gratz, 1964), Slawische Forschungen, ed. R. Olesch, vol. 6.

——, "Eine lateinische Kanonensammlung in Mähren im 9. Jahrhundert," *Orientalia Christiana Periodica,* 18 (1952), pp. 246–269.

——, "Zur Entstehung des glagolitischen Alphabets," *Slovo* 3 (Zagreb, 1953), pp. 35–48.

Letter from the Bavarian higher clergy to John IX in 900. *PL* 131, cols. 34–38.

Lipšič, E. E., "Vizantijskij učenyj Lev Matematik," *Vizant. Vremmenik,* 2 (1949), New series, pp. 106–149.

Loparev, K. M., "Dve zametski po drevney bolgarskoj istorii," *Zapiski russkago arkheologičeskago obsčestva*, 3 (St. Petersburg, 1888), pp. 341–362.

Löwe, H., "Ein literarischer Widersacher des Bonifatius Virgil von Salzburg und die Kosmographie des Aethicus Ister," *Abhandlungen der Akademie zu Mainz*, no. 11 (1951), pp. 903–988.

Lowmianski, H., *Początki Polski* (Origins of Poland) (Warsaw, 1963), 2 vols.

Ludvikovský, J., "Great Moravia Tradition in Tenth Century Bohemia and the *Legenda Christiani*," *Magna Moravia* (Brno, 1965), pp. 525–566.

Maassen, F., *Geschichte der Quellen und der Literatur des canonischen Rechts im Abenlande bis zum Ausgang des Mittelalters* (Graz, 1870).

Majewski, K., *Importy rzymskie na zemiach slowianskich* (Roman Imports in Slavic lands) (Warsaw, 1949).

——, *Importy rzymskie w Polsce* (Roman Imports in Poland) (Warsaw, 1960).

Mandić, D., "Dalmatia in the Exarchate of Ravenna from the Middle of the VI until the Middle of the VII Century," *Byzantion*, 34 (1964), pp. 347–374.

——, *Rasprave i prilozi iz stare hrvatske povjesti* (Essays and Annexes Concerning the Old Croat History) (Rome, 1963).

Mango, C., *The Homilies of Photius, Patriarch of Constantinople*, Dumbarton Oaks Studies, 3 (Cambridge, 1958).

Marasović, T., "Evidence of Byzantine Art in Preromanesque Architecture in Dalmatia," (*XIIᵉ Congrès International des Etudes Byzantines* (Belgrad, Ochrid, 1961), *Résumé des Communications*.

——, "Iskapanje ranosrednjevjekovne crkve sv. Marije u Trogiru" (The Excavation of the Early Medieval Church of Our Lady in Trogir), *Starohrvatska prosvjeta*, 3rd series, 8–9 (Zagreb, 1963), pp. 83–100, with a résumé in French.

——, "Ranosrjednjevekovna crkvica u Ošlju kad Stona" (The Early Medieval Little Church of Ošlje near Ston), *Peristil*, 2 (1957), pp. 85–91.

Mareš, V., "Ceská redakce církevní slovanštiny ve světle Besed Řehoře Velikeho" (The Czech Redaction of Church Slavonic in the Light of Gregory the Great's Homilies), *Slavia*, 32 (1963), pp. 417–451.

Marini, G., *I papiri diplomatici* (Rome, 1805).

Markwart, J., *Osteuropäische und ostasiatische Streifzüge* (Leipzig, 1903).

Markwart, J., and Messina, J., "Die Entstehung der armenischen Bistümer," *Orientalia christiana*, 27, no. 80 (1932), pp. 137–236.

Martini, E., *Textgeschichte der Bibliotheke, Abhandlungen der sachisschen Akademie*, phil. hist. C., vol. 28, no. 6 (Leipzig, 1911).

Marušić, B., "Dva spomenika ranosrednjovjekove architekture u Guranu kod Vodnjana" (Two Examples of Early Medieval Architecture at Guran near Vodnjan), *Starohrvatska prosvjeta*, 3rd series, 8–9 (Zagreb, 1963), pp. 121–149, with résumé in French.

Meester, Pl. de, "Les origines et les développements du texte grec de la liturgie de St. Jean Chrysostom," *Chrysostomica: studi e ricerche intorno a S. Giovanni Crisostomo* (Rome, 1908), pp. 254–357.

Megaw, A. H. S., "The Skripou Screen," *The Annals of the British School of Archeology at Athens*, 61 (1967), pp. 7–32.

Mesesnel, F., "Die Ausgrabung einer altchristlichen Basilika in Suvodol," *Bulletin de l'Institut Archéologique Bulgare*, 10 (1936), Actes du IVe Congrès International des Etudes Byzantines, pp. 184–194.

Meyendorff, J., "Byzantine views of Islam," *DO*, 18 (1964), pp. 115–132.

Meyvaert, P., and Devos, P., "Autour de Léon d'Ostie et de sa Translatio S. Clementis," *Analecta Bollandiana*, 74 (1956), pp. 189–240.

———, "Trois énigmes cyrillo-méthodiennes de la 'Légende Italique,'" *Analecta Bollandiana*, 73 (1955), pp. 374–454.

Michel, A., "Die griechischen Klostersiedlungen zu Rom bis zur Mitte des 11. Jahrhunderts, *Ostkirchliche Studien*, 1 (1952), pp. 32–45.

Mijović, P., "Acruvium-Decatera-Kotor u svetlu novich archeoloskich otkrića" (Acruvium-Decatera-Kotor in the Light of New Archeological Discoveries), *Starinar*, New Series, 13–14 (1962–1963), p. 27 ff., with a résumé in French.

Miller, K., *Itineraria romana, römische Reisewege an der Hand der Tabula Peutingeriana dargestellt* (Stuttgart, 1926).

Millet, G., *L'ancien art serbe, les églises* (Paris, 1919).

Minajeva, T. M., "Archeologičeskie pamjatniki na r. Giljac v verchovijach Kubani" (Archaeological Monuments on the River Giljac at the Riverhead of Kuban), *Materialy i issledovanija po archeologii SSSR*, 23 (1951), pp. 273–301.

Mins, E. H., "St. Cyril really knew Hebrew," *Mélanges P. Boyer* (Paris, 1925).

Mohlberg, C., *Il messale glagolitico di Kiew* (*sec. IX*) *ed il suo prototipo Romano del sec. VI–VII*, Atti della Pontificia Accademia Romana di Archeologia (3rd series), Memorie, 2 (Rome, 1928).

Mohorovičić, A., "Problem tipološke klasifikacije objekata srednjovjekovne arhitekture na području Istre i Kvarnera" (The Problem of a Typological Classification of Medieval Architectural Monuments in the Territory of Istria and Quarnero), *Ljetopis* of the Yugoslav Academy, kniga 62 (Zagreb, 1957), pp. 487–541.

Moravcsik, G., *Byzantinoturcica*, Berliner byzantinische Arbeiten (Berlin, 1958), 2 vols.

———, "Sagen und Legenden über Kaiser Basileios I," *DO* 15 (1961), pp. 61–126.

Moreau, E. de, *Saint Anschaire, missionnaire en Scandinavie au IXᵉ siècle* (Louvain, 1930).

Mošin, V. A., "Christianstvo v Rossii do sv. Vladimira" (Christianity in Russia Before St. Vladimir), *Vladimirskij Sbornik* (Beograd, 1938), pp. 1–19.

Müller, C., *Fragmenta historicorum graecorum*, 5 (Paris, 1883).

Mystakidis, B. A., *Byzantinisch-Deutsche Beziehungen zur Zeit der Ottonen* (Stuttgart, 1891).

Nachtigal, R., "Ot'česky knigy," *Razprave* of the Slovene Academy (Ljubljana, 1950).

———, "Rekonstrukcija treh starocerkvenoslov izvirnih pesnilev" Reconstruction of Three Old-Church Slavonic Original Poems), *Razprave Akademije znanosti i umetnosti v Ljubljane* (Ljubljana, 1943), pp. 43–156.

Nedeljković, O., "Još jednom o hronološkom primatu glagoljice" (Addenda on the Chronologic Primacy of the Glagolitic Alphabet), *Slovo*, 15–16 (1965), pp. 19–38.

Niederle, L., *Slovanské starožitnosti* (Prague, 1906–1910).

Nikolajević, I., "Rapport préliminaire sur la recherche des monuments chrétiens à Doclea," *Actes du Ve Congrès International d'Archéologie Chrétienne* (Paris, 1957), pp. 567–572.

Novak, G., *Povijest Splita* (The History of Split) (Split, 1957).

———, "The Slavonic-Latin Symbiosis in Dalmatia during the Middle Ages," *The Slavonic and East European Review*, 32 (1953), pp. 1–28.

Novaković, S., "Ochridska archiepiskopija u povetku XI veka" (The Archbishopric of Ochrida at the Beginning of the Eleventh Century), *Glas*, The Serbian Academy, 76 (1908), pp. 1–62.

Novotný, B., "The Survey of a Great Moravian Stronghold 'Pohansko' near Nejdek," *Památky archeologické*, 54 (1963), pp. 3–40, with a résumé in German.

Novotný, V., *České dějiny* (Prague, 1912), vol. 1.

Obolensky, D., "Byzantium, Kiev, and Moscow," *DO*, 11 (1957), pp. 21–78.

Oettinger, K., *Das Werden Wiens* (Vienna, 1951).

Okulic-Kazarin, N. F., *Sputnik po drevnemu Pskovu* (Guide to Ancient Pskov) (Pskov, 1913).

Ondrouch, V., *Dohaté hroby z doby rímskej na Slovensku* (Rich Tomb Found in Slovania from the Roman Period) (Bratislava, 1957).

———, *Limes Romanus na Slovensku* (Limes Romanus in Slovakia) (Bratislava, 1938).

———, *Nálezy keltských, antických a byzantských mincí na Slovensku* (Finds of Celtic, Antique, and Byzantine Coins in Slovakia) (Bratislava, 1964).

Orth, E., *Photiana* (Leipzig, 1929).

Ostojić, I., "Benediktine i glagoljaši," *Slovo*, 9–10 (Zagreb, 1960).

Ostrogorsky, G., "The Byzantine Background of the Moravian Mission," *DO*, 19 (1964), pp. 1–19.

———, "The Byzantine Emperor and the Hierarchic World Order," *The Slavic and East European Review*, 35 (1956), pp. 1–14.

———, *History of the Byzantine State* (New Brunswick, 1969), Revised Edition.

———, "Postanak tema Helada i Peloponez" (Foundation of the *thema* of Hellas and Peloponnesus), *Zbornik radova* of the Serbian Academy, 21 (1952), pp. 64–77.

————, "Sur la date de la composition du livre des Thèmes en Asie Mineure," *Byzantion,* 23 (1953), pp. 31–66.

————, "Taktikon Uspenskog i Taktikon Beneševiča," *Zbornik radova* of the Serbian Academy, 22 (1953), pp. 39–59.

Pančenko, B. A., "Katalog molevdovulov" (Catalogue of Lead Seals), *Izvjestija,* 13 (Constantinople, 1908).

Paszkiewicz, H., *The Origin of Russia* (London, 1954).

Pauly-Wissowa, "Panticapaeum," *Realenzyklopädie,* 18 (1949), 2, cols. 780 ff.

Péchayre, A. P., "Les écrits de Constantin le Philosophe sur les reliques de St. Clément de Rome," *Echos d'Orient,* 35 (1936), pp. 465–472.

Pechuška, F., "Řecká předloha staroslovenského textu Skutků apoštolských" (The Greek Prototype of the Old Slavonic Text of the Acts of the Apostles), *Vajs' Festschrift: Slovanské Studie* (Prague, 1948), pp. 60–65.

Peeters, P., "Les Khazars dans la Passion de St. Abo de Tiflis," *Analecta Bollandiana,* 52 (1934), pp. 21–56.

Pelikán, O., *Slovensko a rímské imperium* (Slovakia and the Roman Empire) (Bratislava, 1960).

Perels, E., *Papst Nikolaus I und Anastasius bibliothecarius* (Berlin, 1920).

Pertusi, A., *Costantino Porfirogenito De Thematibus,* Studi e Testi, 160 (Città dell Vaticano, 1952).

————, "Nuova ipotesi sull'origine dei temi bizantini," *Aevum,* 28 (1954), pp. 126–150.

Petricioli, I., "Maketa Zadra u pomorskom muzju Venecije" (Scale Model of Zadar in the Maritime Museum in Venice), *Zbornik Instituta za histor. nauke u Zadru,* 2 (1956–57) (Zadar, 1956).

————, "Neki preromanički spomenici Zadra i okolice u svjetla najnovijih istraživanja" (Some Pre-Romanesque Monuments in Zadar and Its Surroundings in the Light of the Most Recent Research), *Zbornik Instituta za histor. nauke u Zadru,* 2 (1956–1957) (Zadar, 1956).

Pleiner, R., "Slovanské sekerovité hřivny" (Slavic Ax Ironbars), *Slovanská archeologie,* 9 (1961), pp. 405–450.

————, *Staré evropské kovařstvi* (The Smith's Trade in Old Europe) (Prague, 1962).

————, "Velkomoravské železné hřivny jako platidlo" (Moravian

Ax Ironbars as Means of Payment), *Numismatické listy*, 18 (Prague, 1963), p. 134 ff.

————, *Základy slovanského železářského hutnictví v českých zemích* (Foundations of Slavic Metallurgy in Czech Lands) (Prague, 1958).

Pochitonov, E., "Nálezy antických mincí" (Finds of Antique Coins), *Nálezy mincí v Čechách, na Moravě a ve Slezsku* (Finds of Coins in Bohemia, Moravia, and Silesia), ed. E. Nohejlová-Pratová, 1 (Prague, 1955), pp. 85–134.

Pokorný, L., "Liturgie pěje slovansky" (The Liturgy Chanted in Slavic), *Soluňsti bratři* (Prague, 1962), pp. 131–166.

————, "Die slavische Cyrillo-Methodianische Liturgie," *Sancti Cyrillus and Methodius* (Prague, 1963), pp. 118–126.

Polaschek, E., "Noricum," *Realenzyclopädie*, 17 (1937).

Pošmourný, J., "Chrámy cyrilometodějské na Velké Moravě" (Churches of the Time of Cyril and Methodius in Great Moravia), *Umění*, 1 (1953), pp. 42–60.

————, "Církevní architektura Velkomoravské říše" (Church Architecture in Great Moravia), *Umění*, 12 (1964), pp. 187–202, with a résumé in German.

————, "Stavební umění Velkomoravské říše" (The Architectural Art of Great Moravia), *Architektura ČSSR*, 20 (1961), pp. 129–135.

Pošvář, J., "Die byzantinische Währung und das grossmährische Reich," *Byzantinoslavica*, 26 (1965), pp. 308–317.

Poucha, P., *Po stopách dávného Chórezmu* (Prague, 1952), see Tolstov, S. P.

Poulík, J., *Dvě velkomoravské rotundy v Mikulčicích*, Monumenta archaeologica, 12 (Prague, 1963), with a detailed résumé in German (pp. 197–233).

————, *Jižní Morava, zem dávných Slovanů* (Southern Moravia, the Land of Ancient Slavs) (Brno, 1948–50).

————, "Kultura moravských Slovanů a Avaři" (The Civilization of the Moravian Slavs and the Avars), *Slavia antiqua*, 1 (1948), pp. 325–348.

————, "The Latest Archeological Discoveries from the Period of the Great Moravian Empire," *Historica*, 1 (Prague, 1959), pp. 7–70.

————, "Nález kostela z doby velkomoravské v trati 'Špitálky' ve Starém Městě" (The Discovery of a Church from the Great

Moravian Period in the Zone of Špitálky in Staré Město), *Památky archeologické*, 46 (1955), pp. 307–351.

———, *Pevnost v lužním lese* (A Fort in a Wooded Meadow) (Prague, 1967).

———, *Staří Moravané budují svůj stát* (The Ancient Moravians Build their State) (Gottwaldov, 1963).

———, "Vysledky výzkumu na velkomoravském hradišti 'Valy' u Mikulčic" (The First Results of the Investigations Made of the Great Moravian Settlement "Valy" near Mikulčice), *Památky archeologické*, 48 (1957), pp. 241–388, with a résumé in German.

Preidel, H., "Die altslawischen Funde von Altstadt in Mähren und ihre Bedeutung," Stifter Jahrbuch, 4 (1955), pp. 254–277.

———, *Die Anfänge der slawischen Besiedlung Böhmens und Mährens* (Munich, 1954).

———, "Archäologische Denkmäler und Funde zur Christianisierung des östlichen Mitteleuropas," *Die Welt der Slaven*, 5 (1960), p. 62 ff.

———, "Avaren und Slaven," *Südostdeutsche Forschungen*, 11 (1946–1952), pp. 33–45.

———, *Slawische Altertumskunde des östlichen Mitteleuropas im 9. und 10. Jahrhundert* (Graefeling, 1961).

Procházka, Vl., "Le Zakon Sudnyj Ljudem et la Grande Moravie," *Byzantinoslavica*, 28 (1967), pp. 359–375; 29 (1968), p. 112 ff.

Putanec, V., "Refleksi starodalmato-romanskog prodjeva *sanctus* u onomastici obalne Hrvatske," *Slovo*, 13 (Zagreb, 1963), pp. 137–175.

Racek, J., "Sur la question de la genèse du plus ancient chant liturgique tchèque, 'Hospodine pomiluý ny,'" *Magna Moravia* (Brno, 1964), pp. 435–460.

Radojčić, G. S., "La date de la conversion des Serbes," *Byzantion*, 22 (1952), pp. 253–256.

———, "Srpske Zagorje, das spätere Raszien," *Südostforschungen*, 16 (1957), pp. 259–284.

Radoměrský, P., "Byzantské mince z pokladu v Zemianském Vrbovku," *Památky archeologické*, 45 (1953), pp. 109–122, with a résumé in German.

Ramovš, F., and Kos, F., *Brizinski spomeniki* (The Documents of Freisingen) (Ljubljana, 1937).

Rankoff, P., "Die byzantinisch-bulgarischen Beziehungen," *Aus der byzantinischen Arbeit der deutschen demokratischen Republik,* ed. J. Irmscher, 1 (Berlin, 1957), p. 138.

Ratkoš, P., "Die grossmährischen Slawen und die Altmagyaren," *Das grossmährische Reich* (Prague, Academy, 1966).

———, "K otázce hranice Velkej Moravy a Bulharska" (Concerning the Problem of the Boundaries Between Great Moravia and Bulgaria), *Historický Časopis,* 3 (Bratislava, 1955), with a résumé in German.

———, *O počiatkoch slovenských dejin* (On the Beginning of Slovak History), Sbornik, ed. Ratkos (Bratislava, 1965).

———, "Počiatki feudalizmu na Slovensku" (Beginnings of Feudalism in Slovakia), *Historický Časopis,* 2 (Bratislava, 1954), pp. 252–275.

———, "Über die Interpretation der Vita Methodii," *Byzantinoslavica,* 28 (1967), pp. 118–123.

Rauch, G. von, "Frühe christliche Spuren in Russland," *Saeculum,* 7 (1956), pp. 40–67.

Repp, F., "Zur Erklärung von Kap. XV der Legende von Konstantin," *Zeitschrift für Slawische Philologie,* 26 (1958), pp. 114–118.

Riant, P. E. D., *Dépouilles religieuses enlevées à Constantinople* (Paris, 1875).

———, *Excuviae Sacrae Constantinopolitanae* (Genève, 1877, 1878).

Richter, V., "Die Anfänge der grossmährischen Architektur," *Magna Moravia,* Opera Universitatis Purkynianae Brunensis, Facultas philosophica, vol. 102 (Brno, 1965), pp. 121–360.

Ritig, S., *Povijest i pravo slovenštine* (History and Justification of the Slavonic Language) (Zagreb, 1910).

Rogošić, R., *Veliki Ilirik 284–395 i njegova konečna dioba 396–437* (Zagreb, 1962).

Rossejkin, F. M., "Buržuaznaja istoriografija o vizantino-moravskich otnošenijach v seredině IX. v.," *Vizantijskij Vremenik,* 3 (1950), pp. 245–257.

Rubarac, I., *Raški episkopi i metropoliti* (Bishops and Metropolitans of Raška), *Glas* of the Serbian Academy, 62.

Runciman, S., *A History of the First Bulgarian Empire* (London, 1930).

Rutkovskij, N. P., "Latinskija scholii," *Seminarium Kondakovianum,* 3 (1929), pp. 149–168.

Šafařik, J., *Slawische Altertümer* (Prague, 1844).

Sakać, S., "Novissima de Legenda Italica," *Orientalia Christiana Periodica*, 22 (1956), pp. 198–213.

———, "Ugovor pape Agatona i Hrvata proti navalnom ratu," *Croatia Sacra*, 1 (1931), pp. 1–84.

Salajka, A., Bibliographical notices in the symposium *Soluňsti bratři* (The Brothers of Thessalonica) (Prague, 1962), p. 217 ff.

Saria, B., "Dalmatien als spätantike Provinz," *Pauly's Realenzyclopädie*, Suppl. Band 8 (1956), cols. 22–59.

Schaeder, H.H., "Geschichte und Legende im Werk der Slawenmissionare Konstantin und Method," *Historische Zeitschrift*, 152 (1935), p. 232 ff.

Schmid, H. F., *Die Nomokanonübersetzung des Methodius*, Veröffentlichungen des balt. und slaw. Instituts an der Univ. Leipzig (Leipzig, 1922), no. 1.

Schmidinger, H., *Patriarch und Landesherr* (Graz, Köln, 1954).

Schmitz, H. J., *Die Bussbücher und das kanonische Bussverfahren* (Graz, 1958, reprint of Köln, 1898).

Schober, A., *Die Römerzeit in Österreich* (Vienna, 1935).

Schulz, H.-J., *Die byzantinische Liturgie. Vom Werden ihrer Symbolgestalt*, *Sophia*, 5 (Freiburg i.B., 1964).

Schultz, R. W., and Barnsley, S. H., *The Monastery of Saint Luke of Stiris* (London, 1901).

Schwartz, E., *I. Vigiliusbriefe. II. Zur Kirchenpolitik Justinians*, Sitzungsberichte der bayer. Akademie, Phil. hist. Kl. (1940).

Sergheraert, G. (Christian Gérard), *Syméon le Grand* (893–927) (Paris, 1960).

Šetka, J., *Hrvatska kršćanska terminologia* (Sibenik, Makarska, 1940, 1964, 1965), 3 vols.

Ševčenko, I., "The Definition of Philosophy in the Life of Saint Constantine," *For Roman Jakobson* (The Hague, 1956), pp. 449–457.

———, "The Greek Source of the Inscription on Solomon's Chalice in the Vita Constantini," *To Honor Roman Jakobson* (The Hague, 1967), pp. 1806–1817.

Sieklicki, J., "Quidam Priwina," *Slavia occidentalis*, 22 (1962), pp. 116–145.

Simeon Logothete (Pseudo-Simeon), *Chronicon* (Bonn, 1838) (Theoph. Cont.), pp. 603–760.

Šišić, F., *Geschichte der Kroaten* (Zagreb, 1917).

————, *Povijest Hrvata* (Zagreb, 1926).

Skok, P., *Dolazak Slovena na Mediteran* (Split, 1934).

————, *Slavenstvo i romanstvo na jadranskim otocima* (Zagreb, 1950).

————, "La terminologie chrétienne en slave: le parrain, la marraine et le filleul," *Revue des études slaves*, 10 (1930), pp. 186–204.

Skylitses-Cedrenus, *Historiarum Comperdium* (Bonn, 1839), *PG* 121, cols. 23–1166.

Snegarov, I., "B'lgarskiat pervoučitel sv. Kliment Ochridski," *Godišnik na Bogoslovskia Fakultet* (Sofia, 1926–1927).

————, "Černorizets Khrabur," *Khilyada i sto godini s slavyanska pismenost 863–1963*, Sbornik v čest na Kiril i Metody (Sofia, 1963), pp. 305–319.

Šolle, M., "Die Bedeutung des dalmatinischen altkroatischen Gebietes in der Frage nach dem Ursprung der grossmährischen Kultur," *Das grossmährische Reich*, ed. F. Graus, J. Filip, and A. Dostál (Prague, Academy, 1966), pp. 105–107.

————, *Stará Kouřim a projevy velkomoravské hmotné kultury v Čechách* (Ancient Castle of Kouřim and the Influence of Great Moravian Material Culture in Bohemia) (Prague, Academy, 1966).

Soteriou, G. A., "Αἱ Παλαιοχριστιανικαὶ Βασιλικαὶ τῆς Ἑλλάδος" (Early Christian Basilicas in Hellas), Ἀρχαιολογικὴ Ἐφημερίς (Athens, 1929), pp. 198–201.

Soulis, G., "The Legacy of Cyril and Methodius to the Southern Slavs," *DO*, 19 (1965), pp. 19–45.

Spicyn, B., "Archeologija v temach načal'noj letopisi" (Archaeology in the Time of the Early Period), *Sborník v čest' S. F. Platonova* (St. Petersburg, 1922), pp. 1–12.

Srebrnić, J., "Odnošaji pape Ivana X prema Byzantu i Slavenima na Balkanu" (The Relations of Pope John X with Byzantium and the Balkan Slavs), *Zbornik kralja Tomislava* (Zagreb, 1925).

Stanislav, J., *Bolo južne Slovensko bulharské?* (Was Southern Slovakia Bulgarian?) (Bratislava, 1944).

————, "K otázce učinkovania Cyrila a Metoda na Slovensku" (The Question of the Activity of Cyril and Methodius in Slovakia), *Kultura*, 15 (Bratislava, 1943), pp. 449–466, 520–539.

————, "O prehodnotenie velkomoravských prvkov v cyrilometodejskij literature" (Re-estimation of Great Moravian Elements in Cyrilo-Methodian Literature), *Sbornik A. Teodorov-Balan* (Sofia, 1955), pp. 357–363.

———, *Osudy Cyrila a Metoda a ich učenikov v životě Klimentovom* (The Fate of Cyril, Methodius and their Disciples According to the Life of Clement) (Bratislava, 1950).

———, *Životy slovanských apoštolov Cyrila a Metoda* (Slovak translation) (Bratislava, 1934).

Štefanić, V., "Tisuću i sto godina od moravske misije," *Slovo,* 13 (Zagreb, 1963), pp. 1–42.

Stein, E., *Histoire du Bas-Empire* (Bruges, 1949), 2 vols.

Stephen V, Pope, *Fragmenta et Epistolae, MGH Ep* 7, pp. 334–365.

Strabo, *Geography,* ed. H. L. Jones (Loeb, 1923), vol. 2.

Stratonov, I., "Die Krim und ihre Bedeutung für die Christianisierung der Ostslaven," *Kyrios,* 1 (1936).

Stričević, Dj., "La rénovation du type basilical dans l'architecture ecclésiastique des pays centraux des Balkans au IXᵉ–XIᵉ siècles," *XIIᵉ Congrès International des Etudes Byzantines, Ochride 1961* (Belgrade-Ochrid, 1961), rapports VII, p. 179.

Strohal, R., *Hrvatska glagolska kniga* (Croat Glagolitic Books) (Zagreb, 1915).

Strzygowski, J., *Die Altslavische Kunst* (Augsburg, 1929).

Stylianos of Neo-Caesarea, *Letter to Pope Stephen V, Mansi,* 16.

Sullivan, R. E., "Khan Boris and the Conversion of Bulgaria. A Case Study of the Impact of Christianity on a Barbarian Society," *Studies in Medieval and Renaissance History,* 3 (Lincoln, Nebraska, 1966), pp. 55–139.

Svoboda, B., *Čechy a římské Imperium* (Bohemia and the Roman Empire), Acta musei nationalis Pragae, 2, A, Historia (Prague, 1948), with a résumé in English.

———, "Poklad byzantského kovotepce v Zemianském Vrbovku" (The Treasure of a Byzantine Metalsmith Found in Zemianský Vrbovok), *Památky archeologické,* 44 (1953), p. 79 ff., with a résumé in German.

———, "Über das Nachleben der römischen Kultur im mittleren Donaubecken," *Limes Romanus Konferenz Nitra* (Bratislava, 1959), pp. 107–116.

Swoboda, W., "Powstanie panstwa bulgarskiego v Dolnej Mezji" (Foundation of the Bulgarian State in Lower Moesia), *Slavia occidentalis,* 22 (1962), pp. 50–66.

Synaxarium Ecclesiae Constantinopolitanae, ed. H. Delehaye in *Propylaeum ad Acta Sanctorum Novembris* (Brussels, 1902).

Synodicon Vetus, published by J. Pappe in J. A. Fabricius and G. C. Harles, *Bibliotheca graeca,* 12 (Hamburg, 1809).

Syrku, P., *K istorii ispravlenija knig v Bolgarii* (Regarding a Revised Edition of Books in Bulgaria), *Teksty,* 1 (St. Petersburg, 1890).

——, *Liturgičeskie trudy patriarcha Evthimija Tarnovskago* (The Liturgical Works of the Patriarch Euthymius of Tarnovo), *Teksty,* 2 (St. Petersburg, 1880).

Szöke, B., "Über die Beziehungen Moraviens zu dem Donaugebiet in der Spätavarenzeit," *Studia Slavica,* 6 (1960), pp. 75–112.

Szyszman, S., "Les Khazars, problèmes et controverses," *Revue de l'Histoire des religions,* 152 (1957), pp. 174–221.

——, "Le roi Balan et le problème de la conversion des Khazars," *Actes du Xe Congrès International d'études byzantines,* Istanbul (1957), pp. 249–252.

Tafel, L. F., *Via Egnatia* (Tübingen, 1837–1842).

Tarchnisvili, M., "Geschichte der kirchlichen georgischen Literatur," *Studi e testi,* 185 (Città dell' Vaticano, 1955).

——, *Liturgiae ibericae antiquiores, Corpus scriptorum christianorum orientalium,* vol. 123, Scriptores iberici, series I, tome I (Louvain, 1950).

Thalborzy, L., and Jireček, C., "Zwei Urkunden aus Nordalbanien," *Archiv für slawische Philologie,* 21 (1899).

Tiso, F., "The Empire of Samo (623–658)," *Slovac Studies, Historica,* 1 (Rome, 1961), pp. 1–21.

Tkadlčík, V., "Le moine Chrabr et l'origine de l'écriture slave," *Byzantinoslavica,* 25 (1964), pp. 75–92.

Točik, A., "Vyznam poslednych archeolog. vyskumov na Slovensko," *Historický Časopis,* 3 (Bratislava, 1955), pp. 410–421.

Tolstov, S. P., *Po sledam drevnochorezminskoi tsivilizatsii* (Moscow, 1948).

Tunickij, W., *Sv. Kliment episkop slovenskij* (St. Clement, Slavic Bishop) (Sergiev' Posad', 1913).

Turek, R., *Čechy na úsvitu dějin* (Bohemia at the Dawn of History) (Prague, 1963).

——, "Die grossmährische Epoche in Böhmen," *Das grossmährische Reich* (Prague, Academy, 1966), pp. 85–87.

———, "Velkomoravský horizont v českých mohylách" (Great Moravian Horizon in Bohemian Tombs), *Památky archeologické*, 54 (1963), pp. 224–233.

Unbegaum, R. O., "L'héritage cyrillo-méthodien en Russie," *Cyrillo-Methodiana*, ed. Görresgesellschaft (Köln, Graz, 1964), pp. 470–482.

Uspenskij, Th. I., *Vizantijskaja tabeľo rangach*, Mémoires de l'Institut Archéologique Russe de Constantinople, 3 (Sofia, 1898).

Vaillant, A., "Une homélie de Constantin le Prêtre," *Byzantinoslavica*, 28 (1967), pp. 68–81.

———, "Les lettres russes de la Vie de Constantin," *Revue des études slaves*, 15 (1935), pp. 75–77.

———, "Une poésie vieux-slave: la préface de l'Evangile," *Revue des études slaves*, 33 (1956), pp. 7–25.

———, "La préface de l'Evangeliaire vieux-slave," *Revue des études slaves*, 24 (1948), pp. 5–20.

Vaillant, A., and Lascaris, M., "La date de la conversion des Bulgares," *Revue des études slaves*, 13 (1933), pp. 5–15.

Vajs, J., "Il canone del piu antico Messale croato-glagolitico sec. XIV (Codice Vaticano, Sign, Illir. 4)," *Studi e testi*, 125 (Città dell' Vaticano, 1946), Miscellanea Giovanni Mercati, vol. 5, pp. 356–362.

———, "Chrabrova apologie o písmenech," *Byzantinoslavica*, 7 (1937–38), pp. 158–163.

———, "Kanon charvatsko-hlaholského misálu Illir. 4. Protějšek hlaholských listu Kijevských" (The Canon of the Croato-Glagolitic Missal Illir. 4. Counterpart of the Glagolitic *Leaflets of Kiev*), *Časopis pro moderní filologii*, 25 (Prague, 1939), pp. 113–134.

———, *Kritické studie staroslovanského textu biblického* (Critical Studies of the Old Slavonic Biblical Text) (Prague, 1935, 1936).

———, "Kyjevské listy a jejich latinský (římský) originál, stol. VI–VII," *Bratislava*, 4 (1930), pp. 521–527.

———, "Mešní řád charvatsko-hlaholského vatikánskéhonɪ̨ɛ̨sɪ̨u Illir. 4 a jeho poměr k moravsko-pannonskému sakramentáři stol. IX" (The Mass Order of the Croatian Glagolitic Missal of Vatican Ill. 4 and Its Relation to the Moravo-Pannonian Sacramentary of the Ninth Century), *Acta Academiae Velehradensis,* 15 (1939), pp. 89–156.

———, *Najstariji hrvatskoglagolski misal* (The Oldest Glagolitic Missal) (Zagreb, 1948).

———, *Rukověť hlaholské paleografie* (Handbook of Glagolitic Paleography) (Prague, 1932).

———, *Sborník staroslovanských literárnich památek o sv. Vác lavu a sv. Ludmile* (Collection of Old Slavonic Literary Monuments on St. Wenceslas and St. Ludmila) (Prague, 1929).

Vajs, J., and Dobrovský, J., *Cyril a Metod* (Prague, 1948).

Vangeli, V., "Prilog, bibliografijata za Kliment Ochridski" (Contribution to the Bibliography on Clement of Ochrida), *Istorija* III, 1 (Skopje, 1967), pp. 187–197.

Vasić, M. M., *Architektura i skulptura u Dalmaciji* (Belgrade, 1922).

———, "Crkva sv. Krsta u Ninu," *Strena Buliciana* (Zagreb-Split, 1921), pp. 449–456.

Vašica, J., "Jazyková povaha Zakona sudného" (Linguistic Character of Zakon Sudnyj), *Slavia,* 27 (1958), pp. 521–537.

———, *Literární památky epochy velkomoravské* (Literary Monuments of the Great Moravian Epoch) (Prague, 1966).

———, "Origine Cyrillo Méthodienne du plus ancien code slave, Zakon Sudnýj," *Byzantinoslavica,* 12 (1951), pp. 154–174.

———, "Právní odkaz cyrilometodějský" (Cyrilomethodian Juridical Legacy), *Slavia,* 32 (1963), pp. 327–339.

———, "Slovanská liturgie nově osvětlená kyjevskými listy" (The Slavonic Liturgy newly Clarified by the *Kievan Leaflets*), *Slovo a slovesnost,* 6 (Prague, 1940).

———, "Slovanská liturgie sv. Petra" (The Slavonic Liturgy of St. Peter), *Byzantinoslavica,* 8 (1939–1946), pp. 1–54.

Vasiliev, A. A., *The Goths in the Crimea* (Cambridge, Mass., 1936).

———, *The Russian Attack on Constantinople in 860* (Cambridge, Mass., 1946).

Vasiliev, A. A., Gregoire, H., and Canard, M., *Byzance et les Arabes* (Bruxelles, 1935).

Vavřínek, V., "Die Christianisierung und Kirchenorganisation Grossmährens," *Historica,* 7 (1963), pp. 5–56.

———, "K otázce počátků christianisace Velké Moravy" (The Question of the Christianization of Great Moravia), *Listy filologické,* 7 (1959), pp. 217–224.

————, "Předcyrilometodějské missie na Velké Moravě" (Missionary Activity in Moravia Before Cyril and Methodius), *Slavia,* 32 (1963), pp. 465–480.

————, *Staroslověnské životy Konstantina a Metoděje* (Old Slavonic Lives of Constantine and Methodius), *Rozpravy* of the Czech Academy, vol. 73, 7 (Prague, 1963).

————, "Staroslověnské životy Konstantina a Metoděje a panegyriky Řehoře z Nazianzu" (The Old Slavonic Lives of Constantine and Methodius and the Panegyrics by Gregory of Nazianzus), *Listy filologické,* 85 (Prague, 1962), pp. 96–122.

————, "Study of the Church Architecture from the Period of the Great Moravian Empire," *Byzantinoslavica,* 25 (1964), pp. 288–301.

————, "Ug'r'skyj Korol' dans la vie vieux-slave de Méthode," *Byzantinoslavica,* 25 (1964), pp. 261–269.

Večerka, R., "Cyrilometodějský kult v české středověké tradici" (The Cult of Cyril and Methodius in the Czech Medieval Tradition), *Československý časopis historický,* 12 (1964), pp. 40–43.

————, "Grossmähren und sein Kulturerbe in den Arbeiten der tschechischen Philologie der Nachkriegszeit," *Das grossmährische Reich,* Czechoslovak Academy (Prague, 1966), pp. 355–377.

————, *Slovanské počátky české knižní vzdělanosti* (Slavonic Origins of Czech Literary Culture) (Prague, 1963).

————, *Velkomoravská literatura v přemyslovských Čechách* (Great Moravian Literature in Bohemia Under the Dynasty of the Przemyslides), *Slavia,* 32 (1963), pp. 398–416.

Vernadský, G., *Ancient Russia* (New Haven, 1943).

————, "The Beginning of the Czech State," *Byzantion,* 17 (1944–1945).

————, *The Origins of Russia* (Oxford, 1959).

Vernadský, G., and Ferdinahdy, M. de, "Studien zur ungarischen Frühgeschichte," I, Lebedia, II, Almos, *Südeuropäische Arbeiten* (Munich, 1957).

Vlášek, J., "Quelques notes sur l'apologie slave par Chrabr," *Byzantinoslavica,* 28 (1967), pp. 82–97.

Vondrák, V., *O původu kijevských listů a pražských zlomků* (On the Origin of the *Leaflets of Kiev* and of the Fragments of Prague) (Prague, 1904).

———, *Studie z oboru církevněslov. písemnictví* (Studies on Church Slavonic Literature), *Rozpravy* of the Czech Academy, 20 (1903).

Vryonis, S., "St. Joannicius the Great (754–846)," *Byzantion,* 31 (1961), pp. 245–248.

———, "The Slavs of Bithynia," *Byzantion,* 31 (1961), pp. 245–248.

Walden, J. W. H., *The Universities of Ancient Greece* (New York, 1909).

Wallace-Hadrill, J. M., *The Fourth Book of the Chronicle of Fredegar* (London-New York, 1960).

Wartolowska, Z., "Osada i gród w Wiślicy w swietle badan wykopaliskowych do 1962 r." (The City and Sastle of Wiślica in the Light of Excavations Made to the Year 1962), Symposium *Odkrycia w Wiślicy* (Discoveries in Wiślica), the Polish Academy (Warsaw, 1963), pp. 33–45.

Weingart, M., *Bulhaři a Cařihrad před tisíciletím* (The Bulgarians and Constantinople One Thousand Years ago) (Prague, 1915).

———, "K dnešnímu stavu bádání o jazyce a písemnictví církevněslovanském" (Current Results of Studies in the Old Slavonic Language and Letters), *Byzantinoslavica,* 5 (1933–34), p. 419 ff.

———, "Pribina, Kocel a Nitra," *Riša velkomoravská,* ed. J. Stanislav (Bratislava, 1933), p. 319 ff.

Werner, J., "Slawische Bügelfibeln des 7. Jahrhunderts," *Reinecke Festschrift,* ed. G. Behrens and J. Werner (Mainz, 1950), pp. 150–177.

Widajewicz, J., *Państwo Wiślan* (The State of the Vistulanians) (Cracow, 1947).

Wijk, N. Van, "Die älteste kirchenslawische Übersetzung," *Byzantinoslavica,* 7 (1937–38), pp. 108–123.

———, "Dva slavjanskich' paterika," *Byzantinoslavica,* 4 (1932), pp. 22–35.

———, *Studien zu den altkirchenslavischen Paterika* (Amsterdam, 1931).

Woronczak, I., Ostrowska, E., and Feicht, H., *Bogurodzica* (Warsaw, 1962).

Zagiba, F., "Bayerische Slawenmission und ihre Fortsetzung durch Kyrill und Method," *JGOE* 9 (1961), p. 4 ff.

———, "Neue Probleme in der Kyrillomethodianischen Forschung," *Ostkirchliche Studien*, 11 (1962), pp. 97–130.

———, "Zur Geschichte Kyrills und Methods und der bayerischen Ostmission," *JGOE* 9 (1960), p. 268 ff.

Zajączkowski, A., *Ze studiow nad zagadnicniem Chazarskim* (Studies on the Khazar Problem) (Cracow, 1947).

Zástěrová, B., "Avaři a Slované," *Vznik a počatky Slovanů*, ed. J. Eisner, 2 (Prague, 1958), pp. 19–54.

———, "Hlavní problémy z počátku dějin Slovanskych národů" (Main Problems Concerning the Primitive History of the Slavic Nations), *Vznik a počátky Slovanů*, ed. J. Eisner, 1 (Prague, 1956), pp. 28–83.

Zathey, J., "O kilku przepadlych zabytkach rekopismiennych Biblioteki Narodowej w Warszawie" (Remnant of Some Lost Manuscripts in the National Library in Warsaw), *Studia z dziejow kultury polskiej* (Warsaw, 1949), pp. 73–86.

Zibermayer, I., *Noricum, Baiern, und Österreich* (München, Berlin, 1944).

Ziegler, A. W., "Methodius auf dem Weg in die schwäbische Verbannung," *JGOE*, 1 (1953), pp. 369–382.

———, "Questiones Cyrillo-Methodianae," *Orientalia Christiana periodica*, 18 (1952), pp. 113–134.

———, "Der Slawenapostel Methodius im Schwabenland," *Festschrift, Dillingen und Schwaben* (1949), pp. 169–189.

Ziegler, K., "Les 'notices et extraits' des bibliothèques grecques de Bagdad par Photius," *Revue des études grecques*, 69 (1956), pp. 101–103.

———, "Photios," *Paulys Realenzyclopädie*, 39 (Stuttgart, 1941).

Zlatarski, V. N., *Istorija na bůlgarskata důrzava* (Sofia, 1918); vol. I, part 2 (Sofia, 1927).

———, "Velká Morava a Bulharsko v IX st.," *Ríša Velkomoravská*, ed. J. Stanislav (Prague, 1933).

Žužek, I., "Kormčaja Kniga," *Orientalia Christiana Analecta*, 168 (Rome, 1964).

Index

This book was set in Caledonia Linotype and printed by offset on P & S Old Forge manufactured by P. H. Glatfelter Co., Spring Grove, Pa. Composed, printed and bound by Quinn & Boden Company, Inc., Rahway, N.J.